MEDIEVAL LOVE LETTERS

In the Middle Ages, educated people communicated their love in verse letters that revealed at once their personal commitments and their commitments to an established form of literary art. *Medieval Love Letters* reveals the fascinating duality of the medieval love letter as literary art and as life writing by exploring a wide variety of remarkable texts in English, French, German and Latin. These rich texts are made accessible both linguistically, in new editions and translations, and conceptually, by discussing them in a way intelligible to non-specialists. Edited and translated texts include model letters from instructional manuals and fictional verse and actual letters from clerics and lay people, men and women. A substantial introduction explores the interchange and overlap between fact and literary art with reference to a wide range of examples.

Myra Stokes's published work ranges across the languages and literatures of other European vernaculars as well as Old and Middle English. Her books include *Justice and Mercy in Piers Plowman* (1984; reprinted 2020), *The Language of Jane Austen* (1991) and (as co-author) *Studies in the Metre of Alliterative Verse* (2007). With Ad Putter she edited *The Works of the Gawain Poet* (2014).

Ad Putter is a Fellow of the British Academy and Professor of Medieval English Literature at the University of Bristol, where he directs the Centre for Medieval Studies. His publications include *An Introduction to the Gawain Poet* (1996), *The Cambridge Companion to the Arthurian Legend*, co-edited with Elizabeth Archibald (2009), and *North Sea Crossings: The Literary Heritage of Anglo-Dutch Relations, 1066–1688*, co-authored with Sjoerd Levelt (2021).

MEDIEVAL LOVE LETTERS

A Critical Anthology

MYRA STOKES
University of Bristol

AD PUTTER
University of Bristol

Shaftesbury Road, Cambridge CB2 8EA, United Kingdom

One Liberty Plaza, 20th Floor, New York, NY 10006, USA

477 Williamstown Road, Port Melbourne, VIC 3207, Australia

314–321, 3rd Floor, Plot 3, Splendor Forum, Jasola District Centre, New Delhi – 110025, India

103 Penang Road, #05-06/07, Visioncrest Commercial, Singapore 238467

Cambridge University Press is part of Cambridge University Press & Assessment, a department of the University of Cambridge.

We share the University's mission to contribute to society through the pursuit of education, learning and research at the highest international levels of excellence.

www.cambridge.org
Information on this title: www.cambridge.org/9781009398107

DOI: 10.1017/9781009398091

© Cambridge University Press & Assessment 2025

This publication is in copyright. Subject to statutory exception and to the provisions of relevant collective licensing agreements, no reproduction of any part may take place without the written permission of Cambridge University Press & Assessment.

First published 2025

A catalogue record for this publication is available from the British Library

A Cataloging-in-Publication data record for this book is available from the Library of Congress

ISBN 978-1-009-39810-7 Hardback

Cambridge University Press & Assessment has no responsibility for the persistence or accuracy of URLs for external or third-party internet websites referred to in this publication and does not guarantee that any content on such websites is, or will remain, accurate or appropriate.

Contents

Preface	*page* vii
Note on the Edited Texts	ix
List of Abbreviations	x

SECTION I INTRODUCTION: THE ART OF THE LOVE LETTER

1	Art and Actuality: An Overview	3
2	Occasions; Ways and Means; Male and Female Voices	27
3	Clerics and Convents: *Epistolae duorum amantium*; Abelard and Heloise; Baudri of Bourgueil; Regensburg; Tegernsee; Söflingen	65

SECTION II FICTIONAL AND INSTRUCTIONAL MODELS

Text 1	Boncompagno da Signa: *Rota Veneris*	117
Text 2	London, British Library, Harley 3988. How to Pay Court in Anglo-French: A Model Epistle and a Model Conversation	185
Text 3	*The Parliament of Love*	223

SECTION III ACTUAL LETTERS (DRAFTS, COPIES, MISSIVES)

Text 4	The Norfolk Letters: The Abbot to the Nun	241
Text 5	Oxford, Corpus Christi, MS 154: Love Letter from a Woman	280
Text 6	The Armburgh Love Letters	286
Text 7	Pierre de Hagenbach and the Canoness at Remiremont	340
	The Council of Remiremont	428
	Conrad Pfettisheim's Account of Pierre de Hagenbach	454

Select Bibliography	469
Index	481

Preface

Our focus in this book is on art and actuality, on literary and historical instances of the love letter in the Middle Ages, and on the interchange between those two spheres. Section I offers an introductory overview in which different facets of the subject are considered with reference to a miscellany of different epistolary texts. Sections II and III address the topic through a series of editions of texts from, respectively, art and actuality. Section II is devoted to models, instructional and/or literary. Texts 1 and 2 represent material composed to serve as models for actual use: that is, guides to the art of writing (and talking) to the loved one. Text 1 was written c. 1200 in Latin, Text 2 in the early fifteenth century in French. Text 3 is a later-fifteenth-century poem in Middle English, which teaches by example in narrative form: it features a lover choosing to write a letter and gives the text of that letter. Section III presents, also in chronological order, different forms of actual letters. Texts 4 and 5 consist of what seem, pretty certainly, to be drafts of love letters, composed in England in French verse in the fourteenth century, by a man and a woman, respectively. Text 6 is a fifteenth-century series of verse love letters in which existing poems are adopted or adapted, and new ones composed, to serve as letters which were addressed to what appears to be a real woman, and copies of which were entered into the archives of the Armburgh family. Text 7 consists of a set of surviving missives (i.e. actual letters, as opposed to drafts or copies thereof) from a fifteenth-century canoness at the abbey of Remiremont to Pierre of Hagenbach; by way of contrast (in this case) between art and actuality, we add as an appendix to the series two further texts which give literary representations (a) of courtly love at Remiremont and (b) of Pierre himself.

The material is thus varied, as is the relationship between fact and literary art that it reflects. The interchange and overlap between those two categories are evident from the very fact that, in the case of many of the texts discussed in this book, there is or has been critical disagreement as to whether they belong in the one or the other.

We explore the medieval love letter essentially through an anthology of particular texts, presented here either in our own editions (in the case of works not otherwise easily accessible) or in relevant excerpts and quotations from existing editions. We provide side glosses or full translations in all cases. Though we concentrate on material of English provenance, we do not confine ourselves to England or English. Since England was part of a European culture in which Latin and later French were in effect *linguae francae* of scholarly and literary activity, we have included Latin and French texts produced inside and outside England. We give only intermittent attention to varieties of German (in which the love letter is already well served by scholars and critics).

Note on the Edited Texts

In the texts edited by ourselves, our procedures have been as follows. In all cases, abbreviations have been silently expanded. Word division has been normalized, and capitalization, punctuation and diacritics are editorial. In emendations, letters that have been added or altered are enclosed in square brackets. Manuscript practice with regard to the graphs <u> and <v> has been adapted to accord with modern usage. The symbols <ȝ> and <þ> have been modernized to <y> and <th> respectively in Texts 3 and 6, and <ȝ> and <ð> to <z> and <th> respectively in the German verse of Conrad's chronicle at pp. 454ff. Where relevant <i> has been transcribed <j>.

Abbreviations

AND	*Anglo–Norman Dictionary* (online: anglo-norman.net)
AP	*The Armburgh Papers*, ed. Carpenter
BD	Chaucer, *Book of the Duchess*
BL	British Library
BN	Bibliothèque Nationale
BSB, Clm	Bayerische Staatsbibliothek, Codices latini monacenses
CB	*Cent balades*
CBAD	*Cent balades d'amant et de dame*
CT	*Canterbury Tales*
DMF	*Dictionnaire du moyen français* (online: http://zeus.atilf.fr/dmf/)
EDA	*Epistolae duorum amantium*
EETS	Early English Text Society
LGW	Chaucer, *Legend of Good Women*
MED	*Middle English Dictionary* (online: https://quod.lib.umich.edu/m/middle-english-dictionary/dictionary)
PL	*Patrologia Latina*
SGGK	*Sir Gawain and the Green Knight*
STS	Scottish Text Society
TNA	The National Archives (London)
VCR	Victoria County Records
VD	Machaut, *Le livre du voir dit*

SECTION I

Introduction: The Art of the Love Letter

CHAPTER I

Art and Actuality: An Overview

Art in Letters

The letter has always formed an occasion on which ordinary people use language with more attention to formal correctness, euphony and rhetorical effect than they would normally. Hence the appearance of the various medieval *artes dictaminis*, manuals that provided rules and models for the 'art' of 'dictating' a letter (for actual writing was a skill often separate from verbal composition, and many 'authors' of letters did not actually personally inscribe them[1]). The earliest known *ars dictandi* (the *Breviarium de dictamine* by Alberic of Mont-Cassin) appeared about 1087, and the genre peaked over the following two centuries.[2] Few actual letters seem to have modelled themselves on the detailed division into five or more parts set out in many of these manuals (salutation, *captatio benevolentie*, narration, petition, conclusion[3]); but most of them adopted some form of the standard opening salutation and the closing formulae, as well as some of the other locutionary moves that provided the writer with a formal framework within which to unfold his own actual and personal concerns. We will encounter one such model epistolary (devoted to love letters), together with extracts from another, in Section II.

There was also another sense in which the English author of a letter was required to use language less naturally and with more studied art than in other contexts. Until well into the fifteenth century French remained the

---

[1] See pp. 53–9 below.
[2] On the *ars dictaminis*, see pp. 194–268 in James J. Murphy, *Rhetoric in the Middle Ages* (Berkeley, CA, 1974) and pp. 76–103 in his *Medieval Rhetoric: A Select Bibliography*, 2nd edn (Toronto, 1989). The treatises were often accompanied by illustrative letters (real or invented): for examples from England see W.A. Pantin, 'A Medieval Treatise on Letter-Writing, with Examples, from the Rylands Latin MS 394', *Bulletin of the John Rylands Library* 13 (1929), 326–82, and John Taylor, 'Letters and Letter Collections in England 1300–1420', *Nottingham Medieval Studies* 24 (1980) 57–70.
[3] See Catherine Moriarty, ed., *The Voice of the Middle Ages in Personal Letters 1100–1500* (New York, 1990), p. 16; for a summary overview of this and other divisions (and a claim, not entirely convincing, that Margery Brews's letter, given at p. 47 below, can be analysed in its entirety in those terms), see Martin Camargo, *The Middle English Verse Love Epistle* (Tübingen, 1991), pp. 8–13.

standard language for epistolary purposes. Though French had gradually given way to English in many other spheres, in this area it was still the accepted norm.[4] A *donait françois* [French primer] produced by John Barton at the beginning of the fifteenth century justifies its usefulness to his English countrymen by pointing not only to their need to communicate with their French neighbours across the Channel, but also to the facts that French was still the language of English law and of much polite literature and elegant ephemera, and that the gentry chose to write their letters to one another in French: 'les leys d'Engleterre pour le graigneur partie et aussi beaucoup de bones choses sont misez en Francois, et aussi bien pres touz les s[eigno]rs et toutez les dames en mesme roiaume d'Engleterre volentiers s'entrescrivent en romance'.[5] Hence French is the language used in the two fourteenth-century English letters that form Texts 4 and 5 (both draft love letters written on blank spaces in manuscripts devoted to church matters). As the fifteenth century progressed, French started to be replaced by English in letters, and the copies of love letters which form Text 6 (and which date from the second half of the fifteenth century and occur in a roll that otherwise preserves the business correspondence of the English gentleman Robert Armburgh) are in English, not French.

In rhetoric and language, letters were thus usually in any case artefacts rather than spontaneous and unstudied utterances. And yet further art was required of those who wrote love letters, which convention demanded should be in verse. Thus, among the model letters in the French epistolary of Text 2, the love letter alone is in verse. A similar assumption is made with regard to love letters in an epistolary compiled after the Middle Ages had given way to the early modern period, when letter-writing handbooks started to appear in English: William Fulwood, in his *The Enimie of Idlenesse: teaching the maner and stile howe to endite, compose, and write all sorts of Epistles and Letters* (London, 1568; 2nd edn 1578), added to the material derived from his French source a final chapter devoted to twelve model love letters, more than half of them in verse, 'a treatment accorded no other type of model letter in the collection', and in verse apparently of his own composition (see Camargo, pp. 161–2). The lover, then, was expected to aspire to something of the rhetorical and metrical skills of the poet, to

---

[4] 'In letter writing ... English was not an accepted language ... and letters written in England were either in French or in Latin': Herbert Schendl, 'Code-Choice and Code-Switching in Some Early Fifteenth-Century Letters', in *Middle English from Tongue to Text*, ed. Peter J. Lucas and Angela M. Lucas (Frankfurt, 2002), pp. 247–62 (p. 247). Cf. also J.A. Burrow, 'The Languages of Medieval England', in his *English Poets in the Late Middle Ages* (Farnham, 2012), pp. 7–28 (p. 20). For examples, see M. Dominica Legge, ed., *Anglo-Norman Letters and Petitions from All Souls Ms. 182* (Oxford, 1941).
[5] Quoted from the edition by E. Stengel, in 'Die ältesten Anleitungsschriften zur Erlernung der französischen Sprache', *Zeitschrift für Französische Sprache und Literatur* 1 (1879) 1–40 (p. 25).

master rhyme and to select from a repertoire of conceits. And all three of the four actual lovers whose letters figure in Section III obeyed this convention and wrote in verse – though the somewhat uneven command of metre and rhyme scheme indicates that the writers (two male, one female) are novices in this area.

The convention had a cultural context. Composing verses was one of the accomplishments acquired in a gentle or courtly education – one that was displayed to the female in the courting ritual as an act of wooing. It thus appears alongside the other social, cultural and martial skills acquired by the apprentice knight and gentleman in Chaucer's description of the young squire ('A lovyere and a lusty bacheler': *CT* I.80):

He koude songes make and wel endite,
Juste and eek daunce, and weel purtreye and write.   (95–6)

Young men were especially inclined to exercise their greater or lesser skill in this art when in love, which 'naturally', it was supposed, prompted one to 'sing' of or to one's beloved. For making verses is amongst the 'commands' of Love and figures as such among the instructions given by that god to the lover in the *Romaunt of the Rose*:

Among eke, for thy lady sake,
Songes and complayntes that thou make,
For that wol meven in hir herte,
Whan they reden of thy smerte.   (2325–8)[6]

Thus, in Baudet Herenc's *Parlement d'amour*, the lover is ordered by the god to compose a ballade, and being thus 'contraint D'Amours', does so, despite misgivings about his ability, 'pour obeïr a Amours'.[7] To this tradition of thought and behaviour belong Shakespeare's Orlando (who pins verses to Rosalind on 'every tree': *As You Like It* III.ii.9) and the three lovers of *Love's Labour's Lost*, who fall simultaneously both in love and into 'sonneting' – in obedience to 'Dan Cupid, Regent of love-rhymes' (III.i.165–71).

These rhymes were often courtship offerings to the mistress of the lover's heart, part of his efforts to please and impress her. And it seems the ladies were indeed both pleased and impressed by the tributary lyrics – for they evidently enjoyed the prestige of being the inspiration and dedicatee of

---

[6] Quoted from the Middle English translation, in *The Riverside Chaucer*, 3rd edn, ed. Larry D. Benson (Boston, MA, 1987). Quotations from Chaucerian texts other than *Troilus* are also all taken from *The Riverside Chaucer*.
[7] See lines 1–17 of the text as it appears (pp. 127–68) in *Alain Chartier: The Quarrel of the Belle dame sans mercy*, ed. and tr. Joan E. McRae (New York, 2004).

elegant poems and songs more than they feared the talk this might give rise to. Here is Heloise on Abelard's rhetorical gifts and the sex appeal he enjoyed as a result, both for her and for other women:

> You had ... two special gifts with which you could at once win the heart of any woman ... the gifts of composing verse and song ... You have left many songs composed in amatory verse and rhyme. Because of the very great sweetness of their words as much as of their tune, they have been repeated often and have kept your name continually on the lips of everyone ... more than anything this made women sigh for love of you. And as most of these songs told of our love, they soon made me widely known and roused the envy of many women against me ... Your letters came to me thick and fast, and your many songs put your Heloise on everyone's lips, so that every street and house resounded with my name. (Letter 2, pp. 137–41)[8]

Even speaking eloquently on the subject of love was a courtly refinement: it is one of the ingredients, for instance, in the ideal court scene (whose features will be so guessable that the narrator lists them only in negatives, as things he will not describe) in the Knight's Tale: 'Ne who moost felyngly spekech of loue' (*CT* I.2203). This too was a skill that women were assumed to find attractive. Criseyde, for instance, though she does not respond as positively as Pandarus had hoped to the news that a handsome young prince is in love with her, cannot resist asking him how he first discovered Troilus's love, and the question that follows is revealing:

> 'Kan he wel speke of loue', quod she, 'I preye?
> Tel me, for I the bet me shal purueye.' (II.503–4)[9]

Though she hastily covers the question, Pandarus's reaction ('Tho Pandarus a litel gan to smyle': II.505) shows that he has at last detected some interest, an interest he is prompt to feed by shamelessly inventing a little story to act as a frame for a suitably eloquent 'complaint' he fabricates for Troilus (II.523–39). It is Troilus's letter, however, that gives Criseyde her first occasion to form a judgement unmediated by Pandarus's embroidery of his loverly eloquence – though 'unmediated' needs some qualification: Pandarus had suggested the letter and given some anxious directions on certain faults

---

[8] Quotations from and translations of the text of the letters of Abelard and Heloise are from *The Letter Collection of Peter Abelard and Heloise*, ed. D. Luscombe, tr. Betty Radice, rev. D. Luscombe (Oxford, 2013).
[9] Quotations from *Troilus* are from *Chaucer: Troilus & Criseyde*, ed. B.A. Windeatt (London, 1984), where the English text is presented *en face* with that of its source (Boccaccio's *Il Filostrato*).

to avoid in the composition and advised a few tear stains to improve the effect (II.1002–43).

Pandarus is, in fact, sure that he knows how a romance should be conducted, and the fact that he sets store by a letter and how it is written is significant. For the letter occupied a particularly important place in this general area of courtship through rhetorical and/or metrical eloquence. Deservedly well known is the story created in the nineteenth century by Edmond Rostand about the seventeenth-century Cyrano de Bergerac, presented in Rostand's play as a man disfigured through possession of a huge nose, in love with a lady whom he wins for another man by penning the latter's letters for him – for what Cyrano lacks in romantic charm physically he more than makes up for in the rhetorical area. The story is a moving distillation of an idea with a long history: that women are likely to be particularly favourably impressed by skills in the articulation of amorous feeling. Troilus in fact pens his own letter, one not especially influenced by Pandarus's specifications. But Pandarus trusts him to have made a decent job of it. Obviously confident that Troilus's powers will have had their due effect, he snatches a private moment (when they meet again after she has read the letter) to put a question to her:

> 'Now, Nece myn, tel on', quod he, 'I seye,
> How liketh ʒow the lettre that ʒe woot?
> Kan he ther-on? for by trouthe, I not.'
>
> Therwith al rosy hewed tho wex she,
> And gan to homme and seyde, 'so I trowe'.   (II.1195–9)

Criseyde is obviously trying to sound casual, but her blush (like the earlier eagerness she had attempted to cover up) betrays an interest she is embarrassed to admit.

The verse often used in a lover's letter is likewise an indication of the role of verbal art in courtship. However affectionately wives and husbands may write to each other, they do not use verse. In the French model epistolary of Text 2, the lover writes in verse, but the husband in prose – for the latter is not courting. In the *Ancrene Wisse* [guidance for anchoresses], written about 1200, there is a witty allegorical representation of God as the 'wooer' of man's soul: the Old Testament is represented as the time in which he wooed through *sonden* [messengers] and through *leattres isealet* [closed or sealed letters] – a reference to the supposed concealed references to Jesus in the Old Testament – those 'closed' letters then being replaced, when the lover came in person, by the *leattres iopnet* [open letters, letters patent] of the New Testament, written 'in His own blood' and forming '*saluz* to his leofmon [sweetheart] – *luue gretunge* forte *wohin* [woo] hire wiþ & hire luue wealden [possess]'.[10] There is certainly here a reference to the letter as a form of courtship, and probably to the verse letter in particular, for there existed at the time of this text an Anglo-Norman epistolary verse form called the *salut d'amor* [love greeting]: see below.[11]

Letters in Art

Literary art had already itself borrowed from actuality in the area of the letter. Ovid's *Heroides* (a collection of imagined verse letters from legendary women lovers: Penelope to Ulysses, Dido to Aeneas, etc.) had set a classical precedent. Love letters in Latin verse were followed by the emergence of the love letter as a recognizable lyric genre in the Provençal *salutz* and the French and Anglo-Norman *saluts d'amor*, named from the formal 'salutation' to its addressee with which every letter began.[12] Chaucer's *Troilus* is a particularly significant text with regard to the history of the literary love letter in English verse, for the poem was widely known, admired and imitated in the generations following his death. The two sets of letters in *Troilus* belong to two of the most common categories of love letter: the initial declaration of love and the letter occasioned by geographical separation – and we will encounter in Chapter 2 other examples of both types. In his inclusion of these letters, Chaucer was following his source, Boccaccio's *Il Filostrato*, but with some adaptations of his own. He gives only in reported speech the content of the exchange of letters (of which Boccaccio gives the actual texts) that occurs at the beginning of the relationship, when both lovers are still resident in Troy (II.1065–85, 1218–25; cf. *Filostrato* II.96–106, 121–7). He follows Boccaccio in giving the text of the letter Troilus later writes to Criseyde when she has left Troy (V.1317–1421; *Filostrato* VII.52–75), but matches this *Litera Troili* with the text of a *Litera Criseydis* (V.1590–1631) for which there is no equivalent in Boccaccio (though *Filostrato* VIII.5 hints at letters written by her to Troilus), thus producing the epistolary duet which we will notice elsewhere – the letter and its response, in this case the painful earnest of Troilus's letter and the

---

[10] *Ancrene Wisse*, ed. Bella Millett, 2 vols, EETS OS 325, 326 (2005–6), Part 7.2/61–6 (emphasis added).
[11] The word *salut* is not recorded as referring to the verse form in the *MED*, where the other instances are all post-1400 (and so post-Anglo-Norman) or in medieval French (from which *MED* derives it). The *Ancrene Wisse* reference is 200 years earlier and probably reflects Anglo-Norman usage, in which the word does figure in that sense: cf. 'Si fesei[e] les serventeis, Chaunceunettes, rymes, saluz Entre les drues e les druz' (cited by the *AND* from *S Edm* 6).
[12] For examples, see Ernstpeter Ruhe, *De Amasio ad Amasiam: Zur Gattungsgeschichte des mittelalterlichen Liebesbriefes* (Munich, 1975), pp. 22–50, 81–7, 91–7 (Latin), pp. 97–119, 161–70, 208–15 (Provençal), pp. 215–53, 271–4 (French). On Latin verse letters, see further Ch. 3 below.

equally but differently painful prevarications of Criseyde's. And with that latter pair of letters Chaucer produced the first literary love letters to appear in English – though they occupy this position by virtue of the licence of art rather than by reflection of reality, for, of course, in his own late fourteenth century, these letters would have been in French – as is conceded by the extra-metrical subscriptions 'Le vostre T' and 'La vostre C' (V.1421, 1631), which indicate the French language which is to be assumed and from which his readers would be familiar with the epistolary formulae that the lovers use and adapt.[13]

A comprehensive and detailed history of the love epistle as a literary form over the two centuries following the *Troilus* is provided by Martin Camargo (see n. 3 above). Between 1400 and 1568, it became in fact the 'dominant form of the late Middle English love lyric' (Camargo, p. 127). A particularly fine example occurs in the macaronic *De amico ad amicam*, a poem written in alternating French, English and Latin lines, and one which came complete with a *responsio* from the *amica* addressed.[14] Subsequent English examples abound, occurring notably in anthologies connected with particular households and places, for instance, the commonplace book of the Cheshire gentleman poet Humfrey Newton, the collections associated with the Findern and Welles families of, respectively, Derbyshire and Staffordshire, the compilation of love poems made in Scotland by the Edinburgh merchant George Bannatyne, as well as among the so-called 'Suffolk' love poems and in more isolated pieces by known or anonymous poets.[15]

---

[13] These subscriptions do not appear in all manuscripts (though they are unlikely to be scribal): see the textual apparatus in the edition by Windeatt. On the letters and their conformity with prevailing epistolary use, see Norman Davis, 'The *Litera Troili* and English Letters', *RES* 16 (1965) 233–44.
[14] For the most recent edition of this pair of poems see pp. 194–7 in Thomas Duncan, ed., *Medieval English Lyrics and Carols* (Cambridge, 2013).
[15] See Camargo, *The Middle English Verse Love Epistle*, chs. 4 and 5 (pp. 87–163), especially the summary list at pp. 127–8. For texts of love epistles in the collections cited, see R.H. Robbins, 'The Poems of Humfrey Newton, Esquire, 1466–1536', *PMLA* 65 (1950) 249–81, poems II–IV, VII–IX, XI–XV, XVII–XVIII; *The Welles Anthology: MS Rawlinson C.813*, ed. Sharon L. Jansen and Kathleen H. Jordan (Binghamton, NY, 1991), poems 3–5, 11, 13–16, 22, 32–4, 38, 40, 42, 44–7, 49, 53–6, 59; *The Bannatyne Manuscript*, ed. W. Tod Ritchie, 4 vols, STS, 3rd ser., 5, 22–3, 26 (1928–34), 'ballattis of lufe' (vol. 3), poems 253, 255, 259, 264, 266, 267, 287, 294–7, 304–5, 387 (many in ballade form, epistle and ballade-with-envoy being virtually indistinguishable in this collection); *The 'Suffolk' Poems: An Edition of the Love Lyrics in Fairfax 16 Attributed to William de la Pole*, ed. J.P.M. Jansen (Groningen, 1989), poems 6, 14, 17; and items 14 and 31 from the Findern manuscript (see Text 3, pp. 227–38 below). The Welles and Suffolk collections also include poems written in the sister form of the ballade (see pp. 10–12). On the so-called Findern manuscript – an anthology consisting largely of love lyrics (copies and excerpts as well as apparently unique and local compositions) – and its emanation from a south Derbyshire household (only perhaps that of the Findern family), see Text 3, p. 223 below; and on Humfrey Welles and the occurrence of identifiable local persons and places in some items (not the love poems) in the manuscript associated with him, see Edward Wilson, 'Local Habitations and Names in MS Rawlinson C 813', *RES* 41 (1990) 12–44.

Art from Actuality

The autobiographical basis of *Le livre du voir dit*, written in the 1360s by the French poet Machaut, is specifically asserted both in the title (which distinguishes the work from his other first-person narrative *dits* by pointing to the *voir* [true] story it contains) and within the text, which reproduces (doubtless with some editing and polishing) the prose letters exchanged between himself and a young girl called Péronne (the name apparently yielded by a cryptic encoding of it in the rondeau following Letter 35), letters embedded in a connecting (and embroidering) verse narrative and accompanied (with added poems) by verses exchanged between the pair.[16] Machaut here gives rhetorical full dress, complete with dream sequences and personifications, to a body of letters arising from a real liaison. A personal tune was later given similar literary orchestration by Charles d'Orléans (taken prisoner by the English at the battle of Agincourt in 1415), who, while in detention in England, wrote a series of ballades to his absent wife Bonne, and on his grief at her death – a series he later translated into English, adding a second sequence of ballades addressed to a new lady he describes himself as having fallen in love with.[17] Charles's was in fact one of a number of ballade sequences which appeared over the three generations from the late fourteenth to the mid-fifteenth century.[18] He had been preceded by Gower, who wrote in French a sequence of fifty love ballades, and by Christine de Pisan, who later twice went fifty better to produce two sequences, the second of which, *Cent balades d'amant et de dame*, traces a love affair through to its tragic close in the desertion of the lady, a sad story that had also formed the theme of the opening sequence of poems in her earlier *Cent balades*.

Ballades were often in effect a form of verse love letter.[19] This was not only because they addressed the beloved in the second person. In the tradition of love verse, second-person address is in itself not uncommon, and can occur in a number of different verse types. But in most cases, the address is rhetorical: the reader is not required to assume or imagine that the poem was actually presented to the mistress addressed. Conversely (since the language of love was often surprisingly closely imitated in courtly

---

[16] References to the poem are from *Guillaume de Machaut: le livre dou voir dit*, ed. Daniel Leech-Wilkinson, tr. R. Barton Palmer (New York, 1998).

[17] Charles's French poems are cited from *The Poetry of Charles d'Orléans and His Circle*, ed. John Fox and Mary-Jo Arn (Tempe, AZ, 2010), and the English versions of them (and his other English poems) from *Fortunes Stabilnes: Charles of Orléans's English Book of Love*, ed. Mary-Jo Arn (Binghamton, NY, 1994).

[18] On the ballade sequence or cycle, see Helen Louise Cohen, *The Ballade* (New York, 1915), pp. 109–17 (French) and 223 (English).

[19] The close connection between the amorous ballade and the verse love epistle is also remarked on by Camargo (*The Middle English Verse Love Epistle*, p. 36).

compliment from male to female), some poems addressed to named women are or may be mere gallant compliments rather than serious expressions of love, even though it is likely that they were meant to be presented to the lady so celebrated. Chaucer's ballade 'To Rosemounde' would seem to be a poem of this type, since the refrain 'Though ye to me ne do no daliaunce' (which follows assertions that the mere sight of her is a balm, it is happiness enough to love her, and in all events the poet will ever be her thrall) seems designed tactfully to indicate that Rosamund is not being asked to respond (which the poem, notably and unusually, never begs her to do), and to compliment its addressee without embarrassing her. Her name (used at line 15) would not in any case be revealed if there were any real affair (see below, pp. 49–50).

But the amorous ballade resembled the epistle, not only in being (frequently) a second-person address, but also in being at least represented and imagined as actually delivered. One might note the verb used with reference to the ballade in Christine's ironic praise of a carpet knight (*CB* LVIII) whose valour consists in such things as *composing* virelays ('faire virelais': 23) and *delivering* ballades ('baladez baillier': 6).[20] As a metre, the ballade consists of the same rhymes carried through three stanzas with a refrain, followed (in the 'classic' ballade) by an 'envoy' in which the poem is directed to a particular person. But the envoy may be used differently and in fact does not always occur, for poets treated it as an optional alternative to an earlier envoy-less version of the form.[21] Love ballades, in fact, differ considerably in the degree to which they represent themselves – in the poem and envoy, if there is one – as to be delivered, or merely as poems addressed in a looser way to the beloved, if indeed they are addressed to him/her at all, as opposed to being simply poems expressing the feelings of the lover-poet. Their closeness to letters thus varies. In Gower's collection, the envoy in which the poems always terminate regularly acts to 'send' the poem to its destined addressee through such formulations as 'Ceo dit envoie a vous, ma dame' (XXIII) or 'Va t'en, balade, u jeo t'envoierai' (XXXVI). The poems are therefore virtually indistinguishable in form from verse epistles, and indeed 'ceo lettre' figures frequently among the various other terms (*balade, escript, dit, supplicacioun,* for instance) used in self-references.[22]

[20] Quotations are from *Œuvres poétiques de Christine de Pisan*, ed. Maurice Roy, 3 vols (Paris, 1886), vol. 1 (*Cent balades*) and vol. 3 (*Cent balades d'amant et de dame*).
[21] Champion remarks that several of the ballades by Charles d'Orléans lack envoys and that Christine de Pisan had also often favoured 'ce type archaïque dépourvu d'envoi': Charles d'Orléans, *Poésies*, ed. Pierre Champion, 2 vols (Paris, 1971), vol. 1, p. xxxiv.
[22] See II.25, III.23, IV.24, XV.26, XVIII.21, XX.25, XXII.27, XXVII.23, XXXVIII.24, XXXIX.26, XLIV.23. References are from *The Complete Works of John Gower: The French Works*, ed. G.C. Macaulay (Oxford, 1899). *John Gower: The French Balades*, ed. R.F. Yeager (Kalamazoo, MI, 2011) provides an edition with facing translation.

By contrast, Christine's *Cent balades* and the poems of Charles d'Orléans occasionally use other metres and forms, do not all take the form of second-person address to the beloved and do not always consistently assume or maintain the fiction of a missive. Both sequences thus move between meditation and address. Christine's starts by tracing out the same framing narrative as is formed by Charles's French and English ballade sequences – a bereavement that prompts a renunciation of love (a resolve no more 'de faire ami, ne d'amer', *CB* XIX.24; cf. the refrain to Charles's Ballade 76 'Forwhi y am fulle ferre from that purpos'), followed by a second love affair, which ends in Christine's case in the lover losing interest. The two sequences have some historical as well as thematic connection, for Christine belonged to 'le cercle de ménestrels, de musiciens, de rimeurs qui trouvèrent chez Louis d'Orléans [Charles's father] un protecteur',[23] and her *Cent balades* may well have been one of the (conscious or unconscious) models that Charles had for producing ballade sequences that versified personal romantic experience in a form that gave it universal significance.

For the bereavement each refers to is certainly historical, and the subsequent romantic entanglement almost certain in Charles's case, and not improbable in Christine's. Charles's French sequence actually has implicit reference to the autobiographical fact of the death of his wife, and the ballades of his English sequence are addressed to a lady also represented as real. Christine's ballades on the same situation do not have the same pervasive autobiographical *reference*, but they do have an at least partial autobiographical *basis*. Christine was widowed at the age of only twenty-five and left to make her own way in the world as best she could (which she did partly through her pen), and the opening poems in the *Cent balades* certainly refer to this real-life bereavement. As to the subsequent poems, she denies in Ballade L what she claims is an assumption by some that the fact of her writing poems on love (a subject she has chosen because it is one accessible and agreeable to all: 11–13) indicates that she must be in love (which she would be happy to admit, were it true: 19–21). But the specific places and lengths of time that are mentioned in connection with the first lover (XXV.2–4, XXV.6, XXXVIII.10–11, XLVI.4) render that affair more individualized than what emerges from the ballades that follow (which deal with a variety of different love-related subjects, without suggesting any particular narrative or person), and it is difficult to believe that some actuality (observed or undergone) does not underlie it (and perhaps parts of the *Cent balades d'amant et de dame*), though the rest of the sequence is not such as to raise suspicions of that nature. Christine's biographer,

---

[23] Charles d'Orléans, *Poésies*, ed. Champion, vol. 1, p. xxiii.

Charity Canon Willard, sees the sequence as reflecting only the 'trials of widowhood' and 'solitude' that she underwent, a subject Christine certainly did treat elsewhere in her verse as well as in the *Cent balades*: see Rondeau III ('I am a widow lone, in black arrayed').[24] Canon Willard at no point even canvasses the possibility that the liaisons depicted as following the bereavement might also reflect biographical facts. But she is perhaps too ready to rule out (from the almost inevitable lack of hard evidence to the contrary) what is after all not unlikely: that a woman widowed at the age of twenty-five should have had subsequent romantic attachments. Some of Christine's depictions of sorrow and desertion in love, that is, may have been born of painful experience. And Canon Willard's categoric assumption of a virtuous widow, invariably opposed from the first, in practice and in theory, to love outside marriage, is a position that, as we will see, certainly leads to an under-nuanced interpretation of the *Cent balades d'amant et de dame*.[25]

Art for Appropriation

Machaut, like Christine, sought and found wealthy patrons for a prolific output, and both he and Charles involved themselves personally and systematically in the manuscript records of their oeuvre. In these senses, all three were professionals using personal history in the service of an art of which they were notably self-conscious.[26] But the traffic between private experience and professional art could travel in the other direction: for, conversely, writers often assumed readers who might make use of the texts in their own private lives. Love-poets, that is, seem to have been well aware of the porous nature of the boundary between love affairs on and off the page and, indeed, to have advertised the possible relevance of their verse to readers who might wish to appropriate it in order to further their own *amours*. Gower provided marginal notes (appearing beside the end of Balade V and the beginning of Balade VI) to indicate which of his *Cinkante Balades* were relevant to any lover and which were appropriate only to those aiming at marriage: 'Les balades d'amont jesqes enci sont fait especialement pour ceaux q'attendont lours amours par droite mariage' [the ballades up to this point have been composed particularly for those who await fulfilment of

---

[24] *Œuvres poétiques*, ed. Roy, vol. 1, pp. 148–9; the translation is from Charity Cannon Willard, *Christine de Pizan: Her Life and Works* (New York, 1984), p. 57
[25] See Ch. 2, n. 23, below.
[26] The autobiographical element in sequences such as these, and that in the Devonshire manuscript referred to at p. 17 below, is a complex and controversial matter which we intend to discuss more fully in a separate publication.

their love by way of rightful marriage]; 'Les balades d'ici jesqes au fin du livere sont universeles a tout le monde, selonc les propretés et les condicions des Amantz, qui sont diversement travailez en la fortune d'amour' [the ballades from this point to the end of the book are of universal application, describing the various properties and situations of lovers and the different fortunes of love]. And Gower was careful to include both (a) a sequence of ballades (XXXII–XXXVII) specific to the major festivals which lovers were supposed to mark (New Year, Valentine's Day, the advent of May), where the reader-lover could choose between alternative versions expressive of joy or frustration, according to his circumstances ('selonc ... la fortune d'amour'), and (b) to include some spoken in a woman's voice (XLI–XLIV, XLVI), which, again, offer alternative portrayals of a woman happy in a true lover or reviling a false one. He was apparently trying to make the sequence as usably relevant as possible to the different occasions, genders, situations and intentions (marital or otherwise) of his readers, so that all could find appropriate songs to sing (i.e. verses to send).

When Chaucer, in the proem to his *Troilus*, disclaims any personal amorous hopes or ambitions, he adds that he is nevertheless only too glad to think that others may derive some personal real-life benefit from his verse:

Bot natheles, if this may don gladnesse
To any louere and his cause auaille,
Haue he my thonk, and myn be this trauaille.   (I.19–21)

The lines replace Boccaccio's declaration to his lady that, since his love is his muse, though the effort is his, any credit arising from it should be hers ('Tuo sia l'onore e mio si sia l'affanno, s'e' detti alcuna laude acquisteranno' [yours be the honour and mine be the toil, if the writings acquire any praise]: I.5). Chaucer uses his proem to relate the audience both to himself and to the matter, rather than using it, as Boccaccio does, to point to the relation between himself and his beloved that the narrative mirrors. In this new context, 'Haue he my thonk' probably transfers to the putative reader-lover the appreciative credit due to any rhetoric he may borrow from the poem, the phrase 'and his cause auaille' reminding us that love is a *suit* – which, like other suits pursued in the courts or by petition, may stand or fall by how well the suitor pleads it. And the lover who needs to convince his lady of his passion and devotion, in order to move her to respond favourably, may derive, through *Troilus*, some assistance in prosecuting his case or cause. The poem inscribes its sympathetic readiness to be helpful into the person of Pandarus, ever full of plans, of wisdom as to what may 'further' a lover's cause and advice as to how to proceed: how, for instance,

Art and Actuality 15

to plead one's suit by letter (II.1003–29) or in person (II.1368–70). From his sometimes comically practical wisdom on tactics, the lover might learn something, if only to ponder the whole question of the role of strategy and rhetoric in this area. More relevant, however, is the verse in which Troilus's feelings are expressed, which may provide, as well as the psychological solace for another lover of articulation of his own feelings, useful tropes, turns of phrase, or wholesale reusable lines or stanzas, which may 'his cause auaille' when that other lover pleads it. It is certainly the case that *Troilus* became the *lingua franca* of love, in which context it was widely imitated and echoed.[27]

> Go, litill bill, with all humblis
>   vnto my lady, of womanhede þe floure,
> And saie hire howe newe troiles lithe in distreʒ,
>   All-onely for hire sake and in mortall langoure;
>   And if sche wot nat whoo it is, bute stonde in erore,
>   Say it is hire olde louer þat loueth hire so fre, trewe,
>   hir louynge a-lone – not schanginge for no newe.[28]

Thus runs the envoy to one fifteenth-century love lyric, written in the same rhyme-royal stanza as *Troilus*, echoing the envoy Chaucer had used (*Troilus* V.1786: 'Go litel boke, go, litel myn tragedye'), and mimicking the typical posture and language associated with Chaucer's often prostrate and *wo*ful hero, the *trewe* lover of whom the writer claims to be a reincarnation – the 'newe troiles' so often found in those whose causes Chaucer had hoped his poem might 'auaile'.

One of Charles d'Orléans's *chansons* (Rondeau 82: 'Je suis mieulx pris que par le doy' [I am more securely seized than by the finger]) was recorded by him as written 'pour Estampes' (the Compte de Neves, a friend of his), and Charles, by his own account, regularly wrote love verse on others' behalf (see *Fortunes Stabilnes* 4650–735) – thus providing very specific examples of the poet making over to another any real-life goodwill or *thonk* accruing from his *trauaille* in amorous eloquence. The 'I' of love lyrics is a poetic or archetypal 'I' that in fact suggests and invites

---

[27] For a full discussion and extensive bibliography of the afterlife of *Troilus*, see 'Imitation and Allusion, c.1385–1700', in Barry Windeatt, *Oxford Guides to Chaucer: Troilus and Criseyde*, revised edn (Oxford, 1995), and the studies cited by Camargo (*The Middle English Verse Love Epistle*, p. 137, n. 21), which include John Stevens, *Music and Poetry in the Early Tudor Court* (London, 1961), pp. 213–14 and R. H. Robbins, 'The Lyrics', in *Companion to Chaucer Studies*, ed. Beryl Rowland (New York and London, 1979), pp. 380–402 (pp. 382–3).
[28] Lyric no. 190, final stanza, in Rossell Hope Robbins, ed., *Secular Lyrics of the XIVth and XVth Centuries*, 2nd edn (Oxford, 1955); for other examples of poets comparing themselves explicitly with Troilus, see Windeatt, *Oxford Guides to Chaucer*, pp. 371–2.

readerly application to, or writerly appropriation by, any actual empirical 'I'.[29] In the absence of particularizing details, the sentiments can be attributed to or appropriated by any other voice. And those who responded to the prevailing rule or instinct to 'sing' or versify their love might simply send an existing poem – as (with an added quatrain of his own composition: see Text 6, 1.31–4) did Robert Armburgh (if he wrote the poems in the Armburgh Roll) in the case of the fine macaronic poem (see above: p. 9) that seems to have been quite widely known and admired, since it is preserved in two manuscripts (Cambridge University Library, Gg.4.27 fols. 10^v–11^r and London, BL, Harley 3362, fols. 90^v–91^r) – and, as Camargo points out, Middle English lyrics do not commonly appear in more than one copy.[30] For, if one has a cause, it may be prudent to avail oneself of the services of an expert pleader – and poets (especially non-aristocratic ones) were regarded, and regarded themselves, as the scribes or professional exponents (rather than the principals) of amorous *sentiment*.[31] The aim of such borrowings was not to deceive the addressee, who might often recognize the verse as an allusion or a quotation, but to present the beloved with a verbal bouquet of rhetorical flowers. The vocabulary, rhymes and conceits popularized by certain widely circulated poems such as *Troilus* (and perhaps also the Lydgate anthology in London, BL, Sloane 1212[32]) were also in their way looser 'quotes', or roles in which the addressee was expected to recognize a 'new Troilus'. Borrowings from existing art were themselves a form of art, as one extreme example from the Söflingen Letters (1467–84) may illustrate. These letters were written to the Poor Clares of Söflingen (often from the male clerics who were their spiritual 'friends'), and they include an ingeniously derivative love (or at least, loving) letter that is effectively a cento of quotations from a German translation of Piccolomini's prose tale *Euryalus et Lucretia* (1444).[33]

Imitating models devised for and used in actual letters, the verse love letter became in many other ways a site in which art and actuality, reading and writing, the reception and practice of the art could merge. At the height of the popularity of the genre (c. 1500), 'a large part of the audience was engaged in producing as well as reading love epistles', as Camargo points

---

[29] On these two functions of the first-person pronoun, see the seminal article by Leo Spitzer, 'Note on the Poetic and Empirical "I" in Medieval Authors', *Traditio* 4 (1946) 414–22.
[30] See Camargo, *The Middle English Verse Love Epistle*, p. 46, n. 69 (citing J. Boffey, *Manuscripts of English Courtly Love Lyrics* (Cambridge, 1985), pp. 88–9).
[31] See Daniel Poirion, *Le poète et le prince: l'évolution du lyrisme Courtois de Guillaume de Machaut à Charles d'Orléans* (Paris, 1965), pp. 196–9.
[32] See Boffey, *Manuscripts*, p. 14, n. 23.
[33] See Ch. 3, pp. 110–13 below. See also Bert Roest, *Order and Disorder: The Poor Clares* (Leiden, 2013), pp. 193, 233, 275, 315–16.

Art and Actuality 17

out, commenting also on how often the poems show their writers borrowing details and lines from one another and reworking existing material (see Camargo, pp. 129, 136–7). In the Welles anthology, for instance, there is extensive borrowing from Stephen Hawes in items 13–16 and 56 and reuse of a stanza from Lydgate in item 34, while item 38 is entirely made up of recycled material from Chaucer's *Troilus* and item 49 includes a quatrain found elsewhere.[34] Those who collected verse epistles might write their own, and might actualize or personalize sender or addressee: Bannatyne reproduced examples from others (who are sometimes named[35]), including some metrically and rhetorically highly accomplished and artful ones by Scott, but a cryptic signature reveals at least one of them to be probably of his own composition ('Causs Me no*ᵗ ban* þat evir I the indyte *Na tyne* my travel' (287.69–70, emphasis added, with 'Bannatyne' written in the margin in a later hand) – though it includes passages borrowed from Chaucer: lines 33–7, 'No thing of ryᵗ I ask my lady fair … of grace and noᵗ of ryᵗ I craif', are from the Franklin's Tale, *CT* V.1324–6, and lines 41–5, 'And gif þat I be fund to ȝow vntrew / Wilful heichty or … Ielouss vnkind or chengeing for ane new / a vane wantour rebelling to ȝour seruyiss / as tratoʳ is fals', are equally clearly borrowed from *Parliament of Fowls* 428–30 and 456–8. A little later, Humfrey Newton similarly entered into his commonplace book verse love letters that included some which spelled out, acronymically, the names of himself, his wife Elena and (presumably) friends called 'Margaret' and 'Brian'.[36] An interactive mixture of art past and/or public and sharply particularized present is a striking feature of the later Devonshire Manuscript, which was compiled by three gentlewomen attendants of Anne Boleyn (Mary Shelton, Mary Fitzroy and Lady Margaret Douglas). The collection is dominated by poems by Wyatt, but it also includes love poems written by Lord Thomas Howard that almost certainly refer to his love for Lady Margaret (fols. 44ʳ–47ᵛ), whom he married, and also a sequence of poems written by and to one another while the pair were in separate prison rooms as a consequence of their love and marriage (fols. 26ʳ–30ʳ), as well as a poem particularized by acrostic *to* Mary Shelton (fols. 6ᵛ–7ᵛ), verse *by* Lady Margaret (fol. 88ʳ), some poems by less well-known and more amateur contemporaries of Wyatt, and extracts from Chaucerian verse used in an exceptionally interesting way (to reflect personal circumstances, at fols. 29ᵛ–30ʳ and 89ᵛ–92ʳ) to orchestrate a debate between different views of love.[37]

[34] See the editors' headnotes to these poems.
[35] 'ffinis steill' (294), 'q[uod] scott' (295, 296), 'ffinis q[uod] king hary stewart' (305).
[36] Newton poems III, IV, VII, VIII and IX.
[37] References are to the transcription of the manuscript in *A Social Edition of the Devonshire Manuscript (BL MS Add 17,492)*, ed. Raymond Siemens, Karin Armstrong and Constance Crompton (Toronto, 2015), available online at http://en.wikibooks.org/wiki/The Devonshire Manuscript.

Art or Actuality: Arguable or Disputed Cases

Overlap between reality and art is so pronounced a feature of the love letter that it can sometimes be difficult to know whether one is dealing with a copy or draft of an 'actual' communication or an 'artful' and archetypal one.[38] The presence or absence of particularizing details that suggest a specific rather than a representative case is, of course, the most obvious deciding factor. But, since anything that might identify the sender or addressee was avoided in real love letters (see Chapter 2 below, pp. 49–50), and since artful ones aimed for general applicability, there can be difficult cases. Thus in our Text 5, we have interpreted the few lines of French verse that take the form of a love letter found in a flyleaf of Oxford, Corpus Christi, MS 154 (containing material relating to Llanthony Priory in Gloucester) as relating to a 'real' affair, a draft for an actual letter, as the lack of metrical polish and a certain cryptic unease would make it read awkwardly as 'art'.

But the evidence points in a different direction in the case of another little poem scrawled, in a hand later than that of the other contents, on the flyleaf of a manuscript of religious works (London, BL, Royal 6.B.ix):[39]

> Ryht godely, fressh flour of womanhode,
>   My lyues Ioy, myn hertes plesance,
> Example of trouth and rote of godelyhode,
>   And verayly my lyues sustenance –
> And, with al þe hool, feythful obeisance
>   That seruant can thenk or deuyse,
> To you þat haue myn herte in gouernance,
>   Me recomande in all my best wyse.
>   Quod H. Bowesper

The last line indicates the stanza was thought of as formally a letter, and the sentiment, language and rhymes are close to some in the 'actual' fifteenth-century love letters in the Armburgh Roll (see for instance Text 6, 4A.5–6, 9; 4B.1–2; 5B.5–7, 13–16) – though those latter, even when not demonstrably using and adapting existing poems, are often indebted to stand-

---

[38] In the case of actual missives (letters that were in fact sent and received), there will of course be codicological evidence of their actuality: for examples see Ch. 2, pp. 28 and 31 and Text 7 below, and the instances discussed and illustrated in Jürgen Schulz-Grobert, *Deutsche Liebesbriefe in spätmittelalterlichen Handschriften* (Tübingen, 1993), pp. 24–6, 105–15, 128–31.

[39] The poem is assumed to refer to the Virgin Mary by Carleton Brown, who includes it (no. 40) in his edition of *Religious Lyrics of the XVth Century* (Oxford, 1939). We have adopted the corrections made (from the manuscript) by Camargo (*The Middle English Verse Love Epistle*, p. 144) to what Brown misread as 'gvuernance' (line 7) and 'recemande' (line 8).

Art and Actuality

ard literary conceits and topoi.[40] One might thus conclude that this, too, was a draft for a love letter, were it not for the concluding *quod* formula. 'Quod X' was used to indicate attribution to an author or to the scribe who copied out existing text. A number of poems in the Bannatyne manuscript, for instance, conclude in an ascription that takes the form of 'q[uod] chausseir' (283), 'q bannatyne' (284), 'q steill' (289), etc. In the Findern manuscript the formula regularly indicates the scribe who copied out the entry in question. The Langland scribe John Cok used it, not only after a concluding *amen* to indicate his own penmanship of the material copied, but also to indicate quoted material (from Isidore), which he adds to Langland's paraphrase of it and signals the insertion by 'quod Iohannes Cok'.[41] Whether 'Quod H. Bowesper' indicates attribution to or inscription by Bowesper, the formula almost certainly identifies the lines as citation of existing material. But the very fact that such verses occur as manuscript doodles and pen trials is itself significant evidence as to the familiarity most people had with various poems taking the form of amorous address, poems they could quote from memory.

Some of the poems occurring, sometimes as 'fillers', in the Findern manuscript possibly (but disputably) refer to actual situations (see Text 3, pp. 225–7 below). There are other cases in which there is disagreement rather than doubt: each reader makes a fairly confident assumption as to the (non-)actuality of a given epistolary text, on which, however, some or most others may hold a contrary view. Individual critics have, for instance, questioned the authenticity of the letters of Abelard and Heloise, and one or two have argued that the *Epistolae duorum amantium*, written at about the same time, were not actual letters – though it has in each case been demonstrated that the case for authenticity is stronger than for non-authenticity.[42] Conversely, in the course of a useful article establishing the number of and divisions between lyrics (formerly listed as one item) in a fifteenth-century manuscript, Linne Mooney comes to the conclusion that one of these poems (a love epistle in a woman's voice) is 'only explicable in a historical, and therefore autobiographical, context', a hypothesis she bas-

---

[40] The love letter that forms item 14 in the 'Suffolk' poems, a web of amorous clichés and formulae, also finds echoes in some of the verse in the Armburgh Roll (Text 6): see, for example, 3.46, 4A.25–36, 4B.1–7, 5C.13–22.
[41] See pp. 45 and 49 in Simon Horobin, 'John Cok and His Copy of *Piers Plowman*', *Yearbook of Langland Studies* 27 (2013) 45–59.
[42] See John Marenbon's evaluation of the debates over the authenticity of the Abelard–Heloise letters at pp. 19–33, 'Authenticity Revisited', in *Listening to Heloise: The Voice of a Twelfth-Century Woman*, ed. Bonnie Wheeler (New York, 2000), and the comments by Sylvain Piron at pp. 185–99 and 213–18 in his *Lettres des deux amants* (Paris, 2005), in which the Latin text of the *Epistolae* is preceded by a translation into modern French. The standard edition of the *Epistolae* is by E. Könsgen (Leiden, 1974). Both texts are discussed in Ch. 3 below (pp. 65–85).

es on grounds that we find insufficient to support it.[43] The epistle purports to be answering another received from the lover, responding to his request for a meeting (8–14) and to his fear of being made a fool of and incurring 'mokry' (71–2). The lady declares her love, but is firmly uncooperative: she will not consent to any meeting that might bring dishonour or scandal, can offer no hope of one in the foreseeable future, and so can only urge on him the steadfast endurance of delays and difficulties that is the mark of the true and faithful lover (15–49). One of the *Carmina Burana* (70: 'Estatis florigero tempore') presents a not dissimilar dialogue between a passionate male and a woman who, fearful of scandal, enjoins upon him constancy and patience. While Mooney finds the poem 'remarkable in so uniquely expressing a woman's point of view of *derne* love' (p. 243), the female voice and perspective had a tradition of its own (see pp. 59–62 below), with which this poem is in broad conformity. It is certainly not unique in that respect. Nor do the references to specific points raised in a letter to which the present one responds necessarily indicate any underlying exchange of actual letters, as Mooney assumes (p. 244). Reference to a letter received does occur in, and form part of the evidence for, certain or probable actual cases.[44] But the present poem requires no access to its supposed predecessor to be explicable, and it attributes to the lover nothing but standard male complaints. Nor is it unique in representing itself as replying to a letter from the man and stating the specific points to which it responds. There is a poem in the Welles anthology beginning, 'Right best beloved',[45] in which the woman summarizes and replies to some standard male moves made in a letter from him: pleas for her truth, her incomparable beauty, the torments of absence, the fear and self-consciousness that impede expression of his feelings, etc. The woman replying to her lover, it seems, was a received type of epistolary poem, and was a kind of variation on the paired-letter format, a variation in which typical male and female attitudes are condensed into one letter, the woman's reply incorporating the male missive to which it responds, with consequent emphasis on the female (usually guarded) response to male ardour. The Welles poem does not present any departure from the gender stereotypes (the prudent caution of the honourable woman responding to male passion and haste) that might suggest an actual rather than a typical case, though the unspecified charge for which pardon is asked in the

---

[43] Linne Mooney, '"A Woman's Reply to Her Lover" and Four Other New Courtly Love Lyrics in Cambridge, Trinity College MS R.3.19', *MAev* 67 (1998) 235–56 (p. 242). An edited text of the poems is provided by Mooney at pp. 249–56.
[44] See Text 6, 5C.33–6 and cf. line 29 of item 31 in the Findern manuscript, on which see Text 3, p. 227 below.
[45] *Welles Anthology*, no. 59 (pp. 252–4).

Findern poem might do so (see p. 227 below). But Mooney's case rests principally on the final stanza of the poem she discusses:

> But, the second Troyles, as I began
> To be playne unto yow in my sentence,
> And nat the Royal Ox forto be clepyd the swan,
> Ne the swan that ys whyte in existence
> To be cleped Coll – thys ys but apparence,
> As in wordes traversyng the kyng –
> I pray to God, foule fall dissemblyng.   (Mooney's text: ll. 85–91)

Mooney claims these lines are so worded as to suggest a cryptic identification of an actual addressee who must clearly be of the same 'noble birth' and 'royal descent' as Troilus (p. 243) and (given that heraldry seems at least in part to underlie lines 87–9) may well be Henry Bolingbroke (later Henry IV), the ox being associable with the 'bole' [bull] perhaps suggested by his cognomen and the white swan being the badge of his first wife and sometimes borne by him. However, the grammar and sense of lines 86–9 do not imply that the terms listed might be used of the addressee if one was not being 'plain', but that not being plain would involve calling an ox a swan or a white swan by a name used for black things (cf. 'col-blake' in *MED*). The use of these animals in heraldic arms or badges does seem to underlie the lady's designation of them as ones that might be used as code in potentially treasonous discourse. When, for instance, in Shakespeare's *Richard III*, Stanley sends messages of warning to a friend and later to co-conspirators about the king, he refers to him cryptically as the 'boar', which was his heraldic badge (III.2.7–8, IV.5.1–3). But the designation 'second Troyles' is, as we have seen, not singular in itself, and in fact here simply reinforces the steadfastness the lady has urged in the absence of any hope of a meeting – a matter on which she says she has been and will be 'plain': she will not use 'dissemblyng' by giving him false assurances, those 'botmeles bihestes' which, for instance, Troilus found in Criseyde's letters (V.1424–31). Lines 87–91 can thus be paraphrased as: 'I will not say black is white, calling the large and majestic ox a swan or call the white swan black, or use such indirections as are used by traitors when they plot against the king'. She is aligning her plainness with political truth and loyalty, rather than hinting heraldically at the identity of her lover because the political dangers of any relationship force such indirections, as Mooney assumes, and we do not find them inexplicable unless assumed to relate to an 'actual' lover. Yet the lines are somewhat cryptic and illustrate the potentially blurred or arguable boundary in this territory between art and actuality.

The relative proportions of art and actuality in any given case can also be problematic. The woman or wife writing with love and longing to an absent lover or husband was a popular rhetorical topos that figures as an epistolary type in the model love letters of Boncompagno (Text 1, 146/29ff., 154/1ff.) as well as in poems (e.g. 'O, happy dames' at fol. 55[r–v] in the Devonshire manuscript). But she could also, of course, be a real woman. Eleven letters of this type occur scattered amongst the items forming an epistolary formulary from medieval Bohemia. Various specific details strongly indicate the sender to have been the late thirteenth-century Queen Kunhuta writing to her husband Přemysl Otakar II during his absence on a military campaign. But the letters (in Latin), like others in this collection, come without the *superscriptio* that would confirm the identity of sender and addressee, probably in order that they may thereby better serve the purposes of archetypes, which they certainly suggest in many respects, since they are clearly influenced by the amorous rhetoric conventionally pertaining to the situation (quoting, for instance, from Psalm 39: see note to Text 1, 146/31). That the composer of the letter might have felt the influence of the rhetorical tradition would not be surprising. But the special complication in this case is that the wifely devotion expressed is inconsistent (though not absolutely irreconcilable) with the representation of Kunhuta in a contemporary chronicle as a treacherous adulteress. That claim may itself, of course, reflect the influence of another archetype. But it may well be that in the letters 'the actual queen's perspective is reflected through a "shared authorship" which involves different individuals from the composer to the reviser, and knows multiple production stages, from the transcription to the compilation of the collection'. That is the conclusion drawn by Francesca Battista in an essay which gives an excellent account of the case and the problems posed by it and which is contained in a volume with a highly significant title: *Medieval Letters: Between Fiction and Document*.[46]

Reality or Realism?

Ambiguous cases occur throughout the period at issue. Since real love letters were by convention stylized and formulaic and devoid of identifying details, these characteristics alone cannot rule out actuality, and, conversely, the presence of specific details cannot rule out art, especially if they are not such as to confuse (for allusion to the particulars of a

---

[46] *Medieval Letters: Between Fiction and Document*, ed. Christian Høgel and Elisabetta Bartoli (Turnhout, 2015). Battista's essay, 'Queen Kunhuta's Epistles to Her Husband', is at pp. 265–76.

genuine case tends to leave loose ends that suggest a wider story is needed to make full sense of them). The ambiguity, that is, can itself be artful. The following two lyrics may be cases in point. They occur in Humfrey Newton's commonplace book and are numbers XII and XIV in Robbins's edition of the poems therein contained.[47] They may be of Newton's own composition or by a friend or acquaintance, or they may be records of poems he had come across or remembered.[48] They may or may not refer to actual cases, and the initial 'Mittitur' [It is sent] may be simply a generic marker (of a verse epistle: it occurs also with II, XIII, XV and XVII), or it may indicate a poem that was actually delivered to someone. They thus typify the ambiguities that can arise in this area. But their success depends partly on their teasing suggestion of an underlying 'reality' that can only be hinted at indirectly: 'M' in the first suggests a specific person whose name is being deliberately concealed, the concealment (pretended or real) indicating the reality of a 'private' epistle.[49] Both lyrics certainly work by appearing to bring into the 'public' domain a correspondence they simultaneously indicate is importantly and crucially 'private' and whose sender and sendee can thus be referred to only cryptically, by initials and 'tokens':

---

[47] They are also included (as nos. 193 and 194) in Robbins, ed., *Secular Lyrics*. We quote from 'The Poems of Humfrey Newton', ed. Robbins, but have used our own punctuation.

[48] It is generally assumed that Newton was the author of the courtly love poems (fols. 92ᵛ–94), though he has elsewhere copied into the commonplace book verses he certainly or probably did not himself compose: to wit, poems I (*ABC of Aristotle*), XIX (some versified advice on purchasing land, attributed to the jurist Fortescue), XX (six lines of alliterative prophecies), XXI (Richard de Caistre's hymn), XXII (an alliterative poem in a style and metre both older than and very different from the other poems) and XXIII (a copy of a 'nightingale' poem once attributed to, though now thought not to be by, Lydgate: see Deborah Youngs, *Humphrey Newton: An Early Tudor Gentleman* (Woodbridge, 2008), p. 171). It is therefore unsafe to assume he must have been the author of all the courtly love poems (some or all of which may just have been works circulating and/or composed locally), simply because none of them has been found elsewhere, and because he was probably the author of three of the five brief acrostic epistles (those that spell out the names of himself and of his wife Elena: III, IV and VIII); and, if he can be supposed to be also the author of the other two acrostic epistles to 'Margeret' and 'Bryan' (VII and IX), it must be likewise supposable that, conversely, even those on himself and Elena were composed by a friend or acquaintance.

[49] 'M' recurs as addressee in the first line of another of Humfrey's verse letters (XVII: 'Mi Mornynge, M, greues me sore') – which also, like the second poem quoted above, refers to seeing her in church, often mentioned as the likeliest venue in which the lover can be in the physical presence of his beloved, and where he may have seen her for the first time: cf. *Troilus* I.267–73 and *Welles* 13.60–1 ('at þe furst tyme þat I dyd yow mete / In the myddes of þe churche when I dyd yow grete'). In both cases 'M' may well be meant to suggest the name 'Margaret' (abbreviated to 'M' at Text 4, l.1), a very popular girl's name, and one common in the Newton family, where it was given, for instance, to one of Humfrey's daughters and his wife's younger sister (see Youngs, *Humphrey Newton*, pp. 26, 101, 183); it also forms the name spelled out in one of Humfrey's short acrostic verse love letters (VII), where it is probably that of a friend or acquaintance – and it is the name of the addressee and (perhaps) the sender of the actual love letters of Texts 4 and 7, respectively.

Mittitur:

I pray you, M, to me be tru,
    for I will be tru as longe as I lif;
I wil not change you for old ne newe,
    ne neuer lof oþer whiles þat I lif.

and ye be auiset, þis oþer yere,   *and ye be a.* if you remember
ye send me a letter of luf so dere;   *send* sent
I was as glad of youre writynge
as euer I was of any thynge,
for I was sek the day be-fore –   *sek* sick, ill
that letter heyled, I was sek no more.
M, in space
comes fortune and grace;
I trist hit so for to be   I trust that it will so happen
Þat it shall liȝt on you and me.   *liȝht* alight
M, be stidfast and tru in thoȝt,
ffor lof is the swetter the der þat it is boȝt.   *der* dearer
and M I hope securly   *hope securly* certainly think
there is non þat byes it so dere as we.
and in what place so euer ye be,
as oft as ye wil, ye shall me þer se.
þerfor be ye tru tru,   *tru tru* truly true
or ellis sore I mun it rew;   *sore I m. i. r.* I must grieve bitterly for it
be ye stidfast and also true,
ffor y wyl not change for old new.   *change f. o. n.* change the old for the new
and sithen as we may not to-geder spek,
be writynge we shall oure hertes breke.   *be* by; *breke* unload

Mittitur:

Go, litull bill, and command me hertely   *command* commend
Vnto her þat I call my trulof and lady,
be this same tru tokynnynge   By this verifying sign
that sho se me in a kirk on a friday   *se* saw
    in a mornyng,
With a sper-hauk on my hand;
and my mone did by her stond;   *mone* man-servant
and An old womon sete her by
that litull cold of curtesy,   Who was not skilled in courtly ways
and oft on her sho did smile,

to loke on me for a wile. *to* to encourage her to
and yet be this an-oþer token:
to the kirk sho comme with a gentilwomon; *comme* came
euen be-hynd the kirk dore
they kneled bothe on the flore,
and fast thay did piter-pater –
I hope thay said matens togeder! I think they were saying Matins
yet ones or twyes, at the lest,
Sho did on me her ee kest; *ee* eye
then went I forthe preuely,
and haylsed on thaym curtesly.
be alle the tokens truly, *be alle the* by all these
command me to her hertely.

The precise nature of the relationship between art and actuality in these two poems may have been clearer to their original (probably small and local) audience, but their charm still depends on implying such a relationship. Newton's anthology also includes a 'Dear John' verse letter from a woman (XI) whose female voice is certainly not the standard one. The speaker appears to have consented to a (probably arranged) match with another man, and writes to give her lover permission to transfer his affections, should he wish. This cannot have been uncommon news for sweethearts to give or hear, and it must usually have been the women who gave it. The female voice is therefore pertinent here. Such a letter from a woman is included by Boncompagno in his collection of model love letters for various circumstances (see Text 1, 144/25–30). But the self-possessed conciseness of that model is very different from Newton's poem on the same occasion. The poem does not type its speaker in either of the expected ways, as (misogynistically) an example of the infidelity of woman or (sentimentally) as a tragic *mal mariée* (a common figure), but is simply resignedly regretful in tone, affectionate and valedictory simultaneously, and Humfrey obviously composed (or recalled or copied) it for the chord of remembered or recognized sad actuality that it sounds:

fare-well, þat was my lef so dere, *þat was m. l.* you who were my beloved
 and fro her that loued you so well.
ye were my lef from yere to yere –
 wheder I were yours I connot tell.
to you I haue byn trew and lell
 at all tymes vnto this day;
and now I say fare-well, fare-welle:
 I tak my lef for euer and ay. *lef* leave

youre lof, for-soth, ye haue not lost:
if ye loued me, I loued you, I-wys;
Bot that I put you to gret cost,
   þerfore I haue you clipt and kist.   *clipt* embraced
   bot now my luf I most nedes sesse,   *sesse* cease from my love
      and tak me to hym that me has tan.   *take me* betake myself to; *tan* received
   þerfore tak ye anoþer wher ye list: *wher ye list* wherever you choose
      I gif you good lef, sertayn.   *lef* leave, permission

Gif ye me licence to do the same.
   this tokyn[50] truly I you be-tak
In remembrance of my name;
   Send me a tokyn for my sake;
   wheder it be send erly or late,
      I shall it kepe for old qwayntenance.
   and now to crist I you be-take,
      to saue and kepe in whert and sance.   *whert and sance* health and fitness

---

[50] The 'tokens' in this verse are of a different kind from those found in the previous poem (discussed in Ch. 2 below) and refer here to the gift of an object from one lover to the other – a common way of acknowledging a love relationship (cf. Text 4, l.11, ll.54–7 and Text 7, l.3, ll.11).

CHAPTER 2

Occasions; Ways and Means; Male and Female Voices

Letters of Approach

Chaucer, in supplying a *Litera Criseydis* to correspond with his *Litera Troili*, was obeying an instinct which other practitioners shared. A letter from a male lover is the first move in a minor narrative, and it is not just aesthetic symmetry that seems to demand a 'response' of some kind. Boncompagno in his late twelfth-century guide to the love letter regularly alternates between man and woman in the illustrative letters he provides (Section II [1]). Letters do, furthermore, tend to shape the narrative of a love affair as it was portrayed in literature in some very real senses, for they often mark both its inception and its catastrophe. They constitute one kind of standard beginning of a relationship proper, in being the way contact is made, attraction made known and responded to, as with the first of the two pairs of love letters Chaucer included in *Troilus* (II.1065–85, 1218–25). Similarly, in the two series of amorous ballades written by Christine de Pisan, the man characteristically makes known to the lady, through a ballade addressed to her, his love and service – and meets with a positive or negative response (see the juxtaposed *Cent balades* LXV–VII and LXVIII–LXX) or one that at first, like Criseyde's, declares unwillingness to enter into a romantic liaison (*Cent balades d'amant et de dame* II), by whomsoever and in whatever 'letter' the proposal is made ('Qui que m'en parle, *escripse lettre ou brief*': 15, emphasis added).

In this phase of the relationship, the letters fulfil a courting function. Romance heroes such as Euryalus often resort to the letter as a first move.[1] In a less courtly version of the same scenario, the similarly placed Damian likewise launches his likewise successful attempt on another old man's young wife with a note surreptitiously conveyed to her.[2] Given the difficulty of private communication in the social world of the Middle Ages, this probably reflects actual practice. Moving from fiction to fact, we find that a woman too might find a letter the best means of declaring an as yet unconfessed

[1] On this romance, see Ch. 3, pp. 110–12 below.
[2] The Merchant's Tale, *CT* IV.1875–1954.

love. Among the Cely letters there is one from 'Clare' to George Cely, who was at the time based in Calais, where he ran the continental branch of the family's wool-exporting business, and where he took 'a series of mistresses'.[3] Clare's letter was written some time around 1480 (when George was twenty-two):

> Trèschier et especial, je me recomande à vous, Jorge Sely. Sachies que je suy en très bon point et je prye à Dieu que ainsy soiet il de vous. Sachies que je vous ay amé longement, mais je ne le vous ossoye point dire. Sachies que je vous envoye une recomendacion, et je vous prye que il vous souviegne de moy, et je vous en prie que vous m'envoyes une souvenanche ainsy comme je fais à vous par bonne amour. Et je vous laisse savoier que mon coeur n'es mis sur aultre homme que sur vous; mais je pense que votre amour n'est point sur moy. Mais je vous enprie que vous m'envoyes une lettre le plus tos que poes, car mon coer ne sera point à son repos tantque je veray une lettre vena[n]s de vous, car de cest ensaigne que je vous dissoye à la table que je vous envoraye vne lettre. Aultre chose ne vous say que j'escrie pour le pressent, sinon que Dieu soiet garde de Jorge Sely et de Clare.
>
> > Tout le coeur de Clare est à vous, Jorge Sely –
> > tous jour en mon coer
>
> Sachies que j'envoye une ainsaigne à Bietremeulx, votre serviteur. Et se me recomande a lui. Je lui promis caint il estoiet pardecha.
>
> (*dorse*) Desen brief zij ghegeuen tot Jorge Sely[4]

[Dearest and specially beloved, I commend myself to you, George Cely. I can tell you that I am in good health and I pray God that that may be the case with you. I can tell you that I have long loved you, but I did not at all dare to tell you about it. I am sending you a token and I pray that it may remind you of me, and I pray you to send me a souvenir in the same way as I do to you out of love.[5] And I let you know that my heart is given to no man other than you; but I think that your love has not at all fallen upon me. But I pray that you send me a letter as soon as you can, for my heart will not be at rest till I see a letter from you – and this token will prove the letter comes from me: that I said to you at table that I would send you a letter.[6] I do not know what else to write at present, except that may God be protector to George Cely and to Clare.

> All the heart of Clare is yours, George Cely –
> always in my heart.

---

[3] *The Cely Letters*, ed. Alison Hanham, EETS OS 273 (1975), p. xv.
[4] The letter appears as item 54 in Hanham's edition, but our text has been independently edited from TNA, SC1/59/41.
[5] On the exchange of gifts or tokens that may accompany love letters, see below, n. to Text 7, l.3.
[6] On the *enseigne* [sign] or 'token' that verified the identity of the sender (by referring to some facts belonging to a particular time or place that the addressee will remember), see below, n. to Text 4, ll.46.

Occasions; Ways and Means; Male and Female Voices 29

> Know that I have sent a verifying token of myself [as the writer of this letter], to someone who serves you in your affairs, Bietremeulx. And I commend myself to him [requesting him to pass this letter to you]. And I told him I would do so when he was over here.
>
> (*dorse*) Let this letter be given to George Cely]

Clare almost certainly used a scribe or letter-writer,[7] who may also have provided the standard epistolary formulae that here form the framing structure of the letter: opening recommendation, points introduced by 'Sachez' [know, be informed], closing commendation to God. Clare has also arranged with George's 'serviteur' Bietremeulx (= 'Bartholomew') that the letter should be handed to him in the first instance. She made this arrangement with him when he was 'pardecha' [over here], which, as Hanham points out, indicates that she was not in Calais at the time of writing.[8] George frequently travelled out of Calais on business, and had almost certainly met the French-speaking Clare somewhere on the continent other than Calais, which in this period was an English colony and trading post. Though the French-Dutch language border was moving northwards, Calais was still in Dutch-speaking territory in the medieval period, and English households in Calais were served in part by Dutch speakers. Many of George's servants were Dutch,[9] and though the letter written 'over here' is in French, its endorsed instruction that it be delivered to George Cely (who must be 'over there') is in Dutch. Letter and endorsement appear to be written in the same hand, which would indicate a scribe competent in both languages (not unusual in the business communities of these areas[10]).

Clare's offer is unembarrassed, though she does not sound sanguine as to its reception. But the declaration of love by letter seems to have proved successful in this instance, since she is found living with George in Calais by 1480: George refers in two memoranda to a chamber containing pelts, a chamber that lies 'howyr [over] my Lady Clare' (92/4–5, 105/31–3, 41–2), that is a room above the one occupied by Clare. The date of Clare's letter is not known.[11] But it is evident that by the date of these memoranda (June and September of 1480, respectively) she was living with him, presumably as his mistress, 'my Lady Clare' being a locution intended to lend respectability

---

[7] Cf. *Cely Letters*, ed. Hanham, note to item 54. See further pp. 53–9 below.
[8] Alison Hanham, *The Celys and Their World* (Cambridge, 1985), pp. 49–50.
[9] *Cely Letters*, ed. Hanham, p. 262.
[10] Cf. Sjoerd Levelt and Ad Putter, *North Sea Crossings 1066–1688* (Oxford, 2021), p. 16.
[11] Hanham hazards '? Before 26 May 1479', but with slender grounds for doing so (see note to item 54).

to the relationship in communications, the social sense of the phrase functioning as a discreet veil over its derivative amorous sense.

Clare may have some connection with some French scribbles made by George himself. On the dorse of a letter addressed to him (in which no year is given) is found, in his own hand, a series of very amateurish 'practice' French phrases (apparently acquired by ear) with some English glosses, the content consisting largely of songs and sentiments a lover might utter, with some remarks the woman might make:

> Je boy Avous mademoy selle/ Je vous plage movnsenyuevr//
> Poirsse ke vous l estes se belle/ Je boy, etc.
> Je sens lamor rensson estyn selle ke me persse par me
>   le kowre/ Je boy a ... Je voue plege movnsenywr/
> de davns wyth in/ de horse wyth hov[t]e Bosonye besy//
> shavnte// syng/ // vn shavnssovne/ an song
> lere/Rede vn shen an doge/ shovtt hot
> fret covld
> Je le vous hay de kavnt je Raye/ I have sayd yow whan
> I go//
> Je swy hovntesse/shamed Je swy hovntesse//
> I am shamyd   (*Cely Letters* 49/12–22)[12]

> *I drink to you, mademoiselle; I pledge [toast] you, monsieur*
> *Because you are so fair, I drink, etc.*
> *I feel love with its spark piercing me through the heart; I drink to ... I pledge you,*
>   *monsieur*
> dedans: inside; de hors: outside; besogne: busy
> Chant: sing; un chanson: a song
> lire: read; un chien: a dog; chaud: hot
> froid: cold
> Je le vous ay dit quant j'errai: I have told you when I will go
> Je suis honteuse (ashamed), Je suis honteuse: I am embarrassed.

George's efforts in French could be read with Clare[13] and/or with his interest (evidenced by lessons he paid for) in songs[14] – and/or with the section on amorous talk found in a French conversation manual (reproduced at pp. 208ff. below): evidently of a susceptible and/or philandering turn, George perhaps thought, as was assumed by the compiler of that manual,

---

[12] Hanham's text preserves the single and double virgules (represented as slashes) by which the text is punctuated in the manuscript.
[13] Hanham believes Clare might have been George's teacher (note to item 49).
[14] See Hanham, *The Celys and Their World*, pp. 33–5 (and also her article 'The Musical Studies of a Fifteenth-Century Wool Merchant', *RES* 8 (1957) 270–4). The interest in lyrics was common: cf. pp. 46–7 below.

that some French might be useful for making love (to Clare or someone else on the continent).

Between Betrothed Parties

There has survived another, very different, love letter, sent by rather than to a merchant of the staple. It belongs to the year 1476 and is from Thomas Betson, who had entered into partnership with William Stonor in a venture aimed at expanding the latter's wool production into wool trading. The connection between the two men had been formed at the time of Stonor's marriage to the widow Elizabeth Ryche, with whom Betson (who had business and family connections with the Ryches) was closely associated, and whose daughter Katherine Ryche it had plainly been agreed he should marry when she was old enough. Katherine was, at the time he wrote to her from Calais, a mere girl of twelve or thirteen.[15] Such arrangements were not uncommon, though the marriage was usually deferred until the girl reached the age of fifteen or so, and in this case did not take place for a further two years.[16] It was certainly a success by one measure: Katherine bore him five children over the eight years of its duration.[17]

Betson's tone is avuncular, but it is countered by constant anticipations of (and admonishments to) the womanhood that will usher in a different relationship, though these are couched in language suited to a child. The conventional opening reference to the hoped-for good health of the recipient is adapted to urge Katherine to eat up and grow up like a good girl. Betson says he has heard that she is in 'good health of body', God be thanked, and goes on (with a long-winded goodwill characteristic of him):

> And if you would be a good eater of your meat [food] alway, that ye might wax and grow fast to be a woman, ye should make me the gladdest man of the world, by my troth. For when I remember your favour [goodwill] and your sad [serious] loving dealing to-me-ward, for sooth ye make me very [truly] glad and joyous in my heart. And on the tother side again [contrariwise], when I remember your young youth, and see well that ye be none eater of your meat, the which should help you greatly in waxing, forsooth then ye make me very heavy again. And therefore I pray you, mine own sweet cousin [relative, close connection], even as you love me ... to eat your meat like a woman.[18]

[15] These details are taken from *Kingsford's Stonor Letters and Papers*, ed. Christine Carpenter, 2 vols (Cambridge, 1996), vol. 1, pp. xxvii–xxix.
[16] Betson sends regards to Katherine in letters written, to William or Elizabeth, before October 1478, the date of a letter in which Elizabeth refers to 'my son Betson and his wife' (Letter 229).
[17] Betson died in 1486: on his will and his children, see *Stonor Letters*, ed. Carpenter, vol. 1, pp. xxviii–xxix.
[18] We have used Carpenter's text of the letter (*Stonor Letters*, ed. Carpenter, vol. 2, pp. 6–8), but we punctuate differently and have modernized the spelling in all quotations from her edition.

Then come genial pieces of wit, the first of which, however, again includes a reference to the future 'wife' Katherine will be, together with a neatly optative evening up of their age difference. She has been looking after his horse, for which he thanks her, and for which her own elder self (as his wife) will also be thankful:

> I pray you, greet well my horse, and pray him to give you four of his years to help you withal, and I will, at my coming home, give him four of my years and four horse's loaves to amends. Tell him that I prayed him so. And, cousin Katherine, I thank you for him [on his behalf] and my wife shall thank you for him hereafter. For ye do great cost upon him, as it is told me.

There follows an amused correction of some childlike mistake of hers as to where exactly he and Calais are, and then a rather male animadversion on the eccentricities of her clock (a piece of technology still new and still often unreliable), which strikes erratically and is always fast and is to be told that it is putting off visitors and should mend its irritating ways before Betson himself visits her.[19]

Betson's situation evidently created its own category of love talk, and he combines the present child and future wife with some tact. His is, of course, not a letter of approach. Where formal marriage was at issue, the first approaches were usually made – especially, but by no means exclusively, where the lady was a child – to and/or from the woman's 'friends' (i.e. her connections, especially those of status) and often involved brokers or intermediaries. Betson's letter belongs in fact to the category of love letters from or to a formally approved suitor and future husband. Margery Brews's letter (reproduced at p. 47 below) also falls into this category, as does one from the widow Agnes Wydeslade to William Stonor after his application for her hand (following the death of his first wife, Elizabeth) had been approved (*Stonor Letters*, Letter 262: vol. 2, pp. 100–1). The external sanction freed the parties openly to send written messages and letters to each other – something not possible in more clandestine relationships. Thus Betson sends his regards to Katherine, at first tentatively ('if it please your mastership') in a letter to William Stonor (Letter 161) and sends more open, and even cross, messages via Elizabeth (Letter 185), as well as writing to her himself.

The *amours* of the two wool-merchants (George Cely and Thomas Betson) mark the opposing poles of the relationship at this period. The respectable marital home in store for Katherine, in England (where both men found their wives) and complete with such mod cons as the latest tick-tocks,

---

[19] On early clocks, see John Scattergood, *Time's Subjects: Horology and Literature in the Later Middle Ages and Renaissance* (Dublin, 2022), in which Betson's letter is discussed at p. 112.

is separated by more than the Channel from the quarters in which Clare found herself shacked up amid the wool pelts with George, in Calais (which, away from the restraining supervision and observation of family and social connections, offered opportunities for extra-marital liaisons).

Separation

Chaucer gives only a summary of the letter in which Troilus declares his love (*Troilus* II.1065-85), a summary expressed in such a way as to imply a narrator who really cannot be bothered to recreate in all its details a letter which the audience can well imagine. It would take 'muchel space' to repeat Troilus's outpourings verbatim: he called her 'his righte lady' and 'his sorwes leche [physician]' and all that (using 'thise other termes alle, / That in swich cas thise loueres alle seche'), he went on about his unworthiness ('his vnworthynesse *ay* he acused'), and his account of his sufferings was of course 'endeles'. What Troilus would say in this courting letter, even if there were not manuals to follow, would, that is, be utterly predictable and no different from what 'thise loueres alle' say. That, of course, does not stop the feelings from being genuine. Lovers will use the conventional clichés precisely because, intensely personal though the experience may seem, everyone when in love is a walking cliché, brimming over with the same passions and sensations.

But letters occur most characteristically, and most crucially, when the lovers are separated, and absence tends to be something of a crisis in the relationship, a point at which it can end. These more critical letters in *Troilus* Chaucer does not summarize, but gives in full – or two of them (he indicates there were others: from Troilus (V.1583-6) and from Criseyde (1422-30). The standard 'termes' will not now cover the situation, as Troilus finds himself obliged to protest and to reproach, something which so goes against the grain of the 'servant's' proper respect and unquestioning obedience with regard to his 'lady' [mistress] that it can be stated only as a hypothesis:

If any seruant dorst or oughte of right
Upon his lady pitously compleyne,
Thanne wene I that ich oughte be that wight ... (V.1345-7)

Absence forms an equally major test of commitment in Christine de Pisan's two sequences. In the second, a sizeable tranche of the ballades (*CBAD* XLV-LXI) are written against the background of the man's departure on military service overseas, where he remains for a year, and many of the *Cent balades* also involve separation: e.g. LVII ('mon ami s'en vait en Angleterre'), LXXIII-LXXVI. The relationship survives the crisis in the instances cited. But the first and most memorable of the various narrative scenarios outlined in the *Cent balades* concerns a lover who leaves the area (also, it appears, to do military service), and from whom the female speaker vainly waits for; and then despairs of, a letter, eventually assuming he has forgotten her or found a new love (XXXII–XLVIII). This rather harrowing sequence mirrors the sentiments and situation depicted in the letters exchanged in the final book of *Troilus*, where hope deserts Troilus in painfully slow motion following the day designated by Criseyde for her return, when her non-appearance and silence makes it clear that she 'nolde her terme holde' (V.1209), for, as he says in his letter, written after 'His hope al clene out of his herte fledde' (1198), 'ȝe seyden, soth to seyne, / But dayes ten ȝe nolde in oost sojourne – / But in two monthes ȝet ȝe nat retourne' (V.1349–51). Christine's lady undergoes a similar experience:

Helas! doulz loyaulx amis,	Alas, my sweet and true love,
En grant desir attendoie	With great longing I waited for
Le terme que m'aviez mis	The date that you had set for me
De retourner, mais ma joye	For returning, but my joy
Tourne en dueil: tout est cassé	Turns to sorrow: all is fallen away
Le bon espoir que j'avoye,	The good hope that I had,
Puis que le terme est passé.	Since that date has passed.
Vous m'aviez dit et promis,	You had said and promised,
Et aussi je l'esperoie,	And also I had so hoped,
Que deux moys ou trois demis,	That two or three-and-a-half months
Demourriez en ceste voye.	You would spend away. (*CB* XXXVIII.1–11)

Absence thus proves itself to Christine as the true test of true love, for 'Qui bien aime n'oublie pas / Son bon ami pour estre loings' [He who loves well does not forget / a good lover because of distance], but the refrain of the balade that so opens (*CB* LV) is disillusioned and somewhat bitter: 'Car le voyage d'outremer / A fait en amours maint dommage' [For a voyage overseas / Is often most injurious to love].

When Camargo notes that the most common theme of the medieval verse love letter is lament at separation (p. 44), he is in a sense stating the obvious, for lovers would not undertake the complications and risks of having letters written and delivered unless it were necessary – and such necessity generally arose precisely from separation. And separation, as Christine learns, is the rock on which love may well founder. The scenario depicted in her above-described sequence of ballades is one that recurs in the draft letter from the Gloucester lady (Text 5 below), who likewise appears to be a woman vainly waiting to hear from an absent lover, fearing he has forgotten her and appealing to him (as Christine does) as the *garesein*, the doctor who

Occasions; Ways and Means; Male and Female Voices 35

can provide the 'cure' for this emotional *maladie* (21–2; cf. *CB* XLIII 25–8: 'Medecins, de mal suis plaine, / Garissez moy, je mendie / De santé qui m'est longtaine; / Ce me fait la maladie' [Physician, I am full of sickenss: / Cure me, I am in want / Of the health that is far from me; / It is all this that gives me my malady]).

Boncompagno included among his model love letters several that could be used by a lady writing to a sorely missed lover or husband who is in a 'distant region' (see Text 1, pp. 146, 154–6), obviously assuming this was a fairly common occasion for a letter. Further indication of the important part that separation was commonly assumed to play in a love affair is the commonness as a verse type of the farewell poem, addressed to the mistress before temporary departure: see, for instance, the four lyrics grouped together by Robbins in his anthology and entitled 'A Farewell to His Mistress I/II/III' and 'A Lover's Farewell to His Mistress' (Robbins, ed., *Secular Lyrics*, nos. 202–5), Christine's paired rondeaux 'A Dieu, ma dame, je m'en vois' and 'A Dieu, mon ami' (I, Rondeaux XXVII, XXVIII), and the Compleynt 'Now must I nede part out of your presence' in the sequence of love poems commonly known as the 'Suffolk' poems (*'Suffolk' Poems*, ed. Jansen, no. 10). These poems naturally take forms other than that of the verse epistle proper, for they imply that the separation has not yet occurred, whereas a letter indicates that the lovers are apart. In the case of liaisons where marriage was not possible, or not intended, the gap which the letter verbally bridged might not, of course, be one of many miles. But in those cases, prudence might well prompt even a faithful lover to minimize the risks of letter-sending – and, in our actual cases, one meets with both apologies on those grounds for not having written before (as from the Norfolk abbot: Text 4, II.7–11) and (from the writer of the love verses in the Armburgh Roll) with repeated piteous pleas that some time and place for a meeting be fixed by a lady whom the writer dare not visit openly and who is obviously also avoiding the indiscretion of sending compromising messages or missives (Text 6, 3.17–18, 4B.10–12, 5B.59–60, C.50–1, D.89–92).

Retreat and Protest

The avowed pretext for the writing of both of Christine's ballade sequences is a response to a specific request or directive from others.[20] The second sequence is more specifically represented as demanded (by someone universally liked) partly as amends for having advised women against

---

[20] This claim (probably often fictive) was not uncommon: cf. Caxton's assertion that his printing of the tales of Arthur was done at the repeated requests of 'many noble and dyvers gentylmen of thys royame' (Sir Thomas Malory, *Works*, ed. Eugene Vinaver, 2nd edn (Oxford, 1971), p. xiii).

love (Introductory Ballade 19–24).[21] This second series traces the development of a relationship, through the approach of the lover, the overcoming of the lady's initial reluctance, the happiness of each in the other, the way their love survives quite a long absence on the man's part and their joy in their reunion. But the man then starts to make excuses for not having seen the lady recently, and both reader and lady begin to smell a rat. For the reader, some kind of wrong note is struck by the refrain in the very first of these 'apologetic' ballades – a refrain in which a 'petite affaire' [small matter] is repeatedly pointed to as the cause for his having regretfully failed to appear for a few days (LXXXI). The very phrase itself, in its unromantic prosiness, sounds out of place in the refrain of a love poem, where the wrong note it strikes recurs and cannot escape the ear of a reader. He then claims fear of attracting the malicious gossip of 'mesdisans' [ill speakers] and anxiety about her honour are making him cautious (LXXXIII, LXXXV, LXXXVII), and tries to engineer a rupture by turning her mounting suspicions (that there is 'someone else') back on her and saying he has heard that she is favouring another (LXXXXI.15, LXXXXIII). The lady is quick to sense his bad faith – as is Troilus in a similar situation, when he receives a similar missive from Criseyde, which seems to him to herald the infidelity he calls by the softer name of 'change' ('Hym thoughte hit lik a kalendes of chaunge': *Troilus* V.1634), though his love will not suffer this instinctive mistrust to take root in his mind (1635–8).

The word 'retreat' is applied in both French and English to the withdrawal from courtship or from a relationship.[22] Christine and Chaucer give us some idea of how a letter of retreat would look when penned by those who have not the moral courage to write a plain one but do have enough of a conscience to try and hide their own bad faith from the recipient and from themselves. Similarities in the notes sounded suggest a common wisdom as to common recourses. Criseyde also begins by finding an excuse for her non-appearance, though the unspecified 'petite affaire' becomes here the even less specific gesture towards a reason that cannot

---

[21] The similar claim made by Chaucer with respect to *The Legend of Good Women* (purportedly imposed as a penance for the dissuasions from love constituted by his translation of *Le roman de la rose* and by the untruth of Criseyde in his *Troilus*: *Legend of Good Women* F.322–4, 437–41, 479–85) again suggests this too may be one kind of conventional fiction that is not to be taken literally: the claim serves in both cases to draw attention to the ensuing content and to problematize it somewhat. Is an idealistic view of female fidelity as mistaken as, but perhaps a necessary counterpoise to, a cynical one? Do amorous entanglements bring women more trouble than joy?

[22] See Gower's *Confessio amantis* viii.2416 and Machaut's *Voir dit* 7532, 7557 (and L42, an actual letter written in response to actually believed rumours about the lady). References to Gower's poem are to the EETS edn (ES 81 and 82, published 1900 and 1901) by G.C. Macaulay.

Occasions; Ways and Means; Male and Female Voices 37

be spelled out ('But whi, lest that this lettre founden were, / No mencioun ne make I now, for feere': V.1602–3), and then similarly (and somewhat inconsistently) blames fear of *mesdisans* ('ffor that I tarie is al for wikked speche': 1610), and even proceeds into an accusation that is likewise similar to that made by Christine's *amant* ('And beth nat wroth, I have ek understonde, / How 3e ne do but holden me in honde': 1614–15). She is evidently rather clumsily proceeding through some repertoire of moves she knows belongs to the occasion. But Chaucer is dealing with a character, where Christine is tracing a type, and Criseyde is insufficiently callous not immediately to feel the injustice of that last charge and to retract it the moment it has fallen from her pen ('But now no force, I kan nat in 30w gesse / But alle trouthe and alle gentillesse'), so that the letter becomes a web of unconvincing and unconvinced half moves. Christine's *dame* responds to these noises with increasing hurt and accusations. She then finds her suspicions (that her so-called *amant* has lost interest and found someone else) verified (LXXXXVIII), and the sequence ends, significantly, not with a ballade (for communication has ceased), but with a lament by the *dame*: a lament on both the inevitability and the pains of love. So the sequence eventually makes 'amends' for the advice Christine had given women (to avoid love) in a way that the reader had not initially expected: that advice is finally demonstrated to have been 'wrong', not because love can be a wholly positive experience (as the sequence had at first seemed designed to illustrate), but because it had given women counsel it was not in their power to follow, for, as the closing 'Lay' makes clear, no one can defend themselves against love, and to forswear it is like vowing never again to catch a cold.[23]

Chaucer's *Complaint of Anelida* addressed to 'fals Arcite' also ends in soliloquy, though letters play an interesting role in the poem before that point. Anelida's fidelity to Arcite was such, we are told, that

Ther nas to her no maner lettre sent
That touched love, from any maner wyght,
That she ne shewed hit him er hit was brent.   (113–15; cf. 264–5)

This, of course, assumes that writing was a regular way of opening upon the subject. The Complaint itself is introduced by Chaucer as a reproachful letter actually written and sent by Anelida: 'And of her owne hond she gan hit write, / And sente hit to ... Arcite' (209–10; cf. 351–2). The poem is thus

---

[23] The sequence cannot therefore be read as an uncomplicated condemnation of 'love outside marriage', as is assumed by Willard, *Christine*, p. 61.

formally a missive, like the similar complaints from the deserted women who figure among Ovid's *Heroides*. But Chaucer ends by exposing as unreal the idea that women would have the luxury of communicating their grief and anger in this way: the addressee would certainly not respond to, and would probably not even read, these reproaches. The fiction of the letter finally collapses, and Anelida ends, like Christine's betrayed *dame*, who must substitute lay for ballade, in talking to herself. Realizing the futility of her protests, she concludes by turning her first- and second-person letter into a third-person swansong sung to herself:

> I yeve hit up for now and evermore ...
> But as the swan ...
> Ayeins his deth shal singen his penaunce,
> So sing I here my destinee and chaunce,
> *How that Arcite Anelida so sore*
> *Hath thirled with the poynt of remembraunce.* (343–50)

The ladies and their poets know that the only audience for their outcries is the one created by art, not the actual addressee implied by a letter or ballade.

The real psychic need that might be met by such an imaginary letter was recognized early, however. An interesting narrative dream-vision in Latin provides a case in point. In it, a young and rejected lover complains to the god of love, who advises him to write to the girl, which he does, expressing his love and accusing her of infidelity to him. She replies to the effect that she changed him for less callow lovers. He again writes to accuse her of promiscuity and beg her to restore him to her favour. She says the god of love himself should now answer her letter to put an end to a correspondence that is annoying her. The god of love does so, accusing her of cruelty and breach of his command of fidelity and threatens to punish her and all her lovers with the exception of the faithful and true dreamer, who promises to write 'songs of joy' to Love, and wakes to praise the Trinity.[24] Fictional letters are here represented as literally the 'dream' of impotent actuality. Through them the lover has managed to state his case and bring his lady to 'answer' for her wrongdoing and to give authority to a pronouncement of her untruth and his own truth – and imaginary letters are what enable the confrontation and the denunciation.

---

[24] The text (with translation) of this interesting Latin work (in prose interspersed with verse passages), from Escorial, Biblioteca Real, MS T.II.16 (68ᵛ–73ʳ), can be found in Peter Dronke, *Medieval Latin and the Rise of European Love-Lyric*, 2 vols, 2nd edn (Oxford, 1968), vol. 2, pp. 523–34.

Dates to Be Marked by Letters and Verse: New Year, Valentine's Day, May Day

There were three dates which lovers were especially likely to mark by sending a greeting (the equivalent of a modern 'card'), a greeting particularly likely to be in or to contain verse: New Year's Day, Valentine's Day and the beginning of May. Gower's *Cinkante Balades* includes a continuous run of six ballades (XXXII–XXXVII) devoted to these festivals. The relevant day is announced in the first line of each, so that anyone searching for a 'card' to appropriate or excerpt could spot at once which poems were suited to 'Cest aun novell' or 'Saint Valentin' or the 'Mois de Maii'. Two ballades are given for each occasion, the two given for New Year and St Valentine allowing the lover-reader to choose from a plaintive or a celebratory version, as appropriate to his mood or circumstances ('selonc les propretés et les condicions des Amantz': see p. 14 above). Christine's *Cent balades d'amant et de dame* likewise include, in their proper chronological order, male and female ballades for New Year (LXVIII–LXIX) and Valentine's Day (LXXII–LXXIII), and a May ballade by the lady when her lover is away (LXXIX); her *Cent balades* also feature one each for New Year (LXXXI) and May Day (XXXIV). Ballades for all three occasions also figure in the series to and for his wife by Charles d'Orléans.

In the second of the two New Year ballades, Gower's (happy) lover refers to the 'joies que jeo meine / De vous servir' [the joy I have / in serving you] (XXXIII.5–6) – and asks, in the refrain, for the gift of at least a look as a reward for his service ('Si plus n'y soit, donetz le regarder'). He is playing on the fact that New Year was a time when gifts were exchanged, and amatory 'cards' might thus 'give' themselves or the writer's heart and request reciprocation in kind – as in the model New Year love poem which Lydgate, like Gower and Christine, also provided:

I hade leuer a looke alloone withouten any more
Of hir goodely eyen twoo myn *haromes* to restore,   *haromes* harms
Þanne haue alle oþer at my wille I rechche not who hit here.   *w.h.h.* who hears it

I haue no thing to gyven hir at þis gladde tyme,
But myn hert vndeparted, nowe þis firste pryme
Þe which þis day I sende hir al hooly and entier.   (*A Lover's New Year Gift* 45–50)[25]

---

[25] Quoted from John Lydgate, *The Minor Poems of John Lydgate, Part II: Secular Poems*, ed. H.N. MacCracken, EETS OS 192 (1934), pp. 424–7.

Or the 'card' may accompany an actual gift, as in the New Year poem (from a man) that Christine took care, like Gower, to include in her sequence of *Cent balades*, and, like him, to announce as such in its opening line: 'Ce jour de l'an que l'en doit estrener ... Si vous envoy ce petit dyamant, / Prenez en gré le don de vostre amant' [On this day of the new year when one should give a gift ... I send you this little diamond – accept with goodwill this gift from your lover] (LXXXI.1–7). The lovers in her second sequence exchange both literal and metaphorical gifts of various kinds, in fact and in wish, in an elegant synthesis of all the different kinds of giving (of poems, presents, self and love, good wishes, etc.) that might occur in this season:

LXVIII – L'AMANT

Combien que ja pieça toute donnée	Although long ago wholly I gave you
Vous ay m'amour, je la vous represente	My love, I re-present you with it
Avec mon cuer et corps, trés belle née,	Together with my heart and body, fair one,
Ce premier jour de l'année presente,	On this first day of the present year,
Et quanque j'ay, ma doulce dame gente;	Along with all I have, my sweet and gracious lady;
Ce dyamant avec de petit pris	And therewith also this diamond of small value
Prenez en gré, doulce dame de pris.	Please accept graciously, sweet, distinguished lady.
Bon jour, bon an et bonne destinée	Good day, good year and good destiny
Vous envoit Dieux et biens a droite rente,	May God send you and due receipt of goods,
Et que souvent l'un l'autre ceste année	And that we may each other often this year
Nous nous voions en trés joyeuse atente,	See, in expectation of joys,
Et que jamais vo cuer ne se repente	And that your heart may never repent
De moy amer, tout soye mal apris,	Of loving me, despite my lack of *savoir-faire*;
Prenez en gré, doulce dame de pris.	Accept this graciously, sweet distinguished lady.
Ne jamais jour no doulce amour finée	And never may our sweet love
Ne puist estre, ne vous ne soyez lente	Be ended, and may you not be slow
A moy donner joye qui redonnée	To grant me the joy which I hope may be returned
Vous soit par moy a plantureuse vente,	To you through me in plenteous store,
De mesdisans n'ayés ja la tourmente,	And may you have no torment from ill-speakers,
Avec ce, moy, vo serf lige pris,	And, in addition, me, your serf and liege bondsman,
Prenez en gré, doulce dame de pris.	Accept with goodwill, sweet distinguished lady.
De vous servir a ma vie ay empris,	To serve you all my life I have undertaken:
Prenez en gré, doulce dame de pris.	Accept graciously, sweet and distinguished lady.

LXIX – LA DAME

Je te mercy, bon et bel,	I thank you, good and fair one,
De ton trés gracieux don	For the graceful gift
Que m'as de cest an nouvel	Which you have at this New Year
Fait le premier jour, et don	Made me, on its first day, and so
Aussi moy je te redon	Likewise do I give to you in return
M'amour toute et t'en estraine.	All my love and endow you with it as a New Year gift.
Dieu te doint joyeuse estraine!	God grant you a joyful New Year gift![26]

Et cuer, corps par grant revel,	And my heart and body for all pleasure,
Sauf m'onneur, je t'abandon.	Saving my honour, I abandon to you.
Ce rubis en cest annel	This ruby in this ring
Te redonne en guerredon.	I give you in response, in reward.
Ne sçay que plus demandon,	I know not what more there is to settle:
Tu m'as fait de tout mal saine.	You have restored me to health.
Dieu te doint joyeuse estraine!	God grant you the gift of a joyful New Year!

Et en ce doulz renouvel	In this coming lovely time of renewal,
Du temps, ou joye a bandon	In spring, in which joy in plenty
Est, te donray maint chappel	There is, I will give you many a chaplet
De fleurs, mais plus n'atendon	Of flowers, but let us wait no longer
Le doulz baisier; or ça, don.	For sweet kissing; so come here –
Le departir m'est grant paine;	Being apart is great pain to me.
Dieu te doint joyeuse estraine!	God grant you a joyful New Year token!

Je m'en vois de joye plaine,	I go around full of joy:
Dieu me doint joyeuse estraine!	God give me a joyful New Year token!

*

The Valentine's Day poem was effectively put on the literary map by Chaucer and the French poet Granson, whose Valentine poems appeared at much the same time.[27] Both poets assumed a popular myth according to which this was the day on which birds chose their mates ('L'endemain de Saint Valentin, / Que tous oyseaulx vuellent chanter'[28]), and these supposed ornithological origins figure in nearly all medieval and early modern Valentine poems. Granson's Valentine verse includes – as well as narrative (see *Le Livre Messire Ode* 1246, 1996), a *souhait* plus *balade* (pp. 219–23) and

---

[26] An *estraine* was a gift given at New Year as a handsel, or foretoken of good fortune for the whole year.
[27] On the history of Valentine's Day, and the various dates and customs associated with it, see the comprehensive study of Valentine literature by Henry Ansgar Kelly, *Chaucer and the Cult of Saint Valentine* (Leiden, 1986).
[28] *Le Livre Messire Ode* 1246–7 (*N*), quoted from *Oton de Granson: Poésies*, ed. Joan Grenier-Winther (Paris, 2010).

complaintes (pp. 183–7, 368–79 and 515–21) – a *songe* in which the name Isabel figures acrostically (pp. 198–212). One of the complaints illustrates one form often taken by the Valentine or the May poem: a lament in which the lovelorn or bereaved speaker contrasts his or her solitude and misery with the mating of the birds and the general rejoicing attending the renewal of spring in the outer world ('Je voy chanter, rire et dancer. / Mais je me voy seul en tristesse, / Pour ce que j'ay perdu mon per': *Complainte de Saint Vallentin Garenson* 5–7). That speaker's lady has died, and Charles d'Orléans likewise later used a poem set on Valentine's Day for the purposes of making a similar contrast, telling the birds how fortunate they are to 'han yowre makis to yowre gret gladnes / Where y sorow the deth of my maystres / Vpon my bed so hard of noyous thought' (B72.2476–8). Unrequited love may prompt a similar complaint to the saint (and indirectly, of course, to the lady): 'Upon your day doth ech foul chese his make; / And you list not in swich comfort me bringe, / That to her grace my lady shulde me take.'[29]

In England, the seminal Valentine poem was what Chaucer referred to in his retractions of his works devoted to 'worldly vanitees' (*CT* X.1081–92) as 'the book of Seint Valentynes day of the Parlement of Briddes'. One should note that Valentines were chosen for the year, by birds and by humans, though both might be represented as 'renewing' that choice in subsequent years (cf. *Floure of Curtesye* 12–14: 'Some obseruaunce dothe vnto this day, / Your choyse ayen of herte to renewe, / In confyrmyng for euer to be trewe'[30]). Christine refers to the day as the one on which it is customary to choose a love for the year ('Ou mains amans trés le matin / Choisissent amours pour l'année'),[31] and in one of his Valentine rondeaux Charles refers to whoever it was who assigned the addressee to him for the year ('qui estrené / M'a de vous pour toute l'annee': R6.5–6).

Many of the Valentine poems did not in fact take the form of a letter or ballade addressed to the lady. They were quite commonly either (a) narratives or soliloquies *set* on Valentine's Day (such as Chaucer's *Parliament of Fowls* and the above-described melancholy Ballade 72 by Charles) or (b) spoken, not to the lady, but to (or sometimes by) St Valentine (such as Charles's Rondeaux 127–8 and 377). The first English Valentine 'proper' may be the Chaucerian poem 'Compleynt d'Amours', which *is* addressed to the lady and ends:

---

[29] *Complaint to My Mortal Foe* 14–16, quoted from W.W. Skeat, ed., *The Complete Works of Geoffrey Chaucer*, 7 vols (Oxford, 1894–7), vol. 4, pp. xxvii–xxviii.
[30] See also the Valentine ballades exchanged in *CBAD*: 'Ce jour de Saint Valentin ... Je vous retien de rechief' (LXXII.1, 8), 'Je te choisy de rechief et retien ... Je le te reconferme' (LXXIII.2, 6).
[31] *Dit de la rose* 639–40 (*Œuvres poétiques*, ed. Roy, vol. 2, pp. 29–48).

This compleynte on Seint Valentynes day,
Whan every foughel chesen shal his make,
To hir whos I am hool and shal alwey,
This woful song and this compleynte I make ...   (85–8)[32]

Otherwise the honour must belong to a Frenchman writing in England, Charles and his early fifteenth-century Rondeau 6, and an Englishman writing in French, Gower and the two Valentine ballades he provided in his turn-of-the-century *Cinkante Balades*, for which he evidently visualized a readership which would include those who might want to send such a Valentine card. An interesting poem in category (a) above is Lydgate's *Floure of Courtesye*, a narrative set on Valentine's Day, but one which turns into, by incorporating and applying to the lady, a 'quoted' song to the loved one: the narrator sees the birds choose their mates, determines that the day requires him to 'write' something despite his lack of ability to 'ryme' and 'endyte' (99–102), praises his lady in the third person, but feels compelled to address her directly in writing and, despite being no Chaucer and having no talent for verse (225–45), applies his 'quakyng honde' (229) to a 'Balade Symple' in which six lines of direct address are in each stanza followed by the two-line refrain 'Thus herde I foules, in the dawenyng, / Vpon the day of Saynte Valentyne synge' (246–70). The poem interestingly dramatizes the plight of a lover who feels that, though he is no poet, the day requires from him some amorous 'missive', which should be in verse, and the subsequent poem is one represented as a quotation of a ditty by professional songsters. The act of 'borrowing' a poem in order to personalize a love appeal is thus here inscribed into the Valentine narrative.

Gower's two Valentines (XXXIIII and XXXV) are similarly borrowable. Both use the traditional legend of the birds choosing their mates on that day in respectively comparative and contrastive ways. The first tells in the opening verse how each bird 'Eslist' [selects] a companion and begins the second verse thus:

| Ma doulce dame, ensi jeo vous assure | My sweet lady, I thus assure you |
| Qe jeo vous ai eslieu semblablement. | That I likewise have chosen you. |

The second (spoken by a less happy lover, whose sad plight recurs with the refrain) ends:

Chascun Tarcel gentil ad sa falcoun,	Each tercel-gentle[33] has his female falcon,
Mais j'ai faili de ceo q'avoir voldroie:	But I have failed to get what I would like to have:
Ma dame, c'est le fin de mon chançoun,	My lady, this is how my song must end:
Qui soul remaint ne poet avoir grant joie.	He who is alone cannot have any real joy.

*

[32] The poem is included in *The Riverside Chaucer* (pp. 658–9), though it is not attributed to Chaucer in any of its three manuscripts.
[33] Male peregrine falcon.

The major collections of love poems regularly included May poems, as well as New Year and Valentine ones. The advent of May – which '*priketh*' every gentil herte', as Chaucer declares in the Knight's Tale (*CT* 1.1043) – was widely celebrated in courtly circles, and those in love felt especially impelled to mark it: Chaucer's lover Arcite, 'Remembrynge on the *poynt* of his desir' (1501), makes himself a chaplet (1507–8) and gives voice to a song ('May, with alle thy floures and thy grene, / Welcom be thou, faire, fresshe May, / In hope that I som grene gete may': 1510–12). And Gower plainly felt that his readers might want some ideas and themes for May, as well as for the New Year and Valentine's Day, for he follows the pairs provided for those seasons with similar alternatives for May. In the first, he declares that, in this month, when Venus 'poignt l'amant' [pricks the lover, XXXVI.6; cf. 'priketh' at *CT* 1.1043, quoted above, and *Confessio Amantis* 7.1048–50, '[May, when Love] of his *pointure* stingeth ... The youthe of every creature'], he will make his May chaplet of thorns rather than roses (15–16) if his lady does not deign to soothe his distress; the second (XXXVII) plays artfully and elegantly on the conceit of flowers and his lady's garden, from which he is debarred, and the 'douls' [sweet] season that is 'amiere' [bitter] and wintry for him. For, as with Valentine poems, the season can be used in a contrastive way to set off the bereavement, loneliness or frustration in the speaker's amorous life, and when such a poem took the form of a soliloquy and the verse form of a ballade (which classically would have an addressee, who would on Valentine or May Day obviously be the beloved), the loneliness is doubly apparent, the ballade impressing itself as in effect a letter to oneself, and the lack of an addressee telling its own sad story:

Or est venu le trés gracieux moys	Now there has come the most lovely month
De May le gay, ou tant a de doulçours ...	Of colourful May, when there is so much sweetness ...
Ces oisillons vont chantant par degois,	The little birds go singing for pleasure,
Tout s'esjouïst partout de commun cours,	Everything rejoices, in a common course,
Fors moy, helas! qui sueffre trop d'anois,	Except me, alas, I who suffer much grief,
Pour ce que loins je suis de mes amours;	Because I am far from my love;
Ne je ne pourroye avoir joye,	And the season could not bring me any joy:
Et plus est gay le temps et plus m'anoye.	The more splendid it is the more is my grief.
Mais mieulx cognois adès s'onques amay,	But better do I know at this time that I once loved,
Pour la doulçour du jolis moys de May ...	Due to the sweetness of the lovely month of May ...

So runs Christine's *Cent balades* XXXIV, a poem that effectively conveys the simultaneous awakening and thwarting of romantic instincts in this season, if the speaker is lovelorn. In her second sequence, May is similarly marked by a longing solo from the lady (uttered 'seulette' [alone, lonely] before her lover returns: *CBAD* LXXIX), not a duet of ballades (as with the Valentine and New Year poems), beginning 'Ce moys de Mai tout se resjoye ... fors moi, lassette!' [in this month of May, all things rejoice ... except my wretched self].

All three festivals similarly provide motifs developed in this less obvious way in the ballade sequence of Charles d'Orléans, who adapts them to the actuality of his wife's absence and later death. Four May ballades written before the death of his mistress lament his joyless state at this joyous time (17, 42, 48, 53). It is only after the lady's death that all three festivals are marked in the sequence, the days bringing inevitably mournful reminders of the absence of her who would give them point. Charles vows in Ballade 57 that he will serve her in death as in life – through prayers and observances to speed her passage through purgatory; and in a ballade for the following New Year (59) he declares he does not wish to give up his custom of marking the day with a gift to her. In a particularly expressive use of the term *estrenne* [New Year gift], which he here employs as a verb, he states that, in order to show that he has not forgotten her, 'De messes je l'ay estrenee' [I have given her Masses as a New Year gift]. Ballades 61–2 mark 1 May and the following day in an especially moving reference to the courtly game of siding with the flower or the leaf: on 1 May, he chooses to pledge his service for the coming year to the leaf rather than the flower, because he has lost the flower he loved; but the following morning the flower appears to him in a dream to reproach him with faithlessness to her. The sad ballade contrasting the joy of the mating birds with his own grief on St Valentine's Day (French 66/ English 72) has already been mentioned (see p. 42 above).

*

Gower's inclusion of poems in major and minor keys for the three festivals is clearly meant to provide models for verse to mark occasions which no lover could let pass without marking, even if only mournfully or elegiacally. Other forms of literature demonstrably so written as to be adaptable to real specific persons or places certainly existed. A prayer-charm could be so formulated that the user could personalize it by inserting the relevant name into the allotted space, as in Humfrey Newton's commonplace book, in which the names of Humfrey himself and of his wife are entered into, respectively, the 'crux christi' charm and a prayer for pregnant women.[34] The N-Town Plays are so-called because the opening proclamation refers to a performance 'In N-Town', 'N' being replaceable by the name of whatever

---

[34] See Youngs, *Humphrey Newton*, pp. 112–13.

town the cycle was taking place in.[35] And it is worth remembering that love poets may often have composed with possible appropriation of their verse (by their readers) in mind: the lack of specifics and the provision of easily adaptable stereotypes would facilitate this, and would make a virtue of precisely that feature of their style (their conventionality and generality) which often offends the modern taste for concrete detail and individualized characters and situations. It is at any rate certain that the marking of New Year's and Valentine's Day by missives was not merely a literary convention observed by lovers as they were represented in verse: real lovers did indeed avail themselves of such models as poets helpfully provided them with, on those and other occasions. The love letters in the Armburgh Roll include – besides two pre-existing macaronic poems that have been reused by the writer as love letters (Text 6, 1, 2) and a third used as the template for successive versions of another verse letter (5A, B, C, D) – a New Year poem to the lady (4A, B) that almost certainly uses and adapts an existing poem.

And then there is the famous Valentine letter that Margery Brews composed in 1477 and sent to the man she was hoping to marry (her cousin, John Paston III). Margery's mother had written Paston a letter that provides a charming insight into a real love affair in this age of arranged marriages. The letter voices, in a maternally forgiving spirit that is very recognizable, a reproach to him and a complaint about her daughter: she had asked him, she says, not to broach the matter to Margery until the negotiations were further advanced, but he has evidently disobeyed her, and her daughter now presses her on with an urgency that gives her no peace; so she invites John to stay Thursday to Monday over the romantic season ('And, cosyn, vppon Fryday is Sent Volentynes Day, and euery brydde chesyth hym a make') and speak with her husband in order to 'bryng the mater to a conclusyon'.[36] She is evidently on the side of the lovers, pressing their cause on an obviously more reluctant husband, as emerges from Margery's own letter, written a little later – which is thus not strictly a Valentine letter, though it is often referred as such. It is simply a love letter that happens to be written in the aftermath of Valentine's Day and therefore addresses John as her Valentine (because the two had evidently recently chosen one another as their 'Valentines') – and Margery in fact so addresses him in a second (quite unsentimental) letter also written (later in February) in the aftermath of Valentine's Day, though that letter is never called a Valentine.[37] The first runs thus:

[35] See *The N-Town Play*, ed. S. Spector, 2 vols, EETS SS 11, 12 (1991), vol. I, Proclamation 527.
[36] *Paston Letters*, ed. Norman Davis, 2 vols (Oxford, 1971–6), no. 791 (vol. 2).
[37] The two letters are nos. 415 and 416 in *Paston Letters*, ed. Davis (vol. 1).

Occasions; Ways and Means; Male and Female Voices 47

Vn-to my ryght welbelouyd Voluntyn John Paston, squyer, be þis bill delyuered, &c.[38]

Ryght reuerent and wurschypful and my right welebeloued Voluntyne, I recommande me vn-to yowe full hertely, desiring to here of yowr welefare, which I beseche Almyghty God long for to preserve vn-to hys pleasure and ȝowr hertys desyre. And yf it please ȝowe to here of my welfare, I am not in good heele of body ner of herte, nor schall be tyll I here from yowe:[39]

> For þer wottys no creature what peyn þat I endure
> And for to be deede I dare it not dyscure [reveal].

And my lady my moder hath labored þe mater to my fadure full delygently, but sche can no more gete þen ȝe knowe of, for þe whech God knowyth I am full sory.

But yf that ȝe loffe me, as I tryste verely that ȝe do, ȝe will not leffe [leave] me þerfor [because of that]; for if þat ȝe hade not halfe þe lyvehode þat ȝe hafe, for to do þe grettyst labure þat any woman on lyve might, I wold not forsake ȝowe.

> And yf ȝe commande me to kepe me true where-euer I go
> Iwyse I will do all my myght ȝowe to love and neuer no mo.
> And yf my freendys say þat I do amys, þei schal not me let [prevent] so for to do.
> Myn herte me byddys euer more to love ȝowe
> Truly ouer all erthely thing.
> And yf þei be neuer so wroth, I tryst it schall be bettur in tyme commyng.

No more to yowe at this tyme, but the Holy Trinité hafe ȝowe in kepyng. And I besech ȝowe þat this bill be not seyn of non errthely creature safe only ȝourselfe, &c. And thys lettur was jndyte [dictated] at Topcroft wyth full heuy herte, &c.   Be ȝour own M. B.

Of the two passages displayed by the letter's editor as verse, the first, as Camargo points out (p. 5), seems to echo lines found in two lyrics in the Welles anthology (compiled in the sixteenth century): 'but y my mynde yet durst no thyng dyscure / how for your sake I dyd suche woo endure'

---

[38] Medieval letters did not have envelopes, but were folded and sealed; the superscription was written on the back and functioned as an address.
[39] Beadle sees here an inversion of the common epistolary convention of following a hope and prayer for the addressee's prosperity with an assurance of the writer's own good health ('Private Letters', pp. 289–306, in *A Companion to Middle English Prose*, ed. A.S.G. Edwards (Cambridge, 2004), at p. 296); but the 'inversion' in a love letter ('I am not at all well, because I miss you, and shall not be well till I see you again or hear from you') is itself a convention that Chaucer's much-read and imitated *Troilus* may have put into circulation: see *Troilus* V.1359–79, and cf. Newton poem II.5–8 ('If it be likynge you to here / of my welfare, þat is full thyn: / I wos full lusty to my bere [I would have been happy to die] / and I had byn clene out of synne [if I had been in the sin-free state necessary for salvation]' and second stanza of *'Suffolk' Poems* (ed. Jansen), no. 14.

(14.11–12; cf. 56.254, 257). The second Camargo declares also to bear 'some resemblance' to lines 239–43 of the latter of these two Welles poems (a love epistle from a man): 'yet better itt were your frendes were wrothe / then ageynst your mynde ye shulde obey / for then here aftur ye wylbe Sorrye and lothe / that euer they bare the lokke & þe keye / of your mynde'. Yet here the resemblance is much looser both in form and in content: the rhymes and the sense are different, leaving little in common beyond the shared reference to 'frendes' (in the older sense of relative and/or connections) who may be 'wrothe' (i.e. averse to the proposed union of the lovers) – a factor which played a greater part then than today in marriage plans, and which may thus be due simply to a shared cultural background (cf. *Welles* 49.30–31: 'thoughe that all my frendes with me were woode / yet shall I loue hur priuelye'). Neither passage is set out in the manuscript letter itself as verse lines separated from the prose of the rest of the letter. This would not in any case have been expected at the time. But there is likewise no pointing (after rhyme words) in either case to signal verse lines, and this was common practice.[40] So there is no orthographic indication of verse, and it may be that the rhymes in the second passage (the *-o* ones coming at the end of improbably long units, and the *-ing* ones being unpersuasive as intentional rhymes) are accidental or at least ad hoc. We are here dealing with, at the most, adaptation from half memory rather than quotation or appropriation. In one or both instances we find that well-known lyrics provide another kind of relation between literary art and reality that a letter might evince. Resemblances between life and art in this area are almost inevitable. People in love find the popular songs of the day (themselves characteristically based on common idioms rather than uncommon phraseology) come virtually unbidden into their heads. The Norfolk abbot also includes snatches (rather more precisely and recognizably quoted) from popular lyrics in his love letters.[41] In this context, quotation and allusion would by no means be possible only for the learned or the literary – for Margery (though neither ignorant nor uneducated by the standards of the day with respect to laywomen) was neither. But she too evidently feels prompted, in the context of a love letter written in the wake of Valentine's Day, to make some gesture towards the verse (quoted or composed) which was so closely associated with a love letter, but of which there is no hint in any other of her letters.

---

[40] The hand is not Margery's own, but that of her scribe (see below, pp. 57–8) so the formatting (or lack of it) can only provide evidence of how he understood the status of the two passages at issue.
[41] See Text 4, I.26–7, II.39–44 and notes.

Occasions; Ways and Means; Male and Female Voices 49

Communication: Rules and Procedures

We turn now to those conditions and conventions of medieval love letters (and to a certain extent all letters and/or messages) that were relevant to security and confidentiality. Two of them have already been seen in operation in the above-quoted pair of poems from Humfrey Newton's commonplace book (Ch. 1, pp. 24–5 above): the poem addressed to 'M' and the poem expressed through 'tokennynge' (line 3) and 'tokens' (penultimate line). The lady was never named. The troubadours had sometimes used a *senhal*, a 'sign' or code name (such as 'sweet enemy'), to refer to her whose name they thus marked as undisclosable. 'Nomen tamen domine serva palliatum' [let the lover ever keep hidden the name of his mistress] warns the twelfth-century Latin love lyric beginning 'Si linguis angelicis'.[42] It was a cardinal rule of love that 'un vray amant' [a true lover] should never 'publier le nom de sa dame' [make public his lady's name], for she naturally feared being made the subject of gossip, and it was this fear, 'la doubte du parler des gens',[43] which governed her conduct and by which the true lover, on her behalf, governed his own. In many cases, of course, the lady might have a husband or parents or relatives from whom the liaison needed to be kept secret, but even where she was (as with Jehan's lady) a single or (as with Criseyde) a widowed mistress of her own property, the rule of secrecy was strictly observed – though it seems that in those cases it was simply a tenet of amorous propriety and that no real disgrace or social ostracization would have resulted from the affair being known.[44] So, though most normal letters began by naming their addressee and sender ('To *x*, from *y*'), a love letter never named the lady or the writer, and this imperative anonymity is reflected also in those letters that belong to literary art. Camargo (p. 153, n. 69) cites a concluding formula utilized in four of the verse love epistles in the Welles anthology:

froo whens ytt cummethe ytt hathe no name,
but frome hym þat ys nameles;
& whyder ytt shall ytt sayethe the same
by cause they shulde be blameles.[45]

---

[42] Line 6 in the text as given by Dronke, *Medieval Latin*, vol. 1, pp. 319–22.
[43] Quotations are from *Antoine de la Sale: Jehan de Saintré*, ed. Jean Misrahi and Charles A. Knudson (Geneva, 1967), pp. 15, 90. The passages cited are at pp. 12 and 63 in the most recent English translation: *Jean de Saintré: A Late Medieval Education in Love and Chivalry*, tr. Roberta L. Krueger and Jane H.M. Taylor (Philadelphia, PA, 2014).
[44] See pp. 257–8 below.
[45] *Welles Anthology*, ed. Jansen and Jordan, 3.45–8; cf. 5.29–32, 33.43–4, 47.65–6.

Another Welles epistle (no. 207 in Robbins), in a woman's voice, is similarly pointedly 'signed' with 'no name': 'vnto yow I nede nott to wryte my name / for she þat louethe yow best send yow þis same' (45.13-14). An initial might personalize without betraying the parties – and 'M' in the lyric cited above finds a parallel in the letters of Chaucer's *Troilus*, where (as well as avoiding naming the addressee) the writer signs himself or herself only as 'le vostre T' or 'La vostre C' (V.1421, 1631). In a rondel sent to her in the *Voir dit*, Machaut weaves an acrostic of 'Péronne' (9043-50) – a cryptic ingenuity that can be mere artful play with the convention of secrecy in love verse, as with the acrostics of the names of his wife and friends formed by the initial letters of the lines of some of Newton's verse love letters (III, VII, VIII, IX).[46] And then there is the charmingly ebullient Harley lyric beginning 'Ichot a burde in a bour ase beryl so bryht'. It is indirectly signed by Christian name in its last line ('gentil ase Ionas, heo ioyeþ with *Ion*'), and lines 28-30 both indirectly name John and give a winking hint at the girl's name:

hire nome is in a note of þe nyhtegale.
   In Annote is hire nome; nempneþ hit
                              non?
   Whose ryht redeþ roune to Iohon.[47]

      nempneþ h. n. is no one naming it
      (i.e. can't you hear it)?
      redeþ guesses; *roune* let him whisper (it)

The second of the Newton lyrics quoted entire above (pp. 24-5) plays on the epistolary use of 'tokens'. These were references to facts known by the sender and proving that s/he was who s/he claimed to be.[48] They were used for the purposes of verification and identification, though the Newton lyric uses them saucily to be wittily very indiscreet as to how the (probably fictional?) liaison is being carried on while superficially scrupulously avoiding the amatory arch-sin of whistle-blowing (i.e. 'I name no names, but you know who I am and I know what I know ...').

Tokens, seriously and properly used, were in fact very necessary in an age when the recipient of the letter might recognize neither the carrier nor

---

[46] The acrostic was popular and occurs inside (and outside) love verse that is not epistolary in form: see Newton IV and Skelton's 'Dyvers Balettys' (iii), which is cited by Camargo (*The Middle English Verse Love Epistle*, p. 150, n. 55), and in which the name 'Kateryn' is spelled out by the first letters of the successive stanzas.

[47] Cited from poem 3 in *The Harley Lyrics*, ed. G.L. Brook, 4th edn (Manchester, 1968). Editorial capitalization here destroys the playful observation of the rule of *not* naming the lady which the poem is both obeying and breaking, and the editorial title provided ('Annot and John') similarly obscures its witty avoidance of outright naming.

[48] For illustrations, see the note to Text 4, 2.46, where an amatory application of this means of verifying the identity of the sender also occurs (cf. 14-16 of the same letter), as it does in Newton XVI, which ends 'fare-wele, fare-wele ... be this same tru tokynynge / I tellid you how longe I wold abid [stay away from the area] – / ye said, alas, hou shall I do so longe?' See also Clare's letter and postscript at pp. 28-9 above.

the hand (often that of a scribe). For letters, we must remember, did not come by the post. They came by carriers, who were often employees of the sender, or they might be friends or acquaintances or tradesmen travelling in the relevant direction who undertook or were paid to deliver the missive. Letters often referred to the carrier or bearer: the Norfolk abbot refers (at Text 4, III.3) to a message sent 'par Llevelyn mon vallet'. The Paston letters similarly refer to missives brought 'by Yelverton's servant (II.494) 'by Chyttock's son' (I.315), 'by Barney's servant (III.91) 'by Edmund Clere of Stokesby' (I.261). Margery Brews thanks her 'Voluntyne', John Paston III, for 'þe letture whech that 3e sende me be John Bekurton' (I.663), and a letter from Margery Paston's lover Richard Calle reveals the complications that could arise for lovers in this connection, especially when the liaison was an unsanctioned one, as in this case (Richard Calle was the family bailiff, with whom Margery, in the teeth of strong family resistance, eventually contracted a secret marriage):[49]

> I had sent you a letter be my ladde from London, and he tolde me he might not speeke wyth you, ther was made so gret awayte [watch] vpon hym and vpon you boothe. He tolde me John Threscher come to hym in your name and seide þat ye sent hym to my ladde for a letter or a token weche I schulde haue sent you; but he truste hym not, he wold not delyuer hym noon ... My ladde tolde me þat my mastres your modre axyd hym if he hadde brought any letter to you .... (II.499)

A common context in which the bearer may be mentioned is when the recipient is referred to him for further information – a recourse taken especially when the matter was highly confidential or important, or where the sender had not the time, space or patience to go into all the necessary details. The recipient is in these cases told to give trust or 'credence' to the 'bearer', who will expand on the message, and the verb 'croire' and its cognates are semi-technical terms referring to such authorized verbal information. Robert Armburgh's business letters, often concerned with claiming money from tenants, frequently refer to the bearer and/or verbal messages he may deliver: '[I] sent you a letter by William Lenton my servant ... ye sent me but iij mare by the same William ... I pray you yevyth credens to the seid William brynger of this letter and payth hym the remenant' (p. 69); 'yevith credence to Roger Bright and John Rotour bryngers of this letre,

---

[49] For a discussion of these and other instances, see Joel T. Rosenthal, *Telling Tales: Sources and Narration in Late Medieval England* (Philadelphia, PA, 2003), pp. 132–3, and Moriarty, ed., *The Voice of the Middle Ages*, pp. 206, 208.

and ... paieth hem your fermys' (p. 129);[50] cf. 'Miles Walter, portur du cestez [bearer of this letter], vous dira plus pleinement par bouche ... A qi vous plaise ... donner ferme foi et credence de ceo'.[51]

Texts 4 and 5 are drafts in verse, to which the prosaic question of the bearer is both inappropriate and as yet irrelevant. Text 7 consists of actual missives: letters sent by a canoness at the abbey of Remiremont to her lover, the governor of Ferrette. Here the bearer is important enough an issue to form a frequent part of the subject matter. The letters were written by a scribe (see below), but contain the odd postscript in the hand of the lady herself. The first such postscript occurs in Letter I (which is in effect all about bearers) and runs: 'Mon ami de mon ceur, *creés* Humbert de ce qu'il vos diray' [My dear heart, trust what Humbert tells you]. It emerges from the letter itself that the reference is to one Humbert Gille, that there have been other messages both to and from her that he has been commissioned to supplement with material not committed or trusted to paper, and that he is the canoness's 'porteur' [carrier] of choice, of proven 'diligence' and 'foy' [fidelity], and the one she most trusts, for she begs her lover to reply by no other bearer. He is referred to as entrusted with a verbal message likewise in Letters II and VI. Other persons and personnel connected with the abbey also act as bearers, but in no case with a letter that authorizes *credence* of any verbal messages to be delivered to one lover by the other, for which Humbert alone is entrusted with. Only outside the context of her romantic life is any other verbal message from the canoness mentioned: a priest, based (apparently) at Remiremont and used as a carrier for a letter (IV) to the canoness from the 'clerc de la bourse', is referred to as having brought the latter messages from her – in connection with her private affairs, certainly, and her father, but not with her lover.

The prevailing methods of carriage and conveyance obviously meant that lovers wrote to each other at risk of detection. A trustworthy and loyal bearer was of the first importance. Pandarus (the uncle of Criseyde and the friend and confidant of Troilus) is the bearer of the first pair of letters exchanged between the lovers (and of later ones)[52] – though we are not told how or by whom the final letters in Book V are delivered (a small indication of how the affair has by then escaped from the controlling hand of Pandarus, who steers it while he can in the direction of a happy ending).

---

[50] References are to *AP* (see Text 6, p. 286).
[51] Quoted by Schendl, 'Code-Choice and Code-Switching', p. 254; cf. Eileen Power, *Medieval English Nunneries* (Cambridge, 1922), pp. 279–80. On conveyance and carriers and verbal supplementation see further *AP*, p. 2, and Moriarty, ed., *The Voice of the Middle Ages*, pp. 17, 19.
[52] See *Troilus* II.1093–1155, 1226–1323, III.488.

Occasions; Ways and Means; Male and Female Voices 53

And a personal servant of proven discretion and fidelity figures elsewhere as the characteristic carrier of love letters. But letters could never be absolutely secure from interception en route or from the eyes of prying third parties. Hence the avoidance in those letters of any names (of persons or places) that could serve as clues was only prudent, and was strictly observed in fact and in fiction.

The bearer who may expand or supplement the letter marks the thin line that existed between a messenger and the carrier of a letter.[53] Lovers want and receive what they call *nouvelles*, news of one another (*CBAD* LII.25, LIV.1–2). And in age when carriage is personal and ad hoc, whether the messenger bears a verbal account or a written one, or the latter supplemented by the former, is often irrelevant and unspecified (*CBAD* LVI.2–3, LVIII.1–2). The confidentiality and delivery of either are dependent on an agent who can be personally trusted. The ideal was a letter brought by someone who could also tell the recipient about the health, etc., of the sender.

Epistolary communication, then, usually involved at least a third party (the carrier), and in fact regularly a fourth as well, with further reduction to the privacy and confidentiality we take for granted today. For most people employed scribes to write even personal and private letters. Reading and writing were separate skills in this period,[54] and calculations of the general level of literacy are complicated by this fact. The number of those who could and did read far exceeds that of those who wrote, for writing with a stylus on parchment was something only those who did so regularly could do with any ease or pace.[55] Writing was in fact a professional skill, practised by clerics, scribes and secretaries. Nearly all of the best-known letters from the Middle Ages were 'not actually written by the sender but dictated to a scribe', as Catherine Moriarty remarks with reference to her own anthology of medieval letters (p. 15). The manuals of instruction were termed precisely *Artes dictaminis/dictandi* – that is, they concerned the art of *dictandi* [dictating], not of *scribendi* [writing], which was a manual skill quite separate from that of composition.[56] Even such a practised letter-writer as Abbot Gervase of Prémontré (who, like many ecclesiastics, cultivated the

---

[53] See further Giles Constable, *Letters and Letter-Collections* (Turnhout, 1976), p. 53.
[54] See Michael Clanchy, *From Memory to Written Record*, 3rd edn (Chichester, 2013), pp. 13, 47, 126–7, 232.
[55] Many letters may in fact have been written on wax tablets – which Camargo declares (*The Middle English Verse Love Epistle*, p. 1) to have been the 'normal medium' for private letters – though it is, obviously, only those more durably inscribed on parchment or paper that have survived (see further Ch. 3, p. 69 below).
[56] The scribe, however, may in some cases have had a hand in the composition, too, since it appears that he sometimes wrote up the letter from mere general instructions as to content provided by the sender: see Beadle, 'Private Letters', p. 291.

epistolary art and was admired for his rhetorical skills therein) employed what Moriarty calls a human 'typewriter' – in Gervase's case a professional secretary called Hugh, who became his letter-writer because he was 'accustomed to the practice of penmanship from childhood', as Hugh himself put it in a letter in which he draws a distinction between this his own experience in writing (*scribendi usum*) and the compositional skills (*dictandi scientia*) displayed by his dictator Gervase, skills taught in two manuals on the art of *dictamen* which Gervase had given to Hugh.[57] The mystic Catherine of Siena could read but not write, and both her many letters and her treatise *Il Dialogo* (later translated into Middle English under the title of *The Orchard of Syon*) were likewise dictated.[58] Eileen Power reports the similar case of a nun for whom reading her letters, even when they were in Latin, posed no problem, but who could write not at all (p. 245). But in many cases it was simply that the sender could write only with laborious slowness. 'Do not be surprised that I have not written this time as usual with my own hand, for I have recovered my accustomed writer, and am hindered by other trifles',[59] writes an archdeacon whom one might expect, as a cleric, to be better able to write than a layman, but who plainly finds, if he has much to do, that it is quicker and easier to use the scribe whose services are now again at his disposal. 'Scribbled in hast with mine owne hand in default of other helpe' runs an apology from one of Sir William Plumpton's correspondents (c. 1465), who similarly, it is clear, would normally employ an amanuensis.[60]

Margery Brews's love letter to her 'Valentine' was written by a scribe, though she wrote her own initials as a concluding signature and in three later letters (nos. 417, 418 and 420) also penned by a scribe she adds in a 'halting and uncontrolled hand' (*Paston Letters*, ed. Davis, vol. I, p. xxxvii) the subscription 'Be yowre seruaunt (and bedewoman) Margery Paston'; the love letters of the canoness from Remiremont (Text 7) were also written by scribes, but there are likewise two cases (Letters I and VI) in which a final formula was added in her own hand. It is evident, therefore, that these two women were not totally unable to write. Criseyde can and does write to Troilus with her own hand (II.1218), but when the writing of such a letter (in reply to his) is pressed on her by Pandarus, she had exclaimed: '3e, for

---

[57] Letter (1218) from Hugh, a canon of Prémontré, to Simon, a canon of St Mary of St Eloi-Fontaine: quoted from p. 29 of C.R. Cheney, 'Gervase, Abbot of Prémontré: A Medieval Letter-Writer', *Bulletin of the John Rylands Library* 33 (1950) 25–56.
[58] *Women's Writing in Middle English*, ed. Alexandra Barratt (London, 1992), p. 95.
[59] Letter (1443) from Jean de Batute, archdeacon of Saint-Antonin at Rodez (Moriarty, ed., *The Voice of the Middle Ages*, p. 198).
[60] Quoted by Beadle, 'Private Letters', p. 291.

Occasions; Ways and Means; Male and Female Voices 55

I kan so written ... And ek I noot what I sholde to hym seye' (II.1205–6). 'And ek' implies that her second objection (she has no idea *what* to say) is something separate from what is suggested by the obviously sarcastic previous line ('Oh, and I am so well able to write a letter!'), which refers to her lack of experience in penning letters for herself. She had earlier categorically ruled out any epistolary response by her, telling Pandarus he must himself provide any answer he wishes to take back: 'Swich answere as ʒow list ʒoure self purueye, / ffor trewely I nyl no letter write' (1160–1). Pandarus promptly takes up her invitation by offering to be her scribe ('"No? than wol I", quod he, "so ye endite"'), thus jestingly exploiting the usual division of the two labours of composing/dictating and scripting which the action of 'writing a letter' often entailed. When he does urge her for a reply after their meal together, he similarly offers in semi-jest to take on other associated parts of the labour and responsibility involved:

'Myself to medes wol the letter sowe'.
And held his hondes vp and sat on knowe;
"Now, goode Nece, be it neuere so lite,
ʒif me the labour it to sowe and plite"'. (1201–4)

The allusion is to the fact that letters were regularly folded and sewn before being consigned to the carrier: in most surviving missives 'the text occupies one side of the sheet only, which was then folded to form a small packet with only parts of the blank dorse visible from the outside. Tape or thread was passed through small slits in the paper, and the ends were embedded in sealing wax, which sometimes survives to show the impression of the sender's signet'.[61] Troilus had accordingly (II.1085–8) carefully folded and sealed with his signet the letter to which Criseyde replies. The offer of acting as scribe to her dictation Criseyde realizes is a joke (II.1163), and she likewise takes his second offer as unserious (since she does not take him up on it), but she says pointedly of the letter he does thus coax her into writing (by jokingly offering to relieve her of virtually all agency in the matter): 'god help me so, this is the firste letter / That euere I *wroot*, ʒe, al or any del' (1214–15). She would not normally pen her own letters, and what she means is that being forced for once to do so implies possibly embarrassing 'secrets' that cannot be entrusted to a scribe, and that it is Pandarus who has put her in this potentially compromising situation.[62] To have been known to have actually written anything would evidently be as

---

[61] Beadle, 'Private Letters', p. 292; cf. Text 7, p. 357. See also Schulz-Grobert, *Deutsche Liebesbriefe*, p. 23.
[62] On these implications of a woman's acting as her own scribe, see further note to Text 5, 1–2.

damaging as being known to have received a love letter – which has literally to be 'thrust' on Criseyde (II.1155), so shocked is she at the very notion that one should be delivered to her ('scrit ne bille, / ffor loue of god, that toucheth swich matere, / Ne brynge me noon; and also, vncle dere, / To myn estat haue more reward, I preye, / Than to his lust – what sholde I more seye?': II.1130–4). It is significant, however, that she is much less forceful in registering her displeasure at writing a letter than she had been at receiving Troilus's: Pandarus has obviously succeeded in jollying and joking down her propriety to a point where it is not so imperiously unnegotiable.

It is often argued that the use of scribes was something women in particular were reduced to, and that history has thus conspired to muffle or suppress their voices because of a postulated lower level of literacy than was enjoyed by men. But the degree to which this is true can be overstated. Women may indeed often have found it harder to write than non-aristocratic men, since they would generally have been less called on to use the skill in the way of memoranda, accounts, etc., than would professional or business men (who more often wrote their own letters than did aristocratic males), and it is thus certainly the case that, for instance, where the Paston women consistently employed scribes, the Paston men frequently penned their own letters.[63] Betson is cross that Katherine does not write, because she has at hand the scribes he assumes she would need: 'she might get a secretary, if she would' (*Stonor Letters*, vol. 2, p. 28). But the draft letter from a woman that forms Text 5 must be an autograph, and it is clear that some women's letters are in their own hands (as, among the Paston letters, are those from Elizabeth Clere and the Duchess of Suffolk[64]) and their personal hands have been detected on occasion in the letter collections of particular families, even by those who seem disappointed and surprised at the 'exception' thus provided to the suppression of the unmediated feminine hand.[65] Reality and literary art concur in their often being able to write if necessary. Some, that is, might pen their own love letters if there was no scribe to hand whom they could trust with so confidential a document. Criseyde pens her first ever letter in her own hand when so situated: she evidently will trust no one in her household, and apparently would rather not trust even Pandarus (who, though his secrecy could certainly be relied on, might interfere with

---

[63] See *Paston Letters*, ed. Davis, vol. 1, pp. xxxvi–xxxvii.
[64] See notes at pp. 255 and 260 to Barratt's edition of the letters in *Women's Writing in Middle English*.
[65] See, for instance, Rosenthal, *Telling Tales*, p. 105. On female literacy and women's letters, see further the references provided by Beadle, 'Private Letters', p. 292, n. 10, and Youngs, *Humphrey Newton*, p. 177, n. 2, and see also Caroline M. Barron, 'The Education and Training of Girls in Fifteenth-Century London', in *Courts, Counties and the Capital in the Later Middle Ages*, ed. Diana E.S. Dunn (Stroud, 1996), pp. 139–53.

the guarded wording she prefers to keep personal control of). A woman with no or very limited skills might have to use a scribe of dubious proficiency and/or trustworthiness if there was no better one available. Such a woman was Péronne, who apologizes for a letter that may be ill-penned, since she cannot always find a satisfactory scribe (*VD* L43), and when questioned specifically by Machaut about another explains (L46) that it was written 'plus briefment et plus obscurement' than usual, because she cannot always find a trustworthy 'clerc' (i.e. one to whom she could dictate freely).

Writing is an art women exercised, it appears, only in very exceptional cases (cf. *Troilus* II.1214–15): though some gentlewomen could and did sometimes pen their own letters, they were exceptions to the rule of dictation to a scribe.[66] But in that the women differ little from many men for whom the use of a scribe was also normal. If Margery Brews and the canoness at Remiremont confined their personal penmanship to concluding formulae, so likewise did a number of men, for a postscript greeting in his own hand is similarly added in a scribed letter from Jean de Vaudrey to Pierre (Text 7, V), such concluding phrases *manu propria* being in accord with a custom observed by many, including men of high status (who were the likeliest to use scribes as a matter of course).[67]

Margery Brews was fortunate (since her own hand was very wobbly) in having a pre-eminently trustworthy scribe to hand. We know his name, because the hand is the same as that of the Thomas Kela, her father's clerk (and probably a priest), who wrote to John Paston himself in the same February month of 1477 in which Margery's two letters addressing him as her 'Valentine' were penned; and it is evident from this letter that he (like Margery's mother) was 'on Margery's side', privy to all matters relating to the projected match, which he was as anxious to promote as her mother, and equally urgent (cf. p. 46 above) with the prospective groom to negotiate with the father in the full knowledge of not only the mother's, but also his own, support:

> Ryght wurschypfull ser, I recommande me vn-to yowe, lettyng ȝowe knowe as for the ȝonge gentylwoman sche owyth [gives] ȝowe hyr good herte and love, as I know be þe comynicacion þat I hafe hade wyth hyr ...
> And I vndurstand by my lady [Margery's mother] þat sche wold þat ȝe schuld labur þe mater to my maistur, for it schuld be the bettur ... and ȝe be-holdyng vn-to my lady for hyr good wurde, for sche hath neuer preysyd ȝowe to meche [thinks no praise too much for you].

---

[66] Letters from women become increasingly common over the fifteenth century (when the vernacular was increasingly used for those purposes), but holographs are rare before 1500: see Malcolm Richardson, *Middle-Class Writing in Late Medieval London* (London, 2010), pp. 143–54.
[67] 'une pratique générale qui est aussi celle des ducs de Bourgogne' (Werner Paravicini, ed., 'Un amour malheureux au XVe siècle: Pierre de Hagenbach et la dame de Remiremont', *Journal des savants* 1 (2006) 105–81 (p. 122)).

Ser, lyke as I promysyd 30we, I am yowr man and my good will 3e schall
hafe in worde and dede, &c. And Iesus hafe 30we in hys mercyfull kepyng, &c.
Be your man SER THOMAS KELA[68]

Of course, most people in later centuries would not wish to employ a scribe, however discreet, for so private a matter as a love letter. But the different circumstances of an earlier age entailed different standards and kinds of privacy. Love affairs, whether open or secret, regularly involved a go-between, a third party who might be a broker or a friend (Michael Cassio 'who came a-wooing with [Othello]',[69] Pandarus in *Troilus*, Galehot in the *Lancelot*), and the odium today attached to the 'third' ('two is company, three is none') was at this time reserved for the *fourth*.[70] Meetings thus commonly took place under the facilitation, and often in the presence, of a third person (who might sometimes be there to prevent suspicions being aroused by an otherwise 'private' meeting with a man by an unchaperoned woman, as with the duenna in the lyric quoted in Chapter 1 above, pp. 24–5[71]).

The trustworthiness of the scribe was even more important than that of the bearer, and the office of *secrétaire* had some prestige, for it implied the trust of one's superior in one's discretion and diplomacy with respect to confidential matters. The 'secrets' such a man was privy to are, of course, the origin of the term 'secretary'. Several poets indeed are known to have acted as secretaries – a fact that provides a further dimension to the interconnections between the worlds of literary art and of 'real life' letters.[72] Since secretaries often themselves composed the letters of their masters (who would sometimes simply summarize the desired content),[73] they performed an articulatory service analogous to that which love poets might perform for lovers: providing ready-penned formulations which could be sent or delivered in the form of a letter.

---

[68] *Paston Letters*, ed. Davis, vol. 2, no. 792; Kela also scribed no. 773, a letter in March 1477 from Margery's father, Sir Thomas Brews, to John Paston II regarding financial arrangements for the projected match.
[69] *Othello* III.3.71–2.
[70] The undesirable fourth underlies, for instance, the joke made by the Lady of Malehot to Guinevere at pp. 350–1 in Elspeth Kennedy's edition of *Lancelot do Lac: The Non-Cyclic Old French Prose Romance*, 2 vols (Oxford, 1980). On the regular involvement of a third party, see Myra Stokes, 'The Contract of Love Service', *Literaria Pragensia* 9 (1999) 62–83 (p. 77).
[71] Pandarus is thus careful to make it appear that Deiphebus and Helen are present at the first interview between Troilus and Criseyde in an inner chamber, though (unknown to those in the outer chamber) a pretext has been found to get rid of them: see *Troilus* II.1688–1708, 1716–22.
[72] Poirion (*Le poète et le prince*, p. 173) gives examples that include Jean Castel (the son of Christine de Pisan) and Machaut (whose career started with his serving Jean le Bon as secretary and clerk), and he points out that Chartier and Chastellain 'ont occupé des fonctions analogues'.
[73] See Beadle, 'Private Letters', p. 291, where Norman Davis is also cited: 'It is seldom possible to know whether a letter written by a clerk was taken down verbatim at dictation or composed more or less freely on the basis of instructions given by the author' (*Paston Letters*, ed. Davis, vol. 1, p. xxxviii).

The prosaic details of scribe, secretary and carrier can be, and usually are, ignored in the literary love letter. For the practical problems of getting the letter written and delivered are ones which belong to actuality and which art does not need to address. But important exceptions can be found in the art of the personification allegory characteristic of the work of Charles d'Orléans, who is interested in everything to do with written communication and turns to the personnel involved in it to conduct perceptive analyses of, for instance, his relation to love. He can thus represent himself as merely the scribe and secretary of his poems, which are dictated by Love, always represented as his 'master'; and he can also, in a letter to that former master, once Charles has retired from his court, refer him for more information to the carrier, Confort – who is (significantly) a member of Love's own household, to which he returns once he has guided Charles to his new home elsewhere.[74]

The Female Voice[75]

There is a large area of overlap between the genders, but there are also some distinctions, as regards the sentiments and language they may use, in art and reality, in addressing each other when in love. But there is no particular distinction between how they are represented by their own, and how by the other, sex. Gower and Christine, for instance, do not differ significantly in their representations of where female experience and language echo, and where they differ from, those typical of the male.

In general, women do not plead for 'mercy' or 'reward' for 'service', as the male lover insistently does (though a woman may use even that last trope). And they complain more about lack of fidelity than lack of reciprocation. It is truth and fidelity that prompt their praise and celebration (rather than beauty and graciousness), and where the man typically complains of cruelty or lack of reward for his service, the woman typically worries more about disapproving or spiteful gossip, is distrustful of the rhetoric of courtly love, is suspicious of the 'falseness' often found to underlie flowery protestations, which she thinks generally turn out to be lies (*CBAD* IV.16), utters sarcastic verses to and about men who 'fayn' ('Yowre counturfetyng with doubyll delyng ... When that ye do lye, then speke ye so swetely'[76]) and rails against the infidelity and treachery of lovers. Gower's women are as eloquent on that last subject as Christine's. The point in his sequence at which

---

[74] For allegories involving secretary, scribe and carrier, see B25, B30, B50 and *Songe* 479–86, 517–27.
[75] On women as the authors, not of love letters, but of other kinds of letter, see *Dear Sister: Medieval Women and the Epistolary Genre*, ed. Karen Cherewatuk and Ulrike Wiethaus (Philadelphia, PA, 1993).
[76] From a Tudor song edited by Barratt, *Women's Writing in Middle English*, p. 289 (from London, BL, Add. 5465); cf. the Findern poem (fol. 56ʳ) beginning 'What-so men seyn' (Barratt, pp. 268–70).

female-voiced counterparts occurs is revealing. Ballade XL, in which the man hints at promises unfulfilled and which has the refrain 'Loials amours se provont a l'essai' [true love is proved when put to the test], is followed by three ballades in the voice of a woman, one on how men's promises have often been found hollow and a woman should not trust too readily in them, and two that are more emphatically abusive of a man addressed as 'mirour des mutabilitées' (XLII.17) who has proved 'Plus tricherous qe Jason a Medée' (XLIII.1). Being betrayed is obviously a subject on which Gower felt women might have more to say and more vehemently.

Women are not generally represented as falling in love at first sight as men are, but do so only after they have seen proof of constancy and worth (see *Troilus* II.673–9). For women, it was felt, could not afford to be impulsive but must be wary, and *s'aviser* turns out to be a significant verb for Gower's women: 'Bon est qe bone dame bien s'avise' [it is good that a good woman should take careful thought] runs the refrain of XLI, and even when she does give her love, she must likewise be guarded ('Mais pour les gentz tresbien m'aviserai' [but I will take careful thought against being noticed by other people]: XLVI.13). A woman must be on her guard: on her guard against prompting talk that may harm her name, and on her guard against lovers who may betray her trust in their fine words. Her aversion to attracting notice that may damage her status was taken so much for granted that the faithless lover of Christine's later sequence can plead (in his ballades from LXXXIII on) that his staying away from the lady is due to prudent concern for her honour (see e.g. LXXXV), which might suffer from 'mesdisans' [ill-speakers], the very thought of whom had earlier made her tremble and perspire in fear (XVI.14–18). She is found at one point defying all spying eyes and malicious tongues, which she vows will never make her 'recreaunt' to her love (*CB* XXX.5), a posture also taken up at one point in the later sequence (*CBAD* XLII.17–28), but the defiance takes its point from the strength of the deterrent thus over-ridden, and when it appears in art or actuality, it simply marks in reverse the constraints normally operative.

Gossip and the falsity of men are the two specifics that emerge from Criseyde's initial fears of embarking on the 'stormy lyf' (II.778) of the lover:

Also thise wikked tonges ben so preste
To speke vs harm, ek men ben so vntrewe,
That right anon as cessed is hire leste
So cesseth loue, and forth to loue a newe.   (II.785–8)[77]

[77] Though, in the event, it is Criseyde herself who is inconstant, Chaucer's claim at the end of the poem – that his tale constitutes a warning against betrayal that should be heeded as much or more by women as by men (V.1779–80) – is borne out by the frequency with which he elsewhere depicts (with passion and emphasis) the plight of the betrayed female (in *House of Fame, Anelida and Arcite, Legend of Good Women* and the Squire's Tale).

The likewise initially reluctant lady of the *Cent balades d'amant et de dame* gives a similar summary of her fears: 'paour que on m'en diffamast, / Ou que fusse par faulx semblant honnie' [fear that I should be defamed, / Or meet disgrace through falseness] (XII.17–18). And these twin concerns recur throughout Christine's earlier sequence (as well as providing the dramatic catastrophe to her later one). But though her two series come across overall as more stressed, sceptical and bitter than Gower's, she does not differ from him (or from Chaucer) in what she represents as a woman's sentiments, fears and experience (with regard to keeping her name free of scandal and avoiding the danger of betrayal).

In other respects, the standard language and rhetoric of love verse remain largely unchanged in the case of a female speaker. The familiar postures, topoi, conceits and expressions were easily re-genderable. Some poems in the Findern manuscript could be assignable to either gender.[78] And elsewhere it is often only a chance grammatical or lexical indication of gender or a nuance of usage that reveals a female speaker. Two verse epistles from the Welles anthology provide an example. Number 44 begins 'grene flowryng age of your manly countenance', but there is nothing in the rest of the lyric that would be atypical of a male speaker. The next poem begins: 'O resplendent floure prynte þis yn your mynde / how as yet vnto yow I was neuer vnkynde'. 'Vnkynde' indicates a female voice (since, in an amorous context, it was of women that the adjective was characteristically used),[79] and proof of such a voice comes in the designation of the sender in the sign-off as 'she þat louethe yow best' (14) – but the rest of the poem, again, is written in language indistinguishable from that regularly used in verse epistles to women.[80] Poem No. 199 in Robbins (from Douce 95) is also a love letter written by a woman, though the evidence for this has been removed by two small editorial emendations (as Camargo also points out: p. 157): of 'she' to 'he' in line 11 (where the sender writes 'ass she þat is with wo oppressed sore') and of 'manhede' to 'maidenhede' in line 32 (where the writer comments on the 'fressh beaute' that inspired love 'Whan y sawe first your manhede'). One cannot blame Robbins for assuming material so otherwise indistinguishable from standard expressions of male desire must emanate

---

[78] See poems 2, 3, 12, 26, 29 in *The Findern Manuscript: A New Edition of the Unique Poems*, ed. Joanna Martin (Liverpool, 2020).
[79] Used in the positive, it indicated a reciprocating and faithful mistress (cf. *Welles Anthology*, ed. Jansen and Jordan, 59.8, 12), while in the negative it indicated a cold one and was often a transparent euphemism for 'unfaithful' (cf. *Troilus* IV.15–16).
[80] The words 'vnto my mastur' that figure in a strange appended envoy (beginning 'goo little queare') that follows the sign-off cannot be used as unproblematic evidence of a male addressee (the equivalent of a 'mistress'), since this eight-line envoy is repeated verbatim from the envoy to Lydgate's *The Churl and the Bird* (text in EETS OS 192, ed. MacCracken).

from the standard gender. In short, the language of love, developed largely for men, was obviously felt to be equally appropriate to the other sex, to which it could easily be adapted by the odd minor change (which a modern editor can as easily reverse).

Christine (for whom it was something of a mission to give women a voice) in fact also uses for her female speakers many of the same conceits and topoi as do Gower's male speakers. The pains, suffering and oxymorons of love, the peerlessness of the beloved ('Certes c'est cil qui tous les autres passe' runs the refrain of *CB* XXXIII), the 'chain' by which one is 'bound' (XL.1–3), the beloved as the only 'doctor' or 'cure' for the wounds or malady of the lovesick speaker (XLIII): these are all standard conceits and commonplaces that a female speaker is ready to take over virtually unchanged – and that last is also used by the woman who drafted the verse love letter in Text 5 (see lines 21–2 and note). The same applies to the tropes of 'service' (XLIV.2) and lack of 'reward' (LXIII). A male lover may apply these to his beloved or to Love. Christine does not use them in the former way (though there are female-voiced poems that do[81]), but she is happy to use them in the latter. And her *dame* 'yields' and 'humbles herself' to the Love she had vainly supposed herself too wise to be conquered by ('rendre com matée / M'estuet ... il fault que m'umilie' [I must yield myself as overcome ... I must humble myself]: *CBAD* XXII.21–2, 28), as must Troilus, who similarly thought himself so wise in his mockery of Love (I.205, 302–3), who instantly brings him low and reduces him to thraldom (I.231, 235, 439), and as the typical male lover (represented by *l'amant* in the allegory of the *Romaunt of the Rose*) must make a kneeling surrender and 'yelde' himself 'hombly' to the Love who overpowers him with his superior force (1944, 1946). And a lover whose attentions are found to be less than lover-like earns a ballade (*CB* LVI) whose refrain ('Car l'oeuvre loe le maistre' [for it is his work that recommends a master craftsman]) closely matches that of Gower's similar rebuking refrain to a lady who seems likewise to be showing an insufficient degree of interest and commitment ('Loials amours se provont a l'essai', XL).

In general, then, in literary epistles, the sentiments and voices of women are virtually indistinguishable from those of men with regard to expressions of love or praise or longing; but they are represented as perpetually fearful of exposure or gossip that may harm their name and as liable to and fearful of being dumped. The few actual surviving love letters from women only partially bear out this characterization (found in both male

---

[81] See Poem 16 in Martin, ed., *The Findern Manuscript*.

and female poets). Margery Brews does include towards the end of her letter a request that it should come to no one's eyes except John's, and the canoness also several times urges discretion on Pierre, who is evidently less cautious (Text 7, I.10–11, VII.12). But there is also Margery's declaration of readiness to defy disapproval from her relatives and connections (see p. 47 above), and though in her case made in the knowledge that such defiance will probably not be necessary, the statement does remind us that, amongst real women, there were those (like Heloise for instance) who might be rather more heedless and reckless than the men – who, for their part, when they had anything to lose by exposure, were cautious enough: the Norfolk abbot is quite alive to the need to avoid gossip about his affair with a nun (Text 4, II.7–13).

It is also, in our texts, actually the men who reveal themselves as insecure and distrustful about the lady's fidelity – and who, in so doing, confirm a different gender truism often repeated in the literature of the period: that women were likely to suffer from the 'jalousie' of their lovers.[82] Like Péronne in the *Voir dit*, the canoness has to defend herself against suspicions that are, both women claim, quite baseless (Text 7, VII.6–10; and cf. Text 4, 1.3–4). The women themselves do not generally write with any lack of confidence in their positions in the hearts of their men or with any anxious whining on that score.

As far as susceptibility to abandonment goes, Text 5 does sound like the work of a woman who suspects her man has lost interest; and George Cely, who returned in 1482 to England, where he was married in 1484,[83] presumably left behind him a saddened Clare. But modern assumptions may detect Marianas in women who would not necessarily see themselves in that way. Pierre of Hagenbach (who was already a widower in 1471, the year to which the extant letters from the canoness belong) remarried in 1474. But although Paravicini entitled his fine edition of the canoness's letters 'Un amour malheureux au XVe siècle', and although Paul Gerhard Schmidt (in a reference to the correspondence) declares that Pierre 'decided against [the canoness] and married another woman',[84] the implication that the canoness was left jilted and disappointed by the marriage (dictated, like George Cely's and many another's, by considerations other than love) is not borne out by the letters. She reveals no hopes or expectations that the (politically ineligible) liaison with him will lead eventually to marriage and

---

[82] Cf. for instance *Troilus* III.1016–29.
[83] See Hanham, *The Celys and Their World*, pp. 279 (return to England) and 310–11 (marriage).
[84] Paul Gerhard Schmidt, 'Amor in Claustro', in *Medieval Latin and Middle English Literature: Essays in Honour of Jill Mann*, ed. Christopher Cannon and Maura Nolan (Cambridge, 2011), pp. 182–92 (p. 192).

no discontent with her status as an *amie* rather than a wife – for that status was actually one that carried a great deal of (unofficial) weight and even its own kind of respectability, and would not, in many circles, have been regarded as one 'second best' to that of wife.[85] In fact, medieval actualities may often be less in danger of distortion by their refraction in contemporary literary art than by modern assumptions based on sometimes different modern realities.

---

[85] See Stokes, 'The Contract of Love Service', pp. 73–81.

CHAPTER 3

Clerics and Convents

Epistolae duorum amantium; Abelard and Heloise;
Baudri of Bourgueil; Regensburg; Tegernsee; Söflingen

The *Epistolae duorum amantium* consist of extracts from a series of love letters written in Latin and exchanged between a man and a woman in France in about the year 1100. The abridgement was made in 1471 by a Cistercian monk called Johannes de Vepria. He had been commissioned to make an inventory of the manuscripts at the abbey of Clairvaux and in the course of doing so he copied out selected parts of them into a personal anthology. The *Epistolae* occupy fols. 159^r–167^v in this signed and dated florilegium (Troyes, Bibliothèque municipale, MS 1452) and form the only trace of a now lost original manuscript.[1] Johannes evidently kept only what was generally applicable to all lovers, so that the letters could serve as models for the epistolary expression of amorous sentiment. He provided in the margin at the beginning of each letter an initial to indicate whether it was from the man (V[ir]) or the woman (M[ulier]). Their actual names he almost certainly did not know, as names were always scrupulously avoided in amatory correspondence (see pp. 49–50 above). Though it was usually the woman who was especially concerned to avoid exposure, where the man was a cleric (as the *vir* here evidently is), he could show as much or more concern on this score as the woman (cf. the Norfolk Abbot at Text 4.1.14–20, 2.9–15 and notes); and it is almost always the *vir* here who refers to the risks to reputation and the need for caution (Letters 75, 101) in order to avoid the *populi murmura que timeo* (113). The names that did not appear were in any case irrelevant to Johannes's interest in the letters as models – as were all other specifics peculiar to their situation, which he also omitted. He signals his omissions by oblique lines, and what is noticeably absent is all particularizing detail (cf. Piron, pp. 181–2). What remains is sometimes no more than the opening salutation and the *vale* [farewell],

---

[1] See Piron, ed., *Lettres des deux amants*, pp. 177–8 (on the MS) and pp. 194–6 (for the date and place in which the letters were written).

for correctness and stylishness in these areas were of primary importance in epistolary art and etiquette. The regular letter-opening formula has in any case a particular elegance and concision in Latin, consisting of a dative (the person addressed), a nominative (the sender, who is subject of an implied verb 'writes') and an accusative (the blessings that are object of an implied verb 'wishes' or 'sends'), case alone marking the transition and distinction between these three slots (of which the second or third may in this series be omitted). Names would normally appear in the first two slots, but names the lovers cannot use, and they show instead especial skill in the deployment of the formulaic sequence, often playing meaningfully on the strict sense of *salu-* [health] and *vale* [be well] and using elaborately elegant tropes and conceits:

> Preciosissime gemme sue, suo naturali splendore semper radianti, aurum eius purissimum: letissimis amplexibus eandem gemmam circumdare et decenter ornare [...] Vale que me valere facis. (Vir 10)
>
> To his most precious gem, always radiant in its own natural brightness, (he whose faithful love equates to) its setting of purest gold (sends the wish that he may) with his most joyful embraces provide a fittingly ornate encirclement for this gem [...] Farewell to you who makes me fare well.
>
> Amate et semper amande, solitarius in tecto merens, et curis estuans: salutem quam velim tecum habere, et te sine me non habere ... (Mulier 42)
>
> To the one loved and ever to be loved, I sorrowing alone where I dwell and feverish with cares (send) the salutation/health which I would wish to have with you and would not wish you to have without me ...[2]

Quite often the salutation and *vale* may be all the lovers themselves wrote: there are numerous instances where the letter consists of nothing else (39–41, 44, 67–8), but where Johannes does not indicate any omissions. For lovers, indeed, these areas provide slots in which the essence of what they want to say can be expressed (how precious is the beloved, how important his/her welfare, and all that is wished with regard to their love for one another):

> Lumini clarissimo, et solsticio suo, nunquam fuscis tenebrarum labenti, sed semper candoris colorem inferenti, illa quam nullus nisi tu sol uret in die, nec luna per noctem: acrius candescere, splendidius fulgere, in fervore nostri amoris non deficere, salis condimentum habere, conditaque servare. Vale. (M92)

---

[2] Quotations are from Piron, ed., *Lettres des deux amants* (who uses Könsgen's text with minor adjustments); translations are our own. A translation of the complete text is available in Barbara Newman, *Making Love in the Twelfth Century: 'Letters of Two Lovers' in Context* (Philadelphia, PA, 2016).

To the brightest light and her summer solstice, never falling into the shades of darkness, but always bestowing clarity, she for whom no sun except you shines by day, nor moon by night, (sends the wish that he may) ever more keenly shine, ever more brilliantly luminesce, never wane in the heat of our love, possess the preserving power of salt and conserve what has been so preserved. Fare well.

Of the letters that consisted of more, what Johannes kept tends to consist of declarations of love and/or of the excellence and moral virtues of the beloved and the nobly disinterested nature of true *amor* and *amicitia* (see especially 24 and 25) – that is, material of a sentient and sentimental type that all lovers might find useful, applicable or interesting.

The original correspondents evidently took literary pride and pleasure in the very art of composition. They parade to each other their literate Latinity, philosophically and rhetorically sophisticated as it is, embellished with conceits and with learned quotations from and references to Scripture and the classics. Each compliments the other on his/her eloquence in a kind of inverse rivalry that demonstrates their literary self-consciousness. The woman protests her own inarticulacy in face of the wealth of learning (*philosophie*), wisdom (*sapience*) and eloquence she commends in the man (23, 49, 53). He in turn praises her compositional powers (63), and the subtlety of her reasoning on Ciceronian texts convinces him that she is his superior even in the area where, as a man who enjoys the clerical training not open to a woman, he would hope to surpass her, in *facundia* and *ingenium* (50). Furthermore, each sends verses to the other, thus demonstrating mastery of the metrical art which was from the first associated with both love and love letters. The woman, who can write prose that is as learned and stylish as that of the man, similarly shows herself not noticeably inferior to him in verse. The verses they write may be inserted into the letter or the letter itself may take the form of verse, sometimes amounting to an epistolary love poem that incorporates the salutation and farewell formulae:

Flos juvenilis ave, lux et decus imperiale ...
Quot maris undisone, tot tibi dico vale. (M73)

Hail, flower of youth, imperial brilliance and excellence ... I bid you as many farewells as there are sounding waves in the sea.[3]

---

[3] On the *quot ... tot* formula in the farewell, cf. Text 1, 130/22–6 and note, and Text 4, 1.21–3 and note. Elsewhere, the *mulier* includes a poem in 69 and her letter 38b consists entirely of a poem, as, in effect, do 73 (preceded by an extra prose *salve*) and 66 and 82 (each followed by a brief prose *vale*). The *vir* sends verse letters at 38a and c, 87, 108 and 111, and 20 is almost entirely in verse.

Sol meus atque serena dies mea, lux mea, salve ...   (V108)

Hail, my sun and my clear day, my light ...

Item 87 seems (line 2) to celebrate the first anniversary of their love (and is understood to do so by Piron: p. 191), and is in effect an adaptation of the lover's New Year poem (see pp. 39–41 above). The *vir* offers in this new year a new love ('Nunc novus est annus, novus est amor incipiendus'), a love free of the offence he has occasionally given in the past. In another of his poems (20) he laments the absence of the star that guides him ('Sed michi sydus hebet quod me conducere debet'), using a conceit that Chaucer later made famous by adopting it as the theme of his own replacement for the song given by Boccaccio to Troilus after Criseyde has left Troy, a replacement that begins 'O sterre, of which I lost haue al the light' (V.638). The image is a variant of the idea of his mistress as the light of a man's life, a popular conceit much favoured by the *vir*, by whom the *mulier* is often compared to the sun, moon, resplendent gem (4 and 6), etc.[4]

The inclusion of verse is just one aspect of a literary self-consciousness that pervades the present series. The satisfaction the pair derived from, especially, formulating those elegant greetings so central to the letters is evident in the fact that in one letter (109), represented by only a brief extract, the *mulier* declares that, although they are at present able to exchange salutations in person, she cannot resist penning one, composed in the rhyming prose she favours ('Cupio te tamen esse salvum, virtutum decore indutum, sophie gemmis circumtectum, morum honestate preditum, omnisque composicionis ornatu decoratum' [I nevertheless want to wish you to be safe and sound, dressed in the grace of virtues, set in the jewelled circlet of wisdom, endowed with decency of behaviour, graced with adornments of every kind]). The remark forms a revealing exception to a general rule, for the pair elsewhere treat the letter (as other lovers did: see Text 7, I.8 and note) as a poor substitute for the spoken word that personal presence would allow (see 9, 45, 54), the 'viva verba' pithily contrasted by the *vir* (in another example of giving some style to a common topos) with 'vox missa' (110). Each savours the other's letters, which they often refer to in such expressions as 'verba dulcissima' or 'dilectissima' (V110), 'mellita dulcedo' (M49), 'honeyed' words sweet in both content and rhetorical beauty of form.[5]

---

[4] See Dronke, *Medieval Latin*, for detailed discussion of the 'many uses of such images' elsewhere (vol. 1, pp. 123, 125).

[5] For other examples of the topos of 'honeyed speech', cf. Tegernsee IV (quoted below, p. 104) and see Dronke, *Medieval Latin*, vol. 1, pp. 200–1.

Clerics and Convents 69

One of the pair must, moreover, have valued the letters sufficiently to take copies of them – at no inconsiderable cost of time and effort (and perhaps of confidentiality). For it is plain from internal references that the originals were on wax tablets. At this period, those who attached any value or importance to their letters would have them subsequently copied on to parchment, as Baudri de Bourgueil did the verse epistles of which he was so proud, but which he too wrote first on tablets of wax.[6] Such tablets were typically used in pairs joined by a thong (which could be sealed); addressees would return the same tablets with their reply inscribed on the space unused by the sender. Since the man regrets at one point that he could not keep *tabulas tuas* longer, and so pen more as more came to mind (14), it appears that it was the woman who (as Piron argues: p. 184) took copies (or had them taken) not only of the letters sent but also of the replies received.

We are dealing here, then, with correspondents who obviously sought the finest language in which to express the felt fineness of their regard for one another, which all the literary art at their command was pressed into service to convey. Art and actual sentiment thus become inseparable for them. Centuries later, Johannes de Vepria moved their letters decidedly across the always-fluid boundary between art and actuality by editing out all specifics and turning the series into a model (or 'mirror', to use the medieval term) of the art of the love letter: he gave the letters that universal applicability that is the badge of art, producing a glass in which other lovers might see themselves and which they might in turn (by quotation or imitation) reflect into their own actual lives. For it is clear that Johannes was transforming into art by excerpting rather than simply transcribing or abbreviating what was originally already merely a literary exercise as opposed to an actual correspondence.[7] The heading he himself provided was '*Ex* epistolis duorum amantium' (see Piron, p. 179), not 'Epistolae ...', and as we have seen, omissions were indicated by oblique lines. Furthermore, though his editing was done so well as to leave no pervasive bumps or holes in the sense, there are occasions where one encounters felt lacunae or some obscurity even more marked than the now missing particularities that evidently underlie many of the 'misunderstandings, quarrels, alleged infidelities, reconciliations' that figure in the series.[8]

---

[6] See Étienne Wolff, *La lettre d'amour au Moyen Âge* (Paris, 1996), p. 26, n. 32. See also Constable, *Letters and Letter-Collections*, p. 45. On Baudri, see further pp. 86–90 below.
[7] The arguments of those few critics who interpret the series as an 'exercice d'école' are summarized by Piron (who himself argues strongly against them) at pp. 214–17 of *Lettres des deux amants*.
[8] The quoted phrase is from p. 93 of the discussion of the *Epistolae* by Peter Dronke in his *Women Writers of the Middle Ages* (Cambridge, 1984), pp. 92–7; Letters 35, 36, 42, 58–9, 60–1, 72, 74, 76, 95 all refer to some offence taken by the lady. On the more specific gaps in sense that occasionally occur in the letters, see Piron, ed., *Lettres des deux amants*, pp. 187–90.

The other texts copied by Johannes into his personal anthology also testify to a particular interest in the letter as a literary genre – as, in short, an art. For his collection is one almost exclusively composed of letters: an epistolary florilegium centred, as Piron points out (p. 178), on extracts from epistles ancient and modern, patristic, Cistercian and other, together with lengthy excerpts from a humanist 'manuel de lettres'. For letters were valued as a literary mode or genre, and the epistles of the learned (pre-Christian and Christian) were often collected and preserved (either by their authors themselves or by others) as valuable repositories of the wisdom, learning or rhetorical style and elegant Latinity of the writers.[9] An audience considerably wider than the person(s) addressed was often thus intended or acquired by them. So the specific personal addressee typical of an 'actual' letter might widen out to (or be a pretext or cover for) the larger public aimed at by art. Many of the sacred texts and theological authorities cited in learned treatises of the time took the form of Epistles, as is the case with many of the final books of the New Testament, the epistles and epistles general of Paul, James, Peter, John and Jude (often addressed to large groups such as the Colossians, the Ephesians, etc.). Quotations from the Church Fathers similarly often came from their published, or publicly available, epistles – as with the Epistles of Jerome, often cited in his own epistles by that most learned of all lovers, Abelard (1079–1142).

Abelard and Heloise

The best known of Abelard's own epistles was obviously itself meant as a public document, for in it he gave what he clearly intended to be his own authorized version of a professional life and of a love affair that had attracted, respectively, much controversy, including two trials for heresy, and much scandal. Ostensibly addressed to a friend in distress, to encourage him to bear patiently sufferings which could not equal those Abelard had undergone, the letter is known as the *Historia calamitatum*.[10] According to this account, Abelard had, as a scholar and teacher, met with an opposition and enmity (consistently attributed to the 'envy' of rivals) so frequent as to make one suspect that he may have been, despite (or because of) his obviously

---

[9] Cf. Betty Radice, tr., *The Letters of Abelard and Heloise* (Harmondsworth, 1974), Introduction, pp. 47–8, referring to Giles Constable, 'Medieval Letter Collections' (introduction to vol. 2 of *The Letters of Peter the Venerable* (Cambridge, MA, 1967)).
[10] Now available in a separate edition – *Historia calamitatum*, ed. Dag Nikolaus Hasse (Berlin, 2002) – in which the text is followed by a series of essays examining it from different critical perspectives (autobiography, gender, deconstruction, etc.). For contextualization and further explication of Abelard's life, academic career and controversial teachings, see M.T. Clanchy, *Abelard: A Medieval Life* (Oxford, 1997).

real abilities, opinionated and confrontational – and that Matthew 5:10 (to which he is so fond of alluding) may have been a text that enabled such men to interpret hostility as a 'persecution' testifying to their own 'righteousness'. His affair with Heloise is presented as an aberration from his clerical vocation. He frankly avows the deceit by which he persuaded her uncle to give him accommodation that would allow him access to this gifted adolescent, and how he betrayed the trust of this man (for whose gullibility Abelard can hardly hide his contempt), who asked the famous scholar to give lessons to his niece.[11] The relationship is characterized as one of intense physical passion on both sides, resulting in a child born to Heloise and Abelard's marriage to her, but ending in his castration by agents of her uncle (partly due to some mistaken notion that Abelard intended to evade his marital responsibilities by consigning Heloise to a convent), and the taking of vows and retirement to cloistered life by both himself and his wife. The castration he represents as veritably providential: an act of mercy by God to deliver him from a sinful thraldom to the flesh and enable him to resume the clerical career of scholarship and devotion to the church to which he was suited. All his passion, and all real interest in Heloise, died in that instant, and Heloise seems to have been substantially right in the accusation she later represents herself as driven to make (Letter 2, pp. 136–9): that his love had been based simply on carnal lust.

The affair forms neither the chief nor the culminating episode in the *Historia*, for it is on his clerical efforts and struggles that the real focus falls, and the true tragic climax comes, not in his castration (seen by him as a merciful deliverance), but in the moment in which he was forced, after the Council of Soissons in 1121, to burn with his own hand his work on the Trinity, on which he had laboured so long and of which he was evidently so proud. To this incident he explicitly gives more significance than to his castration, an injustice which 'seemed but small in comparison with the wrongs I now had to endure, and I wept much more for the injury done to my reputation than for the damage to my body', for the latter had come about 'through my own fault', but this 'open violence' through the love of truth that had 'compelled me to write' (Letter 1, pp. 72–3). This is perhaps the only moment when *his* pain sears itself into the consciousness of his readers, who generally find their sympathies more engaged by that of Heloise.

When this document came to Heloise's notice, she wrote to Abelard, partly to protest that such a letter should be sent to console a friend, her

---

[11] See Letter 1 (*Historia calamitatum*) in Luscombe, ed., *The Letter Collection of Abelard and Heloise*, pp. 26–9. All subsequent references to the letters are to this edition.

own situation having prompted no word of consolation or counsel from her erstwhile husband (Letter 2, pp. 126–39). Letters 2–6 form the love letters proper of the sequence, but they make painful reading. For Abelard, Heloise can now be only a 'dearly beloved sister in Christ' (superscription to Letter 3, pp. 142–3). He feels none of his old passion for her, and tries to urge on her a similar emotional and spiritual reorientation. Heloise resists this. She entered the cloister, she declares, out of love and obedience to him, not to God (Letter 2, pp. 138–9); the sexual intensity of her love lives on in her mind and memory, which are filled with that, not with God, and the piety she is credited with is a sham, for it is Abelard, not God, who is in her heart (Letter 4, pp. 168–75). These are, in short, strange, thwarted love letters, for not only is the love one-sided, it is also largely retrospective. It is an affair that has been discontinued, and the correspondence lacks the frankness, intimacy and even confidentiality normal in love letters. There is no need for this now estranged husband and wife to conceal their names or identities, for instance; and indeed both write to each other, not only in a somewhat constrained manner (each resisting the role – of lover or pious nun – the other would cast him or her in), but as if they knew that the correspondence would and should be open to the eyes of their respective convents (which all had rules about correspondence) and would form part of publicly available archives.

Heloise eventually accedes to Abelard's terms for the relationship and, partly probably to keep open some kind of correspondence, instead asks him for advice as to what kind of a rule it is suitable for a community of females to follow (the Benedictine Rule having been designed for men). To this Abelard is only too happy to respond (Letters 7 and 8), for it appeals to his clerical abilities and keeps the relationship on the ecclesiastical terms that he wishes. The sequence thus begins and ends with letters (the *Historia* and the so-called 'Letters of Direction') that are not love letters at all, scarcely even letters in the strict sense, and in which the relationship is, first explicitly and later silently, relegated to the past – though the last 'letters' cannot be read without the reader's awareness of the previous relationship and of Heloise's repression of her own still-continuing passion for a man many readers find it difficult, in their sympathy for her, not to dislike intensely.

Where the love of Paolo and Francesca gained mythical status through Dante's representation of it in *Inferno* V, it is their own powers of expression that have endowed that of Heloise and Abelard with what Dronke rightly calls 'a mythic dimension',[12] a product of art that is larger than life. For their 'story' caught the popular imagination almost precisely *as* a story,

[12] Dronke, *Women Writers*, p. 110.

and attracted over the course of time numerous translations and retellings – the best and best-known being Pope's 'Eloisa to Abelard', which responds fully to its potential poetic and narrative power, and which was based on a very free paraphrase by John Hughes (published in 1714). Other poets and storytellers were among its earliest manuscript readers. One of the best extant manuscripts belonged to Petrarch, and marginal notes apparently in his hand indicate he read it with an interest unsurprising in 'the author of the *Secretum* and of his own intensely personal letters',[13] letters to real but long-dead classical authors. Jean de Meun produced a translation in which 'all the headings, which are his own, and his many personal interjections and exclamations' testify to a lively engagement with the material.[14] He also inserted (at lines 8759–8832) into his *Roman de la rose* (as part of the cynical husband's dissuasions against marriage) a recapitulation of the story centred on the arguments against marriage that Abelard attributes to Heloise in the *Historia*. Jean apparently worked from a manuscript earlier than any of those extant.[15] For the story had attracted attention almost at once: there are references to it in the twelfth and early thirteenth centuries,[16] before the date of the earliest surviving manuscripts (none of which antedate the late thirteenth century) – which come with rubrics,[17] and so form texts that have been, even by then, not only copied but also 'edited' so as to facilitate access and reference, and for which a fairly wide interest and potential dispersal was therefore obviously envisaged. (It is almost certainly again the *mulier* who is the ultimate source of the manuscripts: that is, letters from Abelard kept by Heloise along with copies of her own.)[18]

Of especial relevance in the present context is the way in which the worlds of love and of letters constantly impinge on each other throughout the correspondence in a variety of other and more specific ways. The very first 'epistle' belongs to that category of 'public' or 'open' letter described above, in which the addressee is merely a token substitute for the wider audience obviously intended. It is sometimes believed that the friend in trouble was a fiction, though, since Heloise seems to believe in this nominal addressee, he appears to have been a pretext rather than an invention.[19] What is certainly the case

---

[13] Radice, tr., *Letters of Abelard and Heloise*, pp. 48–9.
[14] Peter Dronke, 'Abelard and Heloise in Medieval Testimonies', pp. 247–94 in his *Intellectuals and Poets in Medieval Europe* (Rome, 1992), at p. 275. Jean's translation has been edited by Eric Hicks, *La vie et les epistres. Pierre Abaelart et Heloys sa fame* (Paris, 1991).
[15] Dronke, 'Abelard and Heloise in Medieval Testimonies', p. 254.
[16] Dronke, 'Abelard and Heloise in Medieval Testimonies', pp. 263–8.
[17] Piron, ed., *Lettres des deux amants*, p. 180.
[18] See Radice, tr., *Letters of Abelard and Heloise*, p.47, and Newman, *Making Love*, pp. 54–5.
[19] Jean de Meun's translation indicates that in his manuscript Heloise says she received her copy from Abelard himself and that the 'friend' addressed was a mutual friend (see Dronke, *Women Writers*, pp. 113 and 304, n. 12).

is that the letter was meant for and attained a wider circulation, since a copy does come to Heloise's notice. Epistles of this kind (whether factual or fictional) self-evidently blur the boundaries between the private and specific and the wider public aimed at or implied by literary art. Abelard's essentially literary talents and interests everywhere colour the story of his love as told in the *Historia*, dominated as that text is by the two events he himself represented as mirroring each other, the twin mutilating castrations that deprived him first of sexual potency and later of the book he was forced to burn (see above). When his body had originally started to rebel against his celibate and continent life as a clerk, he chose Heloise precisely because she was an exceptionally learned and literate girl, whose proficiency in Latin was such as to have brought her already to the ears of a scholar such as Peter the Venerable and to her being credited with knowledge also of Greek and Hebrew.[20] Abelard thus thought her an appropriate *amica* for a man such as himself – especially as she would be able to pen eloquent love letters (that composing and receiving of pretty thoughts polished at leisure in which the *duo amantes* had taken such evident delight):

> Knowing her knowledge and love of letters I thought ... that even when separated we could enjoy each other's presence by exchange of written messages [*scriptis internuntiis*] in which we could write many things more boldly than we could say them, and so need never lack the pleasures of conversation. (Letter 1, pp. 26–7)

Abelard's comment reveals the significance of the epistolary expression of love, the artful articulation of the amorous actuality, in an age in which meetings often took place in the presence of others or in snatched moments of fleeting privacy, and in which the letter therefore may, paradoxically, as Abelard indicates, have afforded more opportunity for full and intimate communication than physical rendezvous. We are told of Troilus and Criseyde that 'ther was som epistle hem bitwene / That wolde, as seyth myn auctour, wel contene / Neigh half this book' (III.501–3) – at a period when only hasty and inhibited talk was otherwise possible: 'But it was spoken in so short a wise, / In swich a-wait [watchfulness] alwey and in swich feere, / Lest any wight deuynen or deuyse / Wold of hem two' that they were unable 'To maken of hire speche aright an ende' (III.456–62) or, in meetings that could not be 'often', to have sufficient 'leiser ... hire speches to fulfelle' (509–10).

---

[20] See Radice, tr., *Letters of Abelard and Heloise*, pp. 32 and 36 and the letter of Abelard later sent to Heloise as abbess (translated pp. 277–8).

Abelard, furthermore, wrote love songs Heloise was proud to have addressed to her (Letter 2, pp. 136–7, quoted at p. 6 above) and which he himself mentions as having passed into general circulation, to join that body of art which has become detached from any actuality that inspired it and can be appropriated by others to express their own amorous feelings:

> when inspiration did come to me, it was for writing love songs, not the secrets of philosophy. A lot of these songs, as you know, are still popular and sung in many places, particularly by those who enjoy the kind of life I led [*quos uita similis oblectat*]. (Letter 1, pp. 28–31)

None of these songs survives, but Abelard's musico-poetical abilities are abundantly clear from his compositions for church performance. His six *planctus* were described by Stevens as 'outstanding' examples of that genre, the famous 'Dolorum solatium' being especially skilful and inventive in rhyme and metre.[21] His metrical skills are also well attested in the Hymnary he wrote for the Paraclete (the convent of which Heloise was abbess).[22] He there pioneered, for instance, the use of lines of different length within the same stanza, something uncommon before his time.[23] The collection as a whole has been described as 'one of the glories of medieval Latin literature', the Vespers hymn (no. 29) 'O quanta qualia' as 'one of the most beautiful and also one of the most pathetic of medieval poems', and the Easter hymns as 'an exuberant series of rondeaux – our first examples of the lyrical strophe with internal refrain, which Abelard may even have invented'.[24]

These hymns belong to that body of clerical writing into which Abelard's erstwhile passion transmuted itself, a passion which he had described as having distracted him from his academic career (Letter 1, pp. 28–31). When Heloise conceded to Abelard's insistence on the strictly theological and ecclesiastical terms on which all communication should now occur, she released in him 'a new flood of creativity' (Dronke, *Women Writers*, p. 134) that channelled itself into works written for the Paraclete. He furnished not only lengthy responses to Heloise's queries about the origins of nuns and requests for guidelines or rules for her community (Letters 7–8), but also detailed answers to her forty-two *Problemata* (a series of questions she put

---

[21] John Stevens, *Words and Music in the Middle Ages* (Cambridge, 1986), pp. 120, 127.
[22] See J.S. Szövérffy, ed., *Peter Abelard's Hymnarius Paraclitensis*, 2 vols (Albany, NY, 1975).
[23] F. Brittain, ed., *Medieval Latin and Romance Lyric* (Cambridge, 1951), p. 13.
[24] W.G. East, 'Educating Heloise', in *Medieval Monastic Education*, ed. George Ferzoco and Carolyn Muessig (Leicester, 2000), pp. 105–16 (p. 109); the last two quoted appraisals are also cited by East (pp. 111 and 113) and are from, respectively, F. Brittain, ed., *The Penguin Book of Latin Verse* (Harmondsworth, 1962), p. xxix, and Peter Dronke, *The Medieval Lyric* (London, 1968), p. 52. The hymn O quanta qualia is available, with facing translation (by Helen Waddell), in Radice, tr., *Letters of Abelard and Heloise*, pp. 290–3.

to him on scriptural texts that raised questions for her), a treatise on the six days of Creation (the *Hexameron*), a collection of some thirty-five homilies and the cycle of 133 hymns[25] – all in response to requests by her, for Heloise was now obviously dedicating her formidable powers of commitment and intelligence to her abbatial responsibilities and so preserving yet transferring Abelard's centrality to herself and all she held dear. The relationship in this its last phase forms the most markedly singular instance of the interrelations between art and actuality incident to this affair.

But it is in the letters themselves that the fusion of real love and of literary art and learning is felt most forcibly – particularly in those of Heloise (Letters 2 and 4, and the start of 6), for Abelard cannot and will not now write as a lover. Dronke, remarking how impossible it is 'to demarcate the "artificial" from the "natural" in medieval letters', refers to the 'astonishing passages of rhymed prose' in Heloise's letters, passages which 'are not stylistic exercises', but express 'torrents of emotion in a mode which she had made "second nature"' (*Medieval Latin*, vol. 2, p. 482). And in his essay on 'Heloise' in his *Women Writers of the Middle Ages* he provides an eloquent demonstration of the 'high art' of her 'rhetorically brilliant' letters (pp. 109–10), in which passion and outcry that can reach an 'incandescent' pitch gain their rhythmic resonance from the 'rhetorical shaping' and 'quasi-poetic form' acquired in her schooling (pp. 121, 126), as well as from literary quotations and influences (especially from the *Heroides*: p. 126). But there is a strikingly clear demonstration in the *Historia* itself of how inseparable were her learning and her passion. When people 'out of pity for her youth' tried to dissuade her from taking the veil after the assault on Abelard, she 'broke out as best she could through her tears and sobs into Cordelia's famous lament [from Lucan's *Pharsalia* 8.94]', evidently able at once to find from her well-stocked memory that passage of classical literature most appropriate to her own feelings and situation:

> O most renowned of husbands,
> So undeserved a victim of my marriage, was it my fate
> To bend that lofty head? What prompted me
> To marry you and bring about your fall?
> Now claim your due, and see me gladly pay.   (Letter 1, pp. 48–51)

Her three first letters to Abelard are surely among the literary masterpieces of medieval Latin prose. Heloise was famous in her own day for her command of Latin letters, and shows herself superior in that respect even to her learned clerk husband. Both, as the educated in this period were wont to

---

[25] See *PL* 178.678–730 for Heloise's *Problemata* and Abelard's responses; *PL* 178.731–84 for the *Expositio in Hexameron*; *PL* 178.379–610 for Abelard's sermons.

do, cite biblical and patristic texts very frequently, and also classical texts, which come even more readily to Heloise – whose studies had had a less theological bias than Abelard's, and who quotes freely from Seneca, Lucan, Cicero and Ovid. Though references to classical texts become noticeably rarer as the focus becomes exclusively ecclesiastical (in Abelard's case, after he dedicates himself following his injury to his clerical career, and in Heloise's after she has submitted to write to him only on abbatical and theological matters), the two resemble and outdo the *duo amantes* in ready citation of sacred and secular texts and in the use of the arts of rhetoric (especially parallelism, pairings, contrast and correlation) to give shape and force to their prose. But Abelard (at least in his surviving letters) is writing with the grain of the uses to which Latin was largely put in his day: namely, for the exegetical purposes of theological argument, with exemplification and proof from authorities. There is no breaking of new ground, no conflicting aims, to make demands on his Latin. This is not the case with Heloise, who has unusual, unruly and contradictory feelings to express. She loves Abelard, but she is angry with his relegation of her to a sister in Christ; she is both honest and penitent but also defiant about the persistent sexual orientation of her thoughts; her instinct is to sacrifice her own wishes to Abelard's, as the strength of her love always dictated, and she fears losing contact with him if she persists in the expression of a kind of love he no longer shares, but she is also determined not to let him off the hook by repressing feelings of whose continued existence it is no longer convenient for him to hear – and to make him realize that her love has not and cannot undergo the same permanent power cut as has occurred for him.

There is, in short, nothing easy or glib in her use of the syntactical and rhetorical parallelisms and contrasts of fine Latin. Take the following:

> Si enim uere miserrimi mei animi profitear infirmitatem, qua penitentia Deum placare ualeam non inuenio, quem super hac semper iniuria summe crudelitatis arguo et, eius dispensationi contraria, magis eum ex indignatione offendo quam ex penitentie satisfactione mitigo. Quomodo etiam penitentia peccatorum dicitur, quantacumque sit corporis afflictio, si mens adhuc ipsam peccandi retinet uoluntatem, et pristinis estuat desideriis? Facile quidem est quemlibet confitendo peccata seipsum accusare aut etiam in exteriori satisfactione corpus affligere; difficillimum uero est a desideriis maximarum uoluptatum auellere animum ... [*quotations from Job, Gregory and Ambrose on inefficacy of penance without inner penitence*] In tantum uero ille quas pariter exercuimus amantium voluptates dulces mihi fuerunt ut nec displicere mihi nec uix a memoria labi possint ... Inter ipsa missarum solempnia, ubi purior esse debet oratio, obscena earum uoluptatum phantasmata ita sibi penitus miserrimam captiuant animam ut turpitudinibus illis magis quam orationi uacem; que cum ingemiscere debeam de commissis, suspiro potius de amissis ... Castam me predicant qui

non deprehendunt ypocritam ... Religiosa hoc tempore iudicor in quo iam parua pars religionis non est ypochrisis, ubi ille maximis extollitur laudibus qui humanum non offendit iudicium. Et hoc fortassis aliquo modo laudabile et Deo acceptabile quoquo modo videtur si quis uidelicet exterioris operis exemplo quacumque intentione non sit Ecclesie scandalo ... Atque hoc quoque nonnullum est diuinæ gratie donum, ex cuius uidelicet munere uenit non solum bona facere sed etiam a malis abstinere ...

For if I truthfully admit to the weakness of my most unhappy soul, I can find no penitence whereby to appease God, whom I always accuse of the greatest cruelty in regard to this injustice. By opposing his ordinance, I offend him more by my indignation than I placate him by making amends through penitence. How can it be called repentance for sins, however great the mortification of the flesh, if the mind still retains the will to sin and is on fire with its old desires? It is easy enough for anyone to confess his sins, to accuse himself, or even to mortify his body ... but it is most difficult to tear the heart away from longing for the greatest pleasures ... The lovers' pleasures we enjoyed together were so sweet to me that they cannot displease me and can scarcely fade from my memory ... Even during the celebration of the Mass, when our prayers should be purer, lewd visions of those pleasures take such a hold upon my most unhappy soul that my thoughts are on their wantonness instead of on prayer. I, who should be grieving for the sins I have committed, am sighing rather for what I have lost ... Men call me chaste; they do not know the hypocrite I am ... I am thought to be religious at a time such as this when there is little in religion which is not hypocrisy, when whoever does not offend human judgment is singled out for praise. And yet perhaps it seems in a way praiseworthy and somehow acceptable to God if a person gives no offence to the Church in outward behaviour, whatever his intention ... And this too is a gift of God's grace and comes through his bounty – not only to do good but to abstain from evil ...   (Letter 4, pp. 168–73)

It is instructive to compare Abelard's summary of what, in a verse letter to their son Peter Astrolabe, he calls the constant complaint of 'our Heloise':

Si, nisi peniteat me commisisse priora,
    Salvari nequeam, spes mihi nulla manet.
Dulcia sunt adeo commissi gaudia nostri
    Ut memorata iuventque placuere nimis.

If I cannot be saved without repenting
    of what I used to commit, there is no hope for me.
The joys of what we did are still so sweet
    that, after delight beyond measure, even remembering brings relief.[26]
                                                (lines 19–22)

---

[26] Text and translation from Dronke, *Intellectuals and Poets*, pp. 257 and 280.

The lines are clear, forceful and concise but, though in verse, lack the rhythmic pulse of Heloise's prose, with its insistent use of correlation (*magis ... quam*; *nec ... nec*; *non solum ... sed etiam*), often reinforced by parallelism for the purposes of contrast or pairing (*Facile quidem ... corpus affligere*; *difficillimum uero ... auellere animum* ...; *ex indignatione offendo ... ex penitentia ... mitigo*; *castam ... ypocritam*; *aliquo modo laudibile ... acceptabile quoquo modo*; *bona facere ... a malis abstinere*), the grammatical parallels (because in Latin they are often marked by the same inflectional ending) often having the effect of pararhyme or chime, which gives especial force to that deliberately shocking account of sexual reveries even at Mass (*de commissis ... de amissis*). The learning and careful syntactical organization she brings to her description of false penitence would more naturally serve the purposes of warning and denunciation than that of the spiritual despair of herself they here articulate – a despair which, however, she is likewise too honest and intelligent to revel in and too theologically perceptive not to see is unwarrantable – and that even her confessedly imperfect penitence may not be totally without merit.

We meet again in her last letter this mixture of, or transition between, passion and wisdom, this refusal to give up her love to embrace the resignation dictated by piety, prudence and philosophy, yet the refusal also to indulge in operatic rejection of all compromise and consolation. When she finally agrees to turn her attention and their correspondence to ecclesiastical matters, that being now the only subject into which Abelard can enter, she does so with a masterly poise, expressing a concession and obedience to his will that yet withholds from him the satisfaction (or the sop to his conscience) of supposing her now persuaded or transformed into the state comparable with his own which he has urged on her (that of being ruled by a love of God that frees her from sexual love for a man):[27]

SVO SPECIALITER SVA SINGVLARITER

Ne me forte in aliquo de inobedientia causari queas, uerbis etiam immoderati doloris tue frenum impositum est iussionis, ut ab his mihi saltem in scribendo temperem, a quibus in sermone non tam difficile quam impossibile est prouidere. Nichil enim minus in nostra est potestate quam animus, eique magis obedire cogimur quam imperare possumus. Vnde et cum nos eius affectiones stimulant, nemo earum subitos impulsus ita repulerit ut non in effecta facile prorumpant, et se per uerba facilius effluant que promptiores

---

[27] Dronke also discusses this passage in 'Abelard and Heloise in Medieval Testimonies' (pp. 251–2), in order to refute the critical opinion that Heloise 'came to see the error of her ways' in persisting in her love for Abelard (p. 278).

animi passionum sunt note, secundum quod scriptum est: 'Ex habundantia enim cordis os loquitur' [Matthew 12:34]. Reuocabo itaque manum a scripto in quibus linguam a uerbis temperare non ualeo. Vtinam sic animus dolentis parere promptus sit quemadmodum dextra scribentis.

Aliquod tamen dolori remedium uales conferre si non hunc omnino possis auferre. Vt enim insertum clauum alius expellit, sic cogitatio noua priorem excludit, cum alias intentus animus priorum memoriam dimittere cogitur aut intermittere. Tanto uero amplius cogitatio quelibet animum occupat, et ab aliis deducit, quanto quod cogitatur honestius estimatur, et quo intendimus animum magis uidetur necessarium.

TO HIM WHO IS HERS ESPECIALLY FROM HER WHO IS HIS UNIQUELY

I would not want to give you cause for finding me disobedient in anything, so I have set the bridle of your injunction on the words which issue from my unbounded grief; thus in writing at least I may moderate what it is difficult or rather impossible to forestall in speech. For nothing is less under our control than our mind which, having no power to command, we are forced to obey. And so when its impulses move us, none of us can stop their sudden promptings from easily breaking out, and even more easily overflowing into words which are the ever-ready indications of what is felt in the mind, according to what is written: 'for out of the abundance of the heart the mouth speaketh' [Matthew 12:34]. I will therefore hold back my hand from writing words which I cannot restrain my tongue from speaking; would that a grieving mind were as ready to obey as a writer's hand!

And yet you have it in your power to remedy my grief, even if you cannot entirely remove it. As one nail drives out another hammered in, new thought expels old when the mind, intent on other things, is made to give up or interrupt its remembrance of what went before. The more fully, indeed, any thought engages the mind, distracting it from other things, the more such thought is considered worthwhile and the focus of the mind appears inevitable. (Letter 6, p. 219)

Heloise's very superscription expresses both subservience and rebellion, as does her consent to obey Abelard's commands, for the very style of it makes its own point. Abelard's superscriptions had consistently defined his relationship with her in terms of the God whom each serves: 'DILECTISSIMI SORORI SVE IN CHRISTO ABELARDUS FRATER EIVS IN IPSO' (*Epistola* III), 'SPONSE CHRISTI SERVVS EISDEM' (*Epistola* V). As a bride of Christ, she is as revered by him as the wife of his *dominus* must be by any servant: so he had declared in the letter to which Heloise is replying, a letter which had ended with a prayer to that *Dominus* to marry to

Himself in heaven (*tibi coniungas in celo*) those whom He had joined and then divided on earth (*diuisisti in mundo*). In her own superscription, Heloise refuses to subordinate her relation with Abelard to God or allow God to replace Abelard as the sole lord of her heart: for it is to Abelard that the language of obedience and command is applied in her opening sentence, which implicitly defines *him* as her 'dominus' – a title explicitly conferred on him in the Troyes manuscript (followed in the *PL* text), where the superscription actually, and even more pointedly, reads *Domino specialiter suo*. It is in obedience to the commands of this earthly *dominus* that she turns her attention to ecclesiastical affairs, just as it was in order to serve Abelard, she had insisted, that she entered the cloister in the first place (Letter 2, pp. 138–9; Letter 4, pp. 172–3). But the parallelisms and contrasts of her Latin carefully circumscribe the limits of her compliance. She will refrain in *writing* (*scribendo*) from expressing feeling she could not restrain in *speech* (*in sermone*). In speech, she could not edit her thoughts in advance of delivering them, a task not so much *difficult* (for difficulty she would not shirk to oblige Abelard) as *impossible*. Abelard cannot have the satisfaction of thinking she is as transformed in spirit as he is and has no passion for him left in her. For the language of obedience and command is now transferred to the heart. In obeying Abelard, out of love, she is obeying her heart, which we are *compelled to obey* (*magis obedire cogimur*) rather than *able to command* (*quam imperare possimus*). She quotes Scripture to show that the *mouth* will reveal what the *heart* is full of. She can only refrain her *hand* (*manum*) from words she could not banish from her *tongue* (*linguam*). These distinctions, continued through *animus dolentis* [the mind of the sorrower] and *dextera scribentis* [the hand of the writer], lead on to a new one based on that *dolor* which Abelard can alleviate (*remedium ... conferre*) but not remove (*auferre*). Through the sophisticated doubletting of constructions based on *ut ... sic* and *tanto ... quanto*, she finally moves to the ecclesiastical affairs that may serve to distract her from the thoughts she must not express – distraction in such cases being the more efficacious the more *useful* and the more *worthy* the new matter is perceived to be. Heloise thus gives way with philosophical good grace, but with due retention of the *animus* [the heart, as opposed to the hand or the tongue] that is not at Abelard's nor at her own command and the *dolor* for which discussion with Abelard on matters she cares about can provide assuagement and distraction but not eradication. Heloise's Latin thus imposes controllability on the essential ungovernability of her feelings, which is her perpetual theme.

It is the love she must obey that holds in such perfect poise her obedience to the man she loves and her continued truth to her own feelings. The stylistic and moral 'integrity' that is the result commands respect and belief. Heloise's love is unconditional and unqualified, and gives way not even to God or moral decency. Even her celebrated declaration that she would rather be Abelard's whore than the wife or consort of the grandest man in the world depends on love for its logic – and on the Latin of which she is such a mistress, for that logic is not entirely apparent in translation. *Amica* [lover, mistresss] is the word Heloise first uses to indicate the state that is to her more sacred than that of *uxor* [wife], and it is plainly the word's derivation from *amor* that underlies her reasoning, for it bespeaks a relationship based entirely on *amor* – and can thus bestow even on its more disparaging synonyms (*concubina, scorta*) a kind of dignity; a palliative interjection shows, as it frequently does in Heloise's prose, that she is perfectly aware of the potentially shocking nature of the sentiment she expresses:

> Et si uxoris nomen sanctius ac ualidius uidetur, dulcius mihi semper extitit amice vocabulum aut, si non inidgneris, concubine uel scorti. (*Epistola* II, p. 132)
>
> The title of wife may seem to have more of sanctity and legality in it; but the word *amica* is always sweeter to me – or even, if it does not offend you, that of concubine or whore. (our translation)

Abelard himself, in recording her initial opposition to the marriage he had proposed, had simply put in her mouth the usual clerical arguments against marriage (Letter 1 (*Historia*), pp. 34–43), and the passage was later used by Jean de Meun in *Le roman de la rose* with a similar emphasis, as we have seen (see p. 73 above). But in Letter 2 Heloise goes on to accuse Abelard of failing to put across her chief point, which was the greater value she placed upon a tie consisting entirely in *amor* freely given than upon a legal bond, and so ignoring the real reasons 'quibus *amorem* coniugio, libertatem uincula preferebam' [for which I gave precedence to love over wedlock, liberty over chains] (our italics and our translation). And it is in this context that she defiantly repeats her now explained preference for a status denominated by the disparaging synonym of *amica* over that of wife. And the statement is now ushered in, not with an apology, but with a defiant assertion of the literally sacred seriousness with which she speaks, and concluded with a chiming opposition of *meretrix* and *imperatrix* that gives it climactic emphasis:

> Deum testem inuoco, si me Augustus uniuerso presidens mundo matrimonii honore dignaretur, totumque mihi orbem confirmaret in perpetuo possidendum, karius mihi et dignius uideretur tua dici meretrix quam illius imperatrix.

God is my witness that if Augustus, Emperor of the whole world, thought fit to honour me with marriage and conferred all the earth on me to possess forever, it would seem to me dearer and more honourable to be called not his empress but your whore.[28] (Letter 2, pp. 132–3)

Interestingly, Jean de Meun, in reusing Abelard's version of Heloise's anti-marital stance, could not but give a closing indication that it was misleadingly reductive; remembering this account Heloise herself had given of her reasoning (and, perhaps, her characterization of Abelard's summary of it as inadequate), he paraphrased the above passage in his concluding coda, and in doing so conceded that both she and it were much more remarkable than he has represented them as being: the comment quoted is introduced as 'Une merveilleuse parole' that some even consider crazed (8811–12), and indeed, she was an extraordinary woman 'whose like has never since been seen' (8825–6).

It is in such statements, moreover, that Heloise differs from the lady of the *Epistolae duorum amantium*. It has often been argued that the *duo* are, in fact, Heloise and Abelard. Heloise refers with some bitterness to the many letters Abelard was once ready to write to her (when she expresses her pain at having received no word of comfort or support from him at a time when she most needed it – at her entry into the cloister after the dramatic termination of their marriage) (Letter 2, pp. 140–1). So there were love letters, and the *Epistolae* present us with the circumstance of a highly Latinate female writing to a man she denominates *magister*, the pair being apparently French and living in France. Marrying up the missing letters of the one pair with the missing names of the other obviously provides a neat way of filling two holes in one move, and the identity of the two pairs of lovers is a theory that has both its proponents and its opponents. Suggested by Könsgen (whose edition of the *Epistolae* bore the subtitle *Briefe Abaelards und Heloises?*), the proposition was first seriously argued by Constant J. Mews in *The Lost Letters of Heloise and Abelard*, in which the question mark was in every sense removed, and by C.S. Jaeger.[29] Those who subscribed to it subsequently accepted and added to the precise and wide-ranging grounds on which Mews had based his case, and they include the two scholars who have worked most recently and intensively on the

---

[28] We have retained Radice's 'whore' in the translation (revised into 'mistress' by Luscombe).
[29] C.S. Jaeger, *Ennobling Love: In Search of a Lost Sensibility* (Philadelphia, PA, 1999), pp. 157–73. The second edition of Constant J. Mews's *The Lost Love Letters of Heloise and Abelard* (New York, 2008) includes an additional chapter covering developments in the debate since the first edition appeared in 1999.

Epistolae: Sylvain Piron (pp. 199–213) and Barbara Newman (pp. 59–78), the latter concluding that the ascription to Heloise and Abelard was 'highly probable'. Those specializing rather in Abelard and/or Heloise have been less convinced and have queried some of the grounds on which the case has been argued. Amongst these dissenting voices are those of David Luscombe, the most recent editor of the Abelard–Heloise letters (pp. xxxii–xxxiv); of Peter Dronke, who, in a review of a volume of essays, argued – on grounds of Latin usages and prose style – against the identification of the *mulier* with Heloise remade by Constant Mews in the same volume;[30] and of John Marenbon, who refuted some of the similarities posited by Mews between the philosophical positions of Abelard and the *vir*, and concluded that there were insufficient grounds for identifying the one with the other – a conclusion also reached by Ziolkowski after subjecting the prose of the two to formal stylistic tests.[31]

For us the most powerful argument lies, as we have suggested above, in the contrasting content and style of the two women. Étienne Wolff (p. 24) has rightly pointed to 'l'absence de toute allusion sensuelle' in the *Epistolae*, but the difference goes beyond that. For the *mulier*, God and moral virtue are inseparable from love (3, 38b, 112; 45, 49, 57), on the subject of which she writes with an earnest high-mindedness that could never rise (or sink) to the bold near-blasphemy with which Heloise praises the status of *meretrix* above that of wife, confesses to reliving sexual encounters at Mass, and stops in other ways only just short of conscious profanity, as in her outcries against what appears to be the injustice and cruelty of God – when 'the frantic mind ... angry, as it were [*ut ita dicam*], with God ... O God – if it is right to say this [*si fas sit dici*] – cruel to me in every way! *O inclementem clementiam* [merciless mercy]!' (Letter 4, pp. 160–4). There is here an element of potential sacrilege which the formulaic hesitations show Heloise to have been quite aware of and which has bothered some critics – and which certainly bothered Abelard, who in his reply earnestly deprecated her 'old continual complaint against God' (Letter 5, pp. 178–9).

Nor does the *vir* quite convince as a younger Abelard, who gives the impression of having taken a rather more forceful and less deferential line with his *amica* (from whose 'weaker nature' he confesses to having

---

[30] Review of Wheeler, ed., *Listening to Heloise*, in *IJCT* 8 (2001) 134–9. See also P. Dronke and G. Orlandi, 'New Works by Abelard and Heloise?', *Filologia mediolatina* 12 (2005) 123–77. Dronke believed, as we do, that the *Epistolae* are the work of real lovers who are not, however, Abelard and Heloise: see *Intellectuals and Poets*, p. 270.

[31] J. Marenbon, 'Lost Love Letters? A Controversy in Retrospect', *IJCT* 15 (2008) 267–80; Jan M. Ziolkowski, 'Lost and Not Yet Found: Heloise, Abelard and the *Epistolae duorum amantium*', *Journal of Medieval Latin* 14 (2004) 171–202 (p. 201).

occasionally forced sexual compliance 'with threats and blows': Letter 5, pp. 198–9). Some of the proposed similarities between the two do demand to be weighed, but some are very fragile: the frequent use by the *vir* of images of brilliant light (including the sun) certainly does not, as Piron suggested, indicate a play on the name Heloise (which false etymology connected with the Greek *helios*).[32] Such images, used also by the *mulier* (e.g. 92, quoted above), though deployed in these letters with characteristic virtuosity, are too common elsewhere to be treated as significant in themselves; and Abelard, in his only ascertainable reference to the name Heloise, in fact connects it, not with the sun, but with God's marking her out for Himself by calling her by His own name of Elohim (Letter 5, pp. 203–4) – although that logic would, admittedly, have better suited the pious purposes and emphases of his later self, and does not rule out the solar connection that might come more naturally to the lover. Heloise and Abelard may, that is, have been very different persons before the dramatic and traumatic events that separated them. But this *mulier* has none of the boldly passionate honesty of the later Heloise, and her Latin is more diffuse and less tautly shaped in its parallelisms.

Nor does Heloise furnish the only other example from this period of a woman being as fluent and well-read in Latin as the *mulier* plainly is. There are in fact many recorded instances of high levels of literacy and learning amongst women (especially women religious) in this earlier phase of the Middle Ages, many more than in the fourteenth and fifteenth centuries, which saw a marked deterioration in this respect (see pp. 258–9). From this pre-fourteenth-century period come the many letters collected and translated in *Epistolae: Medieval Women's Latin Letters*,[33] the complex and interesting texts cited and discussed in Peter Dronke's book *Women Writers of the Middle Ages* and a number of other learned and Latinate women occur in his survey of Medieval Latin verse – amongst whom Adela of Blois, the daughter of William the Conqueror, was an especially popular subject for 'clerical panegyrics' (*Medieval Latin*, vol. 1, pp. 209–10). Baudri of Bourgueil, a scholar who wrote instructive poems for inmates of the convent of Ronceray in Angers, in one letter to the Abbess Emma asks her to criticize his verse (vol. 1, p. 217). And although Abelard says that 'a gift for letters [was] so rare in women' as to make Heloise unusual, it is 'the abundance of her learning', in which she stood 'supreme', that he finds truly

---

[32] Piron, ed., *Lettres des deux amants*, p. 205, citing Dronke, who, in attributing to Abelard one of the poems from the *Carmina Burana* (*Medieval Latin*, vol. 1, pp. 313–18), in fact finds the play on the name (proposed by Ehrenthal) implausible.
[33] See https://epistolae.ctl.columbia.edu.

exceptional (Letter 1 (*Historia*), pp. 24–5). The simple fact of her having received the education for which she proved to have such aptitude he attributes to the fact that 'she was so much loved' by her clerical uncle (a canon at Notre Dame) 'that he had done everything in his power to advance her education in letters' (*ibid.*). His logic implies that he assumed educating a daughter, niece, etc., could be one form in which pride and pleasure in her might find expression, and though girls were not usually put to school so rigorously, the phenomenon was for him sufficiently explicable in that way.

Baudri of Bourgueil

Convents in fact included a number of well-born and Latinate women who had entered or retired into them – and who were often in correspondence with clerics whom they had patronized and/or by whom they were admired. There are the endearing verses written by Fortunatus for Radegund and her daughter Agnes, who in turn bestowed gifts, not amatory tokens but creature comforts gratefully received, and who were able to deliver replies in Latin verse.[34] But in such cases the regard expressed might not always be so clearly distinguishable from erotic love. For, as Dronke points out, the languages of *amicitia*, of panegyric and of love shared a common stock of expressions derived from courtly extravagance and flowery *courtoisie*. Commendation and friendship, that is, were often expressed in terms startlingly close to those employed for passionate love, and some documents could today be (and have been) mis-assigned to the wrong category by those unfamiliar with the norms of the time.[35] But the situation is sometimes even more complex – as it appears to be in the case of Baudri of Bourgueil, who sent to nuns verse letters in which the love expressed cannot be fully explained by the *amicitia* to which Dronke would refer such letters.[36] In a verse letter to a genuine *amicus* (Godfrey of Rheims, a fellow clerical poet), Baudri refers (99.183–6) to verse love letters he had written to girls and boys ('virginibus et pueris'), which he clearly feels require some justification. His explanation is essentially literary. He wanted to try what he could do in the way of love verse, rather than express actual love:

> Dicere quid possem, potius temptare volebam,
> Quam quod amauissem, versibus exciperem.   (187–8)[37]

[34] See Dronke, *Medieval Latin*, vol. 1, 202–8.
[35] Dronke, *Medieval Latin*, vol. 1, pp. 192–200.
[36] Cf. Wolff, *La lettre d'amour*, p. 19: 'Avouons que cette explication n'est pas entierement convaincante'.
[37] Quotations from *Baldricus Burgulianus Carmina*, ed. K. Hilbert (Heidelberg, 1979). Part of this letter, as well as those letters discussed below (to Muriel and to and from Constance), are included in the anthology by Wolff, *La lettre d'amour*, pp. 65–91, where texts appear translated into modern French.

That is, it was love that served a desire to versify, not verse serving love.

Love is, after all, a large area for a poet to be debarred from, and the two amatory exchanges of love verse with women to which we will now turn may have involved a species of role-playing on both sides. There was undoubtedly some genuine mutual regard, fostered by a shared pleasure in reading and composing verse (and probably also in giving and receiving elegant assurances of personal worth) – for the ladies were evidently themselves accomplished mistresses of the arts of language. In the poem to Muriel (Poem 137), the compliments to the mistress usual in this context are heavily weighted (2–25) towards her eloquence ('gratia colloquii', 2). The loverly assurances of her specialness also take a literary turn (37–8) – to no other maiden (*virgo*) does he send his *carmina* or pen on his page (*cartula*) a *vale* – as does the *vale* [farewell] itself (43–6): her abundant intellectual gifts will enable her easily to correct defects in his verse ('erratus attenuare meos'), but let her do so in a spirit of sympathy, as will he in his critique of hers ('et tenuabo tuos compatiendo tibi'). And it is in connection with these verses that the amorous topos of secrecy or confidentiality is introduced: they are to be carried or guided by a personified 'taciturna fides' (26).

In this period, the most common way of sharing a critical interest in literature, of reading the production of others and gaining an audience for one's own, was via verse letters of this kind. Baudri's are written in elegiac distichs, and his letters to Godfrey likewise refer to this literary aspect of the act of 'friendship' performed by the exchange of letters. His poetic efforts are to be read by friends ('legatur amicis'), and he will perform the same service for them: 'Carmen amicorum nec minus ipse legam' (99.211–12; cf. 100.1–2). In effect, it is on these grounds that Baudri is excusing himself to Godfrey for writing love letters. It is the friends to whom he writes that always constitute his audience, as he is theirs, so his love verse needed to be sent to women in the form of a letter.

He and Muriel similarly enjoy exchanging 'mutua carmina' (137.25). The relationship, in which the personal and the literary are so inseparable, is also carefully fenced off from the sexual fulfilment a lover would normally be presumed to regard as his dearest wish. The praises include admiration of her rejection of marriage (despite her beauty, status and wealth) for a life of holy chastity ('Propositum sancte virginitatis amas': 18). Her status as a religious is thus incorporated into, rather than flouted by, the love and admiration offered. In this way, Baudri creates or exemplifies a special type of love letter for the enclosed female, which may echo the conventional love letter in all respects except in (or rather with special emphasis on) the assurance that the lady's life of chastity is one of the reasons for the love offered. We will meet this type of love letter again in the Söflingen dossier discussed below. And it is especially well exemplified in the verse letter exchange with one Constance, who was also a nun.[38] Many of the usual topoi of the love letter are present: the opening injunction to secrecy (the letter must not be left open for other eyes to see, or the writer's reputation will suffer: 200.1–2); the top-to-toe description of her beauty (57–66), which agrees precisely with the tactics recommended and exemplified in the model love letter offered by a contemporary *ars dictandi* (see Text 1, 130/27). But there are again the pervasive protestations as to the non-sexual nature of the passion expressed: he honours her virginity and her modesty, to which his love presents no threat (39–40); though he loves vehemently, his love is (74–81) not a lust dictated by the flesh or by illicit desire, but a love of her very virginity ('virginitatis amor'). The pleasures are, in fact, clearly those of amorous rhetoric rather than amorous fact. This is a missive in which love is inseparable from the poem of love ('amor est et carmen amoris': 7), a love that is a response to Constance's muse and her eloquence ('tua Musa ... facundia linguae': 52–3), to her command of letters rather than to her physical charms ('In te sed nostrum mouit tua littera sensum': 51). 'Sit pudor in facto, sit iocus in calamo' [Let shamefastness govern what we do, let our pleasure be in the pen] is an especially significant line (46), given the erotic reference the word *iocus* often had: erotic pleasure has here been transmuted into rhetorical pleasure. And that much of the letter has been an exercise in amorous topoi is implicitly acknowledged in the deprecation offered of the mythological comparisons in which Baudri had indulged (19–24), intrusions of pagan literature ('gentilis pagina': 91) into a letter between committed Christians who cannot take them seriously; the paean to her beauty had been written for the purposes of conveying her moral worth through the medium of exterior comeliness (85–6); and even the opening injunction to the secrecy lovers had commonly to observe is revealed to have been something of a pose, since the conclusion bids her show or hide the letter as she pleases ('Si uis, ostendas, si uis hec scripta recondas': 177), for a good woman has nothing to fear (i.e. Baudri would not mind in the least if his metrical and rhetorical efforts were not hidden away out of a needlessly literal secrecy).

The letter comes with a reply from Constance. There is again much that marks the typical sentiments of *amor* rather than *amicitia*: she has put his letter next to her heart (201.9–10); she is tormented by jealous doubts as to his faith and fidelity (87–8), dreading to lose what she so passionately loves (98: 'Perdere sed timeo, quod uehementer amo', which echoes the phrase

[38] There is another letter to her (Poem 142) entirely devoted to her sacred status and duties as a bride of Christ and, being quite devoid of any amatory language, therefore quite consistent with the *fedus amicitie* (44) referred to as the basis of the relationship.

'uehementer amo' used in Baudri's letter at 200.74); she fears he may prefer another (125); he would come soon if he really loved her and wanted to (138ff.), and they would not lack ecclesiastical pretexts for seeing each other (163), the need for permission from a strict stepmother ('seua nouerca': presumably her superior) preventing her from coming to him (158). But, again, the protestations are neutralized almost as soon as made by the insistence on the inviolability of her status as a bride of Christ: as a *sponsa Dei*, she must love a fellow servant of Christ (115–16), and their love is (121–2) one that breaks no *ius* or *lex*, for their amorous pleasures are sanctioned by their chastity ('Commendet nostros uita pudica iocos', another line in which amorous *ioci* are carefully redefined, here by the juxtaposition with *pudica*). And, again, metrical and rhetorical skills are felt as an essential element in the power of pleasing: would she could write a reply worthy of such eloquence and wisdom as has issued from this second Cicero (19–30), and that what is 'dictated' by the mind of love ('que mens dictabit amantis'), her odes of verse ('carminis oda mei'), may afford him pleasure (107–8).

Constance's reply has been found to have so many similarities with Baudri's own verse as to suggest that it may have been ventriloquized by Baudri himself[39] – though a mixed metaphor (201.48) and a style slightly more effusive and less pointed might indicate a different author, as do the accusations of a certain hollowness in Baudri's expressed urgent desire to see her. Constance herself, however, like Muriel, was undoubtedly a real woman. Dronke, who assumed the reply was her own work, suggested she might be a nun at the convent of Ronceray,[40] for and to which Baudri certainly wrote letters and poems (see p. 90 below), and that theory has been recently persuasively reargued by Belle Tuten.[41] Machaut, in his *Voir dit*, certainly attributed to Péronne (an actual *amie* with whom he exchanged songs) some poems he had composed himself,[42] and Baudri may similarly have created or at least polished a poem for Constance. Whether the response is or is not her work, Baudri took care to keep the two poems as partner pieces of a kind comparable with other fictive paired letters he had composed, notably an exchange (à la *Heroides*) between Paris and Helen (poems 7 and 8) – a comparability that is further evidence of the intricate links between the actual and the literary in his oeuvre.

---

[39] Jean-Yves Tilliette, 'Hermès amoureux, ou les métamorphoses de la Chimère: réflexions sur les Carmina 200 et 201 de Baudri de Bourgueil', *Mélanges de l'école française de Rome* 104 (1992) 121–61 (pp. 139–44); cf. Wolff (note to first line of the letter), *La lettre d'amour*, p. 83; Newman, *Making Love*, pp. 7–8.
[40] Dronke, *Medieval Latin*, vol. 1, p. 217, and *Women Writers*, p. 86.
[41] Belle S. Tuten, 'Who Was Lady Constance of Angers? Nuns as Poets and Correspondents at the Monastery of Ronceray d'Angers in the Early Twelfth Century', *Medieval Perspectives* 19 (2004) 255–268.
[42] See pp. xl–xlvii in Leech-Wilkinson's edition of the *Voir dit*.

Constance's reply reveals that they had not seen each other for a year (63), and it was not unusual for lovers (fictive, real, role-playing, platonic or non-platonic) to experience long separations in which their relationship really was carried on entirely through writing (as in our Text 7). In this case, however, the love seems in any case to have been an entirely rhetorical affair, in which the frisson of a secret liaison and the charms of amorous rhetoric were an end in themselves.

'Regensburg'

Love letters should be seen in the context of the culture of convents and of the courtly relations that often existed between the ladies and the clerics they had dealings with – and by whom they expected to be treated with gallant *courtoisie*. Things may have occasionally gone further than elegant postures. The comic poem *The Council of Remiremont* (reproduced at p. 428ff. below) gives witty expression to the 'religion' of courtly love prevailing in the eleventh century at the abbey of Remiremont, where the God of Love is served by both the canonesses and the clerics by whom they are courted. The pseudo-love letter is an indication of a dangerously fluid boundary. Nuns might receive them from clerical *magistri* (as, with reference to their university learning, they were often termed), as we have seen. But convents contained not only nuns, but also girls receiving a literary education from a clerk (or clerks) who were their *magister* in the more specific sense of the word. And here pseudo-love letters were used, it seems, as a vehicle of teaching.

It was almost certainly to or for the girls being educated at Ronceray that, in the eleventh century, Marbod of Rennes (1035–1123) wrote a series of eleven love poems, which present typical sentiments and situations of men and women in love. A few years later, Baudri of Bourgueil (who knew Marbod and had been, like him, a scholar at the cathedral school of Angers) wrote for the young ladies verses of a more improving kind, preaching piety to them and urging them to write, as exercises in composition, return verses – something also requested by Abelard's pupil Hilarius of Orléans, who in the early twelfth century wrote panegyric verses, in a style 'proche de celui de l'amour courtois', addressed to nuns there.[43]

None of these particular poems suggests any actual amorous or sexual relationship – though they do testify to a culture of literary exchange

---

[43] Wolff, *La lettre d'amour*, p. 19. See poems II, III and V in *Hilarius Aurelianensis: Versus et ludi: epistolae: Ludus Danielis Belouacensis*, ed. Walther Bulst and M.L. Bulst-Thiele (Leiden, 1989). On the verses written for Ronceray by all three poets, see Dronke, *Medieval Latin*, vol. 1, pp. 213–18, and Wolff, *La lettre d'amour*, pp. 15–20. See also Newman, *Making Love*, pp. 5–7.

of Latin verses in which compliments and love were major components. More interesting are the love verses written towards the end of the eleventh century and preserved in Munich, Bayerische Staatsbibliothek, Clm 17142, verses written to each other by the ladies of a convent (nuns and/or high-born girls resident there) and clerics, specifically, Dronke deduced, 'a scholar from Liège, who teaches the liberal arts' there.[44] The abbey in question was possibly (but not certainly) Regensburg.[45] Most of the verses are second-person addresses, and though they do not closely or consistently imitate the epistle in form, the odd opening 'Salve' (42) or closing 'valeas' (41) and references to a messenger (46.18–19) indicate they are often conceived of and perhaps were missives of a kind. They appear to be Latin exercises involving a form of amorous role-playing in which the boundaries of modesty and propriety (and perhaps between fact and fiction) could easily be overstepped.

The items that most explicitly imply sexual love are poem number 3, where a man pleads for sex as the 'medicina' for his fever of love, and the four lines of number 16 where a man tells a lady to come to his bed at dawn in the 'old chapel'. Amongst the most playful is number 5, an insulting couplet on a man's apelike face and unkempt hair. Number 7 (expressing a perhaps similarly playful jealousy) runs thus:

> Corrige versiculos tibi quos presento, magister,
> nam tua verba mihi reputo pro lumine Verbi.
> Sed nimium doleo, quia praeponas mihi Bertham.

> Correct the brief verses I am sending you, master, for to me your words are like the light of the Word. But I am very sad, because you prefer Bertha to me.

Number 9 is a couplet expressing joy that 'me, doctor, dignaris amare' [you, my teacher, honour me with your love]. It is clear that the girls vied for the favour (pedagogic and personal) of the master, and the four lines of number 50 declare that the writer is the object of envy because of being enthroned in his favour, while 39 expresses gratification at the praise she has received of her poetic and metrical skills, praise she takes as evidence of *dilectio*.

---

[44] Dronke, *Medieval Latin*, vol. 1, p. 222 (cf. Poem 40.11). Dronke edits and translates (vol. 2, pp. 422ff.) selections from the poems, which were subsequently edited in full by Anke Paravicini, *Carmina Ratisponensia* (Heidelberg, 1979), whose numbering is retained in the later edition (with translation) by David A. Traill and Justin Haynes in *Education of Nuns, Feast of Fools, Letters of Love: Medieval Religious Life in Twelfth-Century Lyric Anthologies from Regensburg, Ripoll, and Chartres* (Leuven, 2021). Our citations follow the text and numbering in Traill and Haynes, though we sometimes depart from the wording (but not the sense) of their translations.
[45] See Traill and Haynes, *Education of Nuns*, p. 8.

Numbers 11 and 12 are a brief exchange between a woman anxious for the man she loves and his loving reassurance and thanks for what she wrote (*pro scriptis*). Number 13 ('May your letter to me wish to be written, even as mine to you') also refers to mutually welcome letters. Gifts are also exchanged. In the four lines of number 15, a lady is thanked for a vase and a gift of medicinal garlic, and in 24 a girl refers to a gift (of a chain for writing tablets) begged from her, a request which she says puts her vow (*munia voti*) to the test, but which she loves him too much to refuse. The couplet of 27, in which a man refers to a ring he has sent as a *pignus amoris* [pledge of love], is answered by a rebuffing couplet from the lady whose *honestas* refuses to recognize the resulting *foedus* [obligation] he mentions; and in 31 a lady similarly distinguishes between an *honestum ... foedus* and a *privato foedere* [secret attachment] that virtue forbids. Number 44 is a lady's cautious response to praise that included commendation of her beauty, which her illness makes her feel cannot be sincere; and 53 is an outright reproof of praise that is crudely exaggerated (*laudis hyperbolicae ... honore*). There are other signs of distrust: accusations of insincere praise or protestations (numbers 18, 53), words belied by fickleness and infidelity in deeds (17, 49). Thus 62 protests that the writer is being duped by a man who loves another, and she will 'seek out men of more worth'.

Part of one poem from a man ends, interestingly, 'We say farewell before the wings of poetry fail' (34.10). The ladies and cleric(s) are evidently engaging in competitive mastery of Latin verse in the form of flirtation and romance. In 37 the man similarly writes, 'it is no longer safe to vie with you in song' and (laughingly?) gives up both the sentimental and the metrical struggle: 'You surpass me by far, your poems far surpass mine, I confess myself vanquished'. Referring to the fate of Orpheus after 'daring to provoke your sex in his poetry', he gives up the unequal contest ('because I am not equal to you'), for 'men have always been vanquished in their struggles with women'. In number 39, a lady replies to a compliment on her verses, which she deprecates as praise prompted by love and courtesy, and, apparently on behalf of the whole group, sends good wishes in appropriately mythological terms. In 46, a woman breaks off a liaison because, 'When I sent you my carefully polished verses, you did not bother to give me a proper response', even when there was a messenger to hand; 47 is a somewhat irritable response from the delinquent, who says he could not get around to it so immediately. Number 61 asks, 'Is this the reward you give me, oh faithless girl, for my writings [*pro scriptis*] – that you ... refuse to remember how many and how great were the vows of holy love I gave you?' For, in this series, response to composition (of letters and of verses) is a measure of romantic response.

There are also group letters from the women, which deliver, for instance, welcome and salutation, and these present an 'official' attitude that is more demure, warning the man or men that they are nice girls and things should not go so far as to threaten their chastity or modesty. A three-liner sends a welcome from a band of 'vestals', granting 'dominion' on the condition of the honourable treatment demanded by *virtus* (number 6; cf. 10). Number 22 warns that 'men who take pleasure in indecent things should leave our company', for the ladies desire refinement of manners and morals in those who consort with them – and who should therefore 'preen' their plumage in behaviour and speech. The girls plainly expected to be treated and/or wooed with the courtly manners supposed to distinguish clerics and make them pleasant company for ladies (see *Council of Remiremont* 67–77, 149–50). A letter of farewell till the spring teases the addressee with the assertion that he may not be much missed, for 'Sir Hugh's entourage' pride themselves on their dress and talk, and he can only hope that the girls find their behaviour proves unacceptable (number 51). Even when writing on her own behalf, an individual is often conscious of being part of a group, as with the girl offended because her 'smudged lines' have not been answered and who warns the recipient that a wolf like him who harasses lambs should stay well away from their virginal circle (*virgineis ... choreis*: 48). This is, in short, institutionalized lovemaking, centred on literary art, in which the ladies see themselves as a chaste and refined group to be treated with the gallantry and delicacy of *courtoisie*.

These divertingly artful entries reflect a sparring rivalry between young, clever and well-educated girls and the cleric(s). The very fact that they were copied indicates texts with some general interest and relevance, sketching out in an entertaining way the features of a recognizable set of relationships, in which sexuality, high spirits and impudence could be channelled through the academic Latin exercise of the amatory epistle.

They are often lively put-downs. The girls are not to be fooled by flowery compliments on their beauty, are on their guard against promiscuously bestowed male favours, and dislike coarse liberties. They know the dangers of courtly clerics and the way they might use their literary arts. A particularly interesting entry is 40:

```
                cum matre Cupido
qui tibi spe vacua      promisit foedera nostra ...
Sed tamen ille puer      tibi dictat inepta, magister! ...
et vome pestiferam      Veneris puerique cicutam
ridentis flentes       mutilatum foedus amantes!
Denique si tibi se      fautorem Iuppiter ipse
adderet, et cithara     peteret nos Phoebus acuta,
omnibus adiunctis     in vota nefaria divis,
spes tua concideret      et laeto fine careret!
Te non castorum       decepit miles *Amorum*
Ovidius, qui te       persuasit carmen amare
quo subvertuntur       miseri, non erudiuntur ...
```

Cupid and his mother, who promised you my love, was feeding you on vain hopes ... But, master, that boy dictated foolishness to you! ... So disgorge the poisonous hemlock of Venus and of her son, who laughs at lovers weeping over broken vows. Even if Jupiter came to aid you besides, if Apollo petitioned me with his piercing lyre, if all the gods helped you to an unworthy love, your hopes would be dashed and would fail of the joy they promised. Ovid, that knight of the unchaste *Amores*, has deceived you, persuading you to love the poem by which unhappy men are seduced and not instructed ...

Mythological references were among the literary graces by which clerks could dignify love and present it as something courtly and elegant. They were also evidence of proficiency in the rhetoric of classical verse. On the occasion of a temporary absence of their master, the girls write a farewell that is meant to parade their proficiency in Latin rhetoric, the Pierides, Apollo, and Jupiter all occurring within the first four lines (52). Number 40, however, seems not simply to rebuke the man for presumption in mythological terms, but to include in its rebuke the very tactics of mythological rhetoric: he is mistaken if he thinks that talk of Cupid and Venus can disguise attempts on a lady's virtue, for he is invoking a deity who in effect favours rhetorical insincerity and 'laughs ... over broken vows'. The lady would not be impressed if he pressed into service the whole pantheon of classical gods or by any citation from Ovid (famous as the *doctor* [teacher, authority] on amorous matters: see *Council of Remiremont* 27). 'No mythology please, we're good girls' is the message of this entry.

There was one very specific way in which references to the classical gods could be used to grace illicit love. That the gods themselves had literally been brought down to earth in various forms by the power of love demonstrated its cosmic force and inevitability. The argument is used by Chaucer in the Prologue to Book III of his *Troilus*: Jupiter himself was subject to love, which 'amorous him made / On mortal thyng ... And in a thousand formes down hym sente / ffor loue in erthe' (17–21). The most elaborate use of the topos is to be found in an extraordinary poem beginning 'Profuit ignaris', the text of which (with translation) is given by Dronke in *Medieval Latin*.[46] It is addressed to a cloistered nun and to the sexual desires the writer knows she must have. The argument is not used for the purposes of seduction, but is seriously developed in a bold, complex and profoundly thought-provoking way: the *amours* of the Olympians, in which miscegenation occurred between heaven and earth, embody a universal and divine law and necessity requiring the divine to become mortal, the pattern being

---

[46] Dronke, *Medieval Latin*, vol. 2, pp. 452–63; the poem is discussed in vol. 1, pp. 232–8.

repeated when the cloistered have love affairs with lay persons and even in the adulteration of their heaven-directed thoughts with earthly and sensual matters, in which the same kind of descent of heaven to, and marriage with, earth occurs. 'Profuit ignaris' is preserved in a twelfth-century manuscript (Munich, BSB, Clm 19488, pp. 128–30). It was used, very relevantly to our theme here, in an actual love letter, written in verse to a nun, and preserved in another twelfth-century manuscript from Tegernsee (Munich, BSB, Clm 18580, fols. 59^r–64^r).[47] The writer declares that the recipient will know who he is and (since names in a love letter can by convention be only cryptically indicated) includes a broad hint as to the *Nomen mittentis*, which can be found by joining the letters O and T ('Si simul aptata fuerint OT geminata': line 186). Otto appropriates the argument of 'Profuit ignaris' to counter any fears his nun may have as to the sinful nature of their love, for the precedent and the pattern were set by the gods themselves. He also uses other mythological details, as well as a complex allegory based on the anointing of Christ's feet by the Magdalen. We have here an interesting instance of that appropriation of art by actuality that consists in the use of an existing poem for a personal love letter. As well as the particular borrowing from a particular poem, the letter also illustrates other general ways in which the love letter could and often did appropriate literary art of various kinds: it is itself in verse that is further embellished, not only with the mythological references that formed part of the techniques of clerical persuasion to love, but also with the stratagems of Christian exegesis. For sacred sources were as readily exploited as secular ones for these purposes. A conceit used by Jerome in a letter to Rufinus (if only he could, after the manner of Habakkuk, be transported into the presence of his beloved friend) was used not only in a similar letter of *amicitia* by Alcuin (in a letter to Bishop Arno), but also in one of the love verses preserved in another Tegernsee manuscript to which we now turn.[48]

Tegernsee (Munich, BSB, Clm 19411, fols. 69^r–70^r)

Much of the material in this twelfth-century manuscript shows a strong focus on the art of letter-writing, for it consists largely of a collection of official and private letters, and copies of texts that include two *artes dictaminis* (by Adalbert of Montecassino and Adalbert Samaritanus) and a model letter collection (by Henricus Francigena). The verse love letters

---

[47] The information on this poem is based on Dronke's account (*Medieval Latin*, vol. 2, p. 463).
[48] Jerome's conceit and the appropriations of it are referred to by Dronke at *Medieval Latin*, vol. 1, p. 198.

found in this epistle-formulary may well therefore be exercises or models, though they have sometimes been held to be real ones.[49] A group of seven follow Adalbert's *Praecepta dictaminum*, and a further three are included in a collection of letters towards the end of the codex. All are available in editions (with translations) by Peter Dronke: the first seven in *Medieval Latin and the Rise of European Love-Lyric* (vol. 2, pp. 472–82); the other three in an appendix to his illuminating paper 'Women's Love Letters from Tegernsee'.[50] The entire manuscript was edited in 2002 by Helmut Plechl in the Monumenta Germaniae Historica series.

We will consider first the three love letters found later in the manuscript. Before and after them, and between the first and the other two (which appear one after the other), are ones in which sender and addressee are often (as in all ten love letters) identified by initials only, but which apparently (and in some cases certainly) concern real persons and situations associated with the abbey. For instance, a nun R writes to a respected brother C ('domino et fratri suo') and bewails the state of affairs in the cloister, where Abbess 'Elizabet', installed by royal command rather than elected, stands to be excommunicated by the pope (item 192); 'C[onrad] rex Romanorum' commands the Count of Wasserburg to return to the cloister of Tegernsee the wine which the abbot has complained was taken thence (item 194) and Kaiser F[riedrich I] tells the abbot of Tegernsee to obey his previous requests to hand over a benefice to his minister 'W' (item 195).[51] The three love letters thus occur in a context of apparently real letters offering formal and rhetorical models for the kinds of situation and relationship they concern.

We will begin with the first letter (fols. 113^v–114^v), as this appears to be the easiest to interpret. In it, a woman writes to 'H', who may well be her teacher, since the letter is an evidently conscious display of all the literary skills acquired from formal education by a *magister*. She begins in florid verse, simultaneously showing her command of metre and of mythological

---

[49] Anna Grotans summarizes the opposing views in her review of *Die Tegernseer Briefsammlung des 12. Jahrhunderts*, ed. Helmut Plechl with Werner Bergmann, Monumenta Germaniae Historica (Hanover, 2002), *Medieval Review* (Feb. 2003), available online at https://scholarworks.iu.edu/journals/index.php/tmr/article/view/15611/21729.
[50] In Høgel and Bartoli, eds., *Medieval Letters*, pp. 215–45. The ten love letters are also edited by Jurgen Kuhnel, *Dû bist mîn. Ih bin dîn. Die lateinischen Liebes- (und Freundschafts-) Briefe des clm 19411* (Göppingen, 1977), and they are available in translation in Newman, *Making Love*, as are translations of selected 'Regensburg songs'.
[51] Quotations from the manuscript are from Plechl, ed., *Die Tegernseer Briefsammlung*, who, however, prints the love letters at the end of his edition, where they are separately numbered and separated from their context. So, for instance, the first of the three in prose appears as Love Letter 9 on pp. 357–9, the (non-love) letters preceding and following it (in the manuscript) as items 139 and 140 respectively on pp. 170–1.

reference as well as of how to use and vary the formulae of salutation and phrasing of the goodwill the letter sends:

> H. flori florum, redimito stemmate morum ...
> quod Piramo Tispe, tandem post omnia sese,
> hinc iterum sese vel quicquid habet melius se.[52]
>
> To H., flower of flowers, garlanded with virtues ...
> (the writer sends) all that Thisbe (sent) to Pyramus, and after all else herself, herself and whatever she has that is better than herself.

Eloquence and letter-writing then themselves become the subject in the course of a display of a common kind of modesty topos (used also by, for instance, the *mulier* in *Epistolae duorum amantium* 23 and 62), in which points of comparison are again taken from classical literature:

> Dilectissimorum dilectior, si exsuperaret mihi ingenium Maronis, si afflueret eloquentia Ciceronis aut cuiuslibet eximii oratoris aut etiam, ut ita dixerim, egregii versificatoris, imparem tamen me faterer esse ad respondendum pagine elimatissimi tui sermonis.
>
> More cherished than the most cherished, if my talent exceeded that of Virgil, if the eloquence of Cicero or any other outstanding writer flowed in me, or even, I may say, of any famous poet, I would still pronounce myself unequal to a response to the page of your most eloquent speech.

The letter continues to talk about itself, as the typical and chief topic of their correspondence is then specifically stated: the nature of friendship, or *amicitia* – with more classical anchorage, this time in a quote from Cicero, the acknowledged authority on this subject:

> Quia itaque primus et medius et ultimus sermo noster de amicicia semper incessit, de amicicia vera, qua nihil est melius, nihil iocundius, nihil amabilius, dicere ipse rerum ordo concessit. *Amicicia* vera attestante Tullio Cicerone *est divinarum humanarumque omnium rerum cum karitate et benivolentia consensio* [*De amicitia* 6.20], que etiam, ut per te didici, excellentior est omnibus rebus humanis cunctisque aliis virtutibus eminentior, dissociata congregans, congregata conservans, conservata magis magisque exaggerans.
>
> Therefore, since our talk first and last has always been about *amicitia*, true friendship, than which nothing is better, more pleasing or more to be loved, I will continue on this subject. True *amicitia*, as Cicero says, is the accord of

---

[52] Locutions of this kind occur in Boncompagno's model letters: see Text 1, 130/10–21.

all things divine and human in goodwill and *caritas*, and, as I have learned from you, it is more excellent than all other human attributes and greater than all other virtues, bringing together what is apart, conserving what has come together and increasing what has been conserved.

The characterization of friendship that the lady says she has 'learned from you' is actually found elsewhere – in the *Historia Compostellana* 3.51, where it is attributed to Cicero. But her citing of her addressee as a second and immediate source of her knowledge on this subject is strong evidence of his being her *magister* and of disquisition on this subject forming part of the training in expressing sentiment in letters of *amor/amicitia*. For, writing at about the same time, the *mulier* often specifically brings up the subject of *amor* and its nature, which also forms a topic in itself for the *duo amantes*, for whom Cicero is similarly the main authority, and by whom the *De amicitia* is also several times quoted from, as well as *De officiis* (see letters 24–5 and 49–50) and other texts. The lady here now follows up with six more lines (of verse proper) in gnomic praise of friendship. She then returns to the subject of her love and admiration, here inseparable from the command of eloquence, especially in the epistolary art, in which the relationship seems chiefly to lie:

> [F]or I began to love you the first day I saw you: you strongly penetrated into my heart, and for yourself therein, marvellous to say, you prepared a seat of your most pleasing converse (*iocundissime confabulationis*), and lest it be dislodged, with epistolary speech (*epistolari sermone*) a three-legged, nay a four-legged, stool.

There comes further praise of the virtue of fidelity, which she professes and urges on her addressee, and equally fulsome protestations of love – which likewise show only too good a command of that 'copiousness' so often commended as rhetorically stylish and more artfully interwoven quotations from sacred and secular texts:

> You alone are chosen out of a thousand [*ex milibus electus*: Song of Songs 5:104], you alone are received into the inmost place of my mind [*penetrabilibus quoddam penetrale receptus*: Ovid, *Tristia* 1.1.105], you alone are all-sufficient to me, if you do not fail in your love of me. I have done as you have: I have rejected all other joys for your love, on you alone does my being depend, in you have I placed all my faith and hope.

There is then an interesting passage relating to the common topic of the rival claims of knights and clerks as lovers and reflecting the clerical denigration of the former in favour of their own superior amiableness (a prejudice so richly and wittily displayed in the *Council of Remiremont* 67ff.: see below, pp. 434ff.). The present writer accepts that comparative evaluation only with some reservations:

> You certainly do well in persuading me to beware of knights as I would dire portents. I do indeed know what to beware of, and will not fall into that trap. But, saving my faith to you, I do not reject them entirely, so long as I do not surrender to that vice you attribute to them. For it is they from whom, so to speak, the laws of courtliness issue [*iura curialitatis*]. They are the fount of all honour. Let them suffice for such things, provided that they do not threaten our love.

The letter closes with further protestations and elegantly integrated quotes, sentiments then neatly metrified into three more lines of leonine verse, which artfully morph into vernacular verse that continues the theme and the rhyme into another register and another form of quotation (from popular verse) sometimes adopted in the love epistle (see Text 4, I.26–7, II.39–44):

> Semper inherere   statuit tibi mens mea vere.
> Esto secures,   successor nemo futurus
> est tibi, sed nec erit;   mihi ni tu nemo placebit ...
>
> Du bist min, ih bin din, des solt du gewis sin; du bist beslossen in minem herzen, verlorn ist daz sluzzellin, du most och immer dar inne sin.
>
> Always to inhere in you has my mind decreed. You may rest assured there will be no future successor to you; no one but you will please me. [*German:*] You are mine, I am yours, of this be sure. You are locked in my heart, the key is lost, so you will be in it for ever.

This letter, in which there is more art than matter, looks very like a model response from a good pupil, whose mastery of flowery protestations of *amor* and *amicitia*, and philosophical discussion of those virtues, ornamented with literary references, fine Latin and metrical essays are designed to display her epistolary skills, and it was probably copied to serve as a model letter, with a covert warning to any girl so taught not to take too seriously the clerical prejudice against knights (whose company could also be useful to their education in social and courtly skills). It may be genuine in the sense that it was composed by an actual girl for an actual master, and some actual feeling may underlie it, but it seems to have been primarily, and to have been copied to serve as, an exercise and model (which could also teach girls to cultivate courtliness and fine feeling).

It is followed by a letter from a man, who could well be a master responding to a letter that similarly took upon itself, at least in part, to express love and to praise it, in that mixture of sentiment and sententiousness typified in the letters of the *mulier* in the *Epistolae duorum amantium*. He thanks the lady for a letter copious in its praise of faith and friendship (*multiplici laude fidei et amicitiae*), but takes issue with what he sees as some inconsistency in it, which, befitting his role of master correcting a pupil, but perhaps disingenuously, he treats as a rhetorical fault. He could, he says, match her eloquence only by mixing discordant elements in the manner that Horace warned against (in *Ars poetica* I) as the equivalent of adding a horse's neck to a human head or a fish's tail to a comely woman.[53] The text of his epistolary sermon thus comes from a classical treatise on rhetoric, as the writer of the previous item had taken hers from one on friendship (Cicero's *De amicitia*) and as the lady to whom he is replying had taken hers, according to what he says later, from one by Ovid on love. He goes on to reinforce his point with an image drawn from classical mythology: the lady, he says, has produced a sort of rhetorical chimaera (a monster made up of parts of different animals). Her eloquent *words* on love were belied by her conclusion, which in some way refused the *deed* – a mismatch wittily condemned by quotation of the scriptural dictum 'Fides sine operibus mortua est' [faith without works is dead: James 2:26]. He sums up his accusation thus:

> Decet enim priorem literarum tuarum seriem asperum illum epilogum amicicie contrarium omnino abnnuere et, que verbis magnifice exsecuta es, amicabilibus factis adimplere.
>
> For the first part of your letter should properly rule out that unobliging ending, so contrary to friendship, and what in words you so splendidly described should be fulfilled more lovingly in deeds.

He then finds an apt way of making that shift into metre (leonine verse again) that was obviously regarded as a desirable component in a letter: if she is not convinced by his previous words, she may be moved by the present *metrico sermone*; she had taken her exordium (*tua prescripta*) from the truest words of the learned Ovid (*verissima dicta / docti Nasonis*), but her end had belied their content and sweetness. Had the lady indicated that her love was chaste and she would stoop to no foul 'deed', incurring a reply that wittily or with serious displeasure takes her to task for violating a rhetorical rule?

The first of the three love letters in this section of the manuscript is a reply to this letter of the *magister*(?), though in the manuscript it comes (at fol. 100ᵛ) a few pages before it (and the above-described one that

---

[53] The instructions Pandarus gives to Troilus for writing an effective love letter include a similar deprecation of jumbling 'discordant thing yfeere' and paraphrase the same Horatian text (*Troilus* II.1037–43).

precedes it).⁵⁴ It was presumably always possible in this type of pseudo-love letter for one party to transgress a felt boundary, and this the cleric appears to have done. For, whether or not his displeasure was serious, the girl is plainly upset and offended at his words. Her letter begins neatly, 'Suo sua sibi se' [to her own from his own, (sending) to him herself], but gives a reproachful response to his attack, which she represents as an example of male clerical sophistry used to trip up the honest simplicity of a girl – thus voicing (as do some of the Regensburg verses, though in a different way) a certain female distrust of how clerical literary skills might be used to deceive and betray women:

> I wrote to you, as I may truly say, in a familiar way, a thing which no other man has succeeded in inducing me to do. But you clever or, I should rather say, crafty men are apt to entangle in talk [*capere in sermone*: Matthew 22:15] us simple girls, because often, competing with you in the field of words, we are struck by the darts of what you think to be your logic [*iusta ratione*]. So you compared my recent letter to you with certain monstrosities in nature that do not actually exist, but which do not lack some implied signification, and then did not hesitate to put her who loves you [*tuam amicam*] in the wrong. For with too much of an irreverent and impudent mind [Ecclesiasticus 23:6], you let loose the rein of your galloping speech when you equated with chimaeras and sirens words ... proceeding from good conscience and faith unfeigned. [1 Timothy 1:5]

Though her riposte had been preceded by quotations (from Ovid) which showed she was as well able to cite the classics as the writers of the other two letters, it is probably significant that her embedded textual allusions now come from Scripture alone, as if she were consciously or unconsciously thereby asserting her honest piety against the classical learning so open to clerical abuse. And her next allusion goes even further down the scale of simplicity, for it is to a vernacular proverb (about the goat attributing his own vices to other animals), and as she cites it her prose lapses into the German whence it comes and the letter ends in a macaronic alternation between German and Latin phrases:

> Quod aliunde non esse firmissime ducor credere nisi inde, quia *daz der boch*, et exinde, quia putatis, quod post mollia queque nostra dicta transire debeatis

---

⁵⁴ See Plechl, ed., *Die Tegernseer Briefsammlung*, p. 364. Wolff (like Dronke in 'Women's Letters') reads all three letters as forming a single series (*La lettre d'amour*, p. 94), the man's being a reply to the woman's letter that precedes it in the manuscript and prompting a (displaced) response from the same woman; the problems with this assumption are obviated by Newman, who posits (*Making Love*, p. 246) some material missing from the end of the first of the letters found together, material that would account for the man's characterization of that conclusion in the letter immediately following in the manuscript.

ad acta. Sic non est, nec erit: *wande ih mohte dir deste wirs geualle, ob ih mih* prosternerem *in allen, den ich gotlichen zospriche. Wande du mir daz uercheret hast,* notabilis factus es mihi. *Desne soltu du niemere, friunt uolge du miner lere, div nemach dir gescaden nieth. Wande warest du mir nieth liep,* ego permitterem te currere in voraginem, ut ita dicam, ignorantie et cecitatis. *Desne bist abe du nieth wert,* quia in te sunt fructus honoris et honestatis. *Ich habete dir wol mere gescriben, niu wan daz du bist also wole getriben,* quod scis colligere multa de paucis.

Statlich unde salich du iemer wis.

And that, as I firmly believe, issued from nothing but the *ram* [attributing his own vicious intentions to others], and that is why you think that you ought to be able to deduce physical deeds from my expressions of regard. But it is not so, and it never will be: *for I would surely be the less admired by you, if I were to* demean *myself in all ways when I speak in good conscience. That you are twisting my words* I find disgraceful. *If you take the advice I offer as your friend, you will do so no more.* For were you not dear to me, I would let you run on into the whirlpool, as I may call it, of ignorance and folly. *But you are worth better than that,* because in you are the fruits of honour and decency [Ecclesiasticus 24:23]. *I would have written at more length to you, but you are clever enough* to understand much from a little.

May you be ever happy and safe.[55]

The German here pits the girl's untrained sincerity against the Latin that records the man's lying attempts on her honour and the classical image of the whirlpool of moral folly, and the neat Latin *ave* of her opening finally evolves into a simple German *vale* that produces its own kind of chimaera. It sounds very much as if the girl takes the man's criticism to have been an attempt on her honour – to argue that her *mollia* [complaisant] avowals of regard logically implied consent to a carnal 'deed' – which would involve the (Latin) debasement (*prosternerem*) of her (German) innocent speech (*gotlichen zospriche*). The macaronic close, in fact, produced by this 'artless girl' (*simplex puella*) has a kind of literary expressiveness more powerful and complex than the elegantly convoluted tissue of classical rhetoric and reference of the clever master (*vir astutus*) who corrected her.

The German works, at all events, to an effect quite different from that produced at the end of the other female letter. It here suggests an emotion too impatient for the work of Latinization, which is either deferred or rejected. Moreover, the particularity (and opaqueness) of the clerical charge of inconsistency and the emphasis of the response sound 'genuine', at least to the extent that the objection was real and the girl was really upset by it,

---

[55] The italics used to differentiate German from Latin are our own.

Clerics and Convents 103

if only as a pupil. The letters could certainly serve to typify a clerical sally (clever talk aimed at pushing goodwill into something more) and a female refutation which might have been thought by the compilers to be useful and/or interesting to the different genders, and they do seem to record some real relationship and real correspondence involving that shadow love expressed in rhetorical and epistolary training (which might still entail some interest in being liked and admired on either side) or some real feeling of that *amicitia* or *amor* between which little distinction was made in the conventions of epistolary style.

The 'rhythmical prose' that characterizes the above three letters is perhaps even more marked in the seven love letters found earlier in the manuscript. This 'prose that rhymes phrases in pairs, with leonine verses interspersed' was considered by Dronke to be particularly close to the Latin prose style of the *mulier*,[56] which likewise tends strongly towards phrases paired by rhyme or assonance. We quote from Plechl's text, but indicate where line-endings occur in Dronke's text, where they appear as the verse they in many ways suggest.

The first item is headed *Amico amica* [To one she loves from one who loves him] and begins 'S. suo dilecto / omnium cognatorum sibi dulcissimo / H. fidem / et dilectionem' [To her beloved S., sweetest of all her kinsmen, H. sends her faith and love]. His face 'that gives me so much joy' is ever in her mind, and this 'sweetest of lovable men' is begged to return the love of 'one who loves [him] from her heart', etc.

The second, headed *Amico amica derelicta* [From the beloved, abandoned, to her lover] is a grief-stricken love letter accusing the man of the inconstancy women so often bewailed in life and in literature. It begins (likewise naming through initials), 'H. quondam carissimo / nunc autem perfidissimo / N. dignam mercedem / secundum opera sua' [To H., once her dearest, but now her most perjured one, N. (sends) such reward as his deeds deserve]. It ends with a warning against the letter's being seen by a third party ('Cave diligentius, / ne tercius / interveniat oculus'), a plea found elsewhere and paralleled in a real love letter from a real woman (see Text 7, VII.15 and note).

The sixth and seventh are remarkable for being love letters to a woman from a woman.[57] VI begins, 'G. *super mel et favum dulciori* (Psalms 19:10) / B. quidquid amor amori. / O unica et specialis, / cur tamdiu in longinquo moraris? / Cur unicam tuam perire vis, / que anima et corpore te diligit, ut ipsa scis?' [To G., sweeter than honey or honeycomb, B. sends all the

[56] Review of Wheeler, ed., *Listening to Heloise*, p. 137.
[57] These are numbered 7 and 8 in Plechl, who includes amongst the seven pieces a non-love letter (numbered 5). We follow the numeration given in Dronke's text in *Medieval Latin*.

love there is to her love. You who are unique and special, why do you delay so long and so far? Why do you wish your only one to perish, who, as you know, loves you with soul and body?].[58] VII begins, 'To G., her unique rose, from A., the bond of precious love', and later lines prove the feminine gender of both sender ('Quid faciam miserrima?': 356/15) and recipient, than whom there is none so 'amabilis ... et grata' (356/20). Such details as the recollection of kisses (356/14) indicate these letters cannot be unproblematically explained as *amicitia*, which utilized much of the same intense and flowery language as *amor*.

The third and fourth are somewhat exceptional in not using initials in their openings and in forming a pair. A girl writes to a *doctor* (perhaps her *magister*) to respond positively to an offer of love, her honour and chastity excepted:

> Quid dignum digno / valeam scribere, ignoro, / presertim cum doctoris aures pudor sit inculto sermone interpellare ... Durum mihi videtur ac difficile, / quod conaris a me inpetrare, / Scilicet integritatem mee fidei ... Attamen si sciero me casto amore a te amandum / et pignus pudicie mee inviolandum, / non recuso amorem. (348/24–9)

> I do not know if my powers suffice to write anything worthy of your worthy self, especially since it would be embarrassing to bring my uncultivated language to the ears of a scholar ... What you seek to obtain from me seems to me to be hard and difficult – that is, my whole faith ... But if I know I am to be loved by you with a chaste love, and my pledged innocence not to be violated, I will not refuse my love.

The letter ends with a version of the warning plea that ends II, but with an addition that makes it seem not merely a commonplace: 'Take care that no one sees this letter – for it was not written with the permission required for letters [*ex autoritate scripta*]'. Dronke similarly feels that line 25 sounds, not like 'a commonplace of love's anxieties', but more like an awareness that love between parties so situated 'will not be easy'.[59] And this fact is emphasized in what appears to be the man's reply in IV (where the speaker is certainly male), which thanks its addressee for 'Litteras tue melliflue dulcedinis / redolentes aromata summe caritatis' [Your letter of mellifluous sweetness, redolent with the aroma of perfect love] (349/29–30), which was, however, read with some pain, because he saw from it that what he was asking was 'durum tibi esse ac difficule' [troublesome and difficult for you], which seems like a direct echo of III.25 (quoted above). These two items, then,

---

[58] The italics (for the feminine endings) are ours.
[59] Dronke, *Medieval Latin*, vol. 2, p. 482.

bear particular signs of referring to or imagining a veritable (or at least verisimilar) love compact, not least because they eschew the possibly tell-tale initials used in the other love verses.

The fifth love letter (number 6 in Plechl) is the only other one of the seven that is (probably) male-voiced. There is no grammatical indication of the gender of the sender, it is addressed to a woman ('To G., most dearly dear, most sweetly sweet') who is preferred 'pre omni sexu' [before all others of the sex]. The comparisons at 352/29–30 (he sees his lady in his sleep as Boethius did the personified Philosophia) and 353/2 ('prosis velut Io' [may you prosper as did Io]) are, as we have seen, typical rhetorical embellishments associated with the clerical avowal of love. But they are rare in this sequence, occurring in only two items: in this item apparently from a male, but also in the seventh (one of the two woman-to-woman items), which contains the reuse (mentioned above) of the conceit from Jerome ('if Habakkuk's trance-journey were granted me, that I might come to see the face of the loved one': 356/17–18). These learned allusions are signs of the cleric and of girls taught by a cleric, but in general the sequence is less learned and witty, less sophisticated in content and metre, than is its counterpart emanating from (?)Regensburg.

The fifth ends by adding the salutations of the 'convent of young women' (*conventus iuvencularum*), indicating the cloister culture of which verse letters like these seem to have been an integral part and the institutionalization of the art of expressing intense personal feeling ranging across the often-invisible barrier between *amor* and *amicitia*. The titles provided for the first two items would be consistent with exercises personalized by using the initials of an actual writer and addressee, and the two which are both from and to females might show the girls practising their rhetorical arts of love language on each other. The degree of real love (heterosexual and/or homosexual) the passages might also express is unascertainable, and perhaps irrelevant. The headings and the absence of individualizing details (bar the initials) suggest that the entries were preserved because, or rendered in such a form that, they reflected typical rather than peculiar cases, recognizable scenarios that could serve as templates or pedagogic examples.

Söflingen

With the late fifteenth-century Söflingen letters, we turn from the earlier to the late Middle Ages and from Latin to the vernacular. The convent of Clares at Söflingen Abbey had fallen into the ordinary laxities and was taken over by reformers in 1484, after the nuns (and the order of monks associated with them) had long resisted the pressures of the purists. Many of them declined to return to the convent under its new management (though several eventually did), and in the cells of six of the nuns were found items which the Observant reformists considered evidence of the worldliness of their predecessors and confiscated: clothing and accessories, etc., which were unsuitably decorative and a collection of some fifty letters and seven love poems.[60] Both the unreformed abbey and the letters were supposed by many previous scholars to have been much more scandalous than in fact seems to have been the case, according to Max Miller, from whose authoritative edition of the letters the information in this section is largely taken. The infringements of the rule were all of the type common at the time: the enjoyment of personal possessions and money and private space in contravention of the regulations governing communal religious life, and a general worldliness that included more contact with the outer world than was strictly permitted to this austere order. Though access to the inner cloister was hardly ever permitted, there were points of contact at the perimeter (a gate, a passage, a 'Redefenster' [window for talking]) which allowed some interface with the outer world, and the traffic at these points was greater than it should have been (Miller, pp. 109–11). There is, however, no evidence in the records of the reform proceedings or in the letters of any widespread or institutionalized sexual misconduct (Miller, pp. 51–5).

The letters are almost all written *to* the nuns, and often come from other nuns or male clerics, and offer a fascinating insight into the relations of the convent with the world outside their walls: relatives and friends, the exchange of small gifts, purchases, New Year greetings, church news and gossip, pharmaceutical matters, form the most typical subject matter. The letters from the Barfüsser [Barefoot friars] to their sister Franciscans are especially interesting. In this order, female communities were by historical convention overseen by males, and in this case an interesting custom had arisen which is likely to raise some eyebrows today. The monks and nuns often paired up as Gottesfreunde in a kind of 'geistliche Ehe' [spiritual marriage], or religious counterpart to secular conjugality.[61] The Reform movement disapproved of the relationship (Miller, p. 81), and the contact between these Gottesfreunde was certainly greater than strict adherence to the spirit and letter of the regulations would have sanctioned, both as regards correspondence (Miller, p. 110), which the rule restricted and for which permission was required (cf. the close of Tegernsee III,

---

[60] See Max Miller, ed., *Die Söflinger Briefe und das Klarissenkloster Söflingen bei Ulm an der Donau im Spätmittelalter* (Würzburg, 1940), pp. 56–8.
[61] On the history and nature of the relationship between the two communities, see Miller, ed., *Die Söflinger Briefe*, pp. 78ff.

quoted p. 104 above), and in the sorts of peripheral contact described above (Miller, p. 110). That things went further in some cases is a possibility, but there is no evidence of anything improper in the letters (Miller, pp. 85ff.). Some give earnest advice (Letters 39–41), others are full of church news and politics (especially the projected and dreaded reforms), and of the sorts of enmities and friendships that develop in closed and close circles. The most numerous are from Jos Wind to Magdalena von Suntheim and concern his resentment and frustration in his clerical career. The letters often testify to warm affection and solicitude both for the particular addressee and for other sisters in the order. That affection can often be expressed in terms which might suggest love of a kind the letters do not otherwise give any ground for supposing – and which show both the common language shared by *amor* and *amicitia* in epistolary culture and also how closely these particular relationships could thus shadow the secular bond on which they were modelled.

Expressions of regard in the medieval period generally are, as we have seen, often what modern taste finds saccharine, gushy and sentimental (cf. Miller, p. 61), and some of the locutions and endearments (like Wind's 'trwes liebs suzelin' [my true and sweet love]: Letter 32) are those which a sweetheart might use. To Klara von Rietheim (who was his particular favourite amongst other nuns he also cared about) Konrad von Bondort (in a letter otherwise devoted to serious religious adjuration) can express himself as follows:

> Sott wissen in warheit, ye lenger, ye lieber dich han. Diewill du lebest, will ich dich nimer gelon, der tod müsst myn ge dir liebe schaiden, sust niemancz. Ach, wass wolt ich zů wortt nemen! Ich hon an dir alles, dz myn hercz gelangt; du hast dich so tugendklich, frintlich und herczlich menge jar mit mir gehaltten, dz ichs dir nimer mag zů gůttum vergessen … Din wil ich mit trůwen ewig sin, daruff blib festenklich.

> Please know that I hold you the longer the dearer. As long as you live, I will never leave you; death alone will part me from my love of you, nothing else. Ah, what I would like to say! It is in you that all that is dear to my heart exists. You have been for many years so gracious, friendly and heartfelt in your behaviour to me that I can never forget you … Your own will I always faithfully be, of that be sure.[62]

The wording here will be worth remembering when we turn below to another letter to Klara from another cleric expressing worshipping love.

---

[62] Letter 40; the passage is also quoted by Miller, ed., *Die Söflinger Briefe* (pp. 91–2), from whose text (with the omission of some diacritics) all quotations are taken.

The poems are indeed love poems, but they are conventional in sentiment and not personalized – and could only condemn the sisters of worldly and secular literary tastes (for the nuns certainly did often lack spiritual seriousness), although they would not have been unsuitable reading for the girls receiving board and education at the convent. But three of them show an interesting feature that makes them personalizable in the manner of Robert Armburgh, who added a closing personalization to the verses he copied out to send as a love letter (Text 6, 1.31–4). That is, they have a final extra-metrical 'signature'. Appended to Poem I are the words 'din un vergessen von mir unerkant din aigen' [yours without forgetting, your unnamed own one], to Poem IV 'kain zitt aun verlangen' [never without longing], and to Poem II 'alweg gerecht' [ever true], followed by some letters (w e n k j), which may or may not be initials, perhaps those of the person who presented the verses to the nun(s). These addenda could be indications of some actual personal message in the verses, or part of the art of the verses themselves in providing a final sign-off that could suggest or be appropriated by a particular sender, who might (since they are not in metre) add a further hint by means of, for example, his initials. Either way, these semi-subscriptions put the message of the poems on a potentially fluid boundary between art and actuality and provide further evidence of an assumed 'usability' of love poems in actual relationships.

Of the letters themselves, there are five which certainly do to all appearances seem to be love letters. They are grouped together by Miller (who, however, does not consider them to be real love letters: p. 76) as Letters 6–10. The first four are from laymen, probably (according to Miller: p. 76) from members of the gentry, who enjoyed freer intercourse with the nuns than was strictly proper. For the letters are written in hands less adept than those typical of the clerics (Miller, pp. 107–8). Here, the postures and rhetoric are dated and conventional, but provide a superficial courtliness Miller believes to be so at odds with the clumsiness of the letters in other respects (such as the handwriting) as to suggest the wording came from some kind of manual of love letters. There certainly were such things, and one of them (by the twelfth-century Boncompagno) is reproduced in Text 1; many of the *artes dictandi* (the manuals that provided models for letters) in any case included love letters (see Text 2, p. 202).[63] Use of such guides was one kind of indebtedness actuality might owe to art. The first two letters (6 and 7) are signed, but with initials only. C.R., writing to Martha Ehinger, declares that she is his sovereign comfort in this world, 'wan ich doch mich ganz yn uyer truyss hertz ergeben han

---

[63] Cf. Dronke's references to the 'love-declarations' to be found in Matthew of Vendôme's *Epistolarium* and elsewhere (*Medieval Latin*, vol. 1, p. 251).

and mich gar nitz froeen soll dan ir, wan ich der uyer byn' [I have given myself entirely to your true heart and nothing at all can give me joy except you, since I am yours], and his dearest wish is that 'ir woerde soelich liebe erkennen und werden mir uyer truyss hertz mitdayllen, wan ess mir der groesst schatz sin soll, der uff dysem erderrich ist and mich me erfroeren mag' [you would show me the same kind of love and give to me your true heart, since that is for me the greatest treasure that can be found in this world and what can give me joy]; he would have written earlier had a messenger been available, and hopes to receive 'ain früntlich antwirtt, darab min trurigy hertz erfrett mig werden, wan mir min hertz kain mensch nit erfreen mag dan yr' [a friendly reply from which my sad heart may be cheered, since only you can give me happiness]. L.B. (whose sign-off is 'Ich begeren, din ewig zu sin' [I desire to be always yours), writing to A.E. (Adel Ehinger), makes similar protestations:

> Dan ich in rechter warhait nit gefeligers han uf erden wan dich alain und lid fil haimlichen schmertzen an minem hertzen, das ich dich, hertzlieb, nit haben mag nach mines hertzen gier. Dan al welt ist gantz töd in minem hertzen bis alain an dich, hertzlieb.

> For I in very truth have no source of joy on earth except you alone and suffer many inner pains in my heart because I cannot have you, heart's beloved, in the way I desire. For all the world is as dead to my heart except for you, dear heart.

He apologizes, comparably with Letter 6, for not having come on Sunday, and looks forward to being with her the next morning 'und alerlaig mit dier reden, das ich wärlich nit erschriben kan' [and at least say to her what indeed I cannot write].[64] Letters 8 and 9 lack even initials as signatures. Letter 8, to A.A., replying to a letter accusing him of forgetting her because he did not come when he promised and assuring her of his continuing love and faith, sends 'unchanged love and faith' to her 'die ich myr selbs auss ander allen erwellt hab, zu dinen mytt gerechttem, stetter truywen' [whom I have chosen for myself out of all others to serve with real and steadfast truth], and again protests that the 'grost frod' [greatest joy] he has in the world lies in her. Letter 9 delivers to Ursula von Habsperg a May greeting that accompanies a May gift, May Day being (like Valentine's Day and New Year) a date on which lovers and friends felt particularly called on to mark by some missive or physical object and/or verbal greeting or poem (see above, pp. 44–5): 'Wen warlich, alcz dz jecz lebt und gront, kan so lieblich nit sin und dem schemczen so trostlich: min hercz ist noch heher erfred, da ich dich, min

---

[64] The reference is presumably to the window at which the nuns communicated with those from the outer world.

herczlieb, ansach' [Since truly, as all now comes to life and is green, there can be nothing so delightful to the eyes, and the joy of having laid eyes on you makes my heart soar the more], the gift being to betoken his love.

We are plainly here dealing with a common love language that love literature and letter manuals had helped to entrench, whether or not any specific model was used by any of the writers. Letter 10 is especially interesting and has already been referred to above (p. 16). It is addressed to Klara von Rietheim, to whom Konrad von Bondorf wrote the affectionate words quoted above, but, here again, there are not even initials to indicate the sender – who was, however, almost certainly a cleric and quite possibly one of the Barefoot friars. For the writer is clearly educated and literate: his hand ('sehr elegante': Miller's n. 1 to Letter 10) is alignable with the proficient script of letters from the clerical Barfüsser (see Miller, pp. 107–8); and the letter also consists entirely of two word-for-word extracts from a German translation of a major product of the new humanist learning – the story of Euryalus and Lucretia by Aeneas Silvius Piccolomini. The German translation used here was by the humanist Nikolaus von Wyle and had been published in 1478 by Konrad Fyner in Esslingen.

One may recall here the love poem in the Welles Anthology (no. 38) created out of different parts of Chaucer's *Troilus* (see p. 17 above). Piccolomini's story, 'undoubtedly one of the most read stories of the whole Renaissance',[65] was in fact the *Troilus* of its era. This *Historia de duobus amantibus* was written in Latin in 1444. Much copied, printed and translated, it made its way into several English versions, the first of which was published in 1515.[66] Piccolomini was crowned poet laureate in 1442 by the future Emperor Frederick III and in 1556 was elected pope and became Pope Pius II. His early career was as a high-ranking secretary, first in papal employ and then in the imperial chancery. The state visit to Siena made by Sigmund of Luxembourg (in 1432–3) forms the setting of the story in question: Euryalus is a member of his entourage, and the beautiful Lucretia (married to a much older man) is a participant in the city's welcoming ceremonies. The two fall in love at first sight and the tale is concerned with how they manage – with difficulty, ingenuity and danger – to further their adulterous love. Interestingly, excerpts from the story (and the love letters in it) had already been used, often verbatim, by the humanist Hermann Schedelin in what Miller calls his 'lasziven Briefwechsel' [salacious interchange of letters] with Wilhelm von Reichenau.[67] In that case, the original Latin had been quoted, as it could not

---

[65] Æneas Silvius Piccolomini, *The Goodli History of the Ladye Lucres*, ed. E.J. Morrall, EETS OS 308 (1996), p. xv.
[66] This was followed in 1553 by another version, available in Morrall's EETS edition.
[67] Miller, ed., *Die Söflinger Briefe*, Letter 10, n. 1.

be in our Letter 10, where the writer had to use a text that would be intelligible to a nun who (at this date) would not have been Latinate.

The story was originally contained within a letter (dated 1444) written by Piccolomini, when he was in imperial employ, to his former tutor at the University of Siena: the fictional story thus has a factual frame that echoes the German-Siennese axis of the love story and its setting. Significant epistolary elements also occur within the tale. The lovers first make their feelings known to each other in a series of letters, and the affair can thenceforward be carried on for the most part in no other way, meetings being few, dangerous and time-sensitive. Piccolomini, a secretary by profession, obviously found letters came readily to his mind and hand in the conduct of the story, together with the problematics of carriage and delivery attendant on this clandestine affair. Euryalus, furthermore, must rely on the words of others in his initial epistolary efforts, and thus typifies in a rather peculiar way the felt incapacity of many cadet lovers (who often reused existing literary models) to find suitable words of their own: he is hampered by his ignorance of Italian and, until he learns it (which he makes it his business speedily to do), must use an intermediary to compose the wording of his letters.

It is from Euryalus's first two letters that the writer of Letter 10 has created his cento. Euryalus, like Troilus, first announces his love in a letter, and this was often assumed to be the most obvious method of making an amorous proposition, partly because opportunities for private conversation with a lady (especially a married one), who would rarely be alone or unattended, were limited. Letter 10 may itself be intended as a similar opening move. The clerk is more artful than the layman and avails himself of the elegantly eloquent words Piccolomini gave to Euryalus as an opening gambit:

> Ich embutt üch minen gruss und vil *hailles*, allerliepste fraw, wa wir aincher volle wäre dez *hailles*, aber alles *hailles* und aller drost mins lebens hanget ganntz an üch! Ich hab me lieb üch dann mich selbs ...[68]
>
> I send you my greeting – and health, if I myself had a sufficiency of it, but all the health or well-being and comfort of my life are wholly dependent on you. You are to me dearer than myself ...

But although this first letter by Euryalus continued with many always-appropriate loverly topoi, the German writer continues instead with passages from Euryalus's second letter, to which he has to make some small

---

[68] Emphasis added; cf. Troilus at the end of his letter in Book V ('With hele swich that, but ȝe ȝeven me / The same hele, I shal none hele haue': 1415–16) and Criseyde at the beginning of her reply ('How myght a wight in torment and in drede / And heleles, ȝow sende as ȝet gladnesse?': 1592–3).

adaptations. Euryalus, not knowing the town, had resorted to a known bawd to deliver his first letter, and Lucretia (still in denial over her love for him) had made a show of fury that such a woman should deliver her a letter. His second letter is summarized in indirect speech in the *Historia*, which tells how he began by apologizing for the carrier used and continued by assuring Lucretia that he had the deepest respect for her concern for her honour and chastity, which played a large part in his adoring worship of her and which were sacred to him also. The German changes the grammar to direct speech and omits, of course, the apology for the bawd, but uses in full the earnest expressions of regard for the lady's chastity, reputation and honour that had been occasioned by that apology and the culminating assertion that it was the very conjunction of virtue and beauty that had caused her to appear as a goddess in the eyes of her admirer:

> [U]nd dezhalb als ain gottin lobsam erschinent, so hab ich üch lieb gewunnen und dond üch ern und nützet schantlichs von üch begern, och üczet wünschende, daz urern lümden zu dehain weg solt oder mocht verletzen, sunder mich allain begern, üch min gemut wytter zu offnen.

> And your being someone therefore appearing as perfect as a goddess, so I have given you my love and do you honour and desire nothing shameful from you, or wish anything that would or could injure your reputation, but only ask for an opportunity to make known my feeling to you at further length.

He then reverts for conclusion to the ending of Euryalus's first letter:

> Dz wellend dis min geschrifft erfüllen. Wa dz geschicht, so leb ich und sallig, oder aber es erloschet min hercz, daz lieber hat üch dann mich selbs. Domit befilch ich mich in urer gietige antwürt and drwe. Got pflag urer in gesunthait.

> That is what this letter asks. And according to what comes of it, I will live and be joyful, or it will break my heart, which holds you dearer than myself. Therewith I entrust myself to your kind answer and good feeling. God keep you in health.

Like Robert Armburgh, he adds a brief concluding subscription to the material he has borrowed: 'Din dugent min hoffnung' [Your servant in hope].[69]

This is thus indebtedness of a fairly creative and artful kind. The passages have been selected and combined to make a most appropriate and respectful love letter to a nun from a cleric who was probably genuine in

---

[69] Cf. Text 6, I.31–4.

his protestations of a love that did not involve anything deleterious to the lady's honour – as were Troilus and Euryalus. Writing a love letter of an established kind (the platonic love offered a nun: see above, p. 87), he has found common ground between the chaste love of a 'spiritual friend' and the priority over his own desires given by the courtly lover to the lady's honour (cf. for instance *Troilus* IV.568–74). Miller (who argues that the dossier contains nothing incriminating in the way of 'affairs') characterizes the letter as courtly and witty ('hübsch' and 'spielerisch': p. 106). But the overall effect of the letter is one of earnestness. And the declared point, of the missive and the compliments it offers, is to request an opportunity to explain the writer's feelings in more detail: which is exactly the climactic request Boncompagno suggests to the prudent lover in a model letter designed to give a virtuous lady something it might not be too compromising to grant (see Text 1, 140/30–3).

It is difficult to know whether any or all of these five letters should be characterized as love letters or as letters of *amicitia* couched (not untypically) so extravagantly as to suggest a closer bond. The latter usually have some purpose other than the simple expression of devotion. The protestations of love in the first four letters seem to be immediately occasioned by a failure to communicate as and when expected; but the fifth has no other overt purpose except to announce the love of the writer and request he be allowed to express it more fully. The first four obviously presuppose an existing bond, but we cannot know whether Klara responded positively to the request of the fifth for an opportunity for a fuller sentimental avowal. There is no need to assume that there was anything other than sentiment in question in any of the five cases: platonic love between the laymen and the nuns, and what the fifth may well have intended and assumed would be taken as that shadow romance of *Gottesfreundschaft*. But the distinction between romantic love that involved no physical contact and *amicitia* that expressed itself in the same language as romantic love is surely vanishingly small. The very fact of a shared language for expressing both kinds of love (a language which could therefore be used without being in itself improperly suggestive) suggests that non-romantic and romantic love were experienced and classed in the culture of the day as more of a continuum than they are today, when we tend to be conscious of a difference in kind rather than simply degree. Klara would surely assume from her letter that she was being propositioned in the parallel romance realm of *Gottesfreundschaft*, whose distinction from romantic but platonic love would be imperceptible.

However one takes the letters, the influence of literary art on the epistolary expression of love is clear: in the conventional style and phrasing of the first four and in the appropriations of the fifth. Söflingen, in conclusion, gives us another example of a convent in which relationships of *amor* and *amicitia* were actively furthered by an epistolary culture in which expressions of love and regard were fostered and studied. The nuns were not untypical in the high value they are said to have placed on education and polish, qualities they would have found in abundance in the learned and sophisticated order of the Barfüsser.[70] They thus shared the same preference for the company of cultivated clerics (who might become lovers) as is comically represented in the *Council of Remiremont* (see pp. 432ff. below) and is testified to in the interchanges of (?)Regensburg and Tegernsee, which also reflect or play-act relationships always close and sometimes amorous.

[70] See Miller, ed., *Die Söflinger Briefe*, p. 79.

SECTION II

Fictional and Instructional Models

TEXT 1

Boncompagno da Signa: Rota Veneris

Boncompagno

Born c. 1170 in Signa, Italy, Boncompagno began his studies in the three linguistic *artes* (grammar, rhetoric, dialectic) at Florence, but completed them at Bologna, the schools of which city were especially associated with the new branch of rhetoric devoted to the *ars dictandi* (the art of composing letters or epistles). It was in this field that Boncompagno made his name: both as a teacher and in his writings, he devoted himself to publicizing this new discipline, to which he advertised himself as offering an access that dispensed with what he represented as the needless pedantry of the traditional rhetorical training. The two works attended with the most pronounced marks of acclaim were his *Rhetorica antiqua* and *Rhetorica novissima*, both of which were publicly recited in Bologna, in the years 1215 and 1235 respectively, and the first of which was awarded the laurel that constituted graduation towards a master's licence.[1] He attached his name to that former work in a very precise sense, for he called it the *Boncompagnus*, perhaps playing (as he seems to do at the end of the *Rota Veneris*) on the meaning of his name to present his work as a 'good companion' (in a pedagogic sense) to the epistolary art. Circulation for academics in this period often took the form of personal peripatetics, and Boncompagno travelled widely in Italy – and beyond. According to his own report, he had been in Germany, and a knowledge of the German language is certainly evident at a couple of points in the *Rota*.[2] This was probably acquired in the years 1204–15, during which he was employed in the service of Wolfgar of Erla, who acted as emissary and negotiator for the Emperor Otto IV. Boncompagno refers to Wolfgar as his patron in a letter addressed to him in the *Rhetorica antiqua*, which also includes model letters that relate to contemporary German-Italian politics (e.g. letters from Otto and Wolfgar and to the pope).[3]

---

[1] For the facts of Boncompagno's career and a list of his works, see Michael W. Dunne, ed. and tr., *Boncompagno da Signa, Amicitia and De malo senectutis et senii* (Leuven, 2012), pp. 3–11, and the introductions in the translations by Purkart, Garbini, and Wolff (listed at p. 127 below).
[2] See 132/32, 136/22 and notes.
[3] See *Rota Veneris*, ed. and tr. Josef Purkart (New York, 1975), pp. 26–8.

Boncompagno's own self-presentations are the source for much of what is known of his life. From the prologue to his *Rhetorica antiqua*, for instance, we learn that he completed his studies at a young age and took them to doctoral level over the remarkably quick period of sixteen months[4] – and that he had enemies within the scholarly establishment. His claims for and defence of himself take the piquant form of a dialogue between *auctor* [author] and *liber* [book]. The same gift for presenting his material in ways designed to give it life and memorability is evident in the *Rota*, which begins with the appearance of Venus, in obedience to whose command the model love letters that follow are represented as having been composed.

Like Abelard, then (see pp. 70–1 above), Boncompagno was a gifted student whose youthful successes and popularity as a teacher naturally attracted some hostility from older and more conventional scholars – hostility which, like Abelard, he attributed to the 'envy' of his rivals. But the grounds of the opposition he met with were rather different. Whereas Abelard involved himself with complex theology in a thoroughly professional way and met with charges of 'heresy', Boncompagno met with scorn as a popularizer who over-simplified material. The *ars dictaminis* was a branch of rhetoric aimed at practical needs rather than at scholarly speculation, and Boncompagno aimed to free potential users from the task of mastering the complexities of classical rhetoric and the demanding Latin skills it entailed. He therefore carried on a campaign to replace the prevailing dictaminal method (associated especially with Orléans) with a simpler and less Ciceronian kind of prose.[5] He claimed to be totally ignorant of Cicero, and to have found no assistance in the current rhetorical syllabus and its teachers.[6]

This commitment to the art of writing an articulate but unstudied prose was, naturally, calculated to endear him more to students (who would have welcomed speedy acquisition of the letter-writing skills that qualified them for a position as a secretary) than to 'the establishment', who, by his own account, found him lightweight in literary and rhetorical terms (*dicebant me litteratura carere*) and lacking in scholarly seriousness (guilty of *levitas*).[7] There was in Boncompagno an unfortunate streak of the prankster that reinforced this impression of cheap frivolity, however much it did indeed please the crowds. He twice (under the pseudonyms of Robertus

---

[4] See *Rota Veneris*, ed. Purkart, p. 14, quoting from the partial edition of the *Rhetorica* in Ludwig Rockinger, ed., *Briefsteller und Formelbücher des eilften bis vierzehnten Jahrhunderts*, 2 vols (Munich, 1863–4), vol. 1, p. 131.
[5] See *Rota Veneris*, ed. Purkart, pp. 16–19.
[6] See *Rota Veneris*, ed. Purkart, p. 18, quoting from Boncompagno's *Palma*, edited as an appendix in Carl Sutter, *Aus Leben und Schriften des Magisters Boncompagno* (Freiburg, 1894), pp. 105–27 (pp. 105–6).
[7] *Rota Veneris*, ed. Purkart, p. 21, quoting from *Rhetorica antiqua* as edited by Virgilio Pini, *Testi riguardanti la vita degli studenti a Bologna nel sec. XIII (dal Boncompagnus, lib. I)* (Bologna, 1968), p. 33.

and W. Ortonensis) wrote letters against himself in a kind of parody of the procrustean disapproval he met with and arranged public confrontations to which these fictional figures failed to appear, thus making a mockery of the expected public refutation and humiliation of their target.[8] It is little wonder that he was characterized and dismissed as a *joculator*, as he represents himself to have been (in the second of these pseudonymous attacks on himself) and as indeed he was – most notably by the chronicler Salimbene, who introduces him as a kind of street trickster and peddler of quack learning: 'Fuerunt etiam tempore illo trufatores et illusores quam plures ... Ex quibus unus fuit Boncompagnus Florentinus' [There were around at that time many tricksters ... one of whom was Boncompagno of Florence].[9] Salimbene goes on to record the rather sad end (some time before 1250) of this famous *magister* and *dictator* [scholar and epistolarian], now old and impoverished (*factus iam senex ad tantam devenit inopiam*) in a hospice in Florence.

Rota Veneris

The *Rota* appears to have been a relatively early work: Garbini (see p. 127 below) points out that in his *Quinque tabule salutationum* (usually dated to c. 1195) Boncompagno refers the reader to the *Rota* for fuller treatment of amorous epistolary procedures.[10] Love letters had been included in *artes dictaminis*, such as the one written by Matthew of Vendôme,[11] but Boncompagno was unique in composing a manual dedicated exclusively to the epistolary needs of those involved in love affairs.[12] The narrative frame he provided for it gives it both structure and colour: Venus appears to him one day in the spring season associated with love and asks him why he has not used his skills to provide lovers with greetings and locutions, and she reappears at the end to add advice (on intermediaries of which women can avail themselves) not covered by epistolary guidance. This is followed by an epilogue that provides a taxonomy of the bodily gestures which occur as signs and signals in love. This excursus is, as Wolff noted, strictly irrelevant ('hors sujet': p. 29), but it is not felt to be so – nor is Venus' advice on what she explicitly says are matters that fall outside the remit of an *epistolarium*. For Boncompagno has both a focus and a rhetoric that recreates

---

[8] *Rota Veneris*, ed. Purkart, pp. 21–2 and 25 (citing Pini, *Testi*, pp. 33–5 and 35ff.).
[9] Salimbene de Adam, *Cronica*, ed. Giuseppe Scalia, Corpus Christianorum Continuatio Mediaevalis CXXV (Turnhout, 1998), p. 109.
[10] See *Rota Veneris*, ed. and tr. Paolo Garbini (Rome, 1996), p. 10, and cf. his 'Il pubblico della *Rota Veneris* di Boncompagno di Signa', in Høgel and Bartoli, eds., *Medieval Letters*, pp. 201–13.
[11] See Dronke, *Medieval Latin*, vol. 1, p. 251.
[12] Cf. Wolff, *La lettre d'amour*, p. 13.

the larger context (of situations and needs) for his material and gives it life and significance beyond the drily epistolary. He is clearly interested in the whole problem of how lovers conducting an illicit affair communicate. He implicitly treats the husband as belonging to the separate category of epistle assigned to him in the collection of model letters we will encounter in Text 2 (see p. 202 below); for the husband is completely ignored in the *Rota*, in which the lover is always the wooer, the adulterer or the seducer. Communication is thus an issue: the letters cannot be too open, names must be avoided and the message is often cryptically or indirectly given (as in the 'dreams' reported in chapter IV, or the little coded invitation at 152/27). The letters themselves form ways the lovers can 'visit' each other for private conversation (158/15), and the figure of the literal or metaphorical 'messenger' (*nuntius*) unites the two types of non-epistolary communication at the end of the treatise with the previous letters that are the chief recourse of the separated lovers. For one particular letter is actually referred to as a *nuncium* (154/12–13), and the trope is also used of one of the gestural 'signs': the *nutus* is a kind of *amoris nuncius* [messenger used by Love]), who may, again, facilitate mutual revelation of the *secreta* of the heart (160/14–15). And it is, of course, with actual intermediaries that the goddess of love (going predictably to the heart of the matter) concerns herself in her closing instructions to women.

Moreover, the narrative context or sequence always suggested or created by the love letter is here really apparent, for Boncompagno responds with warmth and spirit to the contextual situations he imagines as prompting the letters. After dealing with the non-narrative technicalities (the salutations) as briefly as possible – because he knows this subject could be tedious (end of chapter I) – he declares the importance to the letter of its extra-epistolary context (which phase of love it belongs to: chapter III) and begins his collection with models which form a sequence of interchanges that carry an affair through from the first approach by the man to letters in which full consensual sex is recalled by each partner (chapters III–IV). He advertises the usefulness of his models by bringing the sequence and its underlying narrative to a 'happy ending' for the male, for the 'instruction' takes the form, not only of model letters, but also of intervening commentary and advice very evidently addressed to the man: tell her how beautiful she is, for all women love to be thought lovely (chapters II and III); they all say no at first, so you should attach no significance to an initial negative, for if she answers at all, the omens are good (end of chapter III).

But the charge of 'cynicism' which has (perhaps not unnaturally) been levelled against Boncompagno (Wolff, p. 30) does not really do justice to the breadth of his sympathies or his observation of behaviour and understanding of psychology. The range of reasons he gives for that initial female 'no' demonstrates a clear-sightedness that avoids both sentimentalization of women and reductive anti-feminism. Some women are motivated by feminine perverseness, some by avarice (hoping to gain more in the way of expensive inducements), but many by fear of pregnancy, and others by shame at appearing (in their own and their lovers' eyes) 'easy conquests' or by fear of inspiring distrust of their future fidelity. So Boncompagno can visualize diverse women, actuated by motives variously base, natural and sensible, or even amiable. This is a man who seems to understand women and who neither romanticizes nor belittles them: it would be a very blinkered feminist who would maintain that there are *no* women who are coquettish or mercenary or who would deny that it would be a very rare one who was not pleased to be told she was beautiful, even if she did distrust the sincerity of the compliment (as many did: see Regensburg 44, p. 92 above).

In the letters that follow, which envisage a variety of different situations, many are actually for a woman to send, and it is neither in Boncompagno's interests nor in his nature not to enter into her feelings as much as he does for the man or to be less eloquent on her behalf. The letter from the pregnant woman to her lover (who has 'moved on') is, for instance, quite as tragic and moving as any female could wish such a letter to be (chapter IV, 146/4). All his other women's letters are similarly expressive and effective. Nor is it quite true that he is cheerfully 'immoral' with regard to women because he provides models, for instance, for men wishing to carry on affairs with women who have entered a convent (Wolff, p. 30). It is partly that we are here in the 'alternative' ethical world of love, which, it was often pointed out, spared no man, not even the old or the cloistered, the world of a god who had his own laws.[13] But it is also that such 'immorality' is only half the story. Boncompagno assumes his lovers will make their own ethical choices, and he regularly provides models that cater for differences in conscience as to moral constraints: he provides as eloquent a letter for the cloistered nun who wishes to repel advances as he does for the one who is moved to respond to them (chapter V, pp. 148–50); he pens a nicely pointed letter for a woman writing to end an affair because she has just married another man (chapter IV, 144/25), but he can also craft a naughtily witty one for a wife who wants to tip the wink to her lover that her husband is away and now is a good time (chapter VII, 152/27). He can enter, that is, with that 'negative capability' Keats attributed to the true poet, into any amorous viewpoint or situation.[14]

---

[13] Cf. pp. 256–8.
[14] See John Keats, *The Complete Poetical Works and Letters*, ed. H.E. Scudder (Boston, MA, 1899), p. 277. On the female voice in the narrative contexts of the *Rota*, see further Jonathan M. Newman, 'Dictators of Venus: Clerical Love Letters and Female Subjection in *Troilus and Criseyde* and the *Rota Veneris*', *Studies in the Age of Chaucer* 36 (2014) 103–38.

It will be apparent that this is a warm, spirited and entertaining little tract which manages to be an *epistolarium* with a difference. It 'sets' the letters imaginatively both in a narrative frame and in the larger context of the interesting question of amorous communication of all kinds. For that reason it struck both contemporaries and later readers as going beyond an *ars dictandi* in its relevance to amorous matters and resembling more a manual or handbook on the subject (see below). It certainly shows Boncompagno's gifts for giving flavour and novelty to a literary staple. Few of the ingredients are new in themselves. The spring landscape setting, the appearance of Venus (or of some supra-human female muse like Boethius's Philosophy who can act as muse and give advice and instruction): all these have antecedents, as Baethgen noted in an article devoted to the literary status of this text.[15] The full top-to-toe description of the lady, followed by an account of her excellence of mind (134/19–136/12), follows a pattern already well-established even before it was further popularized by inclusion in Geoffrey of Vinsauf's rhetorical handbook (*Poetria Nuova* 562–99).[16] It is here incorporated into a letter that exemplifies the preceding precept (of flattery, especially commendation of beauty: 130/27–132/2) given by Boncompagno to the hopeful lover. But novelty and originality often consist not in new elements, but in new combinations of those available.[17]

Out of his education in the *artes*, Boncompagno has assembled something unhigh-brow and popular. He puts literary and rhetorical art at the service of the actual needs he foresees that lovers may have. The most common literary borrowing or colouring used within the letters is biblical. Borrowings from sacred literature for the purposes of secular love (especially, of course, from the Song of Songs, which is in fact a love song) is very common throughout the medieval period, and such echoes or quotes would not (except in special cases) have appeared audacious, cynical or parodic. The Bible was simply the best-known (and for many the only) source of eloquent and resonant phraseology and concepts. It was thus freely used in all sorts of contexts, and Boncompagno is not reluctant to avail himself of it to give style and intensity and expressiveness to his epistles. This was an era in which secular and sacred art borrowed freely from one another without

---

[15] Cf. *Rota Veneris*, ed. Purkart, p. 29, citing Friedrich Baethgen, 'Rota Veneris', *Deutsche Vierteljahrsschrift für Litteraturwissenschaft und Geistesgeschichte* 5 (1927), 37–64 (pp. 46ff.). See also *Council of Remiremont*, lines 1 and 37–47 (pp. 432ff. below).
[16] Edited by Edmond Faral in *Les arts poétiques* (Paris, 1923), pp. 197–262; tr. Margaret Nims (revised edn, 1967). See further note to 134/19–136/5 below and cf. Chaucer's *Book of the Duchess* 817–1040.
[17] Cf. Shelley's frequent references to the creative writer as producing new 'combinations' of unvarying aspects of human life and emotions, etc.: e.g. *Shelley's Prose*, ed. David Lee Clark (London, 1988), pp. 312, 328.

any apparent embarrassment: most notably, perhaps, in the sphere of music, where *chansons de geste* and saints' lives were grouped together as characterizing the repertoire of certain minstrels who sang both types of narrative, and where the widespread phenomenon of *contrafacto* (new words to existing melodies) often resulted in liturgical or religious words and verses being set to the tunes of secular songs or love songs to the music of well-known hymns and other kinds of church vocal music.[18] Learned and classical allusions are noticeably absent in the *Rota*, but the biblical allusions and citations add a literary element of an accessible kind. Linguistic and literary art is also apparent, of course, in the Latin language in which the lovers are instructed and which it is assumed they will use. But, similarly, this is Latin of the kind Boncompagno campaigned for in his lifelong furtherance of an epistolary 'art' intended for 'actual' use by non-scholars: relaxed and relatively simple, full of non-classical liberties, but piquant, lively and expressive – a prose in which one can hear an ordinary voice rather than a Ciceronian orator.

Reception, Affiliations, Language

The currency of the *Rota* in the Middle Ages is attested by the nine codices in which it is still extant and by the large portions of it included (in a Franco-Italian translation) in the thirteenth-century compilation *Le livre d'Enanchet*, and its continuing appeal into the early modern era by an incunabulum, brought out, it is surmised, by 'C.W.', a printer known to have been active in Strasbourg in 1473–4. It is this print that forms the basis of the text presented here. It is only in a very few and in very minor details that superior readings could be obtained by following one of the manuscript versions, and there are many features of the print that give it a special interest and a special relevance to our focus in the present volume. In the first place, its existence shows that a market for Boncompagno's work was still confidently assumed to exist nearly 300 years after its composition. In the second place, the print was edited and supplemented so as to provide more signposts for readers who were plainly regarded as potential *users* and to increase the range of potential uses by inclusion of further letters covering other situations: chapter divisions and chapter headings have been introduced, as well as headings for each individual letter, and a space has been left for a large capital (two or sometimes three lines deep) at the start of every such chapter and letter, so that topics and models are clearly flagged by the paratext thus provided; and five further model love letters (from Boncompagno's *Rhetorica antiqua*) have been added just before the epilogue in which Venus

---

[18] See Stevens, *Words and Music*, pp. 235–6 and 143, 181, 183, 193, 248, 395 n. 68, 463, 483.

reappears to give some closing supplementary advice to women. If readers did not actually use the compendium for their own amorous purposes, it is plain that book-producers imagined they might.

Other features of C.W.'s print edition are also of special interest. It is the only one of the witnesses to include the citation of a German proverb (in the opening passage of chapter III), which testifies to Boncompagno's familiarity with the language as well as the land of Germany (which he almost certainly visited: see above, p. 117), a fact for which further evidence is provided by another detail found towards the end of the same chapter (136/22). The German obviously confused nearly all scribes and has disappeared from the other surviving witnesses.

It is also interesting that C.W. also printed the *Tractatus de amore* by Andreas Capellanus.[19] For the *Rota* in many ways extends its *epistolarium* into a manual or handbook of Ovid-like advice:[20] to men on the nature of women (see above, p. 120) and to women on how to conduct clandestine love affairs. The latter counsel is appropriately put into the mouth of a woman: Venus, initially introduced as the tutelary goddess of the work, who has been chosen in preference to Cupid and who reappears at its conclusion, where her gender is exploited in order to put into her mouth some sisterly advice to women of a practical and amoral kind. It may thus be that C.W. was attracted to the *Rota* for its comparability with Andreas Capellanus as a handbook of amorous love – covering tactics, letters, gestures, and (132/25ff.) differing kinds and ranks of lovers – and therefore of wider appeal than might be commanded by a mere *epistolarium* as such, of which there were many, ancient and modern, already available in circulation.

In fact, the coupling of the *Rota* with the near-contemporary *Tractatus* by Andreas, as comparable manuals on love, had occurred soon after the composition of both, for both were extensively excerpted in the *ars amandi* that constitutes the third part of *Le livre d'Enanchet*, a compilation made in French in Italy in the thirteenth century.[21] The *Tractatus* (assumed to date from the last decade of the twelfth century) must have appeared about the same time as Boncompagno's *Rota*. Both were written at a time

---

[19] There is apparently no evidence that the prints of the *Tractatus* and the *Rota* originally formed one volume, as is sometimes stated (as by Garbini, ed., *Rota Veneris*, p. 99): see *Rota Veneris*, ed. Purkart, p. 33. The *De amore* is available with facing translation in the edition by P.G. Walsh, *Andreas Capellanus on Love* (London, 1982).
[20] Cf. the characterizations of the work as a 'bref art d'aimer sous forme épistolaire' (Wolff, *La lettre d'amour*, p. 30) and a 'manuale d'amore in forma epistolare' (*Rota Veneris*, ed. Garbini, p. 12).
[21] The most recent edition of the treatise is by Luca Morlino: *Enanchet: dottrinale franco-italiano del XIII secolo sugli stati del mondo, le loro origini e l'amore* (Padua, 2017). The 1938 edition by Werner Fiebig is available online at the *Scrineum* website (see p. 127 below).

marked by that series of pseudo-Ovidian 'arts of love', or *Minnelehre* to use the German term, that were in one way the precursors of *Le roman de la rose*, completed towards the end of the thirteenth century. The *Facetus* (incipit: 'Moribus et vita') – a manual of behaviour for those who would be thought courtly and respectable – included a section on love that was so popular that it often circulated separately.[22] It appears to have been written in the 1170s.[23] The *Pamphilus, de amore* was a Latin dramatic interlude (written, like the *Facetus*, in elegiacs: that is, couplets consisting of a hexameter followed by a pentameter line), which appeared c. 1200 and in which a lover receives advice from Venus and help from an old woman who acts as intermediary.[24] The epithet 'cynical' (together with 'anti-feminist') can much more deservedly be used of these works than of the *Rota*: the *Pamphilus* dramatizes, and the *Facetus* advises, the use of an old woman who is virtually a bawd and who in effect helps the lover to blandish and entrap the girl into an interview in which intercourse is more or less forced on her.[25] Both works are (as Goddard Elliott points out: p. 28) written in the spirit of Ovid's dictum that, if a girl is willing to give kisses, whoever does not take the rest is not worthy of success (*Ars amatoria* I.669–70) – a sentiment virtually repeated at *Facetus* 301–2. The *Pamphilus* enjoys parading its own mastery of medieval rhetoric (cf. Garbaty, p. 110), and the love-lore of both texts includes much about the arts of language: 'sweet eloquence arouses and nourishes love' (*Pamphilus* 107), so let the lover borrow the arts of the poet (*vatis*) and work on his mistress with 'sweet words' (*Facetus* 304–5). But it is rhetoric used to seduce rather than woo and (unlike the *Rota*, which is concerned to help women express themselves, too) addressed exclusively to men and male sexual desires: 'What you are not you can simulate through ... words', 'Be sure to entice with your words and gifts' (*Pamphilus* 119, 126). But, though the *Rota* is warmer and less crude, a family likeness with such works is occasionally apparent in, for instance, its advice to and identification with the male at 132/22–134/17 and 136/25–36.

---

[22] See p. 27 of the useful translation (facing text as published by A. Morel-Fatio in *Romania* [1886] 234–5) provided by Alison Goddard Elliott in 'The *Facetus*: or, The Art of Courtly Living', *Allegorica* 2 (1977) 27–57.
[23] See Peter Dronke (revising the later date assumed in previous scholarship), 'Pseudo-Ovid, Facetus, and the Arts of Love', *Mittellateinisches Jahrbuch* 11 (1976) 126–31 (pp. 129–30).
[24] For a recent edition of the text (with Italian translation) by Stefano Pittaluga, see pp. 13–137 in *Commedie latine del XII e XIII secolo*, ed. Ferruccio Bertini (Genoa, 1980). Our quotations are from the translation by Thomas Jay Garbaty, '*Pamphilus, de amore*: An Introduction and Translation', *Chaucer Review* 2 (1967) 108–34.
[25] The same nasty little scenario was to recur in subsequent comic and bawdy literature: for thirteenth-century examples in English, see the 'fabliau' *Dame Sirith* (in G. McKnight, *Middle English Humorous Tales in Verse* (New York, 1971)) and the interlude fragment *Cleric and Maiden* (in Bruce Dickins and R.M. Wilson, *Early Middle English Texts* (London, 1951), pp. 132–5).

More generally, it shares with them and with Andreas Capellanus the assumption that love is, as Ovid had represented it to be, an 'art' (the *ars amandi* or *amoris ars* that Andreas claims to expound: e.g. III.1), an art intricately related to courtliness and one to which the *artes* of rhetoric, dictaminal or spoken, are essentially relevant (cf. Andreas 1.6.16: 'Sermonis facundia multotiens ad amandum non amantium corda compellit' [eloquence often prompts love in hearts as yet indifferent]).

The Text

Boncompagno's Latin is, as already stated, consistent with his pitch as a popularizer aiming to make his subject accessible to the interested amateur by stripping it of unnecessary sophistications and pedantry. It is a permissive Latin that does not aim at strict classical authenticity. Besides the predictable innovations at the lexical level (e.g. *bindam* [hairband], *plebescit* [makes common knowledge], *valvasor* [lowest rank of gentry]), the freedoms typical of medieval Latin of this kind include unclassical syntactical simplifications using *quod*, loose sense with conjunctions like *enim* or adverbs like *autem*, substitution of deponent for active forms of verbs or of the indicative or present for harder moods or tenses.[26] To these freedoms, the print has added its own laxities in Latin spellings and forms. Where these involve grammatical errors in case, gender, etc., we have often emended to the more correct form, if it occurs in other witnesses, recording the incunable reading in the apparatus so that those interested may get some idea of the sub-standard or debased kind of Latin that could make its way into print at this date. For the same reason, we have not, unless sense and intelligibility demanded it, corrected the incunable reading to a superior and probably more authentic reading preserved elsewhere.

The standard edition of the *Rota* remains that of Friedrich Baethgen: *Magister Boncompagno: Rota Veneris* (Rome, 1927). It had already been edited entire by Ryszard Ganszyniec (Lwòw, 1925), but that Polish publication is not easily accessible. Baethgen's is thus in effect the only edition available in print of the entire Latin text of the *Rota* – though portions and excerpts have appeared elsewhere. A more recent edition is available online: 'La *Rota Veneris* di Boncompagno da Signa: edizione critica', ed. Luca Core (PhD thesis, University of Padua, 2015). Baethgen's edition is also available online: scrineum.it/scrineum/wight/index.htm, a website which provides editions and translations and a full list of manuscripts for all Boncompagno's works – though the only translation there provided for the *Rota* is into Spanish.

---

[26] For a fuller list of non-standard features in the Latin, see Wolff, *La lettre d'amour*, pp. 30–1.

Boncompagno da Signa: Rota Veneris

There are, however, available in print the translations listed below, all of which we have benefitted from consulting with regard to the translation, information and annotation we offer:

Boncompagno da Signa: Rota Veneris: A Facsimile Reproduction of the Strassburg Incunabulum with Introduction, Translation, and Notes by Josef Purkart (New York, 1975). We have used this facsimile as the basis of the text reproduced here, expanding contractions and supplying our own punctuation, capitalization, paragraphing, etc. Purkart records variants from manuscripts P and (selectively) M (see below).

Boncompagno de Signa: Rota Veneris, edited and translated by Paolo Garbini (Rome, 1996): the translation (into modern Italian) faces the Latin text of Baethgen's edition.

The translation of the incunable text into modern French by Étienne Wolff in *La lettre d'amour au Moyen Âge* (Paris, 1996), in which translations are also provided of the Tegernsee letters, of the *Epistolae duorum amantium* and of poems by Baudri de Bourgueil.

There are a number of witnesses to the treatise. Our own apparatus is highly selective and derivative. Some pertinent variants are recorded from the manuscripts most relevant to the print (P: Paris, BN, Lat. 8654, fols. 101^r–104^v; M: Munich, Bayerische Staatsbibliothek, Clm 14736, fols. 89^v–93^v) and/or from Baethgen's text, based on manuscript S (Siena, Biblioteca Communale, G IX 31, fols. 79^r–82^v). For these variants we are indebted to Purkart (for P and M readings) and to Baethgen's text (for S, cited as /S/ in the apparatus). The variants for the five letters added in from the *Rhetorica antiqua* are from Purkart, who used the copy of the *Rhetorica antiqua* found in Munich, Bayerische Staatsbibliothek, Clm 23499 (M¹), in which these five letters appear on fols. 13, 6^r and 51.

TRACTATUS AMORIS CARNALIS SUBSEQUITUR, ROTA VENERIS NUNCUPATUS, PER BONCOMPAGNUM EDITUS DOCTORUM ANNUENS PRECIBUS

C(apitulum) I:

In principio veris, cum sensibilia et animata quelibet ex aeris temperie revirescunt et germinare incipiunt ex temperancia qualitatum ipsius temporis, que premortua hyemis presencia videbantur: stabam in monticulo rotundo iuxta Ra[v]onem inter arbores florigeras et audiebam iocundissimas et variabiles phylomenarum voces, sicque recreabam animum post laborem. Cum autem sic starem et infra mentis archana plurima revolverem, ecce virgo in vestitu deaurato circumamicta varietatibus ex insperato comparuit, quam natura taliter prepolliverat ut nulla in ea deformitas compareret: ad modum siquidem regine preciosam habebat coronam, regine sceptrum in manu dextra dominabiliter deferendo. Venerat equidem a finibus terre ut singulorum curialitatem et sapienciam scrutaretur. Hanc intuens, facie hylari et iocunda dixi, ut precipere dignaretur. Illa vero interrogata firmiter asseruit se deam esse Venerem, addendo pariter cur salutaciones et delectabilia dictamina non fecissem que viderentur ad usum amancium pertinere.

Stupefactus ad hec, assumpsi stilum propere et hoc opusculum incepi, quod *Rota Veneris* volui nominari, quia cuiuscumque sexus vel condicionis homines amore adinvicem [vincula] colligantur, tamquam in rota orbiculariter volvuntur, et pertimescunt omni tempore plurimum, quoniam perfectus amor continuum parat assidue timorem. Preterea placuit michi virgineum chorum a dextris Veneris collocare; uxoratas, moniales, viduas et defloratas ponere a sinistris; sub scabello pedum ipsius universas ab istis inferius constituo, quia in eis turpissima est voluptas et iocundacio nulla.

Ponam in genere breviter de omnibus exemplum ne prolixitas auditorum pergravet aures:

---

8 temporis] *om* /S/   9 Ravonem] P, /S/; Ranonem   15 regine] regale P, /S/   18 interrogata] non interrogata P, /S/   22 vincula] /S/; *om*   25 parat] parit M, /S/   27 scabello] scabellum P, /S/   31 pergravet] pregravet P, /S/

HERE FOLLOWS A TREATISE ON SEXUAL LOVE, CALLED *THE WHEEL OF VENUS*, BROUGHT OUT BY BONCOMPAGNO IN RESPONSE TO THE PLEAS OF SCHOLARS

Chapter I:

At the beginning of spring, when sentient and living things of all kinds grow green again in the temperate air and, in the season's even mix of the qualities [of hot, cold, moist, dry], start to sprout, having seemed dead while winter lasted: I was standing upon a smoothly rounded elevation by the River Ravone amid blossoming trees and listening to the lovely modulating songs of the nightingales and in this way reviving a mind fatigued by my work. But as I thus stood revolving in my mind many imponderables, behold there appeared out of nowhere a lady whose vestment glittered with gold, enveloped in variously coloured attire, a woman whom nature had made so remarkably superior that there was no blemish to be seen: she bore in fact a splendid crown such as a queen wears, with a queen's sceptre in her right hand in the manner of one who holds dominion. She had come indeed from the bounds of the world in order to examine the courtly refinement and awareness of everyone individually. Looking at her, with pleased and joyful expression I said I hoped she would condescend to treat me as her servant. She indeed, when thus addressed, clearly declared herself to be the goddess Venus, going on at once to ask why I did not compose epistolary salutations and pleasing missives suitable for lovers to make use of.

Struck with wonder at these words, I speedily took up a pen and began this little work, which I decided to call *The Wheel of Venus*, because all people of whatever gender or condition in life are all alike bound by the chain of love and are revolved as if on a wheel round and round, and at all times suffer great fear, because real love unceasingly brings continual fear. Moreover, I decided to picture the band of virgins as at the right hand of Venus, to put wives, nuns, widows and the deflowered at her left, and under her footstool do I set all women of a worse sort, because in them is no joy, but only the basest sensuality.

I will be brief in giving examples that apply to all, to avoid oppressing the ears of my auditors with prolixity:

130   Fictional and Instructional Models

C.II. **Quecumque ergo sit his generalibus salutacionibus potes uti:**

'Nobilissime ac sapientissime domine G de tali loco I seipsum totum', vel aliter, 'In[clit]e ac magnifice domine G committisse, / forma et morum elegancia decorate, G de tali loco salutem et promptum servicium in omnibus', vel 'cum fidelissimo servicio' vel 'quicquid potest'   5
vel 'si aliquid valet salute preciosius inveniri' vel 'quicquid fidelitatis et servicii potest'.

Iste salutaciones locum habent antequam aliquis percipiat quod affectat; postquam vero percepit dicat sic:

'Diligende amice R dulcissime, I seipsum totum', vel 'quicquid sibi   10
[affectat]' vel 'cum diligentissimi amoris perseverancia' vel 'cum indissolubili amoris vinculo' vel 'cum perpetui amoris constancia'; vel aliter 'forma, sensu, genere decorate M, amice dulcissime, I quicquid amoris potest' vel 'seipsum et sua'; vel aliter 'Anime sue dimidio et suorum oculorum lumini G, formosissime ac preciosissime am-   15
ice sue, I animam et corpus ac si plura posset' vel 'quicquid habet et habere videtur' vel 'seipsum et sua'; vel aliter 'Gloriosissime ac preciosissime domine G, amice dulcissime, I salutem et i[llu]d ineffabile gaudium mentis quod aliqua voce vel actu exprimi nunquam potest'; vel aliter 'Super aurum et topasion relucenti domine G, amice dulcis-   20
sime, I quecumque potest et si ultra posse valeret aliquid invenire'.

Consueverunt quidam ponere quandam rusticanam salutacionem qua forte posset quis benivolenciam captare:

'Amice dulcissime G, forma et morum elegancia redimite, I tot salutes et servicia quot in arboribus folia, quot in celo fulgent sidera, et   25
quot arene circa maris littora.'

Et nota quod ferme quasi omnes mulieres appetunt semper de pulchritudine commendari, etiam si fuerint deformes, unde tam in salutacionibus quam in cunctis epistole partibus te oportet benivolenciam a pulchritudine captare. Utaris ergo superlativis et insistas commendacioni,   30
quia muliebris condicio huiusmodi laudibus cicius inflectitur et inclinatur. Ponas ergo quandoque '**sapientissime**', quandoque '**nobilissime et**

---

2 Nobilissime ... potest] *fuller version in* /S/ *(see notes)*   3 Inclite] M, /S/; indice   9 percepit] perceperit P, suum compleverit desiderium /S/   9 dicat sic] hoc modo salutabit amicam /S/   11 affectat] M, /S/; *om*   18 illud] /S/; id   22 quandam] *om* /S/   22 rusticanam] *add* et ridiculosam P, M, /S/   23 quis benivolenciam captare] quandoque benivolentia captari. Hoc enim est /S/   25 in arboribus folia ... in celo fulgent sidera] *transp* /S/   27 ferme] fere /S/   30 ergo] igitur /S/

Chapter II. **So, whoever she may be, you may use these general salutations:**

'To the most noble and wise lady, G., of such-and-such a place, I. [sends] possession of his entire self,' or alternatively, 'To the most celebrated and most eminent G., countess, graced with beauty and elegance of manners, G. of such-and-such a place [sends] greeting and promptitude of service in all things' or 'with most faithful service' or 'all that is possible to offer' or 'whatever, if anything, can be found more valuable than health' or 'all possible fidelity and service'.

These greetings are suitable before one has received the love one wants; once one has received it, he should use words such as the following:

'To the beloved to be cherished, the sweetest R., I. [sends] his entire self' or '[his wishes for] whatever she desires for herself' or 'with the perseverance of most diligent love' or 'with the unbreakable chain of love' or 'with the ever-enduring constancy of love'; or alternatively, 'To the one graced with beauty, wisdom and noble birth, M., his sweetest beloved, I. [sends] all that there can be of love' or 'himself and all he has'; or otherwise, 'To the half of his own soul and the light of his eyes, G., his most beauteous and most precious beloved, I. [sends] his soul and body and whatever more might be possible' or 'whatever he has and may have' or 'himself and all he has'; or alternatively, 'To the most glorious and precious lady G., sweetest beloved, I. [sends] that well-being and ineffable joy that can never be expressed by any word or in any bodily action'; or alternatively, 'To the lady G., more radiant than gold and topaz, his sweetest mistress, I. [sends] all that he can and more, if he can find anything beyond that'.

Some have been accustomed to writing a certain form of salutation popular among the vulgar by which one might be able to win the goodwill aimed at:

'To the sweetest beloved G., crowned with beauty and grace of manners, I. [sends] as many greetings and pledges of service as there are leaves on the trees, stars that shine in the sky and sands on the shores of the sea'.

And note that virtually all women always like to be complimented on their beauty, even if they are ugly, so that both in the salutations and in all parts of the letter it behoves you to acquire her goodwill by means of beauty. You should therefore use superlatives and keep up the compliments, because the female nature is soonest swayed and moved by praises of this kind. Write therefore sometimes '[to the] **wisest**', sometimes '**most noble and most**

Fictional and Instructional Models

illustrissime' (si nobilis fuerit), quandoque '**amantissime**' seu '**splendissime**' vel '**lucidissime**' aut '**jocundissime**'.

Ex hiis autem salutacionibus poteris trahere omnes modos salutandi amicos pro amicis et amic[a]s per amasiis, si revolvere sciveris et mutare mutanda. Nec est aliud necessarium / in variacione nisi permutes adjectiva per sexus, ut ubi posuisti feminum genus pro mulieribus ponas masculinum pro viris. Et licet viri non appetant tantum laudari, de huiusmodi lasciviis cum plurimum letantur. Sed videtur michi quod omnia officia preter miliciam sunt in salutacionibus tacenda, quia ineptum videretur si alicuius clerici dignitas vel negociatoris officium a muliere aliqua diceretur. Nec etiam ipsi debent cum scribunt mulieribus alicuius lascivie causa suas dignitates vel officia nominare, quia male cum antecedenti concordaret illatum, et sic per consequens epistola deluderetur. Clerici autem qui frequenter super nature incude[m] fer[iunt] cum malleo repercussorio, nec vale[n]t motus renum de facili refrenare, ponant in salutacionibus aliqua occulta signa que propria nomina sibi sub ymagine representent. Et est notandum quod tam mulieres quam viri cuiuscumque sint ordinis vel condicionis debent epistole titulum in huiusmodi lasciviis taliter occultare, quod si littere ad aliquorum manus pervenerint, nequeant de facili cognosci.

C.III. Sequitur de generibus commendacionum

Decursis breviter salutandi modis qui possunt ad usum amancium pertinere, duxi quedam narrandi genera ponere generaliter in exemplum, ut dictator quilibet preparatoria inveniat in dicendo. Sed distinguenda sunt amandi tempora et amancium genera. Quidam enim amare incipiunt aliquas nec tamen cum eis colloquium habuerunt; quidam autem post colloquium et parvam familiaritatem amorem qu[a]rundam requirunt; quidam enim quasdam ad amare appetunt quas nunquam viderunt. Tria ergo sunt tempora in quibus hec omnia fiunt. Amancium vero genera duo sunt: layicus videlicet et clericus. Item layicorum alius miles, alius pedes. Item militum alius rex, alius dux, alius princeps, alius marchio, alius comes, alius procer, alius valvasor – quasi valvas, id est januas, serans, quia proverbium est quod 'iunger Hoffman alter portner efficitur'.

1 amantissime] amatissime /S/   4 amicas] /S/; amicos   4 revolvere] volvere /S/   5 variacione] mutatione /S/   5 nisi] *add* ut P, /S/   6 ut] et /S/   7 appetant tantum laudari] tantum l. a. /S/   8 cum] *om* /S/   9 quia] *add* hoc /S/   14 incudem] P, /S/; incude   14 feriunt] P, /S/; fermentur   15 valent] P, /S/; valet   16 sibi] *om* /S/   24 dictator] dictatores /S/   24 inveniat] inveniant /S/   27 quarundam] P, /S/; quorundam   28 quasdam ad] illas /S/   29 ergo] igitur /S/   32 quasi *through to* efficitur] *om all other versions*

illustrious' (if she is of noble rank), sometimes '**most amiable**' or '**most splendid**' or '**most relucent**' or '**most delightful**'.

Furthermore, from the above salutations you will be able to derive all forms of love greeting by a man or woman, if you know how to choose them and make the necessary modifications. Nor is anything necessary by way of adaptation beyond your changing the adjectival endings to agree with the gender, so that where you used the feminine version for women you use the masculine for men. And, granted that men have less desire to be praised, most of them get pleasure from such toys. But it seems to me no vocations except military ones should be mentioned in the salutations, because it would sound absurdly inappropriate if any clerical title or mercantile status should be spoken of by the woman. Nor should they themselves even, when they write to women for some loverly reason, name their positions or offices, because it would be out of keeping with its context if brought in, and will consequently make the letter ridiculous. However, those clerics who use their hammers upon the anvil nature provides, and are not strong enough easily to restrain the promptings of their loins, may use in salutations some cryptic signs in indirect representation of their own names. And it is to be noted that women as much as men should similarly refrain from revealing, in the superscription of letters of this loverly kind, to what rank or condition of life they may belong, to avoid being easily identifiable should the letters fall into the hands of anyone else.

Chapter III. Types of commendation

Having briefly gone through the types of salutation which could be relevant to lovers, it is my plan to set down some kinds of subsequent content [*narratio*], as examples of a general kind, so that any given composer of a letter [*dictator*] may find some preparatory material to hand in composing it. But we should first distinguish between different stages of love and thus of kinds of lover. For some men are beginning on love for women with whom, however, they have not yet spoken; some, on the other hand, are requesting their love after speech and some small acquaintance with them; and others seek to embark on love with those they have never seen. There are thus three different situations in which what we have in hand takes place. As regards lovers, there are two classes: namely, laymen and clerics. The laymen in their turn may be 'knights' or 'foot-soldiers'. Of 'knights', we have king, duke, earl, marquis, count, nobleman and, lowest ranking, 'vavasor' – a word indicating 'one who is locking folding doors (that is, gates)', for the proverb says, 'the young courtier becomes the old porter'.

134   Fictional and Instructional Models

Item peditum alius civis, alius burgensis, alius negociator, alius rusticus, alius liber, alius servus, etc. Clericorum itaque alius prelatus, alius subditus, etc – quia non sunt distinguenda omnes clericorum species ne amoris jura ledantur.

 Ceterum si vellem secundum uniuscuiusque vitam et condicionem genera ponere narracion[u]m, primo deficeret tempus quam sermo. Ergo / sicut humane condicionis natura communis est, ita communia ponam exempla et transcurram opus utiliter inchoatum. Cuiuscumque ergo condicionis aut ordinis sit ille qui amare desiderat, aut amat quam non habuit, aut illam quam iam habuit sed nunc facta est inter eos amoris alteracio, aut illam quam nullo tempore vidit. Ab hiis ergo tribus temporibus, duos narrandi modos ad usum amancium assumam. Primus est ante factum, secundus post factum. Quicumque etiam amorem alicuius mulieris habere appetit debet ven[a]tivas adulacionum blandicias premittere, promittendo que nunquam facere possit, sicut ait Ovidius: 'Quid enim promittere ledit?' In primis namque taliter potest amator exordiri narrare atque petere illam quam desiderat habere:

Commendacio mulierum:
Cum inter gloriosos puellarum choros vos nudiustercius corporis oculis inspexi, apprehendit quidem amoris igniculus precordialia mea et repente me fecit esse alterum. Nec sum id quod eram nec potero de cetero esse: nec mirum, quia michi et universis procul dubio videbatur quod inter omnes refulgeretis tamquam stella matutina que in presagium diei auroram polliceri videtur. Et dum subtiliter inspicerem quanta vos gloria natura dotaverat, pre ammiracione deficiebat spiritus meus. Capilli siquidem vestri quasi aurum contortum juxta coloratissimas aures mirifice dependebant. Frons erat excelsa et supercilia quasi duo cardines gemmati, oculi velut due stelle clarissime, refulgebant, quorum splendore membra quelibet radiabant. Nares directe, labra grossula et rubencia, cum dentibus eburneis comparebant, collum rotundum et gula candissima se directe inspiciendo geminabant pulchritudinem quam nunquam credo potuisse magis in Helena intendi. Pectus quasi paradisi ortulus corpori supereminebat,

---

2 etc] *om* /S/   6 narracionum] M, /S/; narracionem   10 iam] *om* /S/   11 hiis] istis /S/   13 etiam] *om* /S/   14 venativas] P, /S/; *om* M; venetivas   15 sicut ait] quia sic dicit /S/   16 Quid] nil /S/   17 illam] illi /S/   18 corporis] corporeis /S/   21 eram] fueram /S/   23 refulgeretis] refulgebatis /S/   31 candissima] candissima P, /S/   32 magis] *om* /S/

Boncompagno da Signa: Rota Veneris

Then of 'foot-soldiers' we have the city man, the townsman, the merchant, the countryman or peasant, the freeman, the bondsman, etc. The clerics may be prelates or members of the subordinate clergy – for not all degrees of cleric can be specified without injury to the laws of love [which forbid reference to prosaic details of non-chivalric rank].

Moreover, should I choose to give a *narratio* [= main body of a letter] to suit the mode of living and rank of each of the above-named social positions, time would run out before the speech necessary did. Therefore, since the nature of the human condition is common to them all, I will give examples that are similarly common and so proceed expeditiously to end the useful work I have begun. Therefore, whatever the condition or position in life the man may be who writes to further his love, either he loves her whom he has not yet won, or her whom he has won but there has now arisen a difference between them, or her whom he has at no time ever seen. From these three situations arise two kinds of *narratio* which I will adopt and which a lover may use. The first is before the fact [before he has won love], the second after the fact [after he has won it]. But whoever seeks to obtain the love of any woman must start with blandishing adulation in the hunt for the prey, making promises impossible to fulfil, in accord with what Ovid says: 'For how can promising hurt you?' At the outset, therefore, a lover can usher in his *narratio*, and make his attempt to win her whom he desires, in the following kind of way:

Commendation of women:
When the day before yesterday I gazed with my corporeal eyes upon you amidst the glorious bands of maidens, a certain small flame of love took a hold on my heart and suddenly made a different man of me, for I am not now what I was or ever can be again: and no wonder, for to me and to all others it seemed that you unmistakeably shone out from their midst like the morning star which, in presage of day, is seen giving promise of the dawn to come. And as I was busy observing with what glory nature had endowed you my body grew faint. Your hair indeed hung wondrously round your pinkest ears like twisted gold. Your brow rose high and your arched brows, like bejewelled hinges, shone, as did, like two of the brightest stars, your eyes, the light of which gave radiance to every part of your body. Your nose straight, your fullish and ruddied lips were complemented by ivory teeth, your rounded neck and whitest of throats offered to the beholder a doubled pulchritude such as I believe even Helen was never pictured as exceeding. Surmounting your body was your breast, resembling the garden of paradise,

in quo erant duo poma velut fasciculi rosarum a quibus odor suavissimus resultabat. Humeri tanquam aurea capitella residebant, in quibus brachia sicut rami cedri erant naturaliter inserta. Manus longe, digiti exiles, nodi [co]equales, et ungule sicut cristallum resplendentes tocius stature augmenta[bant decorem.

Verum quia primo deficeret commendator] quam vestre pulchritudinis immensitas, stilum verto ad sapiencie vestre magnitudinem, de qua non possum non / admirari – quia multe sunt que licet convenienti pulchritudine gaudeant non cum sapiencia decorantur; sunt et alie quibus sapiencia fuit nature munere concessa et forma corporis denegata. Sed in vos itaque omnia sine defectu aliquo confluxere quod multociens opinio me in hanc trahat sentenciam ut existemem vos aliqua deitate potiri. Magnitudini tandem vestre suppliciter supplico ut michi vestro famulo dignemini precipere, quia paratus sum me ipsum et mea vestre in omnibus exponere voluntati.

Et nota quod hec epistola potest unius dictionis mutacione taliter variari quod cuilibet virgini, maritate, vidue, moniali et deflorate transmitti potest: scilicet, ut ubi dicitur in principio 'puellarum' dicatur 'dominarum'. Nam et moniales debes tam in salutacionibus quam in cunctis epistole partibus 'dominas' appellare, quia si diceres 'monachas' aut 'moniales' pocius ad earum spectaret vituperium quam honorem. Unde in Alamania fere ab omnibus 'domine' appellantur. Et est notandum quod talis epistola non debet transmitti cuilibet, sed magnis et sapientissimis dominabus.

Preterea sciendum est quod unaqueque mulier cuiuscumque sit ordinis vel condicionis negat in primis quod facere peroptat. Unde si aliquo modo [m]i[t]ten[ti] rescribere velit intelligas ipsam concedere velle, licet hoc neget verbis. Ad quod notandum est quod quinque sunt cause quibus mulier denegat quod postulat amans. Prima est ex quadam occulta natura, quia naturaliter omnibus inesse videtur primo negare quesita. Secunda ne si propere tue condescenderet voluntati crederes illam fore communem. Tercia ut postulanti dulcius esse videatur quod sibi fuerat longo tempore denegatum. Quarta ut expectet sibi aliquid elargiri antequam consenciat postulanti. Quinta quia sunt plurime que concipere pertimescunt. Unde si aliqua rescriberet sic mittenti et poneret simpliciter titulum cum salute, posito a[u]te[m] titulo, sic procedere posset:

---

4 coequales] /S/; equales   5 stature *through to* quam] P, /S/; stature augmentatur et quam plurimum   6 vestre] *om* /S/   11 itaque] ita /S/   16 mutacione] permutatione /S/   27 mittenti] P, M, /S/; innitendo   31 fore] P, /S/; fore esse   36 autem] M, /S/; añ P; ante   36 posset] *the sentence* Revertar *through to* modo (140/18–19) *has been wrongly misplaced in the incunabulum to appear here, where it has been adapted to read* Revertar ergo ad propositum et respondebo pro muliere deneganre superiori epistole hoc modo

in which were two apples from which, as from a bunch of roses, the sweetest fragrance was cast. Your shoulders were like golden capitals to the columns of your arms, which were as two cedar branches that Nature had inserted into them. Your hands long, your fingers slender, knuckles in due proportion, and your nails, shining like crystal, added to the loveliness of the whole.

Since indeed the commender would sooner be exhausted than would the great extent of your beauty, I turn my pen to the magnitude of your inner virtues, at which I cannot but wonder. For there are many who, although they may rejoice in harmonious pulchritude, do not have beauty of mind; and there are others to whom wisdom was granted by the gift of nature, but bodily comeliness denied. But into you all things, without exception, are found in such confluence that many times my impressions lead me to such an opinion as to judge you to be in possession of some divine quality. At any rate, to your greatness do I most supplicantly supplicate that you condescend to receive me into your service, for I am ready to devote myself and all that is mine to carrying out your wishes in all things.

And note that this letter can, by altering one word, be modified in such a way that it can be sent to any virgin, married woman, widow, nun or any girl who is not a virgin: that is, by replacing 'maidens' at the beginning with 'ladies'. For you ought to call even women in convents 'ladies' both in the salutations and in all other parts of the letter. Because if you said 'nuns' or 'cloistresses' it would [in a love letter] sound more like condemnation than respect. And therefore in the German lands they are called by nearly everyone 'ladies'. And you should note that this letter should not be sent to just any woman, but only to those who in status are ladies and possessed of good sense.

Moreover, it should be understood that every woman, whatever her condition or station in life, refuses at first what in fact she very much wishes to do. So if she chooses to give any kind of reply at all to the sender, you can assume she wants to accede, even if she denies it in her words. In this connection, you should understand that there are five reasons why a woman refuses what the lover begs from her. The first is out of some obscure facet of their nature, for it seems to be naturally innate in all of them to deny at first what is sought from them. The second is in case you should consider her to be a harlot if she is quick to accede to what you wanted. The third is so that what has been long denied should feel the sweeter to him who pleads for it. The fourth is her hopes of gaining more from him before she consents. The fifth is because there are many who are very much afraid of becoming pregnant. So if she writes anything back to the sender, and just puts a superscription and a greeting, after such superscription, the letter might continue in the following way:

C.IIII. Epistola domine:

In epistole tue serie stilum fatigasti pro nichilo, credens per quedam adulatoria verba et pulchritudinis mee commendacion[em] benivolenciam captare. Sed nichil est quod credis et semina mandas arene: tuo siquidem servicio non indigeo nec volo ut de cetero michi / talia mittere presumas.

Hac siquidem epistola perpendere poterit amans quod suum procul dubio desiderium adimplebit, unde merito sibi talem epistolam transmittat:

Epistola viri:
Vestrarum literarum significatum meam animam pariter et corpus letificavit. Et licet dixeritis me stilum fatigare pro nichilo, credo tamen quod me respicere dignabimini, et si non placuerit vobis ut vivam, precipiatis ut moriar, sic quod post mortem fruar gaudiis paradisi.

Responsio domine:
De tua importunitate non possum non admirari, cum iam penitus denegaverim ne michi literas vel aliquid transmittere auderes, et nunc sic me solicitas ut me credas alterabilem esse. Sed non reperitur nodus in scirpo et flos mirice permanet inviolabilis nec est feno similis quod secatum facile perarescit. Vidisti ergo forte virgulta in deserto et placuerunt tibi pomeria Damasci? Sed non omne quod placet potest ut credis haberi.

Huiusmodi siquidem proverbia, occulte raciocinaciones et similitudines faciunt plurimum ad usum amandi. Ponantur ergo in talibus jocunde transsumpciones et proverbia de quibus possit multiplex intellectus haberi, quia non modicum faciunt amancium animos gratulari. Et non solum milites et domine, verum etiam populares jocundis quandoque transmutacionibus utuntur et sic sub quodam verborum velamine vigor amoris intenditur et amicabile suscipit incrementum. Transumitur enim mulier quandoque in solem, quandoque in lunam, quandoque in stellam, quandoque in palmam, quandoque in cedrum, quandoque in laurum, quandoque in rosam, quandoque in lylium, quandoque in violam, quandoque in gemmam vel in aliquem lapidem preciosum. Vir autem quandoque transmutatur in leonem propter fortitudinem,

---

3 adulatoria] adulancia /S/   3 commendacionem] P, /S/; commendacioni   8 merito] iterato /S/   12 vobis] om /S/   13 sic quod] sicque /S/   20 perarescit] arescit /S/   21 placuerunt] complacuerunt /S/   23 et] similia et /S/   24 ergo] igitur /S/   28 transmutacionibus] transumptionibus /S/   29 amicabile] amabile /S/   34 quandoque transmutatur] transumitur q. /S/

Chapter IV. Letter from the lady:

In the course of your letter you wearied your pen in vain in believing that my goodwill would be gained through some adulatory words and praise of my beauty. But that belief is vain, and you are sowing seeds in sand: I have no need of your service and I do not wish you to presume to write to me ever again in that way.

From this letter, indeed, the lover may have no doubt that his desire will be fulfilled, and he will have good grounds for sending her a letter of this kind:

Letter from the man:
The content of your letter gave me joy in body and soul. And, albeit that you said I had wearied my pen in vain, I nevertheless trust that you will deign to take some notice of me, and if it does not please you that I should live, you may command me to die, so that I may enjoy the delights of heaven that death leads into.

Reply from the lady:
I cannot but wonder at your importunity, since I have already put an emphatic negative on your daring to send me letters or anything else – and you now solicit me in this way as if you believed me to be changeable. But no knot is ever found in the stem of the bulrush, and the flower of the tamarisk lasts unimpaired and is unlike hay, which, when cut, soon dries out. You may perhaps have seen shrubs in the desert and been pleased by orchards in Damascus – but not everything that pleases is, as you believe, to be had.

Indeed, proverbs of this kind, indirect reasoning and similitudes are very often made in amorous contexts. In such things do lovers make pleasing metaphorical transferences and proverbial statements (which can be used with a number of different applications), for these bring no small delight to the amorous mind. And these pleasing lexical transmutations are made not only by knights and ladies, but also occur in popular usage, and beneath this kind of verbal veil is the force of love fostered and pleasingly reinforced. A woman is thus transformed by metaphor sometimes into the sun, sometimes into the moon, or a star, a palm tree, cedar, laurel, rose, lily, violet, or into a gem or some precious stone. A man is transmuted sometimes into

quandoque in draconem propter incomparabilem excellenciam, quandoque in falconem propter velocitatem. Infinitis autem modis fiunt huiusmodi transsumpciones nec possent de facili numerari.

Sed videndum est quid sit transsumpcio. Transsumpcio est posicio unius dictionis pro altera que quandoque ad laudem quandoque ad vituperium 5 rei transumpte red[un]dat. Et est notandum quod omnis transsumpcio est largo modo similitudo, sed non convertitur. / Ceterum dictator ita debet esse providus in transumendo ut semper fiat quedam similitudo vocis vel effectus in transumpcione. Nam si mulierem transsumeres in quercum non esset jocunda transsumpcio. Et si diceres 'collegi glandes' 10 pro effectu amoris alicuius, turpiter transsumeres, quoniam glandes cibaria sunt porcorum. Sed si poneris 'palmam' pro muliere et 'dactilos' pro amoris effectu, bene transsumeres, quoniam palma formosa et dactili dulcedinem exhibent post gustum. Item si virum transsumeres in canem, turpiter transsumeres nisi eum velles taliter dehonestare. 15

Verum quia meum propositum impediretur pretere[o] sub qu[o]dam silencio de transsumpcione; sed alias de ipsa specialem proposui facere tractatum. Revertar igitur ad propositum et respondebo pro amante superiori epistole hoc modo:

Responsio viri: 20
Si regnum essem adeptus et regali dyademate coronatus et non tantum foret [gaudium] cordi meo innatum quantum de vestrarum literarum tenore percepto. Scio quidem quod nodus non reperitur in sirpo, id est, macula non reperitur in facundissimo eloquio vestro; et flos mirice permanet inviolabilis, id est, vestre dilectionis sinceritas 25 non potest aliquatenus violari. Ego autem sum fenum quod secatum facile arescit: nisi me velitis rore vestre gracie irrigare, minus etiam quam fenum aridum potero dici. Vidi tandem virgulta et complacuerunt michi pomeria Damasci, et licet habere nequeam quod placet magnitudinem tamen et curialitatem vestram suppliciter exoro 30 ut michi fidelitatis mee intuitu hoc donarium conferatis, videlicet quod me instruere dignemini quo tempore [vobis] mei cordis secreta valeam aperire.

---

6 redundat] P, /S/; redinidat   13 palma] *add* est arbor P, M, /S/   13 formosa] famosa /S/   14 post] per /S/   16 pretereo] P, /S/; preterea   16 quodam] P, /S/; quadam   18–19 Revertar *through to* modo] P, /S/; *in the print, the sentence is misplaced to end of Cap. II (as in P) and slightly modified*   22 gaudium] P, M, /S/; *om*   27 nisi] et nisi /S/   32 vobis] /S/; *om*

a lion to convey strength, sometimes into a dragon for unrivalled victoriousness, sometimes into a falcon for swiftness. Metaphors, however, can be made in an infinite number of ways which cannot easily be enumerated.

But it should be made clear what metaphor is. Metaphor is the putting of one word in place of another, a word redounding sometimes to the praise, sometimes to the discredit, of the thing it figuratively replaces. And it is to be noted that every metaphor is in a loose sense a similitude (though the converse is not true). So the composer of a letter should see to it that there should always be in his metaphor some similitude or congruence of word or effect. For if you changed a 'woman' by metaphor into 'oak tree', that would not give a satisfying metaphor. And if you used the expression 'collecting acorns' to express an experience of love, you would be using metaphor in a most repellent way, since acorns are the food of pigs. But if you put 'palm tree' to stand for a woman and 'dates' for the experience of love, you would be using metaphor well, since a palm is comely and dates impart sweetness to the taste. Again, if you by metaphor turn 'man' into 'dog', you use metaphor tastelessly, unless you actually wish thereby to rob him of dignity.

Because indeed my present purpose would otherwise be impeded, I shall put metaphor behind me under a certain silence (though I have decided to compose a special treatise in which to say more of that matter). I will now return therefore to my point, and to the last-quoted epistle I will write for the lover a reply, as follows:

Reply from the man:
If I had gained possession of a kingdom and were crowned with a royal diadem it would not engender in my heart any joy to equal that which arose from the perception of the contents of your letter. I am well aware that no knot is found in the reed – that is, that no flaw is found in your most perfect command of articulate eloquence; and that the flower of the tamarisk never fades – that is, how the perfection of your delightfulness cannot to any degree suffer impairment. It is I, however, who am the hay which when cut soon dries out: unless you choose to bedew me with your grace, I will indeed be even less than dry hay. I have however seen those shrubs, and the orchards of Damascus have pleased me, and although I cannot obtain what so pleases me, yet I make humble supplication to your greatness and your courtesy that, in consideration of my fidelity, you would grant me these alms: to wit, that you should deign to inform me at what time I may be allowed to reveal to you the inmost feelings of my heart.

142   Fictional and Instructional Models

Responsio domine:
Credis forte quod labor improbus omnia vincat et pulsanti omni tempore aperiatur. Sed incerte sunt vie hominum et va[n]e cogitaciones e[o]rundem, cum res cuiusque in talibus magis casu et fortuna regatur quam premeditata disposicione. Nolens equidem preces tuas ex toto contempnere ne in desperacionis laqueum trahas exitum, consulo ut in die festo cum domini et matrone templum visitabunt dominicum tuum proicias infra meum pomerium falconem et subito postea currens a familiaribus domus tuam repetas avem. Ego vero illam / tibi faciam denegari dicaturque tibi ab ancillis, 'Recede, non enim tuum est quod petis'. Ad istam siquidem contencionem te vocari faciam, sicque michi tui cordis archana poteris aperire.

Quid plura? Pono quod amans iam perfecerit quod optabat, unde potest et debet post factum aliquas jocundissimas literas ei destinare. Consueverunt autem amantes ad [maior]em delectacion[e]m dicere se vidisse per somnium quod fecerunt, unde talem potest amator sibi epistolam destinare:

Responsio viri:
Dum medium silencium tenerent omnia et dies jocundissimo tempore veris s[u]um perageret cursum, causa venandi quoddam intravi pomerium infra quod duo riv[u]li decurrebant. Erant enim ibi arbores florigere inter quas dulcissimus philomenarum cantus undique resonabat. Fatigatus modicum sub frondosa pinu quievi et cepi suaviter obdormire. Cum autem sic quiescerem ecce comparuit virgo speciosissima cuius pulchritudinem non posset aliquis designare. Apprehendit me per manum et cepit mecum aliquantulum residere. Utebatur primo suavissimis colloquiis et col[o]ratis prefacionibus in dicendo. Post multa siquidem verba plicatis brachiis me suaviter strinxit et suis rubentibus labellis mea comprimens labia contulit michi basia ineffabilia. Post hoc jocundiora et jocundissima exercendo que mille modis gaudium geminarunt, introduxit me tandem in cubiculum suum quod fulcitum erat floribus et undique malis stipatum. Erant ibi cardines eburnei cum capitellis aureis et parietes cristalli

3 vane] P, M, /S/; varie   4 eorundem] P, /S/; earundem   5 equidem] tamen /S/   6 trahas exitum] traharis /S/   7–8 visitabunt dominicum] d. visitant /S/   8 tuum] *om* /S/   10 dicaturque] diceturque /S/   11 petis] queris /S/   13 perfecerit] perfecit /S/   14 post factum] ex postfacto /S/   14 literas ei] *transp* /S/   14–17 Consueverunt *through to* destinare] *om* /P/   15 maiorem delectacionem] M, /S/; amorem delectionem   20 suum] P, /S/; solum   21 rivuli] P, /S/; rivali   24 suaviter obdormire] firmiter dormire /S/   27 colloquiis] eloquiis /S/   coloratis] P, /S/; colleratis   30 hoc] hec /S/   31 geminarunt] geminaverunt /S/   33 et] *om* /S/   cristalli] cristallini /S/

Reply from the lady:
You perhaps believe that dauntless persistence will always conquer and the door will be opened to one who persistently knocks. But uncertain are the outcomes of men's actions and vain are their plans, since any given matter is governed more by chance and luck than by forethought and pre-arrangement. But not wishing to scorn your prayers completely, lest you fall into the snare of despair, it is my decision that on a feast day, when ladies and gentlemen will be at church, you let fly your falcon under the trees of my orchard, and soon thereafter get your household attendants to ask for it. I, however, will order it to be refused, saying (through my attendants), 'Go away, for what you are asking for does not belong to you'. In connection with this disputed point, I will have you sent for, and so you will have your opportunity to reveal to me your inmost thoughts.

What more need I say? For the lover will now have achieved what he was hoping for, so that he can and ought now to write to her some very pleasant *post factum* letters [i.e. letters appropriate where love has been granted]. To add savour to their delight, lovers have adopted the custom of talking about their encounters as if they had experienced them in a dream, and so a lover might send to the lady a letter of this kind:

Reply from the man:
When all was silent, after the day had completed its course in the most lovely time of spring, in the course of hunting I happened to enter into an orchard, beneath the trees of which flowed two brooks. There were trees in flower, amongst which the most sweet song of nightingales was heard all around me. Being somewhat wearied, I rested under a thick conifer and slipped softly into sleep. While I was thus at rest, behold, there appeared the fairest virgin, whose beauty no one could describe. She took me by the hand and placed herself beside me for a time. What she did first was to speak, engaging in the pleasantest conversation and pretty preliminaries. After much talk, having enfolded me in her arms, she embraced me softly and, pressing her ruddy lips upon mine, bestowed upon me ineffable kisses. After this, proceeding to what was even sweeter and then to sweetest, redoubling delight in a thousand ways, she at length took me into her chamber, which was thickly hung with flowers and filled everywhere with soft fruits. There were to be seen there ebony hinges, golden capitals, crystal walls, inscribed with

cum celatura varia sicque radiabant ex gemmarum fulgoribus, ut
michi videretur esse in paradiso deliciarum. Superveniente demum
aurora me sub eiusdem arboris umbra reduxit et repetitis complexi-
bus me innumerabiliter astringens angelicum michi contulit 'ave'. A
sompno quidem tam glorioso salutacionis alloquio excitatus, duxi 5
vestram in hac parte sapienciam consulere ut vestris michi dignemini
literis sompnium explanare.

Et responsio domine:
Jocundari potestis et infra vestre mentis archana inef/fabiliter ex-
ultare quod tam preciosum vobis comparuit sompnium, in quo de- 10
sideratissimos complexus, basia iocundissima et cetera que sequun-
tur magnifice recepistis. Nam si bene memini eadem die ad eiusdem
arboris pedem me recolo sompniasse quod vos ibidem videram hec
omnia facientes. Ab ea siquidem hora excogitavi sedula quomodo
vestre possem magnitudini per omnia et in omnibus complacere. 15
Verumptamen interpretari sompnium non valeo nisi mecum sub eadem arbore quiescatis. Properate ergo ad eundem locum post solis
occasum, quoniam ibi proposui explanare sompnium et referre plura
que literis non audeo annotare.

Responsio viri: 20
Preciosa forma pre filiabus hominum, grates decem milia ex parte
vestri fidelissimi habeatis, scientes procul dubio quod vestri amoris
vinculum me tenet indissolubiliter colligatum. Unde quicquid vobis
precipere placet paratus sum modis omnibus effectui mancipar[e].

Pone quod ista nupserit alii et non velit eum ulterius diligere, taliter scri- 25
bet ei:

Amoris nostri vinculum per effectum operum dissolvatur, quoniam
nupsi viro qui me maritali annulo subarravit, cinxit collum meum
lapidibus preciosis, deditque vestes auro et gemmis plurimum reni-
tentes: unde non possum nec debeo tecum more solito jocundari. 30

Responsio viri:
P[l]orans ploravi nec plangere desistam et in tenebris meum stravi
lectum, quia obscuratum est michi candelabrum quo videbar inter

---

3 umbra] umbram P, /S/   13 pedem] pedes /S/   15 possem] possim /S/   per omnia et in omnibus]
in omnibus et per omnia /S/   17 quiescatis] iterum quiescatis /S/   ergo] igitur /S/   21 Preciosa]
Speciosa P, M, /S/   24 mancipare] P, /S/; mancipari   25–6 taliter scribet ei] unde illi taliter scribit
/S/; unde eidem taliter scribit   32 Plorans] P, M, /S/; *space for enlarged capital* + Orans

designs and glowing with gems, so that I seemed to be in a paradise of delights. When dawn came, she led me back beneath the shade of the same tree, and, resuming her embraces and pressing me close again and again, bid me an angelic farewell. Roused by that word of salutation from so glorious a dream, I thought I would consult your wisdom in this matter, so that you might deign to send a letter interpreting my dream for me.

And a reply from the lady:
You may rejoice and exult inexpressibly in your inmost heart over the fact that there came to you such a precious dream, in which you richly received the most desirable embraces, the most delightful kisses and all the rest that followed. If I remember rightly, on that very day at the foot of that very tree I recollect dreaming that I saw you doing all this there. At that hour indeed I was earnestly studying how I might best give pleasure to your great self in all ways and in all things. But indeed I am not equal to the task of interpreting the dream unless you rest with me under the same tree. Hasten therefore to that same place after the sun has set, for it is there that I propose to explain the dream and to speak of many things that I dare not record in a letter.

Reply from the man:
Most precious in person among the daughters of men, may you have ten thousand thanks on the part of yours most faithfully, and know beyond any doubt that the chains of your love hold me bound indissolubly – so that I stand prepared to give effect to any command it pleases you to give.

Supposing that she marries another and does not wish to continue her love of him, she may write to him a letter of the following kind:

The chain of our love must now be broken through the effect of deeds done, since I have married a man who betrothed me with marital ring, circled my neck with precious stones and gave me vesture glittering with gold and gems in plenty: whence I cannot and ought not take pleasure with you in our accustomed manner.

Reply from the man:
Weeping have I wept and I will not cease to lament and I have prepared my bed in darkness, now that my lampstand is dimmed, by which I shone

gloriosas militum catervas multimode refulgere. Unde sciatis quod si montes et maria cum viro vestro transieritis sequar vos ut quandoque saltem videre valeam desiderium anime mee.

Pone quod antequam nubat efficiatur gravida, sic scribat amico suo:

Eram in domo patris mei tenera et in utriusque parentis conspectu plurimum amabilis quando per venativas adulacionum blandicias me traxisti minus provide in laqueum / deceptivum. Nunc vero non audeo alicui propalare mei vulneris causam et tamen scitur in plateis quod gessimus in absconso: vultus pallet, tumescit venter, reserantur claustra pudoris, fama plebescit, laceror assidue, subiaceo verberibus, requiro mortem. Unde non est similis dolor meo dolori, quia famam et honorem cum flore virginitatis amisi. Nam ad inenarrabilis anxietatis augmentum factus es michi penitus alienus nec illius aliquatenus recordaris cui maria promittebas et montes aureos et universa que celi ambitu continentur. Similibus enim laqueis auceps decepit aves et piscis ex pelago tali trahitur hamo. Sed nichil prodest michi quod refero quoniam qui ex alto cadit irremediabiliter corruit et frustra remedium queritur ubi periculum precucurrit. Succurre michi, queso, tandem et si non vis prebere juvamen inspicias saltem quomodo pro te moriar, et utinam morerer, quia minus malum esset mori quam vivere omni tempore cum pudore.

Responsio viri:
Antequam uxorem acciperem dedignab[a]ris me in virum recipere. Nunc autem qua racione tue possem condescendere voluntati, cum uxorem habeam elegantissimam et multimoda puchritudine decoratam? Cessa ergo a talibus et tecum hec verba retracta, quoniam alium credo esse in causa qui tuam navem fecit ad portum ignominie devenire.

Pone quod aliqua virum vel amicum habeat qui abiit in regionem longinquam nec venire procurat, unde sibi talem potest epistolam destinare:

Expectans expectavi desiderium meum, alteram mei corporis partem, oculorum meorum lumen, primum dilectum et amicum, et iam elapso quinquennio solivaga permansi credens illum corporeis videre oculis sine quo nichil video nec videre potero nisi michi sue

2 transieritis] transiveritis /S/   ut quandoque] M, /S/; transp   4 nubat] P, /S/; vir nubeat sic scribat amico] unde taliter scribit amasio /S/   12 flore] florem /S/   14 aureos] *om* /S/   16 decepit] decipit P, /S/   nichil] nil /S/   18 precucurrit] precurrit /S/   23 dedignabaris] P, /S/; dedignaberis   in virum recipere] recipere in virum /S/   26 ergo] igitur /S/   30 venire] reverti /S/   33-4 corporeis videre] *transp* /S/

conspicuous in the company of the regiments of knights. Know, therefore, that if you cross mountains and seas with your spouse, I will follow you so that I may sometimes be able at least to see my soul's desire.

Supposing that before she can marry anyone she becomes pregnant, she can write to her lover a letter of this kind:

I was still a girl in the home of my parents and dear in the sight of each of them when I, little foreseeing what lay ahead, was lured by you, through blandishments designed to make prey of me, into the snare that deceives. Now indeed there is no one to whom I dare make known the cause of my affliction, and yet what we did in secret is known to all whenever I appear in public: my face grows pale, my belly swells, exposing to view how the gates to modesty have been breached, talk makes my fate common knowledge, I am torn by tongues, I am subjected to their whips, I desire death. So there is no grief like my grief, for along with the flower of my virginity I have lost my good name and my honour. And to add to this indescribable stress you yourself have become very cold towards me and forgetful of her to whom you promised the earth – oceans, mountains of gold and everything contained within the sphere of the heavens. With similar traps does the fowler deceive the birds, and with such a hook is the fish drawn from the sea. But it is useless to speak of the past, for anyone who falls from a great height does not get up again, and in vain does one seek a remedy where the danger has run on ahead to outstrip it. Let me have from you some help at last, and if you do not choose to give me any real assistance, at least consider that it is for you that I will die – and would that I could die, for to die would be a lesser evil than to live in perpetual shame.

Reply from the man:
Before I took a wife, you scorned to accept me as a husband. And what reason could I now have to accede to your request, now that I have a wife of the greatest refinement and with many personal charms? So stop talking like that and weigh your words more carefully, because I believe it is someone else who has caused your boat to arrive at the port of ignominy.

In the case where a lady has a husband or lover who has gone into a distant region from which he cannot soon return, she may write to him a letter of the following kind:

I have waited and waited for my desired one, the other half of my own self, the light of my eyes, the foremost among those dear to and loved by me, and it is now five years that I have lived solitary, trusting to see in the flesh him without whom I see nothing and never can see anything

presencie contulerit claritatem. Rediit ad [No]e columba per fenestram ramum virentis olive in signum leticie reportans. Revertatur, ergo, queso, dilectissimus meus ut illam faciat vivere que pro illo moritur nec mori potest. Alioquin faciam sicut turtur que suum perdidit maritum ad instar cuius amavi semper et amare peropto. Illa quidem postea non sedet in ramo viridi sed gemit in sicco voce flebili / iugiter et aquam claram turbat cum appetit bibere, nullumque nisi mortis prestolatur solacium. Sic ergo vivam sicque moriar si vestra desiderabili non potero presencia prepotiri.

C.V. Qualiter debet mulieribus disuadere ne habitum accipiant monachalem

Vox turturis immo pocius [cuc]uli audita est in terra nostra et resonuit quod huius seculi honore disposito habitum proposuitis recipere monachalem et in claustr[o] cum gibbis, claudis, nas[ic]ur[v]is, strabis mulieribus ducere vitam. Que ergo vobis gloria reservabitur cum vos accendere lampades, pulsare tintinabulum, revolvere libros et cantare altis alleluia vocibus oportebit? Nam cum videbitis puellas plurimas vestimentis preciosissimis exornatas que vobis non possent in pulchritudine coequari stare cum militibus et cantare in timpano et in choro 'Palma nata paridisi redimita floribus', et vos in vestimentis nigris cantabitis 'Requiem eternam', graci[t]ando [psalmos] cum inveteratis. Desistatis ergo a tali proposito, quoniam paratus sum quandocumque placet vos recipere in uxorem.

Responsio domine:
Diu excogitaveram qualiter possem evadere ne habitum susciperem monachalem, sed pater meus hoc me facere compellebat nec inveniebam aliquem qui super hoc michi vellet consulere, unde tristis erat anima mea usque ad mortem nec poteram vivere sine dolore. Placet ergo michi consilium vestrum et parata sum vestre in omnibus obedire voluntati. Quapropter amiciciam vestram effectuose deprecor

1 Noe] P, /S/; me   4–5 perdidit] perdit /S/   8 ergo] ego /S/   9 prepotiri] potiri /S/   10 debet] debeat aliquis /S/   12 cuculi] P, /S/; catuli   13 disposito] deposito /S/   14 claustro] P, /S/; claustra   nasicurvis] P, /S/; nasciturnis   15 strabis] strambis (as also M, /S/); strabi P   ergo] igitur /S/   17 alleluia vocibus] *transp* /S/   19 possent] possunt /S/   pulchritudine] /S/; pulchritudinem   19 militibus] militibus in choreis /S/   21 et vos] *om* /S/   gracitando psalmos] P, /S/; gracidando   22 ergo] igitur /S/   23 recipere] P, /S/; reciperem   27 super hoc michi] m.s.h. /S/   29 ergo] igitur /S/   30 effectuose] attentissime /S/

unless he confer upon me the light of his presence. The dove returned through the window to Noah, bringing back as a joyful sign the branch of an olive in leaf. Oh, let my best-beloved therefore return, so that he may restore to life her who dies deathlessly for him. Otherwise I will do as the turtle dove that has lost her wedded mate, for like her I have loved once and for ever and will continue to love. She indeed, after that loss, chooses no leafy branch as a perch, but groans ever alike with hoarse and tearful voice and, when she seeks to drink, clouds the clear water, waiting for no other solace but death. So will I live and so will I die if I be not given the drink of your desired presence.

Chapter V. How to dissuade women from taking the veil

The voice of the turtle dove, or rather the cuckoo, is heard in our land – and has noised it abroad that you, having laid aside the secular status you enjoy, propose to take the veil and to lead your life in the cloister with hunch-backed, lame, hook-nosed and squinting women. What glory is in store for you from having to light lamps, strike the bell, repeatedly read texts and sing alleluia among those high-pitched voices? For when you see decked out in expensive clothes a crowd of girls who cannot equal you in beauty placed amidst knights and singing to the tambour in the ring-dance 'Palm that has sprung up, adorned with flowers of paradise', you in black clothes will be singing 'Eternal rest' and croaking psalms amidst the aged. Desist, therefore, from such a purpose, for I am ready at any time you choose to make you my wife.

Reply from the lady:
I had long been trying to devise some way of avoiding becoming a nun, but my father made me do it, nor could I find anyone who would help me in this matter. So my soul was grieved unto death and I cannot see that my life will ever be without distress. I was therefore glad to receive your suggestions, and I am ready to do whatever you wish. And therefore I earnestly pray you for the sake of our love to come with haste to

quatinus in proxima nocte ad monasterium cum primum tintinabulum pulsabitur propere accedatis, quia vobiscum veniam quocumque placebit.

Responsio monialis quando petitur pro amica:
Cum sim ipsi desponsata cui angeli serviunt et in primo professionis voto virginitatem meam celesti sponso promiserim, miror quod audes me querere in amicam et presertim cum virginitatis portem sign[um] in vertice, velum videlicet nigrum quo innuitur me quandam speciem assumpsisse mortalitatis, unde tibi ac omnibus / deberem secund[u]m carnis delectacionem procul dubio displicere. Sed, ut video, sic te illaqueavit persuasio dyabolica quod nullius viri lectum violare pertimisceres, ex quo altissimi sponsam exquirere non pavescis. Sed incunctanter scias quod nullatenus dubites quod tue persuasiones contra me non prevalebunt, et si dares que habes et que habere posses in vanum laboras et semina mandas arene.

Responsio viri:
Si per velum nigrum intellegitis mortalitatem vos aliquam assumpsisse, eadem vobiscum desidero mortalitat[e] potiri et familiari vobiscum donec simul aliquantulum revivamus. Sed de avaricie vicio merito reprehend[i] poteritis si michi mortis vestre denegaveritis particulam; ex quo vitam meam in vestra constituo potestate. Et licet velum sit nigrum sub eo tamen membra lacte candidiora intueor, unde mille immo decem milia traho suspiria quod non possum illa gloria perpotiri. Ex eo enim quod asseritis vos illi esse desponsatam cui angeli serviunt et eidem vestram compromisisse virginitatem: dimittere non debetis quin mee con[de]scendatis voluntati, quia celestis sponsus animam et non carnem requirit; unde dicitur 'Celum celi Domino, terram autem dedit filiis hominum'. Sed pro eo quod me dicitis persuasione dyabolica sic esse vinculatum quod nullius viri lectum violare pertimescerem, ex quo altissimi sponsam exquirere non pavesco, respondeo taliter: quod multo forcius illius violarem thorum qui meos consanguineos interfecit, qui dat pluvias, grandines et tempestates quam alicuius viri terreni qui paucos vel nullos offendere potest.

2 pulsabitur] pulsatur /S/   4 *Responsio*] Respondet /S/   5 sim ipsi] illi sim /S/   6 promiserim] compromiserim /S/   8 signum] P, /S/; signo   10 secundum] P, /S/; secundum   18 mortalitate] P, /S/; mortalitati   familiari] famulari /S/   vobiscum] vobis P, M, /S/   20 reprehendi] P, /S/; reprehendere   26 condescendatis] P, /S/; conscendatis   28 Sed pro eo] Super eo vero /S/   32 meos] parentes et *add* /S/

the convent this very night as soon as the first bell is rung, for I will go with you wherever you wish.

Reply from a nun to a man who wants her to become his mistress:
Since I am espoused to Him whom the angels serve and in the first vow of my profession pledged my virginity to that celestial spouse, I marvel that you dare to seek me as a mistress, especially since I bear the sign of chastity on my head – the black veil, that is, by which it is signalled that I have taken on a kind of death, and so unquestionably should not be, for you or for anyone, an object of sexual desire. But, as I see, you have been so caught in the meshes of diabolic temptation that you do not fear to violate the marriage bed of anyone at all, and so have the temerity to seek the spouse of the Most High. But you should know at once that there can be no question of your attempts at persuasion succeeding against me, and were you to give all that you have and might have, you would be labouring in vain and sowing seeds in the sand.

Reply from the man:
If you understand the black veil as a kind of death that you have entered into, then I wish to possess myself, as your associate, of the same death, until we have managed to restore a little life to ourselves. But you will justly be chargeable with the vice of avarice if you deny to me a small share of your own death, when I thus put my own life in your power. And, granting the veil to be black, under it I can picture limbs whiter than milk, which makes me draw a thousand – nay, ten thousand – sighs that I cannot luxuriate in the glory of them. And as to what you say about your being espoused to Him whom the angels serve and having pledged your virginity to Him: that is no excuse for your not conceding to me what I want, since it is the soul and not the body that is required by the heavenly spouse – whence we read in the Bible 'the heaven, even the heavens, are the Lord's: but the earth hath he given to the children of men'. And as to what you say about my being so in the chains of the devil's promptings that I do not fear to violate the bed of any man and so do not tremble to seek the bride of the Most High, I respond thus: it takes a lot more courage on my part to violate the marriage bed of one who has killed my kin and who can visit upon me downpours, hailstorms and tempests than that of some mortal man who can injure few or no people.

152 Fictional and Instructional Models

Responsio monialis:
Verba tua super mel et favum dulciora fuere nec audeo denegare quod postulas, quoniam necessarium proponis et irrefragabile argumentum. Venias ergo et cupitis fruamur amplexibus, co[n]ferendo pariter grata, graciora et gratissima basia que dulciter permisceri solent, labella suaviter committendo. Quod autem sequitur sit secretissimum et fingamus nos ad invicem velle pro re aliqua rixari quatinus nostri amoris integritas occultetur. Hoc tandem / amicicie tue precipere p[ro]posui ut si sponsus meus te aliquo tempore molestaverit in me penam refundas, sciens quod quandocumque potero dabo tibi locum ut tuam valeas iniuriam vindicare.

8ʳ

5

10

C.VI. Matrona mittit litteras alicui qui eam dilexit sed nunc est ab eo derelicta pro quadam domicella:

Si amoris jura diligencius inspiceres non dimitteres grana pro paleis nec rem solidam pro volatili, quoniam qui teneram diligit puellam fructus degustat acerbos neque naturalem percepit saporem qui uvam premere satagit antequam sit matura. Sed scio quod illas diligere consuevisti que suas facies cerusa et ung[u]ento citrino dealbant, que rubent ex apposicione bambacelli e florere videntur ex coloribus appositivis, unde universis deberent plurimum displicere, quia furtivus est color qui non provenit a natura. Est et aliud quod te deberet a talium amore divellere: quia neminem nisi pro munere diligunt, et illa quam tibi credis esse specialem plures, immo plurimi, abutuntur, sicque communis est terminus que[m] speras fore discretum. Revertere ad me igitur et more solito gloriemur, quia in rebus necessariis nullum pacieris defectum.

15

20

25

C.VII. Pone quod aliqua uxorata velit ad se vocare amicum suum quando maritus est absens, dicet sic:

Transmisi vobis violas, nunc autem vasciculum destino rosarum, quoniam amicicie vestre superlativis laudibus conveniunt flores, fructus et frondes: recessit enim aquilo, veniat ergo auster, intret ortum meum et faciat illius aromata suis flatibus redolere.

30

2 fuere] michi fuerunt /S/   4 ergo] igitur /S/   conferendo] P, /S/; coferendo   6 committendo] comprimendo /S/   7 quatinus] quatenus /S/   9 proposui] P, /S/; perposui   18 unguento] P, /S/; ungento   20 appositivis] appositis M, /S/   21 et] etiam /S/   24 quem] P; que   28 dicet sic] *om* /S/   31 ergo] igitur /S/

Reply from the nun:
Your words were to me sweeter than honey and the honeycomb and I do not dare deny what you ask, since you have used arguments necessarily true and irrefragable. Come, therefore, and let us enjoy long-desired embraces, giving on both sides those lovely, lovelier and loveliest kisses that are always so sweetly intermingled with them, and joining our lips sensuously. Let what comes next remain our secretest secret – and let us each pretend to have found some reason to quarrel with the other, and that will serve to keep hidden the fact that our love continues fully intact. I have decided that *I* should be the one to make claims on *your* love, so that if at any time my spouse should molest you, you will be able to exact from me a compensatory penalty, knowing that whenever I am able I will give you the opportunity to avenge your injuries.

Chapter VI. The mistress of a household sends a letter to someone who once loved her but who has now forsaken her for some young woman in service:

If you carefully consulted the laws of love, you would not throw away grain for chaff nor something solid for something fleeting: for anyone who gives his love to a young girl will be offended by the acid taste of immature fruit and anyone who toils at pressing grapes before they are ripe will not taste their true sweetness. But I know that you have always had a taste for those who whiten their faces with lead and citrus ointment, get rosy colour by applying rouge and seem to come out in flower through applied colourings – which should make them unattractive to everyone, since any colour which does not come from nature is a stolen colour. And there is something else which ought to root out from you any love for such women: for they give love only in exchange for remuneration, and she whom you believe to be peculiarly yours is made use of by many, nay by hundreds – so that the boundaries of what you trusted was private property are open to common traffic. So turn back to me, and let us find exultant joy in our old way, for if you do you will find no lack in the essentials.

Chapter VII. If some married woman wants to summon her lover when her husband is absent, she can write as follows:

I have sent you violets in the past, but now I transmit to you a bunch of roses, since flowers, fruit and leafage are the things best suited to celebrate your love in the highest manner: for, now that the north wind has receded, let the south wind come, enter my garden and enhance its aromas with his breath.

De uxore que cum filiis et filiabus maxima premitur egestate, unde maritum revocare intendit:
Vidua sum vivente marito, quoniam vir meus abiit in regionem longinquam, dimisit me cum quinque filiis, quorum adhuc duo jacent in cunis, tres in adalescencia consistentes se ipsos iuvare non possunt nec habent vestes neque corporum alimenta; due filie in etate nubile iam consistunt que nimia egistate coacte corpora forsitan ludibri[o] ded[u]c[e]b[u]nt. Omnes quippe mendicare cogimur et quandoque porcorum siliquas degustare. Sublata sunt nobis pradia fructuosa, distructores multi apparent. Ex hiis quidem inimici nostri per plurimum jocundantur, sed amici non dolent, / quia nullos habemus, unde omnis dolor in me specialius retorquetur. Demum hanc epistolam constitui nuncium specialem, optans ut vobis possit et debeat taliter suadere quod ad propria redire curetis, liberaturi filios vestros et filias qui jacent in tenebris paupertatis et umbra mortis.

De muliere que amicum suum revocare intendit:
Sedens more turturis in ramusc[ul]o sicco gemo assiduo turbans potum cum bibo et mecum voce flebili colloquens traho suspiria dolorosa, quia scire non possum ubi sit quem diligit anima mea immo illum cuius corpori anima est unita. Ille nimirum est qui tenet vite mee claves, sine quo vivere mori esse puto, quia spiritus est amoris, qui precordia mea vivificando regnat et cum deest non sum et donec sum deesse non potest, quia per voluntatem et ineffabile desiderium illum apprehendi et in memoriali meo secrecius teneo circumclusum, ac ipsum velut mirre fasciculum sub quodam spei remedio inter ubera mea brachiis peroptabilis dilectionis astringo. Spes enim est quoddam refugium ymaginarium que multos in calamitate positos revocillat ex eo quod anima in dubiis rebus frequencius exitum felicem expectat nec refrenat corpus licet terminum ignorat quesitum. Sed audite, filie grecorum et adolescentule regni [ty]ronensis: vos forte putatis dilectum et desiderabilem meum inter brachia retinere. Sed fallimini, quia semper cum sopori sum dedita intrat per hostia thalami, ponit levam sub capite meo, dextra suavius tangit renes et pectus et compre[s]sis labellis me dulcius osculatur. Transfert me super ulnas in pomerium florigerum in quo suavis est rivulorum decursus, in eodem philomene a[c] diversa genera volucrum dulciter

---

5 adalescencia] adulescentia M¹   7–8 ludibrio deducebunt] ludibrio deducabunt M¹; ludibria dedificabant   17 ramusculo] M¹; ramusco   22 qui] M¹; quia   25 spei] spēi   28 revocillat] refocillat M¹   30 tyronensis] M¹; aronensis   34 compressis] M¹; comprensis   36 ac] M¹; ad

The case of a wife who, together with her sons and daughters, is oppressed by the greatest need and wants to persuade her absent husband to come back:
I have become a widow while my spouse yet lives, for my husband has departed into distant regions and has forsaken me with five sons, who, two being yet in the cradle and three still young, cannot support themselves and have no clothes nor food; the two daughters are of marriageable age, but, under the compulsion of intolerable need, will perhaps give over their bodies to prostitution. We are all forced to beg and sometimes to eat mast like pigs. Our arable lands have been taken from us, and our buildings are being torn down. At these things our enemies indeed much rejoice, but, since we have no friends to grieve at them, it is on me alone that all of the grief falls. I have at last appointed this letter to act as a special messenger who, I hope, may and should be able to persuade you to take steps to return to your own affairs, in order to liberate your sons and daughters, who lie in the darkness of poverty and the shadow of death.

The case of a woman who wants to persuade her absent lover to come back:
Seated like the turtle dove on a dry branch, I weep continually, defiling the water I drink, and in tearful soliloquy I draw grief-stricken sighs, because I have no knowledge of the whereabouts of him whom my soul loves, or rather him in whose person my soul exists. For it is he indeed who keeps the keys of my life, without whom life is to me death, because he is my inner spirit of love, who animates the heart he reigns over, and when he is not there I do not exist and while I exist he must be there: for through will and ineffable desire I have taken hold of him and keep him enclosed in the privacy of my memory and, in remedial hope, I press him close between my breasts like a bundle of myrrh in the much-longing arms of love. For hope is a kind of asylum of the mind, reviving those placed in dire trouble, in that the mind beset by anxiety often waits for some happy end, of which it allows the sensation, even though it has not pictured to itself what form the desired outcome might take. But hear me, you daughters of Greece and young women of Tyre: you perhaps think that you hold in your arms my beloved and desirable one. But you are mistaken. For every time I fall asleep he enters through the doors of my bedchamber, places his left hand under my head and with his right touches my belly and chest and presses sweet kisses upon me. He carries me in his arms into a flowering orchard in which there is the gentle flow of rivulets and where nightingales and

modulantur. Sunt ibidem omnia genera odoramentorum sicque amplexibus et colloquiis peroptatis divicius ad invicem fruimur in tam desiderabili paradiso et istud inenarrabile michi gaudium in omni sopore occurrit. Cur ergo illum revocare optarem ex quo tam desiderabiliter non desinit visitare, presertim cum sciam quod sine me vivere non poterit neque [mori]?

De excusacione alicuius ad illam que altera Venus reputabatur in terris:

/ De medulla cordis et vena doloris verba mea procedunt quia firmiter intellexi quod aliquot viri dolosi quibus ora fetentur et nascitur agriffol[i]um inter dentes aures datatis vestre mendaci[is] fatigarunt me dixi mendaciter asserentes quod amoris vestri privilegium obtinebam, quod procul fuit ab omni spe veritatis quoniam illud vel simile numque ascendit nec descendit in cor meum nec aliquo tempore cogitavi. Sed invidi[e] livore proscripti ex familiari colloquio et ascensione gracie plenioris loquuntur opinabiliter ut me possint benivolencia vestra privare. Sed omnes qui aurum dilectionis mundum cupiunt ab omni rubigine conservare debent surde aspidis vestigia imitari qu[e] unam aurem in terram defigit et reliquam sumitate caude obdurat ut non audiat vocem venifici sapiencius incantantis.

C.VIII. Suasio pro muliere propter habundanciam diviciarum:

Cuilibet est propensius consulendum ut talem recipiat in uxorem de qua peccuniam possit habere, nec est curandum de nobilitate vel prosapia generosa: quoniam peccunia facit hominem generosum, qui habet denarios, cui affluentur, nobilis efficitur et famosus. Unde uxorem recipere peccuniosam non postponas quantumcumque turpis fuerit vel deformis et etiam si esset vetustissima vetularum et cui jam omnes dentes cecidissent ex ore et sole remansissent gingi[v]e cum salina fluida et spumosa.

Disuasio contra virum propter senectutem:
O vesania inaudita! O stulticia muliebris! Quomodo potuisti audire [n]edum intelligere quod tali viro copulari debeas qui jam senecta et senio est consumptus, cuius oculi jam caligant, immo, quod est abhominabilius, assidue producit lacrimas que guttatim cadunt in

---

6 mori] M¹; dormire   10 fetentur] fetent M¹   11 agriffolium] agriffolum; agrifolium M¹   mendaciis] M¹; mendaciter   15 invidie] M¹; invidii   19 que] M¹; qui   28 gingive] M¹; gingine   32 nedum] M¹; ve dum

other birds sing in sweet symphony. All varieties of spices are there. And thus in so desirable a paradise we luxuriate the more richly in the embraces and colloquies so dear to us. And this indescribable joy befalls me whenever I sleep. So why should I try to get him to come back, when he never fails to visit me in so desirable a manner? – especially since I know that without me he can neither have nor lose existence.

The case of a man who needs to excuse himself to a woman spoken of as a second Venus:
From the core of my heart and from the very soul of grief do my words proceed. For it has become clear to me that a certain number of men who distort the truth, whose mouths stink and between whose teeth there is gall, have with their habitual lies abused your ears by falsely asserting that I have boasted that you have granted me amorous rights over you – which is far from any hope of truth, for there never arose nor dropped into my mind any such thought, which never at any time entered my head. But prejudiced by the malice of envy they give utterance to conjectures they have formed from familiar talk and the increasing good favour in which I stand with you, intending to deprive me of your goodwill. But all who want to keep the gold of love pure and free from tarnish must follow the example of the deaf asp, who presses one ear to the ground and uses the tip of its tail to block the other, so that it cannot hear the voice of the snake-charmer uttering his skilful spells.

Chapter VIII. Persuading someone to marry for money:

Everyone would be well advised to take a wife who will bring him money and not to care about her nobility of lineage or gentle birth: because a man can acquire gentility through money – anyone who has pennies and to whom cash is plentiful turns himself at once into a man of rank and standing. So do not belittle wealth, but take a rich wife, however base of birth she may be or ugly, and even if she is the most aged of old women, whose teeth have all fallen out of her mouth, in which there are now only gums and frothy saliva.

Dissuading from marrying an old man:
What unheard of madness! What stupidity in a woman! How could you even hear of, much less think about, coupling yourself to a man already eaten away by old age and decrepitude, whose eyes are already clouding and, what is even more repulsive, continuously ooze tears that drop

vinum dum potat et in c[i]pho relinquitur de saliva dum comedit. Screat, eructat et mucilagines em[u]ngit de naso que tergit sepe ad mantile. Preterea cum vadit ad lectum dormit, stertit, pedit et fetissimas trullas emittit. Porro cum excitatur a sompno tus[s]it, spuit, suspirat, conqueritur, ingemescit, et virga eius velut plumbi fistula jacet 5
super mentulam ponderosam. Hic osculabitur vos osculo oris sui qui caret dentibus, / sed cum gingi[v]is marcidis praebebit vobis oscula salivosa. Preterea huiusmodi senes zelotypie vicio proscribuntur et super mala de suis uxoribus suspicantur. Unde licet non deliquant non minus cum suspecte habentur. Insuper prevignos habebis et pre- 10
vignas a quibus assidue laceraberis, quia raro vel numquam accidere consuevit quod inter prevignos et novercas possit concordia reperiri.

C.IX. Loquitur Venus universis mulieribus hoc modo:

'Jocunda sunt vobis verba in Rota nostra proposita quibus amantes valeant se ad invicem visitare suorum cordium revelando secreta. Nos 15
autem in eminenciori amoris speculo consistentes quendam in hac parte consideravimus defectum quem ex officio nostro volumus in integrum supplere: videlicet docere vos invenire oportunitatem amandi et per quas personas hoc facere possitis. Unde breviter hanc vos doceo r[egula]m que non fallit. Matrone per se ipsas, moniales et viduas sub obtentu re- 20
ligionis, uxorate per matronas et ancillas, puelle per omnes supradictas possunt multimode lascivire. Item est notandum quod non est aliquis adeo sagax qui mulieris propositum valeat omni tempore impedire.'

His dictis damnavit Sa[rdo]s [et] universos qui zelotipie vicio proscribuntur, addendo pariter quod quicumque dubitat et vult sibi con- 25
scius esse cornutam adipiscet coronam procul dubio in qua scribitur versus cuculi et depingitur cucurbita ortulana. Finito itaque generali edicto abiit dea Venus. Nec dico quod taliter abierit ut non sit ubique potencialiter presens. Ego autem solus remansi et cepi cogitare mecum omnia que causa lasciv[i]e conscripseram et ve[r]eri plurimum ne forte 30
moderni et posteri me crederent nimis fuisse lascivum, unde opus de-

1 cipho] M¹; cpho   comedit] cōmedit   2 mucilagines emungit] M¹; muscilagines emangit   4 tussit] M¹; tuscit   7 gingivis] M¹; ginginis   13 *Loquitur*] Nunc loquitur /S/   15 valeant] valent /S/   suorum] suorumque /S/   16 speculo] specula /S/   18 invenire] proposuimus invenire /S/   19 regulam] M, /S/; rationem P; rōm   21 matronas] matronas et matres /S/   24 Sardos et] P, /S/; saēdos oñs M; sacerdotes   26 coronam procul dubio] procul dubio coronam /S/   scribitur] scribetur /S/   27 versus cuculi] cuculi versus /S/   depingitur] depingetur /S/   itaque] siquidem /S/   30 lascivie] P, /S/; lascive   vereri] /S/; veteri

into his wine when he drinks and who leaves spittle in the bowl when he eats. He hawks and spits and mops mucus from his nose, which he frequently wipes on his napkin. What is more, when he goes to bed, he sleeps and snores, breaks wind and emits the foulest farts. Next, when his sleep is broken, he coughs, spits, sighs, complains and moans; and his nether rod lies as heavy as a pipe of lead. This creature will kiss you, with kisses from a mouth that lacks teeth, but with his withered gums he will give you slobbering kisses. Moreover these kinds of old men are notoriously given to the vice of jealousy and suspect their wives. So, even when women have done nothing wrong, they are nevertheless held in suspicion. On top of all this, you will have stepsons and stepdaughters to be tormented by, since rarely or never has it been seen that concord reigns between stepmothers and stepchildren.

Chapter IX. Venus speaks as follows to all women in general:

'Words to be welcomed have been set forth for you in this *Rota*, or wheel, of ours, writings by which lovers can as it were visit each other and reveal to one another those feelings not to be revealed to others. We, however, with our superior knowledge of love, have found what We consider to be a defect in the treatise, a defect which in our official capacity We wish to make good: to teach you, that is, how to find an opportunity to engage in love and through which persons this can be done. So I give you briefly these general principles that you can trust in. Mistresses of their own households through their own agency, nuns and widows through some religious pretext, married women through mistresses of households and female attendants, and unmarried girls through all the above can by various means manage to have a good time. Moreover you should note this fact: that there is no one so clever that he can manage forever to stop a woman doing what she has a will to do'.

In these last words did she condemn all those who are, like the Sardinians, noted for the vice of jealousy, adding moreover that whoever doubts his wife and seeks certainty will unquestionably simply gain for himself that horned crown in which is represented [such symbols of the cuckold as] the song of the cuckoo and the gourd of the garden. Having concluded her general proclamation, Venus departed. But when I say she departed, I don't mean that she, or her power, is not always present. But I found myself alone, and I began to think about all that I had composed for the furthering of sexual love and to wonder whether I might not be considered improperly preoccupied with it both by those of my own day and by future generations.

struere proposueram ne ad aliorum audienciam perveniret. Condescendi tandem amicorum precibus et Rotam omnibus concessi Veneris quam feceram causa urbanitatis. Unum tandem volo universos et singulos scire: quod plus michi semper placuerunt verba quam facta, quoniam gloriosius est in talibus vivere in spe quam in re secundum sententiam serenissime Capuane.

Quedam oblivioni tradideram que non duxi silencio preterire quoniam in eis subtilis et ardua est theorica, unde vix potest inbecillitas ingenii humani rem per magnitudinem intueri. Inter cunctos equidem amancium gestus hec sunt diligencius et exquisicius / contemplanda, videlicet quid sit nutus, quid indicium, quid signum, quid suspirium, quomodo ista se habeant et qualiter permisceri possunt.

C.X.

Nutus est quidam preambulus [amoris] nuncius qui quodam inenarribili actu cordium secreta revelat. Vel nutus est quedam amoris ymago que representat quid jam fecerint amantes aut quid facere velint. Vel nutus est veri vel falsi amoris indicativus, quia multociens per ipsum trahuntur in laqueum deceptivum. Fit enim actu, cum mulier in momento aperit dextrum vel sinistrum oculum aliquantulum subridendo, unde amatorum cordibus quoddam inenarrabile gaudium nascitur, pro quo extra seipsos multociens traducuntur; et hoc magis proprie dicitur [nutus]. Fit etiam nutus actu, videlicet quando mulieres digito qui vocatur index albissimam gulam demonstrant, unde amantes amoris igniculo comburuntur. Fit etiam actu quando ille que pulchros habent capillos manum circa tempora ponunt sublevando drapel[l]um vel binda[m] ut amantes respiciant puchritudinem capillorum, unde ad amorem non modicum provocantur. Fit etiam actu quando mulieres brachia extendunt revolvendo pelles et permutando ut amatores statum respiciant et personam, unde amoris vigor multimode augmentatur. Multis autem modis fit nutus actu quos numerare non possum propter consuetudinum diversitatem. Nam sagaces mulieres in chorea latentes faciunt nutus, licet ab omnibus percipi non possint. Fit autem actu quandoque in elevacione capitis, quandoque in declinacione, risu, manu et passibus tortuosis.

---

1 aliorum] aliquorum /S/   9 per magnitudinem] pre magnitudine /S/   14 preambulus amoris] P; preambolus amoris /S/; preambulius   15 amoris ymago] *transp* /S/   17 trahuntur] plurimi trahuntur /S/   19 aliquantulum] *om* /S/   21 nutus] P, /S/; *om*   22 nutus] *om* /S/   23 demonstrant] demonstrat /S/   25 drapellum] P, /S/; drapelum   bindam] P, /S/; binda   31 in chorea latentes] in choreis saltantes /S/

So I resolved to destroy this work before it could come to the ears of others. I deferred in the end to the pleas of friends and gave to the public the *Rota* of Venus that I had produced, as an amusement for the sophisticated. One thing I do in the end want one and all to know: that it is the language rather than the deeds that have always interested me in this area, in which, as the great lady of Capua says, the glory lies in any case more in the hopeful anticipation than in the actuality.

I had put to one side subjects which I did not want to leave untreated, deciding to forget about them for the moment, since they involve very subtle and abstruse matters, which the crudeness of the human mind can scarcely get into focus, so wide an area does the subject cover. There are non-verbal communications in love, gestures and body language, amongst which the following deserve especially thorough and particular examination: to wit, what a *nutus* is, what an *indicium*, what a *signum*, and what a *suspirium*, in what they consist and in what way they merge into one another.

Chapter X.

A 'nod', or *nutus*, is a kind of messenger, a herald of love to come, which with a certain wordless action reveals the hidden feelings of the heart. Or it may be a kind of sign of the love the pair have already engaged in or wish to engage in. Or it may be given to indicate a love which may be true or may be false, a 'glad eye' by which people are often deceived and entrapped. It may occur in the gesture of a woman when she briefly opens one or the other eye a little wider while smiling, something which rouses in the hearts of lovers an indefinable joy, and at which they often become transported out of themselves; and this is what is most appropriately called a nod. It can occur in another kind of gesture when women point with the finger called the index to that snowy white throat of theirs, at which a spark of love sets lovers ablaze. It may similarly occur in another kind of gesture by which those women who have beautiful hair every so often lift their hands to raise their head-coverings so that their lovers can see the beauty of that hair, something which rouses love to no small degree. It can also occur in the gesture by which women extend their arms to turn or adjust their fur wraps so that their lovers can see their figures, something by which love is made keener in all sorts of ways. This kind of gestural 'nod' can occur in ways too numerous for me to list them all individually, for there is much diversity in personal usages. For intelligent women can make such a nod even when concealed among other women in a dance circle, although it will not be noticed by others. For the gesture can occur sometimes in a raising of the head, sometimes in a lowering of it, in a smile, in a movement of the hand or in swaying steps.

Indicium est quedam latens revelacio secreti pro qua indicatur nobis quid facere debeamus. Verbi gracia: quedam enim formosa monialis vidit iuxta januas templi transire amasium suum, unde statim accepit librum et incepit canere 'sol fa mi re, sol fa mi re, so-la sum, so-la sum'; hoc erat indicium, quia indicebatur ei per tales voces quid facere deberet. Et est differencia inter nutum et indicium, quia nutus fit multum latenter, indicium aliquantulum expresse. Item nutus fit tantum actu, indicium vero actu et voce. Item est notandum quod omnis nutus est largo modo indicium, quia per ipsum semper aliquid indicatur. Sed non convertitur. Indicium enim dicitur quando mulieres frequenter aliquos nominant, quia indicatur quod eos diligant vel diligere velint. Indicium est ut si aliquis frequent[et] [h]oram alicuius mulieris et ultra quam consueverit se incipiat perpollir[e], quia indicatur quod eam habeat / vel habere affectat. Innumerabilibus enim modis tam voce quam actu fiunt indicia, quorum diversitates non posset aliquis plenarie assignare. Et est notandum quod omne indicium est coniectura.

Signum est quo secretum qu[andoque] perpenditur, ut cum aliquis vel aliqua pallet vel rubet repentino motu, pro quo significatur verecundia vel ira. Et non accipio hic signum nisi quantum pertinet ad amorem, quoniam signi accepciones infinite sunt. Preterea largo modo potest signum indicium dici et e converso.

Suspirium est passio anime innata ex spirituum suspensione vel suspirium est ingens inspiracio cum vehementi spirituum suspensione vel suspirium est vehemens spirituum passio ex valida cogitacione vel suspirium est repentinus ac inopinatus spirituum sonus proveniens ex anime labore. Dicitur autem suspirium a spirituum suspensione quoniam cum anima reducit ad memoriam felicitatem quam habuit aut doloris immensitatem, vel immensum gaudium vel contrarium, seu futurum incomodum, suspenduntur spiritus, quia constringitur cor ex eo quod anima obliviscitur virtutis operative, unde quando cor incipit postmodum dilatari revertuntur spiritus ad principalem sedem et ex ipsa reversione oritur quidam sonus qui suspirum nominatur. Verumtamen sunt quam plures qui ex prava consuetudine vel morbo suspirant. Mulieres autem quandoque suspirant ut decipiant amatores. Nam et ipse multociens

---

5 indicebatur] indicabatur /S/   Et est] Est enim /S/   9 quia] quoniam /S/   12 frequentet] /S/; frequentur   horam] P /S/; coram   13 perpollire] /S/; perpolire /P/; perpolliri   habere] /S/; haberem   affectat] affectet /S/   15 diversitates] diversitatem /S/   Et est] transp /S/   17 quandoque] P, /S/; qum̄   25 sonus] sonitus /S/   28 vel¹ ... seu] seu ... vel /S/   29 suspenduntur] suspenditur /S/   31 revertuntur] revertitur /S/

An indication, or *indicium*, is a kind of covert disclosure relating to some secret matter, a sign which indicates to us some response we should make to it. For instance: a certain comely cloistress saw her lover passing by the doors of the church, at which she at once took up her Psalter and began to sing 'do, re, mi, fa, *sola* [alone] I am, *sola* I am'; this was an indication, or *indicium*, because it indicated to him by these words some responsive action on his part. And there is a difference between a *nutus* and an *indicium*, because the *nutus* gives a message imperceptibly, whereas an *indicium* does so a little more distinctly; and a *nutus* occurs in a gesture alone, while an *indicium* can be something said as well as done. And it should be noted that every *nutus* is in a broad sense an *indicium* in that something is indicated through it (although the reverse is not true). In that broader sense, it is called an *indicium*, or 'indication', when women repeatedly name men, because it indicates that they love them or would be willing to do so; and it is similarly an 'indication' if some man is frequently to be found in the vicinity of some woman and begins to spruce himself up more than usual because it indicates that he has gained her as his mistress or desires to do so. Indications of this kind, in word or behaviour, can occur in countless ways, too numerous for anyone to categorize the different varieties. And it should be observed that every 'indication' leads to an inference that is made from it.

A *signum*, or sign, is that by which something inner or private becomes outwardly apparent, as when a sudden emotion causes a man or woman to go pale or red in the face, which is a sign of self-consciousness or anger. The word can be used of an infinite number of things, but here I use it only as it pertains to love. Moreover, in the broader senses of the words, every 'sign' could be called an 'indication', and vice versa.

A *suspirium*, or sigh, indicating emotion, is a temporary suspension of suspiration (breathing), or a strong inhalation that is followed by marked suspension of suspiration, or strongly marked suspiration arising from intense thought about something or a sudden and unexpected sound of suspiration arising from some disturbance of mind. Now a *suspirium*, or sigh, takes its name from the suspension of suspiration, because when the mind is focused upon happiness it once had or on the greatness of present pain, on great joy or its contrary, or on some impending trouble, breathing is suspended, because the heart is constricted, vital functions being neglected by an organism under stress, so that when the heart starts after a time to re-dilate, breathing recommences, as the vital spirits return to their principal seat in the heart, and from that return of suspiration arises a certain sound which is called a *suspirium*, or sigh. There are, however, many who sigh for base reasons or from illness. Women sometimes feign sighs to deceive their lovers, for they themselves are often

Fictional and Instructional Models

suspiriis deluduntur. Suspiria quidem largo modo possunt dici nutus, indicium et signum. Porro per suspiria plurima indicantur. Profecto cum quidam miles non longe a quadam virgine sederet, vehementer suspiravit. Interrogatus tandem ab ea quare suspiraverit, respondit: 'Non enim audeo vobis mei cordis desiderium aperire.' Illa vero notabile sibi verbum proposuit dicens: 'Non videtur habere virilem animum qui mulieri suam dubitat patefacere voluntatem dummodo loquendi oportunitas adsit.'

Licet autem plura que lasciviam ostendere videntur in hoc opere posuerim, non tamen est credibile me fuisse aut velle fore lascivum, quia Salomon, qui meruit assistrici Dei, id est eius sapiencie, copulari, multa posuit in Canticis Canticorum que secundum literam magis possent ad carnis voluptatem quam ad moralitatem spiritus trahi. Verumptamen sapientes dubia in meliorem partem interpretantur, dicentes sponsam vel amicam Ecclesiam fuisse, sponsum Jhesum Christum. Credere autem debetis quod Boncompagnus non dixit hec alicuius lascivie causa sed sociorum precibus amica[bi]liter condescendit.

2 suspiria] suspirium /S/   4 enim] *om* /S/   12 moralitatem] /S/; carnis spiritum P; mortalitatem   14 Ecclesiam] P, /S/; ecclesiasticam   16 amicabiliter] P, /S/; amicaliter

deceived by such sighs. Sighs, indeed, in a general sense, could be called a 'nod', 'indication' or 'sign'. For many things can be indicated by them. For instance, when a certain knight sat close to a certain maiden, he gave ostentatious sighs. When she at last asked why he sighed, he replied: 'Because I do not dare to disclose to you the desire concealed in my heart'. She in fact made a noteworthy response to this, saying: 'It looks rather unmanly to lack the courage to reveal one's heart to a woman when presented with an opportunity for doing so'.

Although I have in this work set down many things that might seem to indicate lasciviousness on my part, it does not follow that I have been lascivious in fact or intention, for Solomon, who merited union with her who acts as co-assessor with God (that is, His wisdom), set down many things in the Song of Songs which, if read on the literal level, could be taken to relate more to the lust of the flesh than to the morality of the spirit. But the learned choose to interpret those things that look dubious in the way that has most propriety, declaring the bride or beloved to be the Church and the bridegroom Jesus Christ. You should similarly believe that Boncompagno has spoken, not with lascivious motives, but to accede in a spirit of friendship to the prayers of his colleagues.

NOTES TO BONCOMPAGNO, *ROTA VENERIS*

DOCTORUM ANNUENS PRECIBUS Such claims were common. Cf. Caxton's assertion in his preface to Malory's tales of Arthur that this 'hystorye' was produced at the urgent request of 'many noble and dyvers gentylmen of thys royame' (Malory, *Works*, ed. Vinaver, p. xiii).

128.6–20 For the appearance of Venus in the springtime setting as an introduction to material related to love, cf. *Council of Remiremont* (reproduced pp. 432ff. below) 1, 37–54. Such a setting was common for amorous matter. Greenness (*revirescunt*), blossom (*arbores florigeras*) and new shoots (*germinare*) are of course common elements in descriptions of spring (cf. *SGGK* 508, 512, 518), as is birdsong (*SGGK* 509, 514–15) – here, specifically, the especially musical song of nightingales (*phylomenarum voces*), which do in fact sing by day as well as by night.

128.8 *que premortua hyemis presencia videbantur*: cf. 'In May ... That fresshe floures ... Ben quike agayn, that winter dede made' (*Troilus* II.50–2).

128.8–9 The Ravone is a watercourse near Bologna. Boncompagno (B) is referring to a place which was the focus for much of his teaching and scholarly activities, as is pointed out by Garbini ('Il pubblico', pp. 207–11), who quotes from the incipit to the *Notule auree* that appear as an appendix to B's *Tractatus virtutum* (c. 1197): 'Cum in rotundo monticulo iuxta Ravonem operam in rhetorica sedulus exhiberem' [While I was, on a small hill near the Ravone, methodically expounding a work on rhetoric]. The place here offers relief from the professional *labor* of which it was the chief site as it switches from its role as a classroom to its present function as a *locus amenus*, a familiar rhetorical topos to which it here gives topographical and biographical specificity.

128.10–11 *recreabam animum post laborem*: the effect (not uncommon in springtime contexts) is to create a parallel between the human spirit and the outer world in their common re-vivification (cf. 128.6–8).

128.12–17 *virgo in vestitu deaurato ... scrutaretur*: the Venus of the *Council of Remiremont* is described in similar terms (as is that of Andreas at 1.6.E.253): a *virgo regia* (43; cf. *virgo ... regine ... regine*), whose costume is splendid with variety of colour and glitter (*vestis coloribus* 40, *Gemmis ... auro* 41; cf. *vestitu deaurato circumamicta varietatibus*), whose regalia bespeaks a *domina* (*cardinalis domina* 37; cf. *dominabiliter*), with authority over a world to which she is entitled to issue commands and which she has entered for the purposes of inquisitorial visitation (*vitam inquirere* 53; cf. *scrutaretur*).

128.12, 16 *vestitu deaurato circumamicta varietatibus*: cf. **Psalm 44:10, 15** (*regina ... In vestitu deaurato, circumdata varietate ... circumamicta varietatibus*). *a finibus terre* (8): cf. **Matthew 12:42** (*Regina ... venit a finibus terrae audire sapientiam Salamonis*). Many of the biblical echoes in this treatise are, as here, a matter of stylistic influence on phrasing rather than allusions or citations proper. The former, showing the influence of the Vulgate as a well-known repository of dignified, resonant or eloquent locutions, are more pervasively significant with regard to the literary texture they help to create. We have in these notes signalled all references to biblical wording, whether loose or exact, by emboldening the biblical book reference with citations in bold, to make discernible the extent and variety of those references.

128.16–17 *curialitatem et sapienciam*: this valorizes the amorous observances that are Venus' sphere by connecting them with courtly sophistication of mind and behaviour. The association was deeply rooted in the amorous culture of the Middle Ages. For love as both issuing from and resulting in 'courtesy' or 'gentilesse', cf. *Troilus* I.1079–85, III.5 (on which see further *Riverside* note), and Andreas 1.6.A.49, E.Rule XI, F.305, H.412. Courtliness and courting is thus a link that is commonly made: in the *Council of Remiremont* the *curialitas* and *sapiencia* of the clerks are cited as proof that they make the best lovers (73, 194). *Sapiencia* in these contexts often has a social-behavioural sense (i.e. 'decorum', 'discretion').

128.17–18 *ut precipere dignaretur*: cf. *Troilus* III.139–40: 'And that 3e deigne me so muche honoure Me to comaunden aught in any houre'.

128.19–20 For the device of introducing a work on love as having been written at the behest of its deity (a device related to the claim of commission or request by a great man or great men), cf. Chaucer's representation of his *Legend of Good Women* as a collection composed on the orders of Alceste, on behalf of the god of love, who accompanies and endorses her command (Prologue F.479–94, 556–77). In *Le roman de la rose*, Cupid is represented as assisting Guillaume de Lorris so that the latter can begin the *roman* which will contain all Cupid's laws and commands (10,549–50) and which will in due course be completed by Jehan Clopinel (the writer, in fact, of this very passage), who will give maximum publicity to this manual of love in the vernacular (10,641–3). B and Jean de Meun will, in effect, by giving useful advice and instruction in love, serving the deity in a capacity similar to that in which such clerks might serve great men – by putting their compositional skills and learning at their service.

128.22 *Rota Veneris*: commentators generally assume some transference here to Venus of the wheel more commonly attributed to Fortune, and it is certainly true that Fortune's wheel often occurs in amatory contexts (cf. *Troilus* IV.1–11), that Venus could be characterized as inherently changeable ('geery Venus': *CT* 1, 1536) and pictured as incorporating the contrasts usually associated with Fortune (cf. the 'variant' figure, with a laughing and a weeping eye, depicted in Henryson's *Testament of Cresseid* 219–31). But the emphasis here is not on the ups and downs of love, but on being 'bound' (cf. *vinculo*) to a mechanism that brings unceasing stress (cf. *omni tempore ... continuum ... timorem*). The image, then, is not of the wheel of Fortune, but of the wheel as an instrument of torture, familiar from both classical legend (the wheel of Ixion) and from Christian hagiography (the martyrdom of, most famously, St Catherine of Alexandria): see *rota* 2b in Lewis and Short, and *whēl(e* n. (1) 3 in *MED*. That wheel had already in late antiquity been used as an image of the experience of love – in Plautus's *Cistellaria* 205–8 (cited by Garbini, p. 11): 'I am beaten, tortured, pulled about, tormented and whirled up and down by the wheel of love'.

128.24-5 *pertimescunt omni tempore ... perfectus amor continuum parat ... timorem*: the fear inalienably annexed to love was axiomatic. Ovid's dictum 'Res est solliciti plena timoris amor' (*Her.* 1.12), echoed in the 'rules' of love listed by Andreas (II.8.47: 'XX. Amorosus semper est timorosus'), is cited in that same treatise (III.14) in the course of an enumerative analysis of those various fears (listed also at 1.1.2-8) and quoted by Chaucer as a commonly known attribute of love ('men rede / That loue is thyng ay ful of bisy drede': *Troilus* IV.1644-5), of which he himself therefore used the expressive oxymoron 'dredful joye' (*Parliament of Fowls* 3, *Troilus* II.776).

128.26 *virgineum chorum*: *chor-* was often used as a collective for *virgines* (cf. Regensburg, Poem 48, cited at p. 93 above) or maidens. A general sense of 'band, multitude' had already developed in classical Latin for the words *chorus* and *chorea*, and the basic sense of both [dance(-circle), round], as well as the medieval sense of 'choir', reinforced the application to 'virgins' in particular, since song-dances were a typical pastime for girls, and maidens were often found as pupils or nuns in convents.

128.26, 27 *a dextris Veneris ... sub scabello*: cf. **Psalm 109:1** (*Dixit Dominus Domino meo: Sede a dextris meis, Donec ponam inimicos tuos scabellum pedum tuorum*) and **James 2:3**, where *sub scabello pedum meorum* again indicates the humblest place.

130.2-7, 1-21 /S/ has slightly fuller versions. *Salutaciones* were important in providing the formal openings to letters, thereby announcing the literate competence of the writer in this register, and especially studied salutations can occur in love letters (as in *EDA*: see pp. 66-7 above). B later wrote a whole treatise devoted to the subject (*Quinque tabule salutacionum*), but he here gives it relatively little space and attention – knowing, presumably, that in the present context lists of salutations could 'oppress the ears' (128.31) of an audience more likely to be engaged by the potential narrative interest of the main purpose of the letter (as stated in that part of it which was in fact called the *narratio* in the dictaminal *artes*: see 132.22-4 and note). He would probably, therefore, not much have minded that these lists have been even further reduced in the P tradition – as a result of a series of scribal eye-skips occasioned by the repetitive wording within the two groups of model salutations, whose original form is evidently better preserved in /S/.

130.20 *Super aurum et topasion*: the comparison comes from **Psalm 118:127** (*dilexi mandata tua Plus quam aurum et topazion*) and is found elsewhere transferred to other contexts: cf. 'schewingis ... swettir to vs þan gold and topazion' (Pecock, *Rule* (EETS 171) 424). The topaz was 'sonnyssh bright' (Lydgate, *Churl and Bird* 250) and was described in lapidary literature as a stone 'yleke to golde' (*English Medieval Lapidaries* (EETS 190), p. 58).

130.22-6 This *tot ... quot* formula could evidently already be found, by a dictaminal professional like B, hackneyed and unsubtle: *rusticanam* and (as the variants agree) *ridiculosam*. It remained nevertheless a standard feature of a typical lover's letter, whether dictaminal model (see Text 2, IC.3-6), actual (Text 4, 1.21-2) or fictional, as at *Troilus* V.1322-3 – where it takes an uncommonly abstract turn that gives the number a logical infinitude derived from Aristotelian physics: 'I ... As ofte as matere occupieth place, / Me recomaunde vnto 3oure noble grace'. If

Boncompagno da Signa: Rota Veneris 169

Troilus's is the most interesting and thoughtful example (as suits the tragic seriousness of the context), the most extended is Machaut's virtuoso 70-line elaboration of the formula in the *Voir dit* (8941–9010). See further Hans Walther, 'Quot-tot. Mittelalterliche Liebesgrüsse und Verwandtes', *Zeitschrift für deutsches Altertum* 65 (1928) 257–89.

130.23, 29–30 *benivolenciam captare*: a technical rhetorical term for methods of gaining the goodwill of the audience. In the dictaminal field, it was one of the distinct parts of a letter (see n. to 132.22–4).

130.27–132.2 B repeats this wisdom and this advice in *Rhetorica novissima*: 'Since all women are from inherent weakness given to vanity ... even if she is old or ugly [*deformis*], her person should not be passed over [in your praises], from which progression can be made to wisdom [*sapientiam*] and character [*mores*]': see *Boncompagni Rhetorica novissima*, in *Bibliotheca Iuridica Medii Aevi*, ed. Augusto Gaudenzi, 3 vols (Bologna, 1892; repr. Turin, 1962), vol. 2, pp. 249–97 (p. 286). Verbal flattery is also recommended by Andreas (1.6.A.25–6) on the same grounds ('Women ... almost all delight in praise of their persons') and praise as a courting stratagem is common in dictaminal *artes* (Wolff, p. 27).

132.8–13 An interesting passage: though status and official position would normally be specified, B plainly thinks that, in a love letter, such job descriptions are almost comically prosaic and unromantic, unless they are chivalric. 'To/from the knight ...' is not inappropriate, that is, but any other designation would apparently sound ludicrously bathetic ('epistola deluderetur').

132.13–17 Clerics are here permitted sometimes to use some cryptic means of identifying themselves, because, presumably, the lady might not otherwise guess the identity of her admirer and might assume (like the lady at Andreas 1.6.H.478–80) that clerics should not woo. That they were nevertheless subject to the same sexual urges and romantic interests as other men was a commonplace of the topos of the universal power of love and is a point Andreas also makes: 'prone to lapses of the flesh like others', they too feel 'the prick of the flesh and the incentive to sin' (1.6.H.481) and so may make professions of love. The hammer and the anvil is found elsewhere as an image for sexual intercourse, and was probably made especially familiar by its occurrence in the *De planctu Naturae* by Alanus ab Insulis (*PL* 210.456).

132.17–20 These lines deal with the more practical reasons for omitting designations of social position which might (in providing a clue as to identity) indirectly violate the rule of anonymity in love letters. Andreas also points out that the law of secrecy is, in letters, breached by the use, not only of names, but also of anything else that might serve to identify the parties: 'all lovers are bound to keep their love hidden. Likewise if lovers keep in touch by letter, they should refrain from writing their own names ... Nor should they stamp letters sent to each other with their own seals, unless they have secret ones known to none other except themselves and their confidants' (2.7.xxi.51).

132.22–4 *salutandi ... narrandi ... dictator*: these are all technical epistolary terms. The *dictator* (literally 'dictator') is the composer of the letter (who would not always be his own scribe, or *scriptor*), and the letter itself was divided into parts, most commonly *salutatio, captatio benevolentiae, narratio* (explanation of reason for writing), *petitio* (what is asked from the addressee) and *conclusio*. On the first three, see further 130.2–21, 23, 29–30 and notes.

132.25–8 Life was more exclusively public in the Middle Ages, and a lover might lack the opportunity for private conversation with the lady he had lost his heart to. So it was not unusual to assume it is in a letter that he would announce his love – as do Troilus and Euryalus (see p. 111 above). That he might announce it to someone he had not even seen might sound to us highly improbable, but it appears to have been thought perfectly possible in a world in which identity was determined more by a public self (one's reputation and standing) and when there was less notion of a separable private one. Such love is not uncommon in romance, but can also be met with in what purports to be real life: Péronne had never seen the Machaut to whom she wrote offering a love that has been aroused by his reputation and his musical works (*VD* 103–202 and Letter 1). The twelfth-century troubadour Jaufré Rudel was said to have fallen in love with the Countess of Tripoli 'without ever seeing her' (*ses vezer*) on account of the goodness he heard her praised for (*per lo ben qu'el n'auzi dire*): cited by Waddell (*Wandering Scholars*, p. 206) from p. 21 of *Les chansons de Jaufré Rudel*, ed. Alfred Jeanroy (Paris, 1915).

132.32 *valvasor*: the lowest-ranking among those of *gentil* birth, figuring last in similar lists (cf. 'kyng ne Emperour, Duke ne kny3t ne vauesour', *Laud Troy Book*, ed. J. Ernst Wülfing, EETS OS 121, 122 (1902–3) 7311–12), and so sometimes represented as indigent (cf. Chrétien de Troyes's *Erec* 509–11). On the German saying – which is found only in the incunabulum and testifies to B's acquaintance with Germany and German (see p. 117 above) – it presumably refers to the fact that the office of porter was thought of as appropriate to an older man, no longer strong, and thus to a low-ranking *gentil* unable to find a comfortable retirement on his own estates.

134.15 *sicut ait Ovidius*: see *Ars amatoria* 1.441.

134.19 *puellarum choros*: see n. to 128.26. The verb *apprehendere* – found elsewhere with subjects such as *tremor, dolor*, etc. – implies an emotion strong enough to be physically felt.

134.22–136.5 The rhetorical top-to-toe *descriptio* occurs in other near-contemporary works in the context of epistolary and verbal wooing in order to flatter the lady: *Facetus* 215–34, Baudri's Poem 200 (which, however, being a letter of chaste love to a nun decorously confines itself to the head and descends no lower than the lips: 57–64). The most significant parallel in English is the similarly systematic description of his lady by the mourning knight in Chaucer's *Book of the Duchess* 817–960 (itself heavily indebted to Machaut's *Roy de Behaigne* and *Remede de Fortune*).

134.23 *tamquam stella matutina*: Baudri's epistolary *descriptio* contains a similar comparison: 'Non rutilat Veneris tam clara binomia stella, Quam rutilant ambo lumina clara tibi' (200.55–6). The reference is to the planet Venus, prominent in the night sky as both the evening and the morning star, and commonly figuring as a simile (in a usage that is biblical in origin: cf. **Ecclesiasticus 50:6**, *Quasi stella matutuina*) for excellence that 'shines out': cf. 'Seintes, þe whiche

Boncompagno da Signa: Rota Veneris 171

as morowe-sterres schyneden in the dirke ny3te of þis worlde' (*Orologium Sapientiae*, ed. C. Horstmann, *Anglia* 10 (1885), 353/29). Comparisons between greater and lesser luminaries were a common way of asserting the superiority of the lady's beauty over that of other women, and Chaucer introduces his description of Blanche in a similar way: 'Among these ladyes thus echon ... That as the someres sonne bryght Ys fairer, clerer, and hath more lyght / Than any other planete in heven ... so hadde she / Surmounted hem alle of beaute' (817–26).

134.25–6 *deficiebat spiritus meus*: cf. **Psalm 76:4**: *Memor fui Dei ... et defecit spiritus meus.*

134.26 *aurum contortum*: i.e. gold wire (or *fildor*), commonly used to convey the beauty of fair hair in a female; cf. 'Hir sonnyssh here, bri3ter þan gold were' (Lydgate, *Temple of Glas*, ed. J. Schick [EETS ES 60], 271); cf. *Susannah* (in *Scottish Alliterative Poems*, ed. F.J. Amours [STS 27, 38; 1892, 1897] 192). The descending descriptions in Baudri and *Facetus* likewise start with golden hair: 'Crinibus ... fulvum minus arbitror aurum' (200.57), 'Aurea cesaries tibi' (215).

134.28 For the eyes like stars, cf. Baudri 200.55–6.

134.30 *labra grossula et rubencia, cum dentibus eburneis*: cf. 'Labra tument modicum calor et color igneus illis' (Baudri 200.61), 'Labra tument modicum rubeo perfusa colore ... candent albedine dentes' (*Facetus* 221, 223). *collum rotundum et gula candissima*: cf. 'gula ... plus nive candet' (*Facetus* 225), 'Hyr throte ... Semed a round tour of yvoyre' (*BD* 945–6).

136.1–2 The breasts are regularly mentioned in these descending itemizations: cf. 'pulchra mamilla' (*Facetus* 229), 'Rounde brestes' (*BD* 956).

136.2–5 The shoulders, arms, hands and nails are more briefly summarized in *Facetus* (232: 'Brachia cum manibus laude probanda vigent'), and even Chaucer has run out of rhetorical steam by that point (*BD* 952–5: 'Ryght faire shuldres ... and armes ... Fattyssh, flesshy ... Ryght white handes, and nayles rede'). B has not, his enriching comparisons continuing at full pitch; moreover, his crystal nails that shed radiance over the whole body provide a less perfunctory link into the concluding generalities as to the rest of the physical person (*tocius stature*) than occurs in *Facetus* (233: 'Cetera membra quidem proprio funguntur honore') and *BD* (959: 'al hir lymmes ... pure sewynge'), ensuring that the finale of 'and all the rest' is a shining climax rather than a diminuendo.

136.6–15 The coupling of beauty and *sapientia* in compliments to or eulogies of women was standard (cf. Andreas 1.6.G.323–4), and descriptions such as the present one regularly include a similar transition from outer pulchritude to social-moral excellence (designated in Latin by *sapientia*); cf. *BD* 985ff. ('To speke of godnesse, trewly she ...'), and see Text 3, n. to 43–71.

136.13 *aliqua deitate potiri* (cf. *Rhetorica novissima* p. 286: 'unde videmini obtinere quandam speciem deitatis'): claims that the woman was excellent enough to seem a goddess were common; cf. Knight's Tale *CT* I.1101–2 ('I noot wher she be woman or goddesse ...') and *Troilus* I.101–5.

136.13–15 *supplico ... precipere*: this was the standard initial request of the courtly wooer; cf. *Troilus* III.131–46.

136.21–2 *in Alamania*: see n. to 132.32 above.

172 Fictional and Instructional Models

136.25-8 The lover is similarly encouraged to ignore the initial negative the woman will almost invariably give at *Pamphilus* 75-6 ('She ... may first most harshly refuse you. But this tartness is of little importance') and *Facetus* 183-4 ('Forsitan imprimis dabit aspera verba puella, / Sed cito que prius est aspera mollis erit').

136.28-35 On these five 'causes', see pp. 120-1 above.

136.33-4 Cf. Andreas III.66: '[I have never heard of] any woman who did not pressingly demand gifts ... and who did not impose delay on a love already begun if there were no full tally of gifts'. At a time when women of gentle status had few ways of adding to their personal wealth, it is not unlikely that such acquisitive motives did sometimes show themselves.

138.2-4 Women are often represented in medieval literature as reacting sceptically to praise of their beauty; cf. Andreas I.6.A.28 and p. 92 above.

138.4 *semina mandas arene*: the expression had become proverbial; it had been used with similar amorous application by Ovid ('quid arenae semina mandas?': *Her.* 5.117) and is also so used at *Pamphilus* 561 ('Who but a lunatic will cast his seed in the sand ... his plaint sees no relief').

138.13-14 Love was often treated as a religion parallel to that of Christianity and the man here implies that, in dying for his 'goddess', he will die a martyr's death, and thus go straight to heaven (without preliminary purification in purgatory). For similar references to amorous martyrdom, cf. e.g. *Troilus* IV.623, *Romaunt of the Rose* 1875.

138.17-20 The images are meant as figures of, or comparisons for, the lady's unwavering resolve: the stem of the reed was a proverbial image for smooth regularity (Walther, *Proverbia* I.7136b, III.17081), and the tamarisk that flowers even in the desert was familiar from **Jeremiah 48:6** ('salvate animas vestras, Et eritis quasi myricae in deserto') as an image of what does not wither, and so to be contrasted with hay, an image (similarly familiar from biblical usage) of what quickly dries and dies ('quasi foenum ita arescet': **Isaiah 51:12**; '[evil-doers] tanquam foenum velociter arescent': **Psalm 36:2**).

138.20-2 That is, the existence of things that please by their unlikelihood should not encourage the man to hope for an equally improbable change of heart by the lady. 'Les prunes [dates] de Damas étaient notamment réputées' (Wolff, n. 21, p. 42).

138.23-140.15 On B and *transumptio* (tropes, especially metaphor), see further pp. xxvi-xxxi in Core's 'La *Rota Veneris*'. See also pp. 135-6 in Rita Copeland, *Emotion and the History of Rhetoric in the Middle Ages* (Oxford, 2021).

138.26-9 B, a popularizer who aimed to make rhetoric available to the non-elite on the social and educational scale, is interestingly alert to different levels of socio-literary sophistication. Cf. 130.22-6: there he refers to a usage perhaps a little naïve or plebeian ('rustica'), but perhaps also sometimes effective; here he emphasizes metaphor as belonging to a more or less universal rhetoric of love and therefore not confined to, or only appropriate in, courtly circles.

140.4-6 Wolff (n. 23, p. 42) points out that Quintilian, *Institutio oratoria* 8.6.23-4 is the source of this definition.

140.17-18 *specialem ... tractatum*: the reference is almost certainly to the essay that appears as Book 9.2 (*De transumptionibus*) in the *Rhetorica novissima*, where the

Boncompagno da Signa: Rota Veneris 173

same and similar examples and points as occur at 138.29–140.6 can be found (ed. Gaudenzi, p. 281).

140.23-9 The *vir* takes up the lady's figures but, ignoring the signification she had attached to them (her unshakeable resolve not to respond to his amorous overtures), gives them a new application as flattering compliments on her beauty, eloquence and attractiveness. There is a kind of rhetorical game or battle being played here, a display of tactical skills in the use of rhetorical arts.

140.27 *rore vestre gracie*: an example of the amorous appropriation of religious language: dew was a common symbol of grace in Christian theology (see *deu* n. 2 in *MED*, where the citations include several examples of the common expression 'dew/deu/deuh of grace').

140.31 *donarium*: the word was applied in ecclesiastical usage to endowments, offerings, oblations, etc., and so has theological connotations.

140.31-3 This request, worded so as to give the lady something she can consent to without overt compromise to her honour, shows knowledge of the literature of love letters, real or actual: cf. Euryalus's request and its imitation in the Söflingen letter discussed at pp. 112–13 above.

142.2 'Labor omnia vincit' was a familiar expression, though B is evidently aware of its source in Virgil's *Georgics* ('labor omnia vincit / improbus': 1.145–6), which likewise occurs with reference to shameless persistence in attempts on a lady's virtue at *Pamphilus* 71 (in the assurance given by Venus that 'labor improbus omnia vincit'). It is here implied to give false reassurance of success and is coupled with an image of attempted access (the knocking at the door), whose use in the Bible, the lady implies, might similarly have encouraged over-reliance on the assurance of admittance there given ('to him that knocketh it shall be opened': **Luke 11:9, Matthew 7:8**; cf. **Song 5:2**). The *domina* uses the same dialectical tactic at 138.20-2.

142.3-9 The *domina* borrows from biblical wisdom and theological principles. The *vane cogitaciones* are an echo of **Psalm 93:11** (*Dominus scit cogitationes hominum, Quoniam vanae sunt*). But then the man's tactic is represented as working, and in granting (at 142.11–12) his request merely for an interview (cf. 140.31–3), she gives as her reason her duty to save him from the toils of despair (*desperacionis laqueum*: 142.6). Despair of God's mercy was well known as the last and most dangerous stage of sin (specifically the sin of spiritual sloth), and the priest who rebuked sin had always to prevent the sinner falling into any consequent *wanhope* or *despair* (cf. *Piers Plowman* B.V.279–81, 442–5), for that was a 'dampnable synne', especially 'horrible' and 'perilous', 'it is cleped synnynge in the Holy Goost' (Parson's Tale, *CT* X.693–4).

142.7-12 Such elaborate devices for making communication look innocent and casual are not uncommon in fictional love affairs (such as that of Euryalus and Lucretia) and reflect the more public life of the age and the resulting lack of opportunities for private meetings.

142.14 *post factum*: i.e. after love has been gained (see 134.8–13), which, B knowingly implies, can now be assumed.

174 Fictional and Instructional Models

142.14–16 Lovers exchanging recollections of their encounters as if they were dreams is something explained by B, not as a nod to the need for some secrecy in love letters, but to the enhancement of the delight of love by the rhetorical embellishments lovers enjoy using. The pretty indirection of the dream can be compared with the *jocunde transsumpciones* of metaphor (138.24), and both to the more general luxuriating in amorous language, whether spoken (*suavissimis colloquiis*: 142.27) or written (*jocundissimas literas*: 142.14), that B points to and shares. Real lovers recognized the charm of this oneirological game: the letters of Machaut and Péronne include a similar exchange of apparently psychic dreams (*VD* L29, L31).

142.19–144.2 A highly literary passage, in which the gorgeous scene-painting constitutes an exercise in *descriptio* on a common topos comparable with that used in the rhetorical evocation of beauty at 134.19ff. The opening biblical allusion contributes to the beautification a special note that reaches full resonance in the comparison at 7.3 (itself a biblical echo) to the earthly paradise: *Dum ... cursum* recalls **Wisdom 18:14** in the version familiar from the Introit to the Mass for the octave after the Nativity: *dum medium silentium tenerent omnia et nox in suo cursu medium iter haberet* (*Missale Romanum* ed. Robert Lippe, 2 vols (London, 1899), I, 27). The beloved encountered in her sensuously exotic *cubiculum* is a topos found in both sacred and secular literature: cf. *Sir Launfal* 263–348, and the Cambridge Song (on which see Dronke, *Medieval Latin*, vol. 1, pp. 271ff.), cited by Purkart (n. 45, p. 101): 'intra in cubiculum meum / ornamentis cunctis onustum' (stanza 1, 3–4).

142.20 *causa venandi*: an appropriately romantic rationalization. Hunting and/or hawking was a rhetorical topos in itself. A favourite diversion among the gentle classes, its associations with courtly pastime caused it to be often selected as a setting (for a dream or other adventure: cf. *Somer Soneday* 1–39), an event to initiate or develop a narrative (cf. *SGGK* Fitt III), or a pretext (cf. 6.14–17 above).

144.1 *celatura varia*: the phrase has biblical resonance, as it occurs in the account of Solomon's temple: *parietes ... variis caelaturis* (**3 Kings 6:29**), *in angulis autem columnarum variae caelaturae* (**3 Kings 7:31**).

144.2 *paradiso deliciarum*: biblical in both form and content: *In deliciis Paradisi Dei fuisti* (**Ez. 28:13**). See further nn. to 152.29–32, 154.34–156.4.

144.21 *Preciosa* (all MSS: *Speciosa*) *forma pre filiabus hominum* is from **Psalm 44:3** (*Speciosa forma prae filiis hominum*).

144.28–9 Echoes liturgical expressions used of virgins married to Christ: cf. 'anulo fidei suae subarrhavit me ... et collum meum cinxit lapidibus pretiosis', 'anulo subarrhavit me Dominus': (quoted by Garbini (n. 35, p. 93), following Purkart (nn. 51 and 52, pp. 101–2), from, respectively, the service for St Agnes, *Breviarium Romanum* (Rome, 1923), pp. 934–5, and the consecration of virgins in *Pontificale Romanum* (Turin, 1941), p. 118).

144.32–3 *Plorans ploravi ... in tenebris meum stravi lectum*: from **Lam. 1:2** (*Plorans ploravit*) and **Job 17:13** (*Et in tenebris stravi lectulum meum*).

146.5ff. The lament of the pregnant girl is a topos found elsewhere, and one version which contains material similar to that found here occurs in *Carmina Burana* no. 126 (cited by Purkart, n. 56, p. 102).

146.9-10 *reserantur claustra pudoris: claustrum pudoris* occurs with reference to the virgin birth in a hymn for Christmas Eve by Saint Ambrose (pp. 91-2 in Brittain, *Penguin Book of Latin Verse*): 'Alvus tumescit virginis, / Claustrum pudoris permanet' (lines 9-10). The expression obviously refers to the hymen.

146.11 *non est similis dolor meo dolori* is a quotation from **Lam. 1:12** (*videte Si est dolor sicut dolor meus*), a verse especially well-known because used in the service for Good Friday as if spoken by Christ (*Sarum Breviary*, col. dcclxxxvii) and so often elsewhere likewise attributed to Him (see e.g. Lyric I, 99 in Duncan, ed., *Medieval English Lyrics and Carols*).

146.14-15 *maria promittebas et montes aureos et universa que celi ambitu continentur*: ultimately from Sallust ('maria montesque polliceri coepit': *De coniuratione Catilinae* 23.3), but the application to amorous blarney, together with the epithet *aureos*, occurs also in the thirteenth-century rhetorician Conrad of Mure: 'Quando vir scribit uxori ... utatur ... yperbolicis verbis ... promittat aureos montes, aurea flumina, aurea secula': *De Summa de arte prosandi*, ed. W. Kronbichler (Zürich, 1968), p. 122. The phrasing is also influenced by **Esther 13:10** (*fecisti ... quidquid celi ambitu continentur*).

146.15 The catching of fish (an activity more familiar because practised by a wider range of persons than today) was an image often used of amorous entrapment (cf. *Pamphilus* 85), and Andreas actually associates the word *amo* with *hamo* [fishhook] (1.3.1-2). The image is here reinforced by that of bird-catching (another activity common in an era when supplies of fresh meat were limited and one often referred to in contemporary literature: cf. *LGW* F.130-9).

146.23 B evidently (and interestingly) assumes that, if an affair did not result in marriage, it may well have been not because the man was simply amusing himself and did not desire to marry the lady, but because the woman herself refused his offer, considering that her interests were better served by marriage with someone more eligible (144.25) or by entry into a convent (148.23).

146.3ff The woman left vulnerable and anxious during a prolonged absence of a man was a situation commonly portrayed in the literature of love. The plight is here assumed to be as incident to the wife (cf. Franklin's Tale, *CT* V.806-61) as to the mistress, though model letters or codes of love do not usually concern themselves with marital relationships (cf. n. to 154.1-156.6 below and to husband's letter at Text 2, 1B on pp. 204-5 below).

146.31-2 Adapts (as often) biblical phrases to amorous purposes: cf. **Psalm 39:1** (*Exspectans, exspectavi Dominum*) and **Psalm 37:11** (*Dereliquit me ... lumen oculorum meorum*). *desiderium meum*, as used of a beloved, is also a literary usage (and occurs, as Garbini points out (n. 44) in Cicero and Catullus). The opening phrase from Psalm 39:1 occurs also in one of Queen Kunhuta's letters to her absent husband (see p. 22 above): 'Expectans expectavi cor nostrum cum gaudio vestrum reditum' (Battista, 'Queen Kunhuta's Epistles to Her Husband', p. 275).

148.1-2 The reference is to **Genesis 8:10-11**.

148.3-4 The reference is to an emotional death that is denied the relief of physical death: cf. '[I] euere dye and neuere fulli sterve' (*Troilus* IV.280).

148.4 (cf. 154.17-18) This example of the legendary fidelity of the turtle dove is, as Wolff points out (n. 36, p. 49), from one version of the *Physiologus*, which

176 Fictional and Instructional Models

was a medieval compilation of the supposed habits (and their moral-allegorical significance) of different creatures – and in which the turtle dove was always characterized as true to death to a single mate (see *The Middle English Physiologus* (ed. H. Wirtjes, EETS OS 299), 515 and cf. Chaucer's *Parliament of Fowls* 577–88). The comparison B here gives to his female writer was used by other women: Péronne uses it in a letter to Machaut (*VD* L29) and it also occurs, in a form very similar to B's, as Wolff observes (n. 9, p. 101), in the sixth of the verse love letters in the Tegernsee MS (on which see p. 103 above).

148.9 Rome, Biblioteca Angelica, MS 505 here inserts a further *revocatio*, from a wife to a husband, followed by the husband's reply. The former letter has borrowings from the *Rhetorica antiqua*. The same MS inserts another pair of letters at 150.3 below. An additional letter is also found at the end of the *Rota* in MSS M and S. All these added letters are edited by Josef Purkart: 'Spurious Love Letters in the Manuscripts of Boncompagno's *Rota Veneris*', *Manuscripta* 28 (1984) 45–55. Like the additions in the present text (see p. 123 above), they testify to an instinct to pad out an evidently popular work which was widely imitated and plagiarized (Purkart, 'Spurious Love Letters', p. 47).

148.12 An allusion to **Cant. 2:12** (*Vox turturis audita est in terra nostra*), with the superimposition of another bird (*immo pocius cuculi*) with less romantic associations (with exposure or unwelcome news). The resulting effect of mock solemnity is of a kind only achievable through this sort of literary allusion and adaptation.

148.17–22 A multiple contrast in few words – between an out-of-doors, youthful, secular, colourfully clothed, courtly and melodious world and a black-clad, aged, enclosed and grating one – enhanced by the two types of song associated with the two scenarios: the psalms 'croaked out' and the words announcing the Requiem Mass for the dead (*Requiem eternam*) on the one hand and, on the other, the burgeoning plant life figured in the festive song 'Palma nata paradisi redimita floribus' – which has not been identified, and for which editors have given different translations. Wolff, commenting that 'l'allusion est peu claire' (n. 38, p. 50), translates 'Palmier né au paradis et ceint de fleurs' and suggests (unconvincingly) that this may be a metaphor for a lady and introduce a love song. A metaphor it would certainly seem to be, but of a type more commonly associated with the Virgin Mary and other biblical matter, and the line may well indicate a lyric sung in celebration of some religious holiday. Purkart simply leaves the Latin untranslated, but his punctuation (with a comma after *paradisi*) suggests he construes it similarly. Garbini, however, translates 'Nata da una palma, ornata dei fiori del paradiso' (which is grammatically sounder with regard to *paradisi*).

148.20 *in timpano et in choro*: the phrasing is suggested by **Psalm 150:4** (*Laudate eum in tympano et choro*), but the reference is to a contemporary pastime especially associated with courtly life: the carol or dance (often circular) performed to a song with refrain (see Stevens, *Words and Music*, pp. 162–71 and 196).

148.27–8 The expression is biblical: the words are those Christ utters in the Garden of Gethsemane (*Tristis est anima mea usque ad mortem*: **Matthew 26:38, Mark 14:34**).

Boncompagno da Signa: Rota Veneris 177

150.1–2 *cum primum tintinabulum pulsabitur*: in an age when timepieces were rare, the hour of day was often identified by the bells for the various church services: cf. *CT* VI.661–3 and, in an amorous context, I.3653–5 ('And thus lith Alison and Nicholas / In bisynesse of myrthe and of solas, / Til that the belle of laudes gan to rynge').

150.3 The Rome MS here inserts (in an inappropriate context) a pair of letters in which a man who declares his longing to see her receives a brief response from a woman assigning a place and time. See n. at 148.9 above.

150.4–34 *monialis ... petitur pro amica*: the wooing of nuns is something Andreas strongly deprecates as contrary to all laws, divine and human (I.8.1–6), though he registers awareness of a rhetoric assumed to be of avail in seducing them. B too assumes that some men do address nuns – and that there is a rhetoric which may serve them: the pair of letters here in fact has parallels with the dialogue *Me tibi teque mihi (De clerico et moniali)* and belongs to a tradition for discussion of which Purkart (n. 70, p. 103) refers to H. Walther, 'Zur Geschichte eines mittelalterlichen Topos', in *Liber Floridus*, ed. B. Bischoff and S. Brechter (St Ottilien, 1950), pp. 153–64. B is not writing a manual or rulebook of love, and his stance is more morally neutral than that of Andreas: he provides models by which a nun may deliver an indignant refusal (150.5–15) and/or a capitulation (152.1–11). See further p. 121 above.

150.5–9 Her pledge of poverty (renunciation of personal property), chastity and obedience was the prime feature of the profession made by the *monialis* if and when she effected the transition from novice to professed nun. Her status as a 'bride of Christ' (cf. *desponsata ... celesti sponso*) and her 'death to the world' signalled by the *velum nigrum* ('velamen sacrum quo cognoscaris mundum contempsisse': Consecration of Virgins in *Pontificale Romanum*) were well-known facts assumed to have a reality rather more than metaphorical, for they were (and often still are) ritually effected in a virtual marriage ceremony, including bridal white dress and receipt of a ring, and in echoes of the burial ceremony (once involving such things as a shroud and the singing of the funeral chant of *De profundis*), which reinforced the reminder still given that she must henceforth be 'dead to the world, to your parents, and to yourself': see Danielle Rives, 'Taking the Veil: Clothing and the Transformation of Identity', *Proceedings of the Western Society for French History* 33 (2005) 465–86.

150.5 The expression derives from the liturgies associated with holy women: cf. 'ipsi sum desponsata, cui Angeli serviunt' in the Consecration of Virgins at *Pontificale Romanum*, p. 118 and in the service for St Agnes at *Brevarium Romanum*, p. 935.

150.15 See n. to 138.4, where the idiom *semina mandas arene* is similarly used by the woman to deprecate a persistence by the man which does in fact (as it does here) bear the fruit of results declared to be so impossible. The proverb is here coupled with an expression which has biblical resonance: cf. *In vanum laboraverunt* (**Psalm 126:1**).

150.16–152.11 The exchange constitutes a rhetorical triumph for the man (in countering a negative from the woman) similar to that represented by the paired letters at 140.21–142.12. It is dialectic skills that are here on display. He gives a witty counter to the woman's points, which he picks up one by one, beginning with her interpretation of the *velum nigrum*, and signalling his response to other points by the formula *Ex/pro eo quod asseritis/dicitis* (150.24, 28–30). The woman acknowledges the dialectic game when she declares herself beaten by the *necessarium ... et irrefragabile argumentum* his answer has constituted (152.3–4). Her capitulation to the witty riposte from the man is, here and in the earlier exchange, marked by her arranging a subterfuge (152.6–8; cf. 142.6–11) under which they can meet – a subterfuge that satisfies the conflicting demands of both her public honour and her private desires. Each mini-sequence thus forms a little narrative whose conclusion is projected into a picturable future devised by feminine wiles. It is consistent with the popular stereotype of woman as innately duplicitous (cf. Wife of Bath's Prologue, *CT* III.399–402). It is typically she rather than her lover who forms the schemes: it is May who devises the ingenious ploy in the Merchant's Tale (*CT* IV.2107–216), and the concluding moral drawn to a *fabliau* with a similar plot runs 'Et en tiel manere le seignour fust deceu par coyntise d'une femme, qar ... toutz les femmes de monde sont plains de maveistee et tresone' (Kristol, *Manières de langage* 15/35–7: see p. 194 below).

150.21-2 Cf. *Facetus* 227–8, where the catalogue of visible charms leads to the declaration 'Hec mihi significant quantum sint candida membra, / Que tegis interius vestibus ipsa tuis'. The numerous parallels in points and wording between *Rota*, *Facetus* and *Pamphilus* indicate the writers were working within a shared amorous rhetoric and stock of topoi, whether or not the work of any of them was actually known to the other(s).

150.26-7 *celestis sponsus animam et non carnem requirit*: the witty use of the principle to justify carnality has parallels elsewhere: cf. *Decameron* III.8 (cited by Purkart, n. 73, p. 103) 'la santità ... dimora nell'anima e quello che io vi domando è peccato del corpo'. The biblical quotation that follows is from **Psalm 113:16**.

152.2 Cf. **Psalm 18:11** (*Iudicia domini ... super mel et favum*), which is given the same amorous application in the opening addresses of Tegernsee VI and *EDA* Letter 39 ('Dilecte sue super mel et favum dulci'), both of which are cited by Wolff (n. 45, p. 53).

152.4 *cupitis fruamur amplexibus*: the phrasing is again biblical, the words being those attributed to the *meretrix* at **Prov. 7:18** (*fruamur cupitis amplexibus*).

152.9-11 For the joking reference to sex as a currency in which payment can be made, cf. Shipman's Tale: 'For I wol paye yow wel and redily / Fro day to day, and if so be I faille, / I am your wyf; score it upon my taille ['tail'; tally], / And I shal paye as soone as ever I may' (*CT* VII.414–17).

152.17-21 The use of cosmetics – to enhance or fake the red-and-white complexion of the typical medieval beauty – was always highly deprecated, and the more mature woman here indirectly disparages the superior charms of her rival by referring to them as created by these means. Garbini (nn. 56 and 57, p. 94) points out that B deals again with the cosmetic properties of the *cedrus* [cedar, citrus] at the beginning of his *Cedrus* (see p. 121 in the edition provided in Rockinger, *Briefsteller und Formelbücher*) and that *bambacelli* are defined in the *Dizionario etimologico italiana* (Florence, 1975) as cloths for the application of rouge.

Boncompagno da Signa: Rota Veneris   179

152.29-32 See p. 121 above on this little gem of a letter, in whose one expressive sentence witty naughtiness comes packaged in imagery of exotic beauty. The orchard setting and the images of flowers and fruit recall the sensuous associations of love with flowers and fruit at 142.32 and at 154.35 ff, associations strengthened by the *Canticum Canticorum* (in which the beloved is figured as a *hortus conclusus*: 4.12), a seminal text in the rhetoric of love, and one which is echoed in the conclusion to the letter (cf. **Cant.** 4:16: 'Surge, aquilo; et veni, auster; Perfla hortum meum, et fluant aromata illius') – where, however, the effect is more impish, since, in deference to the code of secrecy observed in love letters, the winds are used as code for the husband (the chill north wind) and the lover (the more genial south wind).

154.1-158.12 These five letters appear only in the incunabulum, where they have been added in (before the epilogue at 158.13) from B's *Rhetorica antiqua* (see p. 123 above).

154.1-156.6 These two letters are from a sequence in the *Rhetorica* entitled 'De revocacionibus', and have been included here obviously because the situation of the woman writing to an absent husband/lover was one common in life and literature, and a model letter for her had already been included in the *Rota* (at 146.31 above). The picturing of a woman so circumstanced as a wife (whose tragic plight may be aggravated by a property and children to support) forms the only occasion on which (here and potentially at 146.31) a marital letter is included in the *Rota*, since romantic love was regarded as quite separate from marital relations (however affectionate) and as involving a separate epistolary rhetoric. There are no other letters to a husband in the *Rota* and none at all to a wife. Cf. n. to 146.31.

154.15 *in tenebris paupertatis et umbra mortis*: the biblical echo lends solemnity to the pathos of the letter (cf. **Psalm 106:14**: *Et eduxit eos de tenebris et umbra mortis*).

154.17-156.6 This fine letter was rightly admired by Dronke, who edited it (from MS P) in vol. 2 of his *Medieval Latin* (pp. 483-4) and discussed it in vol. 1 (pp. 251-3).

154.17 *turbans potum*: i.e. with tears. Cf. 148.7, where the same detail occurs in the course of the same comparison with the turtle dove, on which see n. to 148.4.

154.19 *quem diligit anima mea:* the expression is biblical (see **Cant.** 3:1, 3).

154.25-6 *ac ipsum ... astringo*: Wolff (n. 51, p. 56) speculates there may be allusion to some kind of picture (pressed to the heart, presumably), though it would seem to be an 'image' in the psychological sense that is at issue and the wording is actually indebted to **Cant. 1:12** (which both she and Purkart cite): *Fasciculus myrrhae dilectus meus mihi! Inter ubera mea commorabitur*. He translates *ipsum ... sub quodam spei remedio* as 'son image bienfaisant', which is not a convincing rendering of that last phrase (which Purkart translates 'aided by a little hope').

154.30 *tyronensis* is the emendation suggested by Purkart of *aronensis*, which Wolff (n. 52, p. 56) defends, explaining 'adolscentule regni aronensis' as 'women of the realm of Aaron', i.e. of Palestine.

154.33-4 B is expanding with strongly imagined sensual specificity **Cant. 2:6** (repeated at **8:3**): *Laeva eius sub capite mea, Et dextera illius amplexabitur me*. B uses this and another borrowing from the *Canticum* (at 3–4) to evoke an inner world that is more real and more sensuous even than the sensible outer one.

154.34–156.4 The orchard setting and its attendant details (rivulets, fruit, flowers, birds, fragrance) recall the similar 'dream' recounted in the earlier letter (see 142.20–3) and the invitation sent at 152.29–32, all three passages reflecting the common association between love and the sensual delights of the earthly *paradisus* [garden] (*paradiso* at 13; cf. *paradiso deliciarum* at 7.3), an association strengthened by the imagery of the *Canticum canticorum* (see n. to 152.29–32), whose whole world (as reflected in the orchard encounter) has been introduced, it seems, by the two passages from it on which the present letter is structured (see nn. to 154.26 and 154.33–4).

156.5–6 The bold statement of the strictly impossible prompts one to ask whether or not this is simply one of the hyperboles typical of the rhetoric of love. It does in fact follow from the foregoing points, which have vividly evoked and explored the power of the imagination to create its own inner reality in defiance of outer facts – and love does indeed tend to centre precisely on an inner 'image' of the beloved rather than his/her actual person. This image is the 'he' (*illum*) that here lies firmly enclosed (*circumclusum*) in the heart (154.24–5) and which prompts the definition of 'hope', the hoped-for scenario made present to the mind, as a *refugium ymaginarium* (27). The vivid inner image (created from memory and desire: 23) then takes the form of a nightly dream of a union claimed to be more real than that enjoyed by other women in an actuality whose reality is deceptive (*Sed fallimini*: 32). The imagination is thus asserted to create a reality that is independent of outer facts – and independent even of the lover (and the infidelities the woman both assumes and is untroubled by: 30–1). His image within her is part of her life, not his, and this 'he' lives or dies with her and her love (156.5–6). Self-sufficient independence (from the lover himself as from all else) is reflected in the form of the piece, which quite escapes the constraints of a supposed letter and the second-person address proper to an epistle. The lover is never present in the second person, but only in the third, for the piece belongs to an 'I' alone, who needs no 'you' for her love. The only second-person address is the rhetorical one to the women who think they enjoy him (154.32) – an address which in fact makes no sense in the context of a supposed letter to the lover; and the last sentence even negates the supposed purpose of 'revocation' under which heading the letter appears (see n. to 154.1–156.6), since the speaker virtually declares that it makes no difference whether he comes back or not: he will always and infallibly be with her.

156.7–20 A letter relevant to love has again been picked out from a sequence relating to a more general category in the *Rhetorica antiqua* (cf. n. to 154.1–156.6), where this one occurs as the second epistle under the heading *De excusacionibus*. To brag about favours enjoyed was a cardinal sin against courtly love, for it breached the rule of secrecy that protected the lady's name and honour. On the sin of such 'avaunting' see *Troilus* III.295–302, a passage which represents the offence as common and as often based on untruths ('And, for the more part, al is vntrewe / That men of ȝelp': 306–7). B here provides a model letter for a man

Boncompagno da Signa: Rota Veneris 181

so accused – rightly or wrongly we do not know, and the question is irrelevant to the epistolary needs B aims to serve. This model astutely advises the defendant to take refuge in the common outraged denunciation of slanderous tongues and malicious gossip (see pp. 60–2 above). A model letter for the same occasion (from Paris, BN, Lat. 8654, fol. 10) is cited by Waddell (*Wandering Scholars*, p. 144): 'To his lady, that it has come to the ears of her goddess-ship that he boasts of her favours – far be it from him'.

156.11 *agriffolium* is explained as a medicinal herb by Purkart (n. 89, p. 105), who cites Forcellini, *Totius latinitatis lexicon*. But the context seems to require something more baneful, and Du Cange's *Glossarium* gives 'Gall, pomme épineuse'; there may also be some conflation in sense with 'acrifolium', a reputed 'tree of ill omen', according to Lewis and Short.

156.18–20 The trait here ascribed to the asp belongs to the bestiary tradition (see n. to 8.22–4) and to its basis in **Psalm 57:5–6**: *Sicut aspidis surdae et obturantis aures suas, Quae non exaudiet vocem incantantium Et venefici incantantis sapienter*. Wolff (n. 55, pp. 57–8) further cites p. 105 in Gabriel Bianciotto, *Bestiaires du Moyen Âge* (Paris and Stockholm, 1980) and, on this and B's other references to the asp, Sutter, *Aus Leben und Schriften*, p. 99, n. 1; Purkart (n. 90, p. 105) refers, for 'extensive references', to Virgilio Pini, 'Scheda per Boncompagno', in *Dai dettatori al novecento* (Turin, 1953), p. 61, n. 3.

156.21–158.12 These two letters have been taken from a section in the *Rhetorica antiqua* headed *De suasionibus et dissuasionibus in matrimoniis contrahendi* in which they are letters 22 and 34. They have been selected to offer alternatives between gender applicability and between representing the repulsiveness of an aged partner as perfectly bearable (for the sake of money) and as quite unbearable. The matter is thus again one on which the manual itself remains neutral, simply catering for the rhetorical needs of contrary stances on the part of potential letter-writers: cf. n. to 150.4–34.

156.24–5 A forcefully succinct and contextually apposite formulation of a piece of cynical wisdom (that everything comes down to money) not in itself uncommon; Purkart (n. 91, p. 105) compares Horace, *Satires* 2.iii.94–8.

156.32–158.9 B returned in more serious mood to the ills of old age in his last work, *De malo senectutis et senii* (written some time in the 1240s). See the sections headed *De penis senum et miseriis* and *De uxoribus senum* (cited by Purkart, n. 92, p. 105) at pp. 55–7 in Francesco Novati, ed., *Rendiconti della Reale Accademia dei Lincei*, ser. 5, vol. 1 (1892). The repulsive bodily traits and sexual impotence of the old husband is a frequent topos: for comparable details in a late and especially vivid example, see Dunbar's *Tua Mariit Wemen and the Wedo*: 'ane bag full of flewme ... ane scutarde behind ... Bot soft and soupill as the silk is his sary lume ... With gor his tua grym ene ar gladderit all about / And gorgeit lyk tua gutaris that war with glar stoppit' (91–9).

158.6 *osculabitur vos osculo oris sui*: the phrasing comes (with pointed irony) from **Cant.** 1:1 (*Osculetur me osculo oris sui*), a verse that describes a kiss sweeter than wine and fragrant oil.

158.8–9 Old husbands were indeed regularly represented as inevitably jealous: cf. 'Jalous he was, and heeld hire narwe in cage, / For she was wylde and yong, and he was old / And demed hymself been lik a cokewold' (Miller's Tale, *CT* I.3222–4).

158.13ff. The epilogue by Venus serves not only to complement her initial instigation of the *epistolarium* (128.18–20), and so complete the narrative frame B has given it, but also to put it into the larger context of communications between covert lovers: unpacking a comparison found elsewhere (cf. Heloise 'crebris me epistolis visitabas': Letter 2, p. 140), Venus points to the letters as substitutes for the 'visits' often not possible (158.15) and implicitly equates them with the personal intermediaries listed at 20–1. Her words are followed by an epilogue by B in his own voice, in which those kinds of message are followed by the 'messages' (cf. 160.14) conveyed by gestures. See further p. 120 above.

158.18–22 Intermediaries were indispensable in covert liaisons and are regularly included in representations of archetypal love affairs in the persons of, for instance, Ami in *Le roman de la rose*, Pandarus in *Troilus* and Brangaene in *Tristan*. Venus here lists those available to women in particular.

158.22–3 The sentiment (that no amount of even Argus-eyed watch can prevent a woman from contriving at some point to enjoy the union with her lover she is set on) is found elsewhere – 'ffor who may holde a thing that wol away?' (*Troilus* IV.1628; cf. *CT* IV.2107–24, IX.144–53).

158.25–7 That is, jealous watchfulness – regularly thought of as not only pointless but also perverse (cf. *CT* I.3158–66) – deserves to obtain the assurance it seeks of the infidelity it suspects. It was represented as an uncourtly and churlish vice: cf. the description of the Sardinians in B's *Palma* (where they are treated, as here and in the *Rhetorica antiqua*, ed. Rockinger, *Briefsteller und Formelbücher*, vol. 1, p. 143, as typifying jealousy): 'Sardos zelotipie vitio et conditione servili esse proscriptos totus predicat orbis' (ed. Sutter, *Aus Leben und Schriften*, p. 122). The three symbols of the cuckold listed here – *cornua* [horns], *cuculus* [cuckoo], *cucurbita* [gourd] – are all discussed (under the heading *De transumptionibus*) in the *Rhetorica novissima* (ed. Gaudenzi, p. 284), where B speculates on what logic may underlie the signification (as does Wolff, n. 58, p. 60).

160.1–3 Publication was regularly represented as the consequence of urgent pleas by others: cf. 'DOCTORUM ANNUENS PRECIBUS' (and note thereto) in the initial heading given to the *Rota*.

160.3–6 Wolff (n. 59, p. 61, and n. 5, p. 71) cites Ovid's *Tristia* 2.353–4, Catullus's Carmen XVI and Martial's Epigram I.4.8 (all insisting on a distinction between the writer's continence in life and the licentiousness of his matter), as well as the appropriation of the last by B's contemporary Baudri of Bourgueil in his verse letter to Godfrey of Rheims (see p. 86 above): 'Musa iocosa [bawdy] fuit moresque fuere pudici' (99.197). But B's point is, I think, a little different and more relevant to our own present focus of interest: as a rhetorician, he derives pleasure from the verbal representations rather than the deeds of lovers, and he interestingly links that pleasure with a feature of love itself, in which representations in the imagination often give a keener pleasure than do the carnal actualities.

160.5–6 The *serenissime Capuane* remains unidentified.

160.8–12 Garbini points out (p. 18) that B claims in the *Amicitia* and in the *Rhetorica novissima* to have written an entire treatise on gestures and movements of the body. His disquisition here supplements his interest in verbal communication. He evinces an acute awareness of a whole language of the body, at work in both the signs and gestures lovers give to each other (160.14–162.5) and the outer bodily and behavioural evidence by which their love may be detected by others (162.11–13). For the importance of signs and gestures in amorous relationships and the sense of them as an alternative or auxiliary 'language', cf. *Facetus* 192: 'Nutibus et signis sepe loquatur ei' [let him speak to the girl often in nods and signs].

160.14–33 *Nutus* is used in *Facetus* to refer to a sign made by a man to the girl (see previous note), but in B's more investigative taxonomy it is applied to small movements made typically by *women* and expressing or inviting sexual interest in various subtle ways. Some of these little gestures are minutely observed, as is the pleasure taken (by the displayer and the viewer) of such charms as a white throat, pretty hair or a good figure. This close observation of female behaviour matches the psychological insights made in the categorization at 136.25–35.

162.1–16 *Indicium* is used in a narrower sense at 2–5 (where it refers to a 'signal' inviting action: 5) than at 10–13, where it is an 'indication' in the more general sense – something by which a lover involuntarily betrays his love to the outside world. In that larger sense, *indications* are equivalent to the *signs* lovers may unconsciously give of their feelings, as B acknowledges (8–9). Wolff uses the word 'symptom' to render the latter type of 'sign'.

162.12 Garbini (n. 62, p. 95, citing Du Cange) points out that *hora* (the reading in /S/) could have spatial reference to 'district, vicinity'. The incunable reading *coram* yields non-sense.

162.29–32 *spiritus* (a fourth-declension noun) could be singular or plural. The word has in this passage occurred before this point only but consistently in the genitive plural *spirituum* (22–6); so the plural verbs (*suspenduntur, revertuntur*) are perhaps more likely to be correct than the singular forms found in /S/. Assuming the noun is plural ('breaths' = 'breathing'), it may indicate conflation or confusion with the *spiritūs* [spirits] that, in medieval physiology, were 'þynne sotil bodies' generated in 'þe fume of blood in þe hert', and thence circulated as a vitalizing force to other parts of the body (*The Follower to the Donet by Reginald Pecock*, EETS 164, 41/29). For it is of *spiritūs* in that sense that the heart is the source and 'principalem sedem' [principal seat]: cf. 'Hys sorwful hert gan faste faynte / And his spirites wexen dede' (*BD* 488–9). Some conflation of *spiritus* = breath with other senses of the word [life force; rarifed and quickening medium] may well explain the assumed connection here with the heart (rather than the lungs): cf. 'The herte ... ʒeueþ to euery member of þe body blood, or lijf, spirit, or breeþ, and hete' (MS Welcome 564 34b/a: cited in *MED spirit* n. 6).

162.33–164.1 (cf. 160.16–18) It is noteworthy that B represents body language as no more reliable than words: it is quite as capable of abuse and deceitful intention.

164.2–7 The true lover typically finds himself tongue-tied in the presence of his mistress and unable to deliver any speech he has carefully prepared in advance (cf. *Troilus* III.83–4). But B was not alone in feeling it absurd that he should, because of such amiable bashfulness, entirely let slip his opportunity to speak. Purkart and Garbini compare Andreas 1.6A, where he similarly describes lovers so at a loss 'that they forget those carefully devised remarks which they have arranged ... in their minds', but adds that it is simple *fatuitas* in anyone manly and educated (*audacem et sapienter instructum*) to remain silent in such circumstances. B's little anecdote here does not, like that at 162.2–5, illustrate the usefulness of the sign under discussion, but the inappropriateness of relying on it when plain speech is possible. As a rhetorician, he believes in words, and by temperament brings some gamesmanship to love, as does Chaucer's Pandarus, who similarly believes that it is silly and spiritless to be so overcome as to neglect one's chances to speak (*Troilus* II.1499–1500). The lady's rebuke is thus introduced as one to be noted (164.5).

164.9–10 Solomon was always regarded as epitomizing wisdom, and the wording here echoes one of the books attributed to him: *Da mihi sedium tuarum assistricem sapientiam* [Give me wisdom that sitteth by thy throne] (**Wisdom 9:4**).

164.10–16 Lines 13–14 refer to what was indeed the standard way of sanitizing the sexual love that was clearly recognized to be the actual subject of the Song of Songs. Cf. the *Regula* of Leander of Seville (cited by Purkart): 'Cantica canticorum ... carnalem illecebram terreni amoris insinuant ... per species actionis Christi et Ecclesiae charitatem figurant' (*PL* 72.884). This kind of allegorization was well known, since it was regularly applied to the whole of the Old Testament. But the argument here is not, I think, that B should escape the charge of lasciviousness by such figural readings as had served to exonerate Solomon's Song (but which it would be difficult to impose on the *Rota*); the logic is rather that the pious principle which prompts such allegories – the principle of interpretation *in meliorem partem* (13), i.e. putting the best possible construction on dubious matter – should prompt in his case acceptance of the excuse he has already given: that the *Rota* was circulated in response to the prayers of friends (*sociorum precibus*; cf. 162.1–3 and n.). The apology is, however, surely somewhat playful, and B's reference to himself in the third person probably involves some contextually appropriate play on the sense of his name ('Good companion'), which he has lived up to by obliging his friends *amicabiliter* and in a racy manner.

MSS M and S add at the end of the *Rota* a letter of longing from a man. See n. to 148.9 above.

TEXT 2

London, British Library, Harley 3988.
How to Pay Court in Anglo-French: A Model Epistle and a Model Conversation

Instruction in French

The first of the literary arts required for writing a love letter in medieval England was, as we have seen, the mastery of a foreign language. The European lovers envisaged by Boncompagno in the twelfth century were expected to school their tongues to Latin in their letters to one another. Things might have become a little less difficult for English letter-writers when Latin was replaced in the epistolary realm by French, which was the main medium for private, commercial and official correspondence over the thirteenth and fourteenth centuries and into the fifteenth. French had entered English culture with the Norman Conquest, when it became the language of the ruling class, and the gentry remained familiar with Anglo-Norman for some time – but increasingly less so. Instructional aids became increasingly common, and these reached a kind of culmination over the turn of the fifteenth century.[1] At this time there appeared some especially significant codices in which model conversations formed a new type of instructional aid now regularly added to teaching material of a more established kind, such as formularies (collections of actual letters serving as compositional examples) and model letters (both regularly preceded by a treatise on letter-writing), *nominalia* (French vocabulary sets) and treatises on French grammar and orthography.[2]

---

[1] On the different kinds and categories of teaching material, see pp. 340–47 in Andres M. Kristol, 'Le début du rayonnement parisien et l'unité du français au moyen âge: le témoignage des manuels d'enseignement', *Revue de linguistique romane* 53 (1989) 335–67; on the history of their emergence, see Douglas A. Kibbee, *For to Speke Frenche Trewely: The French Language in England 1000–1600* (Amsterdam, 1991), with findings summarized in Christel Nissille, *'Grammaire floue' et enseignement du français en Angleterre au XVe siècle: les leçons du manuscrit Oxford Magdalen 188* (Tübingen, 2014), pp. 42–96, 186–8; and for a full list of 'matériaux didactiques', arranged under the eighty-odd relevant manuscripts, and chronological and generic tables, see Andres M. Kristol, 'L'enseignement du français en Angleterre (XIIIe–XVe siècles): les sources manuscrites', *Romania* 111 (1990) 289–330.

[2] On the ten manuscripts containing these conversations, see pp. xi and xvii in *Manières de langage*, ed. Andres M. Kristol (London, 1995). References are to page and line number of the texts as they appear in this edition.

The contents of Oxford, All Souls, MS 182 may serve as a preliminary illustration. The items date from the late fourteenth and early fifteenth centuries. The first half (fols. 1–190) is in Latin and comprises a copy of the *Registrum epistolarum* of Archbishop Peckham and other ecclesiastical letters. The second part (fols. 191–375) is in Anglo-French and consists of instruction in and models of French. Under the first heading one finds a treatise on writing and pronouncing French by one 'Coyrfully', an interestingly detailed discussion which distinguishes *inter alia* between different regional varieties of French (e.g. Gascon, 'Gallic' and 'Romanic' [Picard]) and which was used by Barclay in his *Introductory to wryte and to pronounce Frenche* (1521). This tract was of demonstrable service to at least one other contemporary scholar in this area: it was used by the author of another item in the manuscript – the interestingly titled *Donait françois*, a French grammar compiled by one John Barton in the early fifteenth century. 'Donet' was the term used for the standard basic Latin primer, and what is here presented as its French equivalent indicates an assumed market amongst those for whom French was now as foreign as Latin but who felt that French, like or in some ways instead of Latin, was now the educational and cultural entrée into worldly and social success. The *Donait françois* is accompanied by lists of French verbs and their principal parts, and similar lists of conjunctions, adverbs and particles also occur in the manuscript, as does a copy of the vocabulary aid composed in octosyllables by Walter Bibbesworth, c. 1245.

In the category of models or examples of French in use, one finds two sets of proverbs (the second from classical and biblical sources); a safe conduct of 1399 (added at the end in a later hand); a little allegorical analysis of love as a castle, a *Chastel d'Amurs* (with, for instance, foundations and walls of, respectively, *amer lealment* and *Celer sagement*); a number of petitions (to, amongst others, the King, the Chancellor, and the Archbishop of Canterbury); and letters (relating to regal and governmental affairs and to the administration of the archdiocese of Canterbury) dating from the years 1390 to 1412. The letter collection consists largely of files or registers compiled by Roger Walden (the King's Secretary 1392–5), supplemented by files from the correspondence of the Prince of Wales (later Henry V) and from the archdiocesan office. These letters – which include correspondence relating to, for instance, Richard II's second marriage and the Glyndŵr campaign – are of some significance for the history of public affairs. The Latin and French parts of the manuscript confirm the linguistic situation in the epistolary realm at this date: though Latin might still be selected in some contexts, especially for ecclesiastical affairs, French is now the normal medium in most spheres (governmental, administrative, clerical, private, commercial).³ Actual letters assembled into formularies are one aspect of the many imbrications of art and actuality to be found with regard to medieval letters: the correspondence collected in this manuscript is clearly 'being used for the instruction of outsiders',⁴ as guides to form and expression.

In the same category of items that provide 'examples' of French usage are two versions of the new kind of instructional aid mentioned above: model conversations aimed at illustrating what is termed the 'manere de parler' in various circumstances. There are extant three different versions of such 'French conversation' manuals: one written (according to a colophon found in the best copy: see below) in 1396 at Bury St Edmunds; another compiled c. 1399; and a third produced in 1415, which is presumably the work of one William Kingsmill, whose school (for teaching French) is advertised in one dialogue (76/19–77/11).⁵ The Oxford All Souls manuscript contains the compilation of 1396 and also the only complete version of the 1399 compilation, which appears elsewhere only in bilingual fragments.⁶

The situations represented in the model dialogues indicate not only that mastery of French was assumed to be an asset within England and in dealings between Englishmen (as well as with Frenchmen in travel or business on the continent), but also that speaking in French was not confined to the upper classes, in what Kristol aptly calls 'conversation soignée' (*Manières de langage*, p. xix), but might occur in the contexts of the working life of those who provided goods and services. It clearly indicated education and respectability in all sorts of circles. The school of William Kingsmill advertised at the conclusion of the 1415 manual offers its services to adults as well

---

³ Cf. *Anglo-Norman Letters*, ed. Legge, p. ix.
⁴ *Anglo-Norman Letters*, ed. Legge, p. xvii.
⁵ On Kingsmill, see further M. Dominica Legge, 'William of Kingsmill: A Fifteenth-Century Teacher of French in Oxford', in *Studies in French Language and Medieval Literature Presented to Mildred K. Pope* (Manchester, 1939), pp. 241–6.
⁶ The foliation for the manuscript items (parts of some of which have been displaced) is sometimes discontinuous: for the order and folio location of the contents see p. x of Legge's *Anglo-Norman Letters* and cf. pp. 33 and 40 of the seminal paper by Stengel ('Die ältesten Anleitungsschriften'), in which were published most of the linguistic items (Barton's *Donet*, the 1399 manual of French vocabulary and model dialogues, Coyrfully's treatise and the list of conjugated French verbs). Barton's *Donet* has since also been edited by Thomas Städtler: *Zu den Anfängen der französischen Grammatiksprache: Textausgaben und Wortschatzstudien* (Tübingen, 1988), pp. 128–43. The proverbs were published by J. Morawski, ed., *Les diz et proverbes des sages* (Paris, 1924). Bibbesworth's manual was available in William Rothwell, ed., *Walter de Bibbesworth: Le tretiz* (London, 1990). The *Chastel d'Amurs* is found in a number of manuscripts and has been partially edited by Meyer in his 'Notice et extraits du MS 8336 de la Bibliothèque de Sir Thomas Phillipps á Cheltenham', *Romania* 13 (1884) 497–541 (pp. 504–5); see item 227 in Ruth Dean, *Anglo-Norman Literature: A Guide to Texts and Manuscripts* (London, 1999). For the conversation manuals, see Kristol's *Manières de langage*, where all three versions are edited. Extracts (with translations) from Bibbesworth and Barton are included in *Vernacular Literary Theory from the French of England*, ed. Jocelyn Wogan-Brown *et al.* (Cambridge, 2016), pp. 52–6 and 73–4.

as children and to those in domestic service or trade as well as to gentlefolk (76/27–33, 79/3–18), and the huge range of possible students (though probably exaggerated in order to attract custom) is consistent with that of the situations and speakers of the dialogues in the manuals. There was, of course, a practical need as well as a cultural advantage at issue. Commercial transactions and other business might have to be conducted across the Channel and/or among French speakers. In fact, the earliest example of French conversation for teaching purposes occurs in the dialogues included in a manual on French usage which was intended precisely for tradesmen: entitled *Le livre des mestiers*, it was originally composed in Dutch c. 1340, and later translated into English by Caxton, who plainly assumed there would be a market for it.[7]

The French in the *Manières de langage* has the usual Anglicanisms that constitute what Kristol defines as a regional variety of French closely related to its origins in Anglo-Norman (*Manières*, pp. xx, xxvi–xxx). But though he is himself careful to avoid any suggestion of a bastard French, it is clear that contemporary Englishmen who were familiar with continental French were not so scrupulously unsnobbish and did look down on what Chaucer calls French from 'the scole of Stratford atte Bowe' as being not the authentic 'Frenssh of Parys' (*CT* I.125–6). The author of the 1396 version takes care to assert at the opening to his colophon (quoted below, p. 193) that the French he has illustrated is that spoken 'es parties dela le mer' [in the regions across the Channel].[8] His manual is in fact, in vocabulary and syntax, richer and more diverse than are the two slightly later ones (see *Manières*, pp. xxx–xxxi, xlviii), and it is from the 1396 version that our own excerpt comes. His overt concern is to impart, not just the basic 'parlez-vous' competence offered by the subsequent redactions of the manual, but also some appreciation of the elegance of authentic 'douce francés', as he terms it in his exordium, where the expression is followed by a relative clause that trumpets its superiority: 'qu'est la plus beale et la plus gracious langage et la plus noble parler après latyn de scole que soit en monde et de toutz gentz melx preysé et amee que nulle autre' (3/9–11).[9] His advertisement, that is, stresses not just the utility, but the intellectual sophistication (comparable with 'school Latin') that comes with a mastery of French. One of his dialogues scripts a meeting with a Frenchman, to whose speech his

---

[7] *Dialogues in French and English by William Caxton*, ed. H. Bradley, EETS ES 79 (1900).
[8] Similar, though less earnest, claims to 'authentic' French are found in other manuals and are reflected in the adaptation (occurring over the fourteenth century) of distinctively Anglo-Norman spellings to their continental counterparts (though the anglicized pronunciation was unaltered): see Kristol, 'Début', pp. 348–65. The regularization to continental norms, however, often went no further (see next note).
[9] There are, however, some very Anglo-French and uncontinental forms here: the errors and inconsistencies in gender and /e/ for /ie/ in 'melx'. See pp. 197–8 below.

interlocutor responds with enthusiastic compliments ('Vous parlez bien et graciousement doulx franceys') and assertions of the consequent pleasure of conversing with him in what is again described as 'vostre beal langage, quar est le plus gracious parler que soit en monde et de toutz gentz meulx preisés et amee que null autre' (32/26–9). When he is in turn complimented on his own proficiency, he explains that he has been used to speak 'entre lez gentils de ce pais ycy'.[10] The perhaps rather snobbish enthusiasm for French that distinguishes this manual from its successors is here again evident, and one notes the implication that it offers its readers a French that will not be scorned by speakers of 'Frenssh of Parys' (the city from which the *monsieur* hails: 32/22). It also confirms that communication in French was a mark of gentility; and since the fashions of the 'gentils' were regularly aped by those who worked for their living, and who were anxious to court the custom of their social betters by suggesting some comparable genteelness, it was evidently also used in those circles, which are also well represented in the dialogues of this manual.

London, BL, Harley 3988

The best copy of the 1396 *Manière de langage* appears to be the one in London, BL, Harley 3988 (*Manières*, p. xxi). This manuscript is another codex devoted to French instruction and/or models of the type commonly found in this period. It consists of the *Manière* of 1396 (fols. 1–23ᵃ), which is followed (fols. 23ᵃ–24ᵇ) by four brief items in French verse and prose (three of which are also found associated with this *Manière* in the Oxford manuscript described above) and (fols. 25ᵃ–26ᵃ) the aforementioned dialogue with the Frenchman (which appears as part of the *Manière* in other manuscripts),[11] and, after some blank pages, some evidently originally separate material (fols. 28–67) consisting of a French treatise on letter-writing and a collection of model letters (plus one or two bills and petitions), also in French. As in the Oxford manuscript, therefore, the Harley 3988 *Manière* is found alongside model letters (in this case specially devised to serve as models; in the other actual letters put together into a formulary), the combination providing two forms of interpersonal communication (oral and written) assembled for the non-specific general audience to which art addresses itself.

---

[10] The text in the manuscript used by Kristol has 'gentz' for 'gentils'. We quote from the version in Harley 3988 (the manuscript on which we focus here in Text 2), where the section is amongst items found after the colophon (see below); 'gentils' is also the reading in the dialogue as it appears in the Oxford All Souls manuscript (see Stengel, 'Die ältesten Anleitungsschriften', 7/5–6).

[11] See items 135, 283 and 284 in Dean, *Anglo-Norman Literature*, where the Oxford manuscript references follow the later of the two folio numerations.

The *ars dictaminis* (the treatise and the models) is the work of one Thomas Sampson, whose *opera* were written during a period extending over the second half of the fourteenth century and into the reign of Henry IV in the fifteenth. He was a teacher associated with the University of Oxford, where it is clear that many students were by now engaged in career-oriented courses in correspondence, the composition of deeds, how to keep lay courts and to enter pleadings. Sampson (who taught both Latin and French and took private pupils) provided instruction in all these areas, as well as offering beginners' courses in Latin, arithmetic and also French. College statutes of this period required French to be used at mealtimes and in ordinary conversation, and there also emerged a rule that Latin should be construed by turns into English and French. Among the model-letter collections Sampson composed are some in which the items come in paired Latin and French versions, and these must have served as teaching exercises. Students were also required to copy out model letters and to memorize them for recital.[12] So model letters were intended to serve the purposes of education towards clerical careers as well as for use by or on behalf of persons actually placed in the relationships and circumstances they portray. For teaching in the *artes dictaminis* had always been especially relevant to students who might hope to begin or develop their careers by gaining posts as secretaries, a large part of whose duties lay in composing and writing letters.[13]

Treatises on letter-writing and/or model-letter collections (in Latin and/or in French) by Sampson are preserved in many manuscripts, all of which are surveyed and excerpted by H.G. Richardson in his *Letters of the Oxford Dictatores* (pp. 360–439). According to him, the treatise in Harley 3988 is closely related to an earlier one by Sampson (preserved in Cambridge University Library, Ee.iv.20),[14] itself a later revision of the one found in London, BL, Harley 4971, which is the earliest extant version (c. 1355). The recast in our manuscript (Harley 3988) probably dates from the 1380s.[15] The model letters which follow are basically those which follow that earliest version of

[12] The information here given on Sampson and on university teaching practice is drawn from H.G. Richardson, *Letters of the Oxford Dictatores* (Vol. II of *Formularies Which Bear on the History of Oxford*, ed. H.E. Salter, W.A. Pantin and H.G. Richardson (Oxford, 1942)), pp. 333–6. For a full account of him and his work (together with a useful bibliography), see also Martha Wetterhall Thomas, 'Medieval Origins of Corporate Communication: Sampson of Oxford and the *Method of Letter-Writing*', *Corporate Communications* 13 (2008), 112–23.

[13] Cf. Waddell, *Wandering Scholars*, p. 136: '[dictaminal teaching] guaranteed, without the fatigues of classical scholarship and the long discipline of the law, to make a young man an admirable secretary'. See further Ian Cornelius, 'The Rhetoric of Advancement: *Ars Dictaminis, Cursus* and Clerical Careerism in Late Medieval England', *New Medieval Literatures* 12 (2010) 289–330 (especially pp. 293–4, 305–9).

[14] There are excerpts (with translations) from this earlier treatise by Sampson in Wogan-Brown *et al.*, eds., *Vernacular Literary Theory*, pp. 62–8.

[15] See Richardson, *Letters of the Oxford Dictatores*, pp. 360–3 (Harley 4971), 370–6 (Ee.iv.20), and 408–10 (Harley 3988) for an account of and excerpts from the Sampson material in these manuscripts.

the treatise in Harley 4971, which is a Bury St Edmund's manuscript containing a miscellany of material relevant to the business and administration of the abbey, including instruction in French language and French correspondence. Those letters (all of which come paired with a *responsio*) are arranged in order of social rank (beginning with royalty and descending down to burgesses, merchants, etc.) and divided into three sections: laymen; church officials; and (interestingly) women. That third category consists of letters that might be received or sent by *dominae*, women who are the mistresses of households. The last item in this section is a request received by such a woman from her sister: a request for temporary accommodation to escape her father's efforts to push her into an unwanted marriage alliance. The collection unfortunately breaks off at this point, though it is evidently incomplete. The close of the letter comes in a partial line introduced by a bracket in the right-hand margin, a habit regularly observed by the scribe when the close of a letter comes at the close of a gathering. But a gathering has plainly been lost, for the next begins, not with the *responsio* that otherwise regularly follows each letter, but with the next item in the manuscript (on the conjugation of French verbs). The equivalent series in Harley 3988 has a *responsio* to the sister's letter, together with seven further letters.

The letters between the sisters are reproduced below, together with the two that follow in Harley 3988: a husband's letter to his wife, and a letter from a lover (which takes the form of verse). We have included the sisters' and husband's letters partly for the purposes of contextualization of the lover's, and partly because those of the sisters contain matter relevant to our subject, and the husband's provides a useful illustration of the different models considered appropriate for the married man (to his wife) and the lover (to his beloved).

In the Harley 3988 redaction of the Bury series, there are some additions and omissions, and within the letters that are shared, though the main points and key expressions are substantially the same, the wording is often different – slightly, but sufficiently so to show that they cannot have been copied direct from the earlier version in Bury St Edmund's. The changes often involve additions and expansions, so that the letters are frequently a little longer than their earlier counterparts. Moreover, the collection is supplemented at the beginning by a series of (genuine) privy seal and signet letters, whose contents indicate that they were added c. 1396[16] (the same year the *Manière* gives in its colophon). So it is a fuller collection that is often dif-

---

The treatise found in London, BL, Royal 17B.47 (fols. 42ʳ–48ʳ), *Modus dictandi brevis et utilis datus a Sampsone* (which has cognates in other manuscripts), has been edited by Martin Camargo at pp. 148–68 in his *Medieval Rhetorics of Prose Composition: Five English 'Artes Dictandi' and Their Tradition* (Binghamton, NY, 1995).
[16] See Richardson, *Letters of the Oxford Dictatores*, p. 408.

ferently worded and slightly expanded as regards the shared items – though the series does for the most part reproduce the same letters in the same order and with the same content. At the point where the Bury St Edmund's manuscript breaks off, Harley 3988 continues, as indicated, with a reply to the sister's letter, letters from a husband and a lover, and five further letters (before a colophon announcing that the letter series has now been completed and bills and petitions will follow: fol. 64^r): from a *domicella* [gentlewoman, attendant] to a *domina*, from a sister to an armigerous brother, from a *mercator* to an *officiale*, from an *armiger* to a bishop, and from a bishop to a vicar.

There are good reasons for doubting that the Bury collection originally continued (after the *responsio* to the sister's letter) with the same seven letters as follow in Harley 3988. The last three do not involve a female sender or recipient and so would not belong under the heading governing the letters at the point at which Bury breaks off; moreover, all seven letters come without *responsiones*, and lack of *responsio* otherwise occurs only in items added by Harley 3988 and not found in the Bury manuscript. So we cannot assume that the love letter also appeared in Bury. This is unfortunate, for love letters do not seem to have had a regular place in the model collections intended for Oxford students. They do occur in Latin collections with other affiliations, however. In the Orleanese models, the section devoted to letters between fellow students is 'often followed by a group of correspondence between lovers – *amicus amice, amasius amasie*, etc. The lady is warned to beware of the boys (*ne credat iuuenibus*); under the name of Thisbe, she is exhorted to elude her guards by night'.[17] But no love letters occur in the anthology from the Oxford *dictatores* provided by Richardson, and none are mentioned by him in his comprehensive survey of the corpus. The epistolary exercises he does reproduce, and the relationships reflected in them, are by no means without human interest, but where such interest arises from private or personal bonds it comes mainly in what is by far the most common type of letter it was assumed (by all *dictatores* everywhere) that a student would write on his own personal account: a letter to members of his family begging for funds. The typical student is envisaged as likely to find himself in financial difficulties, 'and many were the models which the *dictatores* placed before him in proof of the practical advantages of their art'.[18] They were written largely to fathers, but mothers, sisters, brothers and uncles are also asked to intercede or supply funds 'sanz escient de mon piere' [without my father knowing].[19]

---

[17] Charles H. Haskins, *Studies in Medieval Culture* (New York, 1929), p. 31 (with manuscript and printed sources listed in n. 2).
[18] Haskins, *Studies*, p. 8.
[19] Richardson, *Letters of the Oxford Dictatores*, p. 391, no. 46B.

The models assembled by Sampson contain many examples of such funding crises, and one cannot but relish the compiler's appreciation of the situation of young men let out on a long leash for the purpose of studying, of the scapegrace and profligate habits characterizing their time of life – and of the likely responses to their applications. For to such letters, the *responsio* follows a predictable pattern. The fathers reply with anger and displeasure, the mothers send a little something 'your father does not know about' (*sans escient de vostre pere*) and a married sister may likewise afford some succour, 'but don't tell my husband'.[20] There is in fact more recognizable human nature in these exchanges than in the love letter, which is (intentionally) a mere tissue of standard phrases and conceits that each and any lover might use.

As to the Harley 3988 copy of the *Manière* of 1396, it is unique in two important particulars. It alone preserves the above-mentioned colophon, whose opening claims 'authenticity' for the compiler's French, which has been informed by residence in France:

Mon treshonouree et tresgentil sire, ore Dieux en soit regraciez, j'ay achevee cest traitis au reverence et instance de vous, et a mon escient je l'ai traitee et compilee sicomme j'ay entendu et apris es parties dela le mer. (*Manières*, p. 45)

Honoured and good sir, I have now, God be thanked, brought to an end this treatise written in your honour and at your request, and to the best of my ability have I composed and compiled it in accordance with what I have heard and learned across the Channel.

This afterword resembles a letter (as dedications often do) in being a written second-person address (to the man who had commissioned the work) and ending with what was called the 'date' (the place and time of writing): 'Escript a Bury Saint Esmon en la veille de Pentecost l'an du grace mil trois cenz quatre vinz et sesze' [Written at Bury St Edmunds on the eve of Pentecost in the year of Our Lord 1396]. Here, then, we have (by coincidence or otherwise) another connection with Bury St Edmunds.

This version of the *Manière* of 1396 also contains some passages in which the content diverges to a fairly significant extent from the counterparts in other manuscripts.[21] Amongst these is the passage edited below, in which a man taking *hostel* requests the company of his hostess's young daughter,

---

[20] The father-son pair in Harley 4971 is reproduced by Richardson (*Letters of the Oxford Dictatores*, pp. 360–1), as is its variant in Harley 3988 (pp. 409–10); for the mother-son pair that also occurs later on in the series, see pp. 363 (Harley 4971) and 410 (Harley 3988). For the sister's letter, see Paris, BN, Lat. 1093, fol. 82ᵛ (referred to by Waddell, *Wandering Scholars*, p. x). For comparable father-son correspondence in other epistolary models composed by Sampson, see Richardson, *Letters of the Oxford Dictatores*, pp. 367–8, 370–1, 377–8, 389–90, 397, 401–2, 418–19, 421–2; for mother-son correspondence, see pp. 374–5, 390–1, 422–3; and for application to siblings, see pp. 403 and 404–5, and to an uncle pp. 425–6.

[21] Kristol edits in an appendix (*Manières de langage*, pp. 37–43) the scenes from Harley 3988 that differ from those found in the tradition represented by his base text (Cambridge University Library, Dd.12.23).

chats her up and takes her to bed with him. In the counterpart to the scene in other manuscripts, he sends for the hostess to keep him company, and his 'conversation' with her consists in his recounting to her a bawdy story, a typically racy and witty *fabliau*.[22] The *conte* itself, like some poems and songs that also appear here and there in the treatise, represents an interesting instinct to include in the manual the *bones choses* (literary *divertissements*) which, according to Barton's *Donait*, were amongst those matters whose medium was characteristically French and which therefore made a knowledge of French useful to the Englishman.[23] In such areas, where love is a common theme, there naturally occur incidental models for the expression of romantic sentiment or eloquent phraseology for wooing or compliment. The drinking song sung by the traveller in Harley 3988 is replaced in other versions by a love song developing a standard conceit:

> Tresdoulx regarde amerousement trait
> Tant de douçour fra mon coer entrer,
> Quant lez miens oilx te poent y acountrer,
> Que tout mon sank me fuit et vers toy trait.   (Kristol, *Manières*, 9/6–9)

> When my eyes find you before them, the sweetest sight draws such sweetness into my heart that all my blood flees from me and towards you.[24]

The adulterer in the naughty tale told to the hostess can give his lustful desires a similar courtly flourish:

> Ore, dame ... mes que vous ne desplese, je su si dolourosement naufré au coer de l'ardant amour que pieça j'ay eu et enqore ay devers vous que je ne puisse pas longement endurer ne vivre sanz consolacion de vostre tresgraciouce persone. Pur quoi, ma tresdouce dame ... eiez pitee de ma dolour ou autrement vous serrez cause de ma mort.   (Kristol, *Manières*, 13/35–9).

> My lady ... if it does not displease you to hear it, I am so grievously wounded at heart by the burning love that I have long had and still have for you that I cannot long survive without the solace of your most gracious person. So, my dearest lady, have pity on my pain or otherwise you will be the cause of my death.

More relevant to the passage we reproduce below, however, is the specific space twice allotted in the 1399 dialogues to how to 'come on' to a bar-

---

[22] For this scene, see Kristol, ed., *Manières de langage*, pp. 12–17.
[23] Stengel, 'Die ältesten Anleitungsschriften', p. 25/5–6.
[24] The song survives with music in Modena, Biblioteca Estense Universitaria MS α.m.5.24 (Lat. 568, *olim* IV.M.5): see Elizabeth Eva Leach, 'Learning French by Singing in Fourteenth-Century England', *Early Music* 33 (2005) 253–70, esp. pp. 256–8.

maid or a girl plainly of lower status than a courtly *dame*. The language in those passages is pretty crude, no attempt being made in that manual at the courtly conceits the earlier one (with its love of 'doulx franceys') deploys even for the hostel girl. The first (headed by Kristol *Conter fleurette à une demoiselle*) reads:

> Ditez, demoiselle, parlez a moy. Damoiselle, ou demourez vous? Voullez estre refete? Je vous ay veu aileurs. Ditez moy, que est vostre nom? Damoiselle, vuillez vous aler ovesque moy et vous serrez m'amye? Et que vous donnerey je pour estre m'amye? Damoiselle, ditez en bonne foy. Certes, vous ne averez plus pour moy. (Kristol, *Manières*, 55/1–5)
>
> Come on, talk to me, damsel. Where do you live? Can I get you a drink? I have seen you somewhere before. Tell me, what is your name? Will you come with me and be my girlfriend? And what shall I give you to get you as my girlfriend? Tell me honestly. But certainly, you won't get any more out of me than what I've offered.

And, under Kristol's heading *Faire la cour*, one finds a second little tip on how to proposition in French:

> —Damoiselle, bien soiez vous trouvez. Ou fustez vous nee? Ditez moy, que est vostre nom? Damoiselle, ou demourez vous? Dites, ou serrés vous trouvez? Damoiselle, n'avés vous point nul amy? Voulez vous estre m'amye? Damoiselle, je vous purroie bien aymer.
> —Sire, vous plaise il a boire? Sire, je le vous donrey volentiers.
> —Damoiselle, a Dieu vous commande. (Kristol, *Manières*, 56/15–20)
>
> —Damsel, it's nice to meet you. Where do you come from? Tell me, what's your name? Where do you live? Tell me where I can find you. Do you have a boyfriend? Do you want to be my girlfriend? I could treat you well.
> —Do you want a drink, sir? I'll serve you one gladly.
> —I bid you goodbye, damsel.

In fact, in the situations portrayed in the manuals, we are not dealing with courtly or romantic love proper – which figures (as fact or sham) only in the inset song in the earlier manual and among those of *gentil* rank in its inset *conte*. The love-talk in the model dialogues themselves is addressed to the female personnel of a hostelry. The manuals frequently concern themselves with hostelry, how to purchase amenities there, organize comforts, etc.; and it is pretty clear that procuring some female company (and whatever more can be got from her) comes under the heading of how to make oneself comfortable in a hostel – which is the context in which the courting dialogues occur. One will need to be able to order food, arrange a fire and sweet-talk the girls. The *damoiselle* in these dialogues belongs, that is, in the conceptual set of hostel comforts. This is most apparent in the manual of 1415: a good fire, various drinks and a list of dishes figure in the dialogue with the patroness, whose list of goodies leads into a verse passage beginning:

Et puis dez oues, bone candelle,
Et a vostre lyt une damy[se]le beal. (Kristol, *Manières*, 73/31–2)
And then eggs, a good candle and a pretty girl for your bed.

By comparison with the 1399 manual, the man in the passage below reproduced (from the Harley 3988 version of the 1396 manual) is, as indicated above, provided with talk of a courtlier kind, including a poem and a song, in his smarming. The compiler clearly wants to provide some models of stylish gallantry (and Kristol actually heads the episode *Aventure galante*). But neither that title nor the courtly blarney (what is termed in the passage itself 'parl[er] ... tout courtoisement') can disguise the shameless exploitation of a young girl or the lowness of the man's aim, which is explicitly said to be to charm her into bed with him: 'd'amourasser la damoiselle ... pour avoir ... sa pucellage' [to make up to the girl in order to deprive her of her virginity]. No matter how hard one tries to read the scene in the ethical context of its own time, it cannot but prove deeply offensive to a modern sensibility, anachronistic though it may be to judge it by such standards. The girl is in every way at disadvantages that preclude opposition: she is evidently very young (lines 208.13–20), socially inferior, on unequal terms with his superior status (which forms an intimidating and overawing whole of which his courtly talk is simply one element), taught to be complaisant to her superiors and compliant to guests. She says very little beyond 'A vostre comandement, mon signeur' or the equivalent. It is impossible to suppress the distress and indignation with which everyone today will respond to the scene. So much for *doulx franceys*. The replacement of the scene in other manuscript copies by one marginally less offensive may indicate that the compiler himself – or his redactor(s) – experienced or feared distaste. The bawdiness of the *fabliau* is a characteristic of the genre, and any repugnance caused by it results from consciousness of the one woman who is its specially summoned audience, something which makes it come across with a nasty masculine leer. The woman herself, however, even when questioned as to her response, reacts with remarkable sang-froid or worldly wisdom, and registers neither shock nor giggly coyness nor embarrassment. She copes very well: but she is a grown-up and probably experienced in the ways of such guests.

Whether or not the variant reflects some dissatisfaction with what seems to have been the original version of the scene, the fact remains that the compiler – who so prides himself on the refinement and polish testified to in his *doulx franceys* – obviously thought the scene represented one occasion for which his readers might predictably welcome some command of appropriate French – just as Sampson (or someone supplementing his series of model letters) thought something appropriate for the lover should be included. Both passages, that is, in different ways, assume that a degree of acquired verbal art will be thought desirable in the expression of feeling in this sphere. The use of verse in both is particularly significant in this respect, since this was the medium especially indicated in amorous contexts. The lover's is the only letter in the series to be put into verse, verse being the form conventionally taken by love letters in this period (see pp. 4–6 above). And the seducer (or child-abuser) of the model dialogue obviously thinks verse and song should be included in the process of courting *courtoisement*.

The Texts

The consecutive letters from Harley 3988 (the sisters', husband's and lover's) were included (along with the mother–son exchange) in the selection edited by Stengel in his paper of 1879. The scene from the *Manière de langage* 1396 was edited by Andres M. Kristol (pp. 39–43) in an appendix containing the scenes that diverge from those found in the manuscript tradition of his own text. We have re-edited the texts from the manuscript, and the translations are our own; and we have edited from Harley 4971 the earlier version of the sister's letter that appears there as the last item of the model letters before the series breaks off at that point in that manuscript (see above, p. 191). Where it is doubtful how manuscript abbreviations would have been spelled in the text we have expanded to standard forms and give the supplied letters in brackets.

Many of the spellings that had consistently distinguished Anglo-French from continental French (e.g. /aun/ for /an/ and /oi/ for /ei/) were regularized in English scripts to 'graphies continentales' in order to make the French at least appear more 'authentic' (see p. 188 above). Only occasional traces, therefore, of Anglo-French spellings remain: e.g. 'maunder' (in Harley 4971, line 6), beside 'mander' elsewhere, 'vei' [see] for 'voie' (208/10) and 'foin' [oats] for 'fein' (216/3). Anglo-French was nevertheless characterized by more licence in forms and spellings than occurred in standard or continental French.[25] In the letters, this is more evident in the text as written in Harley 4971. The non-standard feature most likely to strike a modern reader is, however, the neglect of gender agreement. The root cause of this

---

[25] Some or all of the non-standard features we list here may of course be scribal.

neglect was the loss of gender (and consequently of any innate sense of its logic) from the first language of the community of users of Anglo-French, though accelerants may have been provided by the increasing instability in Anglo-French of the pronunciation of final -*e* (and a consequent weakening of gender distinctions) and the levelling of 'le' and 'la' to 'le' in Picard.[26] Hence in Harley 4971 'nul chose' ('nulle chose' in Harley 3988) at line 3 and 'malencolie ... soit ensuagé' ('essuagée' in Harley 3988) at line 7, and in Harley 3988 'un mariage' ('une mariage' in Harley 4971) at A.2, 'il est ... coroucée' at A.7–8, 'sustenu' (feminine past participle) at A.18–19, and 'bons nouvelles' at B.2. Lack of concord is only slightly less flagrant in the purportedly 'continental' French of the conversation: e.g. 'grant joye' (208/11), 'tresbelles et ... entailléz' (208/15–16), 'escuelles fais' [bowls made (out of)] (214/14–15).[27]

---

[26] Picard exercised an early and ongoing influence on Anglo-Norman, whose 'picardismes' are usefully summarized in Kristol, 'Début', pp. 363–5; see also Serge Lusignan, *Essai d'histoire sociolinguistique: le français picard au Moyen Âge* (Paris, 2012).
[27] On gender inaccuracies in Anglo-French, see especially Richard Ingham, *The Transmission of Anglo-Norman* (Amsterdam, 2012), pp. 91–6.

I: LETTERS

Harley 4971

22ᵛ *De sorore ad sororem*
Saluz ove tant d'amour come coer poet altre mander. Purceo que mon s[eigneu]r moun père m'ad procuré une mariage grandement en contre ma volonté, quar c'est une lede personne, et pour nul chose de monde il ne fra james copulacion entre nous: purceo, ma tresch[iere] soer, jeo vous prie cherement, come jeo m'affie en vous, que vous emparles a vostre maistre que luy pleise ma 5
maunder un des chivaux que jeo puis demourer en vostre compaignie deus jours ou treis tant sa malencolie soit ensuagé, qar il corusse devers moy purceo que j'ay son comandement refusé. A dieu, tresch[iere] soer, etc.

5 ma] *error for* me

Harley 3988

59ʳ *A. De sorore ad sororem*
Salut et bon amour, treschiere et tresamée soer. Vueillez savoir que mon père m'a enprocurée un mariage grandement encontre ma voulantée, car c'est une leede personne et pour nulle chose de monde il ne fera jamais copulacion entre nous. Pour ce, ma treschiere soer, je vous pri chierement comme je m'affi de vous que vous enparlez a vostre s[eigneu]r qu'il me vue- 5
ille envoier un de ses chivalx que je puis demourer deux jours ou trois en vostre compaignie tanque sa malencolye soit essuagée et abessée, car il est forment coroucée avecque moy pour ce que j'ay son comandement refusée. Ma treschiere et tres amée soer, je pri a Dieu qu'il vous doint bonne vie et longue et gracious fyn. Escr, etc. 10

Responsio
Ma tres chiere soer, je vous salue par maintes fois de cuer. Et sachiez qu'il me poise grandement de ce que vous avez ainsi mespris contre nostre père. Et pancez bien, ma treschiere soer, qu'il est vostre soverain aide et vous aidera qant tous voz amys vous lerront, et abessez vostre cuer et ne soiez mye si 15
hautayne ne si orguillouse ne rebelle de respons contre nostre père comme vous estes, car se vous refusez sa compaignie par aventure vous devendrez folle, pour ce que vous n'avez rien de quoy vous pourrez vivre ne estre sustenu. Et ramembrer vueillez de ce que le sage dit: mieulx vault la verge que plie que ne fait cely que rumpe. Aultre respons ne vous say mander qant a 20
present. A Dieu, qui vous eit en sa garde. Escr, etc.

20 say] fay *Stengel*

I: LETTERS

Harley 4971

From one sister to another
Greetings, together with as much love as one heart can send to another. Because my lord and father has arranged for me a marriage that is greatly against my will (for the man is most unattractive, and under no consideration will I allow him ever to make a match between us), I therefore earnestly entreat you, my dearest sister, for I am relying on you, to speak to your lord and husband and get him to send me one of his horses, so that I can stay with you for two or three days, until his displeasure has abated, for he is angry with me because I have refused to obey his commands. Goodbye, dearest sister, etc.

Harley 3988

From one sister to another
Greetings and much love, dearest and beloved sister. Please be informed that my father has arranged for me a marriage that is greatly against my will, for the man is most unattractive, and under no consideration will I allow him ever to make a match between us. Therefore, my dearest sister, I entreat you, for I am relying on you, to speak to your lord and husband and ask him to send me one of his horses, so that I can stay with you two or three days, until his displeasure has abated and lessened, for he is much angered with me because I have refused to obey his commands. My dearest and most beloved sister, I pray God to grant you a good life and a long one and a gracious end. Written, etc.

Reply
My dearest sister, I greet you from my heart many times. I must tell you that it grieves me greatly that you have thus offended our father. Bear in mind, dearest sister, that he is your trustiest source of aid and will come to your aid when all your other friends desert you. So humble your heart and do not be so proud of spirit and self-willed and rebellious as you are being against our father. For if you dissociate yourself from him, that will perhaps turn out to be madness, for you will have no source of livelihood. And remember the proverb that the pliant stick that bends fares better than the one that breaks. I can at present reply to you in no other way. I commend you to God, whose safekeeping I hope may be extended to you. Written, etc.

B. De viro ad eius uxorem

Ma tres chiere et tres amée famme, je vous salue si souvent fois comme je say ou puis, desirant tous dis d'oier bons nouvelles de vous et de vostre bon estat et santée, que Dieu vueille maintenir / et accroistre a sa louange. Et endroit de le mien, vueillez savoir que a la faisance de ces lettres j'estoy bien aisé et en bon point, beneoit soit Dieux. Et sachiez que Marsdy derrain passée je m'en alay hors de la citée de Londres devers la mer. D'aultre part, ma tres chiere famme, sachiez que je doy a W.B. de Londres, cordewaner, xx s. vi d., le quel argent vous pri que vous luy paiez an plus brief que faire se pourra bonnement pour l'amour de moy. Et saluez bien souvent depar moy tous noz bons amys et voisins; et vous pri faire bien et sagement en m'absence. Tres chiere et tres amée compaigne, Dieux vous eit en sa garde et vous doint grace de bien faire. Escript en hast, etc.

7 cordewaner] cordewanier *Stengel*

C. Littera amorose composite

<pre>
    A m'amie tres belle et chiere,
    En qui est toute ma pensere:
    Saluz vous mande milles cent
    Et moy a vostre comandement.   4
    Tant des fois vous mande saluz
    Comme foilles sont ou bois et plus,
    A tant de fois vous salue chierment
    Comme estoiles / sont en firmament.   8
    Il n'y a famme que tant desire,
    Combien que de vynt pourroi eslire.
    Vous estez ma mort, vous estez ma vie;
    En vous est toute ma druerye.   12
    Et se rien soit que vers moy vueillez,
    Prive[e]ment a moy mandez.
    Aultres ne vous say mander,
    Mais grant desir vous ai parler.   16
    Pancez de moy, comme je de vous,
    Que loyal amour soit entre nous.
    Jhesu Crist vous donne honours
    Et saut de mal tous jours.   20
    Plus vous dire ne say je mye,
    Mais vous comande a filz Marie.   Escript, etc.
</pre>

6 bois] boais   10 pourroi] porroi *Stengel*   14 Priveement] Privement   17 de² *added above line*

From a man to his wife

My dearest and beloved wife, I greet you as many times as I can, and am ever desirous to hear good news of you and to hear news of your well-being and good health, which may God maintain and increase, in magnification of His own name. And with regard to my own, please be informed that at the time of writing this letter I was without trouble and in good health, God be praised. And be informed that on Tuesday last I left the city of London to go to sea. Furthermore, my dearest wife, be informed that I owe to W.B. of London, cordwainer, 20 shillings and 6 pence, which sum I beg you to pay him as soon as you well can for my sake. And greet well on my behalf all our friends and neighbours, and manage things well and prudently in my absence. Dearest and beloved wife, may God have you in his safekeeping and grant you the grace to act well. Written in haste, etc.

Letter composed in the fashion suited to love

To my beloved, most fair and dear, who is the sole object of my thoughts: I send you a hundred thousand greetings and also myself, at your command. As many times do I send you greetings as there are leaves in the wood, and more; as many times do I greet you from the heart as there are stars in the heavens. There is no woman I so much desire, even if I could choose from twenty. You are both my death and my life; in you is all my love. And if there be anything I can do for you, send in secret to me. I don't know what else to write, other than that I have a great desire to speak with you. Think of me, as I do of you, so that true love may subsist between us. May Jesus Christ grant you all honours and ever deliver you from evil. I do not know what else to say to you, except to commend you to the son of Mary. Written, etc.

204   Fictional and Instructional Models

NOTES TO MODEL LETTERS

A

The occurrence of this letter-pair in a model epistolary indicates that the request and the reply must have been regarded as predictable responses to a situation likely to arise. It depicts a daughter attempting to resist an arranged marriage by appealing for hospitality from a married sister. The compiler obviously assumes that the preferred response will be negative: the sister will not want the trouble and expense of housing the renegade. The reply furnished therefore urges obedience to parental authority and provides the respondent with a form of words which, without giving a direct negative to the request, makes it clear that no alternative home is on offer (17–19). The defence of the father, however (14–15), would not have sounded unlikely, and the modern European distaste for arranged marriages probably leads one to forget that it was the daughter's best interests, and not their own, that parents consulted in this matter. And the lady of Remiremont provides an example of a real daughter not inclined, even when in love, to forget that her father is indeed what the married sister here represents a father to be – her truest and most disinterested friend, his advice (even when disobeyed) proving him to have been precisely the wise and careful parent here described: see Text 7, I.7, 10–12, II.7, IV.12–13 (and notes thereto).

The rewording (in Harley 3988) of the earlier version of the letters (preserved in Harley 4971) tends to involve some expansion, though, in the case of the four letters here reproduced, this can be illustrated only from the first of the sisters' letters, for the Harley 4971 series breaks off at that point (see p. 191 above).

A similar complaint by one sister meets with a similar response from the other in a later Oxford textbook (composed c. 1415), *Regina sedens rhetorica*, in which the exchange (almost certainly suggested by Sampson's) is conducted in rather more rhetorically sententious terms: for the text, see pp. 203–5 in Camargo, *Medieval Rhetorics*.

10 *gracious fyn*: i.e. death in a state of grace. *Escr[ipt]* introduced the 'date' (place *x* and time *y*), and that is obviously omitted in models, where the letters characteristically end simply with *Escript*.

19–20 Proverbs are often marked as such by the formula *le sage dit*. For the one quoted here, cf. *Troilus* I.257–8: 'The 3erde [rod, stick] is bet [better] that bowen wole and wynde / Than that that brest' (i.e. compliance is better than pointless resistance, which will be crushed); cf. Whiting B484.

B

It is interesting to compare the sort of letter a husband is assumed likely to write with the model provided for the lover. The husband's is in prose, not verse, for verse is associated with courtship and wooing (see pp. 4–5 above), which a husband, even a loving one, has no occasion to engage in. Andreas in fact categorically denied that a husband could feel love of the courtly or romantic kind for his wife: the Countess of Champagne (when a disagreement is referred to her arbitration) is represented as ruling that love proper is not possible between married persons (*Andreas Capellanus*, I.6.G.397), and the author himself later declares that, though one talks of love between husband and wife, the polysemy of the word is misleading, as in that context it indicates something which is quite separate from romantic love (II.7.IX.21) and which partakes more of the attachment represented by such expressions as 'family love', etc. Whether or not this view was generally held in quite such precisely formulated terms, it was certainly assumed that marriage was no longer primarily a romantic relationship (if indeed such had ever subsisted between the parties) and that its underlying bond was based not on passion, but on mutual interest and commitment to the household, estate and children. It is on such practical matters that real husbands, when absent from home, wrote to their wives: one of his letters to his wife Margaret is classed by John Paston I specifically as a memorandum of household instructions, each of which is introduced by the word 'Item', the letter to be kept, he tells her, as a list, from which she is to cross through items as she deals with them (*Paston Letters*, ed. Davis, vol. 1, p. 144 (Letter 77.163–6)). Husbands and wives followed no particular epistolary form in such letters, beyond obeying the conventions as to opening salutations and closing formulae, and in this case it is the model that takes its cue from actual letters, rather than vice versa. Since wives acted as bursars for a husband in his absence, correspondence would often concern itself with finance and disbursements, with which Paston's letter is in fact almost exclusively concerned; and the specific purpose of the husband's letter in the present model is to arrange for payment of a debt he has not had time to settle before an obviously unplanned trip abroad, for his credit was important to any man of business.

2 *desirant*: the present participle is typical epistolary syntax, and the construction occurs in verse letters, actual and real: cf. Text 6, 3.10, 17, 4B.14, 5B.17, 5C.33, 5D.17 and notes thereto.

12 *Escript en hast*: the formula is common at the conclusion of letters, especially those communicating some urgent request or information; cf., for instance, the end of the letters (from Richard Kingston to Henry IV) quoted by Schendl, 'Code-Choice and Code-Switching', pp. 252–6.

C

The usual heading for a model love letter is *De amico/amasio ad amicam/amasiam*, which is an adaptation of the standard *De x ad y* formula (used in the title for all the other letters in this as in other series). That usual heading, and even the *De ... ad* frame are here, however, replaced by *Littera amorose composite*, where *amorose* seems to mean precisely 'in verse'. For this is the only letter in the formulary to be versified, and that fact and the title furnish a remarkable demonstration of the strength of the contemporary assumption that love letters should be in verse and that the lover must therefore become for the occasion an amateur poet, verse being an essential element in courtship (see p. 197 above and cf. *Love's Labour's Lost* IV.3.1–182). Real lovers (like the Norfolk Abbot and Robert Armburgh in Texts 4 and 6) did indeed become rhymesters in writing love letters, as the model here implies they should, and did in fact use many of the topoi suggested in this model (which is a series of standard amorous locutions): see nn. to 4, 5–8 and 13–14 below.

The verse form here suggested for amateur use is the octosyllabic couplet, for this was the simplest rhyme scheme to master (and it is used by the Norfolk Abbot in Letter II after his first irregularly rhymed efforts in Letter I). In this metrical letter, final *-e* is, interestingly, stable and regular, even though it was often lost in Anglo-French. But the lines as they stand are nevertheless not all octosyllabic. Assuming monosyllabic 'comme' throughout, there are six regular lines with feminine rhymes (1–2, 9–10, if one assumes uncontroversial elision in *y a* and *pourroi eslire*, and 21–2) and six regular masculine lines (3, 5–6, 16, 17, 19). But there are three short lines: seven-syllabled ones at 14 (where, however, MS *Privement* should be, and here has been, emended to the more regular *Priveement*) and 15 (easily regularizable by insertion of *je*), and a six-syllabled one at 20. And there are nine syllables in lines 4, 7, 12, 13 and 18, and ten in 8 and 11. That last should perhaps read 'Vous estes ma mort et ma vie'. Fairly simple emendations would be devisable for the other non-octosyllabic lines, but it is not beyond doubt that they are inauthentic. Other Anglo-French compositions in this verse form show some variation in syllable count, the late twelfth-century *Le petit plet* yielding proportions similar to those found here. In that poem, 'only 952 of the 1780 lines of the base manuscript can be considered regular octosyllabics', according to its editor (Brian S. Merrilees, ed., *Le petit plet* (Oxford, 1970), p. xxvii). Some of the irregular ones are clear or probable errors – but certainly not all. In fact, it may be that some licence in syllable count was thought by some poets to be permissible (especially for the amateur assumed in this model). Much couplet verse in English in this period (at least in the extant copies) observes rhyme much more strictly than syllable count, and it may well have been assumed that it was the rhyme which created the verse, evenness of line length being a norm rather than a rule – especially since it is possible that the English inherited a system in which syllable count was to some degree influenced by the position and nature of the caesura (see Merrilees, ed., *Le petit plet*, p. xxviii), which played a more significant part in French than in English verse, and this may have led their ears to tolerate occasional irregularities in this area.

4 The feudal posture ('I am at your commandment') is conventional and is taken up repeatedly by Robert Armburgh in his verse love letters apparently composed for an actual lady: see, e.g., Text 6, 4A.5, 5D.21–4.

5–8 This model letter is happy to suggest the salutation device Boncompagno labelled as an affectation of the vulgar. Known as the *quot ... tot* formula (from the form it takes when used in Latin), it was especially characteristic of love letters, whether real or fictional (cf. Text 4, I.21–3 and *Welles Anthology* 49.5–8), although not in fact restricted to them (it occurs, for example, in correspondence between nuns: see Power, p. 684). See n. to Text 1, 130.22–6 above.

London, British Library, Harley 3988

11 Such life-and-death-deciding power is commonly attributed to the lady in the epistolary rhetoric of love: cf. for instance, the end of Troilus's letter at *Troilus* V.1417–21 (and V.1413).

13–14 The invitation to send word if there is any assistance the writer can render is standard and is used by the Norfolk Abbot in the draft for what is almost certainly an actual love letter: see Text 4, II.36–7.

22 *a filz Marie*: the circumlocution was common and similarly provides a rhyme at the conclusion of *Le petit plet*: 'Requerez le fiz seinte Marie / Ke il garisse la vostre vie' (1769–70).

II: FROM *LA MANIÈRE DE LANGAGE*

8ʳ Et par cel temps sera venu le signeur a son hostel. Lors venra la dame de l'ostel (ou la damoiselle) et dira en ce maniere a signeur:
—Mon signeur, vous estez tresbien venu. *Vel sic:* Mon signeur, bien soiez venu. *Si vero tuizaveris aliquem, hoc modo responsionem tuam procul dubio reserabis:* Bial amy, bien sois venu.
—Dame, comment vous est il? *Vel sic:* Dame, comment faitez vous? *Vel sic, si sit domina*: Ma dame, comment vous avez vous portée depuis que je ne vous vi mais?
—Tresbien, mon signeur, Dieu mercy et la vostre, et mieulx que je vous vei en bonne santee du corps.
—Vrayement, j'en ai grant joye.
—Hé, mon signeur, il y a grant piece que je ne vous vi mais.
—Vrayement, m'amie, vous ditez verité. Ore, belle dame, me ditez vous: n'avez vous poynt de belles filletes comme vous soloiés avoir?
—Mon signeur, s'il vous plaist, j'en ai deux tresbelles et tresbien et graciousement entailléz du corps et aussi gresles que vous les porez enpoigner entre voz deux mains.
—Hé, me faitez venir devant moy tost celles filletes, car je ne descenderai ja de mon chival avant que je les avrai veu.

8ᵛ / Doncques viennent avant les filletes ou presence du signeur. Fait le signeur:
—Ces sont les plus belles fames et mieulx entailléz du corps, ce m'est m'avis, que j'ay veu pieça, et pleust a Dieu [que je les eusse avec moy] demourans a mon manoir de N. Je les donnroi de l'or et de l'argent et d'autres biens et chateux assés!
Doncques descent le signeur de son chival et demande les noms de les filletes et dit ainsi:
—Mes tresdoulces amies, comment avez vous a noms?
Et doncques respont la plus veile pucele et dit ainsi:
—Mon signeur, s'il vous plaist, j'ay a nom Isabelle.
Puis dit l'autre:
—Mon signeur, j'ay a nom Margarete.

19 de mon] *Kristol*; de de mon   23 que je les eusse avec moy] *Kristol*; avecque homme

II: FROM *LA MANIÈRE DE LANGAGE*

And by now the master will have arrived at the hostel. Then the mistress (or the daughter) of the house will come and will speak in this way to him:

—Sir, you are most welcome here. *Or thus:* **Sir, welcome be you.** *If it is someone to whom you would use the informal 'thou', you will doubtless receive him in this way:* **Fair friend, welcome be thou.**

—Madam, how are things with you? *Or thus:* **How are you, madam?** *Or thus, if she is a lady in her own house:* **My lady, how have you been since I last saw you?**

—Very well, sir, I thank God and you, and the better for seeing you in good health.

—Truly, I am glad to hear it.

—Oh, sir, it is a long time since I last saw you.

—That is true, my friend. Now, fair madam, tell me, have you got any of those pretty girls you used to have?

—Sir, if it please you, I have two, very pretty, with lovely figures, and so slim that they would fit between your two hands.

—Oh, bring them to me at once, those little girls, for I won't get off my horse till I see them.

Then the girls come into his presence, and the gentleman says:

—These are the loveliest women and the shapeliest, it seems to me, that I've seen in a long while, and would to God that I had them living with me at my house in X. I'd give gold, silver, and plenty of other goods and chattels for them!

Then the gentleman dismounts from his horse and asks the girls' names, saying:

—My sweet friends, what are your names?

And then the elder girl replies and says thus:

—Sir, if it please you, my name is Isabel.

Then the other says:

—Sir, my name is Margaret.

—Ore je prie a Dieu qu'il vous donne grace de bien faire. Isabelle, vien ça, vien. *Vel sic:* Venez a moy, ma tresdoulce amie, hardiement, car je vous promette que je ne vous fera ja de vilaynie, ains vous ferai, s'il Dieu plest, de bien et de l'oneur.
—Voulantiers, mon signeur, a vostre comandement. 5
Doncques fait le signeur acoler et doulcement baiser la damoiselle en la bouche. Et puis il li dit gracieusement, de bon et fervent amour et par maniere d'amourasser, les paroles qu'ensuient:

> M'amie doulce et graciouse,
> De bien et de courtoisie plaintivouse, 10
> A qui j'ay donnée m'amours,
> Car de toutes les floures arousée
> Vous estez soveraine a mon gree,
> Et comme la rose entre lilie flours.

Vel sic:

> Ma dame gentille de pourtraiture, 15
> En vous j'ay mis toute ma cure et m'amour
> Et toute plaisance, je vous ensure,
> Comme de toute beautee la flour.

Et puis le signeur li mene par la main vers la sale et li dit ainsi:
—Damoiselle, vous souperez avecque moy? 20
—Grant mercy, mon signeur.
A/donques il appelle son varlet par nom, ainsi luy disant:
—Janyn, est nostre souper tout prest encores?
—Oil, mon signeur. Alez vous seoir quant vous plerra.
Fait le signeur doncques et soi regart tout environ et dit: 25
—Que dea, encore est la table a mettre!
Et soy comence pour estre marri vers ses soubgis et siergeans, ainsi leur disant:
—Malle semayne a vous soit mise tout deux. *Vel sic:* Je pri a Dieu qu'il vous puist mescheoir du corps: amen! Qu'avez vous fait depuis que je 30 venoi ciens? Vous ne faitez que sounger et muser. Mettez la table tost et aportez nous une fois a boire de vin claret, ou de vin blanc, car j'en ai tresgrant soif et aussi tresgrant fain avecques.
—A vostre comandement, mon signeur. 35

29 pri] prie *Kristol*; du] de *Kristol*

—Now, may God give you the grace to lead good lives! Isabel, come here, come here. *Or thus:* Approach, my sweetest beloved, don't be nervous, for I promise you that you will get from me no harm, but rather, please God, profit and advantage.
—Happily, sir, if that is what you wish.

Then the gentleman embraces the girl and tenderly kisses her on the mouth, and then utters gracefully, and in the loving manner of a man who woos, the following:

>My sweet and gracious beloved,
>Plenteously endowed with goodness and courtly graces,
>To whom I have given my heart,
>For of all the flowers that receive the dew
>You are sovereignly agreeable to me,
>Like the rose among lilies.

Or this:

>My lady fair of form,
>In you have I placed all my love and care
>And all my pleasure, I assure you,
>As you are the flower of all beauty.

And then the gentleman leads her by the hand towards the main room and says this to her:
—Mademoiselle, will you sup with me?
—Thank you very much, sir.

And then he calls his servant by his name, speaking thus to him:
—Johnny, is our supper completely ready yet?
—Yes, sir. Take your seat whenever you like.

The gentleman moves to do so, and looks around and says:
—Dear God, the table is not even in position yet!

And he begins to get angry with his inferiors and officials, speaking thus to them:
—A bad time come to you both! *Or thus:* I pray God that something bad happens to you! I really hope so! What have you been doing since I got here? Nothing but dream and gape! Set up the table at once and bring us, can't you, some red or white wine to drink, for I am very thirsty for it, and I'm very hungry too.
—As you wish, sir.

Et quant il avra bu et la damoiselle aussi, il li dira en ce maniere:
—M'amie, venez vous en, car vous seirez icy devant moy en une chaier.
—Mon signeur, s'il vous plaist, non ferai.
—Par Dieu, si ferez.
—Vostre mercy, mon signeur.
Et puis après le signeur et la damoiselle seront serviz de moult bonne viande a souper. Doncques le signeur li fait tresbon chere et tresgrant desduit, ainsi li disant:
—Damoiselle, que chere faitez vous?
—Mon signeur, tresbon chere, Dieu mercy et la vostre.
—Vrayement, j'en ai grant joye, car vous m'estez aussi bien venuz comme aucune fame de monde, et pleust a Dieu que je eusse de viande que vous pourroit plaiser.
—[Si] m'ait Dieux, mon signeur, si est assés, Dieu mercy.
Et doncques dit le signeur a la damoiselle:
—Quoy ne mangez vous doncques?
—Par Dieu, si fais je, mon signeur, vostre mercy.
—Ore il parra.

9ᵛ /Et sitost qu'ils avront soupez, le signeur comencera d'amourasser la damoiselle; et pour avoir son amour et sa pucellage, il fait pour le grant brasier d'amour qu'il en a envers li le plus gracious et le plus amerous chanson qui peut estre en tout le monde, en ce maniere disant, ou autrement chantant tresgracieusement:

cantus patet   Tresdoulz regart amerousement trait
 Tant de doulceur fera mon cuer entrer,
 Quant les miens yeulx te pevent racontrer,
 Que tout mon sang me fuit et vers toi trait;
 Et tant me plaist ton gracious atrait
 Que de veoir je ne me puis saouler.
 Je t'ai pour tant si en mon cuer pourtrait
 Qu'autre pansee ne t'en pourroit ouster,
 Et tel plaiser fait dedans moy entrer
 Que jamais jour tu n'en seras retrait.

Et sic finitur cantus dulcissimus. Et quant le signeur avra achavée sa chanson, il parlera a la damoiselle tout courtoisement en ce maniere:
—M'amie, enne ai je bien et parfaitement fait cest chanson?
—Oil, vrayement, mon signeur, tresbien a poynt, car vous m'avez enravoiée tout le cuer et le sang.

14 Si m'ait] Kristol; mait   24 *cantus patet*] *in left margin in smaller script*

And when he and the damsel have had a drink, he will speak to her in this manner:
—My dear, come on, you're going to sit opposite me in a chair.
—Oh, sir, I could not do that!
—Indeed you will.
—Thank you, sir.
And then the gentleman and the damsel will be served a supper of very good dishes. Then the gentleman will be very attentive to her and to her comfort, speaking thus to her:
—Mademoiselle, is everything to your satisfaction?
—Yes, indeed, sir, I thank God and you.
—Truly, I am very glad to hear it, for I would rather be in your company than in that of any other woman in the world, and God grant I may have food that would please you.
—So help me God, so it does, sir, very much, God be thanked.
And then the gentleman says to the girl:
—Why are you not eating up?
—By God, sir, so I am, thank you.
—Let me see you do so.

And as soon as they have supped, the gentleman will begin to come on to the damsel; and to win her love and take her virginity from her, he will, through the great fire of desire that he has for her, perform the most elegant and the most amorous song that he knows, uttering prettily the following or some other song:

A song appears here: A sweet glance directed in a love-inspiring way
Makes so much sweetness enter my heart,
When my eyes have the opportunity to encounter you,
That all my blood flees from me towards you;
And the attraction of your lovely person so delights me
That I cannot satisfy my hungry gaze.
And your image is thus so firmly printed in my heart
That no other thought can ever dislodge you from there,
Filling me with such pleasure
That you will never be withdrawn from within me.

And here ends the sweetest song he knows. And when the gentleman has brought the song to its conclusion, he will speak in a most courtly manner to the girl in this way:
—My dearest, have I not well and properly sung this song?
—Yes, truly, sir, most perfectly, for you have quite enchanted me, body and soul.

Doncques prent le signeur la fillete par la main et s'affiance overtement de la foy de son corps qu'il n'avra ja autre fame que li durant sa vie, ainsi disant:
—M'amie, je vous prenne icy a ma compaigne, et sur ce je vous affiance.
Et puis le signeur s'esbat et esjoit atant avecque s'amie que tout maniere de solace, desduit et esbatement son cuer s'embat. Et il donne a dame de l'ostel 5 et a tous ses siergeans, chambreres et bais/selletes biaucoup de biaus douns: c'est a savoir, a la dame de l'ostel une tresbelle ceinture de fyn soye vert, et a chascun des siergeans trois souldz et quatre deniers d'esterlings, et a chascun de les baisseletes une bourse de vert velvet bien appareillié et fort cordeillée de fyn soye rouge et douzse deniers d'esterlings. Doncques le signeur 10 et s'amie et toute la gentille compaignie avec luy s'esbatent et s'esjoient atant que c'est mervailles. Et le signeur comande ses escuiers et officers de l'aporter des espices et de boire. Et tost après viennent avant ces escuiers et officers ov grant cop de cierges bien entour cinnquant, et l'aportent de tresbelles escuelles fais des pierres precieuses a guise et manere des Sarrazins, trestout 15 plains des tous maniers des espices; et puis ils aportent de tresbonne cervoise et des bons vins – c'est a savoir vin claret, vermaille et blanc. Item de vins doucetes, comme de vin de Grece, ipocras, montrose, rumney, vernage, malvoisin, osey, clarrey et pyement et de tous autres vins que l'en peut avoir, aussi des aultres boires comme de syser, poyrye et bragote. Doncques vien- 20 nent avant ou presence du signeur ses corneours et clarioners ov leur fretielles et clarions, et se comencent a corner et clarioner tresfort, et puis le signeur ov ses escuiers se croulent, balent, dancent, houuent et chantent de biaux karoles sanz cesser jusques a mynuyt. Et quant ils seront trestout si entravaillez et las qu'ils ne se pourront / ja a cel temps plus longuement danc- 25 er, lors le signeur dira a toute la gentille compaignie luy environ ainsi:
—Mes amys, il est haute heure de nous aler coucher maishuy, car il est deja bien pres une heure après mynuyt. Et pour ce alons tost coucher, car se je fus couchée ou lit, je dormis tresvoulantiers. Et Janyn, amenez m'amie a chambre et li deschausez et devestez et que elle soit tout 30 prest encontre ma venu pour aler coucher avec moy.
Et puis venra le signeur et se couchera avecque s'amie en tresgrant joye et esbatement, et se comence de li baiser et acoler, et boute un de ses bras desoubz le col et li fait trestout la courtoisie et maniere de esbatement et desduit qu'apartient au marit faire a sa fame espousée. 35

---

5 desduit] desduyt *Kristol* et a tous ses siergeans, chambreres et baisselletes] *repeated but struck through after* dame de l'ostel *in line 20* 12 l'aporter] l'apporter *Kristol*

Then the gentleman will take the young girl by the hand and will explicitly pledge himself to have no other love but her for all his life, saying thus:

—My dearest, I take you here for my companion, and pledge my faith to that.

And then the gentleman will have such a happy time with his girl that all manner of comfort, pleasure and joy will fill his heart. And he will give many nice gifts to the mistress of the house, and to all her menservants, maids and serving-girls: that is to say, a pretty belt of fine green silk for the mistress of the house, and to each of her officers three sous and four deniers in good coin, and to each of the maidservants a purse of nicely worked green velvet, closed firmly by means of a fine red silk cord threaded through it, and twelve deniers in good coin. Then the gentleman and his girl and all the goodly company amuse themselves and have a wonderfully good time. And the gentleman orders his squires and officers to bring wine and spiced confections. And straightaway the squires and officers come forward with a large number of wax candles, about fifty, and bring in beautiful dishes set with precious stones, after the eastern manner of the Saracens, filled with all manner of spiced confections; and then they bring ale and good wines, that is, claret and red and white wines. There are also sweetened wines and cordials, such as Greek wine, ipocras, Gironde wine, Romney, vernage, malmsey, osey, clary and piment, and all other wines that can be had, as well as other beverages such as cider, perry and bragot. Then his minstrels with their wind and brass instruments come forward and begin to play their horns and clarions with a will, and then the gentleman and his squires jig and dance and whoop and perform song-dances until midnight. And when they are all so exhausted with the physical exercise that they can dance no more, the gentleman will say to the whole courtly company around him:

—My friends, it is high time we should retire to our beds, for it is already nearly an hour after midnight. And so let us go to bed, for once there I will fall asleep instantly. And, Johnny, bring my *amie* to my room and help her take off her shoes and clothes and see that she is ready to go to bed with me by the time I come.

And then the gentleman will go to bed with his *amie* with great joy and delight, and he starts to kiss and cuddle her; and he puts an arm under her neck, and treats her with all that courtly attention, and enjoys with her pleasure and delight of the kind that a married man has with his wedded wife.

11ʳ	Et quant il venra au matinee, il soi levera sus bien matin ... / ... **–Janyn, baillez ça mon pigne, que m'amie me pourra pigner la teste, et comandez mon garcon qu'il face abuvrer mes chivalx et puis les donne du fein**
11ᵛ	**et des aveines** ... / ... Doncques le signeur se monte a chival et baise la fillete
12ʳ	/ sa compaigne et li baille trent francs a paier pour ses despens et li dit courtoisement ainsi:

 —Ma tresdoulce amie et treschiere compaingne, a Dieu vous comande jusques a revois. Car je m'en irai pour esbatre a Aurilians un poy de temps, mais je n'aresterai guaires.

Et puis le signeur s'en chivalche sur son chemyn, et quant il venra ou mylieue la vile ...

And when the morning comes, he will get up in good time ... [he dresses and washes, and tells the landlady who comes to enquire whether he spent the night well that he did, but is rather tired and hungover and proceeds to give his servant instructions for their departure] ... **Johnny, hand me my comb, so that my *amie* can comb my hair, and tell my lad to water the horses and give them hay and oats** ... [he orders and eats his breakfast, gets directions from the landlady on the route to his next intended destination and takes leave of her] ... Then the gentleman mounts his horse and kisses his little companion and gives her thirty francs in payment for the expenses incurred by the hostel and speaks to her with courtliness as follows:

—**My sweetest *amie* and dearest companion, I commend you to God until I see you again. For I am going on a visit of pleasure to Orléans for a time, but I will not stay there long.**

And then the lord rides off on his way, and when he gets to the centre of the city ...

NOTES TO EXTRACT FROM *LA MANIÈRE DE LANGAGE*

Though model love poems and love letters were common in the Middle Ages, models for the spoken as opposed to the written expression of love are rare outside fiction. The direct addresses and dialogues in Andreas function rather as arguments *pro* and *contra* in the situations specified (e.g. that of a man requesting love from a lady of higher status than his own) and thus contribute to the quasi-forensic nature of a text in which questions of love are deliberated and referred for 'judgement' to named ladies; they are not really suggestions as to how a man might actually express himself to the lady, a purpose for which the text is actually unsuited, since it is typically polemical rather than tender in register.

The only orthographic signposting provided in the present manuscript is the underlining of the Latin annotations to the French. Changes of speaker are usually indicated in the text, but, where they are not, they are not signalled by any orthographic mark or new line; verse is not differentiated from prose, though the second poem assigned to the *signeur* is signalled by a marginal *cantus patet*.

208/1 *le signeur*: the repeated designation of the 'lover' in this scene as *le signeur* marks his superiority in rank to that of the girl to whom he makes love. Though we have usually translated it as 'gentleman' (its nearest English equivalent as a reference to social status), it here has its stricter sense of 'overlord, master', since the previous section has featured purchases for his supper made in advance of his arrival by one of his servants. For the manual is plainly intended for the use of those in service or commerce (cf. next note) – who might have to attend their employers across the Channel or transact business there – as well as for their *gentil* masters and clients.

208/3–5 The manual here aims its instruction at the hostess, who may be running a commercial *hostel* (and would use the polite *vous* form to her clients) or a lady of status in her own residence (who might use the informal *tu* form if the visitor was of lower status than her own and/or was, as is assumed at 6, already known to her). Either way, she is assumed to wish to use French with her *gentil* guest.

208/6–8 Here again (as at 3–5) an alternative is provided for what is assumed to be a perfectly possible case: that the *signeur* has applied for hospitality at the house of a lady of rank known to him. In an age when travel was without its modern facilitations, it was a matter of honour amongst *gentils* to make travellers welcome and to display the amenities of their homes: even a king could proudly refer to his court as a *hostel* when welcoming a stranger (*SGGK* 253). If that is the scenario in the present *hostel*, the *signeur* is advised to use the more polite 'Ma dame' (rather than the bare 'Dame' used to the mistress of a commercial establishment), and it is assumed that the house in which he is applying for shelter is one at which he is already known.

208/13 In direct address, *ami(e)* was used in condescension by a superior signalling affability to an inferior (cf. 5, 28), as was *bel(le)*. The words here thus indicate that the scene proceeds on the assumption the hostess is not a *domina* (the possibility indicated at 7–8).

208/18–19 A mock or real threat to ride on if the girls are not made available? The *signeur* is certainly insisting (as a customer) on the girls – and his assertion serves the subsidiary purpose of illustrating future and future perfect tenses: for the range of constructions and verb forms introduced into this French conversation manual is noticeably greater than in the two subsequent ones (cf. the subjunctive alternative given for the indicative greeting at line 3 and the subjunctive, optative and conditional forms at 23–4).

210/1–3 When addressing this girl alone, the *signeur* at first uses the familiar singular imperative appropriate to her inferiority in status. But in the alternative greeting, he at once switches to the polite *vous* form, which he uses henceforth and which consorts with his casting himself in the role of courtly lover and the girl in that of the courtly mistress – though his previous linguistic assumptions of superiority at 208/28 (see n. to 210/13) and 210/1 mark the fakeness of this courtly respectfulness.

210/2 *amie* was conveniently fluid in application. In its more general sense of 'friend', it could be used in downward condescension to female inferiors simply as the feminine equivalent of the downward *ami* (see n. to 208/13), as at 208/28. But it could also be used in an amorous sense of a 'beloved', of the courtly or non-courtly kind. It here morphs from the first sense into the second, becoming applicable to the courtly mistress, addressed in the opening line of the courtly poem that now follows as *M'amie doulce*, a vocative anticipated by the *ma tresdoulce amie* in line 2. With the possessive alone in direct address (212/2, 36) the term is ambiguously poised between the downward and the amorous application, though in the latter usage it would not normally be used to a courtly mistress without a complimentary adjective of some kind (note that in third-person references without adjective it is equivalent to 'his/my girl/sweetheart', with no especial implication of courtly status: 214/4, 11, 32). Used without adjective in direct address, it certainly sounds a little presumptuous, as does the instatement of the *amie* as his *compaigne* at 214/3, though the latter term is meant to imply some equality and to tip *amie* from its condescending to its amorous application. The lady's permission is not asked for the liberty to use either term of her. Both words are coupled with an adjectival enhancer when the gentleman takes his leave, when he is especially anxious, of course, to imply the respect and love that would dictate the return journey to which he gives an evidently hollow promise (216/8–9). Altogether, his exploitation of the fluidity of the term simply reveals the social power of the *signeur* masquerading as the respectful lover.

214/6–7 *acoler ... baiser ... en la bouche*: throughout this scene, the manual gives behavioural as well as verbal instruction in playing the courtly lover. It here shows the *signeur* taking advantage of behavioural norms which (like the linguistic ones governing *amie*) allow similar traffic between the friendly and the amorous register. Kissing between the sexes was common in social intercourse (by way of greeting or as marks of favour or obligation or friendship), and the kisses permitted went much further than the modest pecks to which the modern equivalents are restricted. There is a *chanson* by Charles d'Orléans that reveals the superficial similarity yet distinction between these public kisses ('cossis dowche [sweet]' given 'for a countenaunce [in polite displays of goodwill]' to make people feel welcome) and amorous ones ('prive [private] cossis of plesaunce'): *English Book* R37 (translated from French Ch37). Under cover of such social kisses, lovers could thus kiss each other in public with some warmth (cf. the public kiss given by Guinevere to Lancelot in *Lancelot of the Lake*, tr. Corin Corley (Oxford, 1989), pp. 409–10).

210/9, 212/24 The songs reinforce the casting of the girl in the role of courtly mistress, picking up the respectful pronoun *vous* and the use of *amie* together with enhancing adjective (used at 210/2): 'M'amie doulce ... Vous estez ...'. The address 'Ma dame' likewise implies a lady of status seen as the feudal superior of the lover ('she who can command me'), for it was used, by contradistinction from simple 'dame', to ladies of rank (see n. to 208/6–8). It is an indication of the important role played by verse in the realm of elegant wooing that a courtly poem should constitute the very first move of the *signeur*, once he has adopted the pose of courtly lover, in wooing the girl, a poem he recites 'par maniere d'amourasser' (210/8).

210/22–35 Cf. Franklin's Tale *CT* V.1209–17. The orders for and hurrying on of the meal are, like the account of the revelries at 214/3–26, standard scenes of courtly domestic life that occur most typically in romances in scenes of *herbergage* (where the protagonist is received and entertained by a host anxious to show off his *politesse* and the facilities of his home). Though the *signeur* here is a guest at, not the lord of, this *hostel*, he is in effect hosting the evening's jollities at his own expense and with his own provisions, and is as anxious to impress the girl as hosts in romance are their chivalric visitors – though from lower motives. See further n. to 214/3–26. The two passages are part of the courtly costume in which this grubby little scene plays itself out.

212/2–5 This again apes a detail in scenes of courtly *herbergage* where the visitor is accorded a place of honour at the meal. Gawain, for instance, is seated at the high dais next to the hostess (*SGGK* 1001–5). Individual chairs were in fact a luxury of some rarity at this period, when seats were usually benches, stools or couches (see n. to *SGGK* 877).

212/24–33 The importance of song and verse to courtly wooing is again apparent (cf. 210/9) and is underlined by the marginal note that marks the poem and the exchange that follows it (212/36–8). The *signeur* is instructed to choose *le plus gracious* song he knows (212/21), the manual providing an example of the sort of elegant composition he should perform. The physiological conceit of the arrow that shoots love into the heart through the eyes (cf. Knight's Tale *CT* I.1096–1100, and *le trait* [shot] *de doulz regard* in the opening line of Chanson LI in *Poetry of Charles d'Orléans*, ed. Fox and Arn) and the inner image of the beloved created in the heart (cf. *Troilus* I.365–6) were conventional figures of courtly amorous rhetoric, serving here to typify a *gracious* chanson. These courtly lyrics were often as elegant in metre as in rhetoric, and this one is artfully constructed around only two rhymes, one of which consists of an elaborate kind of *rime riche* (a play on different parts of speech or senses or forms of the same word: here *-trait*).

212/35 *courtoisement*: a key word in this scene, in which the wooing and the love-making are presented as exercises in the art of *courtesy* in word and deed (cf. 214/34, 216/5). The word *gentille* is similarly insisted on in the revelry that follows (214/11, 26).

214/1-3 Though this pledge would be assumed to be sincere in a courtly romance, it provokes disbelief here – and illustrates how the courtly dress provided for this encounter simply reveals rather than conceals the underlying reality for which it is a less than perfect fit.

214/3-26 On the repeated word *gentille*, see n. to 212/35. The scene in fact recreates the depictions of luxury, revelry and largesse found in courtly romances when the guest is entertained after his meal with dancing, minstrelsy and refections of wine and spices (see next note). But it is here a guest putting on the Ritz for his servants and his commercial (rather than private) hosts, and this anomaly exposes the element of fakeness in the refined luxury of it all. As host, the *signeur*'s motives are less disinterested than is normally the case, and the female charms and favours that are an invariable item in the aggregated desirables are something that, as guest, he is in effect paying *for* rather than being treated *to*. The manual is, of course, on one level expanding this incident of 'gallantry' simply so as to provide an array of courtly incident and associated vocabulary, something for which the otherwise largely practical nature of the scenes offers limited opportunity. It therefore provides the *signeur* with models of courtly behaviour as well as speech, and so comes in this passage sometimes to resemble a courtesy book (as it is today called), a manual on courtly etiquette, especially as it concerned the central courtly rituals of eating and drinking, such as the *Boke of Nurture* (EETS OS 32).

214/5-10 This is veiled instruction as to what kinds of tips or gifts are appropriate for whom. Here, the female domestics receive elegant accessories as well as money, the men simply money. It is significant that here, as elsewhere in this passage, the parallels that spring to mind are with the scenes of courtly life so vividly painted in that most iconic of romances, *Sir Gawain and the Green Knight*. For a green silk girdle as a fashionable accessory for ladies, cf. *SGGK* 1830-3. However, beneath the parallels with courtly largesse, and the material marks of goodwill or appreciation given in courtly circles to household staff, or as New Year gifts, etc., there is a less honourable parallel that suggests itself: the gifts given by a would-be seducer to ingratiate himself with the household of the woman he has his eye on; the monk in the Shipman's Tale (who lusts after the merchant's wife) uses gifts thus to ingratiate himself with the household (*CT* VII.46–51). The manual in this passage hovers between a primer, a courtesy book and an *ars amandi*.

214/11-12 *la gentille compaignie ... esjoient atant que c'est mervailles*: cf. the festivities in *SGGK*, in which '*Wonderly* thay woke [stayed up to party marvellously]' (1025) with entertainments conducted with '*manerly* mirthe' (1656). *des espices et de boire*: wine and spiced confections served in the late evening are a regular feature of courtly life and pastimes: cf. 'Spyces that unsparely men spede hem to brynge, / And the wynnelyche wyne therewith uche tyme' (*SGGK* 979–80). *grant cop de cierges*: candles and wax were expensive, and their presence and number are regularly mentioned as a measure of the luxury and brilliance of the entertainment (cf. *SGGK* 1649–50). *tresbelles escuelles fais des pierres precieuses a guise et manere des Sarrazins*: splendid tableware is also a regular feature of courtly partying; cf. *Cleanness* (in *Works of Gawain Poet*, ed. Putter and Stokes) 1405–11 (and 1456–76), where the feast of the eastern potentate Belshazzar includes highly ornate and bejewelled vessels, for the *Sarrazin* east was especially associated with such rich ornateness of vessels and trappings (see the accounts of the courts of Porus in *Wars of Alexander*, ed. Hoyt N. Duggan and Thorlac Turville-Petre, EETS SS 10 (1989), 3794ff. and of the Great Chan in Jean de Mandeville, *Le livre des merveilles du monde*, ed. Christiane Deluz (Paris, 2000), pp. 373–4).

214/16–20 The very full list of wines and beverages is obviously an oenological *vocabulaire*. The closest parallel occurs, significantly, in the *Boke of Nurture*, a courtesy book which, in the course of teaching courtly behaviour and routines, provides a vocabulary of the types of drinks attendants will need to be familiar with ('The namys of swete wynes y wold þat ye them knewe': 117), while our *Manière* in effect does the reverse. The *Boke*'s list likewise includes *Vernage*, *pyment*, *Rompney*, *O3ey*, *Greke*, *Clarey*, *Malvesyn* and a recipe for *Ypocras* (118–21). Where any of these wines are listed elsewhere, it is typically in the context of feasting: cf. 'in reuel ... And dyuers drynkes ffor solas, / Romney, clarre, ypocras, / In malvesyn and in Oseye, / The longe nyht I daunce and pley' (John Lydgate, *Pilgrimage of the Life of Man*, ed. F.J. Furnivall, EETS ES 77, 83, 92 (1899–1904), 12828–32). All are sweet wines or cordials, and of the other beverages mentioned, bragot was made of ale and honey, found in the *Boke* too as an accompaniment to spiced sweetmeats: 'Spised cakes ... with bragot & methe [mead]' (816–17; cf. 'Hir mouth was sweete as bragot or the meeth' at *CT* 1.3261).

214/21–4 The clarion was a kind of curved trumpet (see *The Earliest English Translation of Vegetius' De re militari*, ed. Geoffrey Lester (Heidelberg, 1988), 113/32–6). The wine, minstrelsy, dancing and singing of carols (ring-dances performed to songs with refrains) is a typical scene of *gentille* revelry: cf. 'wonderly thay woke and the wyne dronken, / Daunced ful dryly with dere caroles' (*SGGK* 1025–6; cf. 1654–5).

214/34 *la courtoisie:* see n. to 212/35. The absorption of the sexual exploitation of the girl into the courtly world of romance and recreation is here at its most evident.

216/1ff. The girl is virtually dismissed by both the *signeur* and the text as soon as morning comes and the attention of both author and character is claimed by the new subject of preparations for leave-taking, into which she is absorbed in the two fleeting references to her. She appears in connection with the account of his morning toilet in the order to Janyn regarding her combing of his hair, an order which is coupled with another for the feeding and watering of the horses (3–4) and then figures as an addendum to the leave-taking from the landlady.

216/5–11 The 'courtesy' of the *signeur* here makes its final appearance: as a tender farewell pending a reunion which, like the promise of fidelity at 214/1–3, is obviously a courteous fiction. The girl is never mentioned again, as both *signeur* and text immediately move on, almost literally, to a new place and the practical and linguistic needs it brings.

TEXT 3

The Parliament of Love

Lovers might also find advice and models for their letters in literature, especially in narratives (such as those of Troilus or Euryalus) where they would encounter recourse to a letter and how to compose one enacted and exemplified. Such a poem occurs in the so-called Findern Manuscript, which itself provides a marked instance of how, in a manuscript culture (particularly with respect to household anthologies and commonplace books), literary text and actual readers are inextricably interlinked.

The Findern Manuscript (Cambridge University Library, Ff.1.6) is a fascinating anthology put together in the mid- to late fifteenth century.[1] Scattered among the entries are names and memoranda relating to the neighbouring households (in south Derbyshire) of Hungerford, Coton, Francis, Shirley and Findern. Many of the names are those of women, and the contents strongly suggest an assemblage made by and/or for a female readership: the texts are all in the vernacular, are courtly rather than clerical or learned in tenor, predominantly concern courtly love and often feature women. Those who commissioned, compiled, owned and read the manuscript have thus left upon it the imprint of their own tastes as well as of the personal and household particulars recorded in their jottings – from two of which (from the sixteenth century) the manuscript gained its sobriquet: the name Findern occurs in a memorandum of expenses (f. 59ᵛ) and a list of household linen and utensils (fol. 70ᵛ).[2] Such marginalia are in manuscripts less visibly differentiated from texts than they would be in a modern printed book. Literature is in form and content here inseparable from actual particular readers.

---

[1] The manuscript was first described by Rossell Hope Robbins, 'The Findern Anthology', *PMLA* 69 (1954) 610–42. His account was corrected and expanded in a seminal article by Kate Harris: 'The Origins and Make-up of Cambridge University Library MS Ff.1.6', *Transactions of the Cambridge Bibliographical Society* 8 (1983) 299–333. Significant subsequent articles include Ralph Hanna, 'The Production of Cambridge University Library MS Ff.1.6', *Studies in Bibliography* 40 (1987) 62–70 and Michael Johnston, '*Sir Degrevant* in the "Findern Anthology"', *Studies in Bibliography* 59 (2015) 71–84.
[2] See the facsimile reproduction of the manuscript: *The Findern Manuscript: Cambridge University Library MS. Ff.1.6*, introduced by Richard Beadle and A.E.B. Owen (London, 1977).

The compilers must have shown a lot of initiative in entering the texts. No less than forty different scribes figure over its sixty-two items and the nine booklets which comprise them.[3] Many of these scribes write only briefly and/or infrequently. Though some of them are at least semi-professional, writing explicits or scribal signatures such as 'quod W Caluerley', 'quod Leweston',[4] there are, according to Beadle and Owen, no signs (such as catchwords or running titles) of the professional scriptorium, and the hands are all those of 'workaday' or 'amateur' scribes (p. xi).[5] Some may thus have been scribally competent members of household staff (and perhaps even of the families), but the ladies must have used considerable resourcefulness, and perhaps some arm-twisting, to conscript into service, often for only very short stints, so many ever-changing hands.

Chaucer's *Parliament of Fowls* (fols. 29^r–42^v), for instance, is divided in a curious manner between two scribes, the second of whom took over briefly from 36^v–37^r, from line 25 of 37^v to line 2 of 38^r, and from line 6 of the same page to the end, where he showed he had at least some scribal training by adding 'explicit parliamentum avium / Quod W Caluerley'. He was, plainly, however, not available to do the whole text at a stretch, but had to intermit it, perhaps with other household business. Pressure of time and/or impatience evidently prompted some ad hoc arrangements that are not untypical of this manuscript and force one to speculate on the particular actualities underlying the business of inscription. And in this area, too, such questions include those of gender.

For, at the end of *Sir Degrevant*, which is also divided between two scribes, there appear written out, in the beautiful hand of its second scribe, two names: 'Elisabet Koton', in a rectangular box, and underneath that 'Elisabet frauncys' (fol. 109^v). In the earliest study of the manuscript, Robbins made the deduction that immediately occurs as the most obvious: that these were the names of the two scribes who wrote out the romance.[6] But subsequent scholars have found it difficult to believe that any woman from the named Derbyshire households could have acquired so trained a hand as that of the second of these scribes. It is least possible, however, that these names are those of the scribes.[7] If not, they may identify the two women who oversaw or arranged for the copying of the two respective parts, 'the

---

[3] See Johnston, '*Sir Degrevant*', p. 75. For an enumeration of the scribes (and of the items each entered), see Harris, 'Origins and Make-up', appendix III, pp. 331–3.
[4] See Robbins, 'Findern', p. 629.
[5] *Findern Manuscript*, introduced by Beadle and Owen.
[6] Robbins, 'Findern', p. 628.
[7] Simone Celine Marshall, 'Manuscript Agency and the Findern Manuscript', *Mitteilungen* 108 (2007) 339–49 (p. 347).

commissioners or future owners' of the text.[8] There is, at any rate, some interaction evident here between the literary text and the actual Derbyshire household(s) who owned and used the particular manuscript in which it is here recorded.

The texts themselves certainly suggest female tastes, as we have already remarked. They include not only, for instance, selected stories from Gower's *Confessio Amantis*, Chaucer's *Parliament of Fouls*, the story of Thisbe (from the *Legend of Good Women*), *The Complaint of Venus* and Clanvowe's *Cuckoo and Nightingale*, but also two famous feminist polemics in which male views of women are subjected to female critiques: Hoccleve's adaptation of Christine de Pisan's letter from Cupid, wherein Cupid responds to the complaints of women in a letter patent that upholds their cause against the wrongs and deceits of false lovers and the slanders of male literati;[9] and *La belle dame sans merci*, a translation by Sir Richard Roos of a French poem, by Alain Chartier, in which a lady refuses to be argued into compliance with her lover's protestations.[10]

There are also a considerable number of lyrics, and it is mostly of these that the many items unique to this manuscript consist.[11] Booklet VII (in Johnston's numeration) was 'certainly produced locally'[12] and consists entirely of lyrics, almost all of them found only in this manuscript. It is formed from individual bifolia added accretively into a single composite quire, which suggests lyrics were added as they came to hand, and were perhaps contributed (and possibly sometimes authored) by friends, visitors or members of the household(s). The same may be true of the shorter poems found in the other booklets (sometimes entered as fillers in the gaps between items or at the end of gatherings). Audience and text thus become in these cases yet more interinvolved. Here, too, the issue includes the matter of gender, for some of these lyrics have female voices (and so very probably female authors[13]). Some of the poems may conceivably have been prompted by actual circumstances. Be that as it may, one may note how often one was assumed to write of or to the loved one, not simply because one felt in a lyric mood, but because s/he could not be addressed in person.

---

[8] Julia Boffey, 'Women Authors and Women's Literacy in Fourteenth- and Fifteenth-Century England', in *Women and Literature in Britain 1150–1500*, ed. Carol M. Meale (Cambridge, 1996), pp. 159–82 (p. 170).
[9] For editions of both Hoccleve's *Letter* and Christine's *Epistre*, see Thelma S. Fenster and Mary Carpenter Erler, *Poems of Cupid, God of Love* (Leiden, 1990).
[10] The poem was edited from this manuscript (collated with its two other witnesses) by F.J. Furnivall, *Political, Religious and Love Poems*, EETS OS 15 (1903), pp. 80–111.
[11] See *The Findern Manuscript*, ed. Martin.
[12] Johnston, '*Sir Degrevant*', p. 76.
[13] *Pace* Boffey, 'Women Authors', pp. 170–1.

There might have been a quarrel or 'varyaunce' (items 32, 36, 51[14]); or the addressee is ill (item 11[15]). But by far the commonest theme of all the love lyrics is separation, that most typical of occasions for a love letter or poem.

The very first of the shorter unique lyrics (a ballade in direct address) provides a case in point. It begins

> I may well sygh, for grevous ys my payne
> Now to departe fram yow thys sodenly   *thys* thus

and its refrain runs, 'Alas, for woo, departynge hath me slayn!'[16] By contrast with the preceding Lydgatian triple ballade, opposite which it appears (and which also bewails the absence of the beloved), with its stagy envoy to the 'Princes of beaute' (item 6), this poem strikes by its simplicity: it says virtually nothing but the 'I miss you' expressed in the refrain, but sounds very much more natural.

Item 23 (a filler) has a female speaker, and though not in direct address, it is another lyric that testifies to absence as the most common (real or assumed) occasion for writing poems to or about the beloved: the first stanza ends, 'Longe absens grevyth me so', the next begins, 'For lakke of syght nere am I sleyn' and the fourth declares the only possible solace to be 'the syght of hym agayn / That cawsis my woo'.[17] Item 34, which does occur elsewhere,[18] is in the voice of a lover 'ferre [far] from hire [her]' (4), in the third person alternating with the second now that he is 'out of your sight' (6). Item 35 is another unique love poem, whose six quatrains were again declaredly written in response to lack of 'sight' of the beloved (1–8), to whom, again, fidelity unto death is vowed (9–24).[19] And item 37, in direct address, is likewise occasioned by 'your partynge' (line 6).[20] In item 52 (in

---

[14] Item 32 is no. 10 in Martin, ed., *The Findern Manuscript*, and appears also in *The Early English Carols*, ed. R.L. Greene (Oxford), 1st edn (1935), p. 301; 2nd edn (1977), pp. 269–70; item 36 is no. 13 in Martin and no. XXXVI in Robbins, 'Findern'; item 51 is no. 26 in Martin and no. 167 in Robbins, ed., *Secular Lyrics*.
[15] No. 4 in Martin, ed., *The Findern Manuscript* and no. 164 in Robbins, ed., *Secular Lyrics*.
[16] The poem was included (under the title 'A Lover's Plaint II') by Robbins in *Secular Lyrics*, p. 158. It is Poem 1 in Martin, ed., *The Findern Manuscript*.
[17] Edited by Robbins in 'Findern', pp. 633–4; by Alexandra Barrett in her anthology of *Women's Writing in Middle English*, where it appears (pp. 270–1) among other short poems from the Findern manuscript; and most recently by Martin in *The Findern Manuscript* (poem 8).
[18] Bodleian MS Ashmole 191: see J. Copley, *Seven Songs and Carols of the Fifteenth Century* (Leeds, 1940), pp. 12–13. The Findern text appears in T. Wright and J.O. Halliwell, *Reliquiae antiquae*, 2 vols (London, 1845), vol. 1, p. 25, and in H.A. Mason, *Humanism and Poetry in the Early Tudor Period* (London, 1959), pp. 169–70.
[19] The poem is no. 167 (pp. 156–7) in Robbins, ed., *Secular Lyrics*, and poem 12 in Martin, ed., *The Findern Manuscript*.
[20] Item 37 is in Robbins, 'Findern', p. 636 and is Poem 14 in Martin, ed., *The Findern Manuscript*.

the seventh booklet), the speaker is female, names 'Departyng' as her chief sorrow and turns from third- to second-person reference at her conclusion:

> Syns that ȝe nedys moste departe me fro,
> It ys to me a verry dedly woo.[21]   *verry dedly* truly mortal

Item 54 (in direct address) again contextualizes itself as occasioned by a parting (line 4), a point given culminating significance in the last couplet:

> When y thing on you and am absent: *thing* think
> Ffor, alas, departyng hath my hert schent.[22]   *schent* destroyed, broken

The unique items, however, include only two letters proper, one from a woman and one from a man. The woman's (item 31, fols. 135^r–136^r) occurs at the end of a quire and consists of some fifty lines of verse written in a hand that occurs only here.[23] The poem (which begins, 'Welcome be ye, my sovereine') takes the form of a letter/address to a beloved who has been absent, but is now returning or returned. It includes (lines 27–32) an apology for some 'chiding' of which the beloved complained in a 'letter' received. Since neither of these things is given any explanation, which we would expect in a 'generic' verse letter or a fictional situation, we may be dealing here with some real circumstances. The narrative adumbrated by the poem is also unclear, the situation and sequence of events being just obscure and unexplained enough to feel 'real'. The apparent quarrel may act partly to type or 'explain' the letter, since it seems to have been assumed that a written approach might be necessary in order to pave the way for, or because of probable avoidance by the addressee of, an interview. Boncompagno mentions 'amoris alteracio' as a common occasion for a letter between lovers,[24] and apologetic regrets following an apparent tiff were certainly part of the repertoire of love-verse motifs, as we have seen above (p. 226). But that does not mean that poems which trace out this sequence are necessarily simply conventional; the convention probably reflects the fact that actual lovers did have quarrels and resorted occasionally to writing to patch them up, and the existence of the verse motif may in turn have prompted a similar recourse in actual cases.

---

[21] The poem is no. 27 in Martin, ed., *The Findern Manuscript*, and no. LII (pp. 638–9) in Robbins, 'Findern'. (They preserve MS 'moste nedys', but metre supports the transposition we make here.)
[22] The poem is no. 168 (pp. 157–8) in Robbins, ed., *Secular Lyrics*, and no. 29 in Martin, ed., *The Findern Manuscript*.
[23] The poem is available in Robbins, 'Findern', pp. 634–5; Barrett, *Women's Writing in Middle English*, pp. 271–3; Martin, ed., *The Findern Manuscript*, no. 9.
[24] See Text 1, 134.10–11 above.

The man's letter occurs in the narrative poem to which we now turn (item 14). It was edited by Furnivall under the title *The Parliament of Love*.[25] We have retained that title for the sake of consistency, though it is perhaps not an apt one, as will become apparent from our discussion of the poem (which we defer until its story has been told to those encountering it for the first time).

---

[25] Furnivall, *Political, Religious and Love Poems*, pp. 76–9. The poem is no. 5 in Martin, ed., *The Findern Manuscript*. Where we have emended, the MS reading is retained in Furnivall and Martin unless otherwise indicated.

THE PARLIAMENT OF LOVE

What so evyr I syng or sey,
My wyll is good too preyse here well.　　　　*here* her

Now yee that wull of lovë lere,
I counsell yow that ye cum nere.
To tell yow now is myne entent
Houth Love made late his parleament,
5　And sent for ladyes of every londe,　　　　*ladyes* high-ranking women
Both mayde and wyf that had housbonde,
Wythe gentyll wymmen of lower degré,　　　　*gentyll* well-born
And marchauntz wyfës grete plenté,
Wythe maidenes eke that were theym undre,　　　　*that were theym undre* in their households
10　Of wyche there were a rygthe grete number;
And all tho men þat lovers were,
They had there charge for too be there.　　　　Received their summons to attend
And when they were assembled all,
Yf I the werré soth sey schall,　　　　*werré* very, veritable
15　Within a castell feyre ande stronge,
And as I lokyd them amonge,
I sawe a rygth grete company
Of gentill wummen that were thereby,
The whyche, as the[n] the custom was,
20　Songe a balad stede of the Mass　　　　*balad stede of* ballade instead of
For goode spede of thes folkys alle
That where assemblede in the hall;　　　　*where* were
And yf ye lyst ley too yowre ere,　　　　And if you wish to lay your ear to it
Ryght thys they songe, as yee schall here:　　　　*thys* thus

25　'O, god of love, wyche lorde hart and soverayne,　　　　*hart* art
Send downe thy grace amonge thys loverys all,
Soo that they may too thy mercy ateyne;
At thys parlament most in asspeciall　　　　*parlament* (pronounced 'parl'mènt')
As thu art ourë juge, so be egall　　　　*egall* equitable
30　Too every wyght þat lovyth feythefully
And aftyr hys dyssert grante hym mercy'.　　　　*aftyr hys dyssert* according to his deserts

19 as then the] as the twas the; as the *Furnivall, Martin*

52ʳ   And whan this songe was songe and done,
      Then went these ladyes everyschone
      Untoo a schambyr, where thay scholde
35 Take theire places, yonge and olde,
      Like as that they where of astate,   According to their ranks
      For t'escheue all maner debate.   In order to avoid all disagreement
      There sawe I first the goddesse of love
      In here see sitte rigth ferre above,   *here see* her seat
40 And many othyr þat ther where.   *where* were
      Yitt for to tell wh[o]m Y sawe there   *whom* all those whom
      It passit now rigth ferre my wytte.   *passit* would surpass
      But among all I sawe one sitte
      Whiche was the feyryst creature
45 That ever was furmyd by Nature;   *furmyd* formed
      And here beauté now too dyscryve
      Ther can noo mannës [w]ytte aly[v]e.   No living man's wit is able
      Yett as ferre as y can or may
      Of here beauté sumwhat too say
50 I will applye my wittës all:
      For here I am and ever schall.   *here* hers; *schall* shall be
      Too speke of schape and semelynesse,
      Off stature and of goodlynesse:
      Here sydës longe, with myddyll smale;   *Here* her
55 Here face well coulord, and not pale,   *coulord* coloured
      With white and rode ryth well mesuryd; With white and ruddiness in appropriate proportions
      And thertoo schee was well emyred,   *emyred* admired
52ᵛ   And stode in every mannës grace,
      This goodly, yong and fresche of face.   *This* this person
60 And too speke of condicïon,
      Coude noo man fynde in noo region
      One of soo grete gentillnesse,   *gentillnesse* graciousness
      Of curtaisé and lowlynesse,   *lowlynesse* modesty
      Of chere, of port and dalyaunce, –   Of (good) manner, bearing and speech
65 And mastres eke of all pleasaunce,   *mastres* mistress; *all pleasaunce* all that pleases
      Allsoo welle of secretenesse,   *welle* fountainhead; *secretenesse* discretion
      The werray merroure of stedfastnesse;   *werray* true; *merroure* mirror, epitome

36 of] oft   41 whom] whem   42 now] ferre now   46 dyscryve] dyscryvye   47 wytte alyve] vyttes alywe   49 Of] Oof   53 of] oft   56 rode] rede *Martin*

	Of onest merth sche coude rith m[u]sche –	*onest* decent, socially acceptable; *musche* much
	Too daunce and synge and othre suche;	
70	Soo well assuryd in here hert	So well-governed within herself
	That none il worde from here scholde stert.	*il* bad; *scholde stert* could spring from her mouth
	And thus on here Y set my mynde	
	And left all othre thyng byhynde	
	As touchyng too these lovers all,	*As touching too* relating to
75	Whysche on here causes fast kan call.	Who their suits earnestly did plead
	And for too tell theire all cumplayntes,	*theire all cumplayntes* all their grievances
	In sothe too me the matire queynte is,	Truly is a difficult matter for me
	For as too hem I toke none hede,	
	But in myne nowne cause to prosede.	But (heeded) only to further my own suit
80	I drowe me by mysylf alone	I drew myself apart
	And into a corner gan too gone,	
	And there I satte me downe a while	
	A litle bill for too compile	
	Untoo thys lady wych was soo faire	
85	And in here doyng soo debonaire;	*doyng* behaviour; *debonaire* gracious
	And, if ye list too hyre and rede,	*list* wish; *hyre* read
	Th'effect of whych was thus in dede:	*of whych* of it (= the bill)
	'O souvereyn prince[s] off all gentillnesse,	*princes* princess
	Too whom I have and evyrmore schall bee	*have* have been
90	Trewe servant with all maner humblenesse,	
	What peyne I have or what adversyté,	*What ... what* whatever ... whatever
	Yett yee schall evyr fynde suche feyth on me	
	That I schall doo that may be your plesaunce,	*doo that* do that which
	If of His grace God list me so avaunce.	*list me so avaunce* pleases to further my suit that far
95	'And yow I pray as lowly as I can	*lowly* humbly
	Too take my serves, if hyt myth yow please;	
	And if yee list too reward thus yowre man,	
	Than mygth hee say he were in hertis ease.	
	For, by my trouth, Y wulde not yow displease	
100	For all the goode that ever I hadde or schall,	
	By my goode wille, whatever me befall.	*By my goode wille* not willingly

68 musche] mosche   72 thus] that thus   79 cause] causes   80 me by mysylf] *Furnivall*; me(*corrected from* my)sylf me by sylf; myself me by my-sylf *Martin*   81] gan] gang *Martin*   88 souvereyn] *Furnivall*; soueuereyn *MS and Martin*   princes] prince *MS and Furnivall*; princess *Martin*   94 of His grace God] god of his grace   98 ease] *Martin*; easee *MS and Furnivall*

'And if I have seide [an]y thynge amysse,
Too pardon me I yow besech and pray:
For as wischli as ever Y cum too blisse,   *wischli* certainly; *cum* may come
105 My will is goode, whatever Y write or say. –
Go, thow litle songe, thou hast a blisfull day: *day* day ahead of you
For sche that is the floure of womanh[e]de
At her oown leyser schall the syng and rede'.   *the* thee

102 any] *Furnivall*; my *MS and Martin*   107 womanhede] womanhode

NOTES TO *THE PARLIAMENT OF LOVE*

The first couplet is plainly an epigraph: there is a gap between it and line 3, which is preceded by a paraph mark. Paraph marks also occur by the first line of each succeeding page (51ᵛ, 52ʳ, 52ᵛ, 53ʳ), and by the opening line of each stanza of the 'bill' (ll. 88, 95, 102). As to the former set (which we have treated simply as 'continuation' markers, not as internal divisions), Furnivall and Martin mark the first by a gap before line 11, but ignores the others.

1   'of lovë lere': though medial *e* is sounded to give disyllabic plurals and genitive singulars for monosyllabic nouns (e.g. 'wyfes', 'wittes'), the metre does not elsewhere require sounded final *e*. The same is true of the 'filler' lyrics in the MS. This is consistent with the late date to which this poem seems from other evidence to belong (see n. to 57). Since 'Love' in line 4 is monosyllabic, it may be that this one anomaly in line 1 is scribal, and that some monosyllable (such as 'here' or 'now') has dropped before 'lere'.

5–9 The list moves down (within the category of genteel women) through 'ladyes' (aristocrats), 'gentyll wymmen of lower degré' and burgesses' wives, and the girls of good family who were placed in households to serve as attendants and for social education (cf. *CT* VII.95–7 and editorial note). Non-*gentils* do not figure: they lacked the leisure which was considered necessary for courtly love and which, as the personification Oiseuse, acts as the porteress to the garden of love in *Le roman de la rose* ('Ydelnesse' in the English translation: see 574–84, 593–9).

20   'a balad stede of the Mass': love is often treated as a parallel 'religion'; cf. the precepts of Ovid which replace the Gospel reading in a similar 'Parliament of Love' in *The Council of Remiremont* (see p. 432 below) 26–7.

25–31 The ballade (pentameter lines in a rhyme-royal stanza) is set off from the narrative frame (tetrameter couplets) metrically – and graphically, since there is a space between ll. 24 and 25; no space between ll. 31 and 32 is necessary or possible, since the stanza ends at the foot of the page. See further the note on the 'bill' at lines 88–108.

36–8 The iambic beat in the poem is not quite as secure as the syllable count, but is more regular than may appear, being ensured by means which sometimes sound awkward now, but were not uncommon. Hence 48 has two initial reversed feet ('Yett as ferre as y can or may'). Some words can take prefix stress (as at 97, 'And if yee list too rèward thus yowre man') or be stressed on either syllable, hence the beats in 37 are 'For t'èscheue all manèr debate' (whereas 'maner' at 90 takes first-syllable stress: 'Trewe sèrvant wìth all maner humblenesse'). A function word rather than an accompanying open-class word can in some circumstances take stress (as in 101, 'By mý goode wille'). The syllable count may legitimately be reduced by the accepted device of headless lines (as in 62, 66 and 104, which begin 'one of...', 'Àllsoo ...', 'Fòr as ...'); but line 38 has an extra syllable, and is thus one of the few syllabically irregular lines.

43-71 The poet shows himself familiar with common rhetorical moves in the description of female perfection, especially those exemplified in Chaucer's *Book of the Duchess*: the lady as Nature's masterpiece (43-5; cf. *BD* 908-12); the inexpressibility of her beauty, which the lover will nevertheless do his best to describe (46-50; cf. *BD* 898-904); the division of the description into what the rhetoricians called the *effictio* (her physical form) and the *notatio* (her graces of mind and manner), a procedure here made formally apparent by the matching announcements 'Too speke of' (52) and 'And too speke of' (60), and one followed also at *BD* 895-1033.

57 'emyred': the verb 'admire' appeared later than its cognates in other parts of speech and in Middle English is recorded by the *MED* only here and in *The Mirror of Man's Salvation* (c. 1500).

75-6, 79 'here causes', 'cumplayntes', 'myne nowne cause': the language continues the allegory of the 'parleament' (4) of Love; in that not uncommon conceit, love poetry could conflate the specific legal senses the words could have (see *MED cause* n. 7, *compleint(e* n. 4) with the frequent application to love of their more general senses.

76-7 'cumplayntes ... queynte is': the rhyme shows familiarity with Chaucerian verse techniques; cf. e.g. 'werkis'/'derk is' (*CT* VIII.64/66).

88-108 The change in form and metre (from octosyllabic couplets to pentameter rhyme-royal stanza) is signalled by gaps before each stanza and paraph marks by their first lines; cf. n. to 25-31.

89, 100 The same minor grammatical looseness occurs in both lines: 'be' and 'hadde' are treated as if they could supply, respectively, 'bene' after 'have' and 'have' after 'schall'.

*

The poem seems to be late (see nn. to 1 and 57) and so may have been composed (like the shorter poems in the first booklet) at about the same time as the MS was being assembled, perhaps the work of a friend, visitor or local acquaintance, perhaps not. At a time when versifying was a genteel accomplishment, when the reading and writing of love poetry, in particular, was a widely popular (as opposed to a high-brow) pastime, and when few earned money from their poetry or had any special 'literary' training, the distinction between the amateur and professional scarcely existed. The present poet, however, is clearly no crude beginner. He is familiar with rhyming sophistications (see n. to 76-7), with the repertoire of rhetorical moves found in love verse (see n. to 43-71), as well as with the tradition of the 'parliament' in love poems (found, for instance, in *The Parliament of Fowls* and *The Council of Remiremont*). The metre is, like that of many of the unique lyrics of the first booklet, uncommonly regular (in beat and syllable count) for this date, when scansion was often somewhat rough and ready, and is inventive as well as assured: octosyllabic couplets for the narrative frame; rhyme-royal stanzas for the inserted ballade and bill (see nn. to 25–31 and 88–108). The formal polish includes an elegant epigraph to, and in the same regular octosyllabic iambics as, the narrative. Given that the rhyme-royal 'balad' is repeatedly characterized as a 'song' (20, 24, 32) – as, in its envoy, is the rhyme-royal 'bill' (106, 108) – even what looks like a mere alliterating doublet, 'syng or sey' (1), may have an unobtrusive precision, the 'preyse' consisting both of the formal *descriptio* in the octosyllabic frame (43–71) and the hymn in her honour of the rhyme-royal intended to be 'sung' (108). The epigraph is, in fact, recalled just before that envoy:

> And if I have seide any thynge amysse ...
> My will is goode, whatever Y write or say.   (102, 105)[26]

This framing 'apology' implicitly casts the poet as an amateur, suggesting that his 'goodwill' must compensate for the imperfections of his verse tribute – a loverly protestation of inadequacy to the lady's excellence which gives a kind of at least assumed tentativeness to his third- and second-person tribute to her.

The decision to address her in writing is the only significant, as well as the culminating, event in the poem. As in Chaucer's *Complaint unto Pity* (a poem included as item 4 in the present MS[27]), the narrative acts as a proem rather than a frame, for it is not resumed after the 'bill' is rehearsed, each poem thus in effect turning itself into a bill. Our poem, then, becomes a bill, a second-person address, and it seems to have no other purpose except to do so: that is, to enact the lover's decision to write to the lady. The transition from the narrative frame is provided by his appeal taking the form of a 'bill' – which in one way is an anomaly. When a man or woman chose (in fact or fiction) to declare his or her love to its object, since opportunities for private meetings were rare and brief, s/he normally did so by 'letter': as does George Cely's *amorosa* (see p. 28 above) and as do both the fictional Euryalus and the historical cleric who appropriated his letter (see p. 111 above). The petition or 'bill' occurs only in allegorical or mythological contexts and is addressed to a deity or personification. Hence the 'Supplicacioun' composed by the hopeless Amans and presented to Venus in the form of a 'lettre' at the climax of Gower's *Confessio Amantis* (VIII.2184, 2209, 2301) – for a letter in such a context is a petition (i.e. a

---

[26] Metre supports Furnivall's emendation of MS 'my' to 'any' at 103.
[27] In fact, item 3, but we follow the numeration in the 'Contents' list of the facsimile, in which the second Gower extract is (wrongly) treated as two items.

quasi-judicial appeal to a magnate who has executive and judicial powers to grant the request). Hence also the 'compleynt' composed in order to be presented to Pity 'as a bille' (43–4) in Chaucer's *Complaint unto Pity*. Chaucer, not by instinct an allegorical poet, interestingly deconstructs the personification device by the initial narrative, in which he discovers with shock that Pity, to whom he nevertheless addresses his bill, is dead – that is, there is no point in appealing to pity against the experienced absence of it in the lady and in the world. As we shall see, our present poem also, in a different sense, deconstructs its allegorical prelude. In the cases of Gower's Amans and Chaucer's *Complaint*, the 'bill' is the recourse of a lover who feels his case to be desperate, and so, instead of addressing a foredoomed appeal by letter to the lady, he in effect goes over her head by appealing to some authority who can dictate her compliance. Women are also represented, or represent themselves, as presenting similar bills: the (probably, though not demonstrably, female) author of *The Assembly of Ladies* tells how, in a dream, she and other ladies presented their bills to Loyauté – that is, pleaded their rights to success in love.[28]

The 'bill' in the present poem thus belongs to the allegorical context of the Parliament, and would be the form taken by the appeals of lovers to Love himself to further their cause. As a form of address, it is appropriate to Love as a prince presiding over a parliament, not to the beloved: to the 'souvereyn prince' whom, interestingly, the scribe mistakenly indicates as the addressee at 88, though 'princes' [princess] is confirmed both by metrical requirements and by line 84.[29] The decision to address the bill to *her* (and not to Love) is, in effect, an abandonment of the allegory, which disappears at that point and is not resumed. It is thus as much a poetic decision as an amorous one – and amounts to a kind of deconstruction of the allegorical fiction. For the 'target' of any allegorical 'bill' was, of course, the lady implicitly assumed as reading the poem. It is to her that the appeal was 'really' addressed (not Love, etc.). So the poet who cast it all into the artful form of allegory here in effect becomes the lover he 'really' is, addressing the lady who is his 'real' addressee, as the 'she' of the rhetorical *descriptio* becomes the 'you' of the bill.

Similarly, the 'I' develops from a narrator into an actor. The slender narrative is not one to which the poet is much committed. The list of those attending the Parliament begins with, and is more specific in the case of, the women – a detail which may have recommended it to (or been included

---

[28] See *The Floure and the Leafe and The Assembly of Ladies*, ed. Derek Pearsall (London, 1962).
[29] 'Princess (of)' was a common form of address in a love poem: cf. the envoy (to a ballade by Lydgate) cited above at p. 226 and Text 6, 4A.1.

expressly in response to) the female bias apparent in the MS. Though the Parliament is summoned by the god of Love, he never appears, and it is the goddess of Love who figures in it (briefly: 38–9). Men who attend are mentioned much more summarily (11). Some presumably male suitors with suits to prosecute do, however, appear at 75–6 (though the gender of the plaintiffs is not stated). But by this time, the poet (the only male to gain any real presence or attention in his own poem) has lost interest in his own fictional parliament and claims (72–9) he was too preoccupied with his own cause to notice the 'complaints' others made (presumably to Love) and so cannot report or 'tell' anything concerning them (76). What literary critics refer to as an 'omniscient' narrator, who begins quite confident of his ability to 'tell' (3) a story to others interested in love, is now no longer omniscient, for he has become an actor in his own fiction, from the scene of which he represents himself as literally withdrawing into his own private corner (78–81) in order to write his bill, not to Love, but to the lady who preoccupies him.

This lady, in the fiction, is one he has only just seen. But in the bill he speaks as one who has 'evyrmore' been devoted to her (88–90). Here we have another internal anomaly similar to the bill properly addressable to Love rather than the beloved. And the effect is similarly to suggest a 'real' love, for a particular lady, that prompted the fiction. The last lines are an envoy addressed to his versified appeal, an address proper, not to a bill, but to a ballade or letter, which is not infrequently apostrophized in concluding internal or external lines as something due (as here: 108) to be read by the lady (cf. Troilus's address to his own first letter to Criseyde: 'lettre, a blisful destine / The [thee] shapyn is, my lady shal the see' (II.1090–1)). The 'bill' has emerged as what it in effect is: a ballade-letter to the lady, who will, the last line declares, 'syng' as well as 'rede' it.

Here another 'real' purpose suggests itself as emerging. Women liked to sing. In the Devonshire Manuscript (another household anthology), Lady Margaret has written beside one poem 'lerne but to syng yt' (fol. 81ʳ), adding 'and thys' against other items.[30] The affair recorded by Machaut in his *Voir dit* is initiated and sustained by the fact that Péronne likes to sing and Machaut keeps her supplied with *chansons*, love poems for which he composes both the words and the music. What suggests itself at the end of the present poem is a lady of similar tastes by whom the poem could be sung. We may remember the bond created in the poems Beethoven set to music,

---

[30] See further Paul Remley, 'Mary Shelton and Her Tudor Literary Milieu', in *Rethinking the Henrician Era: Essays on Early Tudor Texts and Contexts*, ed. Peter C. Herman (Urbana, IL, 1994), pp. 40–77.

by the songs the lover-musician composes and imagines his far-off sweetheart singing:

> Nimm sie hin denn, diese Lieder,
> die ich dir, Geliebte sang;
> singe sie dann abends wieder
> zu der Lute süßem Klang ...
> Und du singst, was ich gesungen, ...
> Dann vor diesen Liedern weichet
> was geschieden uns so weit.[31]

Receive them, then, these songs that I sang out; sing them back in the evening to the sweet accompaniment of the lute ... and you will sing what I composed ... Then through these things will give way what divides us so widely.

What a lover is to 'lere' [learn] (1) thus turns out to lie, not in allegories about parliaments and personifications, but that he must draw breath – or, rather, pick up his pen – and address the lady. The poem might even suggest or be a way of doing so: a way of smuggling in a letter-ballade to a particular lady by means of that 'corner' created within what appears to be a more public or general poem, and so deliverable to her without the usual risks. In short, all sorts of scenarios inevitably suggest themselves, and that may be the whole point. The poem certainly implies a kind of potential redoubling of itself from the 'I' and 'you' within it to the 'I' and 'you' of a particular author and reader, and that is why it seems to sit teasingly at the border between art and actuality. Perhaps its art is precisely to suggest the particularizable.

---

[31] *An die ferne Geliebte* [To the far-away loved one], VII (lyrics by Alois Jeitteles).

SECTION III

*Actual Letters
(Drafts, Copies, Missives)*

TEXT 4

The Norfolk Letters: The Abbot to the Nun

This chapter concerns drafts of three love letters written from a man who describes himself as an abbot to a woman he addresses as 'Margaret' and refers to as owing obedience to a convent (II.65), and who mentions places in Norfolk in connection with past or projected meetings between the two (II.22, 49; III.4). The letters, dating from the fourteenth century, occur at the end of a manuscript devoted to works of canon law and which the abbot therefore probably consulted for professional reasons: Cambridge, Gonville and Caius, 54/31. The existence of these epistles was first noted by Paul Meyer,[1] and Martin Camargo briefly discussed them in his study of the verse love epistle (pp. 29–32).

The letters are written out on what were originally blank pages after the last item in the manuscript (*Casus novarum constitucionum Innocentii quartii*). The *Casus* ends five lines into the second column on fol. 145[r],[2] and immediately beneath occur eleven lines of a note in Latin. After a gap occupying roughly the second third of the column comes the first of the abbot's letters, which takes up the rest of it. Four originally blank pages follow (145[v]–147[r]). The first pair of facing blanks has been used for law notes in Latin. The abbot's second and third letters fill the first of the two remaining facing blank pages. They are written with the book turned upside-down, and are followed at the foot of the page (as inverted) by a repeated word ('ludr' or 'lndr'), whose significance is unclear, and which, though oddly positioned for it, could perhaps be an initial pen-trial following an ink-dip.

The letters are written in Anglo-Norman, but there are brief register switches into English in the first two letters (I.7–8; II.39–44, 67).[3]

---

[1] Paul Meyer, 'Mélanges Anglo-Normands', *Romania* 38 (1909) 434–41.
[2] Our folio numbering differs from that given by M.R. James, *A Descriptive Catalogue of the Manuscripts in the Library of Gonville and Caius College* (Cambridge, 1907), pp. 47–9.
[3] On intermittent epistolary language change, see Schendl, 'Code-Choice and Code-Switching'. Schendl convincingly describes his chosen examples of English interjections in French letters as associated with 'personalization' and as reinforcing goodwill or urgency (pp. 253–8). But there may be other explanations for the code-switch in these (earlier) Norfolk letters. See nn. to II.39–44 and 67.

The writer (that is, the scribe and author, who are in this case evidently, as rarely elsewhere in recorded Middle English, the same person[4]) is plainly used to writing in both languages. When writing in English, he uses the thorn (þ) regularly employed for the sound /th/ and employs the dropped-three-like symbol in two different ways: as /z/ in Anglo-Norman (in words such as *saluz* and *recordez*) and in his English lines as the letter yogh, which in English represented both the /gh/ in words such as *mighten* and /y/ in words such as *yeve* [give] (see II.41, 44). Whereas the Armburgh love letters (Text 6) appear to be neat copies, these are fairly certainly drafts: there are deletions, though these are fewer than they might be today (for, since writing was more manually demanding, writers tended to think before rather than as they wrote). The deletion of 'jeo m'en irray en Essex' towards the end of Letter II looks less like a copying error than a reconsideration of the journey or its relevance.

The Latin notes were presumably written before the letters, which follow them spatially, the first after the first short note, and the second and third after the longer set of notes. The Latin notes and the Anglo-French letters are in fact written in a very similar hand, and may be the work of the same person, who simply found different uses for those inviting blank spaces in a manucsript which was possibly the personal property of, or had been appropriated by, the abbot, for he would scarcely have risked identification by naming himself as such if he thought the manuscript might well be consulted by others.

The first letter (a greeting) is written out in such a way as to make clear its status as verse. The manuscript line corresponds to what today would be printed as two verse lines, a mid-line point normally occurring after the rhyme word of the first 'line' of verse. So the opening manuscript lines rhyme and are set out and pointed thus: a.a/aa/bc/b.c/d.d/d.-/d.d (the rhyme word 'pucele' that should occur at the end of manuscript line 6 (line 12 below) has slid into the next line, but is followed by the point that marks it as a rhyme word). The two-unit-per-line pattern occasionally fails, being sent awry by a deleted phrase at the beginning of line 9 (MS)/16 (edited text) and by the triplet with imperfect rhyme 'mand'/'sunt'/'cressant' at 21–3 (edited text), but the rhyming words that have as a result been displaced into following lines ('lever', 'gré', 'volenté') are (as in the case of 'pucele') clearly marked as such by a point placed after them. In

---

[4] For discussion and examples of some autograph letters, see Richard Beadle, 'Aspects of Late Medieval English Autograph Writings', Lyell Lectures, delivered in Oxford in 2013; see also Taylor, 'Letters', p. 69.

fact, Meyer's assertion that the letters are written out as prose ('Mélanges', p. 434) is not true of this first letter, where the writer is setting out his lines in such a way as to keep himself on track in the verse which was by convention suited to a love letter and which he aims at producing (and which, though the lines have some irregularity in rhyme scheme and syllable length, is by no means painfully lame).

The second letter is intriguingly circumstantial. It begins with an apology for not having communicated before, but warns that the pair must be circumspect. It goes on to recall a journey made with Margaret to the Cross of Bromholm (in Norfolk), an occasion on which they had evidently enjoyed some intimate conversation, and a meal at Fakenham (also in Norfolk) at the house of a cousin of his and a neighbour of hers (a man called 'Sir Robert'). It consists of twenty-five manuscript lines, and is again in verse, although this time (as in the Armburgh letters) the lines are written out continuously as prose, but with points usually following the rhyme words that mark the ends of the couplet (occasionally triplet or quatrain). After the opening three couplets of complimentary greeting, there is a brief relapse into prose for the specifics of apology and warning; the only pointing that occurs in these lines comes after 'promys', 'langes' and 'vous' (in lines 8, 9 and 11 in the edited text), and it is prose pointing, indicating syntactic pauses, not rhyme words. But the verse (and the pointing after rhyme words) resumes after 'fraunceys', that is, after the rehearsal of a rhyming proverb (warning against slander) that had also been cited in the first letter (II.12–13; cf. I.19–20).

A line drawn across the full width of the page separates this letter from the third, which otherwise follows immediately with no gap. This visual marking-off of the one letter from the other makes it highly unlikely that the two greetings in the second letter (II.39, 45) indicate the beginnings of two separate letters, as argued by Camargo (p. 30). Both these greetings occur within a manuscript line, and there is nothing at all to mark them as incipits to separate pieces. The third letter is written in response to a letter from the lady (cf. Armburgh [Text 6] 5C), which the abbot thanks her for, but tartly remarks that some proverb she had quoted actually makes against her, for she had not come to him at King's Lynn, as he had told her to, and so had broken her promise to him. He becomes slightly less cross as he wittily indicates that, though he will impose a 'penance' for this sin, 'amends' for it lie well within her power. But the displeasure with which he opens the letter is probably the reason why, in this epistle, he makes no attempt at verse, which is associated in the love letter with compliments, homage and humble pleas. There is patterning, but it is that of prose, not verse: there are neat doublets and the parallelism of 'Endreit de la lettre qe vous me mandastes ... mes endreit del proverbe qe vous me mandastes ...'.[5] The abbot, in fact, writes rhythmic and assured prose, which a firm command of subordinating devices renders articulate and pithy. As the man of business a medieval abbot was required to be, he was probably used to writing in prose, though he has plainly read enough verse to be able to acquit himself respectably in that format as well. He was a literate man, and these few manuscript pages show him working fluently in Latin, French and English. There emerges, moreover, a speaking visual contrast between the beautiful copy-book calligraphy of the Latin treatise and the scruffier cursive scripts in which the Latin comments and Anglo-Norman private letters are written. We have here a microcosm of medieval (and modern) life, tidy clerical scholarship and the more contingent concerns of working and amorous life: spiritual, professional and romantic concerns are here integrated into a visual and spatial unity that reflects their unity within a single man, a man who used the same pages to pursue both his professional and his amorous interests, his mind turning from ecclesiastical law to his sex life in an expressive epitome of the contrasting realities of which human existence is composed.

The Norfolk Connection

These letters can be as securely placed on the English map as can those of the Armburgh Roll and of the Corpus Christi manuscript. The association with Norfolk is all-pervasive. The home of the manuscript, Gonville and Caius, Cambridge, was itself founded, in 1348, by a Norfolk man, Edmund Gonville, who had earlier created the collegiate church in Rushworth, now Rushford, in Norfolk.[6] When he died in 1351, he was succeeded as founder by his executor, William Bateman, bishop of Norwich. And from Norfolk donors came most of the College's earliest (i.e. fourteenth-century) manuscripts – chiefly from Walter of Elveden, a canon lawyer who deputized for the bishop of Norwich (as his vicar-general during Bateman's life and as keeper of the spiritualities after his death) and from whom the College acquired a number of works of canon law; and Michael Cawston, also from the diocese of Norwich.[7] From the same diocese (which comprised the

---

[5] Compare, in the prose near the beginning of the second letter, 'qe vous fusez en blame par encheson de moy ou jeo par enchesun de vous' (II.10–11).
[6] A. Hamilton Thompson, *The English Clergy and Their Organization in the Later Middle Ages* (Oxford, 1947), p. 153.
[7] See pp. 237–44 in Catherine Hall, 'The Early Fellows of Gonville Hall and Their Books', *Transactions of the Cambridge Bibliographical Society* 13 (2006) 233–52; on Elveden and his donations, see also the entry by Keith Snedegar in the *Oxford Dictionary of National Biography*.

contiguous counties of Norfolk and Suffolk, which were therefore, in ecclesiastical terms, very much a unity at this period) came some of the College's earliest fellows.[8]

The manuscript in which the present letters occur was apparently one of the canon law works donated by Elveden: 'Elued' is, as James noted, written on the outside of the last cover.[9] The letters must, therefore, pre-date Elveden's death in 1360, since thereafter the manuscript would have been accessible only to inmates of Gonville College, and no abbot figures in Catherine Hall's survey of the early fellows of the College and those recorded in its Register as having borrowed books. This is consistent with the first half of the fourteenth century to which Meyer assigned the abbot's script (p. 434), and with the early-to-mid-fourteenth-century date suggested to us by Richard Beadle (personal communication). It is less consistent with the late fourteenth century to which, citing R.H. Robbins and Ernstpeter Ruhe, Camargo assigned the letters (p. 29) and which is certainly too late a date.

The abbot's two conjurations to obedience ('Loke nou þat hit so be / In obedience': I.7–8; cf. II.67) are too brief to rule in or out a Norfolk dialect (the typical characteristics of which were *xal* and *xulde* for 'shall' and 'should'; 'right', 'might', etc., spelled *ryth*, *myth*, etc.; 'what', etc., appearing as *qwat*, etc.; lowering of *i* to *e*; *ik* alongside *I* for 'I').[10] The absence of such Norfolk features from the longer passage in English proves little, as those lines are almost certainly a quotation (see n. to II.39–44) from a lyric in a dialect which the abbot may only partially have naturalized into his own. If he received elsewhere the education the letters clearly testify to (see note to II.59–60), his own dialect may not in any case have been reflected in his written spellings. But the abbot and his Margaret plainly themselves belonged to Norfolk (or, at least, to the diocese of Norwich), for the letters refer to specific Norfolk locations. He had told Margaret to come to him at King's Lynn (III.4), which need not imply that the house he headed was precisely in or very near that town, since anyone anywhere in the diocese may well have had (or have been able to plead) business to take him to King's Lynn (one of the largest towns in England and a major market and trading centre). The two of them had apparently gone together to 'la croiz' (II.22). Though a number of churches claimed to have fragments of Christ's actual cross, the most renowned of these 'relics' was housed at the

---

[8] Hall, 'Early Fellows', pp. 246–8.
[9] See p. 47 of the account of the manuscript given at pp. 47–9 by James in his *Descriptive Catalogue*.
[10] For a survey and list of manuscripts written by Norfolk scribes, see Richard Beadle, 'Prolegomena to a Literary Geography of Later Medieval Norfolk', in *Regionalism in Late Medieval Manuscripts and Texts*, ed. Felicity Riddy (Cambridge, 1991), pp. 89–108.

Cluniac priory of Bromholm in north-east Norfolk, and a journey to 'the cross' without further specification could really only refer to this famous 'Holy Rood of Bromholm', which constituted a major reference point in the religious world of Norfolk and to which Norfolk folk would be especially likely to make a pious pilgrimage. Langland's Avarice, a Norfolk man (*Piers Plowman* B.V.235), vows at the end of his confession to make two Norfolk pilgrimages: he will go to Walsingham (to the famous shrine of Our Lady at Walsingham Abbey in the north of the county, an especially popular destination for pilgrims) and then (B.V.227) 'bidde the Roode of Bromholm bryng me out of dette', that is, pray to the holy relic there to be forgiven the sinful debt constituted by his immoral gains.[11]

The abbot also refers, in the same letter, to the two of them supping at Fakenham (II.49) at the house of 'Sire Robert', declared to be the 'cosyn' [relative] of the abbot and the 'precheyn vesin' [near neighbour] of Margaret (52–3). Fakenham, in northern Norfolk, lay only a few miles south of Walsingham, and pilgrims to the shrine there could find accommodation in Fakenham (as they did for instance in the guesthouse of the Austin canons at Hempton Priory). Since there were no convents particularly close to Fakenham (the nearest being Blackborough, some twenty miles away), the supper at Fakenham may have been on an occasion separate from the pilgrimage, and the expression 'precheyn vesin' may refer to the neighbourhood of Margaret's family home rather than the religious house to which she belonged. If so, it would imply that she, like her abbot, was an inmate of a house situated in the same diocese in which her family resided. For, since the abbot has a relation dwelling in Fakenham, he seems to have pursued his ecclesiastical career in his home diocese. In fact, both were apparently Norfolk folk as well as members of religious orders in the diocese. This would actually follow the prosopographic pattern suggested by those who have studied the church in Norfolk. Men and women who embarked on the monastic life tended (in this diocese as in others) to enter local houses, which therefore recruited to a considerable degree from the local population.[12]

The house under the abbot's authority must have been an abbey, not a priory (which was headed by a prior) or a friary (since all the fraternal institutions in the diocese of Norwich were headed by a provincial, a prior or a warden). There were eight abbeys in the diocese, and these are shown on Map 1: Benedictine monks at Holm, Wymondham and Bury St

---

[11] On the Bromholm relic, see Francis Wormald, 'The Rood of Bromholm', *Journal of the Warburg Institute* 1 (1937) 31–45.
[12] See Marilyn Oliva, *The Convent and the Community in Late Medieval England: Female Monasteries in the Diocese of Norwich, 1350–1540* (Woodbridge, 1998), p. 56; cf. Norman Tanner, 'Religious Practice', in *Medieval Norwich*, ed. Carole Rawcliffe and R.G. Wilson (London, 2004), pp. 137–55 (p. 155).

The Norfolk Letters 247

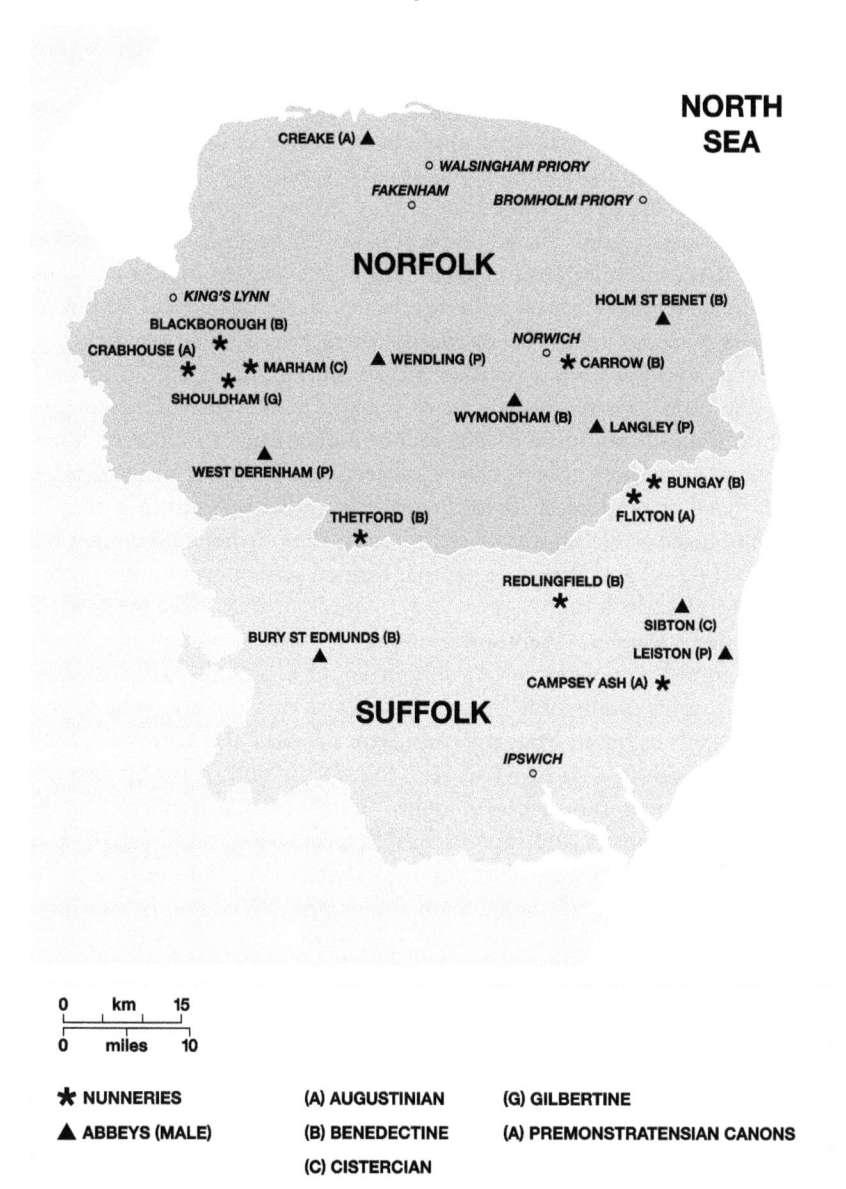

NORTH SEA

NORFOLK

- CREAKE (A) ▲
- ○ WALSINGHAM PRIORY
- FAKENHAM ○
- BROMHOLM PRIORY ○
- ○ KING'S LYNN
- HOLM ST BENET (B) ▲
- BLACKBOROUGH (B) ✱
- NORWICH ○
- CRABHOUSE (A) ✱
- ✱ MARHAM (C)
- ▲ WENDLING (P)
- ✱ CARROW (B)
- SHOULDHAM (G) ✱
- WYMONDHAM (B) ▲
- ▲ LANGLEY (P)
- ▲ WEST DEREHAM (P)
- ✱ BUNGAY (B)
- THETFORD (B) ▲
- ✱
- FLIXTON (A) ✱
- REDLINGFIELD (B) ✱
- SIBTON (C) ▲
- BURY ST EDMUNDS (B) ▲
- LEISTON (P) ▲
- CAMPSEY ASH (A) ✱

SUFFOLK

IPSWICH ○

0 km 15
0 miles 10

✱ NUNNERIES
▲ ABBEYS (MALE)

(A) AUGUSTINIAN
(B) BENEDECTINE
(C) CISTERCIAN
(G) GILBERTINE
(A) PREMONSTRATENSIAN CANONS

Map 1: Abbots and nuns in fourteenth-century Norfolk. Adapted from the map at p. xiv in Oliva, *Convent and the Community*.

Edmund's; Augustinian canons at Creake; and Premonstratensian canons at West Dereham, Wendling, Langley and Leiston. Furthermore, the abbot refers in each of his letters to the 'obedience' Margaret owes him. This was a term with precise and limited application, and it is unlikely that he is referring to his authority simply *qua* abbot (perhaps in the same order as that to which Margaret belonged) or as her confessor, for there is no record of the word being used (in Anglo-Norman or in English) with reference to the confessional relationship. A confessor gave counsel, not commands. The word generally referred to authority in the ecclesiastical hierarchy. All houses (except in the case of specific exemptions) owed obedience to the bishop, who was an ecclesiastical king within his diocese. Within each house, the inmates owed obedience to their head of house, the prior(ess) or abbot/abbess. The house would also owe obedience to a parent house if it were the daughter house of some institution. The abbot must be referring to that last kind of obedience, and it is probably significant that he links the obedience Margaret owes him with the obedience she owes her convent (II.64–5) and her superiors that formed part of every nun's professional vows (III.4–7).

Since there were no Premonstratensian nuns from whom any of the diocese's four Premonstratensian abbeys could claim any kind of obedience, it cannot presumably be to any of those that the abbot belonged. And this claim of his to Margaret's obedience should also serve to narrow down the possibilities as to Margaret's convent. It unfortunately operates to narrow the field almost out of sight. There were ten nunneries in the diocese, six in Norfolk and four in Suffolk (see Map 1).[13] Of the Norfolk convents, four were in west Norfolk, one (Thetford) in the south near the border with Suffolk, and one (Carrow, the nunnery with the highest proportion of well-born entrants from the nobility or upper gentry: Power, pp. 12, 41) in Norwich itself. The four Suffolk nunneries were in the east of that county. Blackborough, Carrow and Thetford (all in Norfolk) and Redlingfield and Bungay (in Suffolk) were Benedictine houses, Crabhouse (in Norfolk) and Campsey Ash and Flixton (in Suffolk) Augustinian, Marham (Norfolk) Cistercian, and Shouldham (Norfolk) was a Gilbertine house in which nuns and canons lived together. Shouldham and Campsey Ash were the most, Crabhouse and Flixton the least, wealthy.[14] Nunneries with male parent houses were, in fact, exceptional, and Power records only four or five in the whole country (pp. 478–81). The Cistercian convent at

---

[13] Oliva's survey (*The Convent and the Community*) includes an eleventh, the Poor Clares at Bruisyard in Suffolk, but that was founded too late (1364) to be relevant here.
[14] See the tables in Oliva, *The Convent and the Community*, pp. 13, 19.

The Norfolk Letters

Marham was technically incorporated into the earliest of the Cistercian houses in England, the abbey of Waverley (Surrey), whose abbot could certainly therefore have claimed authority over the Marham nuns. But Margaret's abbot (with a relative at Fakenham) seems to be a Norfolk man. Thetford Priory had begun as a cell of the Benedictine Bury St Edmund's, but the monks had vacated it and been replaced by a group of Benedictine nuns, who nevertheless 'continued to make annual payments to the abbey which claimed jurisdiction over them' (Oliva, p. 26). A journey via Fakenham from Thetford to Bromholm would have been a circuitous one, and if Margaret belonged to Thetford the supper at Fakenham at the house of a 'precheyn vesin' must surely have been a separate occasion hosted by someone who was a near neighbour of her family house rather than of her convent. This is possible. But Bury St Edmund's is the least probable of the abbeys as a source for the manuscript. M.R. James, who described it, did not include it in his list of manuscripts that apparently belonged at one time to Bury, though he did include others from Gonville and Caius.[15] The abbey and its abbot were, from 1345, in heated and violent dispute with the bishop, from whose authority they claimed exemption, and would have been most unlikely to have had any but hostile dealings with his deputy, Walter Elveden, over that period. If it came from Bury, the manuscript must therefore have passed indirectly into Elveden's hands, or been acquired by him before the dispute began or after it was settled.

The bellicose and active William of Bernham (abbot of Bury St Edumund's from 1335 to 1361), who prosecuted the abbey's case so vigorously, would not on other grounds seem the least likely of abbots to have had an affair with a nun. Apparently from Burnham in Norfolk, and the son of a knight, he was of good birth (*generosus*), he proved himself an effective man of affairs, but was not an especially distinguished divine: the contemporary inmate who described him at his election gave him only so-so marks for literacy (*mediocriter literatum*), referring probably to the abbot's theological learning.[16] And our letter-writer, though plainly educated, appears to be more familiar with Latin proverbs and with courtly love lyrics than with matters scriptural (see note to II.30–2). It is certainly not unlikely that the abbot of so large and important an abbey as Bury, which had property in Norfolk (such as the manor possessed at Wedington by the abbot), should have had business that would take him to King's Lynn.

---

[15] M.R. James, 'Bury St. Edmunds Manuscripts', *EHR* 41 (1926) 251–60.
[16] *Memorials of St Edmund's Abbey*, ed. Thomas Arnold, 3 vols, Rolls Series 96 (London, 1896), vol. 3, p. 48.

Marham and Thetford were the only two nunneries technically subservient to a male abbot. The nuns, like their fellow canons, at the Gilbertine house at Shouldham would have owed obedience to the male head of house, but he was a prior, not an abbot. A male *custos* was sometimes appointed to a nunnery to oversee its financial management, and though the cleric so appointed was not usually an abbot, any abbot acting in that capacity might feel justified in claiming obedience from the nuns; but Power's list of *custodes* (pp. 229–36) does not include any houses in the diocese of Norfolk. Carrow, in Norwich, enjoyed exemption from episcopal control in the election of its prioresses, which it was free to conduct under the supervision of a male patron of its own choice (see Oliva, pp. 32, 164). Since such supervision would normally be conducted by the abbot of a parent house, if there was one, any superior chosen might have felt justified in claiming, for his own ends, 'obedience' from the nuns. Who the supervisors were in the early half of the fourteenth century we do not know, but it seems unlikely that a rendezvous at King's Lynn, on the other side of the county, would be suggested.

The locations of Blackborough and Crabhouse are both such as to make an assignation at King's Lynn plausible. There were Benedictine abbeys at Holm and Wymondham (as well as at Bury), and though Blackborough was not a daughter house, an abbot at one of those abbeys would outrank the prioress and may for some reason have had some perhaps temporary relationship with the nunnery that lent colour to a claim to their obedience. The Augustinian nuns at Crabhouse had links with the Austin canons at Norman's Burrow and Castle Acre,[17] and the Augustinian abbot at Creake (not far from Fakenham) might similarly, legitimately or otherwise, have claimed some authority over the community at Crabhouse. A pause at Fakenham en route to Bromholm (if the supper at the former was connected with the pilgrimage to the latter) would also make sense if the journey started from Blackborough or Crabhouse. Since the conjurations to our Margaret include reference to the obedience she owes her convent (II.65), she was probably not (at least at the time of the writing of the letters) a prioress – though she may later have become one.[18] Further research into the records of the nunneries and abbeys in the diocese may perhaps indicate the possible or probable precise houses to which the abbot and his Margaret belonged.

---

[17] See Sally Thompson, *Women Religious* (Oxford, 1991), p. 66.
[18] Within the relevant period, the VCR records the following prioresses called Margaret: Margaret Costeyn de Lenn, at Crabhouse, 1342–4; Margery Cat and Margery Engys, at Blackborough in the 1360s; and Margaret Bretoun for one year at Thetford, in 1329 (before her death in 1330: see www.british-history.ac.uk/topographical-hist-norfolk/vol2/pp91-95). The VCR also records indults to choose her own confessor at death obtained in 1352 by two nuns called Margaret: Margaret de Hattisle of Crabhouse and Margaret de Bristede of Blackborough. That would be a request (and a year) consistent with the Margaret that emerges from the letters.

The Mores and Morals of the Clergy in Fourteenth-Century England

An abbot and/or a nun engaged in a love affair would, paradoxically, have been less shocking at the period of these letters than it would in present-day England, in which the church has lost so much of its former influence and status. Those who chose life as a recluse were probably motivated by piety alone; but most of the regular and secular clergy entered the profession for quite other reasons. It was the major career path for white-collar work, and ensured varying degrees of income and status to those who could find those things nowhere else. The church was a huge landowner and employer, and its personnel were often valued as much or more for their administrative, social, business or management skills as for their zeal in prayer and devotions. When Chaucer described his worldly, active, well-fed monk as 'A manly man, to been an abbot able' (*CT* I.167), he was playing on the double standards that had consequently emerged – whereby, although godliness might still in theory be the measure of a worthy abbot, it was in fact by more worldly virtues that they were often felt to be especially fitted for the post: by all those qualities, in fact, implied by the word 'manly', which in this context suggests fitness to exercise authority by reason of being 'a man of the world' who is the very opposite of 'bookish or reclusive'.[19] For abbots often ran large, complex and big-budget households.[20] The higher clergy were less learned than those of previous generations (Power, p. 240), though in some respects we are dealing more with a shift (towards the practical) than with a reduction: a large proportion of the books in their libraries were legal works, mostly of canon law (cf. Tanner, p. 144), volumes of the kind in which these letters are transcribed. For abbots could also be much occupied with ecclesiastical politics. William of Bernham, for instance, who was from 1335 to 1361 abbot of Bury St Edmund's (which lay just over the Norfolk border in northern Suffolk), was mostly concerned with conducting an energetic and ultimately successful battle with the bishop of Norwich in order to uphold the abbey's exemption from episcopal authority (and so from any levy he imposed). Much litigious claim and counter-claim, and even distraint and imprisonment, was involved, the abbot eventually lodging an appeal to the pope, who intervened to stop further legal action.[21]

---

[19] See J.A. Burrow, 'Versions of "Manliness" in the Poetry of Chaucer, Langland and Hoccleve', *Chaucer Review* 47 (2013) 337–42 (p. 340). In other contexts, the main implication of the adjective is 'free-spending' (pp. 338–40).
[20] Thompson, *The English Clergy*, p. 168.
[21] For summaries, see VCH volumes for Norfolk (vol. 2, p. 240) and Suffolk (vol. 2, pp. 63–4). For a full account, see *Memorials*, ed. Arnold, vol. 3, pp. 48ff.

A literal discarding of the religious habit in favour of secular attire was the occasional significant result of the secularized habits of thought and action of many of the regular clergy. Breach of the rule of enclosure in the cloister was common, and some monks were accused of indulging in outings in secular dress (Power, p. 360), sometimes with weapons (which clerics were forbidden to carry). Amongst the many complaints made by his convent against one mid-fifteenth-century abbot of Peterborough was that he would leave the cloister to go about in secular clothes and engage in such sports as shooting at the mark 'like a layman'.[22] Sexual liaisons were a charge frequently levelled at male religious (Power, p. 437), and sexual immorality figures frequently in the records of the investigative 'visitations' made by bishops (cf. Tanner, p. 153). So common was it that in itself it was obviously not felt intolerable, and when charges were brought, the sexual misconduct alleged needed to be of an exaggerated grossness, and it is usually possible to detect other factors at work. The abbot of Peterborough was accused of having relationships with the wives of local men and abbey officers, but it is obviously what was felt to be his misappropriation of convent funds and patronage in this connection that was the real issue for his monks – who probably would have objected neither to his womanizing nor to his sporting diversions and expeditions in themselves, and perhaps would have preferred a more macho and non-ascetic superior (since they had themselves been accused of roaming abroad, carrying arms like laymen and mixing with women[23]). The monks of Bury St Edmund's were accused by the bishop of Norwich of similar *scelerum nefandorum* (doffing the habit, carrying arms, leaving the cloister for the purposes of adultery and fornication), the abbot allegedly condoning and participating in this misconduct, being himself guilty of worse enormities.[24] But the bishop was in dispute with the abbey (see above) and had therefore his own reasons for bringing discredit upon the abbot and the convent. It is, however, significant that such charges were assumed not to be so ludicrously heinous as to be implausible.

The worldly abbot given to macho sports and good living and making love to pretty women was in fact a recognizable type, who figures as such in Antoine de la Sale's *Le petit Jehan de Saintré*. This fifteenth-century prose fiction tells the story of the chivalric education and achievements of the eponymous 'petit Jehan', who is brought up at the royal court. A lady at court adopts him as her *ami*, and is the inspiration, funder and instructress of his early years. Her affections are then, however, seduced

[22] See *Visitations of Religious Houses*, vol. III, ed. A. Hamilton Thompson (Lincoln, 1927), p. 296. The full account occupies pp. 285–302.
[23] *Visitations*, ed. Thompson pp. 272, 290.
[24] *Memorials*, ed. Arnold, vol. 2, pp. 65–6.

by an abbot, the head of an abbey of which she is the patroness and which she visits in the course of a retirement to her country estates. The two join in a cruel plan to humiliate 'petit Jehan', who is beaten by the abbot in a wrestling match, but who is easily victorious in an armed chivalric encounter – for 'petit Jehan' is obviously envisaged by the author as still a small man even when grown up, relying on skill and courage, not physical bulk, in his chivalric successes, and thus no match for the abbot (described as a burly and fleshy man) in the more popular sports in which the latter (like the abbot of Peterborough) is more practised.[25] 'Petit Jehan' eventually exposes the infidelity of his lady before the queen and court, and the story ends with her public disgrace. The tale is an interesting variation on a popular theme with a long history: the rival claims of the knight and the clerk, in general – or specifically as lovers.[26] It is itself a noteworthy mixture of art and actuality, in that the knight in the tale is based on two real-life knights who were, in turn, legends in their own lifetimes: the hero is named after an actual fourteenth-century knight ('held to be the best and most valiant knight in France', according to Froissart) and his career shadows remarkably closely that of another historical knight, Jaques de Lalaing (the subject of a chivalric biography, *Le livre des faits de messire Jacques de Lalaing*, which was mainly the work of the Burgundian herald and chronicler Jean Le Fevre).[27] And the world painted in *Le petit Jehan*, though an illuminated and de luxe one, is plainly a product of de la Sale's own first-hand experience of court life and knowledge of social realities among those of gentle birth. The abbot is especially well-drawn and is obviously based on a recognizable type. The son of a 'tresriche bourgoiz de la ville', who had got his son the abbacy through a mixture of money, influence and friends in high places, he is young, 'grant de corps', a master of popular sports involving leaping and throwing, and keeps a liberal and courtly household: 'En toutes joyeusetez se employoit ... larges et liberal ... dont estoit moult amé et prisié de tous bons compaignons' (*Jehan*, p. 244).[28] Like his female counterpart, Chaucer's prioress, who 'peyned hire to countrefete cheere / Of court' (*CT* I.139–40), he cultivates the virtues of the courtly vavasour rather than those of the pious prelate (taking pains to provide good meals, activities

---

[25] Good at sports such as 'wrestling, jumping, casting the bar or throwing the stone', the abbot is 'grant de corps' (Antoine de la Sale, *Jehan* 138, p. 244; *Jean*, p. 163), 'gros et trespuissant de corps' (*Jehan* 173, p. 303; *Jean*, p. 204); a pair of hairy and fleshy white thighs flash memorably into view when he cuts a caper before the lady just prior to the wrestling match (*Jehan* 162, p. 281; *Jean* p. 189).
[26] See, for instance, the *Council of Remiremont* (pp. 428–53 below).
[27] On John of Saintré, see *Jean Froissart: Chronicles*, tr. Geoffrey Brereton (Harmondsworth, 1968), p. 140. On Jacques de Lalaing, see *Jean*, pp. xv and 210 (n. 33).
[28] 'He distributed gifts so generously and freely that he was beloved and highly esteemed by all good fellows' (*Jean*, p. 163).

and entertainments for his female guests). This is reflected in the fact that the vocabulary used of his virtues is precisely that used to commend court personnel (including Saintré) elsewhere in the story – with the exception of that reference to 'bons compaignons', which recurs in an account of his later attention to the lady's comfort and entertainment, where he behaves 'comme tresbon compaignon' (*Jehan*, p. 247). He is plainly a 'boon companion' of a kind, endearing himself especially by that liberality (especially with regard to food and drink) which the adjective 'manly' (by which Chaucer characterized his monk's fitness for abbotship) particularly suggested (see n. 19 above). It is not difficult to see his appeal for the lady (who is missing Saintré and is lonely and at a loose end).

The phenomenon of the lover-abbot was, in short, a familiar one in life and in literature. And plenty would have found such lust – 'Sure ... no sin, / Or of the deadly seven ... the least' (*Measure for Measure* III.1.109–10) – forgivable in itself. For it was frequently pointed out that no one could claim exemption from amorous desire, prelates and clerics regularly figuring in the list of those whom their status and gifts of mind or body failed to protect: popes, cardinals, bishops, archbishops, abbots and abbesses are enumerated in such a list in *Jehan* (pp. 300–1; *Jean*, p. 202).

And if an abbot in love would not have seemed especially unusual or shocking, still less so would a nun. Discipline in fourteenth-century convents was often lax, moral standards low and inmates often there for reasons other than vocation.[29] Some were there following, or even because of, previous sexual misdemeanours (Power, p. 30). Langland refers to spiteful gossip amongst sisterhoods about nuns who had illegitimate children or were the mistresses of priests ('Dame Pernele [is] a preestes fyle – Prioresse worth she nevere, / For she hadde a child in chirie-tyme': *Piers Plowman* B.V.158–9), but there was plenty of well-documented fire behind malicious smoke of this kind. Nuns having babies, or affairs with married or unmarried men, nuns who eloped with their lovers ('as happens to so many', as the thirteenth-century German poem *Helmbrecht* comments of a nun 'who had run away from her convent through a love adventure'[30]) are common occurrences in the annals of the period.[31] Dame Pernele could in fact have cited

---

[29] Power, *Medieval English Nunneries*, pp. 284, 437, 469. For a survey of incontinent nuns who figure in medieval tales, anecdotes, songs, *exempla* and *miracula*, see Schmidt, 'Amor in Claustro'; he refers in particular to *Decameron*, ed. Vittore Branca (Florence, 1965), 3.1 (pp. 318–27), 9.2 (pp. 1030–4); Caesarius of Heisterbach, *Dialogus miraculorum*, ed. J. Strange (Cologne, 1851), vol. 1, pp. 273–4; and the chapter devoted to the love of nuns (*De amore monacharum*) which Andreas Capellanus included in his *De amore*.
[30] The poem can be found in *Readings in European History*, ed. J. Harvey Robinson, 2 vols (Boston, MA, 1904), vol. 1, pp. 418–19.
[31] See Power, *Medieval English Nunneries*, pp. 80, 82, 88, 414–15, 455 (babies), 86, 149 (affairs), 310, 415 (elopements).

precedents for her misconduct amongst prioresses (and abbesses) themselves, who were often unsuited to their office and guilty of incontinence or adultery and sometimes also gave birth to bastard children (see Power, pp. 82, 87, 428, 455, 461). Affairs, pregnancies and apostasy were, in fact, startlingly frequent, as Power demonstrates (see especially pp. 456–74). The men involved might be laymen or lay officials on the convent estates (a bailiff, a miller or a harvest labourer: Power, pp. 88, 149, 660), but were often clerics (Power, p. 399). This is scarcely surprising: since contact with laymen (who, technically, were not supposed to enter the cloister at all: Power, p. 351) was often limited, clerics formed a large proportion of the men the sisters would have come across. Priests and chaplains, in particular, form a large subset in the list of lovers (Power, pp. 53, 82, 87, 88, 233), as do friars and monks (Power, p. 449), suspicion of immoral relations between the nuns of St Mary de Pré and the monks of St Albans forming a particularly notorious example (Power, p. 604). The nunnery of Llansanffraid closed down after the elopement of one of its nuns with the abbot of Strata Marcella.[32] The abbot of St Albans was in 1489 accused of intercourse with nuns (and of keeping a mistress in the monastery).[33] Especially shocking to a modern sensibility is the abuse (by no means uncommon) of the confessional relationship (see, for example, Power, p. 447). Gower's *Vox Clamantis* represents nuns as often led astray by priests who come as confessors or visitors (IV.578–676), and in one of the chansons cited by Power (p. 616), when the girl says she will become a nun, the man saucily responds that he will become a monk, 'Pour confesser la nonne / Dans le couvent'. It was clearly the common view that the relationship could be and was abused for amorous purposes.

But, again, there was available a fairly forgiving perspective on this state of affairs. It remained, naturally, heinous according to official church teaching, which in fact defined any sexual relationship involving an ecclesiastic as incest, and those between nuns and clerics as doubly incestuous (Power, p. 459). But in popular literature, especially in the lyrics known as *chansons de nonnes* (discussed by Power at pp. 604–21), the amorous nun (when not treated, as she often was, as a joke) could be viewed as a type of the *mal mariée* (the girl trapped in a marriage not of her choosing), a caged or cloistered love-bird (see Power, p. 452), whose romantic and sexual yearnings were, again, only natural.

There was, in any case, a whole unofficial romantic code which was often more powerful than official morality, and by which sin and disgrace

---

[32] F.G. Cowley, *The Monastic Order in South Wales* (Cardiff, 1977), pp. 37–8.
[33] See *The Norfolk Antiquarian Miscellany*, ed. Walter Rye, 3 vols (Norwich, 1877), vol. 2, p. 443.

were incurred, not by romantic liaisons, but by infidelity to them. In *Le petit Jehan*, the relationship between Jehan and the lady is conducted with great secrecy, for all extra-marital affairs were regarded as obliging the lover never to reveal the name of his lady or expose her to scandal (cf. *Lancelot do Lac*, ed. Kennedy, 348/32–8 and *Troilus* IV.562–71). It is quite clear, however, that no real disgrace would have attended the lady had the affair been guessed: when the queen ultimately begins to learn the truth about her conduct, she is mildly puzzled, because she had never had any inkling of any liaison with Jehan (*Jehan*, p. 305; *Jean*, p. 205), but there is no implication that she is shocked to learn of it or that her gentlewoman would have lost any respectability in her eyes had such an affair, however officially covered up, come to her knowledge (as she is plainly somewhat surprised that it did not). The lady incurs deep and lasting disgrace, not from her liaison with Jehan, but on the exposure of her infidelity to him, which results in real shame, stigma and public shock and censure of her baseness (*Jehan*, p. 307; *Jean*, p. 206). Similarly with Machaut and Péronne, whose affair had become public knowledge: that several people had guessed her identity does not trouble Péronne; where she shows real distress at prospective disgrace is when she learns of Machaut's suspicions about her and fears she may consequently figure as an untrue mistress (*VD*, Letter 40). A similar truth emerges from Chaucer's *Troilus*. Anxious as Criseyde, the daughter of a traitor, always and naturally is to protect her name and to avoid all scandal, and discreet and secret as Troilus duly is, she acknowledges too late that no real stigma would have attached to the liaison (or even an elopement) in itself, and that she would probably have gained rather than lost status by being the known chosen one of such a man (V.736–42). Her real and lasting disgrace and loss of name is incurred by her infidelity, and she knows it: 'allas, for now is clene ago / My name of trouthe in loue, for euermo! ... of me, vnto the worldes ende, / Shal neyther ben ywriten nor ysonge / No good word ... rolled shal I ben on many a tonge!' (V.1054–61).

The consciences of Margaret and her abbot may, therefore, not have been overly troubled by the fact of their affair. In the pursuance of that affair, they must have sidestepped several subsidiary rules (as well as the major ban on sexual relationships), though these were often not rigorously enforced. Monastic rules forbade the sending or receiving of any letters or gifts without permission of the head of the house, who was supposed to see the contents of any such exchange.[34] The rule was honoured often more in the breach than in the observance, and strict enforcement of it by any prioress would have been much resented (Power, pp. 50, 245). The abbot could, of

---

[34] Power, *Medieval English Nunneries*, citing the Benedictine Rule, ch. LIV (p. 395; see also pp. 96, 408).

course, give himself dispensation, and Margaret would have found it easy to evade the rule. Nevertheless, the pair were, by exchanging letters, and gifts (I.24–5, II.54–7), flouting monastic rules, and their correspondence would have needed to be conducted in a secret manner. Servant-messengers would have had to be trusted ones. The abbot mentions one message (summoning Margaret to a rendezvous at Kings Lynn) as having been delivered by a personal servant of his ('par Llevelyn mon vallet': III.3), but his position may have enabled him to send a verbal or written message like that one fairly openly, under colour of ecclesiastical business. His position of authority with regard to the convent would certainly have facilitated the meetings that had apparently taken place outside it (on a pilgrimage to Bromholm and a supper at Fakenham, which may have been part of the same trip or a separate occasion).

For in leaving their respective cloisters, the pair would again have been infringing some fundamental but loosely enforced convent rules. Such trips abroad were, strictly speaking, forbidden (Power, p. 344), and monks and nuns were not even supposed to leave their convents to go to extra-mural confession (Power, p. 387). All excursions required the permission of the head of the house and were not supposed to include spending the night or eating or drinking away from the convent (Power, pp. 356, 359, 374). The requirements of convent business were one of the few reasons thought to justify exodus (Power, p. 359), and heads of house would be pretty free to come and go as they pleased (Power, p. 367), since they had a variety of secular and administrative tasks to attend to. Pilgrimages were not officially held to constitute valid excuses, and had been specifically ruled out as such at the Council of Fréjus in 791 (Power, p. 373). But these embargoes were widely ignored, and licences for exit were easily obtained. Chaucer treated his Prioress, accompanied by another nun and by three priests, as amongst those to be found in a typical cross-section of pilgrims to St Thomas Becket's shrine in Canterbury (*CT* I.118–64). Norwich (with over seventy pilgrimage centres: Power, p. 371) had a strong local pilgrimage culture, and the abbot's presence and escort would doubtless have been sufficient to render apparently blameless a pious pilgrimage in his company to such a well-known centre as Bromholm. Any nun on leave from the cloister was supposed always to have a companion (Power, pp. 354–5, 359, 384; cf. the nun accompanying Chaucer's Prioress), and (since a trip *à deux* would in any case have attracted gossip) it appears there were other nuns (or at any rate other persons) in the Bromholm party (see II.25).

It is not clear whether the supper at Fakenham took place on the way to/from the pilgrimage or formed a separate excursion, perhaps made by Margaret under colour of visiting her own connections (since nuns licensed to leave the cloister were not supposed to spend the night or dine anywhere but with their own family: Power, pp. 359, 377). Fourteenth-century nuns very noticeably retained their own secular names, identities and connections, and visits to their families could be up to a month long (Power, p. 376); and the designation of 'Sire Robert' as 'Vostre precheyn vesin' [your near neighbour] may refer to Robert's residence near to her own family home rather than to the convent. And at the table of this near neighbour she might plausibly meet a cousin of his: to wit, the abbot (cf. 'Mon cosyn': II.52). Robert, that is, may have had connections with both abbot and nun in their extra-mural identities, and his house would therefore have formed a convenient meeting place. Or Margaret may have combined the pilgrimage with a visit to her own family, and have met the abbot at, or been escorted by him to, this supper at the house of an acquaintance of hers and a relative of his without arousing suspicion of a lover's tryst. It is, at any rate, clear that the rules as to egress, spending the night or dining away from the convent, like the ban on sending or receiving letters or gifts, could easily be sidestepped, especially when the man was a head of house himself and in a position of authority with regard to the house the lady belonged to.

Margaret's conduct was, then, also not very shocking by the standards of the time, nor is the fact that she is apparently not sexually inexperienced (cf. I.12–13). Sexual sins, as explained above, were regarded as the least of the deadly seven, since they had 'nature' to excuse them, and were prompted by the inherent 'frailty' of the flesh ('Pur ceo qe vous estes frele': I.13). For the rest, the abbot may well have found in her in fact rather a superior and classy kind of girl. He describes her as 'mout naturele' (I.9), an epithet often bearing the sense 'well born, courtly in status and manners'.[35] Since convents usually required a dowry of some kind (though they were strictly not supposed to),[36] nunneries were in general 'the refuge of the gently born' (Power, p. 4). And if she was no better morally than many of her peers, the abbot's Margaret seems to have been well above average as regards literacy and was apparently well-educated – which was certainly not the case with nuns in general. The standard of learning had declined sharply among female religious.[37] Practically the only books recorded as possessed in nunneries were

---

[35] See *DMF* A.2.d and cf. *Fergus: Roman von Guillaume le Clerc*, ed Ernst Martin (Halle, 1872), l. 1073.
[36] On the entrance fees for convents in the diocese of Norwich, see Oliva, *The Convent and the Community*, pp. 48–51.

psalters and breviaries and, if the nuns taught children, the odd primer,[38] and it is probably a psalter or breviary for which the abbot sends Margaret the gift of a chemise (a kind of outer jacket) 'Pur vostre lyvre tener' (II.57). Though they were in theory supposed to be literate enough to read and sing the services in choir (which was their chief duty), it is plain that many nuns had not enough Latin even for that (Power, p. 244), and near total ignorance of the language was widespread among them (Power, pp. 246–8). But Margaret apparently has enough to swap Latin proverbs with the abbot (III.2–3) and for him to be able, for instance, to use to her (seriously or otherwise) the word 'fisnomye' (II.48), a topic on which she had apparently conversed with him. Part of her charm for the abbot may well have been that he found in her, not simply a pretty and warm-blooded woman (I.11–13), as many nuns were, but also a 'mout naturele' lady, of good birth and educated intellect, whose elegance may well have been less common, especially in a diocese in which nuns came typically from the minor and parish gentry, rather than from the top echelons of society, who tended to choose convents outside Norfolk and Suffolk (Oliva, pp. 52–61).

We should return briefly, in this connection, to the abbot's gift of a book-covering (II.54–7), described by him as of fine fabric and pure white ('De menu drap ... Il est blanc, il est cler'). The reference is to a chemise, a slip-on cover placed over or attached to the binding of a book and made of leather or (as here) a cloth such as linen or velvet.[39] The textile variety was apparently 'especially prized by noblewomen',[40] an association borne out in the pictorial arts of the period, in which a cloth chemise often accompanies books held by well-born women or by holy women depicted as such – and the white colour of which the abbot is evidently proud appears in Rogier van der Weyden's beautiful depiction (in the National Gallery) of the Magdalen reading, the saint appearing in clothes of quality cloth and holding a book that is plainly a luxury item and has golden clasps and a white chemise.[41] The abbot's gift is thus a compliment to Margaret as a gentlewoman 'mout naturele'.

---

[37] For a survey of the scholarship on nuns' literacy, see Oliva, *The Convent and the Community*, pp. 64–5, n. 135.
[38] On some books (predominantly service books, sometimes such works as saints' lives) recorded as possessed by nuns in the diocese of Norwich, see Oliva, *The Convent and the Community*, p. 65.
[39] See Raymond Clemens and Timothy Graham, *Introduction to Manuscript Studies* (Ithaca, NY, 2007), glossary p. 264.
[40] Clemens and Graham, *Introduction*, p. 57.
[41] Reproduced at p. 443 and as frontispiece in Lorne Campbell and Jan van der Stock, *Rogier van der Weyden: Master of Passions* (Leuven, 2009).

Chemises were obviously not unusual in this area: several of the manuscripts donated (like the present one) by Elveden to Gonville were so wrapped.[42] They were also used as overcovers at Bury St Edmunds; but those chemises were of a different type, being attached by glue and (though also regularly white) made of leather.[43] It cannot therefore be suggested that our abbot would have found to hand in the Bury book department exactly the item he wanted. For the one he sent is of the more informal variety, unsecured and made of cloth. His word for it is 'crisme': a white cloth of the type used for head-coverings and robes in baptism or 'christening' and for altar cloths (see *MED crisme* n. 2 and 3). The abbot's usage is an anglicism in form and sense: no such extended sense of *cresme* [holy oil] is recorded in French or Anglo-Norman. The sacramental associations of the 'crisme' explain his emphasis on whiteness and purity – and relate interestingly to the suggestion that early pictorial images might imply that the origins of the chemise lay in ritual measures to protect a sacred book, or any other holy object, from pollution by direct contact with human hands.[44] It might be that in some quarters some sense of this ritual significance was preserved and dictated a preference for white. So one might after all want to connect the white leather chemises used to protect books in the Bury library with this abbot's decision to send to his Margaret a white cloth for use as a chemise.

---

[42] Hall, 'Early Fellows', pp. 239 and 240.
[43] See Alexandra Gillespie, 'Bookbinding', in *The Production of Books in England 1350–1500*, ed. Alexandra Gillespie and Daniel Wakelin (Cambridge, 2011), pp. 150–72 (pp. 152–6).
[44] Gillespie, 'Bookbinding', pp. 154–5. Gillespie suggests that the leather chemises used at Bury may in part have had this function, as well as a more practically protective one.

I

    M., ma especiele,
    Vous estes bone e bele.
    Gardez qe vous seez lele
4   Aval la mamele:

    Ceo vous mand vostre abé
    De grant reverence;
    Loke nou þat hit so be
8   In obedience.

    Vous estes mout naturele:
    Pur ceo l'en vous apele
    Mergerete la bele.
12 Vous ne estes pas pucele,
    Pur ceo qe vous estes frele.

    L'amour e le especialté
    Entre nous seit privé,
16 Qe nul esclandre pusse lever:
    De ceo vous pri e requer.
    Savez qe dit le fraunceys?
    'Plus enuos est estopée
20 [Plaie de lange qe de espée]'.

    Saluz certes vous mand
    Atant cum erbes sunt
    Entre nous cressant.
24 De vostre bon don vous say grant gré,
    E mout plus de la bone volenté.
    Ey, Mergrete jolie,
    Mon quer sanz fauser, etc.

---

6 *Two letters deleted before* De   14 *A caret mark occurs over the word amyste, which has been deleted after the conjunction* e, especialte *(preceded by caret mark) occurring above the end of the MS line*   16 *Before* Qe, *at the beginning of the MS line, what appears to read* Entre nous seit prive *has been deleted*   19 estopee] estupee *Meyer*

I

M., my specially loved,
You are good and beautiful.
Take care that you also be true
Within your breast:

These words does your abbot send you
In pious admonition;
See that this be so,
According to the obedience you owe me.

You are very much a gentlewoman:
And therefore are you called
Margaret the beautiful.
You are not a maid,
Because your flesh is weak.

The love and special intimacy
Between us, let it remain privy,
So that no scandal may arise:
Of this I beg and require you.
Do you know what the French say?
'With more difficulty is closed up
A wound caused by the tongue than one given by the sword'.

Salutations I certainly send you
As many as there are blades of grass
Growing in the miles between us.
For your nice gift I am very grateful to you,
And even more for the goodwill (which prompted it).
Oh, fair Margaret,
My heart without falsehood, etc.

NOTES TO LETTER I

2 *Vous*: the pronoun is here, as usually elsewhere, abbreviated. Meyer assumes the abbreviated form represents 'vus', but we have expanded to the 'vous' form that occurs on the rare occasions when the pronoun is written out in full.

3–8 The abbot's 'vostre abé' (5) is poised between the amorous and the ecclesiastical sense of the phrase, as he justifies his admonition to fidelity by invoking the *obedience* owed to him as an *abbé* by a nun – on whom he could certainly enjoin *lel*eness (3), for that word too partakes, in this context, of both its amorous sense (fidelity) and its more general one (truth, integrity). His appeal to ecclesiastical rank could be heard as unpleasantly bullying; it is certainly not as clearly playful as is his use of confessional principles at III.8–14. Insecurity in the early stages of an affair with a clearly pretty (10–11) – and perhaps much younger – girl may have led him into what, because context makes its tone uncertain, sounds like an unseemly rather than a witty abuse of his position with regard to Margaret. Worries about the constancy of the other party are a recurrent feature of male love letters (see p. 63 above).

4 Probably a periphrasis for 'at heart': cf. 'Au cuer par dessus la mammele' (*VD* 4815).

7–8 One of the brief switches into English; cf. II.67 and see p. 241 above.

9 See p. 258 above.

10–11 Perhaps an allusion to the meaning of 'Margaret' (= pearl). Similar plays on the Christian name as implying a 'perfect pearl' occur in the near-contemporary poem *Pearl* and the slightly later prose *Testament* by Usk, as well as in a much earlier Latin poem (edited in Dronke, *Medieval Latin*, vol. 2, pp. 384–5) in which a Margarita is said to excel all other *margaritas* [pearls], and where 'M.' is used throughout to reference the personal name (as in the first line here), perhaps in token deference to the rule of non-revelation of the woman's name.

12–13 The constraint of rhyme in what may be one of his first attempts at love verse perhaps leads the abbot into some crudeness or ineptness here. He is plainly running mentally through words in *-ele* suited to the context and, instead of dismissing *pucele*, writes in its inappropriateness in a way that is surely tasteless and ungallant. It is also horribly unfair, if he is referring to a 'frailty' that he has himself led her into and is himself guilty of – though he is more probably alluding to past liaisons which may have been confessed to him or of which, having some authority over the order, he was aware. See p. 248 above. The abbot's use in this context of an admonitory language he might use *qua* abbot to an obedientiary is again (cf. 5–8) rather graceless.

14–20 Though it is more often the woman who enjoins and urges discretion and who fears scandal (*Troilus* II.785–6), and on whose behalf the lover is carefully secretive, exposure would in the present case be as damaging to the abbot as to the nun, if not more so. Cf. II.9–13 and note. Camargo, who does not see the Norfolk letters as 'real' ones, argues that the need for secrecy, like other aspects of the letters, is 'conventional' (p. 31). But there is every reason why a 'real' abbot should be anxious on this score – as the *Epistolae duorum amantium* reveal another real cleric to have been (see *EDA* 54, 75, 101). Reality and convention are not in any case mutually exclusive, and there are too many precise particulars in the second and third letters for the epistles to be plausibly read as relating simply to a representative fiction of an affair.

14 Deleted *amyste* is a word which the writer is content to use at the beginning of his letter of reproach (III.i), but for which he here substitutes what he may have considered the warmer *especialté*.

19–20 The MS contains only the first half of this proverb (line 19), which the abbot is evidently simply cueing in to be expanded when he writes up his draft. Fortunately, he reuses it at II.12–13, so it is obvious how it was to be completed and how it was to rhyme.

21–3 This *quot ... tot* formula was so frequently used as to incur deprecation as trite by Boncompagno in his compilation of exemplary amorous epistles (Text 1, 130.22–6). The abbot's deployment of it is actually quite effective, as the traditionally great number is measured by the very distance between the lovers that the letter and its salutations attempts to counteract; it is thus an intelligent adaptation of that version of the topos in which blades of grass figure as the measure (cf. *Welles Anthology* 4.49–51: 'as many tymes I gret yow / as clarkes can wrytte with papur and ynke / and as money moo as gressys grewe').

24–5 The abbot himself later similarly sends Margaret a letter accompanied by a gift (II.54–7). For love letters referring to or accompanying tokens or gifts cf. Text 7, II.11; the letters from Richard Calle to Margery Paston (p. 51 above); those from Clare to George Cely (quoted on p. 28 above); Camargo, p. 156; *VD* L26.

26–7 As the *etc.* indicates, the abbot is quoting a love lyric. This lyric figures, co-incidentally, amongst other additions to the Latin MSS in Gonville and Caius, which Meyer draws attention to, occurring on a flyleaf (*feuillet de garde*) in Caius College 11/11 (a copy of the Code of Justinian, and so likewise a volume devoted to canon law). It consists of eight stanzas and has a refrain that runs thus: 'E! dame jolyve, / Mun quer sauns faucer / Met en vostre balaye, / Qe ne say vos per' [Oh, lovely lady, / My heart with truth / I put in your possession, / For I do not know anyone equal to you]; see Meyer, pp. 439–41. Meyer himself does not notice that it is this lyric the abbot is citing, though it is pointed out by Camargo (p. 30). The four-line refrain of the lyric was in fact a *refrain* in the medieval French sense of the word: i.e. a tag or form of words found in different poems and contexts. As such, it occurs as a refrain in the modern sense to another poem, a *ballete* in a Lorraine Chansonnier (see Stevens, *Words and Music*, pp. 173–4). The lines are here personalized by the substitution of Margaret's name after the opening 'E!' And it may be that the 'dame' of the *refrain* was regularly subject to such substitution, or represents or invites whatever Christian name is pertinent to the occasion. The appropriation of existing lyrics in love epistles is one aspect of the interconnections between art and actual life those letters demonstrate. Margery

Brews similarly briefly quotes a lyric (see pp. 47–8), and Robert Armburgh appropriates whole poems to send to his lady (see Text 6, poems 1 and 2). For the citation of familiar songs or lyrics in (non-epistolary) poems about or to the beloved, cf. two of the poems (from Cambridge, Trinity College, MS R.3.19) reproduced by Linne Mooney in 'A Woman's Reply to Her Lover': a two-stanza poem ending '... and of her syng thys song where ever I go: "*Ma beele amour, ma ioy,* ever *espiraunce*"' (p. 249), a song identified by Mooney (p. 238) as a slightly imperfect quotation (probably from memory) of one by Charles d'Orléans which begins 'Ma seule amour, ma joye et ma maistresse'; and a five-stanza poem (pp. 255–6) which ends by quoting, more fully than does Chaucer, from the lyric also sung by the mock courtly cock-and-hen lovers at *CT* VII.2879 (and whose wording is perhaps also echoed at VII.2874): '... and for your love evermore wepyng I syng thys song: / "My lefe ys faren in a lond; / Allas why ys she so / And I am so sore bound / I may nat com her to? / She hath my hert in hold / Where ever she ryde or go / With trew love a thousand fold"'.

II

      Mergerete, ma très[chère],
      Qe estes de gentil manere,
      De norture, de porture,
4   E de très bone fesure,
      De c. pson
      De vous saluer ad encheson.

      Jeo vous pri pur l'amor de moy e requer qe vous ne prenz pas a mal
8   qe jeo ne usse avant ces houres a vous mandé com jeo vous promys qe,
      sachez, ne fusent maveyses langes, jeo fuse mesmes a vous venuz; qe
      certes jeo ne vodrey pur nul bien qe vous fusez en blame par encheson
      de moy ou jeo par enchesun de vous. Savez que dit le frounceys?

12 'Mout plus enuuos est estopée
      Plaie de lange qe de espée'.
      Ceste proverbe recordez
      Et de moy donqes soveygnez.
16 Neqedent, si rien voilez qe fere purray,
      Par bone reison fere le dey.
      Kar tiel profre vous me feites,
      Certeynement vous me deites
20 En alant de vostre meson –
      Ceo vint de grant affecion.
      A la croiz od moy alates,
      Grant priveté a moy parlates,
24 Grant amour a moy mostrates
      Qant tote la conpanye refusates.
      Pur ceo, si rien voilez qe fere pusse,
      De bone volenté fere le dusse,
28 A mon poer jeo le fray.
      Si vous volez, mettez en assay.
      Savez qe dit Seynt Escripture?

---

1 *The opening words have been erased and are very hard to read. The first three words follow* Meyer, *as does the conjectured* chère   5 *A small deletion precedes* De   7 Jeo] Je *Meyer* moy] may *Meyer* prenz] pernez *Meyer* 11 ou] ni *Meyer* 21 affecion] affection *Meyer* 22 alates] alastes *Meyer* 25 Qant] Quant *Meyer*

II

My dear Margaret,
You who are of courtly demeanour,
In manners and in bearing,
And of very goodly person,
There is good reason to send you
A hundred salutations.

I beg you for my sake and ask you that you do not take it ill that I have not before this time written to you as I promised, for, be sure, if it were not for evil tongues, I would have come to you in person; for I would certainly not for anything in the world wish that you should incur blame by reason of me, nor I by reason of you. Do you know what the French say?

'With more difficulty is closed up
A wound caused by the tongue than one given by the sword'.
Mark this proverb,
And then apply it to my case.
But, if you want anything that it lies in my power to do,
I should rightly do it.
For you made me that offer,
You explicitly said to me
On the way from your house –
Something that issued from great feeling.
To the cross you were going with me,
You said most confidential things to me,
You showed great love for me
In shunning the rest of the company [for me].
Therefore, if you want anything that it lies in my power to do,
I owe it to you to do it very willingly,
And I will do it to the best of my ability.
Put me to the test if you wish.
Do you know what is found in Holy Writ?

Dilectionis probatio est operis exhibitio:
32 'D'amour la prove est de metre en ovre'.
　　Ceste proverbe recordez,
　　Qe vous la bien sachiez,
　　E de moy donkes remembrez.
36　Si rien vers moy vous plest,
　　Mandez m'en ceo qe vous plest,
　　Com a cely a ki plest, etc.
　　'Have godday nou, Mergerete:
40　Wiþ gret love y þe grete;
　　Y wolde we miȝten us ofte mete
　　In halle, in chambbre and in þe strete,
　　Withoute blame of the contre:
44　God ȝeve þat so miȝte hit be!'
　　Saluz cent mile feiz
　　Par celes enseignes
　　Qe vous tochates:
48　De fisnomye a moy parlates,
　　A Fakenham, a souper, partie mostrates
　　Vostre quer, a la meson ostage,
　　Qi vous apelez outrage,
52　Sire Robert, mon cosyn,
　　Vostre precheyn vesin.
　　Un bel crisme je vous envey,
　　De menu drap, par ma fey:
56　Il est blanc, il est cler,
　　Pur vostre lyvre tener.
　　Savez qe dit le franceys?
　　'Ky poi [me] done vyvre me veut':
60　*Non mihi vult funus modicum qui dat mihi munus.*
　　Ceste proverbe recordez
　　E de moy donkes soveygnez.
　　A Dieu vous rend, qe vous gard cors e alme. Priez pur moy, etc.

64　E veez qe vous seez obedient
　　Al abbé e a covent,
　　E noméement al abbé.
　　Loke nou þat hit so be.

40 y] *replaces crossed-out* ich　42 chambbre] chambre *Meyer*　48] moy] may *Meyer*　53 precheyn] procheyn *Meyer*　59 me(1)] ne *MS*　63 vous rend] me rend *Meyer; written above the line, over a caret mark. After* etc. *the words* jeo m'en irray en Essex, etc. *have been erased*

'The proof of love lies in the testimony of deeds':
The proof of love is putting it into action.
Mark this proverb,
Imprinting it in your mind,
And apply it to me.
If you want anything from me,
Send me word what your will is,
As to one who is pleased [to do your will], etc.
'Have good day now, Margaret:
With great love I greet thee.
Would that we could meet often
In hall, in room, and in the street,
Without incurring opprobrium in the district.
God grant it could be so!'
Greetings a thousand times over
By these verifying tokens
That relate to you:
You spoke to me about Physiognomy
At Fakenham, at the evening meal, and partly showed
Your heart, at the place where we were guests,
Enjoying entertainment that you call excessive,
[From] Robert, my kinsman,
Your near neighbour.
I am sending you a nice piece of cloth
Of fine fabric, by my faith –
It is white and pristine –
To put your book in.
Do you know what the French say?
'Whoever gives me a little something wants me alive':
He who gives me a gift at least does not wish my funeral.
Mark this proverb,
And apply it to me.
I commend you to God; may He guard you, body and soul. Pray for me, etc.

And see that you observe obedience
To the abbot and to the convent,
And especially to the abbot:
Look that it be so.

NOTES TO LETTER II

1–20 Meyer treats this entire passage as prose, and assumes verse only from our line 21 on.

5 MS *c. pson* is obscure.

9–13 See n. to I.14–20, where the same concern is expressed and the same proverb cited. The danger posed to lovers by *maveyses langes* was often cited (cf. the 'wikked tonges' of *Troilus* I.39), the phrase being an echo or allusion to the Male Bouche who figures in the cast list of the archetypal love affair depicted in the famous love allegory, *Le roman de la rose*. The abbot's no doubt genuine fear of them may (in part) be here (as with Criseyde at *Troilus* V.1610) a convenient excuse for a neglect in breach of a promise.

14–15 The same wording and the same rhyme occur with the same sense ('apply this saying to my case') at 33–5 and 61–2.

16–18 (cf. 23–6) Cf. 13–14 of the model love letter (Text 2, 1C, at p. 202 above). The rehearsal of the occasion on which Margaret revealed her private feelings to the abbot is thus introduced and concluded by protestations that in effect give the reason for recalling the incident: it conferred upon him a felt special emotional obligation to her and guarantees the seriousness of his declared readiness to serve her. It is likely that the recollection also acts implicitly, like the other details recalled in the letter, as an *enseigne* (on which see n. to 46) that verifies the identity of the writer by showing knowledge of some past meeting.

20 'Religious house' is a well-attested sense of *maisoun* in Anglo-Norman and the reference here is almost certainly to the convent or religious establishment of which Margaret was a member.

22 The reference is indubitably to the Cross of Bromholm (see pp. 245–6 above) in Norfolk. The pilgrimage would form an occasion or pretext for a journey on which the abbot and the nun (obviously in the company of others: 25), probably already attracted to one another, could be together and enjoy some private conversation en route.

30–2 The saying is from St Gregory (*Homilies on the Gospels* 3.30.1: *PL* 76.1220). It is also quoted in the *Ancrene Wisse*, which interprets it as indicating that true love will show itself in external deeds: 'For luue wule schawin him wiþ uttre werkes' (Part 6: 1, 144/473–4). In attributing the *proverbe* to *Seynt Escripture*, the abbot is either using the phrase 'holy writing' loosely or making an error that demonstrates that, as a man of business *moyen sensuel*, he engaged more readily, like many another abbot, with ecclesiastical law and polite French than with Scripture and the Fathers; his application of the dictum to secular love and the present context is not without wit, and he has certainly remembered or can produce a Frenchification that preserves the internal rhyme of the Latin.

33–5 See n. to 14–15.

38 The 'etc.' indicates that conventional expressions of obligation could be assumed to follow and would be supplied in the final draft by the writer (or mentally by the addressee); cf. 63.

The Norfolk Letters 273

39–44 This is the only register switch into English that does not occur at the opening or closing of the letter (cf. 67 and I.7–8). It is also longer than the other instances, and the abbot is probably quoting what he intends to be recognized as an inserted lyric (as assumed by Duncan, who includes the lines as Lyric II, 16 in his *Medieval English Lyrics and Carols*): the rhyme extending over lines at 39–42 makes the passage stand out to song-like effect, forming a particularly striking contrast with the previous line, whose polite conventionality is indicated by the 'etc.'; there is also the fact that the second-person pronoun used (at 40) is the familiar *þe* [thee], whereas the abbot always otherwise addresses his lady, as all lovers did in their letters, by the respectful *vous* (even when he is displeased with her or joking with her, as in III), and this would also point to a quote (for the form is not uncommon in love lyrics, as opposed to love letters: see, for instance, *Harley Lyrics*, ed. Brook, nos. 5, 24, 25). It is also probably significant that, in l. 40, 'y' (consistent with a Norfolk dialect) replaces deleted 'ich' (inconsistent with it), suggesting adaptation to the writer's own voice. The lyric interjection of expressed feeling again follows a direct address by name ('Mergerete'), as at I.26–7, and it seems that the abbot is again using the Christian name to introduce a lyric protestation of love – either taking advantage of an existing one that used the name to rhyme with or taking advantage of her name to adapt a lyric to her (as at I.26–7). 'Have godday' (39) is an English version of the *Saluz* that marks the resumption of the home language of Anglo-Norman at 45. Salutations were a standard component of the medieval letter, usually found at the beginning (cf. III.1) or at the end (cf. I.21). On Camargo's assumption that the two greetings here marked the start of separate letters, see p. 243 above. The greetings are, in fact, here as in I, part of the closing formulae. The abbot, however, enlarges upon them (by producing a prefatory English lyric version of them and expanding them by introducing – with the phrase 'par celes enseignes ...' – another reminiscence of an intimate moment at 46–53) to a degree that masks their initiation of the concluding phase of the letter. But they are then followed by reference (54) to an accompanying gift (as they were followed by thanks for a gift received at I.24–5), in turn expanded upon (55–62), and by expressions that mark sign-off at 63–7: compare Troilus's '3et pray I God, so 3eve 3ow right good day' (*Troilus* V.1411), which is similarly an early part of the extended closing formulae that end his letter to Criseyde (and corresponds to Boccaccio's letter-closing 'Dio sia teco': VII.75.7).

44 See n. to 67.

46 *enseignes* – referred to elsewhere in the context of letters or messages sent in English as 'signe' or 'token(es)' – were references to an occasion or circumstances which testified to a past or existing relationship between sender and addressee that justified the letter or the message or the approach and verified the assertions and/or identity of the sender; cf. the verbal letter of introduction to Clergy given by Dame Study to the dreamer in *Piers Plowman* ('Seye him this signe: I sette him to scole, / And that I grette wel his wif, for I wroot hire the Bible ... Tel Clergie thise tokens, and to Scripture after, / To conseille thee kyndely to knowe what is Dowel': B.X.170–219). Cf. pp. 50–1 above.

48–53 The meal and conversation here recorded may have occurred during the pilgrimage which is the subject of the first reminiscence (19–25) or, more probably, on a separate occasion, which may also have been a pilgrimage (since there would otherwise be limited opportunities or pretexts for the pair to dine together away from their respective convents), perhaps to the shrine of our Lady at Walsingham, another popular place of pilgrimage which was also situated in Norfolk, north of Fakenham, which formed a lodging place for pilgrims going there (see p. 246).

48 *fisnomye*: the art of judging the nature and disposition of persons by their physical and facial features, a science popular throughout the Middle Ages and one whose origins lay in the treatise *Physiognomonica*, formerly attributed to Aristotle. In the British Isles, Michael Scot compiled a *Liber physiognomiae* in the early thirteenth century, and John Metham produced in the fifteenth century a treatise on the subject, which was one in which Chaucer too interested himself: see J.B. Friedman, 'Another Look at Chaucer and the Physiognomists', *Studies in Philology* 78 (1981) 138–52.

49 *Fakenham*: a town in the northern region of Norfolk, about 19 miles north-east of King's Lynn (referred to at III.4); see p. 246 and Map 1 on p. 247.

51 *outrage*: this is a deprecating compliment; cf. *Le petit Jehan*, where the lady accepts an invitation by the abbot on condition that he moderate the lavishness of his previous hospitality, which was 'outraigeux' (p. 253; 'most extravagant', Jean, p. 170); cf. the abbot's excuse for the lady's initial refusal of an invitation by Saintré, on the grounds that she had feared he would put on 'an extravagant feast with great ceremony' [une grant feste et solempnité *outraigeuse*] (*Jehan*, p. 288; Jean, p. 193).

53 *precheyn*: Meyer reads *procheyn*, but the writer keeps distinct the various contractions for *pro*, *per/par* and *pre/pri*. He consistently uses for *pro-* a downward curl through the descender, whereas the abbreviation employed here is the upward curl used for *pri/pre* (though found in these drafts only otherwise for *pri-*, *pre-* being not elsewhere required). Forms of *prochain* spelled with *pre-* are well attested in the *AND*.

54–7 See n. to I.24–5. On this gift of a baptismal cloth for use as a 'chemise', see p. 259 above.

59–60 Meyer (n. to 59) points out that the proverb occurs elsewhere in French: 'Ki petit me done si veut que je vive' (*Li proverbe au villain* (Leipzig, 1895), p. 8). The Latin version – again (as at 31) in the form of a leonine rhyme – occurs in a schoolbook which survives in two MSS (the fifteenth-century Manchester, John Rylands Library, MS Lat 394, and Oxford, Bodleian Library, MS Douce 52) and which consists of proverbs arranged alphabetically and designed to train boys in Latin composition and metre; on fol. 5ʳ (under *D*) in Rylands can be found eight Latin versions (six in Douce 52) of a proverb given in English as 'He that yeueth me a litel wol my life', the fourth ('Non michi vult funus qui parvum dat michi munus') corresponding to the form in which the saw is cited by the abbot (all eight are quoted by Traugott Lawler, 'Langland Versificator', *Yearbook of Langland Studies* 25 (2011) 37–76, at p. 55). The abbot plainly likes

The Norfolk Letters 275

the rhythmic neatness of Latin proverbs in leonine form (which sit well in the context of rhyming verse and reflect the training in Latin metre exemplified by the above schoolbooks that he would have received as a schoolboy), but he does not cite them without providing a gloss in the form of a French version (cf. 31–2). Women were generally not taught Latin, and Margaret's may have been meagre or shaky (the abbot certainly thinks her own citation of a Latin proverb shows questionable command of its sense: III.2–7), whereas well-born women would naturally be sufficiently familiar with French to use it in letters (where it was the standard language), and would often be familiar with its use in formal documents of various kinds, for it was still frequently preferred as the language of record. Camargo (p. 31) sees in the abbot's use of proverbs (cf. 12–13, used also at I.19–20, and 31–3 above) a reflection of the *dictatores* (who sometimes recommended the use of a proverb or cited material after the *salutatio*: Camargo, p. 10), but in their frequency and random distribution they seem rather to reflect habits of thinking and speaking his education had encouraged.

61-2 See n. to 12–13.

64-6 Cf. I.5–8. Line 66 makes the injunction seem to be given with more of a smile than in the previous letter.

67 Cf. I.7–8. It is noteworthy that both of the brief register switches into English that occur at the opening or close of the letter involve the expression 'Loke nou that hit so be' in connection with an injunction to obedience. The phrase obviously had a formal contextual relevance that resisted translation into its French equivalent and so prompted the register switch (in much the same way as 'Le/La vostre x' would resist translation into English at the close of a letter for which English had been used: cf. *Troilus* V.1421, 1631), although the expression is also useful in supplying a rhyme (the more extended and less formulaic register switch at 38–44 ends, comparably, with 'God 3eve þat so mi3te hit be!').

III

Saluz et chiers amystés. Endreit de la lettre qe vous me mandastes, jeo vous say grant gré, mes endreit del proverbe qe vous me mandastes en latyn, sachiez qe tut est contre vous, kar, par Llevelyn mon vallet, jeo vous priay e en obedience comanday qe vous vensisez par moy de Lynne, 4
e vous certeynement promistes de venir a certeyn jour assigné, al quel jour poynt ne venistes, mes vostre obedience e vostre profession malement avez freynt – par quey le proverbe puet bien estre dit de vous, e pur ceo, qant jeo verray lu e tens, vous averez penance tiele com vous avez deservye. 8
A Dieu, qe vous eit en sa garde e amende vostre estat, nomement en ceo seint tens; e ne seez pas en despeyre, qe certes, si vous volez, vous poez de leger fere les amendes vers Dieu e vers moy en ceste manere – par confession, par contricion, e par satisfaction. Ceste proverbe recordez, que vous la bien 12
sachiez, qe, certes, en ceste manere deit chekun homme sey amender vers Dieu e vers le siecle.

3 Llevelyn] *erased*   vallet] valet *Meyer*   4 moy] may *Meyer*   10 despeyre] despeir *Meyer*   13] homme] hone *Meyer*

III

Salutations and amity. As regards the letter you sent me, it is much appreciated; but as regards the proverb you sent me in Latin, be sure that it goes completely against you – for, by Llewellyn, my servant, I begged and commanded you on your obedience that you should come to me at Lynne; and you certainly promised to come on the day specified, on which day you quite failed to come, but the obedience you owe me and your professional vows badly have you breached, for which reason the proverb can properly be applied to you, and therefore, when I see the right place and time, you shall have such penance as you have deserved. [I commend you] to God, may He have you in His keeping and give you improvement, especially at this holy time; but do not fall into despair, for certainly, if you choose, you can easily make the due amends to God and to me, by way of confession, contrition and amends. Take note of that formula, and imprint it on your mind, for certainly it is by those three steps each man should make amends to God and the world.

NOTES TO LETTER III

2–3, 7 The fact that Margaret could quote Latin at all is, for a woman, noteworthy, even if the abbot thinks she has done so incorrectly (see n. to II.59–60). Margaret is plainly a fairly literate woman (see pp. 258–9 above). She seems to have quoted a proverb about untrustworthiness, which the abbot thinks applies to her own failure to show up when he had expected her; it is probably facts rather than the sense of the Latin that is at issue between the two, however, since some misunderstanding as to arrangements seems to have occurred.

3–4 The erasure of *Llevelyn* indicates the usual care taken in love letters to avoid any proper names that might serve to identify the parties. *mon vallet*: messages, whether verbal or written, always required personal delivery, and a *valet* is often mentioned with reference to communications as the bearer of a letter or a verbal message (see, e.g. *VD*, Letters 26, 36, 46). It is not clear whether the message Llewellyn took summoning Margaret to attend the abbot at Lynne was one intended to be private or whether the abbot could send an open one under pretext of convent business. References to past communications sent 'by my lad' (her lover to Margery Paston: Moriarty, p. 206), 'by Yelverton's man' and by other servants (in the Paston letters: see Rosenthal, pp. 132–3) often serve to identify the communication in question (one which the writer may fear was not received or which was not acted on or responded to by the recipient), and for the implicit accusation of non-compliance with a message whose delivery can be testified to; cf. *AP*, p. 69 (though the message the abbot refers to may have been a verbal one). The prepositions in *par moy de Lynne* are somewhat puzzling: could the sense be 'on my behalf *from* Lynne'?

4, 6 The abbot reminds Margaret of the *obedience* she owes him in each of these three letters (cf. I.5–8, II.64–7), in a way that must strike a modern reader as illegitimately exploitative of his official position in relation to her. The *profession* was the point at which the novice became a professed religious by taking his or her final vows (primarily poverty, chastity and obedience to ecclesiastical superiors, the last being what the abbot is referring to).

8, 10–14 The abbot is playing with confessional doctrine. As her superior (or possibly her confessor), he would be entitled to impose a *penance* (8) for any misdemeanour on her part, though he obviously means he will take her to task as her lover, rather than punish her sin (which her affair with him would constitute). His witty application of the language of confession continues in his injunction against *despeyre* (10) – despair of God's forgiveness being something the penitent sinner was always warned against – and his accompanying reassurance that *amendes* lie well within her power (10–11). He means that she can easily make it up to him in an amorous sense, but he is playing on the penitential amends constituted by the standard three steps of *confession* by mouth, *contricion* of heart and *satisfaction* (i.e. payment for the sin by amends and penance), a well-known triad in confessional doctrine (cf. *Piers Plowman* B.XIV.16–24), which the abbot proceeds to cite (11–14). The confessor anxious to avoid 'despair' on the part of the penitent he rebukes occurs in Langland (*Piers Plowman* B.V.279–80). The need for *amends* or 'restitution' is emphasized by Langland for serious purposes (see e.g. B.V.270–4), by the abbot for playful ones: Margaret must, like any sinner (13–14), make 'amends' to the God and to the world she has wronged, the abbot defining himself as the *world* to which atonement must be made (11, 14). Such witty abuse of the doctrine of amends in an amorous context occurs also elsewhere. See especially the lyric by Charles d'Orléans which begins, 'My gostly fadir y me confesse' (*Fortunes Stabilnes*, ed. Arn, R57, p. 286), in which the poet confesses to having 'stolen' a kiss at a window, but promises to 'restore' it (i.e to 'pay it back'), in effect using the notion of amorous 'amends', as does the abbot, to subvert confessional logic, for in both cases the amends will compound the sin (of lechery), not expiate it. It is noteworthy that playful use of penitential logic is a feature of the behaviour of Antoine de la Sale's parody of an immoral and amorous abbot in *Le petit Jehan* – who will give the lady 'absolution' for partaking at his table during Lent of food that could not be described as Lenten fare (*Jehan*, p. 253; *Jean*, p. 170), and whose power to hear confession and impose penances also figures in the love affair (see *Jehan*, p. 255; *Jean*, p. 171).

9–10 *ceo seint tens*: the most holy time in the Christian calendar was Easter and the period leading up to it (i.e. Lent, the time especially associated with confession and penance), but the reference could be to any of the major festivals.

TEXT 5

Oxford, Corpus Christi, MS 154:
Love Letter from a Woman

Like the manuscript into which the drafts of the Norfolk love letters were written, Oxford, Corpus Christi, MS 154 is primarily devoted to canon law, to which its first six items all relate. These items are followed by a copy of the pseudo-Augustinian *De spiritu et anima* and a life of St Edmund, and the remainder of the manuscript (fols. 191–214) is taken up with a cartulary of the Augustinian Priory of Llanthony in Gloucester. The first pastedown also contains material that relates the manuscript to that priory, for which it was plainly compiled. A preliminary folio provides a table of dates and gives the incarnational year as 1268. The latest date to which items in the cartulary refer is 1282 (fol. 204v).[1] The manuscript can thus be securely assigned to Gloucester and to the late thirteenth century. The draft of the love letter occurs at the foot of the otherwise blank verso of the preliminary folio, opposite the first item in the manuscript (Sicard of Cremona, *Summa decreti*). Though it is in fact verse (as love letters by convention were), the verse lines are written out continuously over six manuscript lines. As would be consistent with a draft, the decision as to metre seems to be one that emerges in the process of composition: the poem starts with three pairs of couplets, but thereafter each couplet is followed by a 'tail' line that rhymes with (an)other 'tail' rhyme(s). The end of a verse line is signalled by pointing at the end of verse lines 4, 7, 9, 14, 15, 17, 19 and 21. As with the Norfolk poems, the amateur (though not incompetent) nature of the verse is reflected in the lack of attempt at regularity in the rhythmic shape or syllable count of the lines and (cf. the first Norfolk letter) in the not-quite-consistent rhyme scheme. The writing is hard to read, but careful and not slovenly, and the lack of deletions suggests (as with the Norfolk letters) that editing was done in the head rather than on the page (something which the manual difficulty of writing with a quill pen would encourage). Since the letter's addressee is masculine (*moun amy*, 5; *frère cher*, 24), the

---

[1] A full account of the manuscript is available in R.M. Thomson, *A Descriptive Catalogue of the Medieval Manuscripts of Corpus Christi College Oxford* (Cambridge, 2011).

letter-writer appears to be a woman, which gives the letter extra interest, as women's writing survives in far fewer examples than does that by men. The participles *envoié* and *grevé*, applied to the speaker at lines 15 and 16, are not, however, inflected for feminine gender. Although neglect of gender agreement was common in Anglo-Norman (see pp. 197–8 above), this means that confirmation of feminine first-person is not provided on the only two linked occasions which the poem affords for grammatical indication of it; and, this being the case, the possibility that the writer was male cannot be discounted entirely.

As it is unlikely that a manuscript containing a cartulary would have left the abbey, the draft may not improbably have been the work of a (lay or clerical) guest at or visitor to the priory. Her lover may or may not have been a cleric: though the address *frère cher* would suit a fellow ecclesiastic, the phrase was used far too generally (see note to line 24) to provide any firm evidence as to the status or relationship of the parties. The writer was almost certainly an Englishwoman, writing in Anglo-Norman (as in the case of the Norfolk abbot) only because that remained the standard language for letters until at least the end of the fourteenth century; and (as with the Norfolk verses) the hand and language also suggest a date well before 1400.[2]

---

[2] Richard Beadle (personal communication) has suggested to us a date of the mid- or late fourteenth century.

　　　　Ore en ey mestre:
　　　　Me couent maunder lettre
　　　　A cely ke ie eym e ameray –
4　　　Ia ne n'en lerray.
　　　　Kar se est moun amy:
　　　　Si ne ce seyt ensi
　　　　　　Trop me peiseroyt.
8　　　Meyntefeye saluz
　　　　Ke ie ne say dire e plus,
　　　　　　Kar certes ben est droyt.

　　　　En bone saunté
12　　　Su e aquainte
　　　　　　Entre bone gent.
　　　　Bien me as envoié,
　　　　Dount mout su grevé;
16　　　Kar fereyt est le vent
　　　　Ke dehors est enfer[m]é.
　　　　Sertes toust est oblié:
　　　　　　Meintenaunt le sent.

20　　　Pur ce y metez la mayn,
　　　　Pu[s]ke vous estes garesein
　　　　　　De nostre maladie.
　　　　De vostre eyde en ey meyster
24　　　Si le vus plest, frère cher;
　　　　　　Ke si noun, poyn ne prie.

17 enfermé] *MS appears to read* enferne　21 Puske] puke

So now I am in difficulty:
I need to send a letter,
To him whom I love and always will –
I will never desist therefrom.
For he is my beloved:
If it were not so,
   It would grieve me greatly.
[I send] many times over salutations
[More] than I can say and even more;
   For certainly it is indeed right [for me to do so].

In good health
I am, and in the company
   Of worthy people.
You have conveyed me well –
At which I am much grieved;
   For cold is the wind
That is locked outside.
Indeed, everything has been forgotten:
   I see that now.

Therefore do something,
Since you are the cure
   For our sickness.
So I have need of your help,
If it please you, dear brother.
   If not, I have no prayer to make.

NOTES TO CORPUS CHRISTI 154

1–2 Separation has necessitated a letter as the only method of communication with the *amy* now possible (see pp. 33–5 above). The letter plainly presents the woman with something of a crisis: it not only requires a manual activity she is not used to (and inscribing on parchment is not easy), but is also (in implying matter not to be entrusted to a scribe) an act compromising in itself (see pp. 55–6 above), as well, of course, as presenting a challenge to her powers of expressing her feelings in writing.

1 The upper-case *O* of *Ore* is preceded by a long /s/, which was often used as a paraph mark, and both incipits and new stanzas could be marked by paraphs: see M.B. Parkes, 'Layout and Presentation of the Text', in *The Book in Britain II: 1100–1400*, ed. Nigel J. Morgan and Rodney M. Thomson (Cambridge, 2008), pp. 55–74, at pp. 68, 70. *mestre* (with *-re* abbreviation in the MS) figures among the variant spellings of *mester* [need, hardship] in *AND*. It here rhymes with *lettre*. It is later written without abbreviation as *meyster*, rhyming with *cher* (23–4). The writer's French is good enough to enable her to make use of variant forms for rhyming needs.

8–13 Having declared herself in something of a quandary at the task before her (1–2), the letter-writer begins by sending the salutations and the news on her own health and welfare that convention required in love letters as in other letters. The writer here connects the two epistolary moves closely (cf. Text 6, 1.4–9), probably (cf. *Troilus* V.1259–72) via a conscious or subconscious awareness that the root of *salutations* is *salu* [health], salutations being strictly good wishes as to the addressee's health, as letter-writers often showed themselves to be aware. The salutations sent in a love letter often involved some conceit indicating numberlessness (cf. Text 1, 130.22–6; Text 2, 1C.3–8; Text 4, I.21–3), a convention the present writer is plainly aware of, but to which she conforms in only a rather perfunctory and dispirited manner.

11–13 *saunté* and *su* are Anglo-Norman variants of *santé* (see p. 197 above) and *sui* (see *AND*). The reference in 12–13 may well be to the company enjoyed in the priory in which the writer is probably at present a resident.

14 *Envoier* [send] could also be used in the senses of 'show the way', 'remove', 'convey'. *me as* is anomalous, as lovers in real or fictional letters addressed each other in the respectful plural (as at 21–4); the more informal form may be due to inattention (to which someone writing not in their first language would be more prone), or may have been prompted by a move from formal salutations to an expression of keener feeling introduced by the statement here made: though *Bien* links back to the previous report on the new and satisfactory surroundings to which the writer has been conducted, the fact of removal from the addressee's presence links forward to the grief nevertheless felt and expressed in the next line.

16 The second letter in MS *f-reyt* appears to be an /e/, which we assume to represent a glide vowel in *freyt*, recorded by the *AND* as a variant of *freid* [cold].

16–17 Removed and perhaps excluded from the presence of the addressee, the speaker apparently compares being shut out from someone's love to the cold wind outside a house whose doors are barred against it. The writer either identifies herself with the excluded wind or imagines herself as exposed to it. The opening and close of the stanza thus present an expressive contrast: safety and social inclusion in outward circumstances versus emotional exclusion (or perhaps remaining problems) pictured as a wintry wind blowing outside.

18 *toust* is not recorded as a form of *tout* [all] in *AND*, but cf. *tust* (recorded as a form found in an Anglo-French letter).

20 The words in this line are very hard to decipher. We are grateful to Richard Beadle for suggesting the reading here adopted. See *AND* for *metre la main* = 'take action'.

21–2 The lines involve the familiar conceit of the beloved as the only cure or *bote* for the emotional wound or sickness of love (cf. Text 6, 2.8 and note). For its use by a woman, see p. 62 above.

21 MS *puke* has been assumed to be an error for *puske* (a recorded form of *puisque*).

24 *frère* is not comparable with Armburgh's use of the term *sister* at Text 6, 4B.24, which does imply a sibling or sibling-in-law. *Frère* in Anglo-Norman was used in direct address to mean 'friend'; since the *AND* records an instance in which it is used by a wife to her husband, it could obviously be used by a woman to a man in the sense of 'dear one, beloved'. As the lady seems to have some doubt about whether the addressee is still her *amy*, the term has a sad cautiousness here.

TEXT 6

The Armburgh Love Letters

The poems here edited are clearly drafts and/or copies of love letters from a man to a woman. They occur in a roll whose other contents are copies of letters and documents relating to the legal affairs of Robert and Joan Armburgh, especially to a dispute concerning land inherited by the latter. The roll has been edited by Christine Carpenter in *The Armburgh Papers: The Brokholes Inheritance in Warwickshire, Hertfordshire and Essex: c. 1417–1453: Chetham's Manuscript Mun. E.6.10(4)* (Woodbridge, 1998). Carpenter's edition of the poems usefully advertises their existence and makes them available in a readable form, but is little more than a transcript (with some errors), for it is largely unpunctuated and unglossed, follows the inconsistent indications of word division found in medieval scripts, and fails to make some obvious emendations for sense.[1] The present edition aims to supply these deficiencies, and provides not only some readings that differ from hers, but also some necessary differences in the line division and layout of the poems, especially those written entirely in English, differences aimed at clarifying the stanza structure of poem 5 (*abab* quatrains in 5B and C, developed into twelve-line stanzas in 5D) and at making visible the rhyming patterns of the other poems. We also supply translation of any Middle English that a modern reader might require and annotations that include identification of exactly which words, phrases and lines are repeated where – since Carpenter's reference to the considerable amount of repetition across the sequence (p. 58) is correct but insufficiently precise. We also provide collation with the other manuscript versions that exist for two of the three macaronic poems.

It is important to make the necessary distinctions between the various items. In the first case, they are not all the compositions of the sender

[1] Letters that look very alike in medieval scripts were often the occasion of miscopying by medieval scribes themselves: long /s/ and /f/; /þ/ and /y/; /e/ and /o/; and /c/and /t/. Thus 'sothe safe', which occurs more than once in Carpenter's text of the prose letters (e.g. at p. 175), is obviously a miscopying by her or the scribe of 'foche safe' [vouchsafe]. For examples of errors occasioned by the above letters in the poems, see notes to 1.13; 4A.9, 34; 4B.2; 5A.10, 16, 26, 28; 5B.50; 5C.49; 5D.90, 104.

himself, though all except the first are treated as such by Carpenter. The three highly artful macaronic poems (poems 1, 2 and 5A in our numeration) were pre-existing poems that the sender has reused. Besides their evident superiority in poetic and metrical terms to the English verse letters – a superiority so marked as to make it virtually impossible that both sets could have been composed by the same man – there are other things that point to productions intended as artful rather than as actual correspondence. Though they take the form of letters, they contain no details that could relate to a particular case (such as the reference to 'my son' and the address to the lady as 'my sister' at 4B.23–4 and the repeated appeals in all four of the English poems that a time be arranged for a meeting) – and, as already indicated, two of them are found elsewhere. The first (poem 1), which alternates lines in French, English and Latin, is the first of a pair (a lover's letter and the lady's reply), of which there are (as Carpenter points out: p. 58) two other manuscript copies: Cambridge, University Library, Gg.4.27, Part Ia(C) and London, BL, Harley 3362, fol. 90^v.[2] Carpenter was unaware that the second (poem 2), which alternates French and English lines, is also found elsewhere.[3] It was edited (from Oxford, Bodleian Library, MS Douce 95) by R.H. Robbins, under the title 'Sweeting, I Greet Thee' (see line 6 of our poem 2), as item 172 in his *Secular Lyrics of the XIVth and XVth Centuries*. Since the Douce version makes it clear that what Carpenter reads as references to *Johan roy* and *Johan tout puissant* in lines 1 and 35 of the Chetham version are respectively her mistranscription of *Jhesu roy* and the scribe's error for *Jesu tout puissant*, Carpenter's suggested identification of this *Johan* with Joan Armburgh – which gender considerations (masculine *roy* and *puissant*) in any case rule out – is erroneous and provides no support for any theory that Joan Armburgh may have been the recipient of these Chetham love letters. The third poem (5A), which follows three composed in English, is, like the first, composed in alternating French, English and Latin lines, and may well have been written by the same poet as the first (poem 1), or in close imitation of it, since line 32 ('Yow sende, grace, joie and honour') is near identical with line 5 of poem 1 ('With grace, joie and honour'). No other versions of this poem have been found, but it too was plainly a pre-existing text that, like poems 1 and 2, is in an epistolary form which

---

[2] The poem has been edited by Thomas Duncan in *Medieval English Lyrics and Carols*, at pp. 194–6.
[3] As noted by Ad Putter, 'The French of English Letters: Two Trilingual Verse Epistles in Context', in *Language and Culture in Medieval Britain: The French of England c. 1100–c. 1500*, ed. Jocelyn Wogan-Browne *et al.* (Cambridge: D.S. Brewer, 2009), pp. 397–408 (pp. 397–8), and Ardis Butterfield, 'Why Medieval Lyric?', *English Literary History* 82 (2015) 319–43 (p. 320).

enabled reuse by the sender as a verse love letter to his own lady. His own English poems contain nothing comparable with the metrical and linguistic virtuosity of these markedly finished macaronic poems. *Humblement magré* at the conclusion of poem 3, repeated at the end of 4B, which closes with a French equivalent ('Escrit de parte le vostre amy ...') of the sign-off in poem 3 ('By youre own suget and servant ...'), constitutes the only venture into French in the poems certainly composed by the sender himself, the conclusion of a letter in French or English being commonly a locus for a brief code-switch.[4]

The English poems are nowhere near as neat and polished as the macaronic ones, though Carpenter's comments on their roughness again fail to make some necessary distinctions. Though she says that 'at times, they turn into prose' (p. 58 and note – to our poem 3 – on p. 157), the only place where the verse is so irregular as to make it difficult to see whether and where there are in fact verse lines is in poem 3, which is markedly less shaped than the other three English poems, and may well represent either a rougher and earlier draft or an apprentice piece, in which the writer was composing in a form to which he was as yet very unused. As to the unusual amount of 'repetition' which might suggest 'successive drafts' (p. 58), it is here, too, possible to be more precise about what is repeated where and which items might be related to which as successive drafts. The sequence of verse letters certainly shows the lover-poet gradually acquiring a repertoire of words, rhymes and phrases that he reuses, and many phrases from poem 3 recur across the other three English poems. But extended and close repetition over several lines occurs only in two cases. Poems 4A and 4B share six to eight lines of good wishes (A.29–36, B.14–20), which incorporate a New Year greeting ('Right good New Yere': 4A.33, 4B.23); though this fact and this link between these two items is not remarked upon by Carpenter, the two poems plainly represent New Year cards, for that was a time when poems (including love poems) were composed and sent – and in this case it may be either that only one of the verse greetings was actually sent, the second (which includes a deprecation of any displeasure caused by the writer's son to the addressee: 5.21–4) perhaps being a revision of the first made in response to some emergent trouble, or that both were sent, perhaps in different years, so that the time gap would make less noticeable the exact repetition of certain lines, which, in the case of formal and standard New Year good wishes, would anyway impress itself as less undesirable than it otherwise might. What is perhaps the likeliest explanation, however,

---

[4] See the letters quoted on pp. 253–5 and 257–8 in Schendl, 'Code-Choices and Code-Switching', and cf. 'Le vostre T' and 'La vostre C' at the conclusion of the letters in Book V of *Troilus* (1421, 1631).

is that 4A was also a pre-existing poem, and was either sent one year and part of it incorporated into an independent poem written for another year, or provided a model that was then adapted and personalized in 4B (which, as already pointed out, refers towards the end to 'my son' and addresses the lady as 'sister': 23–4). 4A is much more finished metrically and contains a more demanding rhyme scheme than any of the other English poems (rhyming *aaaa* and including sixteen lines of syntactically patterned praise, all beginning *Ye be* and all rhyming in *-nesse*, and to that extent reaching heights of virtuosity not otherwise risen to in poems 3, 4B or the English versions of 5), and it has no personalizing specifics that would relate it to an actual as opposed to a representative love relationship – not even the request that the lady should assign a time for a meeting, which otherwise occurs in all the English poems (3.17–18, 4B.10–12, 5B.59–60, C.50–1, D.89–92).

The other case in which material is often and markedly repeated is across what we present as poems 5B, 5C and 5D, as three successive drafts or revisions of the same poem, though Carpenter fails to notice the close relationship between these three items in particular, or between them and what we present as 5A. This last poem, the third macaronic, has plainly provided a template for the following English ones, for the English expands sequentially on the topics of the macaronic: an address expressing love and devotion (5A.1–6, B.1–12), in which the writer commends himself from the heart ('Enterement me commaunde de quer', A.4; 'With hert ... I me comaunde', B.15–16); a hope that he may hear good news as to her state ('Of youre estate I wold fayn here / Corde delectabilia', A.8–9, echoed most closely at C.25–7 'Desyryng ... with hert to here / All thyng that myght be to yow plesaunt'); a complaint that she has caused him to be bound as with a chain to her service until his death (A.16–27, B.29–48: 'Stringor amoris vinculo', A.18; 'ryght strong cheyne ... To love yow best it wol me streyne', B.29–31); and a closing prayer that all blessings may be hers (A.28–45, B.65–87), supplemented by the more distinctive wish that she may live so as to escape the devil's power ('demonis imperio', A.42; 'his tortuouse tyranny', B.84) and gain heaven. The English version was twice revised. The first revision (poem 5C) seems to have been prompted by a letter from the lady which has caused the lover considerable distress (see 5C.33–40): she apparently indicated that the relationship should end or at least gave a negative response to his appeal that she should set a time when he could meet her – an appeal repeated in virtually the same words over all of the English poems (3.18, 4B.10–12, 5B.57–60, C.49–52, D.89–92), except the first of the New Year cards (poem 4A), and one which indicates that a meeting is not a straightforward matter, and thus that the affair is clandestine, one or both of the parties being not free (for, since the man at least is old enough to have a son, one or both of them may be married). The poem is then further revised (poem 5D) with all reference to the lady's letter, and the grief it caused, excised: either the writer thought better of noticing or responding to the letter with such evident woe, or there were further developments that were such as to assuage that woe.

The collection is especially interesting with regard to the meeting point between actuality and art provided by love letters. The transition from the use as personal letters of lyrics already existing in the realm of unpersonalized 'art' to the personal composition of such verse letters for the same purpose is obviously significant in this regard, as is the marked poetical and metrical improvement to be seen in the English verses, as the lover gradually becomes a poet. Though he knows that convention requires a love letter to take the form of verse,[5] he obviously at first prefers not even to attempt his own, though some literary taste and sense is evident in his choice and tailoring of the poems he uses either to send, as with poems 1 and 2, or to serve as a model for his own composition, as with poem 5A (4A belonging, perhaps, to both categories). The epistolary form of the three macaronic compositions makes them suitable for adaptation into love letters, and their macaronic virtuosity and polish lend them a certain clerkly elegance which an amateur could not achieve – and which would in a sense justify the dispatch of such ready-made items, impressive in their professional deftness, but (since the French and Latin elements are not taxing) not being so learned as to be inaccessible. Poem 1 is elsewhere followed by a *responsio* (in the voice of the *Puella*). That *responsio* has been omitted, to suit the use of the poem by a man as a letter to a woman, and the macaronic has been further personalized by a concluding quatrain in humbler English verse:

> He that is youre man,
> I ensure yow, to his laste,
> Sendyth to yow, as he can,
> A rude letre ywriten in haste.

Brief code-switches to English at the end of a letter largely in French are not uncommon, nor are concluding references to haste,[6] which can be implicit self-depreciating apologies for not writing a fuller or more polished letter. The effect here is interesting, since 'rude' and 'hastily written' are epithets in no way applicable to the preceding macaronic poem, though they are

---

[5] See the model love letter in Text 2 and our comments on it (pp. 202, 205–6 above).
[6] Cf. the letters to Henry IV cited by Schendl, 'Code-Choice and Code-Switching', at pp. 252–4.

not inapplicable to the English postscript, and the adjectival and adverbial qualifiers thus serve to draw attention in an apologetic way to the contrast between the poem and its rider, the humble English quatrain which is all the writer can himself manage in the way of verse. There then follows the French-English macaronic (poem 2), and then the first of the English verses (poem 3). Poem 3 apparently belongs to an early stage in the relationship (since it records the writer's resolve upon a love-service which he pleads the lady to deign to accept: 25–45) and is similarly very much an apprentice piece in the role of poet which the writer plainly feels is entailed upon him by the act of writing a love letter. Line lengths and metre are very irregular, though there is some improvement towards the end. The versifying lover complains feelingly of his lack of ability to express himself (14–16, 46–51), a topos that is here uttered with audible sincerity: the beginning of love and the beginning of verse lie equally heavy on his tongue, and the inability to handle the verse medium becomes an expressive focus for the sense (incident to all lovers) of feelings whose force cannot be fully expressed. It is certainly a topos and/or topic to which he recurs elsewhere in the sequence (most feelingly and powerfully at 5B.49–52, D.73–6). If poem 3 was sent without further revision, it must have impressed its recipient less by its poetic merits than by the painful awkwardness that acts in its way to vouch for the authenticity of the feelings expressed.

The two New Year verse salutations that follow (poems 4A and B) show the writer gaining in artistic enterprise and competence. He does not here merely add a personalizing postscript to the model verse letter (4A), but substantially recasts it to write his own poem, and to include matter specific to the particular relationship, around the core of good wishes he reuses (4B.14–20); and his command of metre and rhyme has greatly improved since poem 3. The advance again matches the stage of the relationship, for, though the lover of course expresses himself with the usual humility, he speaks no longer as a petitioner for service, but as *le vostre amy* (4B.28). The third macaronic poem in letter form (5A) leads to even freer and more creative reuse (in poems 5B, C and D), so much so that Carpenter understandably failed to recognize the English as a reworking of the French. The material is substantially recast, expanded, with independent additions and with independence evident even in the appropriations: for instance, a distinctive phrase in the macaronic ('wythout quest or sise' [without inquest or assize, i.e. without any legal formalities]: 5A.38) is reused in a quite different context in 5C.42.

The adaptation of 5A is much the most interesting of the series of adaptations, for, as we have already pointed out, the adaptation in 5B was itself twice revised – and the order of the versions must be the same as that in which they were copied onto the roll: 5C indicates by an 'etc.' ('I pray God that grace, helthe and prudence, etc.') that the poem is to end as does 5B, and must therefore have been composed after 5B; the reference cannot be to the ending as it appears in 5D, where the final blessing begins differently ('I pray God yow graunt, of Hys goodnesse, ...'), so 5D must have been composed before or after 5B–C, and the evidence points almost conclusively in the latter direction (e.g. 5D begins with the equivalent of the third and fourth quatrains of 5B, but follows the expanded version of those quatrains that appears in lines 13–24, of 5C). The revisions are extremely interesting. As already indicated, what seems to have prompted the first is some kind of negative response (5C.33ff.) from the lady, though the writer takes the opportunity to make other alterations and improvements. He also, interestingly, concludes the copy or draft with a quatrain (in the same metre as that in which the letter has been written), which may be compared with the quatrain postscripted to poem 1, the first borrowed macaronic (quoted on p. 290 above). But the postscript in 5C does not, as in poem 1, take the form of an address, and cannot have been meant to be sent along with the rest of the letter, for it in fact quite breaks away from the mode of epistolary address, in order to record as if for a third party the distress the 'answer' received had caused:

As for an answere whan I had notyse,
Althowgh it were womanly and onest,
Downe to my hert as cold as yse
It thyrlyd even thorwghout my brest.

This verse is well written, the rhymes and line-division structuring and pointing its content effectively. It is magnanimous in its woe: the lady's negative response is conceded to have been, not cruel, but 'womanly and onest', despite the woe it caused him – that is, it was that of an honourable (*onest*) woman of right feeling. She presumably expressed regard for him and grateful appreciation of his for her, but refused a meeting (or perhaps terminated the liaison) on the grounds of honour and prudence. And the simple metaphors of the ice and the pierced heart are well used to make an expressive and affecting quatrain. The poet has certainly improved since poem 3. Even more interestingly, his feel for poetry and art in connection with his love has now prompted him to provide a mini narrative frame for the letter, a miniature version of the verse narrative into which Machaut, in *Le voir dit*, slotted a record of the letters he and his lady sent to one another. All reference to the distressing *answere* is, however, removed from the final revision in 5D. The sequence thus ends with some kind of crisis in the affair reached and/or averted. Whether or what progress the poet-epistler made in love we cannot know, but this final poem shows him to have made considerable progress as a poet. Though he never reached the heights of the macaronic he appropriated to his own uses, he now writes verse that is not embarrassingly bad, and his revisions in 5D show him to have warmed to his task, for they are as much and more concerned with improving the poem, reordering the material and selecting between the two previous versions, as they are with altering its content. His increased assurance and competence is especially evident in the increased and increasing metrical skill of poem 5: in the regular stanzaic structure of *abab* quatrains in which 5B and C are written, as opposed to the more random rhyme schemes of the previous English poems, and in the twelve-line stanzas into which these quatrains are transformed in 5D. One can see the transformation occurring: in 5B, one of the rhymes is often carried over into the next one or two quatrains, though not with such regularity as would make for consistent eight- or twelve-line stanzas; in 5C, the poem begins with quatrains that actually do form what could be printed as three twelve-line stanzas rhyming *ababcbcbdbdb* (the rhyme scheme of the twelve-line stanzas in which 5D is actually written throughout), though the introduction of the fact of the distressing 'answer' disturbs this incipient metrical development, and there is certainly no manuscript punctuation (as there is in 5D: see p. 298 below) marking the end of twelve-line units; but the transformation is complete and consistent in 5D. And by this time, his lines are much more regularly (though not invariably) iambic and octosyllabic (with the occasional divergence into a decasyllabic line).

As to the identity of the writer, there is little to go on. The construction of the roll has some relevance to this question.[7] It appears that the original roll consisted of 5–9, and that membranes 1–4 were added later: the material on 5–9 belongs to the years up to 1436, whereas material from the 1440s and 1450s is found only on membranes 1–4, in which there occur no further letters from Robert Armburgh belonging to the years covered by 5–9, although these added membranes 1–4 do contain supplementary material relating to those earlier years as well as carrying on the records, including further letters from Robert, up to about 1450; when the end of membrane 9 recto is reached, the records continue down the verso of membranes 9, 8, 7, 6 and 5, whereas when the end of membrane 4 recto is reached, the succeeding material continues down the

---

[7] The description we give here is much indebted to the perceptive and persuasive account of the manuscript given by Carpenter (*AP*, pp. 54–9).

verso of membranes 1–4, in that order, and down onto membrane 5 verso (i.e. in the opposite direction from the one followed on the verso of membranes 5–9), the two sequences meeting on the verso of membrane 5. The second roll was thus apparently compiled at a slightly later date and was evidently attached to the first after the recto of membranes 1–4 had been completed, so that the scribe could not then turn over to proceed down the verso from membranes 4–1, but had to enter material on the dorse in the direction of membranes 1–4. The scribe who began the compilation (Hand A) writes membranes 5^r–9^r, and is succeeded by Hand B, whose work is briefly interspersed with and followed by that of Hand C, the writing proceeding down the dorse of membranes 9–7, where a further hand, Hand D, takes over, writing down the dorse of membranes 7–6. The love poems then occur down the dorse of membranes 6–5 in Hand A. The added roll (membranes 1–4) is the work of Hand D, that scribe obviously continuing the recording work he had taken over before the compilation came to a temporary halt towards the end of the original roll.

Since the poems are written by Hand A, it appears that the original roll was handed back to that scribe at completion of work and that he used the available space left to make drafts and/or copies of his own or someone else's verse love letters. Since it evidently returned into his hands, he seems to have stood in some kind of supervisory role over it. If Hand A was a secretary or chief scribe commissioned to take charge of the enrolment of pertinent documents, then he used the space left at the end of it when it was returned to him to record love letters either of his own or which he had access to among the papers he was transcribing – which were perhaps not those of Armburgh alone, since the first roll includes a sequence of letters apparently not by him and relating to legal and financial affairs in which he had no known concern (see *AP*, pp. 96–102).

Also possibly relevant is the fact that Armburgh's wife, Joan, took an active interest in the legal proceedings. The first roll contains at least one letter on the ongoing disupute that is certainly by her (see *AP*, pp. 120–3), and the second begins with a document that Carpenter (p. 61, n. 1) thinks may well be by her – as indeed seems very likely. Carpenter describes this entry as 'an account of the case up to c. 1443/8', but it is in fact no such thing, for there is no attempt at systematic or coherent summary or exposition – such as is found, for example, later on in these added membranes in a memorandum (perhaps by Robert) that gives a clear, if naturally partisan, account of the basis of the Armburgh case and the course of the dispute up to 1432 (p. 193). What the opening piece does, by contrast, is to record with triumphant spite all cases in which persons active on the opposite side were overtaken by illness, accident or death (on one or two occasions, it is noted with grim satisfaction, 'without howsell and shrift'). Even given the belief prevalent at the time (and evidently shared by the writer) that such visitations were evidence of divine judgement, this essay makes for very unpleasant reading. It could only have been written by a highly partisan principal in the case, and cannot have been by Robert – for his letters, though often polemical, are cool, factual, practical, expository and business-like. The shrill, histrionic tone of this document is consistent with Joan's style, but not with his. Joan thus herself took an active part in the case and in the production of documents relevant to it, and may thus have taken an equally active interest in the creation of the roll – and it is possible that the love letters were amongst papers of hers available to the scribe, who transcribed them with or without her knowledge. But it is difficult to see them as written either to Joan or from Robert, given that there would have been a high probability that whichever spouse initiated or oversaw the roll must have assumed that the other might well consult it at some point and so see the poems.[8] There is in Joan's case the further problem of how she might have come by earlier drafts of a letter sent to her (that is, poems 5A–C), though scenarios can be imagined in which these might have come into her possession.

The only internal evidence as to the identity of the principals is the writer's reference at 4B.23–4 to an adult son who might have upset the lady whom he addresses as 'Myn owyn lady and sister', and who was thus either a sister (presumably one with whom the writer had not grown up due to differences of age or domicile), a half-sister, stepsister or sister-in-law, for the term could be used of all those relationships (though not of other degrees of kinship, for which the non-specific term would be 'cousin': cf. the letter to Robert Armburgh in which the writer sends his respects 'to my maistrays your cosyn as for a gentil woman that I am most holden to'[9]). 'Sister' could also be used as a general term of address indicating goodwill (see *MED* *suster* n. 3a(b)), but it would not normally be so used by a lover, and in combination with 'lady' is likely to have its narrower sense and to imply a double claim on respect and care. It is certainly in its narrower kinship sense that the word figures in combination with 'lady' when Sir John Fastolf writes to his sister-in-law as 'Worshipful lady and my right welbelouyd suster' regarding documents once left in the hands of 'my brother, your husbonde' (though 'lady' here refers to the actual social status of the addressee, Lady Whytyngham, not to the honorary status she enjoys as 'mistress' of her

---

[8] Since the construction of the roll indicates that the poems were written before the supplementary membranes 1–4 were added (see above), which was probably before Joan died in 1443, the manuscript copy, even if it postdates by some years the affair itself (which cannot, if Robert was the lover, have occurred after Joan's death: see n. 13 below), is unlikely to postdate Joan's demise.

[9] *AP*, p. 183. Carpenter (*AP*, p. 35) believes the reference may be to Lady Ferrars, a high-ranking woman with whom Joan claimed some kind of kinship (pp. 92–3).

lover's heart).[10] Robert Armburgh is not known to have had a son, but he did have a stepdaughter and a stepson, Margaret and Robert Kedington, Joan's children by a previous marriage. There survives a letter, written after her marriage, from Margaret to Armburgh, whom she there addresses as 'dere and welbeloued fadre'.[11] The term 'son' could certainly be used of a son-in-law, and it is therefore possible that Armburgh might use it of his stepson-in-law. The word might also be taken as referring to his stepson, whom, however, in his prose business letters, he never in fact refers to as 'my son', but always as 'my sone in lawe' (*AP*, p. 124) or 'my wyues sone' (pp. 112, 118, 129), though in verse to his mistress he may have preferred a less prosy designation that did not remind the addressee of his wife.[12] And he had brothers whose wives would have been his 'sisters', though no such woman is mentioned in the other letters.

His brother William (who could have addressed Joan as 'sister') had a son called Reynold, who did become embroiled in the legal dispute carried on by Robert and Joan, in which he assisted them; he did later have disagreements with Robert (see e.g. the letters at *AP*, pp. 70–3), but these occurred after Joan's death (in 1443) – when, as the husband of one of her legatees, he claimed a right to property devised by her (see *AP*, pp. 30, 36) – and so there is no obvious reason why there should have been any ill will between him and Joan, though differences can easily arise in families. In connection with these references to 'son' and 'sister', Carpenter (p. 59) points out that Reynold seems to have lived with Robert and Joan for a while; the evidence for this comes in a letter from William to Robert in which Reynold is referred to as currently resident with the latter, a letter dating from about 1443, though Joan was obviously still alive when it was written, since it includes a request to be remembered to 'my suster, your wyfe' (*AP*, p. 186). But poor William should not be charged with fraternal treachery and incest (as it would have been regarded at this time) without stronger grounds than the mere possession of a son. Moreover, the verse epistles, if written out at the behest of the sender or addressee, would most logically have been so recorded if they related to a still ongoing affair. And Joan, by 1436–7 (the years reached by the other preceding contents of this original roll), may well have been rather beyond the age for being a likely recipient of love letters, since she had already been twice married and had a grown-up son when she married Robert in 1420. Since

---

[10] *Paston Letters*, ed. Davis, vol. 2, p. 131. The passage is wrongly cited in the *MED* as illustrating the looser sense of the word 'in direct address to an unrelated woman' (*suster* 3a(b)).
[11] See *AP*, pp. 126–7. See Carpenter's index, *s.v.* Kedington, for further information on Margaret and her husbands.
[12] On Robert Kedington, see *AP*, pp. 9–11.

that son was dead by 1430, 1436 is equally ruled out for a date at which Robert could refer to him as a living 'son'.[13] There is certainly nothing to suggest that the verse love letters and Robert's prose business letters belong to the same idiolect (peculiarly favoured phrases, idioms, constructions or items of vocabulary), although the mode and subject matter of the two sets of letters are so different that little can be concluded from that. There is, in short, little evidence to support, and some problems raised by, any assumption that the letters were written by Robert or to Joan; though those must remain possibilities, they are unfortunately only two possibilities among many others.

The Manuscript Text

The epistolary nature and function of the poems is clear from the manuscript. They are written out as prose, and there is nothing to distinguish them visually from the letters preceding them on the roll – except that they are introduced by a cross in the left-hand margin in the place where 'To + *name*' usually announces the recipient in the case of the other letters. This at once succinctly conveys that these too are letters with a recipient, but that that recipient is not being named. That is in accord with the convention governing love letters: in order to protect the honour of both parties, but especially that of the lady, should the letter fall into the wrong hands, neither the addressee nor the sender was (normally) explicitly named.

Punctuation (a point or slash) is used to clarify metrical structure. In the trilingual poem 1, a point or slash occurs after every Latin word, marking the English-French-Latin triplets in which the poem is written, a point also occurring after the second line of the sender's own appended *abab* quatrain. In the bilingual poem 2, the end of every English line is similarly marked, to clarify the English-French couplet structure (with the addition of a point after one French line, line 35, and the omission, as occurs throughout the poems, of punctuation when the end of a verse line coincides with the end of the writing line at the right-hand margin). In poem 3 (the first and roughest of the sender's own composition), there is (apart from one point at the end of line 6 in our text) no punctuation, and this reflects the lack of metrical finish and focus in this piece and may indicate that it was a mere early draft. In 4A (almost certainly a pre-existing poem used as a template for the New Year card that follows in 4B), nearly all the rhyming words are followed by a point, slash or virgule. In his own adaptation

---

[13] That death of course also rules out the possibility that we are dealing with an affair engaged in after Joan's death in 1443.

of this poem in 4B, the first thirteen lines, which are of his own composition, have punctuation after our lines 4, 7 and 8 only; but verse line-endings are then regularly marked from verse lines 13 to 27 (i.e. through the lines repeated verbatim from 4A and the sender's own closing seven lines). In the pre-existing poem 5A, nearly all verse line-endings are marked. In 5B, the first draft of his own adaptation of 5A, line-endings are again more lightly indicated than for the more tight and complex poems the sender has read rather than written, marks occurring only after lines 8, 12, 40, 46, 50, 56 and 76. But in the revision of 5C, though there is at first virtually no pointing (except after lines 4 and 36), all line-endings from line 40 on are indicated. And in what appears to be the final revision of 5D, not only are all line-endings regularly marked, but stanza-ends are also marked with a double slash at the due twelve-line intervals – even, at one point, at the start of a writing line (the end of our line 96 having occurred at the right-hand margin at the end of the previous writing line). The punctuation of the sender's own successive versions of 5A becomes, in short, ever more regular and minute, and reflects the poet's increasing command of and attention to metre.

A new line is started for each new poem, which opens with a capital letter (upper-case being not otherwise used except for the initial letter of the proper names Jesus and John). In addition, a horizontal S-shape marks the conclusion of some of the poems (2, 3, 4A and 5A).

Carpenter speaks of 'crossings out, almost the only occasion for these in the entire roll, suggesting the agonies of composition rather than the copying that is otherwise going on' (p. 58). But this is misleading, and the manuscript in fact points quite in the other direction. The writing is neat and clear, and there are only three instances of correction, all minor and all in the last poem, where 'I' has been deleted after 'that' at line 85, the writer having presumably at first assumed it was to be the subject of the sub-clause, and 'fo' has been deleted before 'sore' at line 98, the writer evidently having realized he had misread long /s/ as /f/. And eye-skip back to line 91 has perhaps caused the only other deletion: 'And that ye myght' at the start of line 103. Two minor words are entered above caret marks: the numeral 'v' at 5B.67 and the pronoun 'me' at 5D.40. These corrections are evidence of a careful and attentive scribe rather than of the heat of composition. Most tellingly, at 5B.80, the metre (though not the sense) indicates that something is missing, and a gap just large enough to make up the verse line to its normal length has been left for material that was obviously either illegible or did not make sense or was realized to be missing, this gap strongly indicating a copy rather than present composition – and perhaps suggesting that the scribe was not the poet, who might well have been able to remember or make sense of or recompose what a scribe could not decipher.

1

1   A celuy que pluys ayme de mounde,   To the one that I love most in the world
Of all that I have founde
Carissima,   Most dear
Salutz od verray amour,   Greetings with true love
With grace, joie and honour,
Dulcissima.   Sweetest one

7   Sachez bien, plessaunce et bele,   Know well, pleasing and fair one
That I am in good hele,   *hele* health
Laus Christo.   Praise be to God
Mon amour doné vous ay: I have given you my love
As youre man nygth and day
Consisto.   I remain

13   Dishore serray joious et [s]ayne   Henceforth I will be joyful and healthy
If ye will me in certaigne
Amare: Love
Asse[z] serr[oy] joiouz et lé,   I would be very joyful and happy
Ther were nothing that mygth me   *were* would be
Gravare.   Oppress

19   Ma tresdouce et tresamée   My most sweet and most loved one
Ever stedfast that ye will be
Suspiro.   I sigh
Soiez permanaunt et lele   Be constant and true
And in youre hert love me wel,
Requiro.   I beg

25   Jeo vous pray en toute manere   I beg you, in all respects
Theise wordys that be writyn here
Tenete.   Keep in mind
Ore a dieu que vous garde   Now [I commend you] to God, may He keep you
And turne youre hert to me ward: And turn your heart towards me
Valete.   Fare well

31   He that is youre man,
I ensure yow, to his laste,
Sendyth to yow, as he can,   *as he can* to the best of his ability
A rude letre ywriten in haste.   *rude* clumsy; *ywriten* written

NOTES TO POEM I

The poem exists in two other manuscripts (see p. 287 above), and substantive variants from the Cambridge (C) and Harley (H) versions are recorded below. The Armburgh text appears to be a shortened version that has been reconstructed from memory. It is an accomplished macaronic poem, written in lines of alternating French, English and Latin. French comes first, for that was the home language for all correspondence until the end of the fourteenth century, and it here introduces the standard epistolary address and salutations, and initiates conventional topics, which an English line then expands on and a single Latin word rounds off, to complete the syntactic unit the French line had begun. Though no version is absolutely regular in metre, it appears that the French was designed to have seven syllables (with an optional extra unstressed syllable at line-ending), though the first line has eight; the English line was apparently meant to be an iambic octosyllable; and the Latin consists of a single three-syllable word (four-syllable in the opening verse). Its epistolary form was obviously a major reason why this lover chose to use it as a love letter (which convention required should be in verse: see pp. 4–5 above), the chief markers of that form being the opening specification of addressee ('A [to] ...'), followed by the salutation or greeting, and the information that the writer is, God be thanked ('Laus Christo', cf. 'sit deo laus' at 5A.12), in good health (which normally follows a hope that the addressee enjoys health and freedom from troubles), and the farewell commendation to a God whom the writer prayerfully hopes will keep the addressee in His safekeeping (line 28). The poem is not significantly disfigured by the verses the adapter left out, and his omission of the companion poem that, in the other versions, takes the form of a response by the lady is, of course entirely appropriate to his own use of the poem as a real verse love letter to a real lady.

1 *de mounde*: en mounde (C); en munde (H).
2 C and H give a more regular iambic octosyllabic line: 'Of alle tho that I have founde [H: have I fonde]'.
4 *od verray amour*: C and H read 'od treye amour'. Armburgh's *verray* represents scribal substitution of a synonym for some form of the participial adjective *trié* [of best quality]. Though recorded in only a very restricted range of applications in French, and not at all in Anglo-Norman, the adjective was widely used in its Middle English form *tri(e* (variants *tre*, *triʒe*) in the sense not only of 'excellent', but also of 'trusty, faithful', and so could characterize love: 'By-tuixe god and holy folke Loue hys [is] wel trye and riche' (Shoreham *Poems* 56/1575: cited by *MED tri(e* adj. (b)). It would thus be something of an anglicism and has here undergone translation into *verray*. For *Salutz*, Carpenter reads 'Salutez'.
5 Cf. 5A.32 and see p. 287 above. *honour*: 'alle honour' (C, H) yields a more regular octosyllabic line.
7 *plessaunce*: 'pleysant' (C, H) yields more normal grammar and sense. Carpenter transcribes the MS ampersand as 'and' rather than 'et' (as she does also at 13, 16,

19 and 22). In fact, the MS distinguishes between the two languages: the ampersand occurs only in the French lines, whereas 'and' is used in the English lines.
8 *I am in*: H agrees, but 'I am ryght in' (C) provides one of the two more syllables required for what should be an octosyllabic line, and sounded *-e* for dative adjective – 'in goode hele' (the reading of H) – provides the other.
10 *ay*: aye (Carpenter). A line-opening 'Et' in C, H gives the French line its normal seven syllables.
11 'And also thyn owene nyght and day' (C, H). *nygth* (see n. to 2.34): nygyh (Carpenter).
12 *Consisto*: 'In cisto' (C), 'Incisto' (H), meaning 'I persevere'. See Putter, 'The French of English Letters', n. 10.
13–24 These two stanzas have been transposed. In C and H, the stanza equivalent to 19–24 occurs as the third stanza of the poem; it is followed by five stanzas (expressing classic love complaint and longing) that are omitted in the Armburgh version and then by the stanza that corresponds to 13–18.
13 'Tost serroy joyous et seyn' [I would soon be joyful and restored to health] (C, H) gives the normal seven-syllabled French line. *sayne*: MS 'fayne' (followed by Carpenter) must, since a French word is required, be a scribal error resulting from a common misreading of long /s/ as /f/ and by the expectations of an Englishman, for whom the more familiar English word would be naturally suggested as a collocation with 'joyous'.
14 'Yif thou woldest me serteyn' (C, H) shows the *thou* form regularly used in the English lines in the other versions of this poem (by contrast with the *vous* forms used in the French lines). Since our letter-writer is addressing the poem to a lady he is genuinely courting, he consistently uses the polite plural form of the second-person pronoun in both his French and English lines.
16 The opening two words in the MS (retained by Carpenter), 'Assech serra', give a non-French word and a grammatically impossible form of the verb; and the closing one, 'lele', is an obvious error (since *lele* does not rhyme) for 'l(i)é'. The line reads 'Et tost serroy joyous et lé' in C, H.
17–18 Perhaps remembered at 5D.41–4, where the same sentiment is expressed more forcibly.
17 'There nys [is not] no thyng that shal me' (C, H).
19 *Ma*: Carpenter reads 'Mis'.
20 C and H read 'Nyght and day for love of the'. Our letter-writer has altered, misremembered or rewritten to supply a defective memory, in accord with the content of the second half of the stanza – and in accord with the anxiety as to the absent lady's fidelity which issues in similar adjurations and worries from actual lover letter-writers elsewhere (cf. Text 4, I.3–8, Text 7, VII.8) and which perhaps played its part in the Armburgh lover's retention of this stanza and the greater emphasis given to its admonitions towards constancy.
22 *permanaunt*: permaneuant (Carpenter).
23 'Love me so that I it fele' (C, H) gives a smoother iambic line, but is slightly blunter than a real lover might choose to be.

25–30 These lines correspond to the last stanza in C and H, but the two quatrains that there precede it have been omitted: the first of those omitted stanzas is actually quite difficult to construe and may not have been understood well enough to be remembered, and the second adds little.

25–6 *en toute manere* is a tag probably devised to make up for the one the lover has understandably forgotten: 'par charite' (C, H), for which C's version of the next line ('The wordes that here wretyn be'), provides a rhyme, though H ('... ben wryten hyre') in fact has the Armburgh ordering that provides there the 'manere/ here' rhyme.

28 Epistolary closing formulae commonly include such a prayer: cf. *AP*, pp. 103 ('I can no more at this tyme but God haue yow in his kepyng'), 126, 185. *que*: lack of distinction between 'que' and 'qui' was not uncommon in Anglo-Norman. H has 'qui', C has the abbreviation 'q' (expanded, questionably, to 'que' by Duncan, ed., *Medieval English Lyrics and Carols*).

28–9 The lines occur in reverse order in C and H. The usual French-English order of the Armburgh version is obviously correct. The syllable count of this text is less regular than in C and H, and 29 lacks the etymological final *-e* on *herte* that makes the line a regular iambic octosyllable in C, H ('And turne thyn herte me toward'); 'to me ward' was a perfectly idiomatic construction in Middle English. The companion poem (a love letter from the lady to the lover) that follows in C and H is, of course, not used by the Armburgh adapter.

31–5 These lines are added and do not occur in C or H. For the deprecatory 'rude', cf. 'ceste ma rude lettre' (*Die Liebesbriefe Heinrichs VIII an Anna Boleyn*, ed. Theo Stemmler (Zürich, 1988), Letter 3.22; cf. 'ma rude lettre', Letter 4.21).

2

1	En Jhesu Roy sovereigne,	By Jesus, Sovereign King
	My dere love faire and fre,	*fre* noble, worthy
	En fyn amour certeigne,	In true and certain love
	As resoun tellyth me,	As rightness dictates to me
5	Come a mon coer demesne,	Such love being innate in my heart
	Swetyng, I grete the,	*the* thee
	Unquore duraunce en peyne,	(I) still dwelling in torment
	But ye my bote be.	Unless you will be my remedy
9	Care en foy vous dye,	For I tell you in good faith
	I hold none youre pere.	I consider no one your equal
	Desore en vous affye,	Henceforth I will put my faith in you
	As in my trewe fere.	As in my true-hearted mate
13	Tresbone, tresdouce amy,	Most good, most sweet beloved
	Myn owen derling dere,	
	De vostre loiall vie	Of you and your constancy
	Gladly wold I here.	
17	Tresdou[ce] creature,	Sweetest creature
	Myn hert ys wonder wo	My heart is extremely woeful
	Pur vostre long demour,	Through your long stay [away from me]
	That is so ferre me fro.	
21	Ore swetyng lele et pure	Now, sweet one, true and pure
	Let not oure love goo,	Let our love not end
	Car certeigne et sure	For certainly and surely
	I love yow and no mo.	*mo* others
25	Si jeo le ose dire,	If I might venture to say it
	That agayn skyll	It is against reason
	Que chast coer desire,	That a chaste heart should desire
	But ye hit fulfil.	Without your fulfiling that desire
29	De vous quant jeo remembre,	When I remember you
	As faire as flour on hill,	*flour* flower
	Sovent face sup[pi]re,	It could often make me sigh
	I sighe and morne ful still.	*still* quietly, privately
33	Ne poit estre ataunt	It cannot at present be
	As I wol wyth rigth;	As I rightly will it [to be]
	Mais J[hesu] tout puissant,	But may all-poweful Jesus
	Yf yow me sene a sygth.	Grant me to see a sight of you
37	A luy jeo vous comaunde,	I commend you to Him
	As he is most of mygth,	
	Qu'il vous soit ardaunt	That He give you the ardour
	To love hym day and nygth.	

NOTES TO POEM 2

This macaronic poem, written in alternating French and English lines, is, like the previous one, a pre-existing poem the lover has appropriated to send as a love letter to his own lady, because, like the last, it is written in epistolary form – as indicated by the opening sequence of greeting (6), followed by the statement that the sender would be glad to hear positive news about the addressee's circumstances (15–16) and the closing commendation to God (37–40). In this case, there is only one other MS version (Douce 95), and that witness is not clearly superior to the Armburgh version, which is therefore useful in establishing the text as well as being interesting simply in the very fact of its appropriation of a love poem for personal use as a love letter. The variants from Douce recorded below are taken from the edition by Robbins (*Secular Lyrics*, no. 172: see p. 287 above). The Armburgh version again carefully preserves rhyme, but the adapter or the scribe is often less attentive to regularity of line length. It appears that the poem was written in six-syllabled lines, but several presumably corrupt lines of different length occur in both witnesses. The poem is set out in quatrains by Robbins and in three stanzas of unequal length by Carpenter (lines 1–16, 17–24, 25–40), but there seems no reason not to follow the evidence of the rhymes, which indicate the eight-line stanzas we have here assumed.

1 *Jhesu* (Douce: Jesu): Carpenter misreads the MS abbreviation 'Jhu' (with line through /h/) as 'Johan' (which, spelled 'John' with barred /h/, does occur as an error for 'Jhesu' at line 35). See p. 287 above.

2 *My dere love*: since the adjective 'dere' is here weak (following a possessive), and so would have sounded final -*e*, Douce's 'you lady' yields a more regular six-syllabled line.

3 *fyn amour* was a standard phrase indicating true and honourable love, as opposed to passing fancy.

5 *demesne*: the MS in fact appears to have three minims between /s/ and /e/.

6 Since *the* is here needed as a rhyme word, it has been retained in Armburgh; in this and the previous poem the familiar *thou* forms (which figure in the English lines in the other MS versions of the two macaronic poems) are otherwise consistently changed in the Armburgh version to the more respectful *ye* forms. See n. to 1.14.

7 *duraunce* (Douce: durant) shows the same erronneous French as occurs in *plessaunce* at 1.7.

8 *bote* [remedy] is a commonly used metaphor in the context of *fyn amour*, in which the lady was regularly represented as being the only doctor or medicine which could 'cure' the lover's love-sickness. See n. to 3.23–4.

9 *en foy*: printed as one word in Carpenter; the line is a syllable short in both witnesses, unless the -*e* in Douce's *en foye* is not merely graphical and represents a variant available for metrical purposes.

10 *hold*: Douce's grammatically correct 'holde' yields a regular six-syllabled line. The inflectional system was steadily weakened over the fifteenth century, and this would have done nothing to make an amateur realize from his reading of poems that regularity of line length was as important a feature of verse as rhyme.

12 *in*: in in (MS).
13 This yields a better line than Douce's 'Tredoulce tres bien ame' (which does not provide a good rhyme). For *tresdouce*, Carpenter has 'tresdoute' (/c/ and /t/ in this as in other medieval scripts are hard to distinguish).
16 Douce reads 'Blethly wold y here'.
17 *Tresdouce*: tresdout (MS and Carpenter).
19 Armburgh's grammatically correct *long* yields a more regular six-syllable line than does Douce's *longe*.
20 Rhyme shows that MS 'fro me' is an error for what Douce correctly reads as 'me fro'.
21 On Carpenter's erroneous expansion of the ampersand in the MS into English 'and' rather than French 'et', see n. to 1.7. Interestingly, apart from the opening 'Ore' (Carpenter: 'Or'), the line could be an English one, since *swetyng* is an English import, and *lele* and *pure* had already passed into English from French. In fact, the English pronunciation of Armburgh's *lele* provides a more regular syllable count than does Douce's *loial*, though the former derived originally from a disyllabic French *leel*.
23 *et*: and (Carpenter); see preceding note.
25–8 Douce reads 'Si ils le3 ose dire / That is agein skill, / Que chast coer desire / That ye may fulfille'. Armburgh gives a coherent line 25 (for which Douce has an impossible reading), but the sense is not really clear in either witness, and, since both yield lines that are syllabically short, one suspects corruption. The sense assumed in our glosses is consistent with the conventional logic of *fin amour*, where the lover never claimed his passion was platonic, but where the lady was begged to submit to desires that stemmed from a lover careful of her own honour and interests.
29 *De* gives better sense than Douce's *Se*.
30 Douce's 'ffair so flour on hill' is a syllable short.
31 *Sovent face*: Douce has the more intelligible 'sovent foitz' [on many occasions], but agrees on the less perspicuous *supprie*, which rhyme suggests should be emended to *suppire*, a form of *suspire* [sigh]: cf. 'sighe' at 32. But the English generally continues rather than simply translates the sense of the French.
34 Douce reads 'As y wolde with right'. The spellings *rigth*, *sygth*, *mygth* and *nigth* are not errors, but were perfectly possible graphical forms in Middle English.
35 MS *Johan* 'John' (with bar through /h/) must be an error for 'Jhesu'; Douce has 'Jesu' (as in line 1), and lines 37–40 make it clear that the reference is to God.
36 Douce has 'Of you me sende a sight', which makes more sense. The line is corrupt in Armburgh, but was perhaps understood by the scribe and/or letter-writer to involve the not infrequent collocation of 'see' and 'sight'.
37–40 These lines do not occur in Douce, but are indubitably authentic, as four more lines are needed to complete the last of the eight-line stanzas into which the poem organizes its rhyming lines.
39 One would expect *face* here rather than *soit*, which does not yield much sense, but the Armburgh version does have some suspect French. For a closing farewell that includes a wish that the addressee may prove a devoted servant of God, cf. 5A.43–4 and n.

3

Goodlyest of all, as semeth me in myn hert,
And of all other born also the gentilest,   *gentilest* most gracious
Most womanly, thow ye do me smert,   *thow* though
And to ever have be the frendliest,

5   Sethyn the first tyme, of youre goodnesse,   *Sethyn* Since
That yow list to youre service yeve [me] hardynesse   *yow list* it pleased you; *yeve* give
To ateine:
Of my prayer have tendyrnesse
And not disdeigne;   and do not disdain to hear it

10   Besechyng yow of youre goodnesse and benyngnité,
Myn hertys joie and yerthely goodnesse,   *yerthely* earthly
Of youre bontevous grace and mercyfull peté   *Of* out of
Benyngly to helpe and redresse.
And thow it so be that I can not wele expresse   *thow* though
15   The feerefull thougthis wiche I fele in myn hert,
Have ye not the lesse mercy of m[y] smert.

On is that I dare not come in youre sigth   *On* one of my pains
Til it plese yow asigne me a tyme of youre plesaunce,   *of y. p.* that may suit you
Nowithstondyng youre presence makyth me glad and lith,   *Notw.* even though; *lith* light, happy
20   And to all myn hevynesse is soverain allegeaunce.   *is* it is; *allegeaunce* alleviation
Wherefore, sythin in youre service I   *sythin* since
Contynue, and schall withoutyn variaunce,
As ye me brougth into maledy
Now beth gracious and schapyth remedy.   *Beth* be (imperative); *schapyth* arrange, devise

25   Conseyvyng fully that I nothing desire
But fully yow to serve feythfully to my lyves ende,
Withoutyn change soverainly yow chere,
And, I yow ensure, whil I have lyef and mende,   *lyef and mende* life and mind
And ye luste now suche grace me sende   *And ye luste* if it pleased you
30   Of my service nougth disdeigne,   As not to scorn my service
Sithen yow to serve I may not in no wyse me refrayne.

And sithyn hope hath yeve me hardinesse   *sithyn* since; *yeve* given
To love yow best and never to repent,
While that I leve with all my besynesse   *leve* live
35   To drede and serve my will is holy ment,   *holy* wholly; *ment* meant, decided
And hereupon God knowyth min entent –

How I have fully vowyd in my mynde
Soverainly yow to serve, thow I no mercy fynde;
But this is the effect of my preyere finall:
40 Of your benyngne mercy grace for to fynde;
For hert, body, lust, lyf and all,   *lust* pleasure
With all my reson and my full mynde,
And my five wittys, of on assent I binde   *of on assent* in one accord
To youre service, withowtyn ony stryfe,   *stryfe* resistance
45 To make yow princesse of my deth and lyf.

For lak of speche I can now say no more: *lak of s.* want of articulateness
To expresse my mater as I wolde I may not playnly –
My wytte is dulle to telle half my sore,
And nougth I have yit for all my payne.   *yit* as yet
50 For want of wordys I may not now atteygne   *want of w.* lack of vocabulary
To telle half myn hertis hevinesse,
Til it plese yow schewe me sume gladnesse.

By youre own suget and servant, and evere more wil be,   *By* written by; *suget* subject
Wyth all lowlynesse yow to serve, humblement magré.   *h. m.* humbly despite all distress

NOTES TO POEM 3

The poem is very rough (see pp. 289 and 291 above). Verse line-ends are not indicated and have to be deduced from words apparently intended to form rhymes, but the consequent line-lengths and rhythms are very uneven. There is likewise no pointing in the MS (such as occurs for poems 1 and 2: see p. 297) to indicate the end of a group of linked lines; the stanzas into which we have divided the poem are therefore designed simply to show which lines are connected by rhymes, not to suggest that the poem as it stands is written according to any stanzaic plan.

1–4 The poem is written according to the plan of the formal letter (cf. n. to 10 below). It thus begins with an address, to a lady throughout referred to by second-person pronouns (the respectful *ye* forms being chosen, not the more familiar *thou* ones). The rhyme of *smert* and *hert* is part of the repertoire of poetic moves this poem starts to build up, and it recurs at 15–16 and several times in poem 5 (see e.g. 5B.38, 40 and 50, 52). Carpenter divides the lines differently, placing line-endings after *me, hert, womanly* and *smert*.

3 *Thow:* the MS may read 'yow', which is what Carpenter gives, but either or both are an error occasioned by the similarity of /y/ and /þ/.

6 The collocation *yeve* and *hardynesse* recurs at 32 in a line that is then repeated in poem 5; *me* does not figure in the MS but is plainly required.

7 *ateine* becomes a favourite rhyme word: cf. 50 and 4B.12, 5B.37.

9 *disdeigne* is likewise used as a rhyme word at line 30 (cf. 4A.27).

10 *benyngnité*: 'benygnite' in Carpenter, who indicates no line-ending after *goodnesse*. The present participles *Besechyng* and *Conseyvyng* (25) are in imitation of the syntax used in formal letters, where new matter is often introduced by that subordinating device, especially the petitions and information that the letter is designed to express. *Besechyng* is especially common: cf. 4A.27–8, 4B.14 and the verse epistles in Charles d'Orléans ('Bisechyng yow right thus, most goodly fayre', 5776) and in *'Suffolk' Poems* ('Besechyng yow thys lytell byll and I ...', 14.5).

11 *joie and yerthely goodnesse* recurs in poem 5 as *joie and my worldly goodnesse* (B.13).

15 Cf. poem 5, 'The sorefull/noyous thoughtys of myn hert' (B.50, D.74).

16 *my*: MS 'me' is retained by Carpenter.

17–18 This plea for the lady to assign a time for a meeting, for the writer 'dare not' otherwise approach her, recurs, similarly worded, at 4B.10–12 and in 5 (see B.57–60, C.50–1, D.89–92), and indicates that the frustration on this head was real and that the affair was probably an illicit one. For the verb in this context, cf. Henry VIII to Anne Boleyn: '[if you can't write back] assiné moy quelque lieu [for a meeting in person]' (*Die Liebesbriefe Heinrichs VIII*, ed. Stemmler, Letter 3.24).

20 *And* is omitted by Carpenter, presumably accidentally. *allegeaunce* ('alligeance': Carpenter) is a word that figures elsewhere in the language of *fin amours*: cf. 'd'amour aleggement' in the fragmentary love poem, beginning 'Douce Dame',

found on the flyleaf of Oxford, Magdalen College, MS 40 and reproduced in Dean, *Anglo-Norman Literature*, p. 81; it again proves a useful rhyme word at 5B.12 (D.44) and 63.

21 *Wherefore*: Wherfore (Carpenter).

22 *withoutyn variaunce* also provides a rhyming line-ending at 5B.35, and was perhaps suggested by 4A.8 (a pre-existing poem known to the writer), though he could easily have encountered it elsewhere as well: line-ending 'withouten vareance' occurs in line 13 of the Rawlinson poem beginning 'Right best beloved' and discussed by Camargo (pp. 157–8).

23–4 Repeated almost verbatim at 5B.62–4. For the medical logic, see n. to *bote* at 2.8, and cf. 'she is verray rote / Of my disese ... with oon word she mighte be my bote' (Chaucer's[?] *Complaynt d'Amours* 43–5).

25 For the present participle used as an epistolary connective, see n. on *Besechyng* in line 10. Both petitions and facts the writer wished to draw to attention were introduced by formulae such as, in the latter case, 'lyke you to wete that' [may it please you to be informed that] (*AP*, p. 178; cf. 'Sachez bien' at 1.7 above), or, participially, 'doyng you to vnderstande that' (*AP*, p. 138), 'certefying you I haue consaywed your letter' (p. 181), which illustrates also how the verb *conceive* could figure in letters as a more formal equivalent of 'understand' or 'know' (cf. p. 192: 'fynde and conceyve by the sight and examinacion of the seid dedys and munimentz that ...'). *Conseyvyng fully* here means 'please be fully aware'. *fully*: 'full' in Carpenter.

26 Carpenter prints 'to my lyves ende' as a separate line.

27 *chere* here probably provides a rhyme with *desire* (*chire* is a recorded variant of the noun *chere*, and that spelling is found at 5C.28, and *chyr* does occur as a form of the verb *chere*); *MED* does not record the sense 'hold dear' for *cheren* (though that meaning would not be out of line with the range of attested usages), but it does record a participial adjective *chered* to which it assigns the sense 'esteemed, held dear', citing 'Moost chered frendes, dryncketh inwardly' (line 106 of Lydgate's verses on Queen Margaret's entry into London: see Carleton Brown, 'Lydgate's Verses on Queen Margaret's Entry into London', *Modern Language Review* 7 (1912) 226–31).

28 *mende* (a south-eastern form) shows the writer already has sufficient poetic instinct to avail himself (as poets frequently did) of dialectal variants for the purposes of rhyme (here with *ende* and *sende*); contrast *mynde* (rhyming with *fynde* and *binde*) at 42.

31 The whole line is repeated almost verbatim at 4B.13 and the second half of it at 5D.23 and 56.

32 The line (cf. 6 above) is repeated almost verbatim in poem 5 (see B.25).

33 This line (repeated exactly at 4B.7 and 5C.55) shows the writer's familiarity with the language of *fin amours* and love lyric, and perhaps with Chaucerian usage in particular, which probably did much to give currency to the expression: cf. *Complaynt d'Amours* 82–4 ('Alwey in oon to love yow ... is myn entente ... I wol it never repente!') and *Troilus* I.391–2 ('he gan fully assente / Criseyde for to love, and nought repente').

34–5 These lines are treated as four short lines by Carpenter, who puts a period after *leve* and presents *with all* as one word (and *hereupon* in 36 as three).
36–8 The lines recur, slightly rearranged and in combination with 33, at 5C.53–6, as do 36–7 (again in combination with 33) at 4B.5–7. The resolve to commit to love, whatever the outcome, interestingly triggers greater metrical regularity: rhythm and rhyme and line length all gain more pattern and momentum from this point. The expressively decisive 'thow I no mercy fynde' recurs at 4B.27, though the writer is utilizing a phrase and a sentiment not uncommon in themselves (cf. Lydgate, *Floure of Curtesye* 253–4, 'Yet chese I ... To loue you, though I no mercy fynde'; *Bannatyne Manuscript*, ed. Ritchie 253.29–32, 266.34–5).
37 *How*: Carpenter wrongly reads 'Now' here, though she gives 'How' at the comparable lines 4B.6 and 5C.54.
39 A similar line occurs at 5C.49.
40 *your*: 'you' in Carpenter.
41–4 Adapted and abbreviated at 5D.21–2.
45 *princesse of my deth and lyf* is reused at 5B.8. The conceit is common: see *Troilus* V.1417–20, and cf. 'my leche me forto sle or save' (Charles d'Orléans, 5819), 'Both lyfe and dethe, all ys at her wyll' (line 7 of a verse love letter in Cambridge, Trinity College, MS R.3.19: first verse quoted by Camargo, p. 144).
46–52 '(I can) no more at this time' was a common epistolary formula; it is used frequently, for instance, in the Armburgh letters (by Robert Armburgh and by others: see e.g. *AP*, pp. 89, 91, 103), where its status as one of the regular ingredients of closure is indicated by the 'etc.' by which it is followed at p. 133. This formula (used more straightforwardly at 4B.21 and 5A.28) is here interestingly adapted to express the inarticulacy the lover feels (on which see p. 291 above and cf. 3.14–15) – as it is, even more expressively, at 5B.65–72.
47 *To* regularly produced elision before a vowel in verse, a fact often reflected in spelling, so the first two words might be better represented as *T'expresse*. *playnly* should probably be emended to the flat adverb 'plaine' (to rhyme with *payne* and *atteygne*), since the line would otherwise not rhyme with any other.
50–2 These lines recur in rewritten form at 5B.70–2.
51 Cf. 48. *hertis*: Carpenter here as elsewhere expands the abbreviated MS form as 'hertes', but the word always appears as 'hertis' or hertys' when unabbreviated.
53 Probably imitated from the pre-existing poem 4A (lines 5, 36); the conceit itself was common: cf. 4B.26 and Gower's *Cinkante Balades* XI.15–17, XXVI.2 ('Com cil d'amour q'est tout vostre soubgit').
54 *humblement magré* (printed as a separate line in Carpenter) occurs similarly as part of the sign-off at 4B.27. The phrase is perhaps being used as a 'motto': such French phrases used as moral watchwords figure frequently, for example, in *The Assembly of Ladies*, where they are termed 'wordes' and where they figure especially in amorous contexts (in which identification was avoided and in which a normal motto thus could not be used), examples including *Une sans chaungier* (590) and *Entierement vostre* (616).

4A

O princesse of womanhode, enlymnd with all beauté,   *enlymnid* illumined
Youre excellence is fully replete with humilité,
Youre gentilnesse passyth all other in dignité,   *gentilnesse* grace, worth
4   Youre nobles enncrownyd is with all benyngnité,   *nobles* nobleness

    I am youre servant and suget with all obeisaunce,   *suget* subject; *obeisaunce* obedience
Wilfull to fulfille youre hertis plesaunce;   *Wilfull* Wishing
Yow to comende in special remembrau[n]ce   *special* i.e. especially for New Year
8   Is my trew entent withoute variaunce.

    Ye be lady of ladyes, [th]e floure of gentilnesse,   *lady* mistress, queen
Ye be soverne of beauté, ye enlymin all derkenesse,   *soverne* sovereign; *enlymin* illumine
Ye be princesse gracious of all nobilnesse,
12   Ye surmount all creatures in worthinesse,

    Ye be welle of grace, the spring of goodnesse,   *spring* fount
Ye be medicine and cure, helere of all sekenesse,
Ye be comfort and solas of all hevynesse,
16   The beginner and causer of all gladnesse,

    Ye be the fairest of faire, ye be penacle of fairnesse,   *faire* fair ones; *penacle* pinnacle
Ye be that ymage in whom is figurid all stedfastnesse,   *ymage* epitome; *fig.* represented
Ye be habundaunt in vertu and all mekenesse,   *habundaunt* abounding
20   Ye be graunter of grace and gracious of foryevenesse,

    Ye be securable and favorable in all distresse,   *securable* able to give succour
Ye be loser and lisser of all duresse,   *loser* loosener; *lisser* assuager
Ye be reconsiler of all unbuxumnesse,   *unbuxumnesse* impatience under distress
24   Ye be my lady rith full of erthly goodnesse.   *rith* right, completely

    This bref commendacion of my lady soveraigne
Have I made with hert pensiff and payne,   *p. and p.* oppressed by care
Beseching yow that [y]e audience therof not disdeigne,   *audience* hearing; *disdeigne* scorn to give
28   But consider the trew entent of my hert in every veyne.

    Honour, estate, joie and reverence,   *estate* status, rank
Encres of love, vertu in dignité,   *dignité* social standing
Rychesse, wysdom, grace, hele and prudence,   *hele and p.* health and foresight
32   Preysyng, gladnesse, reste and prosperité,   *reste* ease, peace; *prosp.* well-being
Rygth good New Yere, with all felicité,
Be to yow with all myn hert yovyn,   *yovyn* given
As yow best list, ever wele ye levyn.   All that pleases you best, while you live
36   By your servant and sugett and ever more will be.

NOTES TO POEM 4A

The poem was almost certainly a pre-existing one (see pp. 288–9 above), which was sent as a New Year greeting, with part of it (29–35) then being reused for another New Year in 4B (14–20), or which served as a model for the adapted and personalized version that appears in 4B. Metrically and in vocabulary, it is fairly typical of fifteenth-century verse of the more florid and aureate type (*aureate* is a term used to designate a high proportion of Latin-derived polysyllables). The Armburgh verse-letter-writer and lover is, however, beginning to give the existing verse he transcribed for his own use the attention of a practitioner, for, though little in the way of direct verbal echoes occurs in his own verse from poems 1 or 2, he found a use in poem 5C (and the equivalent lines in 5D) for several of the phrases in this poem, as the notes below will illustrate.

1 Reused as two lines at 5C.5–6 and (conflated with 4A.11 below) 45. Cf. e.g. 'Princesse of beautie' in the envoy to Lydgate's *Floure of Curtesye* (267), and 'Princesse / De tout honour' in Gower's *Cinkante Balades* VI.22–3. For *enlymnid*, Carpenter reads 'enkyinnyd'.
2 *replete with humilité*: reused at 5C.2.
4 *enncrownyd ... with ... benyngnité*: reused at 5C.4.
7 *remembraunce* ('remembrance' in Carpenter): the MS word terminates in 'a+two minims+ce'. The abbreviation for a nasal over /u/ has probably been omitted by the scribe or in his exemplar.
8 *withoute variaunce* likewise forms a line-ending and rhyme at 3.22.
9–24 The lines are an orotund extension of a common construction in praise of the lady: with lines 9, 11, 14, and 17 compare, for instance, 'Sur toutes flours la flour, et la Princesse / De tout honour, et des toutz mals le Mire [physician]' (*Cinkante Balades* VI.22–3).
9 *the* ('ye': Carpenter) *floure*: MS 'ȝe' is clearly an error for 'þe'.
10 Carpenter inserts 'sonne' before *soverne*.
11 See n. to 1 above.
12 *creatures*: creaturs (Carpenter).
13 Reused as 'Welle of vertu, spryng of goodnesse' at 5C.9.
14 Reused at 5C.16.
16 Reused at 5C.14.
17 Cf. Knight's Tale, 'Faireste of faire, O lady myn Venus' (*CT* I.2221), which perhaps gave currency to the expression; Carpenter (unintentionally, presumably) omits *the* and retains MS 'fairer', which we assume to be an error for 'faire'.
18–19 Reused at 5C.11–12.
20 *foryevenesse*: Carpenter gives 'forgevenesse', but the word is spelled with a yogh, which is always the equivalent of /y/ in sound and spelling in this text.
22–3 Reused at 5C.18 and 20. *unbuxumnesse*: Carpenter reads 'unbuxomnesse'.
25–6 Printed as one line in Carpenter. *soveraigne* (cf. 4B.1), echoing *princesse* (1), was a term commonly used: cf. 'O excelent Suffereigne, most semely to See' (the

opening of poem 40 in the *Welles Anthology*), 'celle sovereine', 'ma dame sovereine' (*Cinkante Balades* X.17, XIV.1).

27 *ye*: the MS in fact clearly reads 'þe', though it is transcribed 'ye' by Carpenter.

27–8 *disdeigne* provides a rhyme word also at 3.9, and every *veyne* of the heart likewise provides a rhyme for *payne* at 5B.36.

29–36 The lines are repeated in the next letter of New Year greeting (4B.14–20). *Rygth good New Yere* (33) serves to adapt the conventional epistolary closure (wishing the addressee all the blessings they would themselves wish for themselves; cf. 35) into New Year good wishes. See 5B.73–87 and n.

32 *reste*: 'rest' (Carpenter).

34 *yovyn*: rhyme requires 'yevin'. In Carpenter's edition of them, both forms occur in the prose letters (*yeven* at p. 132, *yoven* at pp. 144, 191).

35 *As yow best list* reflects a common formula in epistolary good wishes: cf. 'Right as youre herte ay kan, my lady free, / Devyse, I prey to God so moot it be' (*Troilus* V.1362–3).

36 Cf. 5 above and n. to 3.53, where the same expression occurs and was probably prompted by the present poem.

4B

    To yow that be my soveraigne and maistresse,
    I recommonde me wyth all myn hert and spirit,
        with on assent   *on* one
    Ever to love yow best with all my besinesse,
4   Be my trougth, my will holy ment,   *Be* by; *ment* fixed
    And hereupon God knowyth myn entent, –
    How I have fully vouyd in my mende   *vouyd* vowed
    To love yow best and never to repent.
8   Suffre me nougth, I beseche yowr gentilnesse,   *gentilnesse* graciousness, goodness
    From youre presence be leng absent,
    But certifieth me of youre benyngne hert,   *certifieth* make known
        gracious and patient,
    A tyme of youre plesaunce   *plesaunce* convenience
12 To your presence whan I may atteign,
    Sithyn yow to serve I may nougth ne will me refreine.   *Sithyn* Since

    Besechyng God that honour, joie and reverence,
    Encres of love, vertu in dignité,   *dignité* social rank, status
16 Richesse, wysdom, grace, hele and prudence,   *hele* health; *prud.* foresight
    Preisyng, gladnesse, rest and prosperité,
    Rigth good Newe Yere, wyth all felicité,
    Be to yow, my lady, with all min hert yovyn,   *yovyn* given
20 As yow best list, ever whill ye levyn.   *yow b. l.* it best pleases you; *levyn* live

    More write I not at this tyme, but humbly I yow pray,
    For Hys love that us bothe dere hath bougth,   *dere* dearly; *bougth* redeemed
    What my sonne have seid or in ony wyse schul say,   *have seid* may have said; *ony any*
24 Myn owyn lady and sister, displese yow nougth,
    But serchith wele the treuthe, yf ony faut be sougth.   *faut* fault; *sougth* found
    Y[it] I be as I was, and youre servant perpose ever to be,
    Thow I no mercy finde, humblement magré.   *Thow* Though; *h. m.* humbly,
                                                            whatever happens

28 Escrit de parte le vostre amy,   Written by your lover
    Que vous ayme tant come luy.   Who loves you as much as he loves himself

NOTES TO POEM 4B

This poem reuses (at 14–20) those lines from 4A (29–35) that send good wishes tailored into a New Year greeting (17). The lines are embedded in a new and personalized context, for the poem refers to details specific to the particular relationship (23–5). It may be that 4A (almost certainly a pre-existing poem not composed by the letter-writer) was sent one year, and its relevant lines reused within an independent poem for another New Year, or that 4A was not sent except in the adapted and personalized version of 4B. The latter is perhaps indicated by the fact that 4B takes much more obvious letter form than does 4A, beginning with the formulaic 'To ...' (cf. 1.1, 5A.1), moving through the present participle ('Besechyng ...' at 14) and the formula 'More write I not at this tyme' (21), both typical of epistolary procedure, to the closing 'Escrit de ...'.

1–2 *To yow ... I recommonde me*: the formula is amongst the commonest of those used at letter opening (cf. 5D.1, 12), 'I comaund me to you' occurring in *AP* at the beginning of all kinds of letters (respectful, petitionary, curt or even threatening: see pp. 126, 127, 130, 147, 171).

1–4 The lines are presented as prose by Carpenter, but they include words which could rhyme and which are elsewhere used as rhyme words.

2 *with on assent*: cf. 3.42–3.

4 For participial *ment* similarly applied to *will* at line-ending (and providing a rhyme with *entent* and *repent*), cf. 3.35.

5–7 These lines occur also at 3.33, 36–7.

10–12 A similar plea figures in all the English poems except 4A (which was probably a poem the writer knew or found rather than one he composed). See n. to 3.17–18. It is part of the personalization of the more generalized 4A that occurs in 4B.

12 *atteign* is frequently used as a rhyme word by this amateur love-poet. See n. to 3.7.

13 A line that is repeated in various forms: see n. to 3.31.

14 *Besechyng*: on the present participle as a typical connective in epistolary syntax, see n. to 3.10.

14–20 The lines reuse ones that occur at the end of 4A. See headnotes to 4A and 4B and pp. 288–9 above.

19 *my lady* does not occur in the equivalent line in 4A (34).

19 *yovyn*: see n. to 4A.34.

21–2 These two lines are printed as one by Carpenter, despite the virgule after *pray* that marks the end of a metrical unit (see pp. 297–8 above).

21 *More write I not at this tyme*: a common epistolary formula. See n. to 3.46. Cf. 5A.28.

23–4 There was obviously contact between the writer's 'son' and his mistress, and the writer fears his son may have said something at which the lady might take offence, and may do so again. See pp. 296–7 above.

25 *serchith*: 'sechith' (Carpenter).
26 *Yit*: 'Yf' (MS and Carpenter).
27 *I* is omitted by Carpenter. Cf. 3.38. *humblement magré* is likewise used at the conclusion of poem 3. If it is not a motto (see n to 3.54), it and the French couplet that here follows in 28–9 may have been formulations that the writer found elsewhere rather than invented; the non-macaronic poems contain no other (even common) French phrases.
28–9 Printed as one line by Carpenter.

5A

  A ele que ayme sur tout rien,   To her whom I love above everything
  Of all tho that in this world been,   *tho* those; *been* are
3 Corde meo dure fixa,   firmly fixed in my heart
  Enterement me commaunde de quer, who commands me completely in my heart
  As ye that ben to me most chere   *chere* dear
6 Intra mundi climata: [of all things] within the regions of the world
  Ma tresdouce et treschere,   My very sweet and very dear one
  Of youre estate I wold fayn here   *estate* circumstances; *fayne h.* gladly hear
9 Corde delectabilia.   All things delightful to the heart

  Et je s[u]i saine de corps et cu[er], And I am myself healthy in body and mind
  Yif it lyke yow therof to here,   If it pleases you to hear news of that
12 Sit deo laus altissimo.   Praise be to God most high
  A vous ay doné mon amour,   To you I have given my heart
  As your servant in l[e]all labour,   *leall* faithful
15 Hoc corde et animo.   In heart and soul
  Je s[u]y tout vostre, corps et bien,   I am yours, in body and goods
  Yow to serve over alle that bene   *bene* are, exist
18 Stringor amoris vinculo.   I am constrained by the chains of love

  Sovent en vous ay [sanz] pecché   Often have I, without guilt,
  Founde gret love that causyth me   *Founde* Experienced
21 Vos pre[e]minne amare.   To love you above all others
  Pour ce que vostre tresdouce chere Since your very sweet demeanour
  Hath causyd love betwene us clere,
24 Non permittatis sessare.   Do not allow it to come to an end
  Qar vostre amour me prent si dure For love of you takes hold of me so firmly
  That from min hert, I yow ensure,
27 Mors debet eradicare.   Death alone can eradicate it

  Plus a present ne say que dyre,   More for now I cannot say
  But salue yow wyth hert pure   *salue* greet
30 Ter vicibus quingentis,   A hundred and fifty times over
  Et mon kere en loial amour   And my heart in faithful love
  Yow sende, grace, joie and honour, *Yow sende* I send you, together with …
33 Virtuti[s]que incrementis,   And increase of virtue
  Sancté, lees, prosperité,   Health, joy and well-being
  Be to yow, wyth all felicité,   *Be to yow* Be yours
36 Cum plenitudine mentis.   With fullness of heart

Et Jhesu li tout pusaunt justice,	And Jesus the all-powerful judge
That all schal deme, wythout quest or sise,	*deme* judge; *quest or sise* inquest or assize
39 In maiest[at]is solio,	On the throne of His majesty
Hors de dette et male vous garde	Keep you out of debt and evil
And from all dedly synne yow warde	*warde* defend
42 De demonis imperio,	In the devil's power
Et e[n]sy vous doin[t] ly servere	And grant you so to serve Him
That ye mow come to Hys empere	That you may enter the kingdom of Him
45 Qui sedet in triclinio.	Who sits enthroned

NOTES TO POEM 5A

This accomplished poem is a macaronic that follows the same pattern as poem 1 and may be by the same poet (see pp. 287–9 above): alternating French, English and Latin lines, the French (long the traditional language for correspondence) initiating the epistolary topics, expanded in the English and rounded off by the Latin. The poem occurs only here, and so the errors caused by inattention and shaky command of French and Latin (on the part of the scribe and/or his exemplar) must be corrected by surmise, without the aid of the other witnesses that exist for poems 1 and 2. It is obviously not the work of the letter-writer himself, and (unlike poem 1) was not appropriated as it stood as a letter, but used as a model for the longer English letter (5B, revised in 5C and D), which he composed by following and expanding upon its topics. It thus stands to 5B much as 4A does to 4B: as a pre-existing poem that provides material and pattern for an independent and more personalized verse letter. The text has evidently suffered local corruption, but appears to have been written in eight-syllable lines, the French and English forming a rhyming couplet, and the Latin line changing its grammatical termination after every three triplets: *-a* for three triplets, masculine ablative *-o* for the next three, infinitive *-are* for the next three, *-entis* a further three times, and finally three neuter ablatives in *-io*. The poem thus falls into the nine-line stanzas we have indicated, though it is not divided into stanzas by Carpenter. It was obviously the epistolary form taken by the poem (as with poems 1 and 2) that caused our letter-writer to see it as pertinent to his purposes. The particular features of letter form imitated are the same as for poem 1 and are indicated in the notes below.

1 The opening *A* [To] ... follows epistolary convention (cf. 1.1). Elision would be normal in *que ayme* and yields a line of the eight syllables that seem originally to have been the regular length of all the lines.
2 *been*: 'beene' (Carpenter).
3 Carpenter (following the MS) prints *dure fixa* as one word.
4 *quer*: 'quere' (Carpenter).
5 Second-person forms in the polite *ye* are again used consistently in the English (as is *vous* in the French). In poems 1 and 2, this represented a deliberate change in the Armburgh version to the informal *thou* forms used in the original English lines. Since there are no other witnesses to this poem, it is difficult to know whether the *ye* forms here are (as is probable) likewise deliberate alterations, made because the writer (though he appears to have intended for his letter not this poem itself, but his own version of it in 5B) has in mind his own lady, whom he always addresses with the polite plural *ye* form.
7–12 The lines follow standard epistolary procedure, according to which the opening salutation is followed (immediately or at some later point) by a hope that the addressee enjoys good health and circumstances and a report on the writer's own state, the modest hypothetical clause ('Yif it

lyke yow therof to here') being standard (cf. *Troilus* V.1366–7, 'And if yow liketh knowen of the fare / Of me'; and *Paston Letters*, ed. Davis, vol. 1, p. 662, 'desiryng to here of yowr welefare ... And yf it please 30we to here of my welefare'), as also was the thanks to God offered (12) for the writer's good health (cf. 1.9). See also n. to 5D.12–20.

7 *et*: Carpenter again wrongly expands MS ampersand into English 'and', as also at 10 and 40; see n. to 2.21.

8 Cf. *Troilus* V.1356–8: 'desiryng evere moore / To knowen ... How ye han ferd and don'.

10 *Et je sui* (MS si) *saine de corps et cuer* (MS cure)': Carpenter reads 'and (see n. to line 7) ie fi fame de corps / and euere', which, apart from obvious lack of sense, provides no rhyme for line 10 and yields a hypermetric eleven-syllable line 11; the similariy of long /s/ and /f/ has played a part in her misreading. The collocation 'corps et cœur' was a standard one in French.

14 *leall*: the MS reads 'lall', though it is transcribed 'leall' by Carpenter.

15 *Hoc* gives weak sense and is somewhat suspect, as the line is a syllable short.

16 *suy*: the MS again has 'sy' (cf. 10), which Carpenter, again confusing long /s/ and /f/, again transcribes 'fy'.

19 *sanz*: 'faux' (MS and Carpenter).

21 *preeminne*: MS 'premenne(?)', Carpenter 'preminente'. The poet obviously understands whatever word the MS represents to mean 'pre-eminently' (see 5B.31).

25–7 Cf. Text 2, II.3/7–10.

25 *Qar*: 'Gare' (Carpenter).

26 *from*: Carpenter reads 'frein', confusing /o/ and /e/ and misinterpreting the next three minims.

28–41 See n. to 1.28.

28 *say*: Carpenter confuses /f/ and /s/ and reads 'fay'.

32–6 The listed blessings wished on the addressee are standard: cf. e.g. *Troilus* V.1359–61 ('The whos welfare and wele ek God encresse / In honour swich that upward in degree / It growe alwey').

33 *Virtutis*: MS 'virtututi' (Carpenter 'vurtututi') obviously requires emendation; the line is Englished as 'Encres of vertu' at 5B.74.

37–45 The supplementation of good wishes for temporal prosperity by prayers for eventual spiritual bliss is not uncommon, but the latter are here uttered with a fullness and emphasis that brings the letter to a solemn and resonant conclusion.

39 Metre and sense require the emendation of 'maiestis' (MS and Carpenter) to *maiestatis*.

40 *et*: and (Carpenter; see n. to line 7).

43–5 Cf. the letter-ending in *AP*, p. 100: 'And I pray God of hys infynit mercy he geue yow bothe mygth and grace to serue hym to hys plesaunce'.

43 *ensy:* 'emsy' (MS and Carpenter). *doint*: 'doine' (MS) read as 'dome' by Carpenter. *servere* as a form of *server* is not recorded in the *AND* s.v. *servir*, but does occur s.v. *abbés* and *Cordelier*.

44 *empere*: 'emprere' (MS and Carpenter).

5B

Goodliest of all creature
That beryth lyf in this world so brode,
Gentillest faucone that comyth to lure,   *Gentillest* Noblest; *lure* the 'lure' (see note)
4 Welle of vertu, spryng of womanhode,   *spryng* fount

[Rote] of refute to all manhode,   *Rote* Source; *refute* refuge; *manhode* mankind
Merure to wedowe, mayden and wyf,   *Merure* Mirror (= Model)
Flour of all that ever man bode,   *Flour* Flower; *bode* experienced, met with
8 Princesse of my deth and lyf:

To yow that be my soveraigne blis
And all my ful hertis plesaunce,
My caris leche, my soris lysse,   *caris l.* cares' physician; *soris l.* sorrow's assuagement
12 And my paynes alegeaunce,   *alegeaunce* alleviation

My rightwis joie and my worldly goodnesse,   *rightwis* veritable
Min hele and lyves sustinance,   *hele* health; *lyves* life's
With hert and all that in me is
16 I me comaunde with obeisaunce;   *me comaunde* commend myself; *obeisaunce* obedience

Desiryng with all godlyhede,   *godlyhede* right feeling
As your humill and trewe servant,
Wyth hert, wyth will, wyth thought and dede,   *dede* deed, action
20 All thyng that might be yow plesaunt,   *yow* to you

And pray to God that He yow graunt   *pray* i.e. I pray
Good hele, blisse and prosperitee,   *hele* health
And from the infernall tyraunt   *the infernall t.* i.e. the devil
24 Yow kepe, and all adversitee.   *kepe* keep safe; *and* and from

Sithe hope hath yove me hardynesse   *yove* given
For to discure myn hertis peyne   *discure* disclose
To yow, in triste of summe reles,   *triste* trust; *reles* relief
28 I wol it serche in every [v]eyne.   *serche in e. v.* seek with all my heart

Ye have causyd ryght strong cheyne
Surely fastnede to myn hert rote: *fastnede* to be fastened; *hert rote* heart's root
To love yow best it wol me streyne,   *streyne* constrain, force
32 Whether it so be my bale or bote.   *bale* bane; *bote* cure

In yow it lyth as in balaunce,   *lyth* lies; *in balaunce* in the scales
Whether yow list, my blisse or peyn;   *Whether y. l.* Whichever you please
Min hert is your without variaunce:
36 The cheyne is feste on every veyne.   *feste* tight

Yf [I] ne may your love atteygne,
I cast myself in peynes smert: *cast m. in* will consign myself to
To goddes of love I may complayne   *goddes* goddess; *complayne* make legal complaint
40 With spere of love ye perysshe myn hert.   *With sp.* How, with a spear; *perysshe* pierce

It mevyth me oft handys to wryng,
The godly loke of youre eyne tw[e]yne,   *eyne* eyes
And syk full sadde whan other syng: *syk* sigh; *other* others
44 My lyf may not endure this peyne.

For as a tassel ye me streyne,   *tassel* tercel (falcon); *streyne* grasp tight
Suyn[g] to the hert wyth love talon;   *Suyng to* Falling upon; *love t.* talons of love
In love presone I may not reigne: *love presone* love's prison; *reigne* carry on life
48 Deth wol smert will m[e] rawnsumme.   *wol smert* very painful; *rawnsumme* ransom, deliver

I wold thei were writen in youre syght,
The sorefull thoughtys of myn hert,
And suche pyté were in yow pyght   *pyght* fixed, set
52 That wold asuage my peynes smert.

For grevously into the hert
With love arwes ye thrylle my syde;   *arwes* arrows; *thrylle* pierce
Now ye that be in love expert
56 Takyth cure and hele my woundys wyde.   *Takyth cure* Take heed of me

I dar not come before your face
For to compleyne myn hertis grev[a]unce,
Til it lyke yow of special grace   *it lyke yow* it please you
60 To assigne me a tyme of youre plesaunce.   *plesaunce* convenience

Of my la[n]goure have remembraunce;
Syth ye me brought in maledie,   *Syth* Since
Beth my sorwys allegeaunce   *Beth* Be; *sorwys alleg.* alleviation of my sorrows
64 And graciously schape remedye.   *schape* devise, bring about

More of my peyne I wold discure,   *discure* disclose
But ye beth so empressyd in my mynde   *beth* are
That my five wyttes, I yow ensure,
68 Beth summewhat distract out of here kynde.   *dist.* distracted; *here k.* their nature (= normal operation)

	So that to yow, my lady [h]ende,	*hende* gracious
	I cannot half my sore expresse,	
	Til it like yow of grace me sende	*it like yow* it please you
72	Summe maner tokyn of gladnesse.	Some kind of happy sign

	I pray God that grace, helth and prudence,	
	Encres of vertu and dignité,	*dignité* status, standing
	Honour, joie and reverence,	
76	With all maner felicité,	

	Preysing, gladnesse, prosperité,	
	Encres of love, wysdome and rychesse,	
	Reste, quiete and equité,	*equité* temperance
80	... and all goodnesse,	

	He graunt yow, and so the [fend] venquisse	*so t. f. v.* to vanquish the devil to such a degree
	And his furiouce felonie,	*felonie* wickedness
	With hys malyce and his anguis,	
84	And all his tortuouse tyranny,	
	That it mow be to him annoye,	
	Honour to God, glorie and preysyng,	*mow* may; *annoye* distress
	And blysse to yow perpetually aftyr youre ...	

NOTES TO POEM 5B

The poem is a free variation, expansion and personalization of 5A, which it takes as its template. It follows a much more regular rhyme scheme (quatrains rhyming *abab*) and line length (a norm of eight syllables) than either of the previous poems composed by the letter-writer himself (3 and 4B).

1–16 These lines correspond to 5A.1–6.
1 *creature*, rather than 'creatures' (MS and Carpenter), is required for rhyme and is the form that occurs in the revised version (5C.1).
3 Hawking (a favourite pastime among the gentle-born) supplies figurative expansion of the French both here and at 45–6. The *lure* (a piece of food or feathers attached to a long string) was used to lure the falcon back to the fist. Hawks were considered the equivalent of *gentils* in the bird world: cf. Chaucer's *Parliament of Fowls*, where the falcon is treated as epitomizing the nobly born hawk-kind (323–4, 526–30, 596), and his Squire's Tale, where both the female falcon and her male lover are treated as typifying *gentillesse* of birth (*CT* V.426, 622).
4 For *welle of* and *spryng of* used as figures in eulogy, cf. 4.13. It is one of several phrases from the preceding English poems that here serve to expand upon the French poem (5A) whose outline is being followed.
5 *Rote* (Carpenter: 'B [*sic*]') is supplied from the poem in its first revision (5C.7). The MS, which reaches the end of a line at this point, has simply /b/, followed by 'of' at the start of the next line.
6 *Merure*: 'Mesure' (Carpenter).
8 The line reuses a phrase found at 3.45. See n. to that line.
10 *hertis*: here and at lines 26 and 58, Carpenter has 'hertes'; see n. to 3.51.
11 Carpenter (following the MS) has *care is* and *sore is*; but these are obvious errors for the genitives required by sense and confirmed in the revised versions (5C.15, 5D.3).
12 For *alegeaunce* (Carpenter: 'alegaunce') used in this application and in rhyme position, cf. 63, 3.20 and 5D.44.
13 *rightwis* appears as two words in Carpenter (who, as usual, reproduces the MS word division); for *worldly goodnesse*, cf. *yerthely goodnesse* at 3.11. After the word 'and', the scribe moves from the back of membrane 6 to the back of membrane 5 (see p. 294 above).
15–17 See n. to 5D.12–20.
17–20 These lines correspond to 5A.7–15 (though the correspondence is clearer in the revised versions: see 5C.25–8, 5D.13–16). *Desiryng* represents the epistolary use of present participles to connect separate parts of the discourse: cf. 3.10 and 25 and 4B.14.
19 A condensed version of the trope used at 3.41–3.
20 *All*: 'al' (Carpenter).

21–4 These lines anticipate the rendering of 5A.32–42 that occurs in the proper place, at the close of the letter, at 73 ff. It may have been prompted by the fact that a commendation to God and the prayer for His blessings, though characteristically part of the closing formulae in epistolary convention, could also often be found following the hope that the addressee is at present happy and healthy (cf. the valentine of Margery Brews, quoted at p. 47 above), but this anticipation of the later lines was removed in the final revision (see 5D.13–16).

23–4 These figure as a single line in Carpenter.

25–8 The quatrain is independent of the French and acts to personalize the poem, expressing a sensation the lover has referred to before – that of having committed to love, of having put his shoulder to the wheel: 25 is a line reused from 3.32.

26–48 *-eyn(e)* here provides one of the two rhyming sounds over five successive quatrains, and is a particularly marked example of the repetition of rhyme sounds over successive stanzas that the poet not uncommonly produces (cf. e.g. 58–63).

26 *discure*: the MS reads 'discuu*ere*', but the contracted form better fits the basically octosyllabic metre, and rhyme proves that MS 'discuvere' definitely represents 'discure' at 65.

28 *veyne*: 'peyne' (MS and Carpenter). Cf. the rhyme of *peyn* and *veyne* at 34/36 below, and at 4A.26/28, which probably suggested it to this apprentice poet.

29–48 These lines correspond to 5A.16–27 and expand upon the image of the chain of love and of being held fast in love's grip there found (18, 25–7).

29–31 *cheyne ... streyne*: prompted by 'Stringor amoris vinculo' (5A.18).

29 *Ye*: MS 'yene(?)' is read by Carpenter as *Youe* (which is ungrammatical: the subject form in Middle English was *Ye*, for which *youe* is not easily explicable as a scribal error). Though she otherwise provides hardly any punctuation for the poem, Carpenter also, oddly, has a quite ungrammatical comma after *causyd*.

31 *To love yow best* reflects 'Vos preeminne amare' at 5A.21.

35 *without variaunce*: 'without ony variaunce' (MS and Carpenter). 'ony' is extra-metrical and does not figure in the equivalent line (absent from 5C) in the revision of 5D.55; the phrase is likewise used to provide a rhyme at 3.22 and was probably imitated from 4A.8.

37 *Yf I ne*: 'Yf ne' (MS and Carpenter). For *atteygne* as a rhyme word, see n. to 3.7; *smert* and *hert* (38/40) is likewise a rhyme that the poet often uses (see n. to 3.1–4).

39 On *complayne*, see n. to 5D.60.

42 *tweyne*: 'twyne' (MS and Carpenter).

45–8 The expressive image of the falcon's talons (see n. to 3 above), like that of the 'prison', gives more concrete reinforcement to the metaphor of the 'chain' (29) than does the equivalent French line ('vostre amour me prent si dure': 5A.25).

46 *Suyng:* 'suyn' (MS and Carpenter).

48 *will me rawnsumme* ('wol me ransumme' in the revised version of the poem: 5D.71): 'will my rawnsumme' (MS and Carpenter). The line is the equivalent of 5A.27. See also n. to 5D.71.

49–64 These stanzas are independent additions to 5A, and contribute personalization and force to the verse letter, for the topics are those about which his other poems show him to have had particular anxiety (his inability to express himself and the uncertainty as to when he may see his lady).

49–50 The poet has before expressed his painful sense of being unable to articulate his feelings (see n. to 3.46), but the present lines, in their simplicity and naturalness, are paradoxically eloquent in conveying his frustration on that head. Both originality and what Samuel Johnson called 'nature' make this a memorable couplet.

50 *sorefull*: 'forefull' (Carpenter).

52 *asuage*: 'a suage' (MS and Carpenter).

55–6 *expert* here refers primarily to medical expertise, since the couplet is a variation on the familiar idea of the lady as the only physician or remedy available for the lover's sickness or wounds (see n. to 2.8); but in context it suggests also her skill in causing amorous distress (see 5D.80 and 83 in the revised version). In conceit, logic, rhetorical and syntactical structure, it is thus an independent variation on 62–4 below, whose pithiness it effectively imitates.

57–60 A plea repeated in similar words in all the poems composed by the letter-writer himself, but one which does not figure in the existing lyrics which he appropriated or used as models. See n. to 3.17–18.

57 *before*: 'be fore' (Carpenter, again following the erratic word division of this as of other medieval scripts: cf. n. to 52).

58 *grevaunce*: 'greuance' (Carpenter).

61 *langoure*: Carpenter has 'lagoure', reproducing the MS, in which the nasal abbreviation over /a/ has plainly been omitted.

62–4 See n. to 3.23–4, repeated here almost verbatim and expanded by a phrase in which *allegeaunce* is, as elsewhere, pressed into service as a rhyme word (see n. to 3.20).

62 *Syth*: MS *syȝth* ('Sygth': Carpenter). *maledie*: 'maladie' (Carpenter).

63–4 These lines appear as a single line in Carpenter.

65–72 5A.28 (cf. 65) is here expanded in the same way in which the epistolary closing formula ('no more at this time') is expanded in poem 3 (see n. to 3.46–52): to express inarticulacy and plead for some communication from the lady (concerns which have already been the subject of additions and which are characteristic of the letter-writer); the phrasing of 70–2 is essentially the same as at 3.48, 51–2. 65–8 may be compared with *Welles* 42.25–6 ('no more to yow I wryte for lacke of scyence / my mynde ys nott my owne So Sore I am destresyd').

65 *discure*: MS 'discuu*ere*' (see n. to line 26).

67–70 Cf. Troilus's pre-emptive apology for any clumsiness in his letter to Criseyde, which is to be attributed to 'my cares colde / That sleth my wit' (*Troilus* V.1342–3).

68 *distract*: 'distratt' (Carpenter).

69 *hende*: ende (MS and Carpenter).

72 *maner tokyn* (cf. 5D.108): 'mark tokyn' (Carpenter).

73–87 These lines correspond to 5A.29–45, expanded at 73–8 by material reused from the New Year good wishes of poem 4 (A.29–33, B.14–20), adapted to fit the shorter (octosyllabic) lines of the present poem. The expansion of the blessings and the rewording into a more specific prayer (81) are in accord with other instances of the good wishes common at the close of a letter or verse epistle or ballade address. Cf. lines 33–6 of the second ballade addressed to the king in Gower's *Cinkante Balades* <II>: 'Honour, valour, victoire et bon esploit, / Joie et saunté, puissance et seignurie ... [God] Doignt de sa grace ...'.
78 *and* is extra-metrical and should perhaps be regarded as scribal.
79 *Reste*: 'Rest' (Carpenter).
80 Some material has evidently dropped from the beginning of this line. What remains of it follows a gap or space left for the missing material in the MS.
81 *fend* does not figure in the MS (or in Carpenter); but sense and metre require a monosyllabic word for the devil referred to in the equivalent prayers in the source poem 5A.41–2, and at 23–4 above and 5C.31–2. *venquisse*: 'vengnisse' (Carpenter).
85 *annoye*: an noye (Carpenter, following the MS).
87 The last line (which does not rhyme and is too long) is not in verse form. This version of the poem was apparently aborted: *youre* stands at the start of an MS line, the rest of which is blank, 5C (beginning, as usual, with a capital letter) following in the next line.

5C

    Goodlyest of creatur,
    Fully replete with humilité,
    Gentel as faucon that comyth to lure,
4 Enncrounyd with benyngnité,

    O princesse of womanhode,
    Enlymnyd with all beuté,   *Enlymnyd* Illuminated
    Rote of refute to all manhode,
8 Enpressyd with perdurable pyté,   *Enpressyd* Imbued; *perdurable* inexhaustible

    Welle of vertu, spryng of goodnesse,
    Excellyng all other in bounté,   *bounté* goodness
    Flour and figure of stedfastnesse,   *Flour* Flower; *figure* model
12 Habundant in grace and equité:

    To yow that be my soveraigne blisse,
    Begynner and causer of my gladnesse,
    My cares leche, my sorwys lysse,
16 And cure, helere of my seknesse,

    My ryghtwos joie, myn hertis plesaunce,   *ryghtwos* true
    Reconnciler of all myn hevynesse,   *Reconnciler* Pacifier
    My goodly lyves sustinaunce,
20 Loser and lysser of [all] duresse,   *Loser and lysser* Loosener and soother

    Relever of all my peynes smert,   *smert* smarting
    And full [of] erthly goodnesse,
    Enteerly wyth all myn hole hert,
24 I comaunde in all maner humb[l]esse;   *comaunde* commend myself; *maner* manner of

    Desyryng, as youre humble servaunt,
    Effectualy with hert to here   In all sincerity to hear
    All thyng that myght be to yow plesaunt,
28 And comfort, solas, gladnesse or ch[e]re;

    Gode hele, blysse and prosperité,
    I pray God yow graunt of Hys empere,   *empere* imperial power
    And kepe yow from all adversité
32 And from tortuose serpentis power.   *tortuose* sinuous, twisted

Thankyng with humble hert
Of your graciouse and goodly answere,   *answere* answering letter
Notwithstondyng that wounder smert   *wounder smert* very keenly
36 It perysshyth myn [hert] thorwe as a spere.   *perysshyth* pierces

With syghyng sad and mornyng stille,   *mornyng stille* continuous lament
With hevy chere, withoutyn reste,   *chere* demeanour
For love in poynt myself to spill,   *in poynt* ready; *spill* destroy
40 As man that knowyth not what hym is best,   *what hym is b.* what is his best course

For love I dye – but ye take cure –   *but ye t. c.* unless you take heed of me
Withoutyn juge, dome or queste,   *dome* judgement; *queste* legal process
Of feith and trought I yow ensure;   *Of* In
44 Were never hope, my hert wold breste.   *Were never* If it were not for; *breste* break

Now, princesse gracious of womanh[e]de,
As ye that of pyté ben rote and rynde,   *ben* are; *rote and r.* root and bark, the totality
Let on me your mercy spryng and sprede,
48 And out of all bytter bales me unbynde.   *bales* miseries

This is the entent of my request finall,   *entent* purport
That of grace suche gladnesse ye wold me sende
That I myght onys yow see and speke wythal   *onys* once; *speke wythal* speak with
52 Or love me bryng to sorwfull ende.   *Or* Before

For God knowyth al myn entent
How I have fully vowyd in my mynde
To love yow best and never to repente,
56 Thowe I nevere grace ne mercy fynde.

I pray God that grace, helthe and prudence, etc   *[see 5B.73–87]*
As for an answere whan I had notyse,
Althowgh it were womanly and onest,   *notyse* notification
Downe to my hert as cold as yse   *onest* honourable
61 It thyrlyd even thorwghout my brest.   *yse* ice
    thyrlyd pierced

NOTES TO POEM 5C

This poem is a revised version of 5B, of which the first six quatrains are here reworked in the first eight quatrains (1–32), mainly through the insertion of further material from the New Year poem (4A) which the letter-writer had not used in his own version (4B). But the rest of the poem diverges from 5B, plainly in response to some answer received from the lady (see lines 34 and 58) which has distressed the lover and which may have been received while he was revising 5B, since the alterations in 1–32 are stylistic, whereas they are substantive at 33ff. The notes deal only with the alterations and divergences from 5B; on material shared with 5B, see notes to that poem.

1–12 These lines expand the first two quatrains of 5B into three, the expansion being mainly due to the insertion of phrases borrowed from 4A: lines 2, 4, 5–6, 11 and 12 are from 4A.2, 4, 1, 18 and 19, respectively.
1 *creatur*: 'creatures' (Carpenter). See n. to 5B.1.
5–6 These lines appear as a single line in Carpenter.
13–24 These lines expand into three quatrains the corresponding two quatrains in 5B (7–12), most of the new material again coming from 4A: with lines 14, 16, 18 and 20, cf. 4A.16, 14, 23 and 22, respectively.
15–17 Carpenter mis-indicates line-endings, which she places after *leche, cure, seknesse, joie* and *plesaunce*, producing five lines out of the three indicated by the rhyme of the quatrain stanza form (not observed in her text).
17 The material is in 5B, but combines half-lines from different quatrains (5B.13a with 5B.10b).
22 *of* does not figure in MS (or Carpenter).
23 *Enteerly wyth all myn hole hert*: cf. 'De tout mon coer entier' (*Cinkante Balades* 26.6) and 'I pray you entierly' in a letter from Robert Armburgh (*AP*, p. 103).
24–33 See n. to 5D.12–20.
24 *humblesse*: 'humbesse' (MS and Carpenter).
25–32 These lines correspond to 5B.17–24.
25 *servaunt*: 'servant' (Carpenter); cf. 5B.18.
26 *here* makes the quatrain more consistent with 5A.8–9 and therefore more logical than was the previous rendering in 5B.17–20.
28 *chere* (cf. 5D.16): 'chire' (MS and Carpenter); see n. to 3.27.
30 *I*: omitted in Carpenter. 'emprere' (MS and Carpenter) we have assumed to be an error for *empere*.
32 *tortuose serpentis power* rephrases 'the infernall tyraunt' (5B.23); 'tortuous serpent' was a standard epithet for the devil (see *MED tortuous* (b)) in which the adjective seems to be used in the sense it normally had in Middle English ('coiled, twisted'), but may be starting to acquire also its post-medieval sense of 'malign'.
33–4 These lines appear as one line in Carpenter. The present participle *Thankyng* reflects epistolary syntax: see n. to 3.10. The *answere* referred to is plainly one that distresses its recipient and causes the poem from here on to abandon 5B.

The Armburgh Love Letters 331

35 *Notwithstondyng* appears as two words in Carpenter (who follows MS word division).
36 Reused for the new emergency from 5B.40. *hert* has been erroneously omitted in the MS (and Carpenter).
38 *withoutyn* appears as two words in Carpenter (who follows the MS).
39 *spill*: 'spille' (Carpenter).
40 The words occur at the beginning of an MS line in a smaller script (and perhaps different pen) and may have been inserted later into a gap left for what was missing or undeciphered; cf. n. to 5B.80.
42 The line is borrowed from the macaronic poem, but is reused in a very different application. Christ is a judge above formal earthly courts (5A.38), whereas the point here is that the lover is condemned to death unjustly, without 'due process'.
44 The reference to *hope* now comes in to very different effect from that which it had in the line repeated from 3.32 at 5B.25.
45 Cf. 4A.1 (also used at 5C.5) and 12. *womanhede* (the form required for rhyme) appears as 'womanhode' in the MS and Carpenter.
46 *rote and rynde* is an expression that occurs elsewhere in the sense of 'completely' or 'sum total': cf. 'Envye, thou arte rote and rynde ... of mykyl myschefe' (*Castle of Perseverance* 1135).
48 *all* is redundant to sense and metre and should perhaps be deleted. (Line length varies from eight to ten syllables in 5C, but seldom exceeds that.)
49 *finall*: cf. 3.39. Carpenter reads 'small'.
50–1 This is a version of the pleas the writer makes in all the verse letters he composes for himself: see n. to 3.17–18. Carpenter prints *wythal* as two words.
53–6 A reorganization of lines used at 3.36–7, 33, 38.
53–4 Carpenter treats these lines as one line, despite the MS slash (indicating a verse line-end) after *entent*.
57 MS *etc* indicates that the verse letter is to end as at 5B.73ff.
58–61 On this quatrain and its account of the effect on the letter-writer of the *answere* received from the lady, see p. 292 above. Though he had not reached the edge of the page, the scribe starts a new line for this stanza, indicating that it does not form part of the letter proper.

5D

    To yow that be my soverain blisse,
    Bygynner and causer of my gladnesse,
    My cares leche, my sores l[i]sse,   *leche* physician; *lisse* alleviation
4 And cure, heler of my seknesse,
    My rigthwos joie, myn hertys plesaunce,
    Recounceler of all myn hevynesse,   *Recounceler* Reconciler, Pacifier
    My goodly lyves sustenaunce,
8 Loser and lysser of my duresse,   *Loser and lysser* Loosener and assuager
    Releser of all my peynes smerte,
    And my full erthly goddesse,
    Enterly with all myn hole hert   *Enterly* Entirely, Wholly
12 I comaunde me with all maner humblesse: *comaunde me* commend myself

    Desiryng with all the besynesse   *besynesse* anxious solicitude
    Of hert effectuely to here   *effectuely* sincerely; *here* hear
    All thyng that myght do yow gladnesse,
16 Comfort, solas, plesaunce or chere.
    Thankyng yow wyth all lowlynesse,
    Myn owne soverain lady dere,
    Of youre bountuouse goodnesse
20 And wele noble undeserved chere.   *chere* treatment, behaviour
    I bynde me holly to your service,
    Hert, body, strength, wyth will and lust in fere; *lust* pleasure; *in fere* together
    I may me in no maner wyse refreyne:
24 I am your man with all my full power.

    For I know [none] myght be your pere   *myght be* who could be; *your pere* your equal
    Of whomanhode semyng to me: *semyng* shown
    Ye ben so gentill, so goodly of chere,   *gentill* gracious; *chere* manner
28 Ye be replet with humilité;
    Ye be wele womanly of countenau[n]ce,   *wele* most; *countenaunce* manner
    Ye be soverain of all beauté,
    Ye be the rote of all plesaunce,   *rote* root, source
32 Ye be full [of] benyngnité;
    Ye be welle of vertu, spryng of goodnesse,
    Ye excellyn all other in bounté,
    Ye be flour of stedfestnesse,   *flour* flower
36 Ye habounden in grace and equité.   *habounden* abound, possess in plenty

    Now glad myght hc and lusty be   *lusty* joyful
    That of youre love myght have plesaunce;
    None erthly good, I say for me,   *for me* for my part

40 Myght in this world me so avaunce.	
For thowgh I were wounded to the hert,	
Yt wold relese all my grevaunce,	
And of all my peynes smert	
44 It were soverain allegeaunce.	*were* would be (subjunctive); *allegeaunce* allayment
Myn owen lady, of gentilnesse	*of gentilnesse* out of graciousness
Lat me not lyve in disperaunce,	*disperaunce* despair
But lat peté youre hert inpresse,	But allow pity to make an impression on your heart
48 And beth my lyves sustinaunce.	*beth* be (imperative)
For in yow lyth as in balaunce,	
Whether yow lyst, my blisse or peyne;	*Whether yow lyst* Whichever you please
I put me holly in your governaunce:	
52 Ye be my lady and my soverain.	
Whether it me ese or do grevaunce,	*me ese or do g.* gives me ease or causes me pain
Love hath me bounde fast in his cheyne;	
My hert is your wythout variaunce:	
56 I may yt in no wyse refreyne.	
In byttyr balys I am ybounde,	
Yf I ne may your [love] atteyne.	
With swerde of love sore ye me wounde:	*sore* sorely, grievously
60 To the goddesse of love I may complayne.	
Oft myn hert enduryth peyne	
Whan I thenke on your fresly face;	*fresly* fresh, radiant
For as a tarsell ye me strayne:	*tarsell* tercel, falcon; *strayne* grip tight
64 With love talon myn hert ye race.	*love talon* love's talons; *race* lacerate, tear
Whan all other ben mery and glade,	*ben* are
Harpyn, daunce and make solace,	*Harpyn* Play the harp
For yow I morne and syghe wel sadde;	
68 Whan other syng, I say 'Alas!'	
Thus love me bynt in hys presone:	*bynt* binds; *presone* prison
Fro thens to scape ther is no place,	
Til deth wele smert wol me ransumme.	
72 Myn owen lady, where is your grace?	
I wold thei were wryten byfore your face,	
The noyous thoughtes of myn hert,	*noyous* painful
And in yow were roted such grace	*roted* rooted
76 That wold asuage my peynes smert.	
For grevously ye makyn englyde	*makyn* cause to; *englyde* pass
The dartes of love thorwghout myn hert.	
Wyth pyté hele my woundys wide,	
80 Now ye that be in love expert.	
So faste love bynt, I most abyde,	*bynt* binds; *most* must

Thowe I were wyld as is an herte;   *herte* hart
Love hath yow made so syker a gyde   *syker a gyde* sure a 'guider [of arrows]'
84 That from the deth I may not stert.   *stert* jump away

Now wold God that of your hert
Peté had the governaunce,
And of all my paynes smert
88 Ye had a special remembraunce,
Or ellys ye of your special grace   *ellys* else
Had syned me a tyme of youre plesaunce   *syned* assigned; *of y. pl.* at your convenience
That I mygth come before your face
92 For to complayne my hertis grevaunce.
Now ye that ben cause of my maladie,   *ben* are
Puttyth me in summe maner wey of esperaunce,   *Puttyth* Put (imperative); *esperaunce* hope
And graciously schapyth remedy,   *schapyth* devise, ordain
96 Of my sorwys allegeauns.   *Of* And of; *allegeauns* alleviation

More I wold of my grevaunce
And of my sore to yow expresse,
But I have yt not in remembraunce
100 Half, for all my besynesse: By the half, despite all my efforts
So fast ye have myn hert in hold
And surly ye yt possesse,   *surly* (so) surely, firmly
That ye me bynde in carys cold
104 And my five wyttys sore ye oppresse,   *sore* sorely
So that I may never have full m[e]nde   *full mende* all my faculties
To complayne half myn hevynesse,
Til it like yow of grace me sende   it like yow it may please you
108 Summe maner token of gladnesse.   Some kind of sign that you are not displeased

I pray God yow graunt, of Hys goodnesse,
Good lyf, blysse and prosperité,
Encres of love, wysdome and rychesse,
112 With reste, quiete and equité,   *equité* temperance
Preysyng, gladnesse, grace, hele and prudence,   *hele and prudence* health and foresight
Encres of vertu and dignité,
Onure, estat, joye, reverence,   *estat* status
116 With all maner of felycité;
And so yow governe He graunt yow grace   And grant you the grace to conduct yourself in such a way
Amonges thys wordly adversyté   *wordly* earthly
In heven that ye mow se Hys face,   That you may see His face in heaven
120 There He sitt in Hys magesté.   *There He sitt* Where He sits

NOTES TO POEM 5D

The poem is a further revision of 5B/5C, the quatrains now organized (by the regular repetition of the rhyme sound of the second line) into twelve-line stanzas, rhyming *ababcbcbdbdb*: a single slash marking line-ending is now supplemented by a double slash after every twelfth line. Though there is some rewriting and some additional material, the poem basically follows 5C as far as the reference to the distressing *answere* from the lady, of which no mention at all occurs in this revision (see pp. 292–3 above), though it starts with the fourth quatrain of 5C, which it follows for seven quatrains, and then returns to the material from the first three quatrains of 5C. Most of the revisions of 5C occasioned by the *answere* are then omitted, and the poem then returns to the material from 5B that had been displaced by those revisions, with some admixture from 5C and with some reordering and additions. The notes below deal only with alterations, additions and reordering of the material shared with the previous versions, on which see notes to 5B and 5C.

1–20 These five quatrains correspond to the fourth, fifth, sixth, seventh and ninth quatrains of 5C. They represent a rationalization of the verse letter, so that it begins in the standard manner with *To* ... (cf. 1.1, 4B.1, and the first line of 5A, which provided the model for the successive rewrites in 5B, C and D), the quatrains of praise that had opened the letter (in 5B and C) being shifted to a later point (29ff.). The eighth quatrain of 5C (the sixth in 5B), since it is an anticipation of the closing blessings that is both redundant and out of place (see n. to 5B.21–4), is now removed.

3–4 Carpenter (diverging from the line-divisions marked in the MS: see pp. 297–8 above) places a line-end after *cure* and retains MS *lesse*; *lisse* is required by rhyme and confirmed by the reading in the previous versions (5B.11, 5C.15).

5 *rigthwos*: 'rightwus' (Carpenter).

9–10 *Releser* (cf. 42) replaces *Relever* at 5C.21, and *my full erthly goddesse* replaces *And full [of] erthly goodnesse*, possibly correcting and/or improving or perhaps misreading the previous lines.

11–12 *hert*: MS 'hert hert' (followed by the slash that marks the end of all verse lines). Carpenter reads 'hert / Here', again ignoring the MS indications of where line-ends fall (cf. n. to 3–4 above). The poet's insertion in line 12 of *me* (which did not figure in the previous version) improves both rhythm (obscured by Carpenter's addition of an extra syllable to the line) and sense.

12–20 See n. to 5A.7–12 on this formulaic sequence of commendation followed by hope of hearing good news of the addressee's health and welfare. The present participles that characterize the English version (*Desiryng*, 13; *Thankyng*, 17) regularly occur in the prose letters of several different senders in the Armburgh Roll: cf. 'I commaunde me (un)to you desiryng to here of your prosperite and welfar(e)' (*AP*, pp. 184, 187 and the almost identical wording at p. 181 and in the valentine of Margery Brews); 'I comaunde me to you, desyryng to here of your welfare and prosperite, thankyng you of the greet chere that ye made me ...' (*AP*, p. 186).

13–16 The lines introduce slight improvements to the wording of 5C.25–8; the changes include the introduction of the word *besynesse*, a word that in Middle English characterizes a mental state of anxious diligence or agitation and one which the writer has used before in his own verse (3.34, 4B.3).

17–20 The removal of reference to an upsetting *answere* has occasioned rewording of the corresponding quatrain in 5C (33–6), where that *answere* was first referred to. The changes include *soverain lady*, an expression often used by this as by other lovers of the period (cf. e.g. 4B.25, 4C.1), and *bountuouse* (used at 3.12). Except for the odd line or phrase, 5C.34ff. (recording the answer and its effects) is not used in this revision, the remainder of 5C being replaced by 5B or by new material.

21–8 This is new material, 21–3 consisting of lines and phrases recycled and rearranged from poem 3 (cf. 1.31, 41–4).

24 *I am your* [Carpenter: 'youre'] *man* was the characteristic claim of the courtly lover, whose posture to his 'lady' [mistress] was that of the feudal vassal who owed her allegiance, her liegeman: cf. 21, 4A.5, and *Cinkante Balades* VIII.17–18 ('Qu'a vous servir j'ai fait ma retenue / Come vostre amant et vostre Chivaler' [for I have bound myself to your service as your retainer, as your lover and your knight]), XXIII.5–7 ('jeo l'ai ma foi plevi, / Sur quoie ma dame ad rescue moun hommage, / Com son servant' [I have pledged my faith, upon which my mistress has received my feudal homage, as her subordinate servant]).

25–7 These three lines are transcribed as only two lines by Carpenter (the first ending at her *whomanhode*), who ignores the slashes that in the MS mark line-endings.

25 *none* has been supplied. The line as it stands in the MS (and in Carpenter) does not make sense. Carpenter's reads *pere* as 'pore'; /e/ and /o/ look very alike in this script, but *pere* is indicated by both rhyme and sense.

28 This line (from the first quatrain of 5C) introduces the commendations this revision had omitted from the beginning of 5C and which are now instead introduced here.

29–36 These eight lines are a rewritten version of the opening quatrains of 5C, from whose first quatrain is preserved only its second line (5D.28) and the word *benyngnité*, and whose second survives only in the words *woman-, beauté* and *rote* in the quatrain beginning at 5D.29–32, but whose third quatrain is reused with only minor changes in 5D.33–6.

29 *countenaunce*: the word in the MS (read by Carpenter as 'countenance'), with only two minims between /a/ and /c/, is probably 'countenauce' with omission of the contraction over /u/.

32 *of*: omitted in the MS (and in Carpenter).

33 The occasional ten-syllable line (cf. 12, 29, 36) does intrude into what is by now a more regularly octosyllabic metre than were the poet's earlier efforts.

35 *stedfestnesse*: 'stedfastnesse' (Carpenter).

The Armburgh Love Letters

37–44 This has been expanded from the reference to *hertis plesaunce* and *paynes alegaunce* in the third quatrain of 5B (in a passage equivalent to the one just revised from 5C). The sense (cf. 1.13–18) and emphasis are, however, different, and the quatrains show the writer now able to write fluent, metrically regular and not unforceful verse of his own composition. On the rhyme words *smert*, *hert* and *allegeaunce*, see notes to 3.1–4 and 3.20. Carpenter's text arranges the lines in twelve-line stanzas only from this stanza on, although stanza-ends at 12 and 24 are marked in the MS by the same double slashes as occur to signal stanza-ends at the subsequent twelve-line intervals.

40 *me*: entered over a caret mark in the MS.

42 *grevaunce*: 'grevance' (Carpenter).

44 *allegeaunce*: 'allegaunce' (Carpenter).

45–8 The quatrain is a free re-rendering of the appeal for pity found at 5C.45–8.

45 *gentilnesse*: 'gentilesse' (Carpenter).

46 *disperaunce*: 'desperaunce' (Carpenter).

47 *inpresse* is written as one word in the MS, but represented as 'in presse' in Carpenter. See *MED impressen* 4(b), especially, *Troilus*, II.1371: 'For in good herte it mot som routhe impresse ...'.

48 *sustinaunce*: 'sustenaunce' (Carpenter).

49ff. The revision now essentially follows 5B.29ff.

49–56 These two quatrains rewrite the two quatrains of 5B.29–36, from which come the image of the *cheyne*, and the wording of 49–50 (cf. 5B.33–4) and 55 (cf. 5B.35). Line 56 is one which is often recycled in the verse of the letter-writer's own composition (cf. 23 and 3.31, 4B.13).

51 *your*: 'youre' (Carpenter).

57–60 A slight rewrite of 5B.37–40, with 57 being an adaptation of a line used at 5C.48.

57 Carpenter prints *ybounde* (past participle) as 'y bounde'.

58 Carpenter follows the MS, in which 'love' (cf. 5B.37) has been omitted.

59 *sore*: 'for' (Carpenter).

60 *complayne* reflects a conceit popular in the verse of courtly love; the word had legal connotations, and the lover's 'complaint' was essentially an accusation of injuries unjustly inflicted (cf. 59); cf. *Confessio Amantis* VIII.2217ff., where the lover 'complains' in a 'supplication' or 'bill' (2324–6) presented to 'Venus, the goddesse' (2274) of what he represents as suffering undeservedly endured against the laws of nature.

61–72 These three quatrains are a fairly free revision of two in 5B (41–8), 65–8 representing an expansion of a single line in 5B (43) and the next quatrain (69–72) a development of two lines at 5B.47–8.

61–2 This is the same sentiment as at 5B.41–2, but reworded. For *fresly face* (62), cf. 'her fresshly face' (Lydgate, *Siege of Thebes* 3956) and 'ȝoure freschly face' ('Bi a forest' (Add 31042) 111: cited in *MED freshli* adj.).

64 *race*: 'trice' (Carpenter).

65 *mery*: 'mary' (Carpenter).

71 *ransumme*, like 'rawnsumme' at 5B.48, requires emendation to the well-attested form in *-on(e* for rhyme.
72 A nice forceful rhetorical question that illustrates the writer's improving technique.
73–80 These quatrains are a slightly reworded version of the two at 5B.49–56.
73 *byfore*: 'by fore' (MS and Carpenter).
81–4 This is added material. For the verb *abyde* and the contrast with the *wyld* deer whose instincts are quite the reverse (81–2), cf. *Pearl*, 'For thogh thou daunce as any do [doe], / Braundysch and bray thy brathes breme [fierce impetuosity], / When thou no ferre [further] may, to ne fro, / Thou most abide that [what] He schal deme' (345–8).
85–96 These three quatrains revise, reorder and expand the material of the two quatrains at 5B.57–64.
85 'I' has been deleted between *that* and *of*.
86 *the*: 'ye' (Carpenter). The line preserves in a minor and passing fashion the personification typical of the rhetoric of courtly love lyric, personification which, in the hands of more practised and sophisticated poets, could be highly elaborate and studied, and in which an especially key role was given amongst the *dramatis personae* to Pity; for a particularly marked and extended allegory, see Chaucer's 'Complaint unto Pity'.
89 *your*: 'youre' (Carpenter). Carpenter often reads the upward curl of a final /r/ in 'your' as a final /e/, but final /e/ is not written in that way in these poems.
90 *syned*: 'fyned' (Carpenter). The verb is plainly the aphetic form of 'assign', which is used at the equivalent point at 5B.60 (as also at 3.18). For *plesaunce*, Carpenter has 'pleasuance'.
92 *hertis*: 'hertes' (Carpenter; see n. to 3.51).
94 This plea (to be given some 'hope') inserted into the revised version recalls 5C.44, where the writer's distress at the *answere* had caused him to realize its importance in preventing him from not falling to pieces entirely. It is one of the few features of the C revision after C.34 to be detectable in any form in D.
97–108 These three quatrains again correspond to two in 5B (65–72), the extra quatrain being occasioned by expansion of the writer's sense of love robbing him of the power to express the feeling it occasions (cf. n. to 3.46–52, 5B.49–64, 5B.65–72).
98 *expresse*: 'expressen' (MS and Carpenter). Before *sore*, 'fo' (read as 'so' by Carpenter) has been deleted.
100 *besynesse*: the sense in Middle English is 'anxious solicitude', here with regard to what words to use.
103–4 Carpenter places a line-ending after *bynde* and represents 103b–104 as one line. She also reads 'cavys' for *carys* in 103 and 'fore' for *sore* in 104. Before *That ye me bynde* the words 'and that ye myght' have been deleted, and were perhaps accidentally written because of eye-skip to 91 when reading the exemplar.
107 *it*: 'ye' (Carpenter).

109–16 The first two quatrains of the three-quatrain closing prayer-blessing reverse the order of the equivalent quatrains in 5B.73–80, but otherwise, apart from some minor rewording and reordering, follow 5B fairly closely.

116 *maner*: 'manere' (Carpenter, who, however, always otherwise expands the abbreviated form of the word in the MS as 'maner').

117–20. Since the last quatrain in 5B had broken off, and the close of the poem in 5C had been indicated simply by an 'etc' (indicating it was to be as in 5B), this is the first time the close of the macaronic poem 5A (which formed the groundplan for 5B) has appeared in the successive versions of the English poem it prompted. The reference to triumphing over the devil (5B.81–5, corresponding to 5A.41–2) has disappeared and been replaced by what was missing from the truncated end of 5B: an equivalent to the last triplet of 5A (43–5), praying that the addressee might come to heaven where God sits enthroned. Those lines are here rather well rendered in terms that recall the sixth beatitude ('Blessed are the pure in heart: for they shall see God': Matthew 5:8; cf. 'se Hys face' at 119) and so imbue with extra resonance and solemnity the final prayer of 5A, here transformed into a prayer that the addressee may enjoy the beatific vision of God seated *in Hys magesté*, a scene of peace and grandeur further enhanced by the contrast with *thys wordly adversyté* at 118.

TEXT 7

Pierre de Hagenbach and the Canoness at Remiremont

Amongst the papers of Pierre de Hagenbach, a general in the service of Charles the Bold, duke of Burgundy from 1467 to 1477, were found a series of eleven letters, eight of them from a canoness at Remiremont Abbey (in southern Lorraine), five of those eight being evidently and confessedly love letters to Pierre (I, II, VI, VII, IX), the other three (VIII, X, XI), from 'nous' [we], not evidently so. Two of the remaining letters (III and IV) are addressed to her as bursaress at Remiremont and are from the clerk attached to that office (Nicolas de Bruyères); and the remaining one (V) is to Pierre from a fellow commander in the Burgundian army (Jean de Vaudrey) and concerns military matters underway in the area of Remiremont and incidentally answers a query the writer had received from Pierre about 'dames' [ladies] at Remiremont.[1] The letters were edited in 2006 by Werner Paravicini,[2] who provides comprehensively informative annotation and contextualization, and whose introduction – though it comments on how few actual (as opposed to literary) love letters have survived from the Middle Ages – includes a useful summary and survey of the relevant scholarship with regard to the surviving private letters in French and German and the emergent interest in those countries, as in England, in the letters of women in particular (pp. 138–9).

The letters from the clerk (III, IV) and from Jean de Vaudrey (V) give the day of the month, and belong to the winter of 1470–1. And of the three letters (from 'nous') which do not present themselves as love letters, VIII gives the precise date of 17 August, the year (owing to internal references to, especially, the recent battle of Buxy in 1471) being assumed; no time at all is, unusually, included in the closing formulae of X, but XI again gives a precise date (1 September 1472). The love letters proper avoid, evidently on principle, such potentially tell-tale specificity and substitute time of day and/or day of week (I, late Sunday evening; II, early on Tuesday; VI, early Sunday morning; VII, Sunday morning), only the last (IX) giving the day

---

[1] The letters are conserved in the Tiroler Landesarchiv at Innsbruck as Acta Sigmundiana I.80.
[2] Werner Paravicini, ed., 'Un amour malheureux au XVe siècle: Pierre de Hagenbach et la dame de Remiremont', *Journal des savants* 1 (2006) 105–81.

of the month (19 August), and none of them giving the year; but their close connections with dated ones (especially I and II with III and IV and IX with VIII) show they cannot be far separate in time from the latter, and the whole sequence can be confidently assigned to the years 1470–2, despite the temporal reticence of the five love letters contained in it.

Nor, of course, does the canoness subscribe herself by any name that would serve to identify her, for that was almost always avoided in the love letters both of art and of actuality (see p. 48 above). But in two of the letters (I and VI) she refers to herself in the sign-off as '[voustre] leale Gayrrie'. 'Gayrrie' may well be a pet name whose logic is unrecoverable. Paravicini thinks it is quite possibly an abbreviation of 'Marguerite' (p. 113), though it is unrecorded as such elsewhere. 'Margaret' was especially common as a Christian name in the Middle Ages and was the name of the nun to whom the Norfolk abbot addressed his love letters (Text 4, I.11, 25, II.39).

However, these present letters *from* a female religious who perhaps had the same name *to* her lover do not provide the mirror image of that affair they may at first seem to do. This is not an affair between two clerics who are both breaking their religious vows. Pierre was only too squarely secular in status and career (see below) – and a canoness differed importantly from a nun. At Remiremont, only the abbess took the full monastic vows that bound a professed religious to permanent observance of poverty, chastity and obedience. For the others, the prebend (the lodging and entitlements attached to a canonry) served simply to provide these well-born women with genteel and secure accommodation. Originally part of a double monastery (a female community paired with a male one), the sisterhood had, over the eleventh to the fourteenth centuries, gradually transformed themselves from nuns following the Benedictine Rule into canonesses, and as such claimed and enjoyed the right, not only to exit the convent in order to marry, but also to live in their own private dwellings with their own servants, and to retain their own private wealth.[3] The Second Lateran Council had attempted to curb these latter liberties, so plainly at variance with the whole spirit of the communal life nominally espoused by canonesses (and with the monastic rule officially observed by what came to be termed 'regular' canonesses, as opposed to 'secular' ones, not bound by any such rule).[4] But at Remiremont (a famously grand and prosperous establishment), the canonesses, mostly from well-to-do Burgundian families, continued to

---

[3] On the early history and subsequent secularization of Remiremont, see Françoise Boquillon, *Les chanoinesses de Remiremont* (Remiremont, 2000), esp. pp. 11 and 51. On the privileges enjoyed by canonesses, see J.K. McNamara, *Sisters in Arms: Catholic Nuns through Two Millennia* (Cambridge, MA, 1996), p. 179.
[4] See Carolyn Muessig, 'Learning and Mentoring in the Twelfth Century', in *Medieval Monastic Education*, ed. George Ferzoco and Carolyn Muessig (Leicester, 2000), pp. 87–104, p. 94.

assume their right to live in their own individual houses (see Letter IV.10), retain personal possessions and wealth, and (as Letter III demonstrates) leave the cloister for long or short periods whenever they wished, as well as to marry if they chose.[5] A canoness was thus more secular in status, life-style and social perception than was a nun, and her commitment to chastity and celibacy did not have the same permanently binding force; and so, though G's affair with Pierre was extra-marital and could not therefore be openly conducted, it was not obnoxious to the special scandal that attended relations with a professed religious.

G exists as a historical entity only in these letters of hers, but the same is not true of her lover, Pierre de Hagenbach, who gained some notoriety before and after his death for the harshness with which he was perceived as acting when *bailli* of Upper Alsace and Ferrette, an office to which he was appointed by Charles the Bold in 1469.[6] Pierre in fact played a not insignificant part in Burgundian history in this period, and some account of that history will therefore here be necessary – especially for English readers, most of whom will be unfamiliar with the status and extent formerly enjoyed by a territory known today merely as a region of 'France'. Indeed, at the time of the letters at issue, Louis XI of France would give no official recognition to the ruler by whose extensive territories he found himself encircled, but who consistently refused to acknowledge French suzerainty, and whom Louis therefore referred to pointedly as 'Charles, soi-disant duke of Burgundy'.[7] For the dukedom had in 1363 been conferred by Jean II of France on a younger son, Philip, the brother of Charles V of France, the great-grandfathers of Charles the Bold and Louis XI, respectively. In 1369 Philip married Margaret of Flanders, who brought with her a huge territorial dower, and Burgundian domains had been further added to since then.

The French-speaking areas of Lorraine and Brittany, likewise today forming part of France (which was then a smaller entity than it now is), were then similarly virtually independent duchies. But of these bordering duchies Burgundy had become much the most significant: for its territories now ringed France to the north and east, comprising as they did large parts of the Low Countries as well as the modern districts of Burgundy and Franche-Comté that constituted the duchy and county of Burgundy ('the two Burgundies'). The seats of government for these two swathes of territory were, respectively, Bruges and Dijon (see Map 2). Charles the Bold, the last of the great Valois dukes of Burgundy, nicknamed in his own time

---

[5] Cf. Michel Parisse, 'Les chanoinesses de Remiremont: des religieuses singulières', in *Christliches und jüdisches Europa im Mittelalter*, ed. Lukas Clemens and Sigrid Hirbodian (Trier, 2011), pp. 153–66.
[6] The most recent biography is by Gabrielle Claerr-Stamm: *Pierre de Hagenbach: le destin tragique d'un chevalier sundgauvien au service de Charles le Téméraire* (Altkirch, 2004).
[7] See Richard Vaughan, *Charles the Bold* (Woodbridge, 2002), pp. 67, 73.

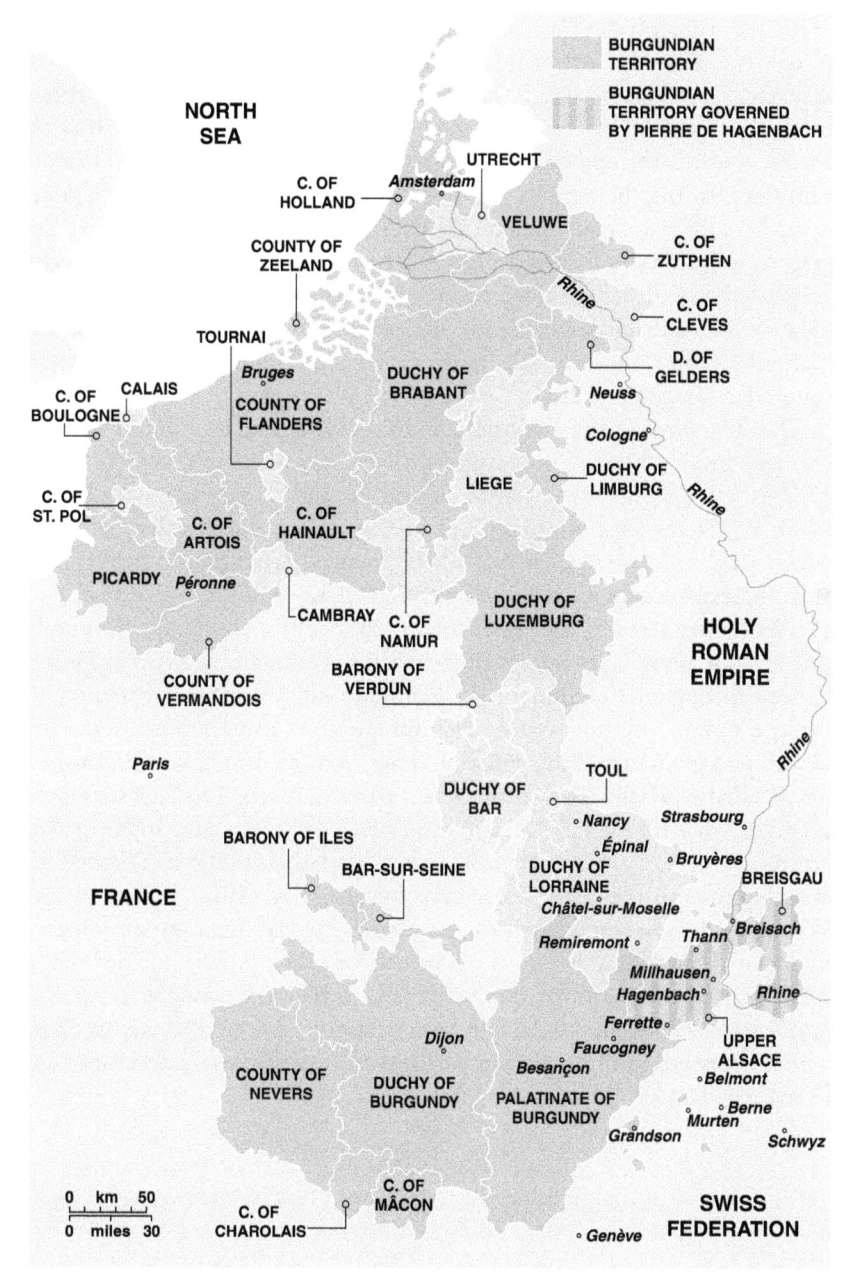

Map 2: Burgundian territory, c. 1470, and Lorraine.

'le Hardi' [brave] and 'le Travaillant' [politically crafty] (Claerr-Stamm, p. 50), was a capable ruler and soldier, with considerable interest in military science and history – and he managed to extend his lands even further by the conquest of Guelders and Zutphen in the north (to which may be added, towards the end of his reign, the acquisition and brief retention of Lorraine), so that in 1476, at the zenith of his own and his duchy's grandeur, he could, a month before his death, style himself 'Charles, by the grace of God duke of Burgundy, of Lothier, of Brabant, of Limbourg, of Luxembourg and of Guelders, count of Flanders, of Artois, of Burgundy palatine, of Hainault, of Holland, of Zeeland, of Namur and of Zutphen, marquis of the Holy Empire, lord of Frisia, of Salines and of Malines' (quoted in Vaughan, p. 226).

The splendour of the Burgundian court was legendary even in its own day, and those otherwise unfamiliar with Gallic history may well be aware of it as a then important centre of culture and of the arts – and have admired, for instance, the paintings of Rogier van der Weyden, amongst which are a beautiful study of Isabella of Portugal, Charles's mother (Fig. 1), and fine portraits of Charles himself and of his half-brother Anton and of a half-sister (two of his father's many illegitimate children).[8] Burgundy was also the home of the prestigious chivalric Order of the Golden Fleece, famous throughout Europe for its grand and often royal membership and for the pomp, pageantry and splendid insignia associated with it. The wealth and grandeur of the court he inherited were in no way diminished under Charles – who knew how to get married or stage-manage state proceedings with breath-taking sumptuousness.[9] He was more interested in armies and less in the arts than had been his father, Philip the Good: his contributions to the ducal library, for instance, lay mainly in such works as the translations undertaken for him from classical literature on military figures such as Alexander and Caesar (see Vaughan, p. 163). He devoted a great deal of time, and of innovative and intelligent thought as well as resources, to the composition and organization of his own forces, amongst which a contingent of English archers was consistently a valued component (Vaughan, p. 216).

---

[8] The portrait of Charles (used as the jacket illustration by Vaughan) is in the Gemäldegalerie, Berlin; those of Antoine and Isabella in, respectively, the Royal Museum of Fine Arts, Brussels, and the Getty Center, California. There are two very similar portraits of what is believed to be the half-sister, one in the National Gallery, London, the other in the National Gallery of Art, Washington.
[9] See e.g. Vaughan, *Charles the Bold*, pp. 50–3 (the marriage to Margaret of York) and pp. 140–7 (the meeting with Emperor Frederick at Trier in 1473). A first-hand account of the Burgundian court in this period is provided by the famous description written in 1474 by Olivier de la Marche: *L'estat de la maison du duc Charles de Bourgogne*.

Fig. 1: Isabella of Portugal, duchess of Burgundy (c. 1450): workshop of Rogier van der Weyden (Getty Museum Collection).

There were other even more significant links with England. Charles's mother, Isabella of Portugal, was a granddaughter of John of Gaunt, and Charles took care to inform himself of the facts of his genealogy on her side, so that, should circumstances ever favour making a claim on the English throne, he might represent himself as the most direct descendant of the ousted Lancastrian dynasty (see Vaughan, p. 72). He did not do so, but instead was sedulous in creating and maintaining links with the Yorkist king of England. For Edward IV, whom Charles assisted against the Duke of Warwick, was among the neighbouring powers with whom he carefully built up a network of alliances – to prevent their aiding the French king, Louis XI, in the event of conflict between these two rival princes, between whom there existed permanent hostility and distrust. Charles's alliance with the English royal house was sealed when in 1468 he took as his third wife Margaret of York, Edward's sister. Margaret was a bibliophile who played a small but significant part in the history of English literature and letter-writing. It was she who, after her marriage, commissioned from William Caxton, then governor of the English merchants at Bruges, the translating and printing of *The Recuyell of the Hystories of Troye*, the first printed book to appear in English; and it was her wedding, celebrated with true Burgundian lavishness, that John Paston III sent his mother an account of (*Paston Letters*, ed. Davis, vol. 1, pp. 538–40) – a wedding which, even while it was still in the mooting, represented an alliance grand enough to catch the English imagination and entail an element of improbability, for it is used as the basis of a financial speculation by John Paston II, who in 1467 offered to pay 80 shillings for a horse if Margaret married Charles within two years, but only 40 shillings if she did not (*Paston Letters*, ed. Davis, vol. 1, pp. 397–8).

Though Louis figured in Charles's mind as the chief threat he faced, there was in fact an uneasy truce between the two rulers for much of Charles's brief reign, during which his opponents on the field of battle were not chiefly the French (though they were the indirect object of much of his strategic and military plans). France did, however, launch an offensive, not only in 1475 (see Vaughan, pp. 346–7), but also, earlier, over 1471–2, precisely the period covered by the letters here at issue. There were incursions into Burgundian territory and military engagements which included a defeat for the Burgundians at Buxy and a success outside Remiremont – actions referred to in Letter VIII.[10] The letter to Pierre from the Burgundian commander Jean de Vaudrey (Letter V), written early (February) in 1471, refers explicitly to a pending war (imminently inevitable due to the French raids) and to Burgundian preparations for it.

But the most serious military reversals which Charles suffered were later, towards the end of his reign, and were the result, not of engagements with the French, but of strategies and interventions with regard to his German borders. Like most rulers with land (as opposed to sea) boundaries, he attempted to secure those boundaries from falling under the dominion or influence of hostile powers by creating and supporting allies there and gaining influence or territorial footholds of his own in those areas. He once defended himself against complaints (voiced by the Order of the Golden Fleece) that he overburdened his subjects with wars by claiming what he himself probably thought was true: that he undertook war only to defend his allies or protect his own subjects and kingdom and that there was no man who desired or needed peace more than he (Vaughan, p. 178).[11]

It was thus his alliance with and support of Archbishop Rudolph of Cologne which led to the protracted, expensive and ultimately abortive siege of Neuss in 1474–5, and it was his attempts to protect Savoy, and thereby make of it a puppet state of his own (and not of France), which led to a series of defeats in that area, notably at Grandson and Murten, in 1476 (see Vaughan, pp. 359–98). His opponents in these cases were German-speaking powers, in the latter case principally the 'Swiss' – a term which was

---

[10] On the French invasions and the battle of Buxy, see Vaughan, *Charles the Bold*, pp. 70–1.
[11] In a practice somewhat similar to that of monks in chapter, the Order encouraged public criticism (and response to it) on the part of its members.

only just emerging and derived from the name (Schwyz) of one member of a group of cantons and communities which had formed a league among themselves in what at the time was referred to as 'Upper Germany'. They had forged an alliance against him with Austria and other towns and powers on the Upper Rhine, and these same forces also came to the assistance of Duke René of Lorraine after Charles had conquered Lorraine (with which, until the accession of René, his relations had been governed by peace treaties), and he died at the ensuing battle of Nancy in January 1477.

Charles had first attracted the active enmity of the Swiss in relation to another enterprise on his borders. Duke Sigmund of Austria was in need of money to prosecute his own wars against the Swiss. And in 1469, in the Treaty of Saint-Omer, he mortgaged a parcel of land on the Upper Rhine to Charles in return for 50,000 Rhenish florins and a promise of military assistance (see Vaughan, pp. 85–6 and 129). Charles never in fact gave up the latter, but acquired the lands and placed himself by the transaction in opposition to the Swiss, who had allies and interests in the territories mortgaged (which included Upper Alsace and the county of Ferrette on the west bank of the Rhine as well as Black Forest towns on the east bank) – a mortgage which Charles evidently assumed should amount or lead to a virtual annexation (Claerr-Stamm, p. 114). It was of these regions that Pierre de Hagenbach was appointed governor, his official title being 'grand bailiff of Ferrette and Alsace'. 'Ferrette' was 'the usual Burgundian name for all the rights and possessions in and near Upper Alsace mortgaged to Charles ... by Sigmund' (Vaughan, p. 289 n. 1), and in the address on the outside of G's letters to him – except VIII and IX, where the address is to 'mon esliance' and 'mon garie', respectively (see Notes), and X, which lacks address – he is designated as 'le Bailly' (I, VI) or as 'le Bailly de Fairette' (II, VII, XI), although his territorial titles are more fully and formally given in the communication from Jean de Vaudrey (V), where the address is to Pierre as 'chevalier' and 'seigneur' of Hagenbach, Ferrette and Alsace. And, since Pierre had taken up his appointment only in September 1469 (Vaughan, p. 89), the title was still, presumably, being used with some deliberateness and conscious awareness of the new status conferred on him.

Pierre was, in fact, by birth a member of the lesser nobility of Alsace, and the ancestral home of Hagenbach, as well as his father's château at Thann, lay squarely within the territories later mortgaged to Charles (see Vaughan, pp. 255–6). But much of his childhood was spent at his mother's château of Belmont in the Franche-Comté (i.e. in Burgundian territory), where he received his education. He therefore grew up able to speak and write fluent French. He had served Charles's father, Philip the Good, and entered the service of Charles while the latter was still count of Charolais (that is, before his accession to the dukedom at the death of his father in 1467), and to him Pierre in 1462 early endeared himself by exposing a plot against his life (Claerr-Stamm, pp. 38–40). In the field, he served Charles as his master of artillery (Claerr-Stamm, pp. 43–4), and by 1460 (when he was about forty years old) had been elevated to the seniority and status signified by the title *maître d'hôtel* (a title conferred upon only four of the most important and trusted officers of the ducal household: see Claerr-Stamm, pp. 54–5). He was, primarily, a tough and loyal soldier. He had not only participated in all of Charles's campaigns, but had several times earned himself special recognition for distinguished service, one of his earliest and most significant achievements being the seizure (in October 1465) of Péronne (Claerr-Stamm, pp. 41–2), one of the towns on the Somme which France and Burgundy competed to control and possess.

Pierre's bilingualism also made him useful to Charles in negotiations and diplomatic missions involving German-speaking powers and princes. He had in 1465 negotiated an alliance between Charles and the Count Palatine of the Rhine (Claerr-Stamm, p. 43), and it was on returning from one of the embassies to Sigmund on which he was sent in 1472 (to discuss a military alliance against the Swiss)[12] that he was for a short time held captive, the news of which incident naturally occasioned such alarm to G (VIII.10–11, IX.6).[13] In 1472–3 (the year covered by the last of G's letters to him and the months following), he was also to play a major part in the negotiations for the projected marriage of Charles's only child, the sixteen-year-old Mary, to the fourteen-year-old son of Emperor Frederick III, acting as ambassador, messenger and interpreter to Frederick and others (Vaughan, pp. 135–52).

A tough nut of proven loyalty and fluent in both French and German, he was therefore the obvious candidate for bailiff of the territories mortgaged – a region familiar to him, where he would occupy a position earlier held by his own great-uncle (who had also been *bailli* of Ferrette: Claerr-Stamm, p. 25), and in which lay Thann, of which his father had been *bailli*, and where Pierre, as *bailli*, maintained two houses, one of which had long been in the Hagenbach family (Claerr-Stamm, p. 116). He seems, however, to have been heavy-handed in the exercise of his office in word and deed (and especially in word), opposing in the area the influence and interests of the Swiss, whom he hated (as did many of the nobles of Alsace, who feared or had suffered, as had the Hagenbach family, reprisals at their hands[14]), and repressing there the urban privileges and the whole independent urban

---

[12] See Vaughan, pp. 267 and 271–2.
[13] Paravicini, ed., 'Un amour malheureux', p. 132.
[14] See Claerr-Stamm, *Pierre de Hagenbach*, p. 30; the château of Pierre's own cousin had been destroyed by the Swiss in reprisals for his siding against them: p. 27.

culture espoused by the Swiss. He was, in short, implacably anti-Swiss and anti-urban and by all accounts used crude insults and threats as well as some force in imposing Burgundian authority on the cities subject to his control (see Vaughan, pp. 96–7, 271, 277).

The Swiss, unhappy with Burgundian control of the area and loathing Pierre, began to form alliances aimed at removing both (Vaughan, pp. 267, 271, 278–9). Charles would by 1471 have known of these measures, and Jean's letter to Pierre at the beginning of 1471 warns Pierre of war brewing on his German front as well as against the French invaders (V.10). The league against him gradually consolidated itself further, and Sigismund was loaned the money to redeem his mortgaged lands (Claerr-Stamm, p. 161).

Swiss-Austrian intervention was in the event anticipated and precipitated by a rebellion against Pierre within one of his towns that lay across the Rhine: Breisach, where the citizens, angered at his suppression of civic liberties, supported a mutiny by a contingent of Pierre's soldiery (Alsatian troops resentful of what they saw as privileged treatment of Picard ones: Claerr-Stamm, p. 164). This took place in 1474 (some time after the last letter in the present series, which was written in September 1472). Pierre was taken captive and put on trial by the Swiss for the 'crimes' he had committed in office. The trial was simply a show-trial, for Pierre's enemies were judge and jury in their own cause, and the outcome was foreordained. The accused was tortured before it and summarily executed after it.[15]

The charges brought against him included suppression of civil liberties and institutions and the execution of burghers after a rebellion – violence which was pretty minor by the standards of the times and, in terms of 'crimes against humanity' (to employ an anachronistic concept), certainly nowhere near in atrocity those on record in his day (see, for example, Vaughan, pp. 316, 370) and committed by the Swiss themselves against their enemies when they had the chance (Vaughan, pp. 305, 393, 425, 429), even their own authorities being moved to protest (at the sack of Estavayer) at barbaric savageries 'which might move God and the saints against us in vengeance'.[16] Otherwise, the charges consisted of rumoured planned atrocities and sexual offences (see Vaughan, p. 285; Claerr-Stamm, p. 177). It is in fact clear from an earlier official list of complaints against him (Vaughan, pp. 281–3) that it was chiefly his 'attitude' that had caused the intense hatred he inspired: bullying threats, crude insults, scornful intransigence, along with some physical violence against officials, was what he had then

---

[15] See Vaughan, *Charles the Bold*, pp. 284–6 and Claerr-Stamm, *Pierre de Hagenbach*, pp. 173–90 for accounts of the torture, trial and execution.
[16] Quoted by Vaughan, *Charles the Bold*, p. 363, from E. von Rodt, *Die Feldzüge Karls des Kühnen*, 2 vols (Schaffhausen 1843–4), vol. 1, p. 531.

chiefly been accused of. There had also been allegations about unspeakably lewd behaviour, legends of atrocities largely traceable to enemies he had made (Claerr-Stamm, p. 123). The sexual misconduct with which he was now charged included the violation of nuns. This last might be of interest to readers of the letters here reproduced, were it not for the fact that such accusations were commonly added to a charge sheet by political enemies in order to present the person targeted as a regular mother-fucker, as it were, of whom no good could ever be expected.[17] But even his complainants and subsequent prosecutors themselves could describe, in the complaints earlier levelled and in the charges now brought, nothing worse than a crude and bullying braggart rather than a monster guilty of unheard-of enormities: 'a bully, a braggart, a man of violence, but scarcely a criminal', as Vaughan put it (p. 285).

Pierre defended his conduct in office by claiming he was acting essentially on orders from his liege lord (Claerr-Stamm, pp. 180–2), and responded to the sexual charges simply by asserting that 'he had never used force and had done only what many others in the courtroom had done' and paid good money for it, too – a response which has the ring of truth to it. But his death had been decided on by his enemies, who were also responsible for his post-mortem reputation: for until relatively recently he lived on, in legend and in literature, only as the archetype of the wicked and tyrannical enforcer of 'a detested foreign regime' (Vaughan, p. 286). Charles sent forces which (led by Pierre's brother Étienne/Stefan), after massing at Remiremont, indulged in a four-day orgy of punitive raiding and looting in Alsace (Claerr-Stamm, pp. 193–4); but Burgundian rule was never restored over the territory, territory now as lost to enemy control as was the image of Pierre in history. His trial had been conducted under the authority of Archduke Sigmund, who proceeded to confiscate all his assets (Claerr-Stamm, p. 182), and it was thus into the archives of Sigmund that even Pierre's documentary profile – that is, his papers (and the love letters they included) – was absorbed, and from which it had to be retrieved. And, with regard to the larger picture of him, that geographical dislocation to an Innsbruck and Sigmundian context of the manuscripts that at present concern us (Innsbruck, Tiroler Landesarchiv, Acta Sigmundiana I.80) is paralleled in the viewpoint of his enemies that determined his subsequent image – and it is difficult to know how much to discount (as due to prejudice) in the hostile characterization to which currency was given. The hatred

---

[17] Compare the charges brought against the abbots of Peterborough and Bury (see above, p. 254); cf. the Italian mercenaries (a regular component of Charles's armies) who were captured in 1474 (at the seizure of Héricourt by the Strasbourgers) and were burnt as heretics 'after being accused of sodomy, rape, sacrilege and other unspeakable crimes' (Vaughan, *Charles the Bold*, p. 296).

he inspired and the charges levelled against him suggest he may have been, at best, blunt and uncompromising, and probably coarse and bludgeoning.

*

Recently widowed (his first wife having died in 1468 or 1469: see Paravicini, pp. 120–1), newly raised to the power and dignity of the office that represented the peak of his career, and certainly a man of strong and commanding ways, Pierre in 1470 may not have been without a certain charisma. At fifty, however, he was no longer a young man, and, even making allowances for the hostile bias in the accounts of him that emerge from other contexts, it must remain surprising to find this man, of all men, in the role of a Romeo. Of the lady who nevertheless evidently found him an attractive rather than a repellent figure, nothing can be known beyond what emerges from the letters themselves, a summary survey of whose contents is at this point in order. The dossier begins with two letters whose main purpose is to respond to a proposal of Pierre that she should travel to Burgundy to join him. She has consulted her father and declares she must wait on his decision (I.6–7). The second letter announces that decision, which is negative, and therefore they must wait for more propitious times (II.7–8). The third and fourth letters are addressed to her as bursaress of the abbey and are from her official clerk, Nicolas, who must also be an old friend, since he is plainly in her confidence and addresses her with a not disrespectful but somewhat avuncular familiarity. From these it emerges that she has a sister in whose company she made some journey with Nicolas just before Christmas 1470, that she had then proceeded to disobey her father and travel to Pierre, that her father was very displeased to hear this and that, on reading his letters, it now appears to Nicolas, too, that it was imprudent (IV.8–12). The fifth letter (dated February 1471) is from Jean de Vaudrey, a commander in the Burgundian army, addressed to Pierre as a brother general, and concerns war brewing both with France (and consequent movements of Burgundian troops in which he and Pierre are and will be involved) and on the German-speaking borders; the writer adds that he does not know the answer to Pierre's question as to whether the 'dames' [ladies] have or have not left Remiremont, in the vicinity of which Jean at present is (V.9). The sixth, from G to Pierre, is a brief letter assuring him of her continuing love and fidelity. In the seventh, she says that the journey he is still urging her to make remains impossible, and replies with considerable feeling and indignation to a suspicion he had apparently voiced that she was detained by an affair with someone else, perhaps a priest (VII.6–10). The remaining four letters are also from G to Pierre, but three of them use the first-person plural and contain no assertions of the

352   Actual Letters

love avowed in her previous four letters. The reason for this in the eighth is clear: there are Burgundian officials at Remiremont after the battle there, and one of Pierre's letters to 'us' has been intercepted by a Burgundian official (VIII.6), and 'we' are now writing to the *bailli* to express 'our' friendly interest in his news and 'our' concern at hearing he had been taken prisoner, which was communicated to 'us' by persons who thought they were giving good news (VIII.10). The ninth, written two days later, refers in more loverlike and personal terms to the distress that news had caused the canoness, who now writes in the singular and as a lover. The tenth and eleventh are again (or purport to be) letters from 'us' to the *bailli*, regretting that the journey 'we' had planned is not possible and protesting 'our' goodwill; as with Letter VIII, the writer plainly either feared interception of her letters or could not find a scribe she trusted, and so writes as if neither the goodwill nor the journey result from any personal or romantic liaison with Pierre – for neither of these final letters (like Letter VIII, but unlike Letters I, II, VI, VII and IX) express any amorous feeling or use any amorous endearments. In the last, she refers to illness and the state of the times as alike preventing the journey 'we' would like to make and which Pierre is plainly still urging (XI.4).

From this material some facts emerge which seem as if they could serve as clues to G's identity. She was perhaps called Marguerite, was *boursière* or treasuress at Remiremont and had a sister also resident there, whose name was probably Catherine (see Letter IV.11 and Note).[18] But Remiremont records are patchy for the years in question, and one is reliant on chance mentions in them or elsewhere, and Paravicini (who canvasses previous theories and surveys other possibilities: pp. 114–19) was unable to turn up any promising or convincing candidate by pursuing these clues. Since it is vain to hope to succeed where such a judicious and thorough scholar has failed, any chance of identifying G must come as a result of new evidence or of pursuing different avenues of enquiry – for it is by no means certain that 'Gayrrie' is a diminutive of 'Marguerite' (see p. 341 above), nor is the Catherine referred to at IV.11 unquestionably to be identified with the sister referred to at III.5.

But there are things about her which are more knowable. She was plainly of gentle birth and rank, for Remiremont was an exclusive institution, whose canonesses were women of wealth and family: in fact, anyone seeking entrance was required (by a papal bull secured by the abbey at the

---

[18] On the office of the *bourserie* at Remiremont, see Boquillon, *Les chanoinesses de Remiremont*, p. 90. On the family networks that were the rule among the residents there (where hardly any canoness would be without relatives at the establishment), see pp. 36–7 and 129–34.

beginning of the fifteenth century) 'to establish unblemished nobility over four generations and two hundred years in both maternal and paternal lines'.[19] The home of her clerk, Nicolas of Bruyères (whom Paravicini did succeed in finding mention of elsewhere: see n. to IV.18), might provide some clue as to the whereabouts of her own family home, since he is obviously an old friend, who knows her and her father and her family circumstances well (IV.11–12). Bruyères lies to the north-east of Remiremont, both places belonging to the modern *département* of Les Vosges. And other relevant facts do emerge about G and her situation in Remiremont with regard to her affair with Pierre. Her father must have had Burgundian sympathies, since he knows of the liaison with Pierre, does not disapprove of it in itself and objects to G's making a journey to him simply on account of the dangers posed by the hostile relations among the local powers. Indeed, though Remiremont itself was in Lorraine, its canonesses came predominantly from the Franche-Comté area of Burgundian territory (Boquillon, p. 161). Paravicini points out (p. 126) that when, in connection with a legal matter in relation to some property, Charles had raised it as an issue that the canonesses were in Lorraine, the ladies themselves had remarked in reply that in fact most of them came from the duke's own Burgundian territories. Pierre himself, in common with many Burgundian families of any standing, had connections with the abbey: he had endowed an 'anniversary' there for himself and his first wife, Marguerite d'Accolans; he had relatives among some of the families to which the canonesses belonged; his own daughter Marie – who married (some time after 1473) Antoine de Farrette, a resident of Remiremont mentioned at XI.8 – retired after being widowed in 1503 to a canoness-ship there;[20] and a Katherine de Hagenbach (perhaps Marie's sister) is also recorded as a 'dame' there by 1474 (see Paravicini, p. 121, n. 80). G says in her second letter that the missive is to go with one the sacristan is writing to Pierre, since (for obvious reasons) she prefers to use a bearer or messenger who does not appear to come from her personally (II.10): and the sacristan at this period was Charlotte de Montjustin, a relative of Pierre (Paravicini, p. 123, n. 93).

It is not surprising, therefore, that one gets the impression from the letters that the affair was to a certain extent known to and condoned by other inmates of the Abbey, many of whom had links with Burgundy and/or Pierre. Charlotte, at least, is explicitly said to have known that G was writing to Pierre. And, since G passes on to him at VIII.16 a request from a

---

[19] Reuben Richard Lee, ed., 'A New Edition of *The Council of Remiremont*' (unpublished PhD dissertation, University of Connecticut, 1981), p. 48; Boquillon, *Les chanoinesses de Remiremont*, pp. 9, 39.
[20] See Paravicini, ed., 'Un amour malheureux', p. 120; on Antoine, see further Claerr-Stamm, *Pierre de Hagenbach*, pp. 32–3.

sister canoness, Clemence d'Husier, for a safe conduct for a friend of hers, and makes a similar request on behalf of perhaps the same man at XI.8 (the last letter, also from 'nous'), she must have been known by other inmates to have had influence with him. Clemence is also mentioned as the bearer of Letter VIII, and though both that and Letter XI are amongst the letters in which G is careful to write not as a lover, but as a spokesman for 'nous' to 'our' friend Pierre, and Clemence may therefore not knowingly carry a love letter, she must at least have assumed that it might have some significance that G was acting as the spokesperson for the friendly greetings and request proferred by 'nous'.

Remiremont, then, was not a place that apparently did or was likely to frown upon a useful liaison between one of its members and a powerful representative of the Burgundian interest most of them espoused. But the situation was not, it seems, quite that simple. G certainly fears public knowledge of the affair, begs Pierre to be more discrete in his arrangements for delivery of letters to her (I.9), and talks of the great 'charges' [burdens and/or accusations, reproaches] she has to bear at Remiremont because of her love for him (I.9, VII.11, IX.5). She is obviously under stress by reason of a felt need for secrecy and/or recrimination and accusations from those around her. Since she was not a nun, and the emergence of the actual fact of an *ami* would probably not have been that damaging in itself (especially since her relatives, i.e. her father and her sister, clearly already know of it: see for instance IV.10–11), her fears (of gossip, exposure, disapproval) are likely to have had, at least in part, a socio-political basis. And since she says she heard the news of Pierre's temporary captivity from those who assumed they were retailing good news (VIII.10), there must have been some pro-French or at least anti-Burgundian elements either in the abbey or in the town. This would not have been surprising. The town was situated in the far south of Lorraine (an independent duchy, not part of Burgundian territory), and its abbey certainly recruited from Lorraine as well as from Burgundy.[21] Though non-aggression pacts had been agreed on by the two powers, and there was official peace and even alliance between them until the accession of Duke René II of Lorraine in 1473 (see Vaughan, pp. 103–7), official peace is one thing and general feeling on the ground is another. The formally non-hostile relationship meant that Charles could transport his troops through Lorraine (which divided the two swathes of Burgundian territory), that is, he enjoyed transit rights which were later explicitly formalized (in treaties in 1472 and 1473: see Vaughan, pp. 103, 107). Just such a mass passage of

---

[21] M. Parisse, 'Le Concile de Remiremont', *Le Pays de Remiremont* 4 (1981) 10–15 (p. 11); Boquillon, *Les chanoinesses de Remiremont*, p. 161.

Burgundian troops throughout the full length of Lorraine is described by Jean in his letter to Pierre (V.4).

The movement of large numbers of troops tends in itself to be a somewhat invasive procedure not likely to be welcomed by the terrain affected (cf. Vaughan, pp. 404–5) and in this case would probably have been exacerbated by a general distrust of Burgundian ambitions, in furtherance of which Charles would obviously have found it useful to incorporate Lorraine into, and thus unite, his own twofold domains. This indeed he was later to do, though it was not until the spring of 1475 that a number of factors (including 'depredations of Burgundian troops in Lorraine which Charles was powerless or possibly unwilling to stop': Vaughan, p. 307) led Duke René to declare a war on Charles which led to a briefly enjoyed conquest of Lorraine by the latter. Another cause of dissension arose from the powerful Burgundian family of Neuchâtel, who came from the Franche-Comté, but who had acquired titles to property in Lorraine. They had in 1467 attacked Épinal (a few miles from Remiremont) in pursuance of a claim to an overlordship which the inhabitants had refused to accept (Vaughan, p. 101). In April 1471, just prior to Letter VIII (with its reference to information of Pierre's capture received from those who thought they were giving tidings of joy: VIII.10), Pierre had himself led forces to raise a siege laid to Châtel-sur-Moselle, the most notable of the Neuchâtel fiefs in Lorraine, Henry de Neuchâtel being the commander-in-chief of this relief force (Paravicini, p. 131).[22] Thus engaged on Neuchâtel business, Pierre was not in fact present at the battle of Buxy (March 1471), which had led to Burgundian casualties that had alarmed G on his behalf (VIII.3). The Neuchâtels were signally associated with Charles and the Burgundian state in a military and political, as well as a geographical, sense. Thibaud de Neuchâtel had been marshal of Burgundy when Charles became duke; his brother Jean was lieutenant general in the Franche-Comté and commanded the forces in Burgundy in 1471 and in 1475, his son Henry was lieutenant general on the German-speaking frontier, and Henry's younger brother Claude commander in Luxembourg. The family was thus well known as the one from which Charles drew the commanders-in-chief of all his various territories, and Letter V (from Jean de Vaudrey to Pierre in February 1471) refers to Jean de Neuchâtel lieutenant general in the Franche-Comté area) as one who should be informed and consulted with reference to the military manoeuvres ahead (V.6–7); and it was indeed he who commanded the Burgundian forces at the battle of Buxy (referred to at VIII.3) in March.[23]

---

[22] The mission was successfully accomplished according to Paravicini ('Un amour malheureux', p. 120), abortive according to Claerr-Stamm (*Pierre de Hagenbach*, p. 104).
[23] On the family and their military roles, see Vaughan, *Charles the Bold*, pp. 70 and 256–7.

It was likewise a family whose members were supported and promoted by Charles, who was prepared to use his armies and his influence on their behalf (see Vaughan, pp. 101–3, 256–7).[24] Their unwelcome intrusions into Lorraine space would certainly have been seen as strong-armed on the part of Burgundy in general and perhaps of Pierre in particular.

The official peace with Lorraine could not, in short, guarantee the friendly feeling of Lorrainers, who figured among the enemy troops (an army of 'Francois, Lorrains et Liegeois': Paravicini, p. 131) defeated by the Burgundians in the engagement at Remiremont in April 1471, a few weeks after their setback at Buxy, both battles being referred to in Letter VIII.3 and 17. The two powers knew that each was a potential enemy of the other, and Lorrainers might well have harboured no very friendly feelings towards Pierre, a man evidently known as Charles's tough guy in that region. In this situation, G's socio-political and amorous attachment to the Burgundian commander (neither of them a bond that could be openly avowed in all company) would have interacted with and reinforced each other, and the interconnections between the two are evident throughout the letters, instances being registered in the Notes. The romantic relationship by turns conflates itself with, expresses itself through, or hides behind the 'nous' of, a political allegiance. When G writes those letters that purport to be from 'nous' and do not avow any love, it is not quite clear whether the 'we' is a dual (and the letter masquerades as one coming from herself and her sister) or a more plural one (referring to other canonesses friendly and/or related to Pierre). In the first case, she would be hiding her love behind some family tie or acquaintance with Pierre, which would entail a politico-social alliance of a larger sort that would also be implied in the second case: 'mon esliance' [alliance] is the term she repeatedly uses in direct address to him in the first of these *nous* letters, as if to advertise – to any Burgundian official who might (as she has good ground to fear: VIII.5–6) intercept the letter – that it is from those loyal to the Burgundian cause and allied with it. That 'alliance' is both mirror to and mask for her love.

It is certainly the political situation that keeps G from joining her lover rather than any fear of discovery of an affair evidently already known to her father, her sister, her clerk and at least one (and probably more) of her fellow canonesses. It is the want of 'peace' to which she attributes her father's ban on the journey (II.9), and it is the unfavourable disposition of 'the times' that she cites as continuing to prevent it (VIII.15, XI.3). For the

---

[24] In the period following the last letter (dated September 1472), the Neuchâtels consented to render homage to the duke of Lorraine for their possessions in the duchy (Vaughan, *Charles the Bold*, pp. 103–4), and so became less of a source of aggravation there.

fate of this love affair, like others in both art and actuality, is defined and determined by the geo-political context in which it occurs. Like Paris and Helen (joined and then separated by Greek–Trojan hostilities), like Troilus and Criseyde (separated by that same conflict), and like Charles d'Orléans, divided by the English Channel from his wife Bonne, whom he never saw again after being taken captive at the battle of Agincourt in 1415, G is separated from Pierre by the politics of the Gallic world she inhabits – and, like Charles d'Orléans, can counter this separation only by writing, and we know of her love only because these adverse circumstances denied her the face-to-face communication she frequently expresses a longing for and for which the letters are, for her and Pierre, a poor substitute, just as Charles yearns to speak by *bouche* rather than by the awkwardly ventriloquist pen, which must leave so much unexpressed (see n. to Letter I.8 below).

*

The letters were closed by a strip of paper passed through slits cut in the margins, then sealed (over the strip), so that no one could open them without leaving the evidence of a broken seal to betray that fact, and were then folded down to a size (about 80 mm x 40 mm) in which they could easily be carried imperceptibly about the person.[25] Their physical form thus guarded their contents from prying eyes as effectively as G kept her own secrets in the dictation, never giving her real name and often disguising even her identity as a lover under a group 'nous'. The remaining traces of the seal which might have helped to identify her are too fragmentary to be of any assistance (Paravicini, p. 122), and it is somehow not inappropriate that circumstances should have conspired to continue, on her behalf, to frustrate the researches and surmises as to her identity made by the third parties she took such precautions to conceal it from. One half hopes that her privacy may remain unviolated, as it probably will, though the details were undoubtedly known to several trusted persons at the time – amongst whom must be numbered three different scribes.

For, as was not uncommon, she did not pen her letters personally, but dictated them to an amanuensis. As has been pointed out (pp. 53–8 above), writing was a skill separate from reading, and, though men engaged in business that required them to keep books and accounts, etc., might be practised enough in the art to write out their own letters, those whose lives did not necessitate much use of the pen (notably, women and aristocratic men)

---

[25] These details are from Paravicini, ed., 'Un amour malheureux', pp. 121–2. Letters were characteristically closed in this way: folded and punched with holes or slits through which some string was passed and then sealed (Constable, *Letters and Letter-Collections*, p. 47); see also p. 55 above.

habitually used scribes. Margery Brews, it will be recalled, used a scribe for her Valentine letter, though both she and G sometimes both add short addenda to their letters (see p. 54 above and Letters I and VI below) that prove they could write, if only clumsily and slowly, and that it was lack of practice rather than illiteracy in the strict sense that prevented them doing so. G could certainly read (see VIII.9 and cf. IV.11–12). But three different hands appear in the love letters: Scribe 1 in Letters I, II and VII; Scribe 2 in Letter VI; Scribe 3 in Letter IX. Interestingly, the less confidential letters from 'nous', which are not superficially love letters and make no mention of love, are written by other scribes (Letter VIII by Scribe 4, Letter IX and X by Scribe 5 and 3 respectively), with only one overlap between the two groups (IX and XI are both penned by Scribe 3: see preliminary n. to XI). Letter V (from Jean de Vaudrey) was, naturally, penned by quite another scribe (Scribe 6), as were the two letters to G from Nicolas de Bruyères (III and IV: Scribe 7), both written in the same hand, which may well be his own (see first n. to III).

But if G, like most women of all ranks, did not write often enough to pen her own letters, she could certainly read and was clearly an educated woman, by the standards of the times. She was certainly also culturally literate and linguistically fluent. She is in command of the opening and closing epistolary formulae and can play graceful variations upon them (see for instance I.2, 15), and she indites with easy and educated coherence, with wit, charm and tact, with intelligent imagination enough to invent the indirection of the strategic 'nous' and (though her manner is neither learned nor rhetorically elaborate) with sophistication: she can allude with some wit to common theological principles and deploy them expressively (see for instance nn. to VIII.9, 14 and IX.8). We cannot know her age, but she does not to our ears write like a girl. There is a self-possession here that bespeaks a woman of mature years. She is neither awed nor flustered by the love of a man such as Pierre, nor cowed by his imperiousness or urgency as a lover. She is capable of standing up to him and of disobeying her father, though she loves Pierre and clearly respects and reveres her father (see for instance I.7). She can be firm in refusal and deliver a rebuke with pleasantness and affection (as at I.9–11). She is a loving mistress and a dutiful daughter who nevertheless manages to retain her independence. She is plainly courageous, faithful and genuine (though never obsequious) in her love. One is reminded by her of the face of Isabella of Portugal (Charles's mother) as Rogier van der Weyden had recently depicted it (see Fig. 1, p. 345): for something of the same refined sensitivity and smiling responsiveness – in the face of a mature woman who has not hidden from realities or sufferings, but has not been soured by them – emerges from G's

Pierre de Hagenbach and the Canoness at Remiremont 359

epistolary style. That Pierre should have loved and have been loved by such a woman provides probably the most powerful evidence possible that the unattractive character that emerges from 'history' should be regarded as largely a one-sided and untrustworthy projection created by those prejudiced against him.

When and how the affair ended, and if the last of the present letters (XI) in effect marks its end, we cannot know. Pierre remarried in January 1474, but that by no means necessarily implies that he tired of or betrayed G, as Schmidt seems to assume in referring to the marriage as showing that she was eventually disappointed in her hopes with regard to Pierre (see p. 63 above). As has already been pointed out, there is no indication G was assuming or hoping for marriage with Pierre and no evidence that she would have been unhappy with the status of *amie* that, at this period, was felt to be an honourable and privileged one, though it entailed discretion (see p. 64 above). It was a month after the last letter that Pierre's deputy, Bernard de Ramstein, wished him, on 2 October 1472, 'joye de vous amours'.[26] This might refer to a still-ongoing affair with the canoness, but, since that was a matter that was not generally known about, it more likely relates to initial moves towards Pierre's second marriage, a plan which might well have been in the public domain. And that marriage of January 1474 (following a formal proposal made in May 1473: Paravicini, p. 136) may have been the result, rather than the cause, of the end of the liaison with G. That is, it looks as if Pierre did not think of a new wife until the affair (to the continuance of which no further letters testify) was over. The logistical difficulties that continually frustrated the pair were clearly severe and may in the end have proved overwhelming. Pierre perhaps got tired or angry at the repeated deferrals of the journey he urged on G. But perhaps not. Both of them seem to have been persons not easily deterred from what they had set their hearts on. And it is possible that G died (perhaps from the 'malladie' mentioned in her last letter). Pierre did not, evidently, destroy her letters, though whether they survived because he treasured them or because he forgot about them we of course cannot know. And he made no recorded moves to remarry until after the date of that last letter.

He was, nevertheless, within only a few months embarked upon a new and a splendid union. Barbara de Tengen was young, apparently beautiful and from a rank of the nobility higher than that in to which Pierre had himself been born (see Paravicini, p. 136; Claerr-Stamm, p. 152). The

---

[26] See Paravicini ('Un amour malheureux', p. 136), whose n. 155 cites H. Brauer-Gramm, *Der Landvogt Peter von Hagenbach* (Göttingen, 1957), p.171, and Innsbruck, TLA, Schatz-Archiv, Urk.I, 8208.

wedding celebrations were conducted with huge éclat, lasting six days in Thann and extending into carnival festivities in Breisach in Febrary (Claerr-Stamm, p. 154). Invitations went far and wide throughout Pierre's domains, and the partying lived on in local report as a scandalous affair (Paravicini, p. 137). Scandal will exaggerate, of course, but it does seem that some of the high jinks were high indeed, and that the lads got very drunk and did some very laddish things (cf. Claerr-Stamm, p. 154).[27] The nuptials certainly show Pierre to have been in a state of triumphant elation which provides further testimony to both his ability to enter into the role of lover or bridegroom and to find some success in this area.

If the last letter does herald G's death, it would simply reinforce the strong sense one is left with of the fated transience of human affairs. A state of things that seemed so intense and solid vanished suddenly without warning. The moral Chaucer drew from his *Troilus* was that love – an experience the most treasured and powerful and one which elicits protestations and convictions that it is 'forever' and is indestructible – does after all share in the tragic finiteness of all human affairs: it, like all things in this world, 'passeth soone as floures faire' (V.1841). The love and the world of Pierre and Gayrrie, so intensely present to both and so vividly present to the reader who follows it in the letters, was soon to disappear 'swa hit no wære' [as if it had never been], as the Anglo-Saxon elegists put it, speaking of love (*Wife's Lament* 24) as of other things (*Wanderer* 96). The all-engrossing affair and its attendant preoccupations, and possibly G herself, were evidently soon to be over.

Equally without warning, Pierre himself, and the solid and secure success and the rude health he seemed to enjoy, would likewise be gone within two years, when the jolly bridegroom of January became the wretch executed in May. And the geo-political entity of Burgundy that had formed and defined the existence of the two was virtually over, again without warning, in four years. The modern type of historical analysis represented by school essays on 'The Causes of ...' seems in this case less appropriate than what the medieval world, and G herself (see II.8), saw as the chief determining factor in historical processes and outcomes: the turns of Fortune's wheel. Gabrielle Claerr-Stamm entitles that section of her biography devoted to events preceding Pierre's execution (pp. 121ff.) 'L'inexorable chute de Pierre de Hagenbach'.

---

[27] This should be seen in the context of fifteenth-century marriage celebrations between persons of rank: to these occasions a tone and focus more frankly sexual than romantic was felt to be appropriate, to a degree that can seem lascivious and crude to modern readers; see, for instance, Willard's comments on Froissart's account of the marriage festivities of Charles VI and Deschamps's poem on the marriage of a son of the Duke of Burgundy (*Christine*, p. 81).

But in truth the postulated 'inevitability' seems more like hindsight. The end was not foreseeable until it was imminent.

Claerr-Stamm points out that the charges brought against him at his trial involved almost exclusively very recent events (p. 177). In fact, bludgeoning in manner and speech though Pierre had often been felt to be, his rule over the years 1470–4 was not accompanied by any such extraordinary massacres or physical brutality, and did not until the last moment cause such violent or concerted opposition as might herald what was to come (cf. Claerr-Stamm, p. 202). His difficulties were in large part financial and administrative. The territories he had taken on were left hopelessly disorganized and fragmented by many years of war, and their different components were mostly heavily mortgaged to a patchwork of different creditors and lordships. Especial problems were posed by Mulhouse, whose debts were particularly heavy, but which was allied with the Swiss, who made repeated efforts to redeem those debts in order to prevent Burgundy buying its way into power over the place. It was in connection with suchlike complications that Pierre suffered the brief captivity which caused G such alarm when she heard of it (VIII.10–11, IX.6). For, as one of the creditors of a fortress the Burgundians had possessed themselves of, his captor had been made an offer of compensation which he found unacceptable, and refused to release Pierre till the latter had agreed to a greater sum.[28] At any rate, during his first couple of years as *bailli* (the years covered by the present letters) Pierre had been largely engaged in the prosaic but demanding business of rescheduling debts, arranging redemptions, restoring a measure of order and setting up centralized institutions and systems of administration and justice – tasks which he addressed with some intelligence and success (see Claerr-Stamm, pp. 86–96, 97–104 and 111). But the towns did not, predictably, cooperate in the loss of their independent privileges and customs to the Burgundian control he was determined to impose, and discontent did break occasionally into open and violent insurrection. Pierre did execute the ringleaders of downright rebellions; and there was one unpopular tax (on wine) that caused especial resentment (Claerr-Stamm, p. 124). But such discontents were almost everyday occurrences in his time, and many rulers were much more extreme in their reactions to them. So it was not until well into 1474 – after confrontations with two or three towns in particular (notoriously, Swiss-allied Mulhouse, Breisach and Landser: see Vaughan, pp. 95–9) – that hostilities escalated to the point where Pierre sensed real

---

[28] Pierre was seized on his return from a journey to consult, and bearing the unsatisfactory offer from, Charles the Bold, according to Claerr-Stamm (*Pierre de Hagenbach*, p. 94), on his return from an embassy to Sigismund (see p. 348 and n. 13 above) according to Paravicini.

danger to his power and personal safety and appealed to Charles. But even then Charles was not immediately convinced that a few revolts in Alsatian towns heralded any inevitable complete loss of the region, let alone Pierre's death in the process, and he did not judge the situation dire enough to merit prioritizing (Claerr-Stamm, p. 159).

Nor does G herself mention any concern for his safety with respect to potential opposition in the territory he governed. Apart from the alarm caused her by news of his imprisonment (by she appears not to know what enemy), which she refers to in Letters VIII and IX, her anxieties about, and references to, his political and military life relate rather to Burgundian actions against France: the battle of Buxy at VIII.3 and at XI.5–6 Pierre's departure at the head of troops destined for the Somme in 1472.

France had seemed to Charles, too, the likeliest source of serious danger to himself and his Burgundian dominions. His defeats and setbacks in 1474–6 – at Murten, Grandson and Neuss, and in Lorraine – were essentially peripheral affairs, none of them likely or expected to strike at the heart of Burgundian power. The crisis came with his own unexpected death at the battle of Nancy. Since neither Charles nor Pierre were carpet knights, they were always likelier than many to die suddenly and not in their beds. But the when and the how of their deaths would always therefore be unpredictable and would resemble a stroke of Fortune. Pierre, who faced execution bravely (as even his enemies agreed: Claerr-Stamm, p. 188), had declared himself not unprepared for death, but unprepared for the manner of it, since he expected to die 'les armes à la main' (Claerr-Stamm, p. 186). To die by violence that cannot be resisted, out of armour and swordless, was a death all knights dreaded as derogatory to their status,[29] and in that respect Charles, who died on the field, was luckier than Pierre. But the death of a still active and relatively young man in his forties will always be unexpected, and that of Charles brought with it the end of Burgundy as his contemporaries knew it. For he died without male heirs, and the marriage in 1477 of his only daughter, Mary, to Maximilian, the son of the Hapsburg Emperor Frederick III, meant the end of the Burgundy Charles had defended and extended with such zealous commitment: the duchy itself passed into the power of the French, and the remainder of the territories became a base for Hapsburg power (Mary herself dying suddenly in 1482 after a fall from a horse). And with G's closing reference in her last letter to Antoine de Montreux (XI.8), who was by 1473 the husband of Pierre's daughter Marie, that next generation seems ready to succeed to the present one.

---

[29] Cf. "'Alas!' seyde sir Launcelot, "in all my lyff thus was I never bestad that I shulde be thus shamefully slayne, for lake of myne armour'": Malory, *Works*, ed. Vinaver, p. 676.

Burgundy had provided the seemingly permanent co-ordinates of the lovers' world. The ducal council at Dijon (VIII.6) must have been to G as much a fixture as the Houses of Parliament seem today. And there is also the reference by Jean de Vaudrey to a member of the powerful Neuchâtel family (V.6), major and famous players on the Burgundian stage, from whose ranks Charles typically chose all his district lieutenant generals. These familiar features of the Burgundian state emphasize the defining political context of the love affair. The intense realities of both the passion and its context were soon alike to disappear – like Troy and Troilus, for the reader inevitably brings his knowledge of the doom of that city to his reading of the hero's end. In the reader's similar knowledge of the imminent deaths of Pierre and of Charles the Bold, the same effect is created in G's last letter, as one senses the coming end of their love and of the Burgundian world they knew, in all its power, colour, wealth and solidity. The pair thus seem to join the list of other famous lovers of (hi)story, whose names provided Thomas of Hales with illustrations of the mortality shared by love and lovers with all things mortal: 'Hwer is paris & heleyne, / þat weren so bryht & feyre on bleo [face], / Amadas and dideyne [Idoine], / tristram, yseude and alle þeo ...? Heo beoþ i-glyden vt of þe reyne [they have passed imperceptibly out of this rainy world] / so þe schef is of þe cleo [as the sheaf has passed from the slope where it grew]'.[30]

*

There exists another link between G's letters and literary art – a connection less abstract and less fundamental, more precise and coincidental, and therefore more piquant. The *Concilium in Monte Romarici*, a twelfth-century Latin poem, takes the form of a mock church council held at Remiremont, on the question of the relative merits of knights and clerks as lovers. The theme was a popular one (see p. 253 above) and here forms the subject of a *concile d'amour*, such *questions d'amour* (amorous topics used as debating points) being a popular category of courtly love literature. The poem comes down in favour of clerks, and is plainly meant to come across partly as a witty reassurance given to the sisterhood by the clerks of the diocese as to their discretion, fidelity and gallantry as lovers. But centuries later Remiremont was, as we have seen, to prove the real setting for a real woman who had taken an *ami* from the opposing camp. When P voices suspicions that she may be detained at Remiremont by interest in another man, some priest or other (the category of male a canoness was most likely

---

[30] 'Friar Thomas de Hales' Love Ron': *English Lyrics of the Thirteenth Century*, ed. Carleton Brown (Oxford, 1932), 43.65–72.

to encounter), G is deeply offended that she should be suspected of a liaison with a class of person so totally without social standing (VII.8–9). Her indignation is plainly primarily social: she reacts as if she had been accused of an affair with the gardener. Had P suspected her with an archbishop, she would have defended herself with the same angry pride, no doubt, but not with such contempt for the class of the lover posited. P is a knight, and in status more than that, but above all he has that minimum qualification for honour and respectability that, in her eyes, qualifies him as an *ami* eligible for a lady of her status. And, in the same letter, she can remind him of the sacred honour of a knight that he would shame should he ever betray her confidence by revealing her love to anyone else (VII.15). This *dame* of Remiremont, then, assumed her *ami* should be and behave as a knight and was deeply shocked at the thought of a 'priest'. She thus thought somewhat differently from the ladies of the *Concilium*, who are full of praises for the discretion characteristically shown by clerks. The coincidental common factor of Remiremont thus reveals some discrepancy between the canoness and her earlier counterparts in literary art.

But the differences go much deeper than that. The earlier poem plays with the whole courtly conceit of a 'religion' of love, centred on a god and goddess of love, in this case wittily set off against the Christian religion the women have espoused and the Benedictine Rule they have committed themselves to observe. This notion of the religion of love is, as often with works that show its influence, treated partly with earnest seriousness, partly with conscious witty audacity, and the romantic priorities of the nuns are presented partly with seriousness, partly with amusement, in a spirit poised between gallant sentimentality and smiling anti-feminism. It is a world away from the stresses of the later canoness, struggling with serious problems of logistical and political realities in an affair with a lover who shows none of the suavity and discretion the poem attributes to clerical Romeos, and whom she is forced to rebuke for his lack of caution in communicating with her (I.9–11, VII.12). This is love in fact, not in theory, passion complicated by realities, desire by social and political practicalities.

Pierre, too, has an even more direct reflection in literary representation. But what emerges is even more evidently something created by the agenda of the writer rather than prompted by reality. For it is in chronicles composed by the opposing German-speaking camp who hated him so much that he and his deeds are recorded. The counterparts in literature of real persons like G and P (as represented in the nuns of the *Concilium* or the Pierre of the chronicles) may thus turn out to reveal more about the prejudices of the writer and/or the genre than about the relevant persons. But the texts at issue are given after the Letters, so that readers may reflect for themselves on the distortions possible in both poetic fictions and historical accounts, which have their own purposes and agendas to fulfil.

The Text

Our text is from the facsimiles of all the letters provided by Paravicini. The accents and cedillas are those which Paravicini supplied in his edition. Paravicini retained the internal numbering observed in previous scholarship, and we also have retained it, though we have corrected the occasional errors in his numbering. We also noted a few cases in which he had neglected to supply the editorial slash (/) used (by him and by us) to signal the end of a line in the MS. In one other minor detail, we have departed from his practice: MS 'qui' often represents 'qu'il', and where it does so he emends to read 'qu'i[l]'; but the absence of <l> is so frequent as to suggest a phonetic or accepted spelling, not an 'error' the scribe would have corrected had he noticed it; MS 'qui' is therefore here transcribed either 'qui' or 'qu'i'. Otherwise our transcription agrees almost entirely with his, though we occasionally punctuate a little differently.

I: TO PIERRE FROM THE CANONESS

A mon tres honoré seigneur / Monseigneur le Bailly

[1] Mon treshonoré seigneur et amy de mon ceur, [2] tant et si humblement comme je puis je me recom/mande a vostre bonne graice, sans laquelle je ne pouroye vivre, [3] vous tousiours remerciant / les gracieuses lettres que m'avés envoyé et tous les biens que me presentés. [4] Et de ce / que vous estes bien amerveilliés de ce que j'avoye ditz a Ymbert Gille / et comment je vous tenoye si laiche de couraige, [5] certe, mon amis, je vous prometz que / l'on m'avoit ditz, maix je n'ay garde de en rien croyre, car je scey bien que / vous ne donneriés, car, ce je n'avoye grant amour a vous, je ne vous en heusse rien / mander. [6] A regard que me mandés par Ymbert Gille de en aller en Bourgogne, [7] certe / je ne vous en sçaveroye rien mander jusques a tant que je aray ici ouyr nouvelle / de mon pere, car vous scavés que je n'oseroye partir sans son congier; et du / plus toust que je en saray nouvelle, je le vous manderer [8] – car je vous promés par ma / foy que le plus grant desir que j'aye en monde, c'est de parler a vous, car je suis celle / qui veult tousiours ce que vous voulrés. [9] Maix je vous prie, mon amy de / mon ceur, que, a moing comme vous pourés, que vous envoyés par de desay, car c'est / une grant charge pour moy et ne sçavés pais les maulx que j'en dure. / [10] Maix toutes fois que vous ilz envoyrés, n'envoyés point d'aultre que Ymbert / Gille, car je vous promés par ma foy qu'i fait tresbien son debvoir. Et ce prant / grant diligence pour vous, et si me semble qu'i vous aimme bien. [11] Je vous prometz / ce j'estoye en bon propos que ilz m'en feroit bien boutter feurt par ces parolles. / Maix je l'y a fait jurei et promettez qu'i seroit secrez, et je cuide que ainsy seroit ilz. / [12] Or scey, mon amis, vous me pouvés tousiours mander et commander tout ce que vous / voullés que je faisse, car vous sçavés que je feroye plus pour vous que pour homme / qui soit en moinde, et vouldroye que vous seussiens la grant amour verita/blement que j'ay en vous. [13] Et suis bien joyeuse, mon amy, que restetz en bonne / santei, car je avoye bien ouyr dire que vous estiens eust bien mal dispossei, dont / en estoye bien malcomptante. [14] Or say, mon amy, quelque foix, ce Dieu plait, / reconttrions de nous nouvelles plus a plain que ne vous sçaveroye rescripre. / [15] Et sur ce point je vous ditz 'a Dieu' sans 'adieu', mon tresdoulx amis de / mon ceur. [16] Escript en Palle Chaulx, le diemenche a soir bien tard.

[17] *manu propria* Mon ami de mon ceur, creés
Humbert de ce qu'i vos diray.
[18] *scribe's hand* La toute voustre et plus que voustre / leale Gayrrie

I: TO PIERRE FROM THE CANONESS

On the outside of the letter: To my right-honoured lord, my lord Bailiff

[1] My right-honoured lord and beloved of my heart, [2] as much and as humbly as I can do I commend myself to your good favour, without which I could not live, [3] ever thanking you for the gracious letters that you have sent me and all the nice things you present me with. [4] And in response to your saying that you are very surprised at what I told Humbert Gille, and at how I could consider you so mean at heart: [5] certainly, my beloved, I promise you that was what I heard – but I have no inclination to believe a word of it, for I know well that you would not make such a gift, and if I had not had great love for you, I would not have sent you anything. [6] With regard to your sending me word by Humbert Gille that I should come to you in Burgundy, [7] I certainly would not be able to send you any reply until I have heard from my father, for you know that I would not venture to depart without his leave; and as soon as I have such news, I shall send you word of it – [8] for I promise you by my faith that the greatest desire I have in the world is to speak with you personally, for I only ever want whatever you want. [9] But I pray you, beloved of my heart, that you send as infrequently as possible to me over here, for it puts a great burden on me, and you do not know the trouble it causes me. [10] But whenever you do send, never send by anyone other than Humbert Gille, for I promise you by my faith that he does his duty as a messenger very well. And he is scrupulous on your behalf, and it seems to me that he is very loyal to you. [11] I promise you that it even seemed to me that he would blow the gaff on me by delivering his message. But I have sworn him to secrecy, and I believe that he will keep his promise. [12] Now you know, my beloved, that you can always send commandments to me to do whatever you wish, for you know that I would do more for you than for any other man in the world, and I wish you knew veritably how great is the love I have for you. [13] And I am rejoiced, my beloved, to hear that you remain in good health, for I had indeed heard that you were indisposed, which gave me great distress. [14] Now I am sure, beloved, that at some time, God willing, we will meet to exchange news more plainly than I know how to give you in writing. [15] And on this note, I say 'God be with you', but not 'goodbye', my sweetest beloved of my heart. [16] Written in Palle Chaulx, late Sunday evening.

[17] *sender's own hand* My beloved of my heart, trust what Humbert will add verbally.

[18] *scribe's hand* Your own, and more than your own, faithful Gayrrie.

NOTES TO LETTER I

The scribe is the same as that who writes Letters II and VII. The letters in this series were all folded several times and sewn up, as was common practice (see p. 55 above). The name of the addressee occurs on the outside of the folded whole, and, since it was visible, normally contains only Pierre's official title, without the endearments that occur in the letter proper (a rule to which Letters VIII and IX form, however, partial exceptions). The 'bailly' of a district was the overlord or governor nominated by whoever claimed sovereignty over the area (in this case, Charles the Bold of Burgundy).

3 On the gifts or tokens that often accompanied love letters, cf. Text 4, I.24, II.54–62, Cely Letter 54 (p. 28 above) and Humfrey Newton XI (p. 26 above).

4 Humbert Gille is mentioned also at II.6 and VI.3, 5. He is plainly in the employ of P: G is here responding to a letter from P which Humbert has brought and to which he evidently waits for and carries back a reply. See also n. to 10–11 below.

5 Depending on the interpretation of *en ... mander*, the reference is apparently either to (a) some gift that G has heard P has given (to another woman?) – though she says she did not really believe he would do so and would not have sent the rallying message if she had not loved him, or (b) to some gift she gave him (since the pair plainly do exchange tokens) which she says she has too much regard for him to believe he would give away (though she has heard something that indicates he has) and would not have sent without such regard.

6–7 G's letter is principally structured by response to what came from P, in the way of gifts or points raised in his letter and/or verbal messages accompanying it (cf. 3 and 4). Her father plainly knows of and countenances her liaison with P, which suggests he was, politically, a supporter of the Burgundian side in the conflict between Burgundy and its neighbours.

8 G fears that her reluctance to make the journey without the sanction of her father may be interpreted as her being only lukewarm in her love for P; she therefore hastens to add the reassurance that to speak with P is her foremost desire. Love letters often lament the speech they are treated as a poor substitute for (cf. *Poetry of Charles d'Orléans*, Ballades 20, 21 and 47): compare I.14, II.8, VII.16.

9 G presumably refers to the difficulties of receiving a letter and/or messenger without arousing the notice and curiosity of those around her (and implicitly asks P to take more trouble in weighing the delicacy of her position against his own desire to communicate his passion). Though several members of the community at Remiremont are obviously aware of her liaison (see pp. 353–4 above), it is clearly not public knowledge, and there may have been political as well as social reasons for discretion: Remiremont evidently has an anti-Burgundian faction (see Letter VIII.10), and it might not be advisable for G to be publicly connected with the chief general of the Burgundian forces.

10–11 Humbert is in the employ of P, and G plainly feels that he is more scrupulous about executing his mission from his master (to deliver the letter) than he is about delivering it discreetly so as to shield her from notice and suspicion. But her complaint takes the form of a wry compliment on his loyalty to his master: he was so zealous in executing his commission from P that he nearly let the cat out of the bag with regard to her (the expression *bouter fors* in 11 is plainly a colloquialism whose precise sense is not clear). Throughout the letter, the voice is that of a woman not overawed by the love of a man of rank who is used to being obeyed and is an importunate lover who may be more ardent than considerate. She holds her ground and her independence with charm, affection and wit: her thanks for his gifts are not fulsome; she cannot undertake such a journey as he proposes without the sanction of her father (whose protection she both needs and plainly values, and who might be more alive to the risks – to her reputation and, in the political circumstances, to her safety – than her lover is) and insists on waiting to hear from him; and she would be grateful if her lover showed a little more consideration of her difficulties in his communications, and would make them less frequent and instruct his messenger to consult her best interests as well as those of his master.

12 G is obviously excusing or feeling guilty about an order she is *not* obeying (to come to Burgundy). In the sentence-opening formula *Or scey*, 'scey' is second person singular imperative (cf. II.5), despite the *vous* forms (the plural of respect) which G, in common with most lovers, otherwise uses; cf. Charles d'Orléans, Ballade 48, 'Bien sçay, mon cueur, que faulx Dangier / *Vous* fait mainte paine souffrir' (17–18), translated as 'Myn hert, thou wost ...').

13 *eust* appears to be an error that should have been deleted, according to Paravicini.

14 Cf. 8 above and note.

15 G here (as also at the end of Letter II) plays on the strict sense of *a Dieu* [(I commend you) to God] and the broader one [goodbye] to indicate she neither wants nor intends real 'closure', and so gives some grace and charm to her sign-off.

16 This is the only one of G's letters to give a place of writing other than Remiremont, but we do not know the whereabouts of Palle Chaulx or whether it was near R. See Paravicini, pp. 110–11 for speculations and possibilities – including the one that MS 'en palle chaulx' might mean 'in warm wraps' (which would indicate the writer had needed extra warmth, if it is winter, in order to stay up to write the letter at a time when she could be sure of privacy). It is also possible, I suppose, that it refers to some chamber or room in R. In her love letters (as opposed to those from *nous*), G characteristically gives as the time only the day of the week and the time of day: Tuesday in Letter II, though Sunday (here and in Letters VI and VII, as also in VIII, which is from *nous*) seems to be the day most commonly chosen for writing these confidential letters; 'late' here, but otherwise early in the morning (Letters II, VI, VII) – presumably, that is, either before or after the convent was stirring. Precise dates (and places) are likewise not given in the *Epistolae duorum amantium*, though they too may indicate time of day ('Cum dies in noctem vergeret ...': *Vir* 17), which was not uncommon in non-love letters,

where, however, it was usually combined with day of month and often year: cf. 'From the camp by Neuss, at four hours after dark, 19 March 1475' in the dispatch sent by the Milanese ambassador, Panigarola, from the siege of Neuss by Charles the Bold (see Vaughan, p. 332). That day of week and time of day alone are, in the present instance, a substitute style of dating (used in the love letters) is suggested by the fact that no time of day occurs in the only three of G's letters that give day of the month: 17 August, the Sunday of the Assumption, and 19 August, day of the week unspecified (in Letters VIII, from *nous*, and IX respectively), and 1 September 1472, day of week unspecified, in the last letter (XI, from *nous*), which is the only one to give a precise calendar date – though one of her clerk's letters to her also gives the year (1470: IV.17).

17 For these kinds of supplementary verbal messages vouched for by the sender as entrusted to the bearer, cf. III.9 and see above pp. 51–2. G writes this concluding vouchment in her own hand, which also occurs in the signature to VI – and which proves she could write (the hand is small but neat), despite employing a scribe, as did most women (along with both males and females of high rank), since, though not usually illiterate, they did not write often enough to do so with speed or ease (see pp. 54–7). The subscription was in any case often the only part of a letter written in its 'author's' own hand, and served to authenticate the written and/or spoken message (see Constable, *Letters and Letter-Collections*, pp. 17–18).

18 Paravicini notes (p. 127) that the subscription formula 'la plus que vostre' (cf. VI.9, IX.12) is also used in the same era by Marie de Valois in letters to her husband at the beginning of their marriage (i.e. in the transition period from sweetheart to spouse): *Lettres de Marie de Valois, fille de Charles VII* ..., ed. P. Marchegay (La Roche-sur-Yon, 1875), Letters 1–8 (1458–60). 'Gayrrie' may be a diminutive of the name 'Margaret' (see p. 341 above).

II: TO PIERRE FROM THE CANONESS

A mon treshonoré seigneur / Monseigneur le Bailly / de Fairette

[1] Mon treshonoré seigneur et mon amy de mon ceur, [2] tant et sy humblement comme / je puis je me recommande a vostre bonne graice, sans laquelle je ne / pouroye vivre. [3] Je vous prometz par ma foye que, ce je sçavoye que je fuisse / feurt de voustre graice, je cuide que je moroye de deulx. [4] Car vous / pouhés bien sçavoir, mon amis, que je ne desire chouse en ce moinde / que vous, car vous estes ma joye, ma liesse et tant que j'ayme en / moinde. [5] Or sçay, mon amis, j'anvoye cedit pourteur par devers vous / pour sçavoir de vous nouvelles et pour vous rescripre des myennes. [6] Pourtant que j'avoye dit a Ymbert Gille que je vous rescripré ce / je m'an alloye en Bourgongne, [7] vuellés sçavoir, mon amis, mon / pere m'etz rescript une lettre laquelle ditz qu'i ne veult point que / me partez d'icy tant qu'il me manderay. De quoy je suis bien / desplaisante. Maix je n'y scaveroye metre remyde, maix que tant qu'i nous fault avoir pacience. [8] Sur mon ayme, je voy / bien que Fortune nous court sus de tout part, car nous ne / pouhons parler emsemble. Maix, ce Dieu plait, Fortune tour/neray sa ruez une foix, a l'aide de Dieu et de la voustre, / que nous i parlerons malgrey les ennuyeulx. [9] Helais, / mon amy, vous pouhés bien pancer que j'ay grant desir et / grant voulloir de vous veor. Et quant je pance a la / grant joye et la grant liesse que je y aray une foix quant / je vous voyrei, je prie que ce soit cy toust comme mon ceur / le desire. Je en suis peulz reconffortee en mes dolleurs, assés / ung peultz. Je sçay bien, mon amis, que ce ne seray pais / cy toust comme nous voulriens tous deux. [10] Mon amis de / mon ceur, j'a ditz a madame la / Secreste que j'en envoye par devers [vous], / laquelle vous rescript une lettre, car je ne veult pais que / le messaigier ce reclame de partz moy, maix de madame la / Secreste. Et vous remercie bien tous les biens qu'elle me fait, / car je voy bien qu'elle prant grant painne de moy complaire / pour l'amour de vous. [11] Mon amis de mon ceur, mon desir et / tant que j'ayme en monde, je vous envoye ung petit / chapeaulx duquel je vous prie que veullés pourter pour / l'amour de moy. Je sçay bien, mon amis, qu'i [n'est] pais telz comme / ilz apartient a vous, maix de petit mercyer de / petit pegnier. Certe, mon amis, je l'eusse bien

---

7 point] *inserted above the line; a letter struck through before* nous fault   8 i] *Paravicini;* ilz   9] mon ceur] *see note*   10 devers vous] devers *MS and Paravicini*   11 qu'i n'est] *Paravicini;* qui   maix] *followed by* tout faux *deleted*

II: TO PIERRE FROM THE CANONESS

On the outside of the letter: To my right-honoured lord, my lord the Bailiff of Ferrette

[1] My right-honoured lord and my heart's beloved, [2] as much and as humbly as I can do I commend myself to your good favour, without which I could not live. [3] I promise you by my faith that, if I knew that I was out of your favour, I would die of grief. [4] For you must know, my beloved, that you are the only thing in the whole world that I desire, for you are my joy, my happiness and all that I love in the world. [5] Now, my beloved, I am sending this bearer to you so that I may learn news of you and likewise write my own to you. [6] Although I told Humbert Gille to tell you that I would write again if I was coming down to Burgundy, [7] I must tell you, my beloved, that my father has written to me a letter which says that he does not at all wish me to leave here until he sends word. About this I am truly unhappy. But I know of no remedy other than that we should be patient. [8] On my soul, I see well that Fortune assails us on all sides, so that we are not able to speak personally to one another. But, God willing, Fortune will turn her wheel one day, with God's aid and yours, so that we will speak together despite those who frustrate our wishes. [9] Alas, my beloved, you will well know that I have great desire and wish to see you. And when I think of the great joy and the great happiness that I shall have one day when I do see you, I pray that this may be as soon as my heart wishes it. I am in this thought a little comforted in my troubles – a very little. I know well, my beloved, that the peace will not come as soon as we both would wish. [10] My heart's beloved, I have told my lady the sacristan that I am writing to you, and she will also write you a letter, for I do not wish the messenger to announce himself as coming from me, but from my lady the sacristan. And I am very grateful to you for all the favours she does me, for I see clearly that she takes great pains to oblige me for your sake. [11] My heart's beloved, you who are my desire and all that I love in this world, I am sending you a little hat, which I pray you to wear for my sake. I know well, my beloved, that it is not such as would be fitting for you, but from small means comes a small basketful. Indeed, beloved, I would have made it better, but I wanted to add a colour in remembrance of you amongst the other

fait meilleur, / maix j'a voulus metre de vous couleur entre les autres / couleurs: j'a mis doubleur qui pourte loyaultei en segni/fiant que tout[e] ma vie vous seray loyaule. Et vous prie, / mon treschier et bien amei, que le veullés porter pour l'amour / de moy, en moy tenant louyaltei, et, ce ne veullés tenir / loyaultei, que ne veullés pourter. [12] Et sur ce point je vous ditz 'a Dieu' sanz 'adieu'. [13] Escript hatierement ce mardi bien matin.

11 j'a ... j'a] j'a[i] ... j'a[i] *Paravicini*   couleur] couleurs *Paravicini*   toute] *Paravicini;* tout   le vuellés porter] porter *follows* pourter *deleted*

colours: I have put a lining of that colour which signifies truth, in betokening that I will be faithful to you as long as I live – and I pray you, my most dear and well-loved one, that you consent to wear it, out of love for me, for as long as you keep faith with me too, and, if you no longer choose to keep faith, that you should not wear it. [12] And on this note, I say 'God be with you', but not 'goodbye'. [13] Written in haste very early this Tuesday morning.

NOTES TO LETTER II

The scribe is the same as the one responsible for Letters I and VII. On the outside, at right angles to the address, another fifteenth-century hand, 'selon toute vraisemblance celle de Hagenbach lui même' (Paravicini, p. 114), has written 'memore de une letre de recomandasyon et madame de Masonval'. This once led to assumptions that 'madame de Masonval' was the name of the sender of the letter (the canoness), but, as Paravicini remarks (p. 114), there is no reason to assume that the name has any more relevance to the letter than the words 'letre de recomandasyon', which do not describe its nature or contents. The endorsement is either a memorandum of another matter for which the present letter has provided a convenient surface, or it has been written in error on the wrong letter.

1-4 Cf. Letter I.1-2, where G similarly develops the standard letter-opening *commendatio* into something more earnest and loverlike (her adaptation of both opening and closing formulae in these two letters having a degree of stylishness). The reinforcement of the sentiment by the added sentences at II.3-4 is obviously intended to counter in advance any doubts about her commitment P might feel in hearing she will not be coming to Burgundy, as he had pressed her to do (I.6). These sentences replace what would normally follow the *commendatio* if the sender were replying to a letter from the addressee: i.e. acknowledgement of and response to the message and/or things received (cf. I.3). But G is not here, as in Letter I, replying to P – and for that reason the carrier of choice, Humbert Gille (I.10), is not available as bearer, for he is in the employ of P (not of G, as stated in Paravicini's note to II.6), and so could carry G's previous letter only because he had brought to her a letter from P (I.10-11, 17).

3 For *feurt* [=*fors*], cf. I.11.

5 The bearer is evidently not P's servant Humbert, as G is here initiating, not responding to, a letter (see note 1-4). She writes so that they can exchange 'news', she says – an indication that they will not be able to do so face to face, and that she will not be making the journey to Burgundy.

6 The verbal messages G had sent via UG along with her previous letter (see 1.17) obviously included one to the effect that she would write again if she was going to make the journey down to Burgundy. Hence the concessive clause: 'Although' P might therefore assume a letter from her would herald that journey, the present one is actually to notify him that she cannot come.

7 G had said she must wait to hear whether her father would consent to the proposed journey to Burgundy (I.6-7): his response has now arrived and is unfavourable. His objections are evidently on the grounds of the safety rather than the propriety of the trip, since it is 'peace' that G assumes will remove the obstacles to a meeting with P (II.9). He has in fact forbidden her to go anywhere until he sends word. When she does travel, it is under the escort of her clerk, who appears to have been taking her and her sister on a Christmas visit to his house (and

perhaps to their father: see Letter III). It is worth noting that G utters no word of impatience against her father, whose judgement she evidently trusts and respects. In the face of his ban, she recommends only *pacience* as a recourse, i.e. waiting for the 'peace' that she assumes will remove the grounds for his objections. But she has enough independence and address not only to counter her lover's wishes by an insistence on deference to her father, but also in due course to disobey that father (as Letters III and IV, from her clerk, imply she does) whilst avoiding a rift with him.

8 For lovers separated by political and military conflict (want of 'peace': see II.9), it is to Fortune (as opposed to evil tongues, jealousy, etc.) that their miseries are regularly ascribed. Charles, grieving at the political situation and national hostilities that separate him from his wife, likewise blames chiefly a personified adverse Fortune (see especially B40), who wages war on him (41.9), and who, in a particularly close parallel to G's wording here, 'me vient assaillir / De tous costez' (42.14–15). And he, too, assumes that, where Fortune is foe, the only course open is patience (cf. 7 here), waiting for her wheel to turn (39.21–2, 41.7) and finding friends in Hope and Joyous Thought (cf. 9). For the common image of Fortune's wheel used in such a context, cf. *Troilus* IV.6–11; in that poem, too, the separation of the lovers is caused by politics and war and so is likewise ascribed to the agency of Fortune (IV.1–5, 260–87). G's analysis of the situation, that is, shows the influence of love poetry. The coupling of divine and human agency in such expressions as 'with God's aid and yours' or 'thanks to God and you' (cf. X.5) was a formulaic device on which variations could be played (cf. Charles d'Orléans, *Poetry*, Ballade 14.25), and here contributes to the overall impression of a writer who is articulate and can express herself with grace and clarity. 'speak together': cf. Letter I.8 and note.

9 *mon* in the second sentence, is, interestingly, inserted above the line and follows both a deleted *vostre* and (also above the line) a deleted *nostre*: G evidently wanted to indicate that her compliance with her father's will was not due to her ardour being less than P's, and so progressively changed 'your' to 'our' and then to 'my' – the change being evidently due to the dictator's revision rather than the scribe's correction of an error he has made (such as the insertion above the line in the next sentence of *suis* [am], which is needed for sense). On the 'peace' that G assumes will enable the two to meet, see n. to II.7 above.

10 In the first sentence, *vous* is not supplied by Paravicini, but the prepositional phrase *envoyer par devers* seems to require a following (pro)noun (cf.II.5 above). The point is that the bearer (who, unlike Humbert, is probably not in the know) must appear to come from someone else – the sacristan, who at this date was almost certainly Charlotte de Montjustin, a relative of P on his mother's side (see Claerr-Stamm, p. 25, Paravicini, p. 123, n. 93), who (like P's mother and like many of the canonesses) came from the Franche-Comté area of Burgundy. See further n. to VIII.14. As a relative of P, Charlotte could obviously write to him without attracting suspicion. Since she knows of G's letter and agrees to G's proposal that it should be borne under cover of a letter from herself, and treats G

with special favour for P's sake, she was obviously aware of the liaison and does not disapprove of it. Many incumbents of the abbey (where both P and G had relatives and friends) had Burgundian affiliations and might therefore have been neither ignorant nor censorious of G's affair: see pp. 353-4 above. The duties of a sacristan are described by Abelard in his directions for Heloise's abbey (Radice, Letter 7, p. 214): she acted as treasurer and was responsible for the maintenance of sacred valuables, fixtures and fittings (vessels, the clock, bells, etc.).

11 On the gift-tokens exchanged by the lovers, cf. I.3 and note. G depreciates her own with modesty and style by quoting the proverb *Petit mercier, petit panier* (see Paravicini, p. 130, n. 129), whose sense is roughly the equivalent of 'beggars can't be choosers'. In the phrase *metre de vous couleur*, I have not emended to 'couleur[s]', as does Paravicini, who assumes a reference to P's heraldic colours; for what follows indicates that G is referring to the colour blue by which she has supplemented an existing colour scheme, blue being the colour of fidelity (cf. *CT* V.644-5). This could, however, be interpreted as a separate point from what precedes the colon (which, in such case, should be replaced by a semicolon), and if the latter does refer to P's 'official' colours, then these might be those of his livery (the brown, grey and white in which his soldiers were dressed on the occasion of his marriage in 1474: see Claerr-Stamm, p. 154), rather than the heraldic gules and silver of the Hagenbach arms (quartered from 1473 on, after his mother's death, with the azure-and-silver arms of Belmont: see Claerr-Stamm, p. 148).

12 G ends with the same play on 'adieu' as in Letter I.15, and follows it with the same minimal dating. But as the sheet is now completely full, there is no space for any signature or anything else in her own hand she might otherwise have wished to add.

13 On G's concluding dates, see n. to I.16. Her haste may be due to the need to consign the letter to the sacristan's bearer before the latter departs (cf. III.9), though both the haste and the early hour may be in order to conceal from notice the production and handing over of the missive.

III: TO THE CANONESS FROM HER CLERK

A ma treshonnoree ma dame / la boursiere en le noble / eglise de Remiremont

[1] Ma treshonnoree: [2] cent mil milions de recommendacions premises. [3] Il me semble qu'il a plus / de .C. mil ans que partites d'icy. Pleut a Dieu que y fuissies a present. [4] Les charretons / qui vous en menerent ne m'ont dit quelconque nouvelle de vous. Je ne sçay se estes / morte ou vive ou se vous m'avés si tost oblié. Il me semble qu'il vous souvient / de moy quant vous me veés. [5] Ma dame vostre suer et voz chamberierez et tout vostre / mainnage est en bon point, Dieu l'y vuelle maintenir et acroistre tousjours de / bien en mieulx, aussi je l'ay au cuer comme le mien propre. [6] Ma dame, vous sçavés / que m'avés dit par plusieurs fois et que je vous ay dit aussi, et darrenierement / a vostre departement fuit encore dit: soies ferme en vostre bon propos. [7] Je vous / supplie, ma dame, que, comme je vous ay desja escript par mon frere, vuelliés dire voz / heures tousiours bien et devotement, et que ne lez laxés pour chose qu'aiés affaire; / [8] au sourplus, que gardez vostre honneur, affin que n'aiés cause d'estre reprinse / de Dieu ne du monde. [9] Le porteur de cestes est tant hatis que je n'ay / pas le temps de vous ecripre plus amplement. Il vous dira toutes nouvelles / de pardeça. [10] Je prie a Nostre Seigneur qu'i vous doint accroissement en honneur et / toutes vertus et graice de bien briefment retourner, car certe je le desire / bien. [11] Escript treshastivement ce matin de Noel.

        [12] Vostre treshumble clerc de / la bourse, tout en vostre commandement

---

7 lez] *inserted above line*

III: TO THE CANONESS FROM HER CLERK

On the outside of the letter: To my most honoured lady, bursaress at the noble church of Remiremont

[1] My right honoured lady: [2] a hundred thousand million commendations [of myself to you], in the first place. [3] It seems to me a hundred thousand years since you left here. Would to God that you were here now. [4] The waggoners who conveyed you have given me no news of you. I know not if you are alive or dead, or if [the silence is because] you have quite forgotten about me. I think you remember me [only] when you see me. [5] My lady your sister and your attendants and all your staff are in good health, and may God continue and increase it from good to better even as it is as dear to me as my own. [6] My lady, you know what you have declared to me several times, and what I have said to you, and, most recently, was said at your departure: stand by all your good intentions. [7] I beg you, my lady, as I have done already when I wrote to you via my brother, that you will please always say your hours well and devoutly, and that you do not relax this rule for any business you may have on hand; [8] and, in addition, that you guard your honour so that you have no reason to be rebuked by God or by the world. [9] The bearer of this letter is in such haste that I have no time to write to you more fully. He will give you all the news from here. [10] I pray Our Lord that He grant you increase in honour and in all virtues and the good fortune of a speedy return, for I certainly much desire it. [11] Written in great haste this Christmas morning.

[12] Your most humble clerk, your clerk of the bursary, wholly at your command.

NOTES TO LETTER III

G was evidently the bursaress or treasurer at Remiremont, an office to which an assistant clerk was attached. This and the following letter are written to G by that clerk (who signs himself Nicolas at the end of the second letter). From the tone of the letters, he must also have been an older man and a family friend who had known her well for some time. For, although he signs off as her inferior, his tone is avuncular: the reproach at her having forgotten about him (4) and the admonitions to 'be a good girl' while away, behave properly and say her prayers (6–8) could only come from long familiarity and seniority in years. It emerges from the next letter that he lived at Bruyères (IV.9, 18), a little to the north-east of Remiremont in the same *département* of Les Vosges. He had evidently escorted to his house both her and her sister (who seems also to have been an inmate of Remiremont: cf. IV.11) for Christmas, perhaps so that they could proceed to their father, who may well have lived in the same area as this evidently old family friend (but see notes to IV.10 and 11). But N (who gives Christmas morning as the date of this letter) refers to her departure from himself and her sister, and it seems plain that G had taken advantage of an escorted (and therefore unsuspicious) exit from Remiremont to proceed, not to her father, but to Burgundy and P. For, since N's letters to her were found among the archives of P along with those from her to P, they must have been delivered to her there. Further corroboration of this journey to P is provided by her father's anger, referred to in the next letter (IV.8), which would be a natural reaction at learning that G had undertaken the journey he had forbidden. N's undertaking to help G appease this wrathful parent (IV.12) is another indication of an acquaintance with the father and his family that is evidently of long standing. The hand of this letter, written from N's home, is different from any of those responsible for G's letters, but is the same as that of N's next letter, which was written from Remiremont; the scribe must therefore have been N himself or someone in his employ.

4 G was evidently conveyed to her own destination by vehicles which returned to the area of Bruyères, and whose drivers were solicitously questioned by N about G's safe arrival, etc. His complaint that she has left him not knowing even if she is alive and evidently forgets him as soon as she is out of his sight sounds affectionately mock reproachful rather than seriously offended.

5 When 'sister' refers to a fellow inmate of Remiremont, the term is generally followed by a name. The reference here must be to a blood sister, which would explain why the two were travelling together to the same destination (and perhaps on to the family home) at Christmas. G had obviously been accompanied also by her entourage.

6–8 An endearing passage. N is evidently in G's confidence, knows about the trip and its destination (though her father does not, and N is evidently complicit in the concealment of it from him), and does not rebuke her for it, but simply tells her to take care (while out of the supervision he and her father probably regarded as in some sense *in loco parentis*) to do nothing damaging to her good name and to be regular in her religious observances.

7 N evidently had a brother whose business took him to where G was, and N had entrusted to him a letter to G in which he had already urged her to be regular in saying her hours, a matter evidently more important to him than any risk to her chastity involved in the trip to P. What happened to this letter (and whether or not it reached G) we cannot tell: it was not (as one might assume that it would be) found along with the letters G received from N at what must have been the same address and at roughly the same time. The 'hours' were the readings prescribed for the canonical hours, which would have been read or recited by all religious (as also by a number of pious persons in secular life).

8 'by God or by the world': references to honour/dishonour in this world and the next were common.

9 Such apologies for haste because the bearer is ready to depart are common. This bearer has evidently been entrusted with supplementary verbal messages for whose authenticity the sender here vouches (cf. I.17).

IV: TO THE CANONESS FROM HER CLERK

A ma treshonnoree dame / ma dame la boursierre /en la noble eglise de Remiremont

[1] Ma dame la boursiere, [2] je me recommande a vous. [3] Il a long temps que je ne vous vy. [4] Messire Gerart, / pourteur de cestes, m'a dit aulcunes choses depart vostre noble personne. [5] Tout ce qu'il m'a dit / j'ay acomply de bon cuer de mon petit povoir. [6] Vous sçavés, ma dame, que je suis vostre a vendre, / donner et engagier et en toutes les manieres que on pourroit dire pour acomplir tous voz / bons commandemens. [7] De couvrechiefz n'y a point ehu icy depuis ledit Messier Gerart venu, / mais s'il en vient, on en fera debvoir. [8] Ma dame, il me desplait grandement de ce que / monseigneur vostre pere est mal content de vostre allee. [9] Je revin vandredi de Bruyères, ou j'ay / esté pour le Noel. [10] Si tost que je fuis descendu, je m'en ally veoir en vostre noble maison, / en la quelle il avoit ung messaigier envoié depart mondit seigneur vostre pere, qui avoit apourtée / des lettres. [11] Ma dame Catherine et moy leumes lesdictes lettres, et avons rescript a mondit seigneur / vostre pere en vous excusant. [12] En conclusion, je sçay que, quant verrés lesdictes lettres, / vous meismes serés desplaisant de vostre allee, et non sens cause. Vous et moy, / nous faudra fort estudier pour en faire la pais. [13] Ma dame, vous sçavés / ce que m'avés dit et que je vous ay dit; je sçay bealcop de choses depuis vostre / departement. Neanmoins s'il ne tient a vous, jamais ne vous faudray, pour / lengue qui en saiche parler, ne pour homme ne femme qui vive. Je / vous serés leal, ferme et constant, par ainsi que le soiés aussi de / vostre cousté – je ne vous prie d'aultre chose. [14] Au sourplus, ma dame, je vous envoie mon cheval: / faictes en tout ce qu'il vous plaira, ne l'apargnés point, car il debvient / truant et est aussi fort ou plus qui fuit oncques. Le cheval vous puelt bien / servir, car le maistre vous serviroit volentier, et servira, qui que en groingne. [15] Quant / vous serés icy a l'ayde de Nostre Seigneur, je vous diray dez choses que seroient longues / a escripre. [16] Ma dame, je prie a Nostre Seigneur Qu'i vous doint sa paix, son amour et / sa grace, et en la fin de voz pechiés pardoint vous faice. [17] Escript le / second jour de l'an lxx.

[18] Voz petit clerc et humble serviteur / N. de Bruyeres, clerc de la bourse

11 excusant] *followed by* que *deleted*   13 constant] *followed by* que *deleted*   17] second] *follows* premier *deleted*

IV: TO THE CANONESS FROM HER CLERK

On the outside of the letter: To my right honoured lady, my lady bursaress of the noble church of Remiremont.

[1] My lady bursaress, [2] I commend myself to you. [3] It has been some time since I saw you. [4] The reverend Gerard, the bearer of this present letter, has told me various things on behalf of your noble self. [5] All that he said I have done with goodwill and to the utmost of my small ability. [6] You know, my lady, that I am your man, to sell, give or mortgage, and in all ways one could name, and so an instrument to carry out your respected commissions. [7] As to kerchiefs, there haven't been any available here since the reverend Gerard's arrival, but if any come, I will dutifully obey your wishes with regard to them. [8] My lady, I am much distressed (to tell you) that my lord your father is ill pleased at the journey you made. [9] I came back on Friday from Bruyères, where I spent Christmas. [10] As soon as I had alighted, I went to your noble residence, where there was a messenger, sent from my lord your father, who had brought a letter. [11] My lady Catherine and I read the said missive, and we wrote back to my lord your father excusing you. [12] In conclusion, I know that, when you see the said writings, you yourself will regret your journey, and not without cause. We must, you and I together, put our minds to making your peace with him. [13] My lady, you know what you said to me and what I said to you; but I have learned many things since your departure. Nevertheless, if he will not stand by you, I will never fail you, for any words anyone can say to me, nor for any man or woman alive. I will be loyal, staunch and constant, provided that you, on your side, are as well – that's all I ask of you. [14] In addition, my lady, I'm sending you my horse: use him as you please, do not spare him, for he is becoming able to be used for draft work and is as strong or more as ever any was. Apt will it be that the horse should serve you well, for his master would most willingly serve you, and will serve you, whoever may snarl as a result. [15] When, with the aid of God, you are back here, I will tell you things that it would take too long to write out. [16] My lady, I pray to Our Lord that He grant you His peace, His love and His grace, and give you at your end-day pardon for your sins. [17] Written on the second day of the year '70.

[18] Your little clerk and humble servant, N de Bruyères, clerk of the bursary.

386   Actual Letters

NOTES TO LETTER IV

The hand is the same as for Letter III (to which see preliminary note).

4 *Messire* indicates a priest. Priests named Gerard are recorded among the twelve canons who at any one time served the chapter *in spiritualibus* (see Paravicini's note). *Messire Gerart* has been used as a bearer of news and messages from G and is available as bearer to N because he is to return to that same area. If he does hail from Remiremont (rather than from G's present presumably Burgundian whereabouts), it appears that he may have accompanied G on her journey. N's present (second) letter is dated 2 January, so a week has passed since he last wrote: G has had time to receive the previous letter and to respond by entrusting messages to Gerard, who either makes a special journey or whose professional or personal affairs take him to and from Remiremont (to which N has now returned and from which he writes).

5–7 G's messages obviously included a shopping list on which there figured some feminine items such as kerchiefs (the most common type of head-covering used by women, whose heads convention required to be covered, e.g. by veils, wimples or kerchiefs). With masculine and avuncular, and slightly exaggerated, gallantry, N treats these as orders of the first importance, before going on to the more serious matter he has to communicate.

9 The end of the letter gives a date of 2 January 1470, but, according to Paravicini (n. 203), the numerical year in Lorraine began on 25 March, and he therefore assumes the reference here to be to the Friday after Christmas 1470 (not 1469), which (n. 206) fell on 28 December. But N should not have been travelling till the 29th, as the three days following Christmas Day were *festa ferianda*?

10 G's father apparently did not learn of his daughter's journey from N personally. He may have learned of it from her sister, who (if she is not the Catherine referred to in II.11) may still be with him, or from a letter from N or G. Or it may be that the sister did not see him over Christmas: i.e. that he did not live near N, but thought it safer for his daughters to make only the comparatively short journey to Bruyères for the festive period. *vostre noble maison*: the canonesses had separate houses, situated near the chapter church (Lee, *Council of Remiremont*, p. 21).

11 One might assume that 'my lady Catherine' is the sister of G referred to at III.5. If so, it appears that she also did not see her father over the Christmas period. But N does not mention her as returning with him (the pronoun is *Je*, not *nous*, at II.9). So it is just possible that Catherine is a confidante of G at Remiremont, not her sister.

12–13 It is evident that the father's displeasure is something of a surprise to N, even though he had already explicitly forbidden G to make journeys he plainly thought imprudent in the present political state of things. Either he is angrier than N had thought he would be, or he spells out factors telling against the journey which N had not fully appreciated: the wording seems more consistent with the latter (N says that even G will rue her action when she reads the actual letter, and that he himself has now learned 'many things' since they last conferred, presumably about the journey). It is worth noting that his fatherly attachment to G is almost more unwavering than her actual father's, for he in effect offers to stand by her even in the event that her father will not – if that is what *s'il ne tient a vous* means: or does it just mean, 'if the cause does not come from you/unless you change your mind'?

14 *truant* is apparently a form of 'traiant' (also recorded in the form 'traant', cited by Paravicini), and a 'cheval traiant' was a draft horse. N is telling G that this is a sturdy and strong animal, and she need not feel afraid of 'tanking' it in using it as a vehicle for her baggage. The horse is further evidence of N's attachment: horses were as jealously guarded and as sparingly loaned as cars are today.

16 Ultimate forgiveness of sins was a common form of blessing prayed for, and does not imply any specific current sins that N thinks G is committing.

17 *premier* is deleted before *second*. Did N write the letter on 1 January, but not dispatch it till the next day? On the year, see n. to 9 above.

18 The identity of G's clerk is known only from this sign-off, in which Bruyères is abbreviated as well as his Christian name. But the former is confirmed by IV.9 above and the latter by the recorded possession from 1468 of a canonicate at Remiremont by a *Magister Nicolai de Bruyeris*: see Paravicini's note. The word *petit* [little] epitomizes his tone to G in a way difficult to define: it is not simply a synonym of 'humble', but (as in the modern English expression 'your own little *x*') is used in a cosifying and semi-playful manner that implies the roles of humble clerk and great lady are a kind of game that he enjoys playing.

V: TO PIERRE FROM J. DE VAUDREY

A nostre treschier seigneur et frere, messire Pierre / de Hacambach, chevalier, seigneur dudit lieu / et bailly de Ferrouste et d'Ausoy

[1] Treschier seigneur et frere, [2] je me recommande a vous tant humblement comme je puis, [3] et vous / plaise sçavoir des nouvelles de par deça. [4] Jehan Prevost est yci, a presens arivés ycy, et / vient de Nancey, et a passé par my le pays de Lourainnes, et a vehu grant / nombre de gens d'armes, et vi[n]rent de puis Espinal jusques a Remiermont avec / lui bien deux cent cheval et dix lances, qui estierent desia audit Remiremont,/ [5] et suismes en la guerre toutalement. Car il luy dirent que il nous / vairaent vehors, et lui dirent pluseurs parolles, et pour ce il me samble / que qu'il hust peur faire une entreprinse sur Remiremont. / A l'aide de vous et de vous gens et de votre hartillerie de par devers vous, / nous lui donerens ung grant eschouques, et pour ce je vouldroie bien que bon il / feyst ung bon copt. [6] Et se en escripvés ung puilt a monseigneur de Montagu, il me / samble que il n'y auroit pas grant mal; [7] et il a audit Remiremontes les chevalcheurs / qu'il entrarest son françois, ainsey comme ledit Jehan Prevost me a dit. [8] Et pour ce / il seroit bon d'y faire aucune chose, car il sont pour nous porter du / dommaige desia bien grant. [9] Et au regard des dames que me escripvés, ce / je sçay point qu'elle en soient partye, je n'en sçay riens de vraye. / [10] Et me samble que debvés faire gardé voz pasaige par devers vostre cousté / d'Alemaingne, car je vous assure que nous fusmes en la guerre de tout / coustez. [11] Et pour ce ayez sur ce vostre aviz, et me mandé tousiours de vous nouvelles ou moy mander / s'il l'est chose que pour vous faire puissions, mandé le moy et je la / complirey de tresbon cuer [12] au plaisir de Nostre Seigneur, qui vous ait en sa saincte / garde. [13] Escript a Falcongny ce xve jour de fevrier.

[14] [*manu propria*] Le tout vostre frere, / J. de Vaudrey

---

5 toutalement] *followed by* et pour *deleted*   hust] *followed by* plus *deleted*   entreprinse] *follows* entre per *deleted*   7] Jehan Prevost] *followed by* lui *deleted*   me] *inserted above line*   8 pour nous porter] *follows* en grat *deleted*   9 partye] *followed by* nen ny *deleted*

V: TO PIERRE FROM J. DE VAUDREY

On the outside of the letter: To our well-beloved lord and brother, my lord Pierre of Hagenbach, knight, lord of that place and bailiff of Ferrette and of Alsace

[1] Well-beloved lord and brother commander, [2] I commend myself to you as humbly as possible. [3] And may it please you to know the news from here. [4] Jehan Prevost is here, just arrived, and he has come from Nancy, and he has passed through Lorraine territory and he has seen a great number of armed men: all the way from Épinal to Remiremont did they come up on him, a good two hundred cavalry and ten groups of lance, who are now at the moment at the said Remiremont, [5] and we are now absolutely on a war footing. For they told him that they would join us there, and spoke much with him, and it therefore seems to me that it would be a small matter to make an assault on Remiremont, with the assistance of you and your men and of the artillery you have – we will be delivering a heavy blow, and therefore I would well wish that a good blow should indeed be a good one. [6] And if you will write a few lines to my lord of Montaigu, it seems to me that it would be no bad thing. [7] And he has at the said Remiremont the mounted agents that he could deploy ... as the said Jehan Prevost has told me. [8] And so it would be good to do something there, for they could as things stand at present bring harm upon us. [9] And with respect to the ladies you wrote to me about, as to whether I know at all if they have left, I have no certain information about this. [10] And it seems to me you ought to have your territory guarded on your border with the German lands, for I assure you we have war on all sides. [11] And therefore hold discussions on these matters, and keep me informed or send to me if there is anything we can do for you, and if there is just let me know and I will very willingly get it done, [12] if it please God, whom I pray may have you in His holy keeping. [13] Written at Faucogney this fifteenth day of February.

[14] *sender's own hand* Your brother, wholly, J. de Vaudrey

NOTES TO LETTER V

This letter is from a brother commander in the service of the Duke of Burgundy. It concerns a massing of Burgundian forces and a projected attack by them on Remiremont, and prophesies 'war on all sides' as a result of a French offensive begun in 1471 and leagues being formed by the Swiss against the Burgundian presence in Alsace (5, 10). The letter was preserved with the others here reproduced, probably because it too concerns Remiremont (which had been occupied by the French, according to Claerr-Stamm: p. 107) and mentions a query from P about 'the ladies' there (9). It is dated and signed from Faucogney by J. de Vaudrey. Faucogney, in northern Franche-Comté, lies a few miles south of Remiremont, and the sender appears to be Jean de Vaudrey, an illegitimate member of the Vaudrey family whose name figures in a couple of documents that suggest he was a Burgundian commander and an associate of P (see Paravicini, p. 118, n. 66).

4 Jehan Prevost may (according to Paravicini's note) be from the Prevost family of Besançon (also in Franche-Comté). Prevost has evidently come south through Lorraine territory from Nancy, from which he travels about forty miles south down to Épinal (in southern Lorraine), and then further south to the nearby Remiremont, and thence (moving out of Lorraine into Burgundian territory) a few more miles on down to Faucogney. Remiremont lay at the southern extremity of the duchy of Lorraine, which separated Charles the Bold's territories around the North Sea from those (Burgundy and Franche-Compté) in the east of France, and through which Charles therefore needed the transit facilities that a formal alliance with Lorraine presently afforded him, facilities which he was later to seize the chance of guaranteeing by annexation of the duchy (see pp. 354–5 above). A *lance* was a small group of (most commonly, five or six) soldiers, variously armed, one of whom bore a pennoned lance; a *lance* in Charles's army typically consisted of a nine-man detachment comprising 'a man-at-arms with his mounted page and swordsman (*coustillier*); three mounted archers; and a crossbowman, a culverineer and a pikeman on foot' (Vaughan, p. 206). *estierent* is a form of 'ester' equivalent in meaning to Latin 'stare' and means 'are to be found' (Paravicini).

5 The Burgundian contingents described in 4 are, the writer hopes, to be joined by forces and artillery brought up by P himself (based in Alsace, a few miles to the south of Faucogney). We are presumably dealing here with military manoeuvres prior to the military activity of the spring of 1471, a year in which the French launched an offensive against Burgundy, and in which there occurred engagements that included the Burgundian defeat at Buxy (March) and their victory at Remiremont (April): see VIII.3, 17 and Paravicini, p. 131. Pierre did not in fact participate in the war against France until August, but was dispatched instead in March to lead a relief force to the aid of Châtel-sur-Moselle (a stronghold in Lorraine belonging to the Burgundian Neuchâtel family: see n. to 6 below), to

which siege had been laid by Lorrainers (see p. 355 above). *vairaent* is from the verb 'voier' and *vehors* may be an error for 'dehors' (Paravicini). *eschouques* seems to be related to 'shock' (Paravicini).

6 The present seigneur of Montaigu was Jean II of Neuchâtel, the Burgundian family from which Charles drew all his divisional general commanders, Jean being commander of the forces in Burgundy in 1471 (and again in 1475): see Paravicini, p. 119, n. 71, and Vaughan, p. 256. *puilt* is a form of 'poi', as is *peur* in 5.

7 A *chevalcheur* could refer to a scout or spy, or to a courier or dispatch rider, as well as to a mounted soldier. But we understand neither the grammar nor the sense of *qu'il entrarest son françois*, whether the verb is from 'entrer' (as we assume) or 'entraire/estraire' [take out].

8 The number of deletions and corrections in the letter show that it was written in some haste, and the expression here is a little confused.

9 It is not clear which particular inmates of the church P's query had related to: whether G and her sister had alone been named, or whether other or all canonesses (many of whom were from Burgundian families and may well have had Burgundian sympathies and/or connections or acquaintance with P) and/or perhaps his own cousin (the sacristan mentioned in Letter II) had also been mentioned. He is clearly concerned to hear that specified *dames* are safely out of the projected battle zone, but may not have named G and her sister alone or specifically (and evidently took care not to name G alone).

10 The territory of which P had been made *bailly* bordered modern Switzerland, and it was becoming known at this date that leagues aimed at opposing the Burgundian presence in that territory were being formed by various Rhineland towns and powers. The letter makes clear the grounds for G's father's disinclination to allow his daughter to travel through a potential war zone from Lorraine into Burgundy and to an unpopular Burgundian commander.

13 The year is not given, but Paravicini gives it as 1471.

14 It was common for many noblemen, as well as most women, to use scribes to pen their letters, to which they themselves would sometimes add in their own hands, at the conclusion, some sign-off or authentication of messages from the bearer, etc.: cf. Letters I and VI and see pp. 54, 57 above.

VI: TO PIERRE FROM THE CANONESS

Mon treschier sseigneur / monssiegneur le bailly

[1] Mon treshonoré sseigneur et amy, [2] bien chieremen et de lyal / ceur je me recommande a vous. [3] Je vous marsier / les grasyeuse lestre que m'avés escrip par Inbert, porteur de / ceste, lequel a bien fait son devoier et m'a dit des / chosse asez, doin j'ay esté bien reconfortez. [4] Or sat, mon amy de / mon ceur, me diste en rens, quar, par moi foit, je ne / vous abandonray jamais pour personne qui soit vyvan; / et say bien en mon [ceur] tout les bonne parole que j'ay par / escrip de vous, [5] comme vous diray bien a lon le dit Inbert, / le que[l] vulliez croire comme ma personne. [6] Mon amy de / mon ceur, je vous heusse escrip pleux a lon, mas / en veryté, je n'ay pais clet a ma vollanté. [7] Et a / Dieu, mon lyal amy, a que je prye qu'i vous sevegne / toutjour de moy et vous doin ce que mon ceur / dessire. [8] Escrip se dimanche bien matien d'un ceur qui est voustre.

[9] *manu propria* le bin voustre et leale / amie et plus que voustre

---

3 que m'avés escrip] que *and* escrip *inserted above line* 4 mon amy] mon *inserted above line* mon ceur] *Paravicini*; mon 5 le quel] *Paravicini*; le que 6 escrip] *follows* estrip *deleted* clet] *follows two or three letters deleted* 7 dessire] *follows* de *and another illegible letter deleted at end of previous line* 8 se] *corrected from* ce dimanche] *inserted above line*

VI: TO PIERRE FROM THE CANONESS

On the outside of the letter: My well-beloved lord, my lord bailiff

[1] My most honoured lord and my beloved, [2] most dearly and with loyal heart I commend myself to you. [3] I thank you for the gracious letter that you have written and sent me by Humbert, the bearer of this, who has executed his mission well and has told me many things which have given me much comfort. [4] He has told me enough, point by point, my heart's beloved, for, by my faith, no living person will ever make me give you up, and I have clearly before my mind's eye all the fair words that I have in writing from you, [5] as the said Humbert will tell you in full detail, whom I beg you to believe as if the words came from me personally. [6] Beloved of my heart, I would have written at more length, but in truth my will is under a lock whose key I do not have. [7] And so, my true lover, 'a Dieu', to whom I pray that He keep me ever in your memory and grant you all that my heart desires for you. [8] Written really early this Sunday from a heart that is yours.

[9] *sender's own hand* Your own and true beloved, and more than your own

NOTES TO LETTER VI

The hand is not the same one as for Letters I and II.

1, 2 The coupling of the social title (*sseigneur*) with the romantic one (*amy*) gives the following commendations (made 'dearly' and with a 'true' heart) both a socio-political and an amorous significance. The fusion of the two, not uncommon in love letters, is especially typical of this writer (cf. n. to II.1–4) and may have been an important factor in the bond between the two, in which political and romantic ties reinforced one another (see p. 356 above).

3, 5 This is further confirmation that Humbert Gille was in the employ of Pierre, for he is employed as bearer by G only when he is returning to P after having delivered her a letter from him; see n. to I.4 (and cf. *VD* 3459, 4288, 4736, 6542–9). G again entrusts to him (as she does to no other bearer) some supplementary verbal messages for which she includes a vouchment (cf. I.17 and note), having received from him similar verbal communications with which P has also entrusted him.

3 For the words used to record successful delivery of the message by the bearer (*a bien fait son devoier*), cf. I.10 (*qu'i fait tresbien son debvoir*), the same formula occurring at VII.4 (in respect of bearers who are not entrusted by either P or G with personal supplementary messages and who presumably do not know the nature of the missives they carry between the two).

4 I do not understand *sat. en rens* is explained by Paravicini as meaning 'comme il covient (en bon ordre)'.

7 For the play on the strict sense of 'adieu', cf. I.15, II.12 (and note); similar relative clauses follow the 'adieu' in the *Voir dit* (e.g. 'Adieu ... qui vous doint ... joie ...': L37). The prayer for all blessings that the addressee could wish for himself (or the sender for him/her) is a regular item among epistolary closing formulae (cf. Text 6, 4B.14–20, 5D.109–16).

8 *se dimanche bien matien* [really early this Sunday]: see n. to I.16; like Letter II, the indication of early time of day is unaccompanied by any indication of place, but is presumably in both cases Remiremont (specified in, among the love letters proper, VII and perhaps I).

9 The sign-off is in G's own hand; cf. I.17 and V.14 and notes.

VII: TO PIERRE FROM THE CANONESS

A mon treshonoré seigneur, monsseigneur / le Bailly de Ferroitte

[1] Mon treschier honeré seigneur et maistre de mon ceur, [2] tant et sy humblement / comme je puis je me recommande a voustre bonne graice, [3] car, sur mon / ayme, sans voustre graice je ne sçaveroye vivre. [4] Et ay ce que escript m'avés / par les pourteurs d'ycelle, lesqueulx hont bien fait leur debvoir. [5] A regard / de aller, certainement, mon treshonoré seigneur, il ne m'est pais possible de / y aller quant il n'y vatz aulcune. Car je vous prometz ce ly fut / allee aulcunne, que je il feusse voluntier allee. Car plus grant / chouse je vouldroye faire pour vous. [6] A regard de ce que dittes qu'il y [ait] / aulcunne personne qui m'en destourbe, [7] certes vous avés tord de le pancer, / car il n'y ait homme a Remiremont qui m'en destourbyt oncques; ausy n'en feroye rien / pour eulx, car il n'y ait homme qui le vaille. [8] Helais, mon amy de / mon ceur, vous sçavés que je me suis donnee a vous, et, par ma foy, je me / garderay pour vous; et rebouttez voustre malvaise pancee de dire que j'aimme / ung prebstre. Par Dieu, je ameroy mieulx estre morte que de moy donner / a telz gens. [9] Je voy bien que me tenez assés pouvre de couraige / quant vous me dittez que je me donne a gentz qui ne vaillent rien. / [10] Je vous prometz par ma foy que vous me corossés a la bonne certez / quant je scey que vous i avés ainsy misse voustre pancee. Je vous prie, mon / amy de mon ceur, que vous debouttez voustre pancee aultrement qu'elle n'est. / Vous sçavés, mon amy, qu'i n'y ait homme que j'amoye tant que vous, maix / je cuide que je pert mon temps quant vous pancés que j'aimme ung / homme que ne vault rien. [11] Helais, je souffre tant de malx nuitz / et jour pour vous, car la chouse seroit troupt longue a rescripre. Se vous / sçaviens les grant chargez que l'on me donne pour l'amour de vous, / vous en seriens bien merveilleux. Car vous sçavés bien que le moinde / est cy malvaix, et ce ne vous sçavés detenir. [12] Et pourtant, mon / amy, je vous prie que en l'amour de Dieu que celléz plus voustre couraige / que vous ne faittes. Et que averiens vous gaingnier quant je seroye / deshonnoree pour l'amour de vous? Certes, il vous en desplairait. / [13] Or scey, mon amy et mon tres honoré seigneur, vous serés mardi en grant festes / et je seray en tristesse. Maix toute voye je vous prie et supplie que en / quelque feste que soyéns que m'ayéns tousiours en souvenance; [14] et ne / chaingés point voustre couraige en vers moy. Car ce je n'y voit

6 qu'il y ait] *Paravicini;* qui ly   10 i] *Paravicini;* il

VII: TO PIERRE FROM THE CANONESS

On the outside of the letter: To my right-honoured lord, my lord the Bailiff of Ferrette.

[1] My most dear honoured lord and master of my heart, [2] as much and as humbly as I can I commend myself to your good grace [3] – for, on my soul, without it I could not live. [4] I have received the letter you wrote me from the bearers of this same, who have executed their trust well. [5] With regard to the journey you suggest, indeed, my most honoured lord, no journey is possible when there is no one going there. For I promise you that, if there were any journey being made there, I would willingly join the persons making it. For I would be willing to do a greater thing than that for you. [6] As to what you say about there being someone that is stopping me, [7] you are certainly wrong to think it, for there is no man in Remiremont who could ever stop me – I would not do anything for any of their sakes, for there is no man who would be worth it. [8] Alas, beloved of my heart, you know that I have given myself to you and, by my faith, I will keep myself for you; and please repel the evil thought that makes you say that I am having an affair with a priest. By God, I would prefer to be dead than to give myself to such a person. [9] I see well that you consider me to have little pride when you tell me that I give myself to people of no standing at all. [10] I assure you by my faith that you anger me in all seriousness when I know that you have sent your thought in that direction. I pray you, beloved of my heart, that you put that thought out of your head. You know, my beloved, that there is no man I could love as I do you, but it makes me believe I am wasting my time with you when you think that I love a nobody of a man. [11] Alas, I suffer day and night so many ills for your sake that it woud take too long to set it out in writing. If you knew what accusations are levelled at me because of my love of you, you would marvel at it. For you know that the world is malicious and you cannot stop it from being so. [12] And therefore, beloved, I pray you for God's sake to conceal your feelings more than you do. For what will you have gained if I should lose my honour on your account? That would surely not be in your interest. [13] Now I know, my beloved and my right honoured lord, that you will be enjoying great festivities on Tuesday, while I will be in sadness. But I pray and beg you that, at all events, in whatever festivity you are, you keep me always in your memory. [14] And do not change your heart towards me, for though I do not at present see the possibility, we will certainly find some time the means to speak together.

/ maintenant nous trouverons bien maniere une aultre foix de parler / ensemble. [15] Je vous prie et requier, mon treshonoré seigneur et amy de mon ceur, / que, pour Dieu, personne du monde voye cez lettres; et ce je puis sçavoir que les / monstrés, je diray que serés le plus fault chivallier du monde – car je / scey que ne les pourés monster que je ne le saiche bien. [16] Et pancés, / mon amy, que je parleroye plus voluntier a vous que de vous rescripre, car je vous / diroye beaulcoupt de chouse lesquelles vous scerient troupt longue / a rescripre. [17] Helas, mon amy, vous scerés en joye et je seray en pleurs, / en larmes et en jemysement. [18] Et sur ce je vous ditz a Dieu, aulquel / je prie que vous dont le mieulx avier de vous desirs. [19] Escript a Remiremont / ce diemenche matin.

[20] Voustre leale Gairrye

14 nous trouverons] *follows* je *deleted*

[15] I beg you and call upon you, my most honoured lord and beloved of my heart, in the name of God, to let no one else in the world see these letters; and if I should find that you show them to anyone, I shall say that you are the most false knight in the world – for I know that you won't be able to reveal them without my finding out. [16] And understand, my beloved, that I would much rather speak with you than write to you, for I could then say many things which it would take too long to write to you. [17] Alas, my beloved, you are going to be in joy and I in weeping, in tears and in groans. [18] And on that point I bid you 'a Dieu', to whom I pray that He grant you your dearest wishes. [19] Written at Remiremont this Sunday morning.

[20] Your faithful Gairrye

NOTES TO LETTER VII

The scribe is the same as for Letters I and II.

1–3 This adaptation of the standard salutation (cf. V.1–2) to suit the closer relationship is used also in Letters I.1–2 and II.1–2. See also n. to VI.1, 2.
4 See n. to VI.3. G is, as in I and VI, sending her reply by the same bearers employed by P for his letter to her (though there is no indication that these bearers are in the confidence of the pair or are entrusted with supplementary verbal messages, as is Humbert).
5, 6 *A regard de* introduces G's reply to points raised in P's letter. See n. to I.6–7.
5 Cf. I.6–8. P has again obviously urged her to come to him in Burgundy. G does not here say she must abide by her father's decision on the matter, perhaps because she now knows this would be negative and there is no longer any possibility of her disobeying him (as she seems to have done before: see preliminary n. to III and n. to IV.12–13), since she could not travel alone and there is now no one else going in that direction (probably because the political situation is now such that there is no civilian traffic between Lorraine and Burgundy that she could join); but there may be other reasons for the fact that there is no further mention of her father after Letter IV (see n. to VIII.15). She again softens her non-compliance with assurances that this is not due to any lack of desire to be with P.
6–11 P has plainly suspected that it may be some*one* rather than some*thing* that is making G disinclined to make the journey to him (6) and that (8) she may be having an affair with a priest (for she is unlikely to be thrown much together with men of any other kind). This was evidently a common fear on the part of the man when a romance was being conducted largely by epistolary communication between lovers geographically separated from one another. Christine's model love letter sequence includes a ballade from the man (*CBAD* LXXIV) in which he voices a suspicion that 'un autre' is responsible for a perceived slight decrease in ardour on her part, a ballade answered by one from the lady in which she protests against such groundless 'jalousie' (LXXV). The Norfolk abbot is similarly a little worried about Margaret's fidelity (Text 4, I.3–4). The situation was such that men evidently both were and were perceived to be quick to detect and over-interpret. G's indignation at being suspected of taking a lover of so humble a rank certainly sounds sincere, and the jealousy of Christine's *amant* is equally ill-founded.
11–12 In a further parallel with Letter I (9–11), G refers to the stressful risks she undergoes in receiving missives from P, who does not and cannot fully appreciate them (I.9, *c'est une grant charge pour moy et ne sçavés pais les maulx que j'en dure*; VII.11 *tant de malx ... Se vous sçaviens les grant chargez ...*), and begs him to be more discreet in sending her letters and messengers (with VII.12, cf. I.9). But there is more bitterness to the tone here, since the topic is arrived at via G's sense of the unfairness of his accusations, when she suffers *tant de malx* on his account (VII.11); and whereas there was something playful in her reference in

Pierre de Hagenbach and the Canoness at Remiremont 401

Letter I.11 to the risk of exposure she runs in receiving letters from him, she is now more explicit and serious in pointing to the 'dishonour' she risks (VII.12). On the concern felt by women in fact and in fiction about the danger to their good name and standing entailed in a love affair, see pp. 60–1 above; G's wording again suggests acquaintance with love literature (cf. n. to II.8) – with VII.12 here, compare, for instance, the plea and warning Guinevere delivers to Lancelot after accepting his love: 'Or gardez que la chose soit si *celee* com il est mestiers ... se mes los ampiroit *par vos*, ci avroit amor laide et vilaine' (*Lancelot do Lac*, ed. Kennedy, vol. 1, p. 348).

13 The reference is to the imminent nuptials of P's nephew (married with much éclat at Ensisheim in Alsace in November 1471: see Paravicini, p. 136).

14 This implies that they have at least once already managed a reunion: see n. to III.

15 *le plus fault chivallier du monde*: falseness and treachery were the arch sins of knighthood, and Pierre had already shown himself to be as jealous of his honour on that score as any knight would have been. When in 1448 (as a result of circumstances that are obscure) he had been charged with treachery by the *bailli* of Landser, he had responded with a passionately furious letter to an accuser whom he termed a 'voleur [robber] de l'honneur des chevaliers' and whom he challenged to a duel (Claerr-Stamm, p. 34). For, though 'truth' (the opposite of falseness and treachery) was incumbent on all, it was the prime virtue of knights in particular (see, for instance *SGGK* 619–39 and 2379–82). Pierre's status as a knight (which the external address on Letter V, from Jean de Vaudrey, also attaches to his name) was emphasized in his membership of a chivalric confraternity, that of Saint-Georges, and the grant to him of the right to add the title 'd'Archembault' to his name, a privilege reserved for knights who performed acts of special prowess (see Claerr-Stamm, pp. 32 and 202). G's reference to the rank of knight that P so conspicuously held and which he would shame by untruth or 'falseness' to her is therefore calculated to make an impression. Her words are carefully chosen in another respect: should he betray her by not keeping her letters secret, she will *say* he is the falsest knight alive. Being known to have been treacherous in an illicit love affair was more damaging than the affair itself (see p. 256 above). G's words, that is, threaten P with a disgrace that would more than equal any he brought on her. Cf. the conclusion of the poem in Letter 69 of the *EDA*, where the *mulier* similarly entreats her lover to guard her letters from the fault-finding eyes of the duplicitous; the warning is also found in Latin verse love epistles from both women (cf. 'Cave diligentius, / ne tercius / interveniat oculus' [Take care that no third eye sees this] in the Tegernsee poem discussed at p. 104 above) and men (cf. 'Missa tibi soli multis ostendere noli' [Do not show to others missives meant for you alone]: last line of the poem 'Omnia postpono', available (with translation) in Dronke, *Medieval Latin*, vol. 1, pp. 249–50).

16 In a further parallel with Letter I, G again implicitly reassures P that her refusal to obey his request that she undertake the journey to him is not due to any lack of desire for a more direct form of communication than letters can provide (see note

on I.8.), a desire that here also provides an important counterbalance to her plea to him to be more discreet in writing to her – she wants better communication, not less, and wants it as much as he does, not less.

19 See VI.8 and note and n. to I.16.

20 As in Letter I, the subscription is actually in the scribe's hand. *leale* might be unremarkable there, but is not without polemical point here (G is asserting the faith P has questioned and that he would betray in failing in the same faith to her). The many parallels with the first letter only point up the stresses and strains that have now developed in the relationship and that a love affair carried on by epistolary means entails: it is now suspicions not knick-knacks that P has sent along with his request to G to come to him, and her own protestations of faith and affection now carry a more aggrieved, accusing and warning tone.

VIII: TO PIERRE FROM THE CANONESS

A Mon esliance

[1] Moinseigneur mon esliance: [2] je me recommande humblement a voustre begnine graice, / tresdesirant de sçavoir de vous nouvelles. [3] Monseigneur mon esliance, povez peinser quelz joye / et plaisir que je es ehu durant sez guerres, quant de jours en jours on nous disoit / que les Bourgoungnons estients tous mors – quar on nous certiffioit que devant Bussy n'y avoit / ehu quatre mil dez mors et xiiij^c des printz. Je tien, se ne fust ehu l'ayde de / monseigneur saint Nicolas, j'eusse perdus ceu poc de sençc que Dieu m'avoit prestez. [4] Tous le / papier de Loraingne n'est pas souffisant pour vous escripre lez grantz doulleurs et melancolie / qu'avontz seste annee souffer; [5] et ce qui nous ait fait le pitz, s'est fait le vaillant home Jaquet / de Honecourt, qui nous avoit dictes qu'i tenoit sa vie de Dieu et de vous – [6] et pour vous / en bien recompeinser ilz allit rompre la lettre qui nous envoiet par Jehan de Banville (ce / qu'i n'avoit faict encoires de nulles) et envoiet la coppie a messeigneurs du Conseille. [7] Et ma seur / et moy allimme tantost vers ly ly demander se nous estiens plus malgracieuses que lez aultres / de commencier ceste rigueur a nous. [8] Et ilz nous respondit que, par sa foy, ilz ne sçavoit qu'ilz / avoit dedent et ilz tenoit par le bras celuy qu'avoit coppier nos dictes lettres. Or sa de tous / ce, se ilz nous ait fallus avoir pacience. [9] J'es par pluseurs foy ly que par pacience l'on doit / entrer en paradis, matz je cuide qu'i ne me sereit pas tourner a grant merite, entendutz / que se m'est estei pacience einfflee. [10] Ma bonne et parfaicte esliance, la malle fortunee / heure que fust quant on me dict que vous estiens prins et menei dilac le Rin – quar le plus / et le moins disientz pour nous donner joie qu'on vous fist morir a l'heure que fust printz. / Matz ilz n'en n'avoient patz çeu que leur cour desiroit, ne ja n'amenne. Ilz convienent que, le jour que fust / prins, eussiés faict quelque bonne priere la quelle vous preservet a seste heure. [11] Je vous prie / qu'i vous plaise en moy rescripre bien a long, se vous fust point blessiei ne comment ilz vous / en est. [12] Messire Jehain Gallon nous ait donnei une lettre de part vous et nous ait dict / que ly aviez priei que, se le voulliens envoier par dever vous, qu'i voulsit aller. [13] Nous ne nous / summes oussez mettre a l'aventure de ly envoier, doubstant de le mettre en dongier. [14] Ilz nous / ait fait relacion du biaulz jerdin que ly avez monstrei. Nous en poulrons cognoistre / par oyr dire, mas aultrement non, quar nos eintreprisse sont tournees toutes aultres que ne le/ divisiens – quar l'home propose, mas Dieu dispose.

VIII: TO PIERRE FROM THE CANONESS

On the outside of the letter: To my ally

[1] My lord and ally: [2] I commend myself humbly to your good grace, desiring greatly to receive news of you. [3] My lord and ally, you can imagine what joy and pleasure I could have had during these battles, when day by day we were told that the Burgundians were all dead – for we were informed that at Buxy there had been four thousand dead and fourteen hundred taken captive. I believe, if it had not been for the aid of my lord Saint Nicholas, that I would have lost the little reason that God had given me. [4] All the paper in Lorraine would not suffice to write out for you the great griefs and misery that we have suffered this year; [5] and what has been the worst infliction was something done by the worthy Jaquet de Honecourt, who had told us that he was still alive only thanks to God and to you – [6] and, to reward you(!), he proceeded to break open the letter you sent us by Jehan de Banville (something he had done in no other case) and sent a copy to my lords of the Burgundian ducal council. [7] And my sister and I went at once to him to ask him if we were more ungracious in his eyes than the others that he should subject us to such procedural rigour. [8] And he replied that, by his faith, he did not know what was inside the letter and that he had detained(?) the man who had copied it. Now you can imagine whether or not, amid all this, we were required to exercise patient endurance. [9] I have many times read that it is through patience that one enters heaven, but I don't believe this exercise of it would much redound to my spiritual credit, given that my patience was swelling with inner rage. [10] My good and perfect ally, what an ill-starred hour was it when I was told that you had been captured and taken to the other side of the Rhine – for great and small said, to give us supposedly good tidings, that you had been executed at the time you were taken. But they did not get what their hearts desired, and may they never get their wish. It must be that the day you were taken you made some efficacious prayer which preserved you at that hour. [11] I beg you to please write back to me at length to tell me if you were at all hurt and how things are with you in all this. [12] The reverend Jehan Gallon has given us a letter from you and has told us that you had asked him, if we wanted to send word to you, if he would be good enough to go back. [13] We have not dared to take the risk of sending him, fearing to put him in danger. [14] He has given us an account of the beautiful garden you showed him. We can know of it by thus hearing tell of it, but otherwise not, for what it is possible for us to undertake has turned out to be very different from what we planned – for man proposes, but God has the disposition of things.

[15] Quant je peinse a sestui biaulz vouaige / qu'aviens eintreprins de faire, et la maniere, se m'est maintenant une chosse bien estrainge, vehu / le tempz qui regne – ilz nous faulret dire einsy que dict Monseigneur d'Onzellet: 'Retourne malle, / heureuse retourne.' [16] Monseigneur mon esliance, ma seur Clemence d'Husier m'ait dict qu'elle vous rescrivot / pour avoir ung sacondus pour ung siens bons amis, nostre lieutenant de Remiremont, pour aller ez / Allegmaingnes. Se vous prie, mon esliance, qu'il vous plaise faire a sa requeste. [17] Ilz ne / tient qu'a moy de vous rescrire de plus grant gracieuseté: quar j'es vehu seste annee / lez François qu'avez batalliei sy rudement en noustre ville – mas ilz furetz tant troublei qu'a / penne n'eussiez nous guaire pohu comprandre et eulz n'en eussiens guerre sçeu monstrer. / [18] Ma bonne et doulce esliance, nous povez rescripre bien a plain de vous novelles et seurement, / quar madicte seur Clemence s'en vaidt a lieu de Facongney, la quelle nous reppourterét / vos lettres. [19] Monseigneur mon esliance, sur ce point je vous dys a Dieu, a quelz je prie qu'i / vous doint ancomplissement de tous vos bons et parfait desirs. [20] Escript a Remiremont le diemenche aupres l'Assumption Nostre Dame, xvij^e jour de ce present mois d'aoust.

[21] Voustre humble esliance au tous jour mais

[15] When I think of that fine journey we planned, and how we would make it, it now seems to me to be something quite unreal, in view of the present state of things – we must say as Monseigneur d'Onzellet used to say: 'If bad times come back, good times come back'. [16] My lord and ally, my sister-canoness Clemence d'Husier has told me that she has also written to you to ask for a safe conduct for a good friend of hers, our lieutenant of Remiremont, to go into German territory. And I pray you, my ally, to please grant her request. [17] It is for me alone to write to you with respect to something more diverting: for I have this year seen the Frenchmen you gave such rough battle to in our town, but they were so distracted that they could hardly understand us at all, and we hardly knew how to show them. [18] My good and sweet ally, you can write back to us with all the news concerning you in full detail, for you can do so in complete security, as my said sister Clemence is going to the area of Faucogney, and so she will bring back to us your letter. [19] My lord and ally, at this point I bid you 'a Dieu', whom I pray may grant you fulfilment of all your good and highest desires. [20] Written at Remiremont the Sunday after the feast of the Assumption of Our Lady, 17th day of the present month of August.

[21] Ever your humble ally

NOTES TO LETTER VIII

Letters VIII and IX are the only ones from G to P in which the latter, in the externally visible specification of the intended recipient, is designated in any way other than by his official title as lord or *bailly* of Ferrette. The term *esliance* is explained as 'élu' [chosen one] by Paravicini. But it is recorded as a form of the word 'alliance' in the *DMF*, where it is cited as occurring, significantly, in a Psalter from Lorrain (*Lothringischer Psalter*, ed. Friedrich Apfelstedt (Heilbronn, 1881)), in which 'mi iuroient faisoient conspiration et eslience' translates 'adversum me iurabant' in Psalm 101:9, where 'eslience' matches similar cases of *es-* for *a-* observable in the glossary to Apfelstedt's edition (e.g. 'esprandre', 'esgaitier'). The term *esliance* occurs not only on the outside of the present letter (where a designation that implied a romantic relationship would be unlikely), but repeatedly and ostentatiously within it (1, 3, 10, 16 twice, 18, 19) and in the subscription (21) – and is one G uses for the first (and only) time in this letter (where it replaces the phrase *mon amy de mon coeur* which she had previously chiefly used in vocatives to the addressee). And 'one with whom I am in alliance' seems a likelier sense of *mon esliance* than 'my chosen one', it being more probable that G is using a term that avoids any indication of a romantic liaison but instead advertises her as one of a group of canonesses who are 'allies' of P and non-hostile to Burgundy. For this letter resembles X and XI in its use of the plural form for most of its first-person pronouns and verbs. It is written as if on behalf of two or more canonesses, presumably the same persons as represented by the *nous* of X and XI and as P is mentioned as having enquired after at V.9: perhaps simply G and her sister, referred to in Letter III and below in VIII.7, perhaps also P's relative Charlotte de Montjustin, referred to at II.10, perhaps a larger group of pro-Burgundian canonesses who were friends or relatives or supporters of P. The letter is thus not a love letter as such, and contains little that is personal: G has been made only too aware (see 6–8) that mail might well be intercepted by Burgundian officials put in authority at Remiremont after the Burgundian victory there (referred to at 17). The scribe is not the same as any of those used by G for her love letters: Letters I, II and VII (Scribe 1), Letter VI (Scribe 2), Letter IX (Scribe 3). There are no deletions or insertions, a fact which may indicate that the letter is a fair copy of a previous draft or was dictated with unhasty deliberateness (and perhaps in the presence of others), rather than in the snatched moments in which the love letters proper were written.

1 The commendation lacks the indication of special affection characteristic of G's love letters (see I.2, II.2, VI.2, VII.2–3).

3 The battle of Buxy (14 March 1471), in southern Burgundy, resulted in a defeat for the Burgundian forces (led by Jean de Neuchâtel, mentioned at V.6 in connection with the coming campaign against the French). Hagenbach was not in fact present, having been sent instead to lead troops to the relief of the besieged Neuchâtel fief of Châtel-sur-Moselle (see n. to V.5 and p. 355 above). Remiremont was in

Pierre de Hagenbach and the Canoness at Remiremont 409

the duchy of Lorraine (which was by no means invariably or totally friendly to Burgundian ambitions), and the news of the defeat may well have been assumed (by those from whom the canonesses heard it) to be good news (cf. 10, where the news of P's death and capture is received from those who assumed they were giving 'joy' to the hearers). *Nicolas* was a saint with particular connections with the duchy of Lorraine, where his cult had a well-known centre at Saint-Nicolas-de-Port, on the Meurthe, a little up-river from Nancy in central Lorraine, a place to which pilgrimage was made and which was the site also of major fairs by which its fame would have been further spread (Paravicini, p. 131, n. 138).

4 *Loraingne* was the duchy in which Remiremont was situated; G's phrasing is indicative of how conscious people were of the distinct political entities constituted by what today are simply different regions in 'France' (see p. 342 above). The language of her own letters has a Lorraine colouring (most obvious in the occurrence of *et/ay/ai* for *a*: see Paravicini, p. 113, n. 42) and so indicates scribes from that region.

5–8 Paravicini could find no record of a *Jaquet de Honecourt* (or *Hovecourt*). He was obviously a Burgundian who had been invested with some authority in Remiremont after the Burgundian victory in the battle fought before the town (see n. to 17 below) – authority which he had used to open a particular letter to some of the inmates, a copy of which was then taken by one of his staff and forwarded to the ducal council at Dijon (Dijon was the chief city of Burgundy, and the ducal council was a major arm and instrument of government in Burgundian territories) – presumably because it was felt the council might want to know about a communication that turned out to be from a Burgundian general to persons in enemy territory. De Honecourt himself (who apparently thought that P had at some point helped to save his life) claims he did not know, when he had the letter opened, that it came from P (a fact that would not be obvious from the outside of the letter, where the sender's name did not normally appear) and had not authorized the making of the copy. On opening it, he would not in any case have discovered an evident love letter: it was apparently one addressed to the same (pair or) group of canonesses as the current one presents itself as coming from (cf. *nous envoiet* at 6 and *nos dictes lettres* at 8), for P and G, aware perhaps that mail might be opened by Burgundian officials, seem both to be avoiding anything private and personal.

5 *de Dieu et de vous*: cf. II.8 and note.

6 Paravicini notes that *Jehan de Banville*, the bearer of the intercepted letter from P, was probably a Lorraine man, since 'Bainville' figures in several place names in Lorraine. He would thus have had connections and/or a home that took him (back) to Lorraine and made him available as a bearer of a letter destined for Lorraine.

9 The supreme salvific effectiveness of patience was a well-known theological principle (well demonstrated in, for instance, both the allegory and the discussion of *Piers Plowman* B.XIII–XIV, with its repeated citation of the text *Patientes vincunt* [the patient overcome], from the apocryphal *Testament of Job* 27:10). The verb *ly* (from 'lire' [read]) is significant: we have here one of the several sophisticated

and literate uses of (not especially learned or recondite) texts or quotations (cf. 14 and 15 below) which contribute to the overall impression of an educated and articulate woman, culturally fluent without being high-brow.

10 In July 1471, P had been captured by Reinhard von Schauenburg, who was unhappy with the sum offered him as one of the creditors of Ortenberg (a château in Alsace of which the Burgundians had possessed themselves); but he was soon set free after agreeing to increase that sum (see p. 348 above). It is plain that (as, probably, with the Burgundian defeat and casualties at Buxy in 3 above) the event was told to G in Lorraine from an anti-Burgundian point of view and its gravity exaggerated by those who assumed it would be good news to anyone resident in Lorraine.

12 As the title *Messire* indicates, Jehan Gallon was a priest, and there are records of a priest and canon of that name at Remiremont (Paravicini, p. 123, n. 89); he died in 1512. He was thus available to P as a bearer because he was returning to his own home base, and would bear back replies to P only as a favour – a favour the ladies decline to ask of him (unnecessary journeys between the territories of hostile powers being evidently unadvisable); personal risks to carriers are one of the complications attendant on that need for bearers on which G's letters are so richly informative (cf. 18 below). Again (cf. n. to 5–8 above), the written and verbal messages he brought do not seem to have been of a confidential kind, for the first-person plural used here (as throughout the letter) indicates news treated as of general interest to members of the convent friendly to P and to Burgundy.

14 Whilst 'bailli', P most often chose to reside at Thann (about 35 km north from Ferrette), where his father had lived, and where he now himself had two houses, one of them in the 'grant rue', the other outside the town and surrounded by a garden (Claerr-Stamm, p. 116). *l'home propose, mas Dieu dispose* represents another sophisticated deployment of a well-known theological priniciple (cf. 9 above), which is also, again, cited by Langland, who attributes the proverb to 'Plato': "*Homo proponit*", quod a poete tho, and Plato he highte, / "And *Deus disponit*", quod he, "lat God doon his wille"' (B.XI.37–8).

15 A journey to P had again (cf. I.6, VII.5) been mooted, it appears, but again made impracticable in 'the times as they are now' by military and political developments – a journey to be made by *nous*, which (though it could refer to herself as accompanied by her sister and an escort of some kind) is obviously (here and at X.4 and XI.4–6) simply a device to conceal the personal nature of the projected *vouaige*, in connection with which, in the love letters proper, the first-person pronouns used are always singular, never plural (cf. I.6–7, II.7–8, VII.5). Neither here nor at VII.5 nor at any future point does G refer to her father in the context of a (non-)journey to P (as she had at I.7 and II.7); since a total breach with him seems unlikely (cf. IV.11–12), it is possible that illness or death has removed the authority and influence in this matter he had previously enjoyed, or that she no longer chooses to consult him (see further n. to VII.5). *Monseigneur d'Onzellet* was presumably (as Paravicini notes) a member of the Franche-Comté family of d'Oiselay, to which belonged the grandparents of Charlotte de Montjustin (the

cousin of P mentioned as sacristan at II.10), and which supplied canonesses to Remiremont (two of them called Margaret: Paravicini, p. 115, n. 53). The great families of Burgundy formed a very interconnected world (cf. n. to VIII.16), a fact reflected in microcosm in the abbey of Remiremont, where the canonesses often had connections not only with one another, but also with Burgundy (of which dukedom Franche-Comté was then a part) and sometimes with P (to whose family the d'Oiselays were related: Paravicini, pp. 123–4, n. 93): see p. 353 above and n. to II.10. *Retourne malle, heureuse retourne* is presumably an expression d'Oiselay was fond of quoting rather than one coined by himself; on G's ability to weave in quotations and allusions, and the overall impression of educated fluency created by her epistolary style, see notes to 9 and 14 above.

16 *ma seur Clemence d'Husier*: when *seur* is followed by a full name, the reference is to a sister canoness rather than to a sibling (contrast 7 above). Clemence d'Usie is recorded as having been elected 'decanissa' (second in command after the abbess) at Remiremont in 1487 and as having died in 1515 (Paravicini, p. 116) and must have been relatively young at the date of this letter. She was the youngest daughter of a minor Franche-Comté nobleman whose wife was a Vaudrey (the family of which the writer of Letter V was an illegitimate member): cf. n. to VIII.15. She is here said to be anxious to gain for a friend of hers (the *lieutenant* of Remiremont) a safe conduct to pass through Burgundian forces and lands into German territory (see further n. to XI.8). G's intercession on her behalf, and probably at her request, indicates that Clemence must know of some relationship between G and P (a fact also indicated in 18 below), if not of the affair as such (see pp. 353–4 above). She was thus, probably, one of a group of inmates whose Burgundian origins and/or links with P led to their being in G's confidence (and complicit in the furtherance and concealment of an affair they did not disapprove of).

17 A note in the archives of P records that, after P's successful deliverance from siege of Châtel-sur-Moselle on 22 April 1471, a military action at Remiremont on the following Thursday resulted in a victory for the Burgundians over a combined force of Frenchmen and men from the territories of Lorraine and of Liège ('Le juesdi apres furent ruez jus Francois, Lorrains et Liegeois devant Remiremont': see Paravicini, p. 131). G here records the presence of the defeated French in Remiremont (which Claerr-Stamm states to have been at this point liberated by the Burgundians from French occupation: p. 108), presumably seeking information and directions, but in a distracted state that made them (with their different dialect) unable to understand the words and signs offered them.

18 G's assurance to P that he can be 'full' in the 'news' he sends to 'us' would seem to be a covert indication of a trustworthy bearer for matter of a more personal nature: for, she says, Clemence can also carry his reply on her return journey – from Faucogney (which is presumably where P at present is, and which figures as a base for Burgundian troops at IV.13, on which see n.). Canonesses, unlike nuns, were free to leave the cloister as and when they chose (see pp. 341–2 above).

19 *a Dieu, a quelz je prie ...* (cf. VI.7, VII.18; see also I.15, II.12): G typically plays on the '-dieu' of 'adieu' to incorporate a prayer or blessing into the characteristic grace of her farewells.

20 The date is fuller than that usually given by G and does not contain the indications of early or late hour given in Letters I, VI and VII. The greater openness and formality is evidently related to the less personal relationship indicated by the term 'esliance' (see prefatory note above) and to the fact that the letter is (at least superficially) written on behalf of a group whose relations with P are of a friendly rather than intimate nature. The year is not given, but must be 1471, when the events referred to in 3, 10 and 17 occurred and when Sunday after Ascension Day fell on 18 August. MS *xvij* must be an error for *xviij* (see Paravicini) on the part of the scribe, unless the dictator herself had not moved her mental calendar on from the previous day.

21 The 'signature' is in the hand of the scribe (not in that of G), as at I.18 and VII.20.

IX: TO PIERRE FROM THE CANONESS

Monseigneur et mon garie

[1] Mon tres honnoré seigneur et garie, [2] tant humblement comme je pult me recommande a voustre bonne graice. [3] Long / tempt est que j'ey desiré sçavoir bonne novelle de vous et de voustre bonne prosperitey et santé / et desire bien tous les jour de en sçavoir novelle. Dieu par sa sainte grace vulle qu'elle soient / comme mon cuer le desire. [4] Se de moy vous plait sçavoir, je suis en bonne santei, la mersy / a Nostre Seigneur [5] – maix biaulcop d'affliction es eheu parmy ces gaire, tant de pluseur lenguage / j'ay oir diere. Et je ne vous sçaroie rescripre la tresgrande grif douleur que j'ey eheu et suffry / pour l'amour de vous; et se vous sçaviens les grant charges que on m'ont cudier donner, vous en / seriens bien mervelleux. Maix j'ay tous pourter patiament pour l'amour de vous. [6] Entre tout les aultres / douleur j'an voy une si tairible que je ne sçavoie que je fasoie ne que je disoie: se fuit le jour / quant on me disont que vous estiens pris. Je ne sçay comment je ne mory de deulx celon / la grant angouste que j'avoie, quant j'y pensoie de mes amours que on [m'en avoit] mener. [7] Et vous / sçavés, mon amy, que je vous aimme mieulx que moy meismes. [8] Maix, se Dieu plait, a plaisir de Dieu, / tout les douleur que j'ay souffert me torneront en liesse, quant je pense en la grant joie que j'arey / quant je pourés parler a vous – quar il n'est chosse au monde que je desire tant que de vous / veor. [9] Je vous prie et supplie que me vullés escripre bien a long tout voustre voluntei: a moient / quant vous ne me poés dire voustre volunter, rescripvés la moy pour moy ung peuc recon/forter. [10] Aultre chose ne vous sçay que rescripre, for que je prie a Nostre Seigneur qu'i vous dont accroissement / en tout honneur, bonne vie et longue, et santei, et paradis a la fin, et accomplissement de tous / vous bon desier. [11] Escript a Rmot le xixe jour d'auost.

[12] La tout voustre et plus que voustre, / celle que vous sçavés

6 m'en avoit] me navoit; *Paravicini* me n'avoit   9 voustre¹] voustre voustre

IX: TO PIERRE FROM THE CANONESS

On the outside of the letter: My lord and my protection

[1] My most honoured lord and my protection, [2] as humbly as I can do I commend myself to your good grace. [3] It is a long time that I have been desiring to hear welcome news of you and of the prospering of your affairs and your health, and I continue to desire every single day to hear such news. May God in His holy grace grant that it is all as good as my heart desires it to be. [4] If it would interest you to hear how I am, I am in good health, thanks be to God [5] – but I have had much affliction in these wars, so many rumours have I heard from many quarters. And I would not be able to write out for you the great and grievous distress that I have had and suffered because of my love for you; and if you knew the great charges put upon me, you would marvel at it. But I have borne it all for your sake. [6] Amid all these other griefs, I have had one so terrible that I did not know what to do or say: this was on the day when I was told that you had been taken captive. I do not know how I did not die from the great anguish that I felt, when I thought of my love that has been taken from me. [7] For you know, my beloved, that I love you more than I do myself. [8] But, God willing, if it please Him, all the griefs that I have suffered will yield the equivalent amount of bliss, as I believe when I think of the joy that I will have when I am able to speak to you face to face, for there is nothing in the world that I desire so much as to see you. [9] I beg and implore you please to write to me at length to tell me fully all you want to say: since you cannot say it to me face to face, at least put it in writing to me in order to give me some consolation. [10] I have nothing else to write, except to pray Our Lord to grant you increase in honour, a good life and a long one, and health, and paradise in the end, and the fulfilment of all your fair wishes. [11] Written at Remiremont, the 19th day of August.

[12] Wholly yours and more than yours: you know who

NOTES TO LETTER IX

There are no deletions in this fairly short letter, which is written by a scribe other than those G used for her other confidential letters (i.e. love letters) to P (Scribe 1 for Letters I, II and VII, and Scribe 2 for Letter VI). It is also the last love letter proper, as Letters X and XI are, like the previous one (VIII), written as coming from a pair or group, and do not refer to G's love for P (as this one, like the other non-group ones, does: at 5–7). This and Letter VIII are the only ones in which the addressee is designated on the exterior of the missive in any way other than by his official status as lord or *bailly* of Ferrette. And this is the only love letter in which that designation indicates any personal relationship; G may have felt able to use it because she had found some trustworthy bearer who was in her confidence and would make sure the letter was not seen by anyone but its addressee. But the designation may amount to only a partial 'confession'. The romantic context would certainly suggest that *garie* (repeated in the superscription at 1) means 'cure, remedy' (a sense in which *gar-* was often used in amorous contexts: cf. Text 5, 21–2 and note and the lover as *potens medicina* at *EDA* 21). But nouns bearing that sense in fact derive from the same verb as had the more general signification of 'protect, guarantee', and the word may well bear the alternative or additional sense of 'protection, protector' (cf. *EDA* 23, where *mulier* directs her letter in the salutation to her *presidio* [fortress, protection]). The term thus fuses political and romantic reference in a way characteristic of G's superscriptions in particular and of the often feudal language of love in general, which might frequently mirror or imitate a political or social relationship of lord/lady and dependent (see Stokes, 'The Contract of Love Service', p. 76). In one way, that is, the word is equivalent to the term *esliance* used in the exterior designation of the previous (less personal) letter, advertising to any curious Burgundian official that the letter comes from a Burgundian dependant or sympathizer. G writes superficially and partly as inmate of an institution in Lorraine that has accepted Burgundian 'protection' (as a town or territory was euphemistically said to do when it submitted to a hostile take-over: cf. Vaughan, pp. 95–6, 266) – but also and more critically as a woman whose love has exposed her to all sorts of emotional and social risks and distresses (5–7) against which her lover and his fidelity are her only protection and antidote. G's use of the term on the exterior is pregnant testimony to the grace and subtlety of her expressive powers: it reminds P of her vulnerability, and that she has put herself in his hands in all sorts of senses – the full range of which will be apparent to him alone, beyond the simple political sense intended for the eyes of a bearer not in their confidence and/or someone who caught sight of the unopened letter.

3–5 Good wishes for the health of the recipient, followed by a modestly introduced bulletin on the sender's own good health ('And should you be at all curious about mine ...'), for which God is given thanks, is a standard epistolary sequence (cf. *AP*, p. 187), frequently found in and adapted to amorous contexts, often to somewhat wistful or reproachful effect (love has made the sender actually ill, or s/he is well but sick at heart, etc.): cf. Text 6, 5A.10–12; *Troilus* V.1356–72; *'Suffolk' Poems* 14.8–11 ('And yf ye lyst have knowlech of my qwert [health], / I am in hele, God thankyd mot he be, / As of body, but treuly not in hert, / Nor nought shal be to tyme I may you se').

3 *Long tempt est*: this letter is actually dated only two days after the last, which in fact referred to letters recently received from P (VIII.6, 12). The present speedy follow-up missive indicating a desire for 'news' not yet had provides confirmatory evidence of what is deducible from other facts: G is here writing in a different (personal) capacity and role from that which she had assumed in the previous letter, where she was both sender and recipient of letters coming from and addressed to a pair/group of well-wishers; she now wants to give and receive communication of a more intimate sort (i.e. she is sending and requesting a love letter proper). This is the only one of the love letters proper that does not refer to the bearer, but G must have found one she could trust, since it is evident that she here risks both a letter and carriage of it that, unlike the last, are not ones which any watchful Burgundian official could safely know of.

5 *parmy ces gaire* is explained by Paravicini as '"c'est (na)gaire", récemment', but *affliction es eheu parmy ces gaire* surely forms a close parallel with the little joy *que je es ehu durant sez guerres* at VIII.3. *gaire* must therefore be an error for or form of *guerre(s)* (for which the spelling *gair* does occur in Anglo-Norman). For the *charges* borne for love of P, cf. VII.11 (and I.9). The sense on both occasions may be either 'accusations' (of an extra-marital affair and/or fraternization with a general leading what some in Lorraine might have thought of as an enemy power) or 'burdens, troubles' (in avoiding suspicion). G is presumably referring to stress caused her by disapproval or efforts to avoid attracting it.

6 See n. to VIII.10, where distress caused by news of P's capture is also referred to. Since G has thus already told P of the anxious grief this caused 'us', the present repetition of that point again demonstrates that she writes now in a different capacity: as a lover (cf. *mes amours*), who was obviously even more afflicted than she had indicated both/all P's well-wishers at Remiremont had been.

8 Cf. Criseyde's assurance to Troilus on accepting him into her 'service': 'ffor euery wo 3e shal recouere a blisse' (III.181). The point in fact represents a sophisticated application (to love) of a philosophical/theological principle (that suffering and pains will be counterpoised by the joys for which they are a kind of purchase price: cf. e.g. *Piers Plowman* B.XIV.105–216); cf. notes to VIII.9 and 14. *me torneront*: for the verb used in this context (positives accruing from their opposing negatives), cf. *Piers Plowman* C.V.93–101: 'y haue ytynt tyme and tyme myspened ... Ac ȝut I hope, as he þat ofte hath ychaffard [traded] / And ay leste and loste, and at þe last ... A [he] bouhte such a bargain he was þe bet [better] euere ... So hope y to haue ... a tyme / That alle tymes of my tyme to profit shal *turne*'.

9 All sorrows will be converted to joys only when G can at last 'speak' personally with P (IX.8), for which written letters given and received are regularly regarded as a poor substitute: cf. I.8 (and note) and II.8.

10 For this final blessing, cf. Text 6, 5A.28–45. G, too, has nothing left to say *for que* [except] this blessing, which is (therefore?) fuller than usual and constitutes a valediction that sounds rather significantly marked.
11 An actual date (though not the year) is again given, as in Letter VIII, rather than simply the time of day (as in the earlier letters): see n. to VIII.20. Perhaps G wanted to make it clear that this more private letter was written after the previous one, in which she had not been able fully to express her real feelings.
12 The subscription is again written in the hand of the scribe, not in G's own (see n. to VIII.21). Only in Letter VI is the sign-off in G's own hand, which otherwise occurs only in the postscripted validation of messages entrusted to the bearer in Letter I. The pointed avoidance of a name that would identify the sender and its replacement by a cryptic periphrasis (*celle que vous sçavés*) is common in love letters, actual and artful: see pp. 49–50 above.

X: TO PIERRE FROM THE CANONESS

[1] Monseigneur, [2] nous nous recommandons a vous plus de fois que plumes / ne papier ne sçaroyent porter. [3] Et au regart de nos doloreuses nouvelles, / celle qui est tant pompeuse vous en dira le tout – et créés que / ne avons pas mains que vous. [4] S'il est vray ce que vous / escripvés, et avons bien desir et bonne volunter de assouvir nos / vouyages – quar je vous assure qu'i nous tarde tant que ne / pouhons veoyr l'eure. [5] Orsa, Monseigneur, nous nous recommandons tousjours / a vostre bonne grace; et au regart de la nostre, vous y estes plus / que jamais. [6] Et vous envoyons la cainture de nostre esglise, / la quelle vous prions que la faicte[s] couvrir de cire et / la nous ranvoyrés en deux pipes pour bruler devant nos corps saincts; / [7] et nous prirons Dieu pour vous qu'i vous doing honneur, bonne vie et longue, et grace de nous veoyr bien brief. [8] Escript de par /

        [9] Celles qui sont vostre sans / changer a tous jours mais

---

6 faictes] faicte

X: TO PIERRE FROM THE CANONESS

[1] My lord, [2] we commend ourselves to you more times than pen and paper could suffice to record. [3] And with respect to our sad tidings, she who is so grand will tell you all – and, believe it, we have no hand to help us but yours. [4] If what you have written to us is true, we on our side certainly have the desire and the will to accomplish the journey – for I assure you that we are impatient to be able to see a suitable time for it. [5] So, my lord, we commend ourselves to your good grace; and with regard to our own good graces, you are in them more than ever. [6] And we are sending you a model of our church, which we pray you to have covered in wax, and then send it back to us in two containers, so that we can burn it before our holy relics; [7] and in return we will pray to God for you that He give you honour, a happy life and a long one, and the favour of seeing us very shortly. [8] Written on behalf of

[9] Those who are unalterably and always yours

NOTES TO LETTER X

This brief letter (which bears no address on its exterior) has no deletions and is written by a scribe different from the three who pen G's love letters (I, II, VII; VI; IX) and also different from the other two responsible for the letters in which she writes (or pretends to) as one of a group (or at least a pair) of canonesses, on behalf of a plural 'nous' that might refer to herself and her sister or to a larger group at Remiremont, as here and as in VIII (Scribe 4) and XI (Scribe 3).

3 This would seem to be a reference to one of the canonesses who is making some journey that enables her to act as bearer of the present letter and (since it bears no address) to put it in P's hands herself – and to supplement it by the verbal accounts which letters often mention the carrier as able or authorized to deliver (cf. I.17, VIII.12, 14 and p. 52 above). The light tone of *celle qui est tant pompeuse* suggests that the 'sad news' may not be anything seriously tragic. This reference to the bearer and her message seems, that is, to involve some casual wit that is not untypical of G's fluently readable style.

4 It appears that P has again urged G to come to him (and has claimed that the journey would be feasible or the circumstances propitious), and a response to such a proposal from him constitutes the most common reason (or partial reason) for G's writing to him (cf. I.6–7, II.7–8, VII.5, VIII.14–15, IX.9–10 implying her regret that a reunion is not possible, XI.4–5), even where she can only do so by disguising the personal nature of the trip by referring to it, as here and as in Letters VIII and XI, as one to be made by *nous*, and to herself as spokesman for a pair (with her sister) or a group ('*je vous assure qu'i nous tarde ...*'). The first-person plural nature of this letter (as of VIII and XI), and the suppression in it of any reference to G's love for P, probably indicates that G fears interception of the letter, or is using a scribe (and/or bearer) who is not in her confidence. The scribes used for this letter and for Letter VIII are not used for any of the love letters (see preliminary note above).

6 A model of Remiremont is to be waxed and burnt (like a dedicatory candle) before the holy relics. Paravicini (p. 130, n. 136) explains this ritual as an apotropaic device designed to invoke divine protection for a town or church, but adds that, though P is here requested to have the model covered in wax (and then returned in two pieces), it was common for all churches of any importance to have their own facilities for waxworking. Possibly P had offered to see to the waxing for some reason (and thus to take a stake in the ritual), since it does not sound as if the subject is here being broached to him for the first time. *pipes*: the word was used of barrels employed in transporting goods (see *DMF* B.2).

7 See n. to XI.8–9. The prayer is very similar to that which closes the previous letter (IX.10), but less earnest and emphatic – which is consistent with the different roles adopted by the same writer in the two letters (the lover and the spokesperson for a friendly pair/group).
9 Though the subscription takes a plural form, the pledge of truth it contains is possibly intended to be understood by P as an encoded amorous pledge; cf. XI.11.

XI: TO PIERRE FROM THE CANONESS

A nostre treshonnoré seigneur / monseigneur le ballif de Farreth

[1] Treshonnoré seigneur, [2] tant et de si bon cuer comme nous poions nous recommandons a vous, / [3] vous remerciant voz gracieusez lettres qu'avons darierement recue. [4] De la requeste / que nous faitez de tenir nostre promesse, nous vous supplions humblement que / vostre plaisir soit de nous avoir pour excusee; car nullement ne le povons tenir / pour le present, pour la dispositions du temps que n'est point convenable d'aller, / tant pour malladie comme pour guerre. [5] Certe, nous fuissiens vollentiés allee par dela / avant vostre departement. Et, au plaisir de Dieu, quant serez retournez nous tanrons / noz promesses tellement que serez contant – et vous festeroins si longuement / que vous direz 'allez a Dieu' avant que nous departons de vous. [6] Nous / prions a Dieu de jour en jour qu'i vous doint retourner brief et joieulx, / affin que puissiens acomplir voz gracieusez et doulcez requestez. [7] Il nous / desplait de vostre allee en la guerre, se fare se poioit aultrement, maix / au plaisir vous y averez honnour et profit – comme bien le savons par lez priers / que ferons pour vous a Dieu et a saincte Barbe, aul queulx pour / vous avo[n]s du tout nostre fiance. [8] Treshonnoré seigneur, nous vous suplions / qu'il vous plase a nostre requeste levez le mains tochant lez bien Anthonne de / Fareth, et nous prirons Dieu pour vous et en serons a tousiour maix tenuez / a vous – [9] priantz Dieu qu'i vous doint honnour, bonne vie et longue, paradis / a la fin. [10] Escriptz a Remiremont le premier jour de septembre mil iiij^c lxxii.

[11] Vostre ferme et malgrip / toutez vostre sens contredit

---

6 qu'i (= qu'il) que *Paravicini*   7 avons] *Paravicini*; a vous   9 qu'i (= qu'il) que *Paravicini*   vous] *inserted above line*   10 V[ostre] *is deleted before* Escriptz

XI: TO PIERRE FROM THE CANONESS

On the outside of the letter: To our most honoured lord, my lord the bailiff of Ferrette

[1] Most honoured lord, [2] as much and with as much goodwill as we can do we commend ourselves to you, [3] thanking you for the gracious letters that we last received from you. [4] As to the request you made us to keep our promise, we humbly beg you that it may please you to hold us excused; for in no way can we keep it at this time, because of the present state of things, in which a journey is impracticable, by reason equally of illness and war. [5] We would assuredly have wished to have gone to you before you left the place. And, by God's will, once you have returned, we will keep our promise in such a way as thoroughly to satisfy you – and we will celebrate with you so long that you will wish us 'go, and God be with you' before we go. [6] We pray to God from one day to the next that He grant you to return soon and joyful, so that we may be able to fulfil your gracious and kind requests. [7] We are unhappy about your departure for the war, and would wish it could be otherwise if that were possible, but, God willing, you will gain thereby honour and profit – as we well know you will, because of the prayers we make for you to God and to St Barbara, in whom lies all our trust for your welfare. [8] Right honoured lord, we beg you at our request please to intercede with respect to the property of Antoine de Farrette, and we will raise prayers on your behalf to God and will be forever obliged to you – [9] praying God to grant you honour, a happy life and a long one, and paradise at the end of it. [10] Written at Remiremont the first day of September 1472.

[11] Those who are yours firmly and despite all things yours without any gainsaying

NOTES TO LETTER XI

This (like VIII and X) is another letter in which G does not refer to her personal love for P, but writes as one of a pair or group, evidently in order to disguise the real nature of her relationship with the addressee. The scribe, however, is the same who penned the openly amorous Letter IX. This suggests that G could not write more openly either because there was available to her no bearer she could trust or because she feared the circumstances were such that mail from non-Burgundian territory to P (not now at home, but in the field: XI.5, 7) might fall into the wrong hands (cf. VIII.5–8).

4 See n. to X.4. Since we do not know how soon after the last letter (which was undated) this one was written, it is not clear whether the 'promised' journey is the one G wrote as if she was looking forward to at X.4 or one yet again rescheduled. At any event, the sequence of letters thus begins and ends with G citing politics and war as factors preventing her from joining her lover as he presses her to do. She here, perhaps significantly, adds 'illness' as another impediment. Though this could be her own or her sister's, it probably refers to some prevailing 'epidemic', exposure to which would be dangerous. And since this is the last letter P appears to have received from her, it is possible that she fell victim to the illness.

5–7 *departement* (5), *retourner* (6) and *allee en la guerre* (7): in September 1472 Pierre led a muster of troops from Alsace to march, via Champagne, to Charles the Bold, to reinforce the latter in his war with the French, who in this year went on the offensive (see Claerr-Stamm, pp. 112–13). He returned to Alsace at the end of the year.

5 *nous tanrons ... de vous*: i.e. 'we will come and make such a fuss of you and be such a burden on your hospitality that you will be glad to say "goodbye [God be with you]" to us'; with this graceful pleasantry does G, typically, sweeten a refusal that is actually (4) quite downright.

7 *saincte Barbe*, killed by her own (pagan) father, who was himself immediately afterwards struck dead by lightning, was regarded as providing protection for anyone who worked with explosives (gunners, etc.) and, by extension, anyone so situated as to be in danger of sudden death.

8–9 Prayers were the return offered for a gift or favour the donee could not otherwise repay: cf. *Juan Ruiz: Libro de Buen Amor*, ed. Raymond S. Willis (Princeton, 1972), 1651, 1719; *Piers Plowman* B.VI.121–8. The pledge of such gratefully reciprocative prayers here morphs neatly into the conventional closing blessing. Cf. X.6–7, and see nn. to I.15, II.8.

8 Paravicini says the reference must be to Antoine de Montreux en Ferrette, who lived in Remiremont, though it is not clear why this man (who became P's cup-bearer and married his daughter at some point before 1473: Paravicini, p. 120) could not plead his own cause with P. Paravicini also interprets the 'good friend' of Clemence d'Husier, for whom a safe conduct was requested from P at VIII.16, as a reference to Antoine de Montreux, but does not give his reasons for the

identification. The two passages certainly both show G acting in an intercessionary capacity with regard to a request to P in his official status, in a way consistent with, and giving plausibility to, the non-personal stance adopted in both letters – as spokesperson for a pair/group in friendly *esliance* [alliance: cf. Letter VIII] with P; it does look significant, however, that she seems to have been known at Remiremont to have influence with P.

9 The prayer is almost identical with that which closes IX, a love letter proper penned by the same scribe as writes this present superficially 'plural' letter – which can evidently be decoded into a personal one with much the same purport as IX.

10 *V[ostre]* deleted before *Escriptz*: the error was occasioned, presumably, by anticipation (on the part of the dictatress or scribe) of the subscription that follows (11). The fuller date is more typically used by G in letters in which she does not reveal herself as P's lover, but adopts the role of spokesperson for a pair/group (cf. VIII.20).

11 See n. to X.9.

THE COUNCIL OF REMIREMONT

On this poem, and the contrast between it and the letters of the canoness, see pp. 363–4 above. It is written in leonine verse: rhyming half-lines consisting in this case of seven syllables, scanning trochaically (three trochees plus one more stress). It survives in two manuscripts: Trier, Stadtbibliothek 1081/29, fols. 39ᵛ–42ʳ (T) and Koblenz, Landeshauptarchiv 162, Nr.1401, fols. 156ᵛ–157ᵛ (R). The earliest edition, by George Waitz ('Das Liebesconcil', *Zeitschrift für deutsches Altertum* 7 (1849) 160–7), was based on *T*, as was the text that appears in Oulmont (*Les débats du clerc et du chevalier*, pp. 93–107). The edition by Wilhelm Meyer ('Das Liebesconcil in Remiremont', *Nachrichten von der Gesellschaft der Wissenschaften zu Göttingen. Philologisch-Historische Klasse* (1914) 1–19) was based on both manuscripts, as was the re-edition by Reuben Lee in 1981 (in an as yet unpublished PhD). The present text is also based on the readings of both manuscripts, as provided by Lee, and we have also followed Lee in retaining Meyer's line numbering.

Content proves *R* to have been written after 1216 (Lee, p. 85), but the four hands responsible for the text in *T* belong to the mid-twelfth century (Lee, p. 80), and so the poem cannot have been written after that, but equally does not seem to have been composed much before then. According to Lee's researches into the ladies whose names appear in either or both of the manuscripts (Lee, pp. 69–76), sisters with the relevant Christian names can be found in the abbess-ship of Judith (1114–64), and on the basis of that and other evidence Lee favours 'a mid-twelfth century date for the composition of the *Council*' (p. 76). In its use of the conceits of courtly love, in particular the trope of love as a religion parallel to that of the Christian church, it would appear therefore to be more pioneering and avant-garde than it may seem, for it predates the work both of Andreas Capellanus and of Chrétien de Troyes, and the fashion and currency they gave to these ideas. It may, in fact, 'be the first work of amatory verse in Latin to make explicit mention of courtliness' (Lee, p. 150), though the poem also has evident affiliations with goliardic verse, the earliest of which, interestingly, likewise has connections with Lorraine (Lee, pp. 130, 134).

It is itself an interesting mixture of art and actuality. The mock church council it depicts is obviously fictional and represents a marked instance of the transference of church procedures, rituals, language and theology to love, presented as a church with its own god. But it has the historical abbey of Remiremont as its setting, and the named inmates are obviously real women. It is likely that it was some kind of local joke or witty *jeu*. Since the council decides in favour of clerks as lovers (excommunicating those who prefer knights), and, though no other men are admitted, its gates being open to all the clerks of Toul (the diocese to which Remiremont belonged), it is obviously meant to be assumed that the author was himself a clerk of the diocese. But this internal indication of authorship may be part of the wit, since the effect of indicating a strongly partisan narrator is usually comic – as with the old retainer through whom Maria Edgeworth's *Castle Rackrent* is mediated, and to whose comically obvious partiality she drew attention in her preface to the novel – as making it easier for the reader to identify and quantify the prejudices which *any* biographer or historian inevitably brings to his task.

The joke thus lies mainly in the mock 'directive' issued to the sisterhood that they should give their favours to clerks, rather than in the satiric exposure of any impropriety on their part, although the latter is what tends, somewhat reductively, to be assumed. The predetermined bias towards clerks is what distinguishes the poem from, for instance, the otherwise very similar *Altercatio Phyllidis et Florae* (for the text of which see Oulmont, pp. 107–21). For, although that poem too gives a verdict in favour of clerks, the debate gives equal space to the claims of knights, and so provides a more straightforward example of the topic than does the *Concilium*, which does not even pretend to be impartial, and in which the argument in favour of knights is a mere brief token (109–32). The poem is not so much a mock debate (on knights versus clerks) as a piece of cheeky propaganda (for clerks) directed at ladies who are obviously personally known to the writer(s) and who, it implies, are not so much the target as the audience of a joke delivered by clerks who share (rather than scorn) the amorous preoccupations that, being (like the ladies) members of the church, they ideally should not have. It is a joke shared with the ladies, not a joke on them. So 'satire' is a misleading term when taken, as it often is, to imply a lampoon which 'insults' the sisters (Lee, p. 76) by revealing 'scandalous' things (p. 93) about them. There are other objections to be made to this line of criticism. The secularizing transformation of the inmates from nuns to canonesses had already occurred, having taken place according to Lee in the mid-eleventh century (pp. 20–1; cf. Boquillon, p. 51), although a strict terminological distinction between 'nuns' and 'canonesses' would not have been typical of the earlier period. The poem probably reflects the fact that the sisters were known to follow a more relaxed version of the rule, a relaxation that was in due course formalized by an official change in status to that of 'canonesses' – who as has been pointed out (see pp. 341–2 above) did not take the same vows as did nuns, but were free to leave the cloister whenever they wished and to marry if they chose. This means that Remiremont was one of the very few establishments where the sisters could be represented as the poem does represent them *without* implying the scandal that would attach to fully professed nuns, whose vows were intended to be permanently binding. The ladies would have committed themselves to observing chastity and celibacy in the cloister, and there are deprecating references to such vows in the poem. But the poem is careful to make it clear that those vows, though doubtless breached in spirit, have not been disobeyed in the letter: of fornication and promiscuity the sisters (36) are quite innocent (see below), and the word *virgo* is used of them and the lady who presides over the meeting (25, 44 and perhaps 138).

Proto-canonesses, that is, though they should not of course be chiefly occupied with romantic matters, retained secular identities and options that made secular concerns less disgraceful than in the case of nuns. The evidence which Lee points to for a reputation for laxity at Remiremont needs to be seen in this light. There was papal concern about the community and its over-worldly orientation (Lee, pp. 23–4, 38–9, 68). But these complaints are not phrased so as to suggest they were occasioned by any shocking reports of sexual licence. They are relatively mild, and seem to have been prompted precisely by the inevitably more worldly tone taken on by an abbey once its personnel were secularized into canonesses, canonesses belonging to families of wealth and status – who had joined an institution whose own wealth and property was ever increasing and ever more preoccupying, and the power and prestige of which was at its height under the abbatial rule of Judith (Lee, p. 40). Some carnality was no doubt included in, but does not seem to have been the main focus of, the charges.

Lee also points to the reference to Remiremont that occurs in one of the twelfth-century Latin love poems found in the Spanish manuscript Ripoll 74. A woman-hungry young man is told by Venus to find himself a nice-looking girl of good birth ('Egregia specie generosam quaere puellam': 25), and, when he objects that his locality offers no suitable candidate 'quae mihi conveniat' (42), he is directed to Remiremont, where he will certainly find what he is looking for ('quod cupis': 43), and where he does then indeed discover a lady that fits the bill nicely ('mihi quae bene conveniebat': 47): see Ripoll Poem 19 (pp. 102–6) in Traill and Haynes, *Education of Nuns*. But one should note the emphasis and the logic here. The point is not that Remiremont will provide complaisant women (which, it seems assumed, any locality could afford). What Remiremont guarantees are the desirable adjuncts of good birth and courtly classiness that a 'gentil' would naturally look for in a sweetheart. The present poem is in fact careful to pre-empt any suspicion that the expertise in the *ars amatoria* it attributes to the ladies (35) implies promiscuity (fidelity to a single lover is enjoined on them at 179–80: cf. p. 256 above) or even, in two cases at least, as has already been pointed out, any sexual experience at all (36). Their amorous preoccupations are thus categorized as virginally romantic and sentimental rather than lascivious. This is consistent with a playful joke addressed *to* the canonesses from the clerical author(s) as to an interest in love which the poem represents the abbey inmates as sharing *with* male clerks (who often had equally little vocation for a life in the church similarly dictated in many cases largely by economic and family pressures), not the ribald exposé of sexual incontinence that Lee often suggests (especially in his detection of sexual innuendo in the poem: pp. 109–10).

The poem, in its depiction of love as a religion, hovers interestingly and not untypically between a serious applicability of the conceit (to the ardour, devotion and felt spiritual significance of the experience) and comic extravagance. It is an engaging piece that develops its theme with wit and charm – and with linguistic and metrical competence. The metre is well-handled and the Latin is largely 'correct' by classical standards (Lee, p. 116).

We follow T unless R is plainly more accurate. Insignificant variants between, or evident errors in one of, the two manuscripts are not recorded, and no notice has been taken of what appear to be mistranscriptions by other editors or of emendations we have not adopted.

IDUS APRILIS HABITUM EST CONCILIUM HOC IN MONTE ROMARICI

    Veris in temporibus,   sub Aprilis idibus,
    Habuit concilium   Romarici Moncium
    Puellaris concio   montis in cenobio.
    Tale non audivimus,   nec fuisse credimus,
5   In terrarium spacio;   a mundi principio
    Tale nunquam factum est,   sed neque futurum est.
    In eo concilio   de solo negocio
    Amoris tractatum est,   quod in nullo factum est,
    Sed de evangelio   nulla fuit mencio.
10   Nemo qui vir dicitur   illuc intromittitur;
    Quidam tamen aderant,   qui de longe venerant –
    Non fuerunt laici,   sed honesti clerici:
    Hos honestos senciunt   intus et suscipiunt.
    Janua Tullensibus   aperitur omnibus,
15   Quorum ad solacium   factum est concilium;
    ....
    Puellis amantibus,   illis solis omnibus,
    Janua dat aditum,   ceteris prohibitum.
    Janue custodia   fuit hec Sibilia
20   Que, ab annis teneris   miles facta Veneris,
    Quiquid amor jusserat   non invita fecerat.
    Veterane domine   arcentur a limine,
    Quibus omne gaudium   solet esse tedium,
    Gaudium et cetera   que vult etas tenera.
25   Intromissis omnibus   virginum agminibus,
    Lecta sunt in medium,   quasi evangelium,
    Precepta Ovidii,   doctoris egregii.
    Lectrix tam propicii   fuit evangelii
    Eva de Danubrio,   potens in officio
30   Artis amatorie,   ut affirmant alie.
    Cantus, modulamina,   et amoris carmina
    Cantaverunt pariter   satisque sonoriter,
    De multis non quelibet,   due sed Elizabet.
    Has duas non latuit   quicquid Amor statuit:
35   Harum in noticia   ars est amatoria;
    Sed ignorant opere   quid vir sciat facere.

ON THE IDES OF APRIL [13 APRIL] THIS COUNCIL TOOK PLACE AT REMIREMONT

In the days of spring, around the time of the Ides of April,
A council was held at Remiremont
By a gathering of the maidens in that monastery of the mountain.
We have never heard of, nor do we believe there ever to have been, such a one
5   In the whole world; from the beginning of time,
Such a one not only never was but never will be.
In that council, the only business
Discussed was that of love, which has never figured in any other council,
But there was no reference made to the Gospels.
10 No one describable as a male is officially allowed access,
Though there were some men present, who had come from afar –
Not laymen, but respectable clerics:
These men they consider honourable and allow them admittance.
To all the clerks of the diocese, Toul, the gates are open,
15 To please whom the council has been called;
....
And to all those girls who love, and to those alone,
Do those gates give entrance, being prohibited to all the rest.
The portress of the gates was that lady called Sybil
20 Who, a soldier of Venus from her early youth,
Had willingly obeyed all the commands of Love.
Older women are kept away from the threshold,
For to them joy has become tedious –
Joy and all else that requires youth.
25 All the virgins having entered in procession,
There was read in their midst, instead of a passage from the Gospel,
The precepts of Ovid, that famous authority.
The lectress of such a comforting Gospel was
Eva de Danubrio, well qualified to officiate
30 In the amorous art, as all the others declared.
Choral music, melodies, and songs of love
Were sung in unison and with resonance,
Not by simply any persons among the many there, but by the two Elizabeths.
None of the statutes of Love were unknown to them:
35 The art of love lies within their cognizance;
But they are ignorant of the deeds that a male knows how to do.

　　　　　Post hec oblectamina　　cardinalis domina
　　　　　Astitit in medio,　　　 indicto silentio,
　　　　　Vestita ut decuit,　　　 veste qua refloruit:
40　　　　Hec vestis coloribus　　colorata pluribus
　　　　　Gemmis fuit clarior,　　auro preciosior,
　　　　　Mille Maii floribus　　 hinc inde pendentibus.
　　　　　Ipsa virgo regia,　　　 mundi flos et gloria,
　　　　　..

45　　　　Florens super omnia,　 quasi Veris filia,
　　　　　Hec talis in omnibus　　docta satis artibus,
　　　　　Habens et facundiam　　 secundum scientiam,
　　　　　Postquam cetus siluit,　ora sic aperuit:
　　　　　'Vos quarum est gloria　amor et lascivia,
50　　　　Atque delectatio　　　 Aprilis cum Maio,
　　　　　Notum vobis facimus　　 ad vos quare venimus.
　　　　　Amor, Deus omnium　　　 quotquot sunt amancium,
　　　　　Me misit vos visere　　 et vitam inquirere:
　　　　　Sic Maius disposuit　　 et Aprilis monuit.
55　　　　Vos ergo benigniter　　 et amicabiliter
　　　　　Obtestor et moneo,　　 sicut iure debeo,
　　　　　Nulla vestrum sileat　　que vos vita teneat:
　　　　　Si quid corrigendum est,　vel si cui parcendum est,
　　　　　Meum est corrigere,　　 meum est et parcere'.
60　　　　Convocavit singulas　　 magnas atque parvulas.

　　　　　Elizabet de Granges loquitur
　　　　　'Nos ex quo potuimus　　Amori servivimus:
　　　　　Quicquid ipse voluit,　 nobis non displicuit,
　　　　　Et si quid neglximus　　inscienter fecimus.
　　　　　Sic servando regulam　　nullam viri copulam
65　　　　Habendam eligimus,　　　sed neque cognovimus
　　　　　Nisi talis hominis　　　qui sit nostri ordinis'.

　　　　　Elizabet de Falcon
　　　　　'Clericorum gratiam　　 laudem et memoriam:
　　　　　Hos semper amavimus　　 et amare cupimus,
　　　　　Quorum amicitia　　　　 nil tardat solatia.
70　　　　Clericorum copula:　　　hec est nostra regula,
　　　　　Nos habet et habuit　　 et placet et placuit –
　　　　　Quos scimus affabiles,　gratos et amabiles.
　　　　　Inest curialitas　　　　clericis et probitas:

After these delights, the chief lady
Rose to her feet in the central place, silence having been called for,
Apparelled most fitly in apparel in which she bloomed:
40　This apparel, coloured in many colours,
Was more lucent than gems, richer than gold,
Hung all round with a thousand flowers of May.
This lady, the queen of the virgins, the flower and glory of the world,
．．．
45　Flowering above everything, like the daughter of Spring,
This lady of such a kind, learned in all the arts,
Having likewise eloquence to match her knowledge,
After the chapter had fallen silent, began thus to speak:
'You whose glory lies in love and frolic,
50　And the delights of April together with May,
We herewith make known to you why we have come to you.
Love, the God of all the lovers there are,
Has sent me on a visitation to you to make enquiry into how you lead your lives:
This is what April and May require and demand.
55　With all goodwill and friendship, therefore,
Do I conjure and admonish you, as is my duty,
That none of you should remain silent with regard to your manner of life:
If anything requires amendment, or if anyone is to be pardoned,
The correcting and the pardoning belong to me'.
60　She addressed each of them in turn, great and small.

Elizabeth de Granges speaks:
'We have, since we have been able to do so, given our service to Love:
We followed whatever he willed without any displeasure,
And, if we were remiss in anything, we were unknowingly so.
Accordingly, observing our amorous rule, we choose to have no relationship
65　(Or indeed to become acquainted) with any man
Except such a one as belongs to an order obeying the same rule'.

Elizabeth de Falcon speaks:
'I would like to commend the charm and reputation of clerics:
It is these men we have always loved and whom we wish to give our love,
Men who give a love that brings no alloy of anxiety to pleasure.
70　Union with clerics is the rule we observe,
By which we bind and have bound ourselves, and by which we are and have been pleased to live –
Men whom we know to be possessed of address, charm and loveability.
There is courtliness in clerics and goodness:

    Non noverunt fallere   neque maledicere.
75 Amandi periciam   habent et industriam.
    Pulchra donant munera,   bene servant federa:
    Si quid amant dulciter,   non relinquunt leviter.
    Pro his quos assumpsimus   ceteros postponimus.
    Vota stulta frangere   non est nefas facere:
80 Nulla est dampnatio   sed neque transgressio
    Si votum negligitur   quod stulte promittitur.
    Experto credendum est,   cui bene certum est:
    Certum est et cognitum   quid sit amor militum,
    Quam sit detestabilis,   quam miser et labilis.
85 Per insipientiam   eorum noticiam
    In primis quesivimus;   sed cito cessavimus,
    Dolus ut apparuit   qui in eis latuit.
    Inde nos transtulimus   ad hos quos notavimus,
    Quorum est dilectio   omni carens vicio,
90 Quorum amor utilis,   firmus est et stabilis.
    Quid dicemus amplius   nisi quod ulterius
    Nulla valet racio   a nostro solacio
    Clericos disiungere,   omni gratos opere?'

Agnes:
    'Puellis claustralibus   vobis dico omnibus:
95 Est quaedam abusio   militum susceptio:
    Nefas est et vetitum   et vobis illicitum.
    ....
    ....
    Amplectendo clericum,   sic recuso laicum'.

Berta:
100 'Amor, deus omnium   iuventutis gaudium,
    Clericos amplectitur   et ab eis regitur.
    Tales ergo diligo,   stultos quoque negligo'.

Omnes iste loquuntur:
    'Tali vita vivimus,   in qua permanebimus,
    Si vobis laudabilis   videtur et utilis.
105 Et, si quod peccavimus,   si vultis, cessabimus'.

Cardinalis Domina:
    'Ipsis amatoribus   circumspectis ominibus,

It is not in them to deceive or say offensive things.
They show both skill and commitment in amorous matters.
They give nice presents, they keep to the pacts they make:
What they love tenderly they do not lightly abandon.
In favour of these men, whom we have accepted as companions, do we disregard others.
Breaking stupid vows is not something it is wrong to do:
There is no damnability, nor even transgression,
If a vow which is not wisely made is not kept.
What is to be trusted is experiential knowledge, where one can indeed be certain.
And it is both certain and known what the love of knights amounts to,
How contemptible it is, how base and unreliable.
Out of ignorance, acquaintance with them
Was something we at first sought – but we soon ceased to do so
When the fraudulence that lurked in them revealed itself.
So we then transferred ourselves to those we have spoken of,
In whom is delight lacking all defect,
Whose love is a serviceable love, firm and stable.
What more do we need to say, except to add that
There is no rational way to separate clerks,
Pleasing in all they do, and our happiness in life?'

Agnes:
'To all you maidens who live enclosed in the cloister I say:
Taking up with knights is a type of vice –
It is wicked and forbidden and something not permitted to you.
....
....
In embracing the clerk, I reject the layman'.

Bertha:
'Love, the god of all the joys of youth,
Embraces clerics and is ruled by them.
Such men therefore do I also love, and pass over the fools'.

All three of them speak:
'This is the life we lead and in which we will continue,
If it seems to you praiseworthy and profitable.
And if we have sinned in any way, we will, at your pleasure, desist'.

The superior speaks:
'After consideration of all these lovers,

  Utiles non adeo   amatores video
  Quam istos, quos laudibus   prefertis in omnibus'.

Militares etiam loquuntur:
  'Nos a puericia   semper in familia
110 Amoris permansimus   et manere cupimus.
  Sed est nobis alia   amandi sententia:
  Qui student milicie   nobis sunt memorie'.
  Horum et milicia   placet et lascivia;
  Horum ad obsequium   nostrum datur studium'.

Elizabet Popona:
115 'Audaces ad prelia   sunt pro nostri gratia:
  Ut sibi nos habeant   et ut nobis placeant,
  Nulla timent aspera   nec mortem nec vulnera.
  Tales pre-elegimus,   tales nostros fecimus:
  Eorum prosperitas   est nostra felicitas,
120 Eorum tristicia   nostra turbat gaudia'.

Adeleyt:
  'Semper ex quo potui   sectam illam tenui,
  Et semper desidero,   dum habere potero,
  Servire militibus   mihi servientibus.
  Tale vero studium   magis quam psalterium,
125 Talibus me iungere   placet plus quam legere;
  Propter horum copulam   parvi pendo regulam.
  Nostrum illis atrium   est et erit pervium,
  Et fontem et pascuam   que habemus congruam
  Equis exposuimus   quos eorum novimus.
130 Tali vita vivere   gaudemus summopere,
  Quia nulla dulcior   nullaque commodior,
  Et quia sic novimus   et sancte iuravimus'.

[New Speaker:]
  'Nos parum regnavimus,   parum adhuc fecimus.
  Sed flores colligere,   rosas primas carpere,

I see none so appropriate
As those whom you in all ways praise as preferable'.

Those who favour knights now also speak:
'We are ladies who also, since childhood, always in the household
110 Of Love have remained and desire to remain.
But our feelings on the subject of love are different:
Those who apply themselves to the military art are the ones who occupy our thoughts;
Both the chivalric activities and the pastimes of these men are pleasing,
And it is towards complaisance to them that our zeal is directed'.

Elizabet Popona:
115 'It is to win our favour that they are bold to engage in battles:
In order to win us and in order to please us,
They fear no hardships, neither death nor injury.
Such are the men that we have chosen, such are the men we have made our own:
Their well-being is our joy,
120 Their sorrow clouds our pleasures'.

Adeleyt:
'Ever since I was able to, I have held by that class of men,
And I desire always, as long as I have the capacity to do so,
To give my service to the knights who have given theirs to me.
I am better pleased with such an occupation than with the psalter,
125 And with dedicating myself to such men than to reading that out;
And the bond with them makes me attach little importance to our rule.
Our forecourt is and will remain open to the passage of those men,
And our spring water and any suitable pasture that we have
We have made available for the horses that we know to be theirs.
130 We have supreme joy in living a life of this kind,
Because there is none sweeter and none easier,
And because it is one we have found to be so and are solemnly sworn to'.

[New Speaker:]
'We have as yet enjoyed only too little power and have done only too little.
What we have done is to vouchsafe to gather flowers and pick the new roses

135 His tantum concessimus   quos de clero novimus.
    Hec nostra professio   est, erit intentio:
    Clericis ad libitum   persolvere debitum,
    Quotquot oblectamina   virgo debet femina.
    Idem proposuimus   et voto firmavimus.
140 Quidquic dicant alie   nobis adversarie,
    Clericis nos dedimus   nec eos mutabimus.
    Clericorum probitas   et eorum bonitas
    Semper querit studium   ad amoris gaudium, –
    Sed eorum gaudia   tota ridet patria:
145 Laudant nos in omnibus   rithmis atque versibus.
    Tales iussu Veneris   diligo pre ceteris.
    Dulcis amicicia   cleris est et gloria.
    Quicquid dicant alie,   apti sunt in opere.
    Clericus est habilis,   dulcis et affabilis:
150 Hunc habendo socium   nolo maius gaudium.
    Omne votum utile   firmum sit et stabile;
    Sed quod est illicitum   habeatur irritum,
    Nam stulta promissio   non est absque vicio.
    Vos, quarum prudentia   apta dat consilia,
155 Nunc illud attendite   et bene discernite:
    Amor quarum apcior,   quarum est deterior?'

    [New Speaker:]
    'Militum noticia   displicet et gratia,
    Quibus inest levitas   et stulta garrulitas:
    Gaudent maledicere,   secretum detegere.
160 Hoc ergo consilium   damus et iudicium:
    Ut cunctis odibiles   sint et execrabiles
    Que se militaribus   implicant amoribus.
    Novi vitam omnium   et mores amancium
    ....
165 Novi qui sint mobiles   et nobis inutiles.
    Nulla est felicitas,   sed neque fidelitas,
    In amore militum,   quod multis est cognitum.

135   For those men alone whom we know to be among the ranks of the clergy.
This is our formal pledge and will remain our purpose:
To pay at their pleasure whatever is owed to the clerks
In the way of gratifications that a female virgin owes.
That is what we have determined upon and confirmed by vow.
140   Whatever others who oppose us in this matter may say,
It is to clerics that we have given ourselves and we will not exchange them for others.
The clerks, in their conscientiousness and goodness,
Are always seeking to cultivate the joys of love, –
And indeed the whole land smiles bright at the joys they furnish:
145   They praise us in all their poems and verses.
Such men, by the command of Venus, I love above others.
In the clergy one finds both sweet affection and glory (from their verses in one's praise).
Whatever other sisters may say, everything they do is fit and right.
The cleric is adept, pleasant and urbane:
150   I wish for no greater joy than to have the company of such a man.
Every suitable vow should be observed with firmness and stability;
But when it is an improper one, it should be held null and void,
For a foolish promise is one not free of wrongfulness.
You wiser sisters, whose sagacity provides fitting counsel,
155   Give your attention to the matter and decide properly between the two:
Which sisters love more fittingly, which less so?'

[New Speaker:]
'There is no pleasure to be had in the acquaintance and favour of knights,
In whom there is fickleness and foolish babbling:
They take pleasure in repeating scandal and in revealing confidential matters.
160   This, therefore, is the counsel and judgement we give:
That those who involve themselves in knightly loves
Should be pronounced worthy of the hate and execration of the community.
I am familiar with the habits of life of all lovers and with their characteristic behaviour
         ....
165   I have got to know which are unreliable and unprofitable to us.
There is no happiness, nor even fidelity,
In the love given by knights, as many of us have found out.

　　　　　Hos vitando dicimus　　et iure decernimus
　　　　　Clericos diligere　　bonum est et sapere,
170　　Eorum dilectio　　magna delectatio.
　　　　　Hos tantum suscipite,　　ceteros negligite!'

　　　　　Cardinalis domina:
　　　　　'Quia sic decernitis　　et iure consulitis,
　　　　　Nunc ego precipio　　eas in consorcio
　　　　　Nostre ne recipiant,　　nisi satisfaciant.
175　　Sed si penituerint　　et se nobis dederint,
　　　　　Detur absolucio　　et talis condicio:
　　　　　Ne sic peccent amplius,　　quia nil deterius.

　　　　　Nota aliud dictum:
　　　　　'Hoc mandamus etiam　　per obedienciam:
　　　　　Nulla vestrum pluribus　　se det amatoribus,
180　　Uni soli serviat　　et ille sufficiat.
　　　　　Hoc si qua neglexerit,　　banno nostro suberit;
　　　　　Non levis remissio　　fiet huic vicio:
　　　　　Levi penitentia　　non purgantur talia.

　　　　　Item aliud dictum:
　　　　　'Nunc demum precipio,　　sed non sub silencio,
185　　Ne vos detis vilibus,　　nec umquam militibus,
　　　　　Tactum vestri corporis,　　vel coxe vel femoris;
　　　　　Talibus solacium　　dare vel colloquium
　　　　　Dolor nobis maximus　　est et pudor plurimus
　　　　　...
190　　Militum solacia　　nobis sunt obprobria,
　　　　　Quia cum non creditur　　fama turpis oritur:
　　　　　Quorum ex infamia　　nostra perit gloria.
　　　　　Precor vos summopere　　clericos diligere,
　　　　　Quorum sapientia　　disponuntur omnia,
195　　Totum quicquic agimus　　vel cum nos desipimus;
　　　　　Causas nostras agere　　student atque regere –
　　　　　Quantum possunt etiam,　　per eorum gratiam,
　　　　　Nostra quedam abdita　　numquam erunt cognita.

In ruling them out, we thus declare and justly give it as our decision
That to love clerks is to act wisely and well,
And that great delectation lies in so loving them.
Adopt only these, and ignore the others!'

The superior speaks:
'Because you give this as your decision and your formal recommendation,
I too now rule that those who are not in conformity with it should not be received
Into their company by the members of our order – unless they make satisfaction for their sin.
But if they do repent, and submit themselves to our correction,
Let absolution be given them, on this condition:
That they should not sin in this way any more, because there is nothing worse than relapse.

Note a further clause:
'This also we charge you, on your obedience:
That none of you should give herself to more than one lover,
But should give her service to one alone and one must suffice.
If she fails in any way to observe this injunction, she will suffer our denunciation,
And pardon will not lightly be given to such a vice:
Such things are not to be purged by any small penance.

Again another clause:
'Now finally I rule, in a decree not to be confined to these four walls,
That you should not permit to worthless men, nor ever to knights,
Physical contact with your body, either hip or thigh;
Giving to such men any kind of pleasure or speech
Brings on us the greatest pain and the most manifold shame
....
Favours given to knights are reproaches upon us,
Because they give rise in unforeseeable ways to evil fame:
In the bad name of such men our own good name perishes.
I beg you as earnestly as I can that you should cherish clerics,
By whose good judgement all things are well arranged,
Everything we do and everything we enjoy;
They study how to conduct and manage affairs for us –
And, thanks to them and to their doing their utmost,
Our confidential matters will never be publicly known.

Cardinalis Domina ad omnes:
'Si placent que diximus,   que vobis suggessimus,
200 Horum confirmacio   sit vestra responsio;
Si cui displiceat,   hec nequaquam taceat'.

Omnes respondent:
'Omnis nostra concio   sedens in concilio
Ut vestra prudencia   dictat laudat omnia:
Placet iunioribus,   placet nobis omnibus'.

Item Cardinalis Domina:
205 'Quicquid vestra probitas   firmat et auctoritas
Nuncietur alias   per omnes ecclesias,
Nostrisque sororibus,   puellis claustralibus,
Faciamus cognitum   quid sit eis vetitum:
Omnia que diximus   et que confirmavimus,
210 Non ullo sophismate,   sint sub anathemate,
Sed racionabiliter   fiat et perhenniter,
Nisi sic peniteant,   clericis ut faveant.
Huius banni racio   vestro sit consilio:
Igitur attendite,   "Amen!" tantum dicite.

Excommunicatio rebellarum:
215 'Vobis iussu Veneris   et ubique ceteris
Que vos militaribus   subditis amoribus,
Maneat confusio,   terror et contricio,
Labor, infelicitas,   dolor et anxietas,
Timor et tristicia,   bellum et discordia,
220 Fex insipiencie,   cultus inconstancie,
Dedecus et tedium,   longum et obprobrium,
Furiarum species,   luctus et pernicies!
Luna, Jovis famula,   Phebus, suus vernula,
Propter ista crimina   negent vobis lumina!
225 Sic sine solamine   careatis lumine!
Nulla dies celebris   trahat vos de tenebris!
Ira Jovis celitus   destruat vos penitus!
Huius mundi gaudia   vobis sint obprobria!
Omnibus horribiles   et abhominabiles
230 Semper sitis clericis,   que favetis laicis!
Nemo vobis etiam   "ave" dicat obviam!
Vestra quoque gaudia   sint sine concordia!

The Council of Remiremont

The superior to all the ladies assembled:
'If the things which we have said and proposed meet with your approval,
200 Let confirmation of them be your response;
And if they meet with the disapproval of anyone, she should speak now'.

All reply:
'All those here assembled and sitting in formal council
Give their approval to all that your wisdom decrees:
It is agreed to by the novices, agreed to by all of us'.

The superior again:
205 'All that is thus sanctioned by your probity and authority
Should now be announced throughout all other churches,
And to all the cloistered maidens who are fellow sisters of our order
Let us make known what is thus forbidden to them:
Let all that we have said and ratified,
210 Plainly and without sophism, be under threat of anathema,
Which should rightly and permanently remain in force
Unless the guilty repent and give their favours to clerics.
The legality of this ban should be affirmed by this council of yours:
Therefore listen to it, and then simply say, "Amen!"

Excommunication of the disobedient sisters:
215 'By the commandment of Venus, unto you and to all others everywhere
Who make yourselves subject to the love of knights,
Let there be turmoil, terror and grief,
Toil, unhappiness, sorrow and anxiety,
Fear and misery, conflict and discord,
220 The dregs of stupidity, the festering of inconstancy,
Indignity and irksomeness and lasting opprobrium,
Apparitions of the Furies, torment and ruin!
May the moon, servant to Jove, and Phoebus the sun, born vassal to him,
Deny you their light because of these crimes of yours,
225 So that you may always, without any relief, lack light,
With no feast day ever to give you any holiday from your darkness!
May Jove's anger falling from heaven destroy you wholly!
May the joys of this world be taunts to you!
May you who thus favour laymen ever be to all clerics
230 A source of horror and abomination!
May no one even say "hail" to you when they meet you!
May your very joys be sources of discord!

Vobis sit intrinsecus   dolor et extrinsecus!
Vivatis cotidie   in lacu miserie!
235   Pudor, ignominia   vobis sint per omnia!
Laboris et tedii,   vel pudoris nimii,
Sed si quid residuum   sit vobis perpetuum,
Nisi spretis laicis,   faveatis clericis!
Si qua penituerit   atque satisfecerit,
240   Dando penitentiam   consequetur veniam'.

Ad confirmacionem   omnes dicimus 'Amen!'

Affliction both inward and outward befall you!
May you live daily in the pit of wretchedness!
235 Shame and ignominy be your lot in all things!
Whatever else there remains of toil or hatefulness or of deep disgrace,
Let it be yours in perpetuity,
Unless you spurn laymen and transfer your favours to clerks!
If any such repentance and amends takes place,
240 Pardon, with the assignment of due penance, will follow'.

In confirmation of this, we all say, 'Amen!'

NOTES TO *THE COUNCIL OF REMIREMONT*

'The title appears only in T, and may be a later hand' (Lee, p. 156).

2–3 The abbey took its name from Romary, an ascetic who had in the seventh century founded (originally upon the nearby peak of Saint-Mont) a double monastery (i.e. one consisting of monks and nuns) which observed the Columban rule (Lee, pp. 7–8, 9, 13). By this date, the male community had been discontinued, the Columban rule had been replaced by the Benedictine (Lee, p. 16) and the nuns by canonesses.

5 *a mundi principio*: only in T.

9 In this parallel religion of love, the Gospel is replaced by Ovid as the authoritative text. See 26–8 and note.

10 The present tense implies that men are usually absent from the deliberations of the sisters.

14 Remiremont lay in the diocese of Toul, a town which was actually 110 km away.

15 The line, in pre-announcing the bias of the proceedings that follow, wittily reflects the fact that the poem itself is written to serve the interests of clerics (as suitors).

16 We have, in order to retain Meyer's lineation, inserted blank lines where (rightly or wrongly) he assumed lines to be missing.

19 *Sibilia*: a contemporary of Judith who bore that name is recorded as a donor in the *Liber memorialis* of the abbey (Lee, pp. 75–6).

26–8 See n. to 9. The religion of love shadows that of the Christian church in both procedure (the reading of a Gospel text at the start of proceedings) and language (*precepta* [commandments] and *doctor* [learned man, teacher] were both terms well-entrenched in church discourse). On Ovid's status as a kind of ecclesiastical authority or *doctor* in this parallel church, cf. the near-contemporary reference to him by Heloise (writing as an abbess concerned with the proper conduct of her abbey) as *poeta luxurie turpitudinisque doctor* (*The Letter Collection of Peter Abelard and Heloise*, ed. Luscombe, Letter 6, p. 222).

27–8 Not found in R. *Lectrix* (28) is the emendation suggested by Waitz of T's *litta*.

29 An *Eva* and an *Adeleyt* (cf. 120a) figure in an act of 1151 that was witnessed by the abbess Judith and her *decana* Berta (cf. 99a); *Danubrio* refers to Deneuvre, a village which lies, like the other places figuring in the names of the ladies mentioned, in the vicinity of Remiremont (Lee, p. 71).

30 This line is in both manuscripts followed by what we follow Meyer and Lee in transposing to line 60 (see n. to 60).

31–2 The songs of love replace in procedure and terminology the liturgical chants of church services and rituals. Cf. n. to 26–8.

33 *due ... Elizabet* (R: *Eua et Elizabet*): later named (though only in T) as *Elizabet de Granges* (60a) and *Elizabet de Falcon* (66a). Faucogney (mentioned in Text 6, V.13 and VIII.18 above) lies near Remiremont (see n. to 29), as do several places with names containing the element 'Granges' (Lee p. 75). R and T tend to differ in which ladies they name.

34 *statuit*: cf. *jusserat* (21), *precepta* (27). The notion that the God of Love had 'commandments' equivalent to those of the Christian faith was to become a dominant one in the rhetoric of courtly love: cf. for instance *Roman de la rose* 2038–2581.

36 See pp. 430–1 above on the significance of this line for the nature of the comedy in the poem, which is not a 'satire' exposing sexual improprieties on the part of the nuns, but rather a comic endorsement of their assumed romantic orientation.

37 *cardinalis* [chief] reflects ecclesiastical usage (cf. n. to 48), in which, as a noun, it was used of a 'chief presbyter' (and, of course, became especially associated with the 'cardinals' who formed the papal council) and, as adjective, was applied, for instance, to one of the archdeacons in the diocese of Toul (Parisse, 'Le Concile', p. 11). The lady thus designated as the 'most senior in office' of those present is not the abbess (who would probably be named, as actual residents of Remiremont tend to be in the poem), but an allegorical figure engaged in an ecclesiastical 'visitation', and thus not an inmate of the institution.

39–47 The rhetorical wordplay on *vest-* at 39–40, and on *flos, -flor-* (39, 42, 43, 45) underlines the assimilation, signalled by her colourful and flower-hung clothes, of the *domina* with the spring season in which the poem is set and which requires that observance of the laws of Love the lady is here to check on (52–4). The identification with Flora rather than Venus enables her too to figure as a *virgo* (43), the chaste celibate of the model ecclesiastical superior, who would also be *docta* [learned] in the arts, especially rhetoric (46–7).

44 Meyer assumes a missing line after 43, since otherwise the same rhyme would be repeated from one line (*regia/Gloria*) into the next (*omnia/filia*).

47 *et* does not appear in T or R, and was supplied by Waitz (following Haupt).

48 *cetus* [= *coetus*] is another word with ecclesiastical associations (cf. n. to 37): it was used of a church synod or council (*Mittellateinisches Wörterbuch*), as well as of the 'college' of cardinals (*Dictionary of Medieval Latin from British Sources*).

49 *Vos* (T): R has *Nos*.

52–5 The lady is presented allegorically as on an ecclesiastical 'visitation': sent by the convent's superiors to investigate their conduct and whether it conforms with what God (here, Amor) commands. Interrogations and corrections were supposed always to be made in the spirit of fraternal charity expressed by the adverbs of line 55.

60 In both R and T, the line appears after line 30, 'where it is clearly an interpolation' (Lee). Meyer suggested it belonged here. The transposition may not be right, but it is fairly insignificant and enables Meyer's lineation to be retained.

60a Only in T are lines 61–6 assigned to this named speaker. See n. to 33.

63 *inscienter*: the word contributes to the parallel 'theology' of love, since lack of intention to sin was a mitigating factor in confessional theory.

64–70 *regula* would normally refer in the context of enclosed religious to their monastic rule, and is thus part of the poem's parallel 'religion' of love. *copula* (64; cf. 70, 126) had no necessary reference to sexual coition, but could refer to any bond or assosciation. *nostri ordinis* (66): since church references in the poem usually have figurative rather than literal application, this presumably refers, not to the Benedictine order to which Remiremont belonged, but to compatible men who belong to the same 'order of life' and have the same amorous values as the ladies (i.e. fellow clerics, as the next speech makes clear). Lines 66–70 so precisely explicate exactly what *regula* (64, 70) the ladies observe in deciding what men are suitable for *copula* (64, 70) as to counter-indicate a change of speaker. In fact, the division of the response of the chapter amongst named speakers differs in the two manuscripts, both of which seem to believe that specific women figure, but do not agree as to who they are or when they speak. The assignment of 67ff. to *Elisabet de Falcon* occurs only in T, as does the assignment of 61–6 to *Elizabet de Granges*.

67–9 Omitted in R.

67 *laudem* is Haupt's emendation of T's 'laude', adopted by Waitz and Lee. *memoriam* is translated 'reputation' by Lee, which, though not elsewhere used of the 'fame' of a still living person, seems a not improbable sense in context.

70 *hec* was supplied by Meyer for metrical reasons to R's *est nostra regula*. T reads *non nostra regula* (which would give an emphasis similar to that perhaps found at 79–81). In either case, the point would be that the rule of *copula* with clerics has replaced the monastic rule.

79–81 If this is a reference to monastic vows, it comes in rather oddly, without any relation to what comes before or after, but the same is true of what appears to be a similar reference at 151–3. Explicit reference to the religious rule that should forbid, but has in the poem been replaced by, a theology and rule of love also occurs at 124–6. It may be that the reference here is actually to the justified breach of any foolish pledges (79) once given to knights – for the following lines go on to say that the sisters formerly, through foolish ignorance (85), favoured knights. There is certainly an implied emphasis on *stulta* in 79: clerks are to be commended for *not* breaking their amorous bonds (76), though *stupid* vows should not be treated as equally binding; that point is made even more explicitly in the parallel passage at 151–3.

90 Cf. 77, and contrast *labilis* (84) and *dolus* (87). The greater fidelity (as well as the greater discretion) of the clerks is emphasized. Fear of exposure and fear of betrayal were, typically, the chief anxieties of women in amorous matters (see pp. 60–1 above). Cf. 158–9 and note.

93a *Agnes*: the name occurs here only in R (see n. to 64–70); no Agnes has been found who could be associated with the abbatial rule of Judith (Lee, p. 72).

94–9 The lines wittily apply the moral rule of the cloister to the parallel religion of love: the love of knights is treated as a kind of engagement with the 'lay' rather than the 'clerical' – and so forbidden or *illicitum* in the cloister, where worldly matters were, in theory, rejected.

99a *Berta*: a lady of this name is recorded as *decana* (second in status to the abbess) under Judith (see Lee, pp. 71–2), but her name occurs at this point only in R, as does that of Agnes at 93a. In neither case does the content necessitate an assumption of a new speaker. See n. to 64–70.

100–2 Again the logic is mock religious: the cloistered should love what God loves. There is even perhaps in line 100 (cf. 26) an echo of the opening of the Mass: 'Ad Deum qui laetificat iuventutem meam ...'.

The Council of Remiremont 451

102   Cf. 99. The poet often uses the leonine verse for parallels and contrasts that give shape and emphasis to his discourse.

102a   This indication of change from 'solo' to 'tutti' is, again, found only in R, and is not required by the sense. See n. to 99a.

105   The submission to correction is, again, part of the parallel religion of Love.

105a   Again, the indication of speaker is found only in R (see n. to 102a), but it does here confirm a deduction necessitated by content (the second person plural at 108).

107   *adeo* is the emendation made in Waitz of *audio* in T and R.

108a   Only in R, but here too the lines would cause confusion without the indication as to speakers (see n. to 105a).

109–10   Cf. 61–2.

114a   *Elizabet Popona*: as at 93a, 99a, 105a, 108a and 120a, the indication of speaker is found only in R; see n. to 64–70. She is perhaps the 'Elizabeth. Popo.' Lee refers to as preserved in a necrology of Remiremont (p. 75).

115–17   The lines reflect a sentiment often expressed in courtly and chivalric literature: that love is the inspiration and motivation of knights. Cf. 'And this encresse of hardynesse and myght / Com hym of loue, his ladies thank to wynne' (*Troilus* III.1776–7), and the claim in *Wynnere and Wastoure* that the love of the knight's lady will 'Make hym bolde and bown with brandes to smytte, / To schonn schenchipe and schame there schalkes are gadird' (431–2).

116   It was Waitz who suggested this adoption of the line as it reads in T (where, however, the verbs are singular: *habeat ... placeat*), but with the plural verb forms found in the otherwise less satisfactory version of R (*ut si nos habeant et si nobis placeant*).

120a   *Adeleyt*: an Adeled was *decana* at Remiremont in the time of the abbess Judith (Lee, p. 71; see also n. to 29). The name is found only in R (see n. to 114a), and the lines introduced by it do make better sense if assigned to a new speaker (whose first person is singular, not the plural used so far in the defence of the knights as lovers).

121   Cf. 109–10 and note. The supporters of the knights echo the language and claims of the supporters of clerics.

123   A neatly pointed leonine line is achieved through pithily expressive play on the verb *servire*, which was a key one in amorous and chivalric logic.

124–6   Omitted in R. For such explicit reference to the rule the canonesses are neglecting in favour of the 'church' of Love, cf. 79–81 and note.

126   On *copulam*, see n. to 64–70.

132–63   Omitted in R. Change of speaker (indicated by R alone after 93a) needs to be assumed at 132, since the lines are plainly uttered by a spokeswoman for a different group of women, who favour clerks.

136   *est, erit intentio*: T (the only witness in this section of the poem) reads 'est et intentio erit'.

138   The point seems to be that the delights bestowed are only those compatible with virginity (cf. n. to 36); but *virgo* is emended to *viro* [to a man] in Waitz and Lee.

139 Cf. 132 and *professio* at 136. Love is a parallel monastic 'church', with professed members vowed to observe its rule.

144 *Sed* (emended to *Ad* in Meyer and Lee) may be used in its loose 'climactic' sense.

145 For the gratification women are represented as deriving in being the subject of love songs and poems, see pp. 5–6 above. These compositions are thus one aspect of the ideal lover the cleric is declared to be – along with their discretion, constancy and pretty gifts.

147 T reads *Dulcis amicia clericis est et gloria* (emended by Meyer to ... *amicicia ... est gloria*). The unexplained word *Dane* appears in the margin – and provides only slight grounds for Oulmont's insertion of 'Danu [Eva de]' before 148 to indicate the start of a speech by Eva de Danubrio (mentioned at 29).

151–3 Cf. 79–81 and note. The logic in 152–3 is mock theological: if one has made a promise that should not have been made, observing the promise only compounds the sin.

154–6 Lee follows Meyer in assigning these lines to the *cardinalis domina*. But they could be an appeal by the present inexperienced group (133) to the wiser heads (154) of those who customarily give valuable counsel in chapter.

157–71 Lee follows Meyer in assuming a new speaker for the reply to the question (which they assign to the presiding lady). Certainly 160 and 168 look like a deliberate response to 154–5.

158–9 The knights are accused of being both fickle and indiscreet, and thus exposing their mistresses to betrayal and shame, the two main things women feared from love. See n. to 90 above.

161–2 These lines herald the excommunication that forms the climax of the poem.

167 The second half-line reads *quod nobis est multum cognitum* in T and *quod est multum cognitum* in R.

171a The indication of speaker is found only in R. See n. to 64–70.

172 Cf. 154–5 and 168.

174–7 These lines use the language and logic of sin and confession: following repentence (175) and satisfaction or amends (174), absolution (176) may be given. Line 177 also draws on confessional theory: to return to a sin from which one has been 'cleansed' by absolution was an act often compared with that of the dog that returns to its vomit (Proverbs 26:11) and was considered especially reprehensible (cf. *Cleanness* in *Works of Gawain Poet*, ed. Putter and Stokes, 1129–48).

177a The division of the decree of the *cardinalis domina* into separate *dicta* or formal 'clauses' is found only in R.

178 *etiam* was suggested by Haupt: T has *et* (which R omits). *per obedienciam*: the language is drawn from that of church hierarchy and discipline (cf. Text 4, I.8, II.65–7, III.4, 6).

183a See n. to 177a.

198 The discretion with which the clerks are credited contrasts with the lack of it detected in the knights. See n. to 158–9.

198a, 201a, 204a These rubrications are (like all except the first two at 60a and 66a, found only in T, and the last at 214a) found only in R.

203 *dictat* is the emendation made in Waitz of T's *distat* (in R, the second half-line reads *collaudent per omnia*).

206–8 The literal church and the allegorical church of Love here merge: the dictat comes from the latter, but it is to be promulgated amongst the institutions and cloisters of the former.

210 *sint sub anathemate* occurs only in R (where the first half-line reads *cum nostro sophismate*).

214a *rebellarum* is found only in T and is a non-classical form, slipped in to suit gender, which *rebellum* (the correct genitive plural of *rebelles*) would not reveal.

237 The first half-line is a syllable too short in T (*si quid residuum*) and a syllable too long in R (*sed si quid est residuum*). The missing syllable may be supplied by retaining from R either *sed* (as in Waitz) or *est* (as in Meyer).

241 This appears only in T. R has instead *Militibus victis, cessit victoria clero* [the knights defeated, victory is ceded to the clerk], a line whose content undoubtedly sums up the point of the poem, but which does not conform to its metre (since its half-lines are neither seven-syllabled nor rhyming).

CONRAD PFETTISHEIM'S ACCOUNT OF PIERRE DE HAGENBACH

As Claerr-Stamm points out (p. 201), the introduction of the printing press gave rapid and wide circulation to the negative image of Pierre de Hagenbach recorded in 'history', for that history was based mainly on chronicles written by his German and Swiss enemies. There was the late fifteenth-century account preserved by Johannes Knebel, a chaplain from Basel, whose 'diary' covering the years 1473–9 was edited by Wilhelm Vischer: *Johannis Knebel Capellani ecclesiae Basiliensis Diarium* (Leipzig, 1887). There was the *Breisacher Reimchronik*, a German verse chronicle originating from Breisach, the very town whose hostility and resistance to Pierre's rule had precipitated his death (see pp. 349, 361–2 above), edited by F.J. Mone in *Quellensammlung der badischen Landesgeschichte*, 4 vols (Karlsruhe, 1848–67), vol. 3, pp. 257–417. And there was the short verse chronicle which concerns us here and which is clearly connected with Strasbourg, where it was published in 1477, and to which the poem returns in its closing lines (to describe the public rituals and processions that had been conducted there, in petition for God's protection, in circumstances dealt with earlier in the chronicle), and with which the author can be associated by his dialect and in his name (which he gives in a cryptic signature incorporated into his opening lines, whose initial letters spell out 'Conradus Pfedteshem'): for there was a well-to-do Strasbourg family bearing the name of Pfettisheim, one member of which, a priest who died in 1516, could plausibly be our author, as suggested in the facsimile produced by Lilli Fischel and Rolf Müller, *Geschichte Peter Hagenbachs und der Burgunderkriege* (Plochingen, 1966), pp. 10–11. That facsimile includes a translation into modern German, and there is also available a translation into modern French (by Albert Summer: *Société d'Histoire de Kingersheim*, 1 (1995) 87–93), part of which (i.e. the lines concerning Hagenbach: 23–108 in our numbering) was reproduced by Claerr-Stamm (pp. 212–15). The text below is taken from the facsimile, and the translation is our own.

Conrad's account of the humiliation and death of the powerful Hagenbach is only a prelude to the same fate met over a longer period by his master, Charles the Bold, who then replaces him as the villain of this folk chronicle, whose overall subject is in fact what Conrad sees as the Swiss-German triumphs in a campaign against the mighty Burgundy. The transition comes with an account of how Charles refused the money offered to redeem the mortgaged territory of which Hagenbach had been appointed governor. He will, says Conrad, pay for this *ubermut* [arrogance,

Conrad Pfettisheim's Account of Pierre de Hagenbach 455

overweening]. His fate is thus presented as illustrating the same moral as the story of Hagenbach is introduced as exemplifying: no good ever comes of *hochfart* and *ubermut*, we are told at the end of the prefatory lines (21–2), and it is apropos of that *sententia* that Hagenbach is introduced ('In this connection, note a striking evil / That befell a man called Peter Hagenbach': 23–4), those key terms recurring in the *hochmut* and *ubermut* identified as his defining characteristics (32, 47). Conrad in fact gives consistent patterns and integration to his chronicle, and his simplifications are one kind of literary art: an art by which he gives focus and direction to material that is in fact diverse and complex. Charles's humiliations and defeats at Neuss, Grandson and Murten are followed through with sarcasm, gloating scorn and mockery, while the victories and booty gained by the German and Swiss troops, and the losses inflicted by them, are recorded with triumphant glee and with self-righteous piety, the victors singing hymns of gratitude to the God who has so mercifully protected them. All this aligns the events with the preliminary pieties (with which poems by convention opened and closed), in which those who follow God's law are assured of the same protection He extended to the Jewish nation in the Old Testament (13–14). The divine protection modulates through the Jewish nation into the German-Swiss alliance, in the same way as the penalties of *ubermut* of which the preface warns are evident in the characters and fates of Peter and Charles, giving the shape and unity of a moral *exemplum* to this highly partisan record of the hostilities (see especially 423–54 below and note).

As Conrad moves, in the transition from Peter to Charles, to matter that involves those consistently described as 'our men', his style gathers pace and colour with his increased involvement. The rhetorical art used is that of popular polemic, but it is art nevertheless. It is a kind of wit, a kind to which Fischel and Müller draw attention and of which they give well-chosen examples (p. 11). They point, for instance, to the figure of 'der Strauss' into which the Strasbourgers are generalized and to the figurative force with which military events are described, as he beats on doors and his cannon lays hard eggs; to metaphors involving a wild dance or the 'macabre' image of the 'harvest' gathered by the Swiss in their massacre of fleeing Burgundians; and to the persistent characterization of a blustering Charles as roaring like a lion or bull, with a 'hide' the Swiss can get at. The homely vigour of such personifications and ongoing metaphors enlivens the events, reducing them to the simple shapes of caricatures which nevertheless serve to give bold outline to amorphousness.

The formal shaping as an *exemplum* (illustrating the success enjoyed by nations protected by God and the punishments of *ubermut*) and the racy style: these are the rhetorical counterpart to the metre, which also gives shape, pace and popular appeal to the material. Vernacular chronicles were often written, like Conrad's, in verse. But the signal given by verse in the Middle Ages was not the same as that which it came to give in later times, when it became increasingly associated with a very literary and rarefied kind of art. Many factual works were written in verse, because metre was supposed to sugar their dryness and make them easier and more pleasant to read – the chosen metres tending to be the simpler types, in which short lines and obvious rhyme-schemes impart something of a sing-song quality to the content. Conrad handles metre of this kind fairly well, and his verse (in which couplets give way to experiments with other rhyme schemes) suggests a writer responsive enough to metre to do something other than stick mechanically to the predictable couplet. But verse does make it clearer than would prose, which is today invariably selected for such 'factual' matter as 'history', that such matter is no freer of art and craft than are the more recognizably creative genres of fiction or fable. For, as we have seen, Conrad's matter has been as moulded as the language to fit a predetermined pattern. The historical 'facts' he had received and here retails appear in a form dictated by hostility to the Burgundian leaders portrayed, the features of whose careers have been distorted in the popular imagination to fit those of overweening tyrants. The result is a lampoon of kinds, a song of scorn as prejudiced and predetermined as its opposite, the eulogy or hymn of praise, a history orchestrated in both content and rhythm to play a particular tune. But in literature 'actuality' is never free of some kind of controlling 'art'; all writing must therefore be judged by the canons of both, and Conrad's work has its own kind of interest and entertainment value: it is succinct, memorable, consistent and lively and conveys well one kind of perceived 'reality', as valid in its way as the 'truth' emerging from investigative history – which can also, of course, be ill- or well-handled as an art and from which emerges an actuality no less questionable and no less discernibly fashioned by the tools and skills of the particular category of intellectual craft that has been employed on it. Conrad's art is that of the cartoon or popular song, forms of art in which historical objectivity is not even aimed at or pretended, but it nevertheless records one kind of historical reality – by expressing an unashamed partisanship as energetic and as real as, for instance, the vulgar anti-Nazi songs sung by soldiers in the Second World War, songs in which dispassionate impartiality would be stupidly out of place.

Czu lob und er der Trinnitot
On zwyvel so wurd ich genot
　　Nicht abelossen danck zu sagen.
4　Richt sich darnach by sinen tagen
　　Also der mensch und lobe Got,
Darzu ouch halte sin gebott;
　　Und wan er sinens willen pflicht,
8　So schat im ymer ewig nicht.
　　Priesterschafft die musz er prysen,
Frowlichen stam ouch er bewysen.
　　Ein yder der desz glichem pflicht
12　Der truwe Gott er loszt in nicht.
　　Trostlich half er ouch von mols me
Ein judschen volck der alten e;
　　So dick es sich von sunden kort,
16　Hatt Gott ir stym gar bald erhort.
　　Ein glychnisz hab ich hie verstanden
Maria, die sy uns vor schanden.
　　Man sicht nun wol zu diser frist
20　Was yetz der welt begeren ist:
　　Wann hochfart und der ubermut,
Die tunt den menschen niemer gut.
　　Der merckent bie ein grosse schand
24　Von eim hiesz Peter Hagenbach.
　　Der dorft ein zyt in disem land
Nicht wonen umb sin grosse schand.
　　Er was ein ritter gantz on er,
28　Desz glichen man kum findet mer.
　　Er wonet in Burgund ein zyt,
And meint die wyl er wer so wyt
　　Solt man sin dester e vergessen.
32　Mit hochmut wz sin hertz vermessen.
　　Es macht sich dar noch snelleclich
Herczog Sygmund von Osterich
　　Wolt ein lantvogtig verpfenden
36　Im Sunckow und an selben enden.
　　Do nun der anslag gar geschach,
Gedocht Her Peter Hagenbach:

　　'Der hertzog von Burgund myn her,
40　Wan der dar zu genouget wer,

To the praise and honour of the Trinity
Without doubt it behoved me
Not to omit to give thanks.
4   Man should in the same way be governed thereby in his lifetime
And praise God,
And thereto also keep His commandments.
And when he does His will,
8   He will never come to harm.
Priesthood should he honour,
And show respect for womanhood.
Each man who follows this course
12 May trust that God will never reject him.
He likewise gave comfort and help at one time
To the Jewish people of the Old Law;
As soon as they turned away from sin,
16 God at once heard their voice.
A likeness have I here perceived
To how Mary protects us from evil.
One can see well in these present times
20 What worldly covetousness now really is:
Since arrogance and overweening
Never do men any good.
In this connection, note a striking evil
24 That befell a man called Peter Hagenbach.
He could not for some time in this land
Remain in residence, because of a most shameful deed.
He was a knight, but one wholly without honour,
28 Whose like it would be hard to find.
He lived in Burgundy for a time,
And thought that because he was so far off
He would thereby be forgotten about the sooner.
32 His heart was filled with overweening.
It soon afterward happened that
The Duke Sigmund of Austria
Wanted to pawn an earldom
36 In the Sundgau and neighbouring districts.
When the news of this got about,
Sir Peter Hagenbach thought to himself:

'The Duke of Burgundy, my master,
40 If he were inclined to it,

        Ich hett nicht gar verloren.
        Die lantvogtig ward gut bu[r]gundsch:
        Die sach fugt sich noch sinen wunsch'.
44   Glich bald darnoch kam ufz die mer
        Wie Hagenbach im Suntgow wer
           Ein lantvogt usz herkoren.

        Do herschet er in ubermut:
48   Es was den burgen nicht ser gut
           Zu Brysach und zu Thanne.
        Den bosen pfennig wolt er han,
        And fing vil nuwer schaczung an:
52   Der brot trouff im in pfanne.

        Zum ersten kund er kratzen lyse
        Mit senftickeit zu glicher wyse
           Als wer es im im hertzen.
56   Do er das grassz hergriffen hat,
        Er herscht zu Brysach in der stat:
           Die burger litten smertzen.

        Do nun der schimpf am besten wz,
60   Sin hochfart name ein ende.
        Sie mochtent nymmer gelyden dz,
        Und fingent im behende.

        Sz leiten in gefangen snell,
64   Und machtent in do kallen:
        Man zog in uss, er schrey so hell
        Sin stymm die hort man schallen.

        Er do veriach der boszheit vil
68   Die er vor hat im willen;
        Gotts sy gelobt, im brast der wil:
        Er mocht sie nicht erfullen.

        Do siner boszheit is nicht not –
72   Wan er ist dot –
        Dz ich do von icht melde.
        Man flug im ab sin houbt so trod:

           I would certainly not be the loser.
       It would be a good thing if the territory were Burgundian:
       The business is shaping itself to his own desires'.
44   Pretty soon afterwards there came the news
       Of how Hagenbach had been
           Chosen as governor of the Sundgau.

       Then he lorded it in arrogance:
48   Things did not go well for the citizens
           At Breisach and at Thanne.
       He wanted to have as a tax that 'evil penny',
       And introduced many new levies:
52   It all made for meat in his frying-pan.

       At first, he knew how to curry favour
       With softness in such a way
           As if it came from the heart.
56   Once he had gained their confidence,
       He asserted his lordship in the city of Breisach:
           The citizens suffered sorely.

       When the mischief was at its height,
60   His overbearing received its end.
       They could no longer endure all this,
       And seized him all of a sudden.

       They led him off a prisoner,
64   And made him then cry out:
       On being drawn up, he shrieked so loud
       One heard his voice re-echo.

       He then renounced the great wickedness
68   Which he before had had in his will;
       God be praised, his will was blocked,
       And he was not able to fulfil it.

       Of his wickedness there is no need –
72   Since he is dead –
       That I should speak about that.
       His head was quickly struck off:

```
           Im schach genod
76     Zu Brisach in dem felde.

           Man zalte xiiii.c. ior –
              Jo dz ist wor –
           Do ab im ward gerichtet,
80     Ouch lxx vier gar offenbor.
              Vil welt kam dar;
           Er hat ouch vor gebychtet.

           Gott der tug im genoden schin,
84            Ist er in pin,
           An siner armen selen;
           Er must on zwyfel mussig sin
              By guten win
88     Solt er es als erczelen.

           In diser geschicht ward manig man,
              Ist nicht daron,
           Gar billich ser herfrowet.
92     Also kam Hagenbach darvon.
              Im ward der lon,
           Dem kalb is ouch gestrowet ...
```

[Quoted below are the verses describing the final defeat of the Burgundians and the death of Charles, the line numbers being those they would have by our enumeration: verse lines are not numbered in the early print, and would not tally with the numbers as we give them, by reason of the way in which 71–94 were laid out.]

```
           Es ging im do noch allem wunsch:
424    Von Gott fugt sich das flucke.
           Si rantent under die burgunsch
           Und stochent sie zurucke.

           Herczog Karle den stach man tot,
428    Und mit im uss vier tusent.
           Die vordersten im grosser nott
           Durch flucht gar fyntlich susent.
```

	Things went ill for him
76	On the field at Breisach.

	One counted fourteen hundred years,
	That indeed is the truth,
	When he was executed,
80	And seventy-four more, to be plain;
	A great crowd came there to see it;
	And he had been confessed beforehand.

	May God show mercy for him,
84	If he is in torment,
	On his poor soul.
	A man would have, no doubt about it, to be at leisure
	And with good wine before him,
88	If he were to narrate it all.

	At this event was many a man,
	No doubt,
	Most certainly made joyful.
92	In this way did Hagenbach come to an end.
	He got his reward,
	And the litter was spread for the calf.

	Things went for them [the Swiss] exactly as they would have wished:
424	It was from God that this good fortune came about.
	They stormed among the Burgundians
	And thrust them back.

	Duke Charles was stabbed to death,
428	And with him a good four thousand others.
	The front ranks in great distress
	Rushed along wildly in flight.

432   Er lag al do gar one macht,
       Im ellend wie ein ander;
       Also endt sich die selbe nacht
       Der ander Allexander

       ...

451   Diss ding hat uns verhenget Got
       Und hat fur uns gestritten.
       Syt er uns nun erhoret hot
       Wollen wir in furbasz bitten ...

432 He lay there all powerless,
     In wretchedness like any other ordinary man.
     And thus that night did he end,
     This second Alexander

     ...

451 This thing God ordained for us,
     And He has fought for us.
     Since He has thus heard our prayers in the past,
     Let us continue henceforth to pray to Him ...

NOTES TO CONRAD'S ACCOUNT OF PIERRE DE HAGENBACH

Diacritics appearing in the original print have been ignored. We have retained the indents found in its lay-out, as these are used as signposts to rhyme scheme and metre (to announce the start of, or to mark shorter lines within, a metrical unit), which we have further clarified by dividing into separate stanzas the various verse forms used by Conrad.

1–48 These lines take the form of the short couplet (i.e. eight-syllabled rhyme, not counting the extra final unstressed syllable in feminine rhymes).

1–18 On the acrostic of the author's name formed by the initial letters of these lines, see headnote (p. 454 above). Acrostic signatures of this kind occur elsewhere in medieval verse: the name of the author of another 'historical' work in verse, *The Destruction of Troy*, is inscribed into the opening letters of the Prologue and books I–XXII, which spell out 'M(aistur) I[o]hannes Clerk de Whalele' ('Whalele' being Whalley, in Lancashire), as was pointed out by Thorlac Turville-Petre (*MAev* 57 (1988) 264–9); Usk included his name in a similarly formed acrostic (see *Thomas Usk: Testament of Love*, ed. R. Allen Shoaf (Kalamazoo, MI, 1998)).

13, 17, 29, 33 These lines appear in the print without the indent that elsewhere regularly marks the first member of the couplets used in the opening forty-eight lines.

25–8 Hagenbach had been born in Upper Alsace, but was brought up in Burgundy (see p. 347 above). There obviously remained in German history some awareness of an early residence in the region followed by a return in later life (when he became *bailli* of the lands mortgaged by Sigmund of Austria to Charles the Bold), but these facts have been reinterpreted in the light of hostility to him and are here explained to his discredit (cf. nn. to 39–46 and 53–5): he had committed some crime that caused his banishment or flight from the region.

26 *grosse*: the print reads *gorsse*.

39–47 A new metrical tranche is signalled by an indent. Couplets with masculine rhyme are now interspersed with a shorter (six-syllable) 'tail rhyme' line with feminine ending in a rhyme scheme of *aabccddb*, the tail lines being indented. In German verse, alternation between masculine and feminine line-endings plays as important a part in metrical patterning as rhyme and syllable count, as will be seen in the other schemes used by Conrad.

39–46 Hagenbach is here credited with some Machiavellian deep-laid schemes on how the situation might be made to work to his own advantage: i.e. with an implied plot (of which there is no evidence) to use his influence with Charles to get him to take on the mortgage and to secure his own appointment of the governorship of the lands at issue. Again, the facts are presented in order to make of him the evil anti-hero of the whole chain of events. Cf. nn. to 25–8 and 53–5.

47–58 Two more classic tail-rhyme stanzas (rhyming *aabccb*) here follow the slightly irregular one above, indents marking the tail-rhyme lines, whose feminine rhymes again counterpoint the masculine-rhyming couplets.

47 Cf. 21, 32, 60 and see headnote, pp. 454–5 above.

50 'The evil penny' was the popular term for the much-resented tax on wine that Hagenbach introduced: see Claerr-Stamm, p. 124.

53–5 Hagenbach's administration of the mortgaged lands in 1469–74 had aroused no violent opposition until the fatal chain of events over the weeks leading to his death in 1474 and was in fact characterized by some effectiveness and success (see p. 361 above). These lines look like an acknowledgement of those facts, but with a hostile interpretation of them that again turns Hagenbach into a Machiavellian figure with ulterior motives. Cf. nn. to 25–8 and 39–46.

57–8 It was discontent and rebellion in Breisach that led to Hagenbach's trial and execution by the Swiss in 1474: see pp. 349, 361–2 above.

59 The indent marks a new verse-form: quatrains rhyming *abab*, the *a*-rhymed lines having masculine rhymes and eight stresses and the *b*-rhymed lines having feminine rhymes and six stresses.

64–6 Pierre was tortured prior to his trial, and line 65 refers to the method used: weights were attached to his legs and cords to his arms, and he was then winched aloft by the latter. An illustration occurs in the *Reimchronik* (on which see headnote, p. 454 above), and this is reproduced by Claerr-Stamm, who says (p. 175) that the procedure drew from him cries of pain (cf. lines 64 and 66), but (contrary to what might be suggested by 67–8) failed to elicit from him any admission of misconduct in office.

67–70 The charges against Pierre included the allegation that he had planned to slaughter all the male population of Breisach and had procured leaky boats on which the women and children were to be embarked (Claerr-Stamm, p. 177). Conrad gives pious thanks that he had been unable to carry out plans so laughably monstrous as to testify more to the demonizing of Pierre in the imagination of his enemies than to any credible wickedness on his part.

71–94 There here appears a new metrical form involving the interjection of short lines or 'bobs'. The bobs do not appear on separate lines in the print (which in that respect follows the earlier manuscript tradition, in which bobs had likewise been marked otherwise than by a new line). Instead, slashes appear after the bob rhyme word and its non-bob counterpart in most, but not in all, cases: after *not* and *dot* in the first of the four stanzas that take this form (71, 72), after *wor*, *offenbor* and *dar* in the second (78, 80, 81), after *schin*, *pin*, *sin* and *win* in the third, and after *man*, *daron*, *darvon* and *lon* in the fourth; but not after *genod* (75), or *trod* (74), which occurs at a line-end, nor after *ior* (77); and there is an anomalous slash after *herfrowet* (91). Line-ends out of synch with verse-line ends occur after *Brisach* (76), *Vil* (81), *ouch* (82), *ist* (84) and *By* (87), and throughout the stanza beginning at 89. It is therefore clear that the bobs disconcerted the setters (or the scribe of their exemplar), who either only half understood how they fit into what verse form or were careless, inconsistent or uncertain as to what lay-out to use.

81 On the crowds of German-speaking spectators who came to witness the execution, see Claerr-Stamm, p. 188: they included, for instance, four hundred visitors from Basle, who travelled on specially chartered boats.

82–8 It would have been damnable at this period to wish any harm to the *soul* of anyone, however hated and wicked. And, at Pierre's death, the priest in Conrad takes over from the Strasbourger to note (82) that he had been confessed (a right enjoyed by all condemned men), and so would pay for any sins in purgatory rather than in hell, and (83–5) to pray God to have mercy on his soul if he is still paying his debts there – though the idiomatic wryness of 86–8 is more in his normal style. His equally unsympathetic account of the death of Charles (at 427–34) is likewise followed by a prayer for the duke's soul (not quoted here).

423–54 The diptych presented here, formed by the contrast between humbled *ubermut* and a God-protected nation, follows the moral message announced in the prologue (13–22) and evident also in Hagenbach's fate as here described. See headnote.

431–4 The lines emphasize how the arrogant Charles was 'brought down to size' in his end, which levelled him in wretchedness and death with all others, and which marked the failure of his attempt to model himself on the world-conqueror Alexander (his dedication to the story of whom had been mocked at an earlier point in the poem and is here recalled). The final twenty-four lines (not quoted here) lead into the conventional final prayer, in this instance taking the form of an adjuration to give to God the thanks due Him for granting the deliverance prayed for ('Gott gab den friden offembor: / Dem danchent, lieben kinder' [God gave the peace decisively: give thanks to him, dear children]), followed by the date of composition, given as the year 1477 ('m.cccc.lxx.vii. ior').

Select Bibliography

Primary Sources

Anthologies

Barratt, Alexandra, *Women's Writing in Middle English* (London: Routledge, 1992)
Brittain, F., *The Penguin Book of Latin Verse* (Harmondsworth: Penguin, 1962)
Brook, G.L., *The Harley Lyrics*, 4th edn (Manchester: Manchester University Press, 1968)
Brown, Carleton, *English Lyrics of the Thirteenth Century* (Oxford: Oxford University Press, 1932)
—— *Religious Lyrics of the XVth Century* (Oxford: Oxford University Press, 1939)
Camargo, Martin, *Medieval Rhetorics of Prose Composition: Five English 'Artes Dictandi' and Their Tradition* (Binghamton, NY: Medieval and Renaissance Texts and Studies, 1995)
Copley, J., *Seven Songs and Carols of the Fifteenth Century* (Leeds: University of Leeds, 1940)
Dickins, Bruce and R.M. Wilson, *Early Middle English Texts* (London: Bowes & Bowes, 1951)
Duncan, Thomas G., *Medieval English Lyrics and Carols* (Cambridge: D.S. Brewer, 2013)
Fenster, Thelma S. and Mary Carpenter Erler, *Poems of Cupid, God of Love* (Leiden: Brill, 1990)
Furnivall, F.J., *Political, Religious and Love Poems*, EETS OS 15 (1903)
Greene, R.L., *The Early English Carols* (1st edn 1935), 2nd edn (Oxford: Oxford University Press, 1977)
Legge, M. Dominica, *Anglo-Norman Letters and Petitions from All Souls Ms. 182* (Oxford: Anglo-Norman Text Society, 1941)
McKnight, G., *Middle English Humorous Tales in Verse* (New York: D.C. Heath, 1971)
Moriarty, Catherine, *The Voice of the Middle Ages in Personal Letters 1100–1500* (New York: Peter Bedrick, 1990)

470 Select Bibliography

Newman, Barbara, *Making Love in the Twelfth Century: 'Letters of Two Lovers' in Context* (Philadelphia, PA: University of Pennsylvania Press, 2016)
Oulmont, Charles, *Les débats du clerc et du chevalier dans la littérature poétique du moyen âge* (Paris: Champion, 1911)
Robbins, Rossell Hope, *Secular Lyrics of the XIVth and XVth Centuries*, 2nd edn (Oxford: Oxford University Press, 1955)
Rockinger, Ludwig, *Briefsteller und Formelbücher des eilften bis vierzehnten Jahrhunderts*, 2 vols (Munich: Franz, 1863–4)
Rye, Walter, *The Norfolk Antiquarian Miscellany*, 3 vols (Norwich: Miller & Co., 1877)
Traill, David A. and Justin Haynes, *Education of Nuns, Feast of Fools, Letters of Love: Medieval Religious Life in Twelfth-Century Lyric Anthologies from Regensburg, Ripoll, and Chartres* (Leuven: Peeters, 2021)
Wogan-Browne, Jocelyn *et al.*, *Vernacular Literary Theory from the French of England* (Cambridge: D.S. Brewer, 2016)
Wolff, Étienne, *La lettre d'amour au Moyen Âge* (Paris: NIL, 1996)
Wright, T. and J.O. Halliwell, *Reliquiae antiquae*, 2 vols (London: Smith, 1845)

Other Primary Sources Listed by Author or (if Anonymous) by Title or Manuscript Collection

Abelard, Peter, *Historia calamitatum*, ed. Dag Nikolaus Hasse (Berlin: De Gruyter, 2002)
The Letter Collection of Peter Abelard and Heloise, ed. D. Luscombe, tr. Betty Radice, rev. D. Luscombe (Oxford: Oxford University Press, 2013)
The Letters of Abelard and Heloise, tr. Betty Radice (Harmondsworth: Penguin, 1974)
Peter Abelard's Hymnarius Paraclitensis, ed. J.S. Szövérffy, 2 vols (Albany, NY: Classical Folia Editions, 1975)
Ancrene Wisse, ed. Bella Millett, 2 vols, EETS OS 325, 326 (2005–6)
Andreas Capellanus, *Andreas Capellanus on Love*, ed. and tr. P.G. Walsh (London: Duckworth, 1982)
Antoine de La Sale, *Jehan de Saintré*, ed. Jean Misrahi and Charles A. Knudson (Geneva: Droz, 1967)
Jean de Saintré: A Late Medieval Education in Love and Chivalry, tr. Roberta L. Krueger and Jane H.M. Taylor (Philadelphia, PA: University of Pennsylvania Press, 2014)
The Armburgh Papers: The Brokholes Inheritance in Warwickshire, Hertfordshire and Essex: c. 1417–1453: Chetham's Manuscript Mun. E.6.10(4), ed. Christine Carpenter (Woodbridge: Boydell & Brewer, 1998)
The Assembly of Ladies, in *The Floure and the Leafe and The Assembly of Ladies*, ed. Derek Pearsall (London: Nelson, 1962)
The Bannatyne Manuscript, ed. W. Tod Ritchie, 4 vols, STS, 3rd series, 5, 22–3, 26 (Edinburgh: Blackwood, 1928–34)

Select Bibliography

Barton, John, *Donait françois*, in *Zu den Anfangen der französischen Grammatiksprache: Textausgaben und Wortschatzstudien*, ed. Thomas Städtler (Tübingen: Niemeyer, 1988), pp. 128–43

Baudet Herenc, *Le parlement d'amours*, in *Alain Chartier: The Quarrel of the Belle dame sans mercy*, ed. and tr. Joan E. McRae (New York: Garland, 2004), pp. 127–68

Baudri de Bourgeuil, *Baldricus Burgulianus Carmina*, ed. K. Hilbert (Heidelberg: Winter, 1979)

Bibbesworth, Walter de, *Le tretiz*, ed. William Rothwell (London: Anglo-Norman Text Society, 1990)

Boncompagno da Signa, *Amicitia and De malo senectutis et senii*, ed. and tr. Michael W. Dunne (Leuven: Peeters, 2012)

Palma, in Carl Sutter, *Aus Leben und Schriften des Magisters Boncompagno* (Freiburg: Mohr, 1894), pp. 105–27

Rhetorica novissima, in *Bibliotheca Iuridica Medii Aevi*, ed. Augusto Gaudenzi, 3 vols (Bologna, 1892; repr. Turin: Bottega d'Erasmo, 1962), vol. 2, pp. 249–97

Tractatus amoris carnalis subsequitur rota veneris nuncupatus per Boncompagnum editus sociorum annue ([Strasbourg]: [C.W.], [approximately 1473–4])

Magister Boncompagno: Rota Veneris, ed. Friedrich Baethgen (Rome: Regensberg, 1927)

Rota Veneris, ed. and tr. Josef Purkart (New York: Scholars' Facsimiles, 1975)

Rota Veneris, ed. and tr. Paolo Garbini (Rome: Salerno, 1996)

'La *Rota Veneris* di Boncompagno da Signa: edizione critica', ed. Luca Core (PhD dissertation, University of Padua, 2015), available at www.research.unipd.it/handle/11577/3424707

Testi riguardanti la vita degli studenti a Bologna nel sec. XIII (dal Boncompagnus, lib. I), ed. Virgilio Pini (Bologna: Grafiche Mondo, 1968)

Breisacher Reimchronik, in *Quellensammlung der badischen Landesgeschichte*, ed. F.J. Mone, 4 vols (Karlsruhe: Macklot, 1848–67), vol. 3, pp. 257–417

Breviarium Romanum (Rome: Typos Polyglottis Vaticanis, 1923)

Caxton, William, *Dialogues in French and English*, ed. H. Bradley, EETS ES 79 (1900)

The Cely Letters, ed. Alison Hanham, EETS OS 273 (1975)

Charles d'Orléans, *Fortunes Stabilnes: Charles of Orléans's English Book of Love*, ed. Mary-Jo Arn (Binghamton, NY: Medieval and Renaissance Texts and Studies, 1994)

Poésies, ed. Pierre Champion, 2 vols (Paris: Champion, 1971)

The Poetry of Charles d'Orléans and His Circle, ed. John Fox and Mary-Jo Arn (Tempe, AZ: Arizona Centre for Medieval and Renaissance Studies, 2010)

Chaucer, Geoffrey, *The Riverside Chaucer*, ed. Larry D. Benson, 3rd edn (Boston, MA: Houghton Mifflin, 1987)

The Complete Works of Geoffrey Chaucer, ed. W.W. Skeat, 7 vols (Oxford: Oxford University Press, 1894–7)

Troilus & Criseyde, ed. B.A. Windeatt (London: Longman, 1984)

Christine de Pisan, *Œuvres poétiques*, ed. Maurice Roy, 3 vols (Paris: Firmin Didot, 1886)
Council of Remiremont: ed. George Waitz, 'Das Liebesconcil', *Zeitschrift für deutsches Altertum* 7 (1849) 160–7
ed. Wilhelm Meyer, 'Das Liebesconcil in Remiremont', *Nachrichten von der Gesellschaft der Wissenschaften zu Göttingen. Philologisch-Historische Klasse* (1914) 1–19
'A New Edition of *The Council of Remiremont*', ed. Reuben Richard Lee (PhD dissertation, University of Connecticut, 1981)
Devonshire Manuscript: *A Social Edition of the Devonshire Manuscript (BL MS Add 17,492)*, ed. Raymond Siemens, Karin Armstrong and Constance Crompton (Toronto: Iter, 2015)
Les diz et proverbes des sages, ed. J. Morawski (Paris: Champion, 1924)
Enanchet: Dottrinale franco-italiano del XIII secolo sugli stati del mondo, le loro origini e l'amore, ed. Luca Morlino (Padua: Esedro, 2017)
Epistolae duorum amantium, ed. E. Könsgen (Leiden: Brill, 1974)
Lettres des deux amants, ed. Sylvain Piron (Paris: Gallimard, 2005)
The Lost Love Letters of Heloise and Abelard, ed. Constant J. Mews, 2nd edn (New York: St. Martin's Press, 2008)
Facetus: Alison Goddard Elliott, ed., 'The *Facetus*: or, The Art of Courtly Living', *Allegorica* 2 (1977) 27–57
Findern Manuscript: *The Findern Manuscript: Cambridge University Library MS. Ff.1.6*, facsimile, introduced by Richard Beadle and A.E.B. Owen (London: Scholar Press, 1977)
The Findern Manuscript: A New Edition of the Unique Poems, ed. Joanna M. Martin (Liverpool: Liverpool University Press, 2020)
Froissart, Jean, *Chronicles*, tr. Geoffrey Brereton (Harmondsworth: Penguin, 1968)
Geoffrey de Vinsauf, *Poetria Nuova*, in *Les arts poétiques*, ed. Edmond Faral (Paris: Champion, 1923), pp. 197–262
Poetria Nuova, tr. Margaret Nims, intr. Martin Camargo, revised edn (Toronto: Pontifical Institute, 2010)
Gower, John, *The English Works of John Gower*, ed. G.C. Macaulay, EETS ES 81, 82 (1900–1)
The Complete Works of John Gower: The French Works, ed. G.C. Macaulay (Oxford: Oxford University Press, 1899)
The French Balades, ed. R.F. Yeager (Kalamazoo, MI: Medieval Institute, 2011)
Granson, Oton de, *Poésies*, ed. Joan Grenier-Winther (Paris: Champion, 2010)
Guillaume de Lorris and Jean de Mean, *Le roman de la rose*, ed. Daniel Poirion (Paris: Garnier-Flammarion, 1974)
Guillaume le Clerc, *Fergus*, ed. Ernst Martin (Halle: Verlag der Buchhandlung des Waisenhauses, 1872)
Henry VIII, *Die Liebesbriefe Heinrichs VIII an Anna Boleyn*, ed. Theo Stemmler (Zürich: Belser, 1988)
Hilarius of Orléans, *Versus et ludi*, ed. Walther Bulst and M.L. Bulst-Thiele (Leiden: Brill, 1989)

Select Bibliography

Jean de Meun, *La vie et les epistres. Pierre Abaelart et Heloys sa fame*, ed. Eric Hicks (Paris: Champion, 1991)
Keats, John, *The Complete Poetical Works and Letters*, ed. H.E. Scudder (Boston: Houghton Mifflin, 1899)
Knebel, Johannes, *Johannis Knebel Capellani ecclesiae Basiliensis Diarium*, ed. Wilhelm Vischer (Leipzig: Hirtzel, 1887)
Lancelot do Lac: The Non-Cyclic Old French Prose Romance, ed. Elspeth Kennedy, 2 vols (Oxford: Oxford University Press, 1980)
Langland, William, *The Vision of Piers Plowman (B Text)*, ed. A.V.C. Schmidt, 2nd edn (London: Dent, 1995)
Piers Plowman by William Langland: An Edition of the C-Text, ed. Derek Pearsall (London: Arnold, 1978)
Lydgate, John, *The Minor Poems of John Lydgate, Part II: Secular Poems*, ed. H.N. MacCracken, EETS OS 192 (1934)
Pilgrimage of the Life of Man, ed. F.J. Furnivall, EETS ES 77, 83, 92 (1899–1904)
Machaut, Guillaume de, *Le livre dou voir dit*, ed. Daniel Leech-Wilkinson, tr. R. Barton Palmer (New York: Garland, 1998)
Malory, Sir Thomas, *Works*, ed. Eugene Vinaver, 2nd edn (Oxford: Oxford University Press, 1971)
Mandeville, Jean de, *Le livre des merveilles du monde*, ed. Christiane Deluz (Paris: CNRS, 2000)
Manières de langage, ed. Andres M. Kristol (London: Anglo-Norman Text Society, 1995)
Memorials of St Edmund's Abbey, ed. Thomas Arnold, 3 vols, Rolls Series 96 (London: HMSO, 1896)
Missale Romanum, ed. Robert Lippe, 2 vols (London, 1899)
Newton, Humfrey, 'The Poems of Humfrey Newton, Esquire, 1466–1536', ed. R.H. Robbins, *PMLA* 65 (1950) 249–81
The N-Town Play, ed. S. Spector, 2 vols, EETS SS 11, 12 (1991)
Pamphilus, ed. Stefano Pittaluga, in *Commedie latine del XII e XIII secolo*, general ed. Ferruccio Bertini (Genoa: Istituto di Filologia Classica e Medievale, 1980), 13–137
Thomas Jay Garbaty, '*Pamphilus, de amore*: An Introduction and Translation', *Chaucer Review* 2 (1967) 108–34
Paston Letters, ed. Norman Davis, 2 vols (Oxford: Oxford University Press, 1971–6)
Le petit plet, ed. Brian S. Merrilees (Oxford: Anglo-Norman Text Society, 1970)
Pfettisheim, Conrad, *Geschichte Peter Hagenbachs und der Burgunderkriege*, ed. Lilli Fischel and Rolf Müller (Plochingen: Müller und Schindler, 1966)
Albert Sutter, 'Von Hagenbach: traduction et étude d'un incunable', *Société d'Histoire de Kingersheim* 1 (1995) 87–93
Piccolomini, Æneas Silvius, *The Goodli History of the Ladye Lucres*, ed. E.J. Morrall, EETS OS 308 (1996)
Historia de duobus amantibus, tr. Nikolaus von Wyle (Esslingen: Fyner, 1478)
Pontificale Romanum (Turin: Domus editorialis Marietti, 1941)

Regensburg letters: *Carmina Ratisponensia*, ed. Anke Paravicini (Heidelberg: Winter, 1979)
Remiremont letters: Werner Paravicini, ed., 'Un amour malheureux au XVe siècle: Pierre de Hagenbach et la dame de Remiremont', *Journal des savants* 1 (2006) 105–81
Salimbene de Adam, *Cronica*, ed. Giuseppe Scalia, Corpus Christianorum Continuatio Mediaevalis CXXV (Turnhout: Brepols, 1998)
Shelley, Percy Bysshe, *Shelley's Prose*, ed. David Lee Clark (London: Fourth Estate, 1988)
Sir Gawain and the Green Knight, in *The Works of the Gawain Poet*, ed. Ad Putter and Myra Stokes (Harmondsworth: Penguin, 2014)
Die Söflinger Briefe und das Klarissenkloster Söflingen bei Ulm an der Donau im Spätmittelalter, ed. Max Miller (Würzburg: Triltsch Verlag, 1940)
Somer Soneday, in *Alliterative Poetry of the Later Middle Ages*, ed. Thorlac Turville-Petre (London: Routledge, 1989), pp. 140–7
Stonor Letters: *Kingsford's Stonor Letters and Papers*, ed. Christine Carpenter, 2 vols reprinted as one (Cambridge: Cambridge University Press, 1996)
The 'Suffolk' Poems: An Edition of the Love Lyrics in Fairfax 16 Attributed to William de la Pole, ed. J.P.M. Jansen (Groningen: Universiteitsdrukkerij, 1989)
Die Tegernseer Briefsammlung des 12. Jahrhunderts, ed. Helmut Plechl with Werner Bergmann, Monumenta Germaniae Historica (Hanover: Hansche Buchhandlung, 2002)
Dû bist mîn. Ih bin dîn. Die lateinischen Liebes- (und Freundschafts-) Briefe des clm 19411, ed. Jurgen Kuhnel (Göppingen: Kümmerle, 1977)
Visitations of Religious Houses, vol. III (Records of Visitations Held by William Alnwick, Bishop of Lincoln AD 1436–1449), ed. A. Hamilton Thompson (Lincoln: Lincoln Record Society, 1927)
Wars of Alexander, ed. Hoyt N. Duggan and Thorlac Turville-Petre, EETS SS 10 (1989)
The Welles Anthology: MS Rawlinson C.813, ed. Sharon L. Jansen and Kathleen H. Jordan (Binghamton, NY: Medieval and Renaissance Texts and Studies, 1991)
Wynnere and Wastoure, ed. Stephanie Trigg, EETS OS 297 (1990)

Secondary Sources and Reference Works

Baethgen, Friedrich, 'Rota Veneris', *Deutsche Vierteljahrsschrift für Litteraturwissenschaft und Geistesgeschichte* 5 (1927) 37–64; reprinted in Baethgen, *Mediaevalia: Aufsätze, Nachrufe, Besprechungen* (Stuttgart: Hiersemann, 1960), pp. 363–84
Barron, Caroline M., 'The Education and Training of Girls in Fifteenth-Century London', in *Courts, Counties and the Capital in the Later Middle Ages*, ed. Diana E.S. Dunn (Stroud: Sutton, 1996), pp. 139–53
Battista, Francesca, 'Queen Kunhuta's Epistles to Her Husband', in *Medieval Letters: Between Fiction and Document*, ed. Christian Høgel and Elisabetta Bartoli (Turnhout: Brepols, 2015), pp. 265–76

Select Bibliography 475

Beadle, Richard, 'Prolegomena to a Literary Geography of Later Medieval Norfolk', in *Regionalism in Late Medieval Manuscripts and Texts: Essays Celebrating the Publication of a Linguistic Atlas of Late Mediaeval English*, ed. Felicity Riddy (Cambridge: D.S. Brewer, 1991), pp. 89–108
'Private Letters', in *A Companion to Middle English Prose*, ed. A.S.G. Edwards (Cambridge: D.S. Brewer, 2004), pp. 289–306
'Aspects of Late Medieval English Autograph Writings', Lyell Lectures, delivered in Oxford in 2013
Boffey, Julia, *Manuscripts of English Courtly Love Lyrics* (Cambridge: D.S. Brewer, 1985)
'Women Authors and Women's Literacy in Fourteenth- and Fifteenth-Century England', in *Women and Literature in Britain 1150–1500*, ed. Carol M. Meale (Cambridge: Cambridge University Press, 1996), pp. 159–82
Boquillon, Françoise, *Les chanoinesses de Remiremont* (Remiremont: Société d'histoire locale de Remiremont, 2000)
Brittain, F., *Medieval Latin and Romance Lyric* (Cambridge: Cambridge University Press, 1951)
Brown, Carleton, 'Lydgate's Verses on Queen Margaret's Entry into London', *Modern Language Review* 7 (1912) 226–31
Burrow, J.A., 'The Languages of Medieval England', in *English Poets in the Late Middle Ages* (Farnham: Ashgate, 2012), pp. 7–28
'Versions of "Manliness" in the Poetry of Chaucer, Langland and Hoccleve', *Chaucer Review* 47 (2013) 337–42
Butterfield, Ardis, 'Why Medieval Lyric?', *English Literary History* 82 (2015) 319–43
Camargo, Martin, *The Middle English Verse Love Epistle* (Tübingen: Niemeyer, 1991)
Campbell, Lorne and Jan van der Stock, *Rogier van der Weyden: Master of Passions* (Leuven: Peeters, 2009)
Cheney, C.R., 'Gervase, Abbot of Prémontré: A Medieval Letter-Writer', *Bulletin of the John Rylands Library* 33 (1950) 25–56
Cherewatuk, Karen and Ulrike Wiethaus, eds., *Dear Sister: Medieval Women and the Epistolary Genre* (Philadelphia, PA: University of Pennsylvania Press, 1993)
Claerr-Stamm, Gabrielle, *Pierre de Hagenbach: le destin tragique d'un chevalier sundgauvien au service de Charles le Téméraire* (Altkirch: Société d'histoire du Sundgau, 2004)
Clanchy, Michael, *Abelard: A Medieval Life* (Oxford: Wiley, 1997)
From Memory to Written Record, 3rd edn (Chichester: Wiley-Blackwell, 2013)
Clemens, Raymond and Timothy Graham, *Introduction to Manuscript Studies* (Ithaca, NY: Cornell University Press, 2007)
Cohen, Helen Louise, *The Ballade* (New York: Columbia University Press, 1915)
Constable, Giles, *Letters and Letter-Collections* (Turnhout: Brepols, 1976)
Cornelius, Ian, 'The Rhetoric of Advancement: *Ars Dictaminis*, *Cursus* and Clerical Careerism in Late Medieval England', *New Medieval Literatures* 12 (2010) 289–330

Cowley, F.G., *The Monastic Order in South Wales* (Cardiff: University of Wales Press, 1977)
Davis, Norman, 'The *Litera Troili* and English Letters', *RES* 16 (1975) 233–44
Dean, Ruth, *Anglo-Norman Literature: A Guide to Texts and Manuscripts* (London: Anglo-Norman Text Society, 1999)
Dronke, Peter, *Medieval Latin and the Rise of European Love-Lyric*, 2 vols, 2nd edn (Oxford: Oxford University Press, 1968)
The Medieval Lyric (London: Hutchinson, 1968)
'Pseudo-Ovid, Facetus, and the Arts of Love', *MLatJB* 11 (1976) 126–31
Women Writers of the Middle Ages (Cambridge: Cambridge University Press, 1984)
Intellectuals and Poets in Medieval Europe (Rome: Edizioni di storia e letteratura, 1992)
Review of Wheeler, ed., *Listening to Heloise*, *IJCT* 8 (2001) 134–9
'Women's Love Letters from Tegernsee', in *Medieval Letters: Between Fiction and Document*, ed. Christian Høgel and Elisabetta Bartoli (Turnhout: Brepols, 2015), pp. 215–45
Dronke, Peter and G. Orlandi, 'New Works by Abelard and Heloise?', *Filologia mediolatina* 12 (2005) 123–77
East, W.G., 'Educating Heloise', in *Medieval Monastic Education*, ed. George Ferzoco and Carolyn Muessig (Leicester: Leicester University Press, 2000), pp. 105–16
Ferzoco, George and Carolyn Muessig, eds., *Medieval Monastic Education* (Leicester University Press, 2000)
Garbini, Paolo, 'Il pubblico della *Rota Veneris* di Boncompagno di Signa', in *Medieval Letters: Between Fiction and Document*, ed. Christian Høgel and Elisabetta Bartoli (Turnhout: Brepols, 2015), pp. 201–13
Gillespie, Alexandra, 'Bookbinding', in *The Production of Books in England 1350–1500*, ed. Alexandra Gillespie and Daniel Wakelin (Cambridge: Cambridge University Press, 2011), pp. 150–72
Grotans, Anna, Review of *Die Tegernseer Briefsammlung*, ed. Plechl with Bergmann, *Medieval Review* (Feb. 2003), available online at https://scholarworks.iu.edu/journals/index.php/tmr/article/view/15611/21729
Hall, Catherine, 'The Early Fellows of Gonville Hall and Their Books', *Transactions of the Cambridge Bibliographical Society* 13 (2006) 233–52
Hanham, Alison, 'The Musical Studies of a Fifteenth-Century Wool Merchant', *RES* 8 (1957) 270–4
The Celys and Their World (Cambridge: Cambridge University Press, 1985)
Hanna, Ralph, 'The Production of Cambridge University Library MS Ff.1.6', *Studies in Bibliography* 40 (1987) 62–70
Harris, Kate, 'The Origins and Make-up of Cambridge University Library MS Ff.1.6', *Transactions of the Cambridge Bibliographical Society* 8 (1983) 299–333
Haskins, Charles H., *Studies in Medieval Culture* (New York: Ungar, 1929)
Høgel, Christian and Elisabetta Bartoli, eds., *Medieval Letters: Between Fiction and Document* (Turnhout: Brepols, 2015)

Horobin, Simon, 'John Cok and His Copy of *Piers Plowman*', *Yearbook of Langland Studies* 27 (2013) 45–59

Ingham, Richard, *The Transmission of Anglo-Norman* (Amsterdam: Rodopi, 2012)

Jaeger, C.S., *Ennobling Love: In Search of a Lost Sensibility* (Philadelphia, PA: University of Pennsylvania Press, 1999)

James, M.R., *A Descriptive Catalogue of the Manuscripts in the Library of Gonville and Caius College* (Cambridge: Cambridge University Press, 1907)

'Bury St. Edmunds Manuscripts', *EHR* 41 (1926) 251–60

Johnston, Michael, '*Sir Degrevant* in the "Findern Anthology"', *Studies in Bibliography* 59 (2015) 71–84

Kelly, Henry Ansgar, *Chaucer and the Cult of Saint Valentine* (Leiden: Brill, 1986)

Kibbee, Douglas A., *For to Speke Frenche Trewely: The French Language in England 1000–1600* (Amsterdam: Rodopi, 1991)

Kristol, Andres M., 'Le début du rayonnement parisien et l'unité du français au moyen âge: le témoignage des manuels d'enseignement', *Revue de linguistique romane* 53 (1989) 335–67

'L'enseignement du français en Angleterre (XIIIe–XVe siècles): les sources manuscrites', *Romania* 111 (1990) 289–330

Leach, Elizabeth Eva, 'Learning French by Singing in Fourteenth-Century England', *Early Music* 33 (2005) 253–70

Legge, M. Dominica, 'William of Kingsmill: A Fifteenth-Century Teacher of French in Oxford', in *Studies in French Language and Medieval Literature Presented to Mildred K. Pope* (Manchester: Manchester University Press, 1939), pp. 241–6.

Levelt, Sjoerd and Ad Putter, *North Sea Crossings: The Literary Heritage of Anglo-Dutch Relations 1066–1688* (Oxford: Bodleian Library, 2021)

Lusignan, Serge, *Essai d'histoire sociolinguistique: le français picard au Moyen Âge* (Paris: Garnier, 2012)

McNamara, J.K., *Sisters in Arms: Catholic Nuns through Two Millennia* (Cambridge, MA: Harvard University Press, 1996)

Marenbon, John, 'Authenticity Revisited', in *Listening to Heloise: The Voice of a Twelfth-Century Woman*, ed. Bonnie Wheeler (New York: Palgrave Macmillan, 2000), pp. 19–33

'Lost Love Letters? A Controversy in Retrospect', *IJCT* 15 (2008) 267–80

Marshall, Simone Celine, 'Manuscript Agency and the Findern Manuscript', *Neuphilologische Mitteilungen* 108 (2007) 339–49

Mason, H.A., *Humanism and Poetry in the Early Tudor Period* (London: Routledge, 1959)

Meyer, Paul, 'Notice et extraits du MS 8336 de la bibliothéque de Sir Thomas Phillipps á Cheltenham', *Romania* 13 (1884) 497–541

'Mélanges Anglo-Normands', *Romania* 38 (1909) 434–41

Mooney, Linne, '"A Woman's Reply to Her Lover" and Four Other New Courtly Love Lyrics in Cambridge, Trinity College MS R.3.19', *MAev* 67 (1998) 235–56

Muessig, Carolyn, 'Learning and Mentoring in the Twelfth Century', in *Medieval Monastic Education*, ed. George Ferzoco and Carolyn Muessig (Leicester: Leicester University Press, 2000), pp. 87–104

Murphy, James J., *Rhetoric in the Middle Ages* (Berkeley, CA: University of California Press, 1974)
— *Medieval Rhetoric: A Select Bibliography*, 2nd edn (Toronto: University of Toronto Press, 1989)
Newman, Jonathan M., 'Dictators of Venus: Clerical Love Letters and Female Subjection in *Troilus and Criseyde* and the *Rota Veneris*', *Studies in the Age of Chaucer* 36 (2014) 103–38
Nissille, Christel, *'Grammaire floue' et enseignement du français en Angleterre au XVe siècle: les leçons du manuscrit Oxford Magdalen 188* (Tübingen: Niemeyer, 2014)
Oliva, Marilyn, *The Convent and the Community in Late Medieval England: Female Monasteries in the Diocese of Norwich, 1350–1540* (Woodbridge: Boydell & Brewer, 1998)
Pantin, W.A., 'A Medieval Treatise on Letter-Writing, with Examples, from the Rylands Latin MS 394', *Bulletin of the John Rylands Library* 13 (1929), 326–82
Parisse, Michel, 'Le Concile de Remiremont', *Le Pays de Remiremont* 4 (1981) 10–15
— 'Les chanoinesses de Remiremont: des religieuses singulières', in *Christliches und jüdisches Europa im Mittelalter*, ed. Lukas Clemens and Sigrid Hirbodian (Trier: Kliomedia, 2011), pp. 153–66
Poirion, Daniel, *Le poète et le prince: l'évolution du lyrisme Courtois de Guillaume de Machaut à Charles d'Orléans* (Paris: Presses universitaires de France, 1965)
Power, Eileen, *Medieval English Nunneries* (Cambridge: Cambridge University Press, 1922)
Putter, Ad, 'The French of English Letters: Two Trilingual Verse Epistles in Context', in *Language and Culture in Medieval Britain: The French of England c. 1100–c. 1500*, ed. Jocelyn Wogan-Browne *et al.* (Cambridge: D.S. Brewer, 2009), pp. 397–408
Remley, Paul, 'Mary Shelton and Her Tudor Literary Milieu', in *Rethinking the Henrician Era: Essays on Early Tudor Texts and Contexts*, ed. Peter C. Herman (Urbana, IL: University of Illinois Press, 1994), pp. 40–77
Richardson, H.G., *Letters of the Oxford Dictatores*, vol. II of *Formularies Which Bear on the History of Oxford*, ed. H.E. Salter, W.A. Pantin and H.G. Richardson (Oxford: Oxford Historical Society, 1942)
Richardson, Malcolm, *Middle Class Writing in Late Medieval London* (London: Routledge, 2010)
Robbins, Rossell Hope, 'The Findern Anthology', *PMLA* 69 (1954) 610–42
— 'The Lyrics', in *Companion to Chaucer Studies*, ed. Beryl Rowland (New York: Galaxy Books, 1979), pp. 380–402
Robinson, J. Harvey, ed., *Readings in European History*, 2 vols (Boston, MA: Ginn, 1904)
Roest, Bert, *Order and Disorder: The Poor Clares* (Leiden: Brill, 2013)
Rosenthal, Joel T., *Telling Tales: Sources and Narration in Late Medieval England* (Philadelphia, PA: University of Pennsylvania Press, 2003)
Ruhe, Ernstpeter, *De Amasio ad Amasiam: Zur Gattungsgeschichte des mittelalterlichen Liebesbriefes* (Munich: Fink, 1975)

Scattergood, John, *Time's Subjects: Horology and Literature in the Later Middle Ages and Renaissance* (Dublin: Four Courts, 2022)
Schendl, Herbert, 'Code-Choice and Code-Switching in Some Early Fifteenth-Century Letters', in *Middle English from Tongue to Text*, ed. Peter J. Lucas and Angela M. Lucas (Frankfurt: Peter Lang, 2002), pp. 247–62
Schmidt, Paul Gerhard, 'Amor in Claustro', in *Medieval Latin and Middle English Literature: Essays in Honour of Jill Mann*, ed. Christopher Cannon and Maura Nolan (Cambridge: Cambridge University Press, 2011), pp. 182–92
Schulz-Grobert, Jürgen, *Deutsche Liebesbriefe in spätmittelalterlichen Handschriften* (Tübingen: Niemeyer, 1993)
Spitzer, Leo, 'Note on the Poetic and Empirical "I" in Medieval Authors', *Traditio* 4 (1946) 414–22
Stengel, E., 'Die ältesten Anleitungsschriften zur Erlernung der französischen Sprache', *Zeitschrift für Französische Sprache und Literatur* 1 (1879) 1–40
Stevens, John, *Music and Poetry in the Early Tudor Court* (London: Methuen, 1961)
Words and Music in the Middle Ages (Cambridge: Cambridge University Press, 1986)
Stokes, Myra, 'The Contract of Love Service', *Literaria Pragensia* 9 (1999) 62–83
Tanner, Norman, 'Religious Practice', in *Medieval Norwich*, ed. Carole Rawcliffe and R.G. Wilson (London: Hambledon, 2004), pp. 137–55
Taylor, John, 'Letters and Letter Collections in England 1300–1420', *Nottingham Medieval Studies* 24 (1980) 57–70
Thompson, A. Hamilton, *The English Clergy and their Organization in the Later Middle Ages* (Oxford: Oxford University Press, 1947)
Thompson, Sally, *Women Religious* (Oxford: Oxford University Press, 1991)
Thomson, R.M., *A Descriptive Catalogue of the Medieval Manuscripts of Corpus Christi College Oxford* (Cambridge: D.S. Brewer, 2011)
Tilliette, Jean-Yves, 'Hermès amoureux, ou les métamorphoses de la Chimère: réflexions sur les Carmina 200 et 201 de Baudri de Bourgueil', *MEFRM* 104 (1992) 121–61
Turville-Petre, Thorlac, 'The Author of *The Destruction of Troy*', *MAev* 57 (1988) 264–9
Tuten, Belle S., 'Who Was Lady Constance of Angers? Nuns as Poets and Correspondents at the Monastery of Ronceray d'Angers in the Early Twelfth Century', *Medieval Perspectives* 19 (2004) 255–68
Vaughan, Richard, *Charles the Bold* (Woodbridge: Boydell & Brewer, 2002)
Waddell, Helen, *The Wandering Scholars*, 7th edn (London: Constable, 1934)
Walther, Hans, 'Quot-tot. Mittelalterliche Liebesgrüsse und Verwandtes', *Zeitschrift für deutsches Altertum* 65 (1928) 257–89
Proverbia Sententiaeque Latinitatis Medii Aevi, 6 vols (Göttingen: Vandenhoeck and Ruprecht, 1963–9)
Wetterhall Thomas, Martha, 'Medieval Origins of Corporate Communication: Sampson of Oxford and the *Method of Letter-Writing*', *Corporate Communications* 13 (2008) 112–23

Wheeler, Bonnie, ed., *Listening to Heloise: The Voice of a Twelfth-Century Woman* (New York: Palgrave Macmillan, 2000)

Whiting, B.J., *Proverbs, Sentences and Proverbial Sayings from English Writings Mainly before 1500* (Cambridge, MA: Harvard University Press, 1950)

Willard, Charity Cannon, *Christine de Pizan: Her Life and Works* (New York: Persea, 1984)

Wilson, Edward, 'Local Habitations and Names in MS Rawlinson C 813', *RES* 41 (1990) 12–44

Windeatt, Barry, *Oxford Guides to Chaucer: Troilus and Criseyde*, revised edn (Oxford: Oxford University Press, 1995)

Wormald, Francis, 'The Rood of Bromholm', *JWI* 1 (1937) 31–45

Youngs, Deborah, *Humphrey Newton: An Early Tudor Gentleman* (Woodbridge: Boydell & Brewer, 2008)

Ziolkowski, Jan M., 'Lost and Not Yet Found: Heloise, Abelard and the *Epistolae duorum amantium*', *Journal of Medieval Latin* 14 (2004) 171–202

Index

Page references for illustrations are in *italics*.

'A Dieu, ma dame, je m'en vois' (poem), 35
'A Dieu, mon ami' (poem), 35
abandonment, 34, 63–4, 103
abbeys, 247, 246–8, 250,
  see also Remiremont Abbey
Abelard, 19, 70–86, 118
  'Dolorum solatium', 75
  and *Epistolae duorum amantium* (Johannes de Vepria), 83–6
  Hexameron, 76
  Historia calamitatum, 70–2, 73–4
  Hymnary, 75
  musical composition, 74–5
  O quanta qualia, 75
  prose writing of, 77, 78–9
  retellings of story of, 72–3
absence, 8, 22, 33–5, 90, 175, 226, 227
acceptance letters, 104
acrostics, 17, 42, 50, 466
actuality
  art based on, 10–13, 95, 253
  art, boundaries with, 108, 290
  art, indebtedness to, 108
  art, merging with, 16–17, 428
  art, relationship with, 18–26, 69, 74–5, 456
  autobiographical, 10, 12–13
  delivery/receipt of letter, 10–11
  fiction, basis for, 111
Adalbert of Montecassino, *Praecepta dictaminum*, 95
Adalbert Samaritanus, 95
adaptation, 18, 111–13
address
  to actual person, 21
  to named women, 11
  second-person, 10, 11, 12, 38, 91, 193, 227
  third-person, 38, 43
  in Valentine poems, 42–3
Adela of Blois, 85
Agnes (daughter of Radegund), 86
Alberic of Mont-Cassin, *Breviarium de dictamine*, 3

Alcuin, 95
allegories, 236–7
allusions, learned, 105
Alsace, 347–51, 361–2
Altercatio Phyllidis et Florae (poem), 429
amicitia (friendship), 86, 98
  vs love, 87–8, 88–9, 113–14
amies/mistresses, 28, 29, 64
amor (passionate love), 86, 98, 114
Ancrene Wisse, 7–8
Andreas Capellanus, *Tractatus de amore*, 124–6, 169, 177, 218, 428
Anglo-French language, 185–9, 197–8
Anglo-Norman language, 241, 281
anniversaries, 68
announcement of love, 8, 170
anonymity, 65, 105, 169, 278, 297
  of clergy, 65, 169
  conclusions and, 49–50
  of women, 49–50
anthologies, personal, 65–6, 70
Antoine de la Sale, *Le petit Jehan de Saintré*, 49, 252–4, 256, 279
apology, 243
approaches, 27–31
appropriation, 13–17, 43, 47–8, 265, 287–8, 288–9
Armburgh, Joan, 286, 287, 294–5, 296
Armburgh, Reynold, 296
Armburgh, Robert, 16, 51, 108, 112, 286, 294, 295, 296, 297
Armburgh Roll, 4, 16, 46, 286–98
  adaptations in, 18
  author's identity, 293–7
  construction of, 293–4
  English poems, 288–9
  macaronic poems, 287–8, 290–2
  quotation/borrowing in, 287–8, 288–9
  scribes, 294
  text, 297–8
  verse form, 297–8

482

Index

Armburgh, William, 296
art
　actuality, based on, 10–13, 95, 253
　actuality, boundaries with, 108, 290
　actuality, merging with, 16–17, 428
　actuality, relationship with, 18–26, 69, 74–5, 290, 456
　actuality's debt to, 108
　literary, education in, 96, 98
　love as, 126
artes dictandi (letter dictation manuals), 3, 53, 108, 119, 122, 185, 189–93
Assembly of Ladies, The (poem), 236
Astralabe, Peter, 78
authenticity, debates on, 19–21
authorship
　of Armburgh Roll, 293–7
　gender and, 59
　shared, 22
autobiography, 10, 12–13

Baethgen, Friedrich, 122, 126
ballades, 10–13, 44–5
Bannatyne, George, 9, 17
Bannatyne Manuscript, The, 9
Barbara de Tengen, 359
Barclay, Alexander, 186
Barfüsser (Barefoot friars), 106, 110
Barton, John, *Donait français*, 4, 186, 194
Bateman, William, 244
Battista, Francesca, 22
Baudri of Bourgueil, v, 65, 69, 86–90, 102, 103, 108
　Constance, letters to, 88–90
　Poems 7 and 8, 89
　Poem 137 (to Muriel), 87
Beadle, Richard, 224, 245, 47
bearers of letters, 50–3, 87, 354
bereavement, 10, 42, 44, 45, 45
betrayal, 59–60
betrothals, 31–3
Betson, Thomas, 31–2, 56
Bibbesworth, Walter, 186
Bible
　borrowings/quotations from, 122–3, 173, 175
　epistolary form in, 70
　references to, 101
birds, 41–2
Boccaccio, Giovanni, 68
　Il Filostrato, 8, 14
Boethius, 122
Boke of Nurture (courtesy book), 222
Bologna, 117
Boncompagno da Signa, 113
　biography, 117–19
　response letters, 27
　Rhetorica antiqua, 117, 118, 179, 180, 181
　Rhetorica novissima, 117
　Rota Veneris, 22, 25, 35, 118, 119–27, 227

Bondort, Konrad von, 107
borrowing, 13–17, 43, 47–8, 265, 287–8, 288–9
　biblical, 122–3, 173, 175
Bourgueil, Baudri of *see* Baudri of Bourgueil
Breisacher Reimchronik (verse chronicle), 454
Brews, Margery (later Paston), 32, 51, 54, 57, 63
Brittain, F., 75
Bromholm priory, 246
Burgundy, 342–51, 354–7, 360–3
Bury St Edmunds manuscripts, 191–2

Calais, 28, 29–30
Calle, Richard, 51
Camargo, Martin, 9, 16, 34, 241
　on borrowing, 16, 47, 48, 49
　on Norfolk letters, 243, 245, 264
Cambridge University Library
　Ee.iv.20, 190
　Ff.1.6 (Findern Manuscript), 61, 223–8
　Gg.4.27, 16, 287
Cambridge University, Gonville and Caius College, 244–5
Cambridge, Gonville and Caius 54/31, 51, 52, 63, 241–8
Canon Willard, Charity, 13
canonesses
　G, of Remiremont Abbey, 340, 341–2, 352–4, 356–7, 358–60, 382
　nuns, difference from, 341–2, 429, 430
Canterbury Tales (Chaucer)
　Franklin's Tale, 17
　Knight's Tale, 6, 44
　Merchant's Tale, 27
　Prologue, 5, 251, 253
　Shipman's Tale, 221
Carmina Burana, 20
Carpenter, Christine, 286, 287, 288, 291, 294, 296, 298
carriers of letters, 50–3, 87, 354
Catherine of Siena, 54
Cawston, Michael, 244
Caxton, William, 188, 345
Cely, George, 28–31, 63
Cely Letters, 28–31
Cent Balades see Christine de Pisan
Chardri, *Le Petit Plet*, 206
Charles d'Orléans, 10, 12, 13, 59
　Ballade 72, 42
　dates/festivals, marking of, 39, 42, 45
　Rondeau 6, 43
　Rondeau 82, 15
Charles the Bold (Charles I), Duke of Burgundy, 342–8, 362, 454–5
Charles V, King of France, 342
Chartier, Alain, *La belle dame sans merci*, 225
chastity, 87, 89, 93
Chaucer, Geoffrey
　Canterbury Tales

Index

Franklin's Tale, 17
Knight's Tale, 6, 44
Merchant's Tale, 27
  Prologue, 5, 251, 253
  Shipman's Tale, 221
Complaint of Anelida, 37–8
Complaint unto Pity, 235, 236
Legend of Good Women, 167
Parliament of Fowls, 17, 41, 42, 224
Romaunt of the Rose, 5
'To Rosemounde', 11
Troilus and Criseyde, 17, 21, 62
  absence and separation in, 33, 34
  anonymity in, 50
  bearers/carriers in, 52
  female voice in, 27
  guiding star metaphor in, 68
  honour/reputation in, 60, 256
  love letters in, 6–7, 8–9, 14–15
  privacy, lack of, 74
  retreat in, 36–7
  writing and scribes in, 54–6
Chrétien de Troyes, 428
Christine de Pisan, 10
  Cent Balades, d'amant et de dame, 10, 11, 12–13, 44
  absence and separation in, 33–5
  approach in, 27
  dates/festivals, marking of, 40, 44–5
  honour/reputation in, 60
  retreat in, 35
  women's voices in, 62
  Dit de la rose, 42
  Epistre au dieu d'amours, 225
chronicles, verse, 98, 454, 456
Cicero, 98, 118
Cinkante Balades (Gower)
  Ballade XL, 60
  dates/festivals, marking of, 39, 43, 44, 45
  marginal notes in, 13–14
  women's voices in, 59–60
Claerr-Stamm, Gabrielle, 360, 361, 454
class *see* social class, 480
classical references, 97, 100
clergy, 251–60, 386
  anonymity, need for, 65, 169
  love letters by, 74
  nuns, relationships with, 51, 52, 63, 86–90, 241–8, 254–6
  as profession, 251
  religious/secular clothing of, 252
  scholarship of, 251
  sexual relationships of, 252–4, 254–6
  see also Abelard
clerks, as lovers, 429
clichés, 33
Clopinel, Jehan *see* Jean de Meun
Cok, John, 19

colophons, 191, 192, 193
commonplace books, 9, 17, 23–6, 45, 50
communication
  gestures, 119
  model conversations, 187–9, 218
  speech, 81, 184
  see also letters; love letters; writing
communication rules and procedures, 49–59
  letter bearers/carriers, 50–3, 87, 354
  letters, folding and sealing of, 55, 357, 368
  secrecy, 49–50
  tokens, 23, 50–1
  see also scribes
Complaint of Anelida (Chaucer), 37–8
Complaint unto Pity (Chaucer), 235, 236
complaints, 37–8
'Compleynt d'Amours' (poem), 42
compliments
  on beauty, 88, 93, 122, 171, 173, 236
  on eloquence, 87
  exchange of, 67–8
  on poetic skill, 91
  rejection of, 92
composition
  mastery, demonstration of, 67–8
  musical, 74–5
Concilium in Monte Romarici (*Council of Remiremont*, poem), 90, 363–5, 428–31
conclusions to letters, 3, 99
  anonymity and, 49–50
  signatures, 108
  subscriptions, 112
  vale (farewell), 65–7
Confessio Amantis (Gower), 235, 236
confidentiality, 53, 56–7, 62–3, 87, 103
Constance (nun), 88–90
contrasts, 77, 176
convents, 72, 75
  courtly culture of, 90–1, 105
  morality in, 254
  Norfolk, 246, 248–50
  Paraclete, 75
  'Regensburg', 91–5
  Ronceray (Angers, France), 85, 90
  rules, contravention of, 105–6, 256–7
  secularization of, 429–30, 430
  Söflingen, 105–14
  worldliness of, 430
  see also nuns; Remiremont Abbey
conversations, model, 187–9, 218
copies of letters, 68–9, 286, 294
  editing in, 65, 69
Core, Luca, 126
correlation, 79
cosmetics, critique of, 178
Council of Remiremont (*Concilium in Monte Romarici*, poem), 90, 363–5, 428–31

Council of Soissons (1121), 71
courtliness/*courtoisie*, 99, 108, 167, 253–4
  accomplishments, 5–7
  convent culture of, 90–1, 93
  seduction and, 196, 221
courtly romances, 221, 364
courtship
  initiation of, 27–31, 32
  religious allegories and, 7
  resistance of, 93–4
  retreat from, 35–7
  rituals, 5–6 *see also* dates/festivals, marking of
  song and verse, importance of, 220
  as suit, 14
  see also love affairs
Cupid, 124, 167, 225

Dante, *Inferno*, 72
dates/festivals, marking of, 39–48
  anniversaries, 68
  May Day, 39, 44–5, 109
  New Year's Day, 39–41, 45, 288, 291
  Valentine's Day, 39, 41–3
dating of letters, 340
De amico ad amicam (poem), 9
death, 10, 42, 45, 360, 362, 454–5
deletions, 242, 280, 298, 391
despair, spiritual, 79, 173, 278
Devonshire Manuscript (London, British Library, Add 17492), 17
dialectic skills, 177
dictation, 53–4, 357–8
disagreements, 227
Dit de la rose (Christine de Pisan), 42
'Dolorum solatium' (Abelard), 75
Douglas, Lady Margaret, 17
drafts, 242, 280–1, 288, 289–90
Dronke, Peter, 85, 86, 89, 91, 94
  on Abelard and Heloise, 72, 73, 75, 75
  on *Epistolae duorum amantium*, 69, 84
  on Tegernsee letters, 96, 103, 104
Dutch language, 29

East, W.G., 75
education
  of girls and women, 86, 90–5, 258–9, 358
  in letter writing, 118, 190, 291, 293
  in literary arts, 96, 98
Edward IV, King of England, 345
Elliott, Goddard, 125
eloquence, 6–7, 67–8, 87, 97
Emma, abbess of Ronceray, 85
emotion, 102
  expression of, 76–7, 79–82
  jealousy, 63, 63, 88, 91, 182
  sorrow, 13, 43

endearments, 107, 107, 352, 368
English language
  first literary love letters in, 9
  letters in, 4, 241
  envoys, poetic, 11
Epistolae duorum amantium (Johannes de Vepria), v, 19, 65–70, 83–6, 100–3
Epistre au dieu d'amours (Christine de Pisan), 225
Escorial, Biblioteca Real, T.II.16, 38
Euryalus and Lucretia story (*Historia de duobus amantibus*, Piccolomini), 16, 27, 110–13
exempla, 455

fabliaux, 178, 196
Facetus (behaviour manual), 125, 183
Fakenham, 246
falseness, 59, 61, 225, 401
'Farewell to his Mistress I/II/III., A' (poem), 35
farewells
  in letters, 93
  vale, 65–7
  verse, 35
feminism, 225
Ferette, 347
fiction
  actuality and, 111
  epistolary, 111
fidelity, 59, 63, 98
Findern manuscript, 9, 19, 223–8
first-person voice, 15, 236–7
Fischel, Lilli, 454, 455
Fitzroy, Mary, 17
flirtation, 92
florilegia, 65, 70
Fortunatus (Venantius Fortunatus), 86
Frederick III, Holy Roman Emperor, 348
French language, 3–4, 9, 9, 29, 30–1, 347
  Anglo-French, 185–9, 197–8
  Anglo-Norman, 241, 281
  primers and instruction, 4, 185–200
  social class/status, marker of, 187, 189
friendship, 86, 106–7
  Gottesfreundschaft (spiritual marriage), 106–7, 113
  vs love, 87–8, 88–9
  vs sexual relationships, 219
Fulwood, William, *The Enimie of Idlenesse*, 4
Furnivall, F.J., 228
Fyner, Konrad, 110

Ganszyniec, Ryszard, 126
Garbini, Paolo, 127
gender
  authorial, 59
  grammatical, 197, 287

Index

manuscript compilation, commission and scribing, 224–6
stereotypes, 20, 63
in verse, 61–3
Geoffrey of Vinsauf, 122
German language, 101–3, 110, 108–10, 124
Gervase, Abbot of Prémontré, 53–4
gifts
  book chemises, 259–60
  exchange of, 40, 92
  May Day, 109
  New Year, 39, 40, 45
  refusal of, 92
  regulation of, in convents, 256–7
  social class/status and, 221
girls, 196–7
  education of, 86, 90–5, 258–9, 358
go-betweens, 58, 120, 125, 182
God, love of, 72, 79, 81
gods, classical, 94–5, 119, 167
Gonville, Edmund, 244
gossip, 59, 60–1, 62–3
Gottesfreundschaft (spiritual marriage), 106–7, 113
Gower, John, 10, 11
  Cinkante Balades
    Ballade XL, 60
    dates/festivals, marking of, 39, 43, 44, 45
    marginal notes in, 13–14
    women's voices in, 59–60
  Confessio Amantis, 235, 236
Granson, Oton de, 41–2
Grotans, Anna, 96
Guillaume de Lorris and Jean de Meun (Jehan Clopinel), *Roman de la rose*, 73, 82, 83, 125, 167

Hall, Catherine, 245
handbooks/manuals, 119, 122
  artes dictandi, 3, 53, 108, 119, 122, 185, 189–93
  French conversation, *Manières de langage*, 186–9, 193–8, 218
  French language, 4, 185–7
Hanham, Alison, 29, 30
Harley Lyrics, 50
Hawes, Stephen, 17
Helmbrecht (poem), 254
Heloise, 5–6, 19, 70–86
  emotion, expression of, 76–7, 79–82
  and *Epistolae duorum amantium* (Johannes de Vepria), 83–6
  Latin prose style of, 76–8, 85
  Problemata, 75
  retellings of story of, 72–3
  rhetorical skills of, 74, 76, 80–2, 76–83

Herenc, Baudet, *Parlement d'amour*, 5
Hexameron (Abelard), 76
Hilarius of Orléans, 90
Historia calamitatum (Abelard), 70–2, 73–4
Historia Compostellana (chronicle), 98
Historia de duobus amantibus (Piccolomini), 16, 27, 110–13
historiography, 456
Hoccleve, Thomas, *Letter of Cupid*, 225
homosexuality, 103–4
honour/reputation, preservation of, 60, 62, 112, 173, 292
Horace, 100
hostelries, 195
Howard, Lord Thomas, 17
Hughes, John, 73
humour, 429–30
husbands, 120, 182
  model letters for, 191, 204–5
hyperbole, 180

imagery
  animal, 21
  dreams, 174
  fishing, 175
  messengers, letters as, 120
  personification, 59
  stars, 68
  wheels, 167
infidelity, 25, 36, 37, 59, 256
initials
  names indicated by, 23, 54, 96, 103, 105
  as signatures, 54, 108
intermediaries, 32, 120, 125, 182
Isabella of Portugal, Duchess of Burgundy, 344, 345, 358
Italy, 117

Jaeger, C.S., 83
James, M.R., 249
jealousy, 63, 88, 91, 182
Jean de Meun (Jehan Clopinel), 73
  Roman de la rose, 73, 82, 83, 125, 167
Jean de Vaudrey, 57, 340, 346, 351
Jean II, King of France, 342
Jehan Clopinel *see* Jean de Meun, 480
Jerome, 95
Johannes de Vepria, *Epistolae duorum amantium*, v, 19, 65–70, 83–6, 100–3
John of Gaunt, 345
Johnston, Michael, 225

Katherine de Hagenbach, 353
Kela, Thomas, 57–8
King's Lynn, 245, 250
Kingsmill, William, 187

kisses/kissing, 125, 219
Knebel, Johannes, 454
knights/knighthood, 98, 253, 401, 429
Koblenz, Landeshauptarchiv 162, Nr.1401, 428, 428
Könsgen, Ewad, 83
Kristol, Andres M., 187, 188, 196
Kunhuta (Kunigunda of Halych, Queen of Bohemia), 22

Lalaing, Jaques de, 253
laments, 34, 37, 42, 75, 76
lampoons, 456
Langland, William, 19, 246, 254, 278
Latin language, 9, 38, 101–3, 126, 186, 259
  prose, 76–8, 85
Le Fevre, Jean
  Le livre des faits de messire Jacques de Lalaing, 253
leave-taking *see* farewell
Lee, Reuben, 428, 429, 430
Legend of Good Women (Chaucer), 167
lesbianism, 103–4
letters
  bearers/carriers, 50–3, 87, 354
  collections, 70, 185, 187
  dating of, 340
  as literary genre, 70
  paired, 204
  public/open, 73–4
  regulation of, in convents, 256–7
  scrutiny/inspection of, 72
  sealing of, 55, 357, 368
  vs speech, 81
  from students, requesting money, 192–3
  writing
    education in, 118, 190, 190, 291, 293
    skills in, 118, 291, 293
  see also communication rules and procedures; love letters; model letters; responses/replies
literacy, 53, 56
Livre d'Enanchet, Le (compilation), 124
Livre des mestiers, Le (French language manual), 188
Livre du voir dit, Le (Machaut), 10, 57, 63, 89, 237, 256
London, British Library
  Add 17492 (Devonshire Manuscript), 17
  Harley 3362, 16, 287
  Harley 3988, 4, 7, 189–98
  Harley 4971, 190, 197, 198, 204
  Royal 6.B.ix, 18
  Sloane 1212, 16
London, The National Archives, SC 1/59/41
loneliness, 44–5
Lorraine, *343*, 347, 354–6

Louis XI, King of France, 342, 345, 346
love
  vs *amicitia* (friendship), 87–8, 88–9, 113–14
  amor (passionate love), 86, 98, 114
  announcement of, 8, 170
  as art, 126
  basis for, 60
  manuals for, 124–6
  vs marriage, 81–2
  as religion, 364, 428
  transience of, 360
love affairs
  condoning of, 353–4
  ending of, 359–60
  extra-marital, 29, 35, 111
  letters, conducted by, 90
  letters written after, 72
  moral code of, 255–6
  risks of, for women, 60–1, 62
love compacts, 105
love letters
  ballades, similarity to, 11
  categories of
    acceptance, 104
    announcement of love, 8, 170
    apology, 243
    approach, 27–31
    between betrothed parties, 31–3
    complaint, 37–8
    farewell, 93
    for nuns/religious women, 87–8
    quarrels, 227
    rejection, 25
    requests for meeting, 113
    retreat, 35–7
    separation, 8, 22, 175, 226
  dates/festivals, marking of, 39–48
  dating of, 340
  drafts, 242, 280–1, 288, 289–90
  headings for, 205
  as literary exercise, 86–7, 87–8
  as literary form, 6–7, 8–17
  vs meeting in person, 68, 74
  paired, 8, 89, 104
  as petitions/'bills', 235–6
  real vs artful, 18–26
  retention of, 69, 73
  revisions,
  risks of, 34, 35, 52–3
  role-playing, 87–8, 90–5
  unread, 38
  verse, demanded for, 4–5
  see also communication rules and procedures; model letters; responses/replies
'Lover's Farewell to His Mistress, A' (poem), 35
Luscombe, D., 84

Index

lust, 71, 72
Lydgate anthology, 16
Lydgate, John, 17
   Floure of Curtesye, 42–3
   A Lover's New Year Gift, 39

macaronic verse, 9, 101–2, 287–8, 289, 290–2
Machaut, Guillaume de, 13
   Le livre du voir dit, 10, 57, 63, 89, 237, 256
Manières de langage, 186–9, 193–8, 218
manuals *see* handbooks, 480
manuscripts
   Bury St Edmunds, 191, 191–2
   Cambridge, Gonville and Caius 54/31, 51, 52, 63, 241–8
   Cambridge University Library, Ee.iv.20, 190
   Cambridge University Library, Ff.1.6 (Findern Manuscript), 61, 223–8
   Cambridge University Library, Gg.4.27, 16, 287
   Escorial, Biblioteca Real, T.II.16, 38
   Koblenz, Landeshauptarchiv 162, Nr.1401, 428, 428
   London, British Library, Add 17492 (Devonshire Manuscript), 17
   London, British Library, Harley 3362, 16, 287
   London, British Library, Harley 3988, 4, 7, 189–98
   London, British Library, Harley 4971, 190, 197, 198, 204
   London, British Library, Royal 6.B.ix, 18
   London, British Library, Sloane 1212, 16
   Munich, Bayerische Staatsbibliothek, Clm 17142, 91–5
   Munich, Bayerische Staatsbibliothek, Clm 18580, 95
   Munich, Bayerische Staatsbibliothek, Clm 19411 (Tegernsee Letters), 95–105
   Oxford, All Souls 182, 185–7
   Oxford, Bodleian Libraries, Douce 95, 287, 304
   Oxford, Corpus Christi 154, 18, 34, 52, 56, 63, 280–5
   Ripoll 74, 430
   Rome, Biblioteca Angelica, MS 505, 176, 177
   Trier, Stadtbibliothek 1081/29, 428
   Troyes, Bibliothèque municipale, 1452, 65
Marbod of Rennes, 90
Marenbon, John, 84
Margaret III, Countess of Flanders, 342
Margaret of York, Duchess of Burgundy, 345
marriage, 31
   arguments against, 73, 82
   arranged, 204
   Gottesfreundschaft (spiritual marriage), 106–7, 113

   vs love, 81–2
   rejection of, 87
   spiritual, 106–7
Mary of Burgundy (Mary the Rich), 348, 362
Matthew of Vendôme, 119
Maximilian I, Holy Roman Emperor, 348, 362
May Day, 39, 44–5, 109
men
   courtly accomplishments, 5–7
   husbands, 120, 182, 191, 204–5
   knights, 98, 253, 401, 429
   monks, 106–7, 110
   scribes, use of, 53, 54, 57
   see also clergy
metre, 11, 75, 100, 233, 291, 455–6
Mews, Constant J., 83, 83, 84
Meyer, Paul, 241, 243, 245, 272, 274
Meyer, Wilhelm, 428
Miller, Max, 106, 108, 113
mistresses/*amies*, 28, 29, 64
model conversations, 187–9, 218
model letters *see* handbooks
modesty, 88, 93, 97
Mone, F.J., 454
monks, 106–7, 110, 255–7
Mooney, Linne, 19–21
Moriarty, Catherine, 53, 54
Müller, Rolf, 454, 455
Munich, Bayerische Staatsbibliothek
   Clm 17142, 91–5
   Clm 18580, 95
   Clm 19411 (Tegernsee Letters), 95–105
music, 74–5, 222, 237–8
mythological references, 94–5, 97, 119, 167

names/naming, 273
   absence of, in letters, 104, 109, 110
   initials, 23, 54, 96, 103, 105, 105
   senhal (code name), 49
   see also anonymity
narrative, 3
   context, for letters, 120
   first-person, 15, 236–7
   love stories, 72–3
   verse, 42, 43
Neuchâtel family, 355
New Year's Day, 39–41, 45, 288, 291
Newman, Barbara, 84, 101
Newton, Humfrey, 9, 17, 23–6, 45, 50
Nicolas de Bruyères, 340, 351, 353
Norfolk, 244–50
   Bromholm priory, 246
   Fakenham, 246
   King's Lynn, 245, 250

Norfolk Letters (Cambridge, Gonville and Caius, 54/31), 51, 52, 63, 241–8
nouvelles (news), 53
'Now must I nede part out of your presence' (Suffolk love poems), 35
N-Town Plays, 45
nuns, 72, 177
  canonesses, difference from, 341–2, 429, 430
  clergy, correspondence with, 51, 52, 63, 86–90, 96–9, 241–8
  education of, 258–9
  friars, spiritual marriage with, 106–7
  laymen, correspondence with, 108
  Poor Clares, 105
  sexual relationships of, 254–6
  vows of, 341, 430, 450
  see also Heloise

O quanta qualia (Abelard), 75
obedience
  in love affairs, 33, 72, 79, 81
  religious, 248, 250, 264
offence, 101, 102
Old Swiss Confederacy, 346–7, 349
Oliva, Marilyn, 249
open/public letters, 73–4
Otto IV, Holy Roman Emperor, 117
Oulmont, Charles, 428
Ovid
  Ars amatoria, 125, 126
  Heroides, 8, 38
Owen, A.E.B., 224
Oxford, All Souls 182, 185–7
Oxford, Bodleian Libraries, Douce 95, 287, 304
Oxford, Corpus Christi 154, 18, 34, 52, 56, 63, 280–5
Oxford University, 190

Pamphilus, de amore (drama), 125
parallelisms, 77, 79
Paravicini, Anke, 63
Paravicini, Werner, 340, 352
Parliament of Fowls (Chaucer), 17, 41, 42, 224
Parliament of Love, The (poem), 48, 223–8
Paston, John, 46
Paston Letters, 46–8, 51, 56, 345
Paston, Margery (formerly Brews), 32, 46–8, 54, 57, 63
Péronne (in *Le livre du voir dit*, Machaut), 57, 89, 170, 237, 256
personalization, 105, 108, 290
personification, 59
Peter of Hagenbach *see* Pierre de Hagenbach
petitions, 3, 113, 235–6
Petrarch, 73
Pfettisheim, Conrad, 454–6
Philip the Good (Philip III), Duke of Burgundy, 344, 347

Piccolomini, Aeneas Silvius
  Historia de duobus amantibus, 16, 27, 110–13
Pierre de Hagenbach, 63, 340–1, 342, 347–52, 353, 355–7, 359–62, 454–6
pilgrimages, 246, 257–8
Piron, Sylvain, 69, 70, 84, 85
Pisan, Christine de *see* Christine de Pisan, 480
Pius II, Pope *see* Piccolomini, Aeneas Silvius, 480
Plechl, Helmut, 96
poetry *see* verse, 480
polemics, 218, 225, 245, 455
Pope, Alexander
  'Eloisa to Abelard', 73
Power, Eileen, 54, 248, 255
prayer-charms, 45
Přemysl Otakar II of Bohemia, 22
presents *see* gifts, 480
privacy, 58
  lack of, 74
  public, boundary with, 23
'Profuit ignaris' (poem), 94–5
propriety, 55, 56
prose, 10, 77, 78–9, 243–4
  Latin, 76–8, 85
  married couples, used between, 7
  rhymed, 76, 103
  by women, 67, 76–8, 85
Provençal language, 8
public/open letters, 73–4
punctuation, 284, 297, 298
Purkart, Josef, 127

quarrels, 227
quod formula, 19
quot ... tot construction, 67, 168, 206, 265
quotation, 13–17, 43, 47–8, 76–7, 98, 265, 287–8, 288–9
  biblical, 122–3, 173, 175

Radegund, 86
Radice, Betty, 73
rape, 125
Recuyell of the Hystories of Troye, 345
regard, expressions of, 107
Regina sedens rhetorica (textbook), 204
Reichenau, Wilhelm von, 110
rejection
  of compliments, 92
  of love or lover, 25, 120–1
  of marriage, 87, 175
religion
  blasphemy, 84
  confession, 255, 278
  love as, 172, 364, 428
  sacrilege, 84
  spiritual despair, 79, 173, 278

Index

spiritual guidance, 75–6
spiritual marriage, 106–7, 113
theological argument, 77
see also clergy; convents; monks; nuns
Remiremont Abbey, 340–2, 352, 353, 363–5, 428–9, 430–1, 448
G, canoness of, 340, 341–2, 352–4, 356–7, 358–60, 382
Remiremont letters, 57, 63, 340–2, 351–62
   bearers/carriers in, 52
   contents of, 351–2
   ending of, 359–60
   scribes, written by, 54, 358–60
   seals/sealing, 357
   text of, 365
René II, Duke of Lorraine, 354, 355
renunciation, 12, 72, 72, 79
reputation
   loss of, 255–6
   preservation of, 60, 62, 112, 173, 292
requests for meeting, 113
responses/replies, 19–21, 27, 69
   as measure of affection, 92
   models of, 99, 191, 191, 204
   from nuns/enclosed women, 88–9
   from women, 5–7
retreat, 35–7
revisions, 242, 280–1, 288, 289–90
rhetoric, 100
   ars dictaminis, 117, 118
   classical, 94–5, 118
   as courtly accomplishment, 6–7
   pleasures of, 88, 89
   skills in, 67–8, 77
Richardson, H.G., 190, 192
Rietheim, Klara von, 107, 110–13
'Right best beloved' (poem), 20
Ripoll 74, 430
risks
   of love affairs, 60–1, 62
   of love letters, 34, 35, 52–3
Robbins, R.H., 35, 61–2, 287, 304
role-playing, 87–8, 91, 90–5, 101
Roman de la rose (Guillaume de Lorris and Jean de Meun), 82, 83, 125, 167
Romaunt of the Rose (Chaucer), 5
Rome, Biblioteca Angelica, MS 505, 176, 177
Roos, Richard, *La belle dame sans merci*, 225
Rostand, Edmond, *Cyrano de Bergerac*, 7
Rudolph, Archbishop of Cologne, 346
rumours, 59, 60–1, 62–3
Ryche, Elizabeth, 31, 32
Ryche, Katherine, 31–2

sadness, 13, 43
Saintré, Jehan de (historical character), 253
Salimbene, 119
salut d'amor (epistolary verse form), 8

salutations, 3, 273, 284, 376
   importance of, 65–7, 168
   models of, 206
salutz (Provençal epistolary verse form), 8
Sampson, Thomas, 190, 193
Schedelin, Hermann, 110
Schmidt, Paul Gerhard, 63
scribes, 53–9, 224–5, 294
   editing by, 65, 69
   multilingual, 29
   quod formula, use of, 19
   women as, 224
seals/sealing, 55, 357, 368
Second Lateran Council, 341
secrecy, 49–50, 62–3, 87, 88, 111, 169, 264
secretaries, 110, 111, 190
seduction, 193, 196–7
separation, 8, 22, 33–5, 90, 175, 226, 227
sex, 94–5
   desire, 194
   instructions for seduction, 193, 196–7, 219
   propositions, 194–6
   in Latin-love letters, 91
   repression of, 77
   sanitization of, 184
sexual relationships, 71
   of clergy and nuns, 252–4, 254–6
   discussion of, 120
   vs friendship, 219
   incest, ecclesiastical, 255
   passionate, 72, 81
sexual violence, 125, 350
sexuality
   exclusion/erasure of, 87, 88
   homosexuality, 103–4
Shakespeare, William
   As You Like It, 5
   Love's Labours Lost, 5
   Measure for Measure, 254
   Richard III, 21
Shelton, Mary, 17
'Si linguis angelicis' (love lyric), 49
Sigmund, Duke of Austria, 347, 350
signatures, 108
   initials as, 54, 108
sin, 173
   blasphemy, 84
   sex as, 258
   spiritual despair, 79, 173, 278
singing, 74–5, 237–8
Sir Degrevant (poem), 224
Sir Gawain and the Green Knight (poem), 221
social class/status, 187, 189, 253
   letters for ranks of, 191
   of nuns, 258
   sexual propositions and, 195
   of women, 233, 259, 430
Söflingen letters, 16, 105–14

soliloquy, 37, 38, 42, 44–5
songs, 74–5, 237–8
sorrow, 13, 43
speech
  need for, despite embarrasment, 184
  vs writing, 81
Stengel, E., 197
Stevens, John, 75
stigma, social, 255–6
Stonor, William, 31, 32
submission, 62
Suffolk love poems, 9
  'Now must I nede part out of your presence', 35
Suntheim, Magdalena von, 107
symbolism
  animal, 21
  dreams, 174
  fishing, 175
  messengers, letters as, 120
  stars, 68
  wheels, 167
syntax, 77, 79, 81

Tegernsee Letters (Munich, Bayerische Staatsbibliothek, Clm 19411), 95–105
Thomas of Hales, 363
Tilliette, Jean-Yves, 89
'To Rosemounde' (Chaucer), 11
tokens, 23, 50–1, 265, 273, 368, 378
tot ... quot construction, 67, 168, 206, 265
Tractatus de amore (Andreas Capellanus), 124–6, 169, 169, 177, 218, 428
transcription of letters, 68–9, 286, 294
  editing in, 65, 69
travel, 351, 352
  conventual restrictions on, 257–8
  pilgrimages, 246, 257–8
Trier, Stadtbibliothek 1081/29, 428
Troilus and Criseyde (Chaucer), 17, 21, 62
  absence and separation in, 33, 34
  anonymity in, 50
  bearers/carriers in, 52
  female voice in, 27
  guiding star metaphor in, 68
  honour/reputation in, 60, 256
  love letters in, 6–7, 8–9, 14–15
  privacy, lack of, 74
  retreat in, 36–7
  writing and scribes in, 54–6
Troyes, Bibliothèque municipale, 1452, 65
trustworthiness, 51, 58
truth, 21, 38, 59
Tuten, Belle S., 89

Valentine's Day, 39, 41–3
van der Weyden, Rogier, 259, 344, *345*, 358
Venantius Fortunatus (Fortunatus), 86

Venus (goddess), 119, 124
verse, 4–6
  appropriation/borrowing of, 13–17, 43, 47–8
  ballades, 10–13, 44–5
  chronicles, 456
  as courtly accomplishment, 5–6
  farewell poems, 35
  laments, 34, 37, 42, 75, 76
  lay-out as, 242
  literary self-consciousness of, 67–8
  love letters, required for, 4–5
  macaronic, 9, 101–2, 287–8, 289, 290–2
  mythological references in, 94–5
  narratives, 43
  readers as writers of, 16
  salut d'amor (epistolary verse form), 8
  salutz (Provençal epistolary verse form), 8
  soliloquy, 42, 44–5
  by women, 67
verse form
  in Armburgh Roll, 297–8
  couplets, 206
  English, 206
  expertise in, 234
  line length, 75, 291
  metre, 11, 75, 100, 233, 291, 455–6
  refrain, internal, 75
  rhyme, 75, 206, 242, 273, 293
  rhyme schemes, 15, 206, 280
  strophe, 75
  syllables, 206
virginity, 88, 196
Vischer, Wilhelm, 454
voice
  female, 19–22, 25–6, 59–64
  first-person, 15, 236–7

Waitz, George, 428
Walden, Roger, 186
Walter of Elveden, 244, 245, 249
warfare, 346, 355–6, 357, 390
Welles Anthology, 9, 17, 47
  anonymising conclusions in, 49–50
  No. 44, 61
  'Right best beloved', 20
Weyden, Rogier van der, 259, 344, *345*, 358
William of Bernham, 249, 251
Wind, Jos, 107
wives, model letters for, 204–5
Wolff, Étienne, 84, 119, 120, 127, 101
Wolfgar of Erla, 117
'Woman's Reply to Her Lover, A' (love epistle), 19–21
women
  Anglo-Norman, use of, 281
  anonymity, preservation of, 49–50

education of, 86, 358
girls, 196–7
handwriting of, 54–5, 56–7
honour/reputation, preservation of, 60, 62, 112, 173, 292
Latin, use of, 76–8, 85, 259
learnedness, 74, 85–6
letters from
  approaches, 28–31
  drafts, 281
  group, 92
  separation, 227
  ventriloquized by male writers, 89
literacy, 85–6
manuscripts, commissioning of, 224
model letters for, 121, 191
psychology of, 121
responses/replies, 5–7
risks of love affairs for, 60–1, 62
as scribes, 224
scribes, use of, 54, 54, 56–7
sisters, correspondence between, 191, 204
voices of, 19–22, 25–6, 59–64
wives, 204–5
writing
  by hand, 53–5, 110, 224, 244, 298
  of letters, training in, 118, 190, 291, 293
  materials, 69, 69
  seals, 55, 357, 368
  and scripts, 53–5, 110, 224, 244, 298
  vs speech, 81
Wyatt, Thomas (1503–42), 17
Wydeslade, Agnes, 32
Wyle, Nikolaus von, 110

yielding to Love, 62

Ziolkowski, Jan M., 84